EXHIBIT 1-9 Financial Statements of Cookie Lapp Travel Design, Inc.

COOKIE LAPP TRAVEL DESIGN, INC.
Income Statement
Month Ended April 30, 2008

Revenue:		
Service revenue		$8,500
Expenses:		
Salary expense	$1,200	
Rent expense, office	1,100	
Rent expense, computer	600	
Utilities expense	400	
Total expenses		3,300
Net income		$5,200

COOKIE LAPP TRAVEL DESIGN, INC.
Statement of Retained Earnings
Month Ended April 30, 2008

Retained earnings, April 1, 2008	$ 0
Add: Net income for the month	5,200
	5,200
Less: Dividends	(2,000)
Retained earnings, April 30, 2008	$3,200

COOKIE LAPP TRAVEL DESIGN, INC.
Balance Sheet
April 30, 2008

Assets		Liabilities	
Cash	$19,900	Accounts payable	$ 200
Accounts receivable	2,000	**Stockholders' Equity**	
Office supplies	500	Common stock	30,000
Land	11,000	Retained earnings	3,200
		Total stockholders' equity	33,200
Total assets	$33,400	Total liabilities and stockholders' equity	$33,400

COOKIE LAPP TRAVEL DESIGN, INC.
Statement of Cash Flows*
Month Ended April 30, 2008

Cash flows from operating activities:		
Receipts:		
Collections from customers ($5,500 + $1,000)		$ 6,500
Payments:		
To suppliers ($600 + $1,100 + $400 + $300)	$ (2,400)	
To employees	(1,200)	(3,600)
Net cash provided by operating activities		2,900
Cash flows from investing activities:		
Acquisition of land	$(20,000)	
Sale of land	9,000	
Net cash used for investing activities		(11,000)
Cash flows from financing activities:		
Issuance of stock	$ 30,000	
Dividends	(2,000)	
Net cash provided by financing activities		28,000
Net increase in cash		19,900
Cash balance, April 1, 2008		0
Cash balance, April 30, 2008		$19,900

*Chapter 16 shows how to prepare this statement.

Color-Coded Accounting Equation

This color-coded accounting equation is a tool you will use throughout your first accounting course. This tool is so important that we have to put it here for quick reference. You may find this helpful when preparing your homework assignments. Each financial statement is identified by a unique color. You will see these colors throughout the chapters when we present a financial statement.

1 The **income statement**, enclosed in the red box, provides the details of revenues earned and expenses incurred.

2 The revenue and expense transactions are then condensed into one number—net income—that becomes part of the **statement of retained earnings**, which appears in the yellow box.

3 Information from the statement of retained earnings flows into the **balance sheet**, shown in the blue box.

4 The **statement of cash flows**, as indicated by the green box, provides details of how a company got its cash and how it spent cash during the accounting period.

Financial and Managerial Accounting

Chapters 12–25

1e

Charles T. Horngren Series in Accounting

Auditing and Assurance Services: An Integrated Approach, 11th ed.
Arens/Elder/Beasley

Governmental and Nonprofit Accounting: Theory and Practice, 8th ed.
Freeman/Shoulders

Financial Accounting, 6th ed.
Harrison/Horngren

Cases in Financial Reporting, 5th ed.
Hirst/McAnally

Cost Accounting: A Managerial Emphasis, 12th ed.
Horngren/Datar/Foster

Accounting, 7th ed.
Horngren/Harrison

Introduction to Financial Accounting, 9th ed.
Horngren/Sundem/Elliott

Introduction to Management Accounting, 13th ed.
Horngren/Sundem/Stratton

Financial and Managerial Accounting
Chapters 12–25

Charles T. Horngren
Stanford University

Walter T. Harrison Jr.
Baylor University

Upper Saddle River, New Jersey 07458

Library of Congress Cataloging-in-Publication Data
Horngren, Charles T.
    Financial and managerial accounting / Charles T. Horgren, Walter T. Harrison
      p. cm.
    Includes index.
    ISBN 978-0-13-156877-8
     1. Accounting.   2. Managerial accounting.   I. Harrison, Walter T.   II. Title.
HF5636.H67   2007
657—dc22   2006103241

Executive Editor: Jodi McPherson
Editorial Director: Jeff Shelstad
Developmental Editors: Claire Hunter, Ralph Moore
Product Development Manager, Media: Nancy Welcher
Executive Marketing Manager: Sharon Koch
Associate Director, Production Editorial: Judy Leale
Permissions Supervisor: Charles Morris
Manufacturing Manager: Arnold Vila
Creative Director: Maria Lange
Cover Design: Solid State Graphics
Illustrator (Interior): BookMasters, Inc.
Director, Image Resource Center: Melinda Patelli
Manager, Rights and Permissions: Zina Arabia
Manager, Visual Research: Beth Brenzel
Manager, Cover Visual Research & Permissions: Karen Sanatar
Image Permission Coordinator: Nancy Seise
Photo Researcher: Diane Austin
Composition/Full-Service Project Management: BookMasters, Inc.
Printer/Binder: RR Donnelley–Willard
Typeface: 10/12 Sabon

Credits and acknowledgments borrowed from other sources and reproduced, with permission, in this textbook appear on appropriate page within text.

Copyright © 2008 by Pearson Education, Inc., Upper Saddle River, New Jersey, 07458.
Pearson Prentice Hall. All rights reserved. Printed in the United States of America. This publication is protected by Copyright and permission should be obtained from the publisher prior to any prohibited reproduction, storage in a retrieval system, or transmission in any form or by any means, electronic, mechanical, photocopying, recording, or likewise. For information regarding permission(s), write to: Rights and Permissions Department.

Pearson Prentice Hall™ is a trademark of Pearson Education, Inc.
Pearson® is a registered trademark of Pearson plc
Prentice Hall® is a registered trademark of Pearson Education, Inc.

Pearson Education LTD.   Pearson Education Australia PTY, Limited
Pearson Education Singapore, Pte. Ltd   Pearson Education North Asia Ltd
Pearson Education, Canada, Ltd   Pearson Educación de Mexico, S.A. de C.V.
Pearson Education–Japan   Pearson Education Malaysia, Pte. Ltd

10 9 8 7 6 5 4 3
ISBN-13: 978-0-13-614302-4
ISBN-10: 0-13-614302-4

Brief Contents

CHAPTER 12 Corporations: Retained Earnings and the Income Statement 596

CHAPTER 13 Long-Term Liabilities 640

CHAPTER 14 The Statement of Cash Flows 690

CHAPTER 15 Financial Statement Analysis 754

CHAPTER 16 Introduction to Management Accounting 806

CHAPTER 17 Job Order Costing 850

CHAPTER 18 Process Costing 900

CHAPTER 19 Activity-Based Costing and Other Cost Management Tools 958

CHAPTER 20 Cost-Volume-Profit Analysis 1006

CHAPTER 21 Short-Term Business Decisions 1056

CHAPTER 22 Capital Investment Decisions and the Time Value of Money 1110

CHAPTER 23 The Master Budget and Responsibility Accounting 1168

CHAPTER 24 Flexible Budgets and Standard Costs 1220

CHAPTER 25 Performance Evaluation and the Balanced Scorecard 1266

Appendix A: Amazon.com Annual Report A-1

Appendix B: Investments and International Operations B-1

Appendix C: Present Value Tables C-1

Photo Credits PC-1

Glindex G-1

Company Index I-1

Contents

12 Corporations: Retained Earnings and the Income Statement 596

Retained Earnings, Stock Dividends, and Stock Splits 598
Retained Earnings 598
Stock Dividends 599
Stock Splits 601
Stock Dividends and Stock Splits Compared 602

Treasury Stock 602
Purchase of Treasury Stock 602
Treasury Stock Basics 603
Sale of Treasury Stock 604

Other Stockholders' Equity Issues 605
Retirement of Stock 605
Restrictions on Retained Earnings 605
Variations in Reporting Stockholders' Equity 606

Decision Guidelines 608
▶ Summary Problem 1 609

The Corporate Income Statement 611
Continuing Operations 611
Special Items 611
Earnings per Share 613
Statement of Retained Earnings 615
Combined Statement of Income and Retained Earnings 615
Prior-Period Adjustments 616
Reporting Comprehensive Income 616

■ **Decision Guidelines** 618
▶ Summary Problem 2 619

Review and Assignment Material 621

13 Long-Term Liabilities 640

Bonds: An Introduction 642
Types of Bonds 642
Bond Prices 643
Present Value 644
Bond Interest Rates 645

Issuing Bonds Payable to Borrow Money 645
Issuing Bonds Payable at Maturity (Par) Value 646
Issuing Bonds Payable at a Discount 646

Decision Guidelines 649
▶ *Summary Problem 1 650*
Issuing Bonds Payable at a Premium 651

Additional Bond Topics 652
Adjusting Entries for Bonds Payable 652
Issuing Bonds Payable Between Interest Dates 653
Retirement of Bonds Payable 654
Convertible Bonds Payable 655
Reporting Liabilities on the Balance Sheet 655
Advantages and Disadvantages of Issuing Bonds Versus Stock 656

■ **Decision Guidelines** 658
▶ *Summary Problem 2 659*
Review and Assignment Material 661

CHAPTER APPENDIX 13A: The Time Value of Money: Present Value of a Bond and Effective-Interest Amortization 679

Comprehensive Problem for Chapters 11–13 689

14 The Statement of Cash Flows   690

Introduction: The Statement of Cash Flows   692
Cash Equivalents   693
Operating, Investing, and Financing Activities   693
Two Formats for Operating Activities   694

Preparing the Statement of Cash Flows by the Indirect Method   695
Cash Flows from Operating Activities   696
Cash Flows from Investing Activities   700
Cash Flows from Financing Activities   701
Noncash Investing and Financing Activities   703

Measuring Cash Adequacy: Free Cash Flow   704

■ **Decision Guidelines**   705

▶ *Summary Problem*   706

Review and Assignment Material   709

CHAPTER APPENDIX 14A: *Preparing the Statement of Cash Flows by the Direct Method*   736

■ **Decision Guidelines**   744

▶ *Summary Problem*   745

CHAPTER APPENDIX 14B: *Preparing the Statement of Cash Flows Using a Spreadsheet*   748

15 Financial Statement Analysis   754

Methods of Analysis   757

Horizontal Analysis   757
Illustration: Google Inc.   758
Horizontal Analysis of the Income Statement   759
Horizontal Analysis of the Balance Sheet   759
Trend Percentages   760

Vertical Analysis   760
Illustration: Google Inc.   761
How Do We Compare One Company with Another?   761

Benchmarking   762
Benchmarking Against a Key Competitor   763
Benchmarking Against the Industry Average   764

▶ Summary Problem 1   765

Using Ratios to Make Decisions   767
Measuring Ability to Pay Current Liabilities   767
Measuring Ability to Sell Inventory and Collect Receivables   769
Measuring Ability to Pay Long-Term Debt   771
Measuring Profitability   772
Analyzing Stock Investments   774

Red Flags in Financial Statement Analysis   776
■ Decision Guidelines   777

▶ Summary Problem 2   779

Review and Assignment Material   781

Comprehensive Problem for Chapters 14 and 15   804

16 Introduction to Management Accounting 806

Management Accountability 808

Today's Business Environment 811

Service Companies, Merchandising Companies, and Manufacturing Companies 812
Merchandising Companies 813

▶ *Summary Problem 1* 815

Manufacturing Companies 817

Ethical Standards 823
■ Decision Guidelines 825

▶ *Summary Problem 2* 827

Review and Assignment Material 828

17 Job Order Costing 850

How Much Does It Cost to Make a Product? Two Approaches 852
Job Order Costing for Manufacturing Products 853
Job Order Costing: Accounting for Materials and Labor 853

Decision Guidelines 859

▶ *Summary Problem 1* 860

Job Order Costing: Allocating Manufacturing Overhead 862
Allocating Manufacturing Overhead to Jobs 863

Accounting for Completion and Sale of Finished Goods and Adjusting Manufacturing Overhead 865
Accounting for the Completion and Sale of Finished Goods 865
Adjusting Underallocated or Overallocated Manufacturing Overhead at the End of the Period 866
Overview of Job Order Costing in a Manufacturing Company 868
Job Order Costing in a Service Company 868

■ **Decision Guidelines** 872

▶ *Summary Problem 2* 873

Review and Assignment Material 876

18 Process Costing 900

Process Costing: An Overview 902
Two Basic Costing Systems: Job Order Costing and Process Costing 902
How Does the Flow of Costs Differ Between Job and Process Costing? 903

Building Blocks of Process Costing 906
Conversion Costs 906
Equivalent Units of Production 906

Process Costing in First Department with No Beginning Inventory 907
Where Costs Are Added in the Manufacture of Calendars 908
Step 1: Summarize the Flow of Physical Units 909
Step 2: Compute Output in Terms of Equivalent Units 910
Step 3: Compute the Cost per Equivalent Unit 911
Step 4: Assign Costs to Units Completed and to Units in Ending Work in Process Inventory 912

- **Decision Guidelines** 914

▶ **Summary Problem 1** 915

Process Costing in a Second Department 917
The Weighted-Average Process Costing Method 917
Steps 1 and 2: Summarize the Flow of Physical Units and Compute Output in Terms of Equivalent Units 919
Step 3: Summarize Total Costs to Account For and Compute the Cost per Equivalent Unit 920
Step 4: Assign Total Costs to Units Completed and to Units in Ending Work in Process Inventory 921
How Managers Use a Production Cost Report 923

- **Decision Guidelines** 925

▶ **Summary Problem 2** 926

Review and Assignment Material 929

CHAPTER APPENDIX 18A: *The FIFO Process Costing Method* 950

19 Activity-Based Costing and Other Cost Management Tools 958

Refining Cost Systems 960
Sharpening the Focus: Assigning Costs Based on the Activities That Caused the Costs 960

Activity-Based Costing 961
Developing an Activity-Based Costing System 961
Traditional Versus Activity-Based Costing Systems: Fischer Chemical Company 962

Activity-Based Management: Using ABC for Decision Making 966
Pricing and Product Mix Decisions 966
Cutting Costs 967

■ Decision Guidelines 970

▶ Summary Problem 1 971

Just-in-Time (JIT) Systems 973
Just-in-Time Costing 973
JIT Costing Illustrated: Mintel Company 975

Continuous Improvement and the Management of Quality 977
The Four Types of Quality Costs 977
Deciding Whether to Adopt a New Quality Program 978

■ Decision Guidelines 980

▶ Summary Problem 2 981

Review and Assignment Material 982

20 Cost-Volume-Profit Analysis 1006

Cost Behavior 1008
Variable Costs 1008
Fixed Costs 1009
Mixed Costs 1010
High-Low Method to Separate Fixed Cost from Variable Cost 1010
Relevant Range 1012

Basic CVP Analysis: What Must We Sell to Break Even? 1013
Assumptions 1013
How Much Must Chan Sell to Break Even? Three Approaches 1013

Using CVP to Plan Profits 1017
How Much Must Chan Sell to Earn a Profit? 1017
Graphing Cost-Volume-Profit Relations 1017

▶ Summary Problem 1 1020

Using CVP for Sensitivity Analysis 1022
Changing the Selling Price 1022
Changing Variable Costs 1022
Changing Fixed Costs 1023
Margin of Safety 1023
Information Technology and Sensitivity Analysis 1024

Effect of Sales Mix on CVP Analysis 1025

■ Decision Guidelines 1028

▶ Summary Problem 2 1030

Review and Assignment Material 1032

CHAPTER APPENDIX 20A: Variable Costing and Absorption Costing 1049

21 Short-Term Business Decisions 1056

How Managers Make Decisions 1058
Relevant Information 1059
Relevant Nonfinancial Information 1060
Keys to Making Short-Term Special Decisions 1060
Special Sales Order and Regular Pricing Decisions 1061
When to Accept a Special Sales Order 1062
How to Set Regular Prices 1064

- **Decision Guidelines** 1070

▶ **Summary Problem 1** 1071

Other Short-Term Special Business Decisions 1073
When to Drop Products, Departments, or Territories 1073
Product Mix: Which Product to Emphasize? 1076
When to Oursource 1079
Sell As Is or Process Further? 1082

- **Decision Guidelines** 1085

▶ **Summary Problem 2** 1086

Review and Assignment Material 1088

22 Capital Investment Decisions and the Time Value of Money 1110

Capital Budgeting 1112
Four Popular Methods of Capital Budgeting Analysis 1112
Focus on Cash Flows 1113
Capital Budgeting Process 1113

Using Payback and Accounting Rate of Return to Make Capital Investment Decisions 1114
Payback Period 1114
Accounting Rate of Return (ARR) 1117

■ Decision Guidelines 1120

▶ Summary Problem 1 1121

A Review of the Time Value of Money 1122
Factors Affecting the Time Value of Money 1122
Future Values and Present Values: Points Along the Time Continuum 1123
Future Value and Present Value Factors 1124
Calculating Future Values of Single Sums and Annuities Using FV Factors 1124
Calculating Present Values of Single Sums and Annuities Using PV Factors 1126

Using Discounted Cash-Flow Models to Make Capital Budgeting Decisions 1129
Net Present Value (NVP) 1130
Internal Rate of Return (IRR) 1140

Comparing Capital Budgeting Methods 1146

■ Decision Guidelines 1148

▶ Summary Problem 2 1149

Review and Assignment Material 1150

CHAPTER APPENDIX 22A: Present Value Tables and Future Value Tables 1164

23 The Master Budget and Responsibility Accounting 1168

Why Managers Use Budgets 1168
Using Budgets to Plan and Control 1171
Benefits of Budgeting 1172

Preparing the Master Budget 1174
Components of the Master Budget 1174
Data for Whitewater Sporting Goods' Master Budget 1175

Preparing the Operating Budget 1177
The Sales Budget 1177
The Inventory, Purchases, and Cost of Goods Sold Budget 1178
The Operating Expenses Budget 1178
The Budgeted Income Statement 1179

▶ Summary Problem 1 1180

Preparing the Financial Budget 1182
Preparing the Cash Budget 1182
The Budgeted Balance Sheet 1185
The Budgeted Statement of Cash Flows 1185
Getting Employees to Accept the Budget 1185

Using Information Technology for Sensitivity Analysis and Rolling Up Unit Budgets 1186
Sensitivity Analysis 1187
Rolling Up Individual Unit Budgets into the Companywide Budget 1188

Responsibility Accounting 1189
Four Types of Responsibility Centers 1189
Responsibility Accounting Performance Reports 1191

■ Decision Guidelines 1194

▶ Summary Problem 2 1195

Review and Assignment Material 1199

24 Flexible Budgets and Standard Costs 1220

How Managers Use Flexible Budgets 1222
What Is a Flexible Budget? 1222

Using the Flexible Budget: Why Do Actual Results Differ from the Static Budget? 1224

- **Decision Guidelines** 1226

▶ **Summary Problem 1** 1227

Standard Costing 1228
Price Standards 1228
Application 1229
Quantity Standards 1229
Why Do Companies Use Standard Costs? 1230
Variance Analysis 1231

How Pluto Uses Standard Costing: Analyzing the Flexible Budget Variance 1232
Direct Material Variances 1232
Direct Labor Variances 1235

Manufacturing Overhead Variances 1236
Allocating Overhead in a Standard Cost System 1236
Overhead Flexible Budget Variance 1237
Overhead Production Volume Variance 1238
Summary of Overhead Variances 1239

Standard Cost Accounting Systems 1239
Journal Entries 1239
Standard Cost Income Statement for Management 1241

- **Decision Guidelines** 1243

▶ **Summary Problem 2** 1244

Review and Assignment Material 1247

25 Performance Evaluation and the Balanced Scorecard 1266

Decentralized Operations 1268
Advantages of Decentralization 1268
Disadvantages of Decentralization 1269
Responsibility Centers 1269

Performance Measurement 1270
Goals of Performance Evaluation Systems 1270
Limitations of Financial Performance Measurement 1272
The Balanced Scorecard 1272
The Four Perspectives of the Balanced Scorecard 1273

■ **Decision Guidelines 1278**

▶ *Summary Problem 1 1279*

Measuring the Financial Performance of Cost, Revenue, and Profit Centers 1280

Measuring the Financial Performance of Investment Centers 1283
Return on Investment (ROI) 1284
Residual Income (RI) 1287
Economic Value Added (EVA) 1288
Limitations of Financial Performance Measures 1289

■ **Decision Guidelines 1292**

▶ *Summary Problem 2 1293*

CHAPTER APPENDIX 25A: Allocating Service Department Costs 1295

Review and Assignment Material 1297

Appendix A: Amazon.com Annual Report   A-1

Appendix B: Investments and International Operations   B-1

Appendix C: Present Value Tables   C-1

Photo Credits   PC-1

Glindex   G-1

Company Index   I-1

To Billie Harrison, who taught me excellence

The *Financial and Managerial Accounting, 1e*, Demo Doc System:
For professors whose greatest joy is hearing students say "I get it!"

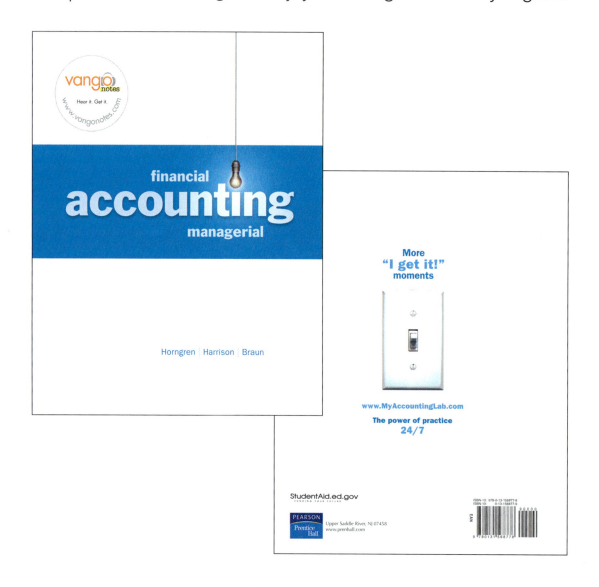

Help your students achieve "I get it!" moments when you're with them AND when you're NOT.

When you're there demonstrating how to solve a problem in class, students "get it." When you're not there, they get stuck—it's only natural.

You deliver the best "I get it!" moments, so our system is designed to support you in the classroom. (Instructor's Edition, Instructor Demo Docs)

But it's the really tricky moments, the ones no one else has zeroed in on—the 2 A.M. outside-of-class moments, when you're not there—that present the greatest challenge.

That's where we come in, at these "they have the book, but they don't have you" moments. The ability of the *Financial and Managerial Accounting, 1e*, Demo Doc System will help in those critical times. That's what makes this package different from all other textbooks.

The *Financial and Managerial Accounting, 1e,* Demo Doc System provides the vehicle for you and your students to have more "I get it!" moments inside and outside of class.

THE FINANCIAL AND MANAGERIAL ACCOUNTING, DEMO DOC SYSTEM

Duplicate the classroom experience anytime, anywhere with Horngren and Harrison's *Financial and Managerial Accounting.*

How The System Works

- The Demo Docs are entire problems worked through step-by-step, from start to finish, with the kind of comments around them that YOU would say in class. They exist in the first four chapters of this text to support the critical accounting cycle chapters, in the Study Guide both in print and in Flash versions, and as a part of the instructor package for instructors to use in class.

- The authors have created a "no clutter" layout so that critical content is clear and easily referenced.

- Consistency is stressed across all mediums: text, student, and instructor supplements.

- MyAccountingLab is an online homework system that combines "I get it!" moments with the power of practice.

The System's Backbone

Demo Docs in the Text, the Study Guide, and MyAccountingLab.

▶ **NEW DEMO DOCS** – Introductory accounting students consistently tell us, "When doing homework, I get stuck trying to solve problems the way they were demonstrated in class." Instructors consistently tell us, "I have so much to cover in so little time; I can't afford to go backward and review homework in class." Those challenges inspired us to develop Demo Docs. Demo Docs are comprehensive worked-through problems, available for nearly every chapter of our introductory accounting text, to help students when they are trying to solve exercises and problems on their own. The idea is to help students duplicate the classroom experience outside of class. Entire problems that mirror end-of-chapter material are shown solved and annotated with explanations written in a conversational style, essentially imitating what an instructor might say if standing over a student's shoulder. All Demo Docs will be available online in Flash and in print so students can easily refer to them when and where they need them.

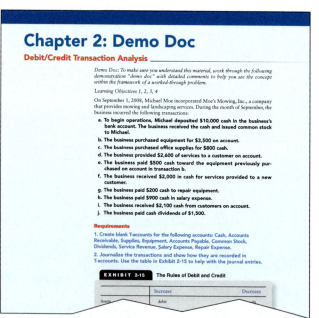

MyAccountingLab – This online homework and assessment tool supports the same theme as the text and resources by providing "I get it!" moments inside and outside of class. It is in MyAccountingLab where "I get it!" moments meet the power of practice. MyAccountingLab is about helping students at their teachable moment, whether that is 1 P.M. or 1 A.M. MyAccountingLab is packed with algorithmic problems because practice makes perfect. It is also packed with the exact same end-of-chapter material in the text that you are used to assigning for homework. MyAccountingLab features the same look and feel for exercises and problems in journal entries and financial statements so that students are familiar and comfortable working in it. Because it includes a Demo Doc for each of the end-of-chapter exercises and problems that students can refer to as they work through the question, it extends The System just one step further by providing students with the help they need to succeed when you are not with them.

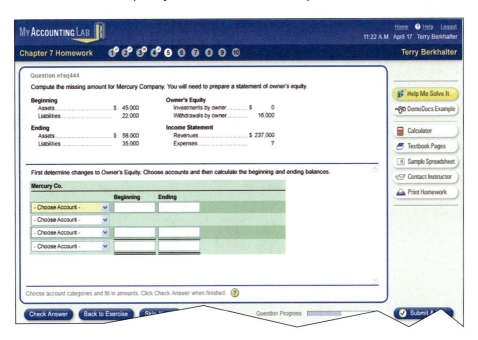

The System's Details

CHAPTERS 1–4 – We know it's critical that students have a solid understanding of the fundamentals and language surrounding the accounting cycle before they can move to practice. To that end, we're spending extra time developing the accounting cycle chapters (Chs 1–4) to make sure they will help students succeed. We're adding extra visuals, additional comprehensive problems, and a Demo Doc per chapter to give students additional support to move on through the material successfully. You'll be able to stay on schedule in the syllabus because students understand the accounting cycle.

CONSISTENCY – The entire package matters. Consistency in terminology and problem set-ups from one medium to another—test bank to study guide to MyAccountingLab—is critical to your success in the classroom. So when students ask "Where do the numbers come from?," they can go to our text **or** go online and see what to do. If it's worded one way in the text, you can count on it being worded the same way in the supplements.

CLUTTER-FREE – This edition is built on the premise of "Less is More." Extraneous boxes and features, non-essential bells and whistles—they are all gone. The authors know that excess crowds out what really matters—the concepts, the problems, and the learning objectives. Instructors asked for fewer "features" in favor of less clutter and better cross-referencing, and Horngren/Harrison, *Financial and Managerial Accounting, 1e,* is delivering on that wish. And we've redone all of the end-of-chapter exercises and problems with a renewed focus on the critical core concepts.

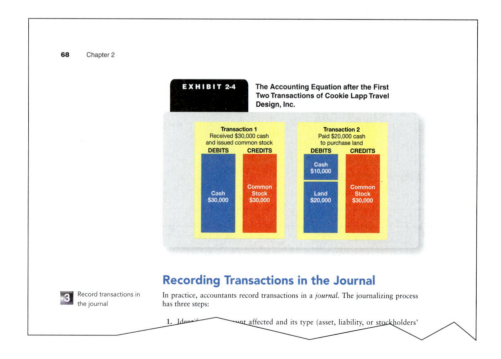

INSTRUCTOR SUPPLEMENTS

Instructor's Edition Featuring *Instructor Demo Docs*

▶ **The New Look of the Instructor's Edition**

We've asked a lot of instructors how we can help them successfully implement new course-delivery methods (e.g. online) while maintaining their regular campus schedule of classes and academic responsibilities. In response, we developed a system of instruction for those of you who are long on commitment and expertise—but short on time and assistance.

The primary goal of the Instructor's Edition is **ease of implementation, using any delivery method**—traditional, self-paced, or online. That is, the Instructor's Edition quickly answers for you, the professor, the question "What must the student do?" Likewise, the Instructor's Edition quickly answers for the student "What must I do?," offers time-saving tips with "best of" categories for in class discussion, and strong examples to illustrate difficult concepts to a wide variety of students. The Instructor's Edition also offers a quick one-shot cross-reference at the exact point of importance with key additional teaching resources, so everything is in one place. The Instructor's Edition includes summaries and teaching tips, pitfalls for new students, and "best of" practices from instructors from across the world.

▶ **The Instructor's Edition also includes *Instructor Demo Docs***

In *Instructor Demo Docs*, we walk the students through how to solve a problem as if it were the first time they've seen it. There are no lengthy passages of text. Instead, bits of expository text are woven into the steps needed to solve the problem, in the exact sequence—for you to provide at the teachable *"I get it!"* moment. This is the point at which the student has a context within which he or she can understand the concept. We provide conversational text around each of the steps so the student stays engaged in solving the problem. We provide notes to the instructor for key teaching points around the Demo Docs, and "best of" practice tid-bits before each *Instructor Demo Doc*.

The *Instructor Demo Docs* are written with all of your everyday classroom realities in mind—and trying to save your time in prepping new examples each time your book changes. Additionally, algorithmic versions of these Demo Docs are provided to students in their student guide. We keep the terminology consistent with the text, so there are no surprises for students as they try and work through a problem the first time.

Solutions Transparencies

These transparency masters are the **Solutions Manual** in an easy-to-use format for class lectures.

Instructor's Resource Center CD or www.prenhall.com/horngren

The password-protected site and resource CD includes the following:
- **The Instructor's Edition with *Instructor Demo Docs***
- **Problem Set C**

- **Solutions Manual with Interactive Excel Solutions**

  The Solutions Manual contains solutions to all end-of-chapter questions, multiple-choice questions, short exercises, exercise sets, problems sets, and Internet exercises. The Solutions Manual is available in Microsoft Excel, Microsoft Word, and in print. You can access the solutions in MS Excel and MS Word formats by visiting the Instructor's Resource Center on the Prentice Hall catalog site at www.prenhall.com/horngren or on the Instructor's CD. You will need a Pearson Educator username and password to retrieve materials from the Web site.

  Solutions to select end-of-chapter exercises and problems are available in **interactive MS Excel format** so that instructors can present material in dynamic, step-by-step sequences in class. The interactive solutions were prepared by Kathleen O'Donnell of the State University of New York, Onondaga Community College.

- **Test Bank**

The test item file includes more than 2,000 questions:
  - Multiple Choice
  - Matching
  - True/False
  - Computational Problems
  - Essay

- **Test Bank** is formatted for use with WebCT, Blackboard, and Course Compass.

- **PowerPoints (instructor and student)** summarize and reinforce key text materials. They capture classroom attention with original problems and solved step-by-step exercises. These walk-throughs are designed to help facilitate classroom discussion and demonstrate where the numbers come from and what they mean to the concept at hand. There are approximately 35 slides per chapter. PowerPoints are available on the Instructor's CD and can be downloaded from www.prenhall.com/horngren.

New *MyAccountingLab* Online Homework and Assessment Manager

The **"I get it!"** moment meets *the power of practice*. The power of repetition when you "get it" means learning happens. **MyAccountingLab** is about helping students at their teachable moments, whether it's 1 P.M. or 1A.M.

MyAccountingLab is an online homework and assessment tool, packed with algorithmic versions of every text problem, because practice makes perfect. It's also packed with the exact same end-of-chapter material that you're used to assigning for homework. Additionally, **MyAccountingLab** includes:

1. A **Demo Doc** for each of the end-of-chapter exercises and problems that students can refer to as they work through the questions.
2. A **Guided Solution** to the exact problem they are working on. It helps students when they're trying to solve a problem the way it was demonstrated in class.
3. A full **e-book** so the students can reference the book at the point of practice.
4. New **topic specific videos** that walk students through difficult concepts.

Companion Web Site–www.prenhall.com/horngren

The book's Web site at www.prenhall.com/horngren—contains the following:
- Self-study quizzes—interactive study guide for each chapter
- MS Excel templates that students can use to complete homework assignments for each chapter (e-working papers)
- Samples of the Flash Demo Docs for students to work through the accounting cycle

Online Courses with WebCT/BlackBoard/Course Compass

Prentice Hall offers a link to MyAccountingLab through the Bb and WebCT Course Management Systems.

Classroom Response Systems (CRS)

CRS is an exciting new wireless polling technology that makes large and small classrooms even more interactive, because it enables instructors to pose questions to their students, record results, and display those results instantly. Students can easily answer questions using compact remote-control–type transmitters. Prentice Hall has partnerships with leading classroom response-systems providers and can show you everything you need to know about setting up and using a CRS system. Prentice Hall will provide the classroom hardware, text-specific PowerPoint slides, software, and support.

Visit **www.prenhall.com/crs** to learn more.

STUDENT SUPPLEMENTS

Runners Corporation PT Lab Manual

Containing numerous simulated real-world examples, the **Runners Corporation** practice set is available complete with data files for Peachtree, QuickBooks, and PH General Ledger. Each practice set also includes business stationery for manual entry work.

A-1 Photography-Manual PT Lab Manual

Containing numerous simulated real-world examples, the **A-1 Photography** practice set is available complete with data files for Peachtree, QuickBooks, and PH General Ledger. Each set includes business stationery for manual entry work.

Study Guide including Demo Docs and e-Working Papers

Introductory accounting students consistently tell us, "When doing homework, I get stuck trying to solve problems the way they were demonstrated in class." Instructors consistently tell us, "I have so much to cover in so little time; I can't afford to go backwards and review homework in class." Those challenges inspired us to develop Demo Docs. Demo Docs are comprehensive worked-through problems available for nearly every chapter of our introductory accounting text to help students when they are trying to solve exercises and problems on their own. The idea is to help students duplicate the classroom experience outside of class. Entire problems that mirror end-of-chapter material are shown solved and annotated with explanations written in a conversational style, essentially imitating what an instructor might say if standing over a student's shoulder. All Demo Docs will be available in the Study Guide—in print and on CD in Flash, so students can easily refer to them when they need them. The Study Guide also includes a summary overview of key topics and multiple-choice and short-answer questions for students to test their knowledge. Free electronic working papers are included on the accompanying CD.

MyAccountingLab Online Homework and Assessment Manager

The **"I get it!"** moment meets **power of practice**. The power of repetition when you "get it" means that learning happens. **MyAccountingLab** is about helping students at their teachable moment, whether that is 1 P.M. or 1 A.M.

MyAccountingLab is an online homework and assessment tool, packed with algorithmic versions of every text problem because practice makes perfect. It's also packed with the exact same end-of-chapter that you're used to assigning for homework. Additionally, **MyAccountingLab** includes:

1. A **Demo Doc** for each of the end-of-chapter exercises and problems that students can refer to as they work through the question.
2. A **Guided Solution** to the exact problem they are working on. It helps students when they're trying to solve a problem the way it was demonstrated in class.
3. A full **e-book** so the students can reference the book at the point of practice.
4. New **topic specific videos** that walk students through difficult concepts.

PowerPoints

For student use as a study aide or note-taking guide, these PowerPoint slides may be downloaded at the companion Web site at www.prenhall.com/horngren.

Companion Web Site–www.prenhall.com/horngren

The book's Web site at www.prenhall.com/horngren—contains the following:

- Self-study quizzes—interactive study guide for each chapter
- MS Excel templates that students can use to complete homework assignments for each chapter (e-working papers)
- Samples of the Flash Demo Docs for students to work through the accounting cycle

Classroom Response Systems (CRS)

CRS is an exciting new wireless polling technology that makes large and small classrooms even more interactive because it enables instructors to pose questions to their students, record results, and display those results instantly. Students can easily answer questions using compact remote-control-type transmitters. Prentice Hall has partnerships with leading classroom response-systems providers and can show you everything you need to know about setting up and using a CRS system. Prentice Hall will provide the classroom hardware, text-specific PowerPoint slides, software, and support.

Visit **www.prenhall.com/crs** to learn more.

- **VangoNotes in MP3 Format**

  Students can study on the go with VangoNotes, chapter reviews in downloadable MP3 format that offer brief audio segments for each chapter:
  - Big Ideas: the vital ideas in each chapter
  - Practice Test: lets students know if they need to keep studying
  - Key Terms: audio "flashcards" that review key concepts and terms
  - Rapid Review: a quick drill session—helpful right before tests

  Students can learn more at **www.vangonotes.com**

Hear it. Get It.

Study on the go with VangoNotes.

Just download chapter reviews from your text and listen to them on any mp3 player. Now wherever you are-- whatever you're doing--you can study by listening to the following for each chapter of your textbook:

Big Ideas: Your "need to know" for each chapter

Practice Test: A gut check for the Big Ideas--tells you if you need to keep studying

Key Terms: Audio "flashcards" to help you review key concepts and terms

Rapid Review: A quick drill session--use it right before your test

VangoNotes.com

Acknowledgments

We'd like to thank the following contributors:

Florence McGovern *Bergen Community College*
Sherry Mills *New Mexico State University*
Suzanne Oliver *Okaloosa Walton Junior College*
Helen Brubeck *San Jose State University*

We'd like to extend a special thank you to the following members of our advisory panel:

Jim Ellis *Bay State College, Boston*
Mary Ann Swindlehurst *Carroll Community College*
Andy Williams *Edmonds Community College*
Donnie Kristof-Nelson *Edmonds Community College*
Joan Cezair *Fayetteville State University*
David Baglia *Grove City College*
Anita Ellzey *Harford Community College*
Cheryl McKay *Monroe County Community College*
Todd Jackson *Northeastern State University*
Margaret Costello Lambert *Oakland Community College*
Al Fagan *University of Richmond*

We'd also like to thank the following reviewers:

Shi-Mu (Simon) Yang *Adelphi University*
Thomas Stolberg *Alfred State University*
Thomas Branton *Alvin Community College*
Maria Lehoczky *American Intercontinental University*
Suzanne Bradford *Angelina College*
Judy Lewis *Angelo State University*
Roy Carson *Anne Arundel Community College*
Paulette Ratliff-Miller *Arkansas State University*
Joseph Foley *Assumption College*
Jennifer Niece *Assumption College*
Bill Whitley *Athens State University*
Shelly Gardner *Augustana College*

Becky Jones *Baylor University*
Betsy Willis *Baylor University*
Michael Robinson *Baylor University*
Kay Walker-Hauser *Beaufort County Community College, Washington*
Joe Aubert *Bemidji State University*
Calvin Fink *Bethune Cookman College*
Michael Blue *Bloomsburg University*
Scott Wallace *Blue Mountain College*
Lloyd Carroll *Borough Manhattan Community College*
Ken Duffe *Brookdale Community College*
Chuck Heuser *Brookdale Community College*
Shafi Ullah *Broward Community College South*
Lois Slutsky *Broward Community College South*
Ken Koerber *Bucks County Community College*

Julie Browning *California Baptist University*
Richard Savich *California State University—San Bernardino*
David Bland *Cape Fear Community College*
Robert Porter *Cape Fear Community College*
Vickie Campbell *Cape Fear Community College*
Cynthia Thompson *Carl Sandburg College—Carthage*

Liz Ott *Casper College*
Joseph Adamo *Cazenovia College*
Julie Dailey *Central Virginia Community College*
Jeannie Folk *College of DuPage*
Lawrence Steiner *College of Marin*
Dennis Kovach *Community College Allegheny County—Allegheny*
Norma Montague *Central Carolina Community College*
Debbie Schmidt *Cerritos College*
Janet Grange *Chicago State University*
Bruce Leung *City College of San Francisco*
Pamela Legner *College of DuPage*
Bruce McMurrey *Community College of Denver*
Martin Sabo *Community College of Denver*
Jeffrey Jones *Community College of Southern Nevada*
Tom Nohl *Community College of Southern Nevada*
Christopher Kelly *Community College of Southern Nevada*
Patrick Rogan *Cosumnes River College*
Kimberly Smith *County College of Morris*

Jerold Braun *Daytona Beach Community College*
Greg Carlton *Davidson County Community College*
Irene Bembenista *Davenport University*
Thomas Szczurek *Delaware County Community College*
Charles Betts *Delaware Technical and Community College*
Patty Holmes *Des Moines Area Community College—Ankeny*
Tim Murphy *Diablo Valley College*

Phillipe Sammour *Eastern Michigan University*
Saturnino (Nino) Gonzales *El Paso Community College*
Lee Cannell *El Paso Community College*
John Eagan *Erie Community College*

Ron O'Brien *Fayetteville Technical Community College*
Patrick McNabb *Ferris State University*
John Stancil *Florida Southern College*
Lynn Clements *Florida Southern College*
Alice Sineath *Forsyth Technical Community College*
James Makofske *Fresno City College*
Marc Haskell *Fresno City College*
James Kelly *Ft. Lauderdale City College*

Christine Jonick *Gainesville State College*
Bruce Lindsey *Genesee Community College*
Constance Hylton *George Mason University*
Cody King *Georgia Southwestern State University*
Lolita Keck *Globe College*
Kay Carnes *Gonzaga University, Spokane*
Carol Pace *Grayson County College*
Rebecca Floor *Greenville Technical College*
Geoffrey Heriot *Greenville Technical College*
Jeffrey Patterson *Grove City College*
Lanny Nelms *Gwinnet Technical College*
Chris Cusatis *Gwynedd Mercy College*

Tim Griffin *Hillsborough Community College*
Clair Helms *Hinds Community College*
Michelle Powell *Holmes Community College*
Greg Bischoff *Houston Community College*
Donald Bond *Houston Community College*
Marina Grau *Houston Community College*
Carolyn Fitzmorris *Hutchinson Community College*

Susan Koepke *Illinois Valley Community College*
William Alexander *Indian Hills Community College—Ottumwa*
Dale Bolduc *Intercoast College*
Thomas Carr *International College of Naples*
Lecia Berven *Iowa Lakes Community College*
Nancy Schendel *Iowa Lakes Community College*
Michelle Cannon *Ivy Tech*
Vicki White *Ivy Tech*
Chuck Smith *Iowa Western Community College*

Stephen Christian *Jackson Community College*
DeeDee Daughtry *Johnston Community College*
Richard Bedwell *Jones County Junior College*

Ken Mark *Kansas City Kansas Community College*
Ken Snow *Kaplan Education Centers*
Charles Evans *Keiser College*
Bunney Schmidt *Keiser College*
Amy Haas *Kingsborough Community College*

Jim Racic *Lakeland Community College*
Doug Clouse *Lakeland Community College*

Patrick Haggerty *Lansing Community College*
Patricia Walczak *Lansing Community College*
Humberto M. Herrera *Laredo Community College*
Christie Comunale *Long Island University*
Ariel Markelevich *Long Island University*
Randy Kidd *Longview Community College*
Kathy Heltzel *Luzerne County Community College*
Lori Major *Luzerne County Community College*

Fred Jex *Macomb Community College*
Glenn Owen *Marymount College*
Behnaz Quigley *Marymount College*
Penny Hanes *Mercyhurst College, Erie*
John Miller *Metropolitan Community College*
Denise Leggett *Middle Tennessee State University*
William Huffman *Missouri Southern State College*
Ted Crosby *Montgomery County Community College*
Beth Engle *Montgomery County Community College*
David Candelaria *Mount San Jacinto College*
Linda Bolduc *Mount Wachusett Community College*

Barbara Gregorio *Nassau Community College*
James Hurat *National College of Business and Technology*
Denver Riffe *National College of Business and Technology*
Asokan Anandarajan *New Jersey Institute of Technology*
Robert Schoener *New Mexico State University*
Stanley Carroll *New York City Technical College of CUNY*
Audrey Agnello *Niagara County Community College*
Catherine Chiang *North Carolina Central University*
Karen Russom *North Harris College*
Dan Bayak *Northampton Community College*
Elizabeth Lynn Locke *Northern Virginia Community College*
Debra Prendergast *Northwestern Business College*
Nat Briscoe *Northwestern State University*
Tony Scott *Norwalk Community College*

Deborah Niemer *Oakland Community College*
John Boyd *Oklahoma City Community College*
Kathleen O'Donnell *Onondaga Community College*
J.T. Ryan *Onondaga Community College*

Toni Clegg *Palm Beach Atlantic College*
David Forsyth *Palomar College*
John Graves *PCDI*
Carla Rich *Pensacola Junior College*
Judy Grotrian *Peru State College*
Judy Daulton *Piedmont Technical College*
John Stone *Potomac State College*
Betty Habershon *Prince George's Community College*

Kathi Villani *Queensborough Community College*

William Black *Raritan Valley Community College*
Verne Ingram *Red Rocks Community College*
Paul Juriga *Richland Community College*
Patty Worsham *Riverside Community College*
Margaret Berezewski *Robert Morris College*
Phil Harder *Robert Morris College*
Shifei Chung *Rowan University of New Jersey*

Charles Fazzi *Saint Vincent College*
Lynnette Yerbuy *Salt Lake Community College*
Susan Blizzard *San Antonio College*
Hector Martinez *San Antonio College*
Audrey Voyles *San Diego Miramar College*
Margaret Black *San Jacinto College*
Merrily Hoffman *San Jacinto College*
Randall Whitmore *San Jacinto College*
Carroll Buck *San Jose State University*
Cynthia Coleman *Sandhills Community College*
Barbara Crouteau *Santa Rosa Junior College*
Pat Novak *Southeast Community College*
Susan Pallas *Southeast Community College*
Al Case *Southern Oregon University*
Gloria Worthy *Southwest Tennessee Community College*
Melody Ashenfelter *Southwestern Oklahoma State University*
Douglas Ward *Southwestern Community College*
Brandi Shay *Southwestern Community College*
John May *Southwestern Oklahoma State University*
Jeffrey Waybright *Spokane Community College*
Renee Goffinet *Spokane Community College*
Susan Anders *St. Bonaventure University*
John Olsavsky *SUNY at Fredonia*
Peter Van Brunt *SUNY College of Technology at Delhi*

David L. Davis *Tallahassee Community College*
Kathy Crusto-Way *Tarrant County Community College*
Sally Cook *Texas Lutheran University*
Bea Chiang *The College of New Jersey*
Matt Hightower *Three Rivers Community College*

Susan Pope *University of Akron*
Joe Woods *University of Arkansas*
Allen Blay *University of California, Riverside*

Barry Mishra *University of California, Riverside*
Laura Young *University of Central Arkansas*
Jane Calvert *University of Central Oklahoma*
Bambi Hora *University of Central Oklahoma*
Joan Stone *University of Central Oklahoma*
Kathy Terrell *University of Central Oklahoma*
Harlan Etheridge *University of Louisiana*
Pam Meyer *University of Louisiana*
Sandra Scheuermann *University of Louisiana*
Tom Wilson *University of Louisiana*
Lawrence Leaman *University of Michigan*
Larry Huus *University of Minnesota*
Brian Carpenter *University of Scranton*
Ashraf Khallaf *University of Southern Indiana*
Tony Zordan *University of St. Francis*
Gene Elrod *University of Texas, Arlington*
Cheryl Prachyl *University of Texas, El Paso*
Karl Putnam *University of Texas, El Paso*
Stephen Rockwell *University of Tulsa*
Chula King *University of West Florida*
Charles Baird *University of Wisconsin—Stout*

Mary Hollars *Vincennes University*
Lisa Nash *Vincennes University*
Elaine Dessouki *Virginia Wesleyan College*

Sueann Hely *West Kentucky Community and Technical College*
Darlene Pulliam *West Texas A&M University, Canyon*
Judy Beebe *Western Oregon University*
Michelle Maggio *Westfield State College*
Kathy Pellegrino *Westfield State College*
Nora McCarthy *Wharton County Junior College*
Sally Stokes *Wilmington College*
Maggie Houston *Wright State University*

Gerald Caton *Yavapai College*
Chris Crosby *York Technical College*
Harold Gellis *York College of CUNY*

About the Authors

Charles T. Horngren is the Edmund W. Littlefield Professor of Accounting, Emeritus, at Stanford University. A graduate of Marquette University, he received his M.B.A. from Harvard University and his Ph.D. from the University of Chicago. He is also the recipient of honorary doctorates from Marquette University and DePaul University.

A Certified Public Accountant, Horngren served on the Accounting Principles Board for six years, the Financial Accounting Standards Board Advisory Council for five years, and the Council of the American Institute of Certified Public Accountants for three years. For six years, he served as a trustee of the Financial Accounting Foundation, which oversees the Financial Accounting Standards Board and the Government Accounting Standards Board.

Horngren is a member of the Accounting Hall of Fame.

A member of the American Accounting Association, Horngren has been its President and its Director of Research. He received its first annual Outstanding Accounting Educator Award.

The California Certified Public Accountants Foundation gave Horngren its Faculty Excellence Award and its Distinguished Professor Award. He is the first person to have received both awards.

The American Institute of Certified Public Accountants presented its first Outstanding Educator Award to Horngren.

Horngren was named Accountant of the Year, Education, by the national professional accounting fraternity, Beta Alpha Psi.

Professor Horngren is also a member of the Institute of Management Accountants, from whom he has received its Distinguished Service Award. He was a member of the Institute's Board of Regents, which administers the Certified Management Accountant examinations.

Horngren is the author of other accounting books published by Prentice-Hall: *Cost Accounting: A Managerial Emphasis*, Twelfth Edition, 2006 (with Srikant Datar and George Foster); *Introduction to Financial Accounting*, Ninth Edition, 2006 (with Gary L. Sundem and John A. Elliott); *Introduction to Management Accounting*, Thirteenth Edition, 2005 (with Gary L. Sundem and William Stratton); *Financial Accounting*, Sixth Edition, 2006 (with Walter T. Harrison, Jr.).

Horngren is the Consulting Editor for Prentice-Hall's Charles T. Horngren Series in Accounting.

Walter T. Harrison, Jr. is Professor Emeritus of Accounting at the Hankamer School of Business, Baylor University. He received his B.B.A. degree from Baylor University, his M.S. from Oklahoma State University, and his Ph.D. from Michigan State University.

Professor Harrison, recipient of numerous teaching awards from student groups as well as from university administrators, has also taught at Cleveland State Community College, Michigan State University, the University of Texas, and Stanford University.

A member of the American Accounting Association and the American Institute of Certified Public Accountants, Professor Harrison has served as Chairman of the Financial Accounting Standards Committee of the American Accounting Association, on the Teaching/Curriculum Development Award Committee, on the Program Advisory

Committee for Accounting Education and Teaching, and on the Notable Contributions to Accounting Literature Committee.

Professor Harrison has lectured in several foreign countries and published articles in numerous journals, including *Journal of Accounting Research*, *Journal of Accountancy*, *Journal of Accounting and Public Policy*, *Economic Consequences of Financial Accounting Standards*, *Accounting Horizons*, *Issues in Accounting Education*, and *Journal of Law and Commerce*.

He is co-author of *Financial Accounting*, Sixth Edition, 2006 (with Charles T. Horngren), published by Prentice Hall. Professor Harrison has received scholarships, fellowships, and research grants or awards from PriceWaterhouse Coopers, Deloitte & Touche, the Ernst & Young Foundation, and the KPMG Foundation.

Financial and Managerial Accounting

Chapters 12–25

1e

12 Corporations: Retained Earnings and the Income Statement

Learning Objectives

1. Account for stock dividends
2. Distinguish stock splits from stock dividends
3. Account for treasury stock
4. Report restrictions on retained earnings
5. Analyze a corporate income statement

Chapter 11 introduced corporations and covered the basics of stockholders' equity. Our feature company was IHOP, the restaurant chain. We saw that a corporation's balance sheet is the same as for a proprietorship or a partnership, except for owners' equity. Chapter 11 began with IHOP's issuance of common stock and also covered the declaration and payment of cash dividends.

This chapter takes corporate equity a few steps further, as follows:

Chapter 11 Covered	Chapter 12 Covers
Paid-in capital	Retained earnings
Issuing stock	Buying back a corporation's stock (treasury stock)
Cash dividends	Stock dividends and stock splits
Corporate balance sheet	Corporate income statement

Chapter 12 completes our discussion of corporate equity. It begins with *stock dividends* and *stock splits*—terms you've probably heard. Let's see what these terms mean.

Retained Earnings, Stock Dividends, and Stock Splits

We've seen that the owners' equity of a corporation is called *stockholders' equity* or *shareholders' equity*. Paid-in capital and retained earnings make up stockholders' equity. We studied paid-in capital in Chapter 11. Now let's focus on retained earnings.

Retained Earnings

Retained Earnings carries the balance of the business's accumulated lifetime net income less all net losses and less all dividends. A debit balance in Retained Earnings is called a *deficit*. Retained earnings deficits are rare because these companies go out of business. When you see a balance sheet, remember this about Retained Earnings:

1. **Credits to Retained Earnings arise only from net income.** Retained Earnings shows how much net income a corporation has earned and retained over its entire lifetime.

2. **The Retained Earnings account is not a reservoir of cash.** Retained Earnings represents no asset in particular. In fact, the corporation may have a large balance in Retained Earnings but insufficient cash to pay a dividend.

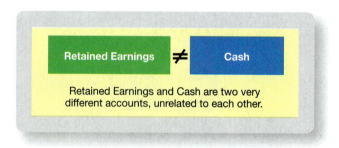

3. Retained Earnings' ending balance is computed as follows (amounts assumed):

Beginning balance	$ 70,000
Add: Net income for the year	80,000
Less: Net loss (none this year)	
Dividends for the year	(50,000)
Ending balance	$100,000

Stock Dividends

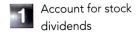 Account for stock dividends

A **stock dividend** is a distribution of a corporation's own stock to its stockholders. Unlike cash dividends, stock dividends do not give any assets to the stockholders. Stock dividends:

- Affect *only* stockholders' equity accounts (including Retained Earnings and Common Stock)
- Have *no* effect on total stockholders' equity
- Have *no* effect on assets or liabilities

As Exhibit 12-1 shows, a stock dividend decreases Retained Earnings and increases Common Stock. A stock dividend is a transfer from Retained Earnings to Common Stock. Total equity is unchanged.

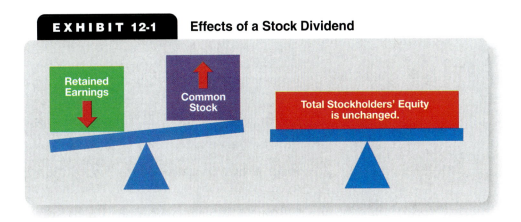

EXHIBIT 12-1 Effects of a Stock Dividend

The corporation distributes stock dividends to stockholders in proportion to the number of shares they already own. Suppose you own 300 shares of IHOP common stock. If IHOP distributes a 10% stock dividend, you would receive 30 (300 × 0.10) additional shares. You would now own 330 shares of the stock. All other IHOP stockholders also receive additional shares equal to 10% of their holdings, so you are all in the same relative position after the dividend as before.

Why Issue Stock Dividends?

A company issues stock dividends for several reasons:

1. **To continue dividends but conserve cash.** A company may wish to continue dividends but need to keep its cash.
2. **To reduce the market price of its stock.** A stock dividend may cause the company's stock price to fall because of the increased supply of the stock. A share of IHOP stock has traded at $50 recently. Doubling the shares outstanding by issuing a stock dividend would drop IHOP's stock price to $25 per share. The objective is to make the stock less expensive and, thus, more attractive to investors.

Recording Stock Dividends

As with a cash dividend, there are three dates for a stock dividend:
- Declaration date
- Record date
- Distribution (payment) date

The board of directors announces the stock dividend on the declaration date. The date of record and the distribution date then follow.

The declaration of a stock dividend does *not* create a liability because the corporation is not obligated to pay assets. (Recall that a liability is a claim on *assets*.) With a stock dividend, the corporation has declared its intention to distribute its stock. Assume that IHOP has the following stockholders' equity prior to a stock dividend:

IHOP CORP.
STOCKHOLDERS' EQUITY (ADAPTED, IN THOUSANDS)

Paid-in capital:	
Common stock, $1 par, 1,000 shares authorized, 200 shares issued..	$ 200
Paid-in capital in excess of par	31,800
Total paid-in capital	32,000
Retained earnings	308,000
Total stockholders' equity	$340,000

The entry to record a stock dividend depends on its size. Generally accepted accounting principles distinguish between

- A *small* stock dividend (less than 20% to 25% of issued stock)
- A *large* stock dividend (25% or more of issued stock)

Stock dividends between 20% and 25% are rare.

SMALL STOCK DIVIDENDS—LESS THAN 20% TO 25% Small stock dividends are accounted for at their market value. Here's how the various accounts are affected:

- Retained Earnings is debited for the market value of the dividend shares.
- Common Stock is credited for the dividend stock's par value.
- Paid-In Capital in Excess of Par is credited for the remainder.

Assume IHOP distributes a stock dividend when the market value of IHOP common stock is $50 per share. Exhibit 12-2 illustrates the accounting for a 10% stock dividend.[1]

EXHIBIT 12-2   Accounting for a Stock Dividend

Small Stock Dividend—For Example, 10% (Amounts in thousands)		
Retained Earnings		
(200 × 0.10 × $50 market value)	1,000	
Common Stock		
(200 × 0.10 × $1 par)		20
Paid-In Capital in Excess of Par		980

A stock dividend does not affect assets, liabilities, or *total* stockholders' equity. A stock dividend merely rearranges the equity accounts, leaving total equity unchanged. Exhibit 12-3 shows IHOP's stockholders' equity after the stock dividend.

---

[1] A stock dividend can be recorded with two journal entries—for (1) the declaration and (2) the stock distribution. But most companies record stock dividends with a single entry on the date of distribution, as we illustrate here.

EXHIBIT 12-3 Stockholders' Equity after a Stock Dividend—IHOP Corporation

IHOP Corporation Stockholders' Equity (Adapted, in Thousands)	
Paid-in capital:	
Common stock, $1 par, 1,000 shares authorized, 220 shares issued ($200 + $20)	$ 220
Paid-in capital in excess of par ($31,800 + $980)	32,780
Total paid-in capital	33,000
Retained earnings ($308,000 − $1,000)	307,000
Total stockholders' equity	$340,000

Observe that total stockholders' equity stays at $340,000.

LARGE STOCK DIVIDENDS—25% OR MORE Large stock dividends are rare, so we do not illustrate them. Instead of large stock dividends, companies split their stock, as we illustrate next.

Stock Splits

A **stock split** is fundamentally different from a stock dividend. A stock split increases the number of authorized, issued, and outstanding shares of stock. A stock split also decreases par value per share. For example, if IHOP splits its stock 2 for 1, the number of outstanding shares is doubled and par value per share is cut in half. A stock split also decreases the market price of the stock.

The market price of a share of IHOP common stock has been approximately $50. Assume that IHOP wishes to decrease the market price to approximately $25. IHOP can split its stock 2 for 1, and market price will drop to around $25. A 2-for-1 stock split means that IHOP will have twice as many shares of stock outstanding after the split as before, and each share's par value is cut in half. Assume that IHOP had issued 200,000 shares of $1 par common stock before the split. Exhibit 12-4 shows how a 2-for-1 split affects IHOP's equity.

EXHIBIT 12-4 A 2-for-1 Stock Split

IHOP Stockholders' Equity (Adapted, in Thousands)			
Before 2-for-1 Stock Split		After 2-for-1 Stock Split	
Paid-in capital:		Paid-in capital:	
Common stock, $1.00 par, 1,000 shares authorized, 200 shares issued	$ 200	Common stock, $0.50 par, 2,000 shares authorized, 400 shares issued	$ 200
Paid-in capital in excess of par	31,800	Paid-in capital in excess of par	31,800
Total paid-in capital	32,000	Total paid-in capital	32,000
Retained earnings	308,000	Retained earnings	308,000
Total stockholders' equity	$340,000	Total stockholders' equity	$340,000

Study the exhibit and you'll see that a 2-for-1 stock split:

- Cuts par value per share in half
- Doubles the shares of stock authorized and issued
- Leaves all account balances and total equity unchanged

Because the stock split affects no account balances, no formal journal entry is needed. Instead, the split is recorded in a *memorandum entry* such as the following:

Aug. 19	Split the common stock 2 for 1. Called in the $1.00 par common stock and distributed two shares of $0.50 par common stock for each old share. Now 400 shares are outstanding.

Stock Dividends and Stock Splits Compared

 Distinguish stock splits from stock dividends

Stock dividends and stock splits have some similarities and differences. Exhibit 12-5 summarizes their effects on stockholders' equity. For completeness, it also covers cash dividends.

EXHIBIT 12-5 Effects of Dividends and Stock Splits

Event	Common Stock	Paid-In Capital in Excess of Par	Retained Earnings	Total Stockholders' Equity
Cash dividend	No effect	No effect	Decrease	Decrease
Stock dividend	Increase	Increase	Decrease	No effect
Stock split	No effect	No effect	No effect	No effect

Treasury Stock

Account for treasury stock

A company's own stock that it has issued and later reacquired is called **treasury stock**.[2] In effect, the corporation holds the stock in its treasury. A corporation such as IHOP may purchase treasury stock for several reasons:

1. Management wants to increase net assets by buying low and selling high.
2. Management wants to support the company's stock price.
3. Management wants to avoid a takeover by an outside party.

Treasury stock transactions are common among corporations. A recent survey of 600 companies showed that 66% held treasury stock. Now let's see how to account for treasury stock.

Purchase of Treasury Stock

Jupiter Cable Company had the following stockholders' equity before purchasing treasury stock:

---

[2]We illustrate the *cost* method of accounting for treasury stock because it is used most widely. Intermediate accounting courses also cover an alternative method.

JUPITER CABLE COMPANY	
Stockholders' Equity [*Before* Purchase of Treasury Stock]	
Paid-in capital:	
Common stock, $1 par, 10,000 shares authorized and issued	$10,000
Paid-in capital in excess of par	12,000
Total paid-in capital	22,000
Retained earnings	23,000
Total stockholders' equity	$45,000

On March 31, Jupiter purchased 1,000 shares of treasury stock, paying $5 per share. Debit Treasury Stock and credit Cash as follows:

Mar. 31	Treasury Stock (1,000 × $5)	5,000	
	Cash		5,000
	Purchased treasury stock.		

Treasury Stock

5,000	

Treasury Stock Basics

Here are the basics of accounting for treasury stock:

- The Treasury Stock account has a debit balance, which is the opposite of the other equity accounts. Therefore, *Treasury Stock* is *contra equity*.
- Treasury stock is recorded at cost, without reference to par value.
- The Treasury Stock account is reported beneath Retained Earnings on the balance sheet, subtracted as follows:

JUPITER CABLE COMPANY	
Stockholders' Equity [*After* Purchase of Treasury Stock]	
Paid-in capital:	
Common stock, $1 par, 10,000 shares authorized and issued	$10,000
Paid-in capital in excess of par	12,000
Total paid-in capital	22,000
Retained earnings	23,000
Subtotal	45,000
Less: Treasury stock, 1,000 shares at cost	(5,000)
Total stockholders' equity	$40,000

Treasury stock decreases the company's stock that's outstanding, that is, held by the stockholders. We compute outstanding stock as follows:

$$\frac{\text{Outstanding}}{\text{stock}} = \frac{\text{Issued}}{\text{stock}} - \frac{\text{Treasury}}{\text{stock}}$$

Outstanding shares are important because only outstanding shares have voting rights and receive cash dividends. Treasury stock doesn't carry a vote, and it gets no dividends.

Sale of Treasury Stock

Companies buy their treasury stock with a view toward reselling it. A company may sell treasury stock at its cost, above cost, or below cost.

Sale at Cost

If treasury stock is sold for cost—the same price the corporation paid for it—then debit Cash and credit Treasury Stock for the same amount.

Sale Above Cost

If treasury stock is sold for more than cost, the difference is credited to a new account, Paid-In Capital from Treasury Stock Transactions. This excess is additional paid-in capital because it came from the company's stockholders. It has no effect on net income. Suppose Jupiter Cable Company resold its treasury shares for $9 per share (cost was $5). The entry to sell treasury stock for a price above cost is:

Dec. 7	Cash (1,000 × $9)	9,000	
	Treasury Stock (1,000 × $5 cost)		5,000
	Paid-In Capital from Treasury Stock Transactions		4,000
	Sold treasury stock.		

Treasury Stock	
5,000	5,000
0	

Paid-In Capital from Treasury Stock Transactions is reported with the other paid-in capital accounts on the balance sheet, beneath Common Stock and Paid-In Capital in Excess of Par, as shown here:

JUPITER CABLE COMPANY
Stockholders' Equity [*After* Purchase and Sale of Treasury Stock]

Paid-in capital:	
Common stock, $1 par, 10,000 shares authorized and issued	$10,000
Paid-in capital in excess of par	12,000
Paid-in capital from treasury stock transactions	4,000
Total paid-in capital	26,000
Retained earnings	23,000
Total stockholders' equity	$49,000

Exhibit 12-6 tracks stockholders' equity to show how treasury stock transactions affect corporate equity.

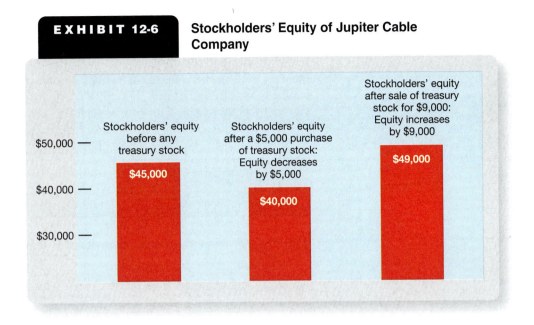

EXHIBIT 12-6 Stockholders' Equity of Jupiter Cable Company

Sale Below Cost

The resale price of treasury stock can be less than cost. The shortfall is debited first to Paid-In Capital from Treasury Stock Transactions. If this account's balance is too small, then debit Retained Earnings for the remaining amount. We illustrate this situation in Summary Problem 1 on page 609.

Other Stockholders' Equity Issues

Companies may retire their stock, restrict retained earnings, and report stockholders' equity in a variety of ways. This section covers these reporting issues.

Retirement of Stock

Not all companies purchase their stock to hold it in the treasury. A corporation may retire its stock by canceling the stock certificates. Retired stock cannot be reissued.

Retirements of preferred stock are common as companies seek to avoid paying the preferred dividends. To purchase stock for retirement, debit the stock account—for example, Preferred Stock—and credit cash. That removes the retired stock from the company's books.

Restrictions on Retained Earnings

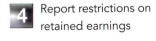

Dividends and treasury stock purchases require a cash payment. These outlays leave fewer resources to pay liabilities. A bank may agree to loan $50,000 only if Jupiter Cable Company limits its payment of dividends and its purchases of treasury stock.

Limits on Dividends and Treasury Stock Purchases

To ensure that a corporation maintains a minimum level of equity, lenders may restrict the amount of treasury stock a corporation may purchase. The restriction often focuses on the balance of retained earnings. Companies usually report their retained earnings restrictions in notes to the financial statements. The following disclosure by Jupiter Cable Company is typical:

NOTES TO THE FINANCIAL STATEMENTS

Note F—Long-Term Debt The . . . Company's loan agreements . . . restrict cash dividends and treasury stock purchases. Under the most restrictive of these provisions, retained earnings of $18,000 were unrestricted at December 31, 2006.

With this restriction, the maximum dividend that Jupiter can pay is $18,000.

Appropriations of Retained Earnings

Appropriations are Retained Earnings restrictions recorded by formal journal entries. A corporation may *appropriate*—that is, segregate in a separate account—a portion of Retained Earnings for a specific use. For example, the board of directors may appropriate part of Retained Earnings for expansion. Appropriated Retained Earnings can be reported as shown near the bottom of Exhibit 12-7.

Variations in Reporting Stockholders' Equity

Companies can report their stockholders' equity in ways that differ from our examples. They assume that investors understand the details. One of the most important skills you will learn in this course is how to read the financial statements of real companies. In Exhibit 12-7, we present a side-by-side comparison of our teaching format and the format you are likely to encounter. Note the following points in the real-world format:

1. The heading Paid-In Capital does not appear. It is commonly understood that Preferred Stock, Common Stock, and Additional Paid-In Capital are elements of paid-in capital.

2. For presentation in the financial statements, all additional paid-in capital accounts are combined and reported as a single amount labeled Additional Paid-In Capital. Additional Paid-In Capital belongs to the common stockholders; therefore, it follows Common Stock in the real-world format.

Retained earnings appropriations are rare. Most companies report retained earnings restrictions in the notes to the financial statements, as shown for Jupiter Cable Company and in the real-world format of Exhibit 12-7.

EXHIBIT 12-7 Formats for Reporting Stockholders' Equity

Teaching Format		Real-World Format	
Stockholders' equity		Stockholders' equity	
Paid-in capital:			
Preferred stock, 8%, $10 par,		Preferred stock, 8%, $10 par,	
30,000 shares authorized and issued	$ 300,000	30,0000 shares authorized and issued	$ 300,000
Common stock, $1 par,		Common stock, $1 par,	
100,000 shares authorized,		100,000 shares authorized, 60,000 shares issued	60,000
60,000 shares issued	60,000	Additional paid-in capital	2,170,000
Paid-in capital in excess of par—common	2,150,000	Retained earnings (Note 7)	1,500,000
Paid-in capital from treasury stock transactions	20,000	Less: Treasury stock, common	
Total paid-in capital	2,530,000	(1,000 shares at cost)	(30,000)
Retained earnings appropriated		Total stockholders' equity	$4,000,000
for contingencies	500,000		
Retained earnings—unappropriated	1,000,000	Note 7—*Restriction on retained earnings.*	
Total retained earnings	1,500,000	At December 31, 2009, $500,000 of retained	
Subtotal	4,030,000	earnings is restricted for contingencies.	
Less: Treasury stock, common		Accordingly, dividends are limited to a	
(1,000 shares at cost)	(30,000)	maximum of $1,000,000.	
Total stockholders' equity	$4,000,000		

Review the first half of the chapter by studying the Decision Guidelines.

Decision Guidelines

ACCOUNTING FOR RETAINED EARNINGS, DIVIDENDS, AND TREASURY STOCK

Retained earnings, dividends, and treasury stock can affect a corporation's equity. The Decision Guidelines will help you understand their effects.

Decision

How to record:

- Distribution of a small stock dividend (20% to 25%)?

- Stock split?

What are the effects of stock dividends and stock splits on:

- Number of shares issued?
- Shares outstanding?
- Par value per share?
- Total assets, total liabilities, and total equity?
- Common Stock?
- Retained Earnings?

How to record:

1. Purchase of treasury stock?
   Sale of treasury stock?
2. At cost? (Amount received = Cost)

3. Above cost?

4. Below cost?

What are the effects of the purchase and sale of treasury stock on:

- Total assets?

- Total stockholders' equity?

Guidelines

Retained Earnings............	Market value	
Common Stock...........		Par value
Paid-In Capital		
in Excess of Par........		Excess

Memorandum only: Split the common stock 2-for-1. Called in the outstanding $10 par common stock and distributed two shares of $5 par for each old share outstanding (amounts assumed).

Effects of Stock

Dividend	Split
Increase	Increase
Increase	Increase
No effect	Decrease
No effect	No effect
Increase	No effect
Decrease	No effect

1. Treasury Stock .... Cost
      Cash .... Cost
2. Cash .... Amt. received
      Treasury Stock .... Cost
3. Cash .... Amt. received
      Treasury Stock .... Cost
      Paid-In Capital from
        Treasury Stock
        Transactions.................. Excess
4. Cash .... Amt. received
      Paid-In Capital from Treasury
        Stock Transactions .... Amt. up to prior bal.
      Retained Earnings .... Excess
      Treasury Stock .... Cost

Effects of

Purchase	Sale
Decrease total assets by full amount of payment	Increase total assets by full amount of cash receipt
Decrease total equity by full amount of payment	Increase total equity by full amount of cash receipt

Summary Problem 1

Simplicity Graphics, creator of magazine designs, reported shareholders' equity:

Shareholders' Equity	
Preferred stock, $10.00 par value	
Authorized—10,000 shares; Issued—None	$ —
Common Stock, $1 par value	
Authorized 30,000 shares; Issued 15,000 shares	15,000
Capital in excess of par value	45,000
Retained earnings	90,000
	150,000
Less: Treasury stock, at cost (2,000 common shares)	(16,000)
	$134,000

Requirements

1. What was the average issue price per share of the common stock?
2. Journalize the issuance of 1,000 shares of common stock at $4 per share. Use Simplicity's account titles.
3. How many shares of Simplicity's common stock are outstanding?
4. How many shares of common stock would be outstanding after Simplicity split its common stock 3 for 1?
5. Using Simplicity account titles, journalize the distribution of a 10% stock dividend when the market price of Simplicity common stock is $5 per share. Simplicity distributes the common stock dividend on the shares outstanding, which were computed in requirement 3.
6. Journalize the following treasury stock transactions, which occur in the order given:
   a. Simplicity purchases 500 shares of treasury stock at $8 per share.
   b. Simplicity sells 100 shares of treasury stock for $9 per share.
   c. Simplicity sells 200 shares of treasury stocks for $6 per share.

Solution

1.	Average issue price of common stock was $4 per share [(15,000 + $45,000)/15,000 shares = $4]		
2.	Cash (1,000 × $4)	4,000	
	Common Stock (1,000 × $1)		1,000
	Capital in Excess of Par Value		3,000
	Issued common stock.		
3.	Shares outstanding = 13,000 (15,000 shares issued minus 2,000 shares of treasury stock).		
4.	Shares outstanding after a 3-for-1 stock split = 39,000 (13,000 shares outstanding × 3).		
5.	Retained Earnings (13,000 × 0.10 × $5)	6,500	
	Common Stock (13,000 × 0.10 × $1)		1,300
	Capital in Excess of Par Value		5,200
	Distributed a 10% common stock dividend.		
6.	a. Treasury Stock (500 × $8)	4,000	
	Cash		4,000
	Purchased treasury stock.		
	b. Cash (100 × $9)	900	
	Treasury Stock (100 × $8)		800
	Paid-in Capital from Treasury Stock Transactions		100
	Sold treasury stock.		
	c. Cash (200 × $6)	1,200	
	Paid-in Capital from Treasury Stock Transactions (from entry *b.*)	100	
	Retained Earnings	300	
	Treasury Stock (200 × $8)		1,600
	Sold treasury stock.		

The Corporate Income Statement

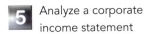 Analyze a corporate income statement

As we have seen, the stockholders' equity of a corporation is more complex than the capital of a proprietorship or a partnership. Also, a corporation's income statement includes some twists and turns that don't often apply to a smaller business. Most of the income statements you will see belong to corporations. Why not proprietorships or partnerships? Because they are privately held, proprietorships and partnerships don't have to publish their financial statements. But public corporations do, so we turn now to the corporate income statement.

Suppose you are considering investing in the stock of IHOP, Coca-Cola, or Pier 1 Imports. You would examine these companies' income statements. Of particular interest is the amount of net income they can expect to earn year after year. To understand net income, let's examine Exhibit 12-8, the income statement of Allied Electronics Corporation, a small manufacturer of precision instruments. New items are in color for emphasis.

Continuing Operations

In Exhibit 12-8, the topmost section reports continuing operations. This part of the business should continue from period to period. Income from continuing operations, therefore, helps investors make predictions about future earnings. We may use this information to predict that Allied Electronics Corporation will earn approximately $54,000 next year.

The continuing operations of Allied Electronics include two items needing explanation:

- Allied had a gain on the sale of machinery, which is outside the company's core business of selling electronics products. This is why the gain is reported in the "other" category—separately from Allied's sales revenue, cost of goods sold, and gross profit.
- Income tax expense ($36,000) is subtracted to arrive at income from continuing operations. Allied Electronics' income tax rate is 40% ($90,000 × 0.40 = $36,000).

Special Items

After continuing operations, an income statement may include two distinctly different gains and losses:

- Discontinued operations
- Extraordinary gains and losses

Discontinued Operations

Most corporations engage in several lines of business. For example, IHOP is best known for its restaurants. But at one time IHOP owned Golden Oaks Retirement Homes, United Rent-Alls, and even a business college. Sears, Roebuck & Co. is best known for its retail stores, but Sears also has a real-estate company (Homart) and an insurance company (Allstate).

Each identifiable division of a company is called a **segment of the business**. Allstate is the insurance segment of Sears. A company may sell a segment of its business. For example, IHOP sold its retirement homes, United Rent-Alls, and its business college. These were discontinued operations for IHOP.

EXHIBIT 12-8 — Income Statement in Multi-Step Format—Allied Electronics Corporation

ALLIED ELECTRONICS CORPORATION
Income Statement
Year Ended December 31, 2008

Continuing Operations	
Net sales revenue	$500,000
Cost of goods sold	240,000
Gross profit	260,000
Operating expenses (detailed)	181,000
Operating income	79,000
Other gains (losses):	
Gain on sale of machinery	11,000
Income from continuing operations before income tax	90,000
Income tax expense	36,000
Income from continuing operations	54,000
Special Items	
Discontinued operations, income of $35,000,	
less income tax of $14,000	21,000
Income before extraordinary item	75,000
Extraordinary flood loss, $20,000,	
less income tax saving of $8,000	(12,000)
Net income	$ 63,000
Earnings Per Share	
Earnings per share of common stock	
(20,000 shares outstanding):	
Income from continuing operations	$2.70
Income from discontinued operations	1.05
Income before extraordinary item	3.75
Extraordinary loss	(0.60)
Net income	$3.15

Financial analysts are always keeping tabs on companies they follow. They predict companies' net income, and most analysts don't include discontinued operations because the discontinued segments won't be around in the future. The income statement reports information on the segments that have been sold under the heading Discontinued operations. Income from discontinued operations ($35,000) is taxed at 40% and reported as shown in Exhibit 12-8. A loss on discontinued operations is reported similarly, but with a subtraction for the income tax *savings* on the loss.

Gains and losses on the sale of plant assets are *not* reported as discontinued operations. Gains and losses on the sale of plant assets are reported as "Other gains (losses)" up among continuing operations because companies dispose of old plant and equipment all the time.

Extraordinary Gains and Losses (Extraordinary Items)

Extraordinary gains and losses, also called **extraordinary items**, are both unusual and infrequent. Losses from natural disasters (floods, earthquakes, and tornadoes) and the taking of company assets by a foreign government (expropriation) are extraordinary items.

Extraordinary items are reported along with their income tax effect. During 2008, Allied Electronics Corporation lost $20,000 of inventory in a flood. This flood loss reduced both Allied's income and its income tax. The tax effect decreases

the net amount of Allied's loss the same way income tax reduces net income. An extraordinary loss can be reported along with its tax effect, as follows:

Extraordinary flood loss....................................	$(20,000)
Less: Income tax saving....................................	8,000
Extraordinary flood loss, net of tax....................	$(12,000)

Trace this item to the income statement in Exhibit 12-8. An extraordinary gain is reported the same as a loss, net of the income tax.

The following items do *not* qualify as extraordinary:

- Gains and losses on the sale of plant assets
- Losses due to lawsuits
- Losses due to employee labor strikes

These gains and losses fall outside the business's central operations, so they are reported on the income statement as other gains and losses. Examples include the gain on sale of machinery reported up in the Other gains (losses) section of Exhibit 12-8. The two graphics on this page illustrate an extraordinary loss and an "other" gain (loss).

Earnings per Share

The final segment of a corporate income statement reports the company's earnings per share, abbreviated as EPS. EPS is the most widely used of all business statistics.

Earnings per share (EPS) reports the amount of net income for each share of the company's *outstanding common stock*. Recall that:

$$\begin{matrix}\text{Outstanding}\\\text{stock}\end{matrix} = \begin{matrix}\text{Issued}\\\text{stock}\end{matrix} - \begin{matrix}\text{Treasury}\\\text{stock}\end{matrix}$$

For example, Allied Electronics has issued 25,000 shares of its common stock and holds 5,000 shares as treasury stock. Allied, therefore, has 20,000 shares of common stock outstanding, and so we use 20,000 shares to compute EPS.

EPS is a key measure of success in business. EPS is computed as follows:

$$\text{Earnings per share} = \frac{\text{Net income} - \text{Preferred dividends}}{\text{Average number of common shares outstanding}}$$

Corporations report a separate EPS figure for each element of income. Allied Electronics Corporation's EPS calculations follow.

Earnings per share of common stock (20,000 shares outstanding):	
Income from continuing operations ($54,000/20,000)	$2.70
Income from discontinued operations ($21,000/20,000)	1.05
Income before extraordinary item ($75,000/20,000)	3.75
Extraordinary loss ($12,000/20,000)	(0.60)
Net income ($63,000/20,000)	$3.15

The final section of Exhibit 12-8 reports the EPS figures for Allied Electronics.

Effect of Preferred Dividends on Earnings per Share

Preferred dividends also affect EPS. Recall that EPS is earnings per share of *common* stock. Recall also that dividends on preferred stock are paid first. Therefore, preferred dividends must be subtracted from income to compute EPS.

Suppose Allied Electronics had 10,000 shares of preferred stock outstanding, each share paying a $1.00 dividend. The annual preferred dividend would be $10,000 (10,000 × $1.00). The $10,000 is subtracted from each of the income subtotals (lines 1, 3, and 5), resulting in the following EPS computations for Allied:

	Earnings per share of common stock (20,000 shares outstanding):	
1	Income from continuing operations ($54,000 − $10,000)/20,000	$2.20
2	Income from discontinued operations ($21,000/20,000)	1.05
3	Income before extraordinary item ($75,000 − $10,000)/20,000	3.25
4	Extraordinary loss ($12,000/20,000)	(0.60)
5	Net income ($63,000 − $10,000)/20,000	$2.65

Basic and Diluted Earnings per Share

Some corporations must report two sets of EPS figures, as follows:
- EPS based on outstanding common shares (*basic* EPS).
- EPS based on outstanding common plus the additional shares of common stock that would arise from conversion of the preferred stock into common (*diluted* EPS). Diluted EPS is always lower than basic EPS.

Statement of Retained Earnings

The statement of retained earnings reports how the company moved from its beginning balance of retained earnings to its ending balance during the period. This statement is not altogether new; it's essentially the same as the statement of owner's equity for a proprietorship—but adapted to a corporation.

Exhibit 12-9 shows the statement of retained earnings of Allied Electronics for 2008. Notice that corporate dividends take the place of withdrawals in a proprietorship. Allied's net income comes from the income statement in Exhibit 12-8, page 612. All other data are assumed.

EXHIBIT 12-9 Statement of Retained Earnings—Allied Electronics Corporation

ALLIED ELECTRONICS CORPORATION
Statement of Retained Earnings
Year Ended December 31, 2008

Retained earnings, December 31, 2007	$130,000
Add: Net income for 2008	63,000
	193,000
Less: Dividends for 2008	(53,000)
Retained earnings, December 31, 2008	$140,000

Combined Statement of Income and Retained Earnings

Companies can report income and retained earnings on a single statement. Exhibit 12-10 illustrates how Allied Electronics would combine its income statement and its statement of retained earnings.

EXHIBIT 12-10 Combined Statement of Income and Retained Earnings—Allied Electronics Corporation

ALLIED ELECTRONICS CORPORATION
Combined Statement of Income and Retained Earnings
Year Ended December 31, 2008

Sales revenue	$500,000
Cost of goods sold	240,000
Gross profit	260,000
Expenses (listed individually)	197,000
Net income for 2008	$ 63,000
Retained earnings, December 31, 2007	130,000
	193,000
Dividends for 2008	(53,000)
Retained earnings, December 31, 2008	$140,000

(Income Statement: Sales revenue through Net income for 2008)
(Statement of retained earnings: Retained earnings, December 31, 2007 through Retained earnings, December 31, 2008)

Prior-Period Adjustments

A company may make an accounting error. After the books are closed, Retained Earnings holds the error, and its balance is wrong until corrected. Corrections to Retained Earnings for errors of an earlier period are called **prior-period adjustments**. The prior-period adjustment either increases or decreases the beginning balance of Retained Earnings and appears on that statement.

In recent years there have been more prior-period adjustments than in the 20 previous years combined. Many companies have restated their net income to correct accounting errors. To illustrate, assume De Graff Corporation recorded $30,000 of income tax expense for 2007. The correct amount of income tax was $40,000. This error:

- Understated income tax expense by $10,000
- Overstated net income by $10,000

In 2008 De Graff paid the extra $10,000 in taxes for the prior year. De Graff's prior-period adjustment will decrease retained earnings as follows (all amounts are assumed).

DE GRAFF CORPORATION
Statement of Retained Earnings
Year Ended December 31, 2008

Retained earnings, December 31, 2007, as originally reported	$390,000
Prior-period adjustment—To correct error in 2007	(10,000)
Retained earnings, December 31, 2007, as adjusted	380,000
Net income for 2008	100,000
	480,000
Dividends for 2008	(40,000)
Retained earnings, December 31, 2008	$440,000

Reporting Comprehensive Income

As we've seen, all companies report net income or net loss on the income statement. There is another income figure. **Comprehensive income** is the company's change in total stockholders' equity from all sources other than from its owners. Comprehensive income includes net income plus some specific gains and losses, as follows:

- Unrealized gains or losses on certain investments
- Foreign-currency translation adjustments

These items do not enter into the determination of net income but instead are reported as other comprehensive income, as shown in Exhibit 12-11. Assumed figures are used for all items.

Earnings per share apply only to net income and its components, as discussed earlier. Earnings per share are *not* reported for other comprehensive income.

EXHIBIT 12-11 **Reporting Comprehensive Income**

NATIONAL EXPRESS COMPANY
Income Statement
Year Ended December 31, 2009

Revenues	$10,000
Expenses (summarized)	6,000
Net income	4,000
Other comprehensive income:	
Unrealized gain on investments	1,000
Comprehensive income	$ 5,000

Decision Guidelines

ANALYZING A CORPORATE INCOME STATEMENT

Three years out of college, you've saved $5,000 and are ready to start investing. Where do you start? You might begin by analyzing the income statements of IHOP, Coca-Cola, and Pier 1 Imports. These Decision Guidelines will help you analyze a corporate income statement.

Decision

What are the main sections of the income statement? See Exhibit 12-8 for an example.

Guidelines

Continuing operations
- Continuing operations, including other gains and losses and less income tax expense

Special items
- Discontinued operations—gain or loss—less the income tax effect
- Extraordinary gain or loss, less the income tax effect
- Net income (or net loss)
- Other comprehensive income (Exhibit 12-11)

Decision

What earnings-per-share (EPS) figures must a corporation report?

Guidelines

Earnings per share
- Earnings per share—applies only to net income (or net loss), not to other comprehensive income

Separate EPS figures for:
- Income from continuing operations
- Discontinued operations
- Income before extraordinary item
- Extraordinary gain or loss
- Net income (or net loss)

Decision

How to compute EPS for net income?

Guidelines

$$\text{EPS} = \frac{\text{Net income} - \text{Preferred dividends}}{\text{Average number of common shares outstanding}}$$

Summary Problem 2

The following information was taken from the ledger of Calenergy Corporation at December 31, 2008.

Common stock, no-par, 45,000 shares issued	$180,000	Discontinued operations, income	$20,000
Sales revenue	620,000	Prior-period adjustment— credit to Retained Earnings	5,000
Extraordinary gain	26,000	Gain on sale of plant assets	21,000
Loss due to lawsuit	11,000	Income tax expense (saving):	
General expenses	62,000	Continuing operations	32,000
Preferred stock 8%	50,000	Discontinued operations	8,000
Selling expenses	108,000	Extraordinary gain	10,000
Retained earnings, beginning, as originally reported	103,000	Treasury stock, common (5,000 shares)	25,000
Dividends	14,000		
Cost of goods sold	380,000		

Requirements

Prepare a single-step income statement and a statement of retained earnings for Calenergy Corporation for the year ended December 31, 2008. Include the EPS presentation and show your computations. Calenergy had no changes in its stock accounts during the year.

Solution

CALENERGY CORPORATION
Income Statement
Year Ended December 31, 2008

Revenue and gains:		
Sales revenue		$620,000
Gain on sale of plant assets		21,000
Total revenues and gains		641,000
Expenses and losses:		
Cost of goods sold	$380,000	
Selling expenses	108,000	
General expenses	62,000	
Loss due to lawsuit	11,000	
Income tax expense	32,000	
Total expenses and losses		593,000
Income from continuing operations		48,000
Discontinued operations, income of $20,000,		
less income tax of $8,000		12,000
Income before extraordinary item		60,000
Extraordinary gain, $26,000, less income tax, $10,000		16,000
Net income		$ 76,000
Earnings per share:		
Income from continuing operations		
[($48,000 − $4,000) / 40,000 shares]		$1.10
Income from discontinued operations		
($12,000 / $40,000 shares)		0.30
Income before extraordinary item		
[($60,000 − $4,000) / 40,000 shares]		1.40
Extraordinary gain ($16,000 / 40,000 shares)		0.40
Net income [($76,000 − $4,000) / 40,000 shares]		$1.80

Computations:

$$\text{EPS} = \frac{\text{Income} - \text{Preferred dividends}}{\text{Common shares outstanding}}$$

Preferred dividends: $50,000 × 0.08 = $4,000
Common shares outstanding:
   45,000 shares issued − 5,000 treasury shares = 40,000 shares outstanding

CALENERGY CORPORATION
Statement of Retained Earnings
Year Ended December 31, 2008

Retained earnings balance, beginning, as originally reported	$103,000
Prior-period adjustment—credit	5,000
Retained earnings balance, beginning, as adjusted	108,000
Net income	76,000
	184,000
Dividends	(14,000)
Retained earnings balance, ending	$170,000

Review: Retained Earnings, Treasury Stock, and the Income Statement

Accounting Vocabulary

Appropriation of Retained Earnings
Restriction of retained earnings that is recorded by a formal journal entry.

Comprehensive Income
Company's change in total stockholders' equity from all sources other than from the owners.

Earnings per Share (EPS)
Amount of a company's net income for each share of its outstanding stock.

Extraordinary Gains and Losses
A gain or loss that is both unusual for the company and infrequent. Also called **extraordinary items**.

Extraordinary Item
A gain or loss that is both unusual for the company and infrequent. Also called **extraordinary gains and losses**.

Prior-Period Adjustment
A correction to retained earnings for an error of an earlier period.

Segment of the Business
One of various separate divisions of a company.

Stock Dividend
A distribution by a corporation of its own to stockholders.

Stock Split
An increase in the number of outstanding shares of stock coupled with a proportionate reduction in the value of the stock.

Treasury Stock
A corporation's own stock that it has issued and later reacquired.

Quick Check

1. A company's own stock that it has issued and repurchased is called
   a. Issued stock
   b. Outstanding stock
   c. Treasury stock
   d. Dividend stock

2. A stock dividend
   a. Decreases Common Stock
   b. Increases Retained Earnings
   c. Has no effect on total equity
   d. All of the above

3. In a small stock dividend,
   a. Common stock is debited for the par value of the shares issued.
   b. Retained Earnings is debited for the market value of the shares issued.
   c. Paid-In Capital in Excess of Par is debited for the difference between the debits to Retained Earnings and to Common Stock.
   d. Net income is always decreased.

4. Stock splits
   a. Decrease par value per share
   b. Increase the number of shares of stock issued
   c. Both a and b
   d. None of the above

5. Assume that IHOP paid $10 per share to purchase 1,000 of its $1 par common as treasury stock. The purchase of treasury stock
   a. Decreased total equity by $10,000
   b. Increased total equity by $1,000
   c. Decreased total equity by $1,000
   d. Increased total equity by $10,000

6. Assume that IHOP sold all 1,000 shares of its treasury stock for $15 per share. The sale of treasury stock
   a. Decreased total equity by $15,000
   b. Increased total equity by $5,000
   c. Decreased total equity by $5,000
   d. Increased total equity by $15,000

7. Allied Electronics in Exhibit 12-8, page 612, is most likely to earn net income of $x next year. How much is $x?
   a. $90,000
   b. $79,000
   c. $75,000
   d. $54,000

8. Which of the following events would be an extraordinary loss?
   a. Loss due to an earthquake
   b. Loss on the sale of equipment
   c. Loss on discontinued operations
   d. All of the above are extraordinary items

9. What is the most widely followed statistic in business?
   a. Gross profit
   b. Earnings per share
   c. Retained earnings
   d. Dividends

10. Earnings per share is *not* computed for
    a. Net income
    b. Comprehensive income
    c. Discontinued operations
    d. Extraordinary items

    Answers are given after Apply Your Knowledge (p. 639).

Assess Your Progress

Short Exercises

Recording a small stock dividend

S12-1 Crestview Pool Supply has 10,000 shares of $1 par common stock outstanding. Crestview distributes a 10% stock dividend when the market value of its stock is $15 per share.

1. Journalize Crestview's distribution of the stock dividend on September 30. An explanation is not required. (pp. 600–601)
2. What is the overall effect of the stock dividend on Crestview's total assets? On total stockholders' equity? (pp. 600–601)

Comparing and contrasting cash dividends and stock dividends

S12-2 Compare and contrast the accounting for cash dividends and stock dividends. In the space provided, insert either "Cash dividends," "Stock dividends," or "Both cash dividends and stock dividends" to complete each of the following statements:

1. _____ decrease Retained Earnings. (p. 602)
2. _____ have no effect on a liability. (pp. 600–601)
3. _____ increase paid-in capital by the same amount that they decrease Retained Earnings. (p. 602)
4. _____ decrease both total assets and total stockholders' equity, resulting in a decrease in the size of the company. (p. 602)

Accounting for a stock split

S12-3 Pier 1 Imports recently reported the following stockholders' equity (adapted and in millions except par value per share):

Paid-in capital:	
Common stock, $1 par, 500 shares authorized 101 shares issued.............................	$101
Paid-in capital in excess of par.............	142
Total paid-in capital............................	243
Retained earnings..................................	656
Other equity..	(235)
Total stockholders' equity.......................	$664

Suppose Pier 1 split its common stock 2 for 1 in order to decrease the market price of its stock. The company's stock was trading at $20 immediately before the split.

1. Prepare the stockholders' equity section of Pier 1 Imports' balance sheet after the stock split. (p. 602)
2. Which account balances changed after the stock split? Which account balances were unchanged? (p. 602)

Accounting for the purchase and sale of treasury stock (above cost)

S12-4 True Discount Furniture, Inc., completed the following treasury stock transactions:

a. Purchased 1,000 shares of the company's $1 par common stock as treasury stock, paying cash of $5 per share. (p. 604)
b. Sold 500 shares of the treasury stock for cash of $8 per share. (p. 604)

continued ...

Journalize these transactions. Explanations are not required. Show how True Discount will report treasury stock on its December 31, 2008, balance sheet after completing the two transactions. In reporting the treasury stock, report only on the Treasury Stock account. You may ignore all other accounts. (p. 604)

Interpreting a restriction of retained earnings

4

S12-5 MG Corporation reported the following stockholders' equity:

Paid-in capital:	
Preferred stock, $1.50, no par, 10,000 shares authorized; none issued	$ —
Common stock, $1 par, 500,000 shares authorized, 150,000 shares issued	150,000
Paid-in capital in excess of par-common..........................	350,000
Total paid-in capital	500,000
Retained earnings	400,000
Less: Treasury stock, 5,000 shares at cost	(30,000)
Total stockholders' equity	$870,000

1. MG Corporation's agreement with its bank lender restricts MG's dividend payments for the cost of treasury stock the company holds. How much in dividends can MG declare? (pp. 602–607)
2. Why would a bank lender restrict a corporation's dividend payments and treasury stock purchases? (pp. 605–606)

Preparing a corporate income statement

5

S12-6 List the major parts of a complex corporate income statement for WRS Athletic Clubs, Inc., for the year ended December 31, 2007. Include all the major parts of the income statement, starting with net sales revenue and ending with net income (net loss). You may ignore dollar amounts and earnings per share. (p. 611)

Explaining the items on a corporate income statement

5

S12-7 Answer these questions about a corporate income statement:
1. How do you measure gross profit? (p. 611)
2. What is the title of those items that are both unusual and infrequent?
3. Which income number is the best predictor of future net income? (pp. 609–611)
4. What's the "bottom line?" (p. 611)
5. What does *EPS* abbreviate? (p. 614)

Preparing a corporate income statement

5

S12-8 PWC Corp. accounting records include the following items, listed in no particular order, at December 31, 2008:

Other gains (losses)	$ (20,000)	Extraordinary loss	$ (5,000)
Net sales revenue	180,000	Cost of goods sold	70,000
Gain on discontinued operations	15,000	Operating expenses	60,000
Accounts receivable	19,000		

continued . . .

Income tax of 40% applies to all items.

Prepare PWC's income statement for the year ended December 31, 2008. Omit earnings per share. (p. 611)

Reporting earnings per share

S12-9 Return to the PWC Corp. data in Short Exercise 12-8. PWC had 10,000 shares of common stock outstanding during 2008. PWC declared and paid preferred dividends of $4,000 during 2008.

Show how PWC reported EPS data on its 2008 income statement. (p. 614)

Interpreting earnings-per-share data

S12-10 Owens-Illinois, Inc. has preferred stock outstanding.

1. Give the basic equation to compute earnings per share of common stock for net income. (p. 614)
2. List all the income items for which Owens-Illinois must report EPS data. (p. 614)

Reporting comprehensive income

S12-11 Use the PWC Corp. data in Short Exercise 12-8. In addition, PWC had unrealized gains of $4,000 on investments during 2008. Start with PWC's net income from Short Exercise 12-8 and show how the company could report other comprehensive income on its 2008 income statement.

Should PWC Corp. report earnings per share for other comprehensive income? (pp. 615–616)

Reporting a prior-period adjustment

S12-12 Statistical Research Service, Inc. (SRSI) ended 2008 with retained earnings of $75,000. During 2009 SRSI earned net income of $90,000 and declared dividends of $30,000. Also during 2009, SRSI got a $20,000 tax refund from the Internal Revenue Service. A tax audit revealed that SRSI paid too much income tax back in 2007.

Prepare Statistical Research Service, Inc.'s statement of retained earnings for the year ended December 31, 2009, to report the prior-period adjustment. (pp. 615–616)

Exercises

Journalizing a stock dividend and reporting stockholders' equity

E12-13 The stockholders' equity of Lakewood Occupational Therapy, Inc., on December 31, 2009, follows.

STOCKHOLDERS' EQUITY

Paid-in capital:	
Common stock, $1 par, 100,000 shares authorized, 50,000 shares issued	$ 50,000
Paid-in capital in excess of par	200,000
Total paid-in capital	250,000
Retained earnings	120,000
Total stockholders' equity	$370,000

On April 30, 2010, the market price of Lakewood's common stock was $14 per share and the company distributed a 10% stock dividend.

continued . . .

Requirements
1. Journalize the distribution of the stock dividend. (pp. 600–601)
2. Prepare the stockholders' equity section of the balance sheet after the stock dividend. (p. 601)

Journalizing cash and stock dividends

E12-14 Martial Arts Schools, Inc., is authorized to issue 500,000 shares of $1 par common stock. The company issued 80,000 shares at $4 per share. When the market price of common stock was $6 per share, Martial Arts distributed a 10% stock dividend. Later, Martial Arts declared and paid a $0.30 per share cash dividend.

Requirements
1. Journalize the distribution of the stock dividend. (pp. 600–601)
2. Journalize both the declaration and the payment of the cash dividend. (pp. 561–563)

Reporting stockholders' equity after a stock split

E12-15 Cobra Golf Club Corp. had the following stockholders' equity at December 31, 2007:

Paid-in capital:	
Common stock, $1 par, 200,000 shares authorized, 50,000 shares issued	$ 50,000
Paid-in capital in excess of par	100,000
Total paid-in capital	150,000
Retained earnings	200,000
Total stockholders' equity	$350,000

On June 30, 2008, Cobra split its common stock 2 for 1. Make the memorandum entry to record the stock split, and prepare the stockholders' equity section of the balance sheet immediately after the split. (p. 602)

Effects of stock dividends, stock splits, and treasury stock transactions

E12-16 Identify the effects of the following transactions on total stockholders' equity. Each transaction is independent.

a. A 10% stock dividend. Before the dividend, 500,000 shares of $1 par common stock were outstanding; market value was $6 at the time of the dividend. (p. 602)

b. A 2-for-1 stock split. Prior to the split, 60,000 shares of $4 par common were outstanding. (p. 602)

c. Purchase of 1,000 shares of treasury stock (par value $0.50) at $5 per share. (pp. 602–603, 605–606)

d. Sale of 600 shares of $1 par treasury stock for $5 per share. Cost of the treasury stock was $2 per share. (pp. 604, 605–606)

Journalizing treasury stock transactions

E12-17 Journalize the following transactions of Austin Driving School, Inc.:

Feb.	4	Issued 20,000 shares of 1 par common stock at $10 per share. (pp. 554–555)
Apr.	22	Purchased 1,000 shares of treasury stock at $14 per share. (pp. 602–603)
Aug.	22	Sold 600 shares of treasury stock at $20 per share. (p. 604)

Journalizing treasury stock transactions and reporting stockholders' equity

E12-18 Mid America Amusements Corporation had the following stockholders' equity on November 30:

STOCKHOLDERS' EQUITY

Common stock, $5 par, 500,000 shares authorized, 50,000 shares issued	$250,000
Paid-in capital in excess of par	150,000
Retained earnings	490,000
Total stockholders' equity	$890,000

On December 30, Mid America purchased 10,000 shares of treasury stock at $9 per share.

1. Journalize the purchase of the treasury stock, and prepare the stockholders' equity section of the balance sheet at December 31. (pp. 602–603)
2. How many shares of common stock are outstanding after the purchase of treasury stock?

Reporting a retained earnings restriction

E12-19 The agreement under which Toshiba Printers issued its long-term debt requires the restriction of $100,000 of the company's retained earnings balance. Total retained earnings is $250,000, and common stock, no-par, has a balance of $50,000.

Requirements

Report stockholders' equity on Toshiba's balance sheet, assuming the following:

a. Toshiba discloses the restriction in a note. Write the note. (pp. 606–608)
b. Toshiba appropriates retained earnings in the amount of the restriction and includes no note in its statements. Follow the Teaching Format on page 607.

Preparing a multistep income statement

E12-20 Cannon Photographic Supplies, Inc., accounting records include the following for 2008:

Income tax saving—extraordinary loss	$ 6,000	Sales revenue	$430,000
Income tax saving—loss on discontinued operations	20,000	Operating expenses (including income tax)	120,000
Extraordinary loss	15,000	Cost of goods sold	240,000
		Loss on discontinued operations	50,000

Requirement

Prepare Cannon's multistep income statement for 2008. Omit earnings per share. (p. 611)

Computing earnings per share

E12-21 Palestine Corp. earned net income of $108,000 for 2007. Palestine's books include the following figures:

Preferred stock, 6%, $50 par, 1,000 shares issued and outstanding	$ 50,000
Common stock, $10 par, 52,000 shares issued	520,000
Paid-in capital in excess of par	480,000
Treasury stock, common, 2,000 shares at cost	40,000

continued . . .

Requirement

Compute Palestine's EPS for the year. (p. 614)

Computing earnings per share

E12-22 Athens Academy Surplus had 50,000 shares of common stock and 10,000 shares of 5%, $10 par preferred stock outstanding through December 31, 2008. Income from continuing operations of 2008 was $110,000, and loss on discontinued operations (net of income tax saving) was $8,000. Athens also had an extraordinary gain (net of tax) of $20,000.

Requirement

Compute Athens' EPS amounts for 2008, starting with income from continuing operations. (p. 614)

Preparing a combined statement of income and retained earnings

E12-23 Good Times Express Company had retained earnings of $160 million at December 31, 2006. The company reported these figures for 2007:

	($ Millions)
Net income..	$140
Cash dividends—preferred......................	2
common	98

Requirement

Beginning with net income, prepare a combined statement of income and retained earnings for Good Times Express Company for the year ended December 31, 2007. (pp. 614–616)

Preparing a statement of retained earnings with a prior-period adjustment

E12-24 Sarah Lou Bakery, Inc., reported a prior-period adjustment in 2008. An accounting error caused net income of prior years to be overstated by $5,000. Retained earnings at December 31, 2007, as previously reported, stood at $39,000. Net income for 2008 was $70,000, and dividends were $24,000.

Requirement

Prepare the company's statement of retained earnings for the year ended December 31, 2008. (pp. 614–616)

Computing comprehensive income and reporting earnings per share

E12-25 During 2009, Newfoundland Corp. earned income from continuing operations of $135,000. The company also sold a segment of the business (discontinued operations) at a loss of $30,000 and had an extraordinary gain of $10,000. At year-end, Newfoundland had an unrealized loss on investments of $5,000.

1. Compute Newfoundland's net income and comprehensive income for 2009. All amounts are net of income taxes. (pp. 614–616)
2. What final EPS figure should Newfoundland report for 2009? Name the item and show its amount. Newfoundland had 57,500 shares of common stock (and no preferred stock) outstanding. (pp. 614–616)

Problems (Group A)

Journalizing stockholders' equity transactions

P12-26A Dearborn Manufacturing Co. completed the following transactions during 2009.

Jan. 16	Declared a cash dividend on the 4%, $100 par preferred stock (1,000 shares outstanding). Declared a $0.35 per share dividend on the 100,000 shares of common stock outstanding. The date of record is January 31 and the payment date is February 15. (pp. 561–563)
Feb. 15	Paid the cash dividends. (pp. 561–563)
June 10	Split common stock 2 for 1. Before the split, Dearborn had 100,000 shares of $2 par common stock outstanding. (p. 602)
July 30	Distributed a 5% stock dividend on the common stock. The market value of the common stock was $10 per share. (pp. 600–601)
Oct. 26	Purchased 2,000 shares of treasury stock at $11 per share. (pp. 602–603)
Nov. 8	Sold 1,000 shares of treasury stock for $17 per share. (p. 604)

Requirement
Record the transactions in Dearborn's general journal.

Journalizing dividend and treasury stock transactions and reporting stockholders' equity

P12-27A The balance sheet of Lennox Health Foods, at December 31, 2007, reported 100,000 shares of no-par common stock authorized, with 30,000 shares issued and a Common Stock balance of $180,000. Retained Earnings had a balance of $140,000. During 2008, the company completed the following selected transactions:

Mar. 15	Purchased 5,000 shares of treasury stock at $7 per share. (pp. 602–603)
Apr. 30	Distributed a 20% stock dividend on the 25,000 shares of *outstanding* common stock. The market value of Lennox common stock was $9 per share. (pp. 600–601)
Dec. 31	Earned net income of $110,000 during the year. Closed net income to Retained Earnings. (pp. 551–552)

Requirements
1. Record the transactions in the general journal. Explanations are not required.
2. Prepare the stockholders' equity section of Lennox Health Foods' balance sheet at December 31, 2008. (pp. 601–603)

Using dividends to fight off a takeover of the corporation

P12-28A Jennifer Vera, Inc., is the only company with a distribution network for its imported goods. The company does a brisk business with specialty stores such as Neiman Marcus, Saks Fifth Avenue, and Nordstrom. Vera's recent success has made the company a prime target for a

continued . . .

takeover. Against the wishes of Vera's board of directors, an investment group from France is attempting to buy 51% of Vera's outstanding stock. Board members are convinced that the French investors would sell off the most desirable pieces of the business and leave little of value.

At the most recent board meeting, several suggestions were advanced to fight off the hostile takeover bid. One suggestion is to increase the stock outstanding by distributing a 100% stock dividend. The intent is to spread the company's ownership in order to make it harder for the French group to buy a controlling interest.

Requirement
As a significant stockholder of Jennifer Vera, Inc., write a short memo to explain to the board whether distributing the stock dividend would make it difficult for the investor group to take over the company. Include in your memo a discussion of the effect that the stock dividend would have on assets, liabilities, and total stockholders' equity—that is, the dividend's effect on the size of the corporation. (pp. 598–599)

Journalizing dividend and treasury stock transactions; reporting retained earnings and stockholders' equity

P12-29A The balance sheet of Morrisey Management Consulting, Inc., at December 31, 2007, reported the following stockholders' equity:

Paid in capital:	
Common stock, $10 par, 100,000 shares authorized, 20,000 shares issued	$200,000
Paid-in capital in excess of par	300,000
Total paid-in capital	500,000
Retained earnings	160,000
Total stockholders' equity	$660,000

During 2008, Morrisey completed the following selected transactions:

Feb. 6   Distributed a 10% stock dividend on the common stock. The market value of Morrisey's stock was $25 per share. (pp. 600–601)

July 29   Purchased 2,000 shares of treasury stock at $25 per share. (pp. 602–603)

Nov. 27   Declared a $0.30 per share cash dividend on the 20,000 shares of common stock outstanding. The date of record is December 17, and the payment date is January 7, 2009. (pp. 561–563)

Dec. 31   Closed the $86,000 net income to Retained Earnings. (pp. 561–563)

Requirements
1. Record the transactions in the general journal.
2. Prepare a retained earnings statement for the year ended December 31, 2008. (p. 615)
3. Prepare the stockholders' equity section of the balance sheet at December 31, 2008. (pp. 601–603)

Preparing a detailed income statement

P12-30A The following information was taken from the records of Mobile Motorsports, Inc., at September 30, 2008.

General expenses	$133,000	Cost of goods sold	$435,000
Preferred stock, $2, no-par, 5,000 shares issued	200,000	Retained earnings, beginning	88,000
		Selling expenses	121,000
Common stock, $10 par, 25,000 shares authorized and issued	250,000	Income from discontinued operations	8,000
Net sales revenue	837,000	Income tax expense:	
Treasury stock, common (1,000 shares)	11,000	Continuing operations	72,000
		Income from discontinued operations	2,000

Requirement

Prepare a multistep income statement for Mobile Motorsports, Inc., for the fiscal year ended September 30, 2008. Include earnings per share. (p. 611)

Preparing a corrected combined statement of income and retained earnings

P12-31A Lisa Sheraton, accountant for Chase Home Finance, was injured in a boating accident. Another employee prepared the accompanying income statement for the year ended December 31, 2008.

The individual *amounts* listed on the income statement are correct. However, some accounts are reported incorrectly, and two items don't belong on the income statement at all. Also, income tax has *not* been applied to all appropriate figures. The income tax rate on discontinued operations was 40%. Chase Home Finance issued 52,000 shares of common stock in 2006 and held 2,000 shares as treasury stock during 2008. Retained earnings at December 31, 2007 was $167,000.

CHASE HOME FINANCE
Income Statement
Year Ended December 31, 2008

Revenue and gains:		
Sales		$362,000
Paid-in capital in excess of par—common		90,000
Total revenues and gains		452,000
Expenses and losses:		
Cost of goods sold	$105,000	
Selling expenses	67,000	
General expenses	61,000	
Dividends	17,000	
Sales returns	11,000	
Sales discounts	6,000	
Income tax expense	20,000	
Total expenses and losses		287,000
Income from operations		165,000
Other gains and losses:		
Gain on discontinued operations		5,000
Net income		$170,000
Earnings per share		$ 3.40

continued . . .

Requirement
Prepare a corrected combined statement of income and retained earnings for 2008, including earnings per share. Prepare the income statement in single-step format. (pp. 273–275, 611, 614–616)

Computing earnings per share and reporting a retained earnings restriction

P12-32A The capital structure of Knightsbridge, Inc., at December 31, 2006, included 20,000 shares of $1.25 preferred stock and 40,000 shares of common stock. Common stock outstanding during 2007 totaled 40,000 shares. Income from continuing operations during 2007 was $105,000. The company discontinued a segment of the business at a gain of $20,000, and also had an extraordinary gain of $10,000. The Knightsbridge board of directors restricts $100,000 of retained earnings for contingencies.

Requirement
1. Compute Knightsbridge's earnings per share for 2007. Start with income from continuing operations. All income and loss amounts are net of income tax. (p. 614)
2. Show two ways of reporting Knightsbridge's retained earnings restriction. Retained earnings at December 31, 2006, was $100,000, and the company declared preferred dividends of $25,000 during 2007. (pp. 606–608)

Problems (Group B)

Journalizing stockholders' equity transactions

P12-33B Maxfli Hot Air Balloons, Inc., completed the following selected transactions during 2009:

Feb. 9	Declared a cash dividend on the 10,000 shares of $1.50, no-par preferred stock. Declared a $0.20 per share dividend on the 10,000 shares of common stock outstanding. The date of record is February 16, and the payment date is February 28. (pp. 561–563)
Feb. 28	Paid the cash dividends. (pp. 561–563)
Mar. 21	Split common stock 2 for 1. Before the split, Maxfli had 10,000 shares of $10 par common stock outstanding. (p. 602)
Apr. 18	Distributed a 10% stock dividend on the common stock. The market value of the common stock was $27 per share. (pp. 600–601)
June 18	Purchased 2,000 shares of treasury stock at $25 per share. (pp. 602–603)
Dec. 22	Sold 1,000 shares of treasury stock for $28 per share. (p. 604)

Requirement
Record the transactions in the general journal.

Journalizing dividend and treasury stock transactions and reporting stockholders' equity

P12-34B The balance sheet of Banc One Corp. at December 31, 2007, reported 500,000 shares of $1 par common stock authorized with 100,000 shares issued. Paid-In Capital in Excess of Par had a balance of $300,000. Retained Earnings had a balance of $101,000. During 2008 the company completed the following selected transactions:

Jan. 12	Purchased 10,000 shares of the treasury stock at $4 per share. (pp. 602–603)
Sep. 28	Distributed a 10% stock dividend on the 90,000 shares of *outstanding* common stock. The market value of Banc One's common stock was $5 per share. (pp. 600–601)
Dec. 31	Earned net income of $73,000 during the year. Closed net income to Retained Earnings. (pp. 551–552)

Requirements
1. Record the transactions in the general journal. Explanations are not required.
2. Prepare the stockholders' equity section of the balance sheet at December 31, 2008. (pp. 601–603)

Purchasing treasury stock to fight off a takeover of the corporation

P12-35B Guatemalan Imports is the only company with reliable sources for its imported gifts. The company does a brisk business with specialty stores such as Pier 1 Imports. Guatemalan Imports' recent success has made the company a prime target for a takeover. An investment group from Mexico City is attempting to buy 51% of Guatemalan Imports' outstanding stock against the wishes of the company's board of directors. Board members are convinced that the Mexico City investors would sell the most desirable pieces of the business and leave little of value.

At the most recent board meeting, several suggestions were advanced to fight off the hostile takeover bid. The suggestion with the most promise is to purchase a huge quantity of treasury stock. Guatemalan Imports has the cash to carry out this plan.

Requirements
1. As a significant stockholder of Guatemalan Imports, write a memorandum to explain to the board how the purchase of treasury stock would make it difficult for the Mexico City group to take over the company. Include a discussion of the effect that purchasing treasury stock would have on stock outstanding and on the size of the corporation. (pp. 602–603)
2. Suppose Guatemalan Imports is successful in fighting off the takeover bid and later sells the treasury stock at prices greater than the purchase price. Explain what effect these sales will have on assets, stockholders' equity, and net income. (p. 604)

Journalizing dividend and treasury stock transactions; reporting retained earnings and stockholders' equity

P12-36B The balance sheet of Oriental Rug Company at December 31, 2008, included the following stockholders' equity:

Paid-in capital:	
Common stock, $1 par, 250,000 shares authorized, 50,000 shares issued	$ 50,000

continued . . .

634   Chapter 12

Paid-in capital in excess of par..	350,000
Total paid-in capital..	400,000
Retained earnings..	100,000
Total stockholders' equity	$500,000

During 2009, Oriental Rug completed the following selected transactions:

Mar. 29	Distributed a 10% stock dividend on the common stock. The market value of Oriental common stock was $8 per share. (pp. 600–601)
July 13	Purchased 10,000 shares of treasury stock at $8 per share. (pp. 602–603)
Dec. 10	Declared a $0.20 per share cash dividend on the 45,000 shares of common stock outstanding. The date of record is December 17, and the payment date is January 2. (pp. 561–563)
31	Closed the $79,000 net income to Retained Earnings. (pp. 551–552)

Requirements
1. Record the transactions in the general journal.
2. Prepare the retained earnings statement for the year ended December 31, 2009. (p. 615)
3. Prepare the stockholders' equity section of the balance sheet at December 31, 2009. (p. 601)

Preparing a detailed income statement

P12-37B The following information was taken from the records of Underwood Company at June 30, 2007:

Selling expenses	$120,000	Common stock, no-par, 22,000 shares authorized and issued	$350,000
General expenses	75,000	Preferred stock, 6%, $25 par, 4,000 shares issued	100,000
Gain on discontinued operations	5,000	Income tax expense:	
Retained earnings, beginning	63,000	Continuing operations	28,000
Cost of goods sold	275,000	Gain on discontinued operations	2,000
Treasury stock, common (2,000 shares)	28,000		
Net sales revenue	565,000		

Requirement
Prepare a multistep income statement for Underwood Company for the fiscal year ended June 30, 2007. Include earnings per share. (p. 611)

Preparing a corrected combined statement of income and retained earnings

P12-38B Jeremy Hawk, accountant for Rainbow International Corp., was injured in an auto accident. Another employee prepared the following income statement for the year ended December 31, 2007:

continued . . .

RAINBOW INTERNATIONAL CORP.
Income Statement
December 31, 2007

Revenue and gains:		
Sales		$733,000
Paid-in capital in excess of par—common		111,000
Total revenues and gains		844,000
Expenses and losses:		
Cost of goods sold	$383,000	
Selling expenses	103,000	
General expenses	91,000	
Sales returns	22,000	
Sales discounts	10,000	
Dividends	15,000	
Income tax expense	32,000	
Total expenses and losses		656,000
Income from operations		188,000
Other gains and losses:		
Loss on discontinued operations		(15,000)
Net income		$173,000
Earnings per share		$ 17.30

The individual *amounts* listed on the income statement are correct. However, some accounts are reported incorrectly, and two items don't belong on the income statement at all. Also, income tax has *not* been applied to all appropriate figures. The income tax rate on discontinued operations is 40%. Rainbow issued 14,000 shares of common stock in 2004 and held 4,000 shares as treasury stock during fiscal year 2007. Retained earnings at June 30, 2006, was $117,000.

Requirements

Prepare a corrected combined statement of income and retained earnings for the fiscal year ended December 31, 2007. Prepare the income statement in single-step format, and include earnings per share. (pp. 273–275, 611, 614–616)

Computing earnings per share and reporting a retained earnings restriction

P12-39B The capital structure of Audiology Associates, Inc., at December 31, 2007, included 5,000 shares of $2 preferred stock and 100,000 shares of common stock. Common shares outstanding during 2008 were 100,000. Income from continuing operations during 2008 was $370,000. The company discontinued a segment of the business at a gain of $60,000 and also had an extraordinary gain of $30,000. Audiology Associates' board of directors has restricted $250,000 of retained earnings for expansion of the company's office facilities.

Requirements

1. Compute Audiology Associates' earnings per share for 2008. Start with income from continuing operations. Income and loss amounts are net of income tax. (p. 614)
2. Show two ways of reporting Audiology Associates' retained earnings restriction. Retained Earnings at December 31, 2007, was $160,000, and the company declared cash dividends of $100,000 during 2008. (pp. 606–608)

for 24/7 practice, visit
www.MyAccountingLab.com

Apply Your Knowledge

Decision Cases

Analyzing cash dividends and stock dividends

Case 1. Valley Mills Construction, Inc., had the following stockholders' equity on June 30, 2008:

Common stock, no-par, 100,000 shares issued	$250,000
Retained earnings	190,000
Total stockholders' equity	$440,000

In the past, Valley Mills has paid an annual cash dividend of $1 per share. Despite the large retained earnings balance, the board of directors wished to conserve cash for expansion. The board delayed the payment of cash dividends and in July distributed a 5% stock dividend. During August, the company's cash position improved. The board then declared and paid a cash dividend of $0.9524 per share in September.

Suppose you owned 1,000 shares of Valley Mills common stock, acquired three years ago, prior to the 50% stock dividend. The market price of the stock was $30 per share before any of these dividends.

Requirements

1. What amount of cash dividends did you receive last year—before the stock dividend? What amount of cash dividends will you receive after the stock dividend?

2. How does the stock dividend affect your proportionate ownership in Valley Mills Construction, Inc.? Explain.

3. Immediately after the stock dividend was distributed, the market value of Valley Mills stock decreased from $30 per share to $28.571 per share. Does this decrease represent a loss to you? Explain.

Reporting special items

Case 2. The following accounting issues have arisen at T-Shirts Plus, Inc.:

1. Corporations sometimes purchase their own stock. When asked why they do so, T-Shirts Plus management responds that the stock is undervalued. What advantage would T-Shirts Plus gain by buying and selling its own undervalued stock?

2. T-Shirts Plus earned a significant profit in the year ended December 31, 2008, because land that it held was purchased by the State of Nebraska for a new highway. The company proposes to treat the sale of land as operating revenue. Why do you think the company is proposing this plan? Is this disclosure appropriate?

3. The treasurer of T-Shirts Plus wants to report a large loss as an extraordinary item because the company produced too much product and cannot sell it. Why do you think the treasurer wants to report the loss as extraordinary? Would that be acceptable?

Ethical Issue

Bobby's Bagels just landed a contract to open 100 new stores in shopping malls across the country. The new business should triple the company's profits. Prior to

continued . . .

disclosing the new contract to the public, top managers of the company quietly bought most of Bobby's Bagels stock for themselves. After the discovery was announced, Bobby's Bagels stock price shot up from $7 to $52.

Requirements

1. Did Bobby's Bagels managers behave ethically? Explain your answer.

2. Identify the accounting principle relevant to this situation. Review Chapter 6 if necessary.

3. Who was helped and who was harmed by management's action?

Financial Statement Case

Corporate income statement, earnings per share

Use the Amazon.com financial statements in Appendix A at the end of this book to answer the following questions.

Requirements

1. Show how Amazon.com computed basic earnings per share of $0.87 for 2005.

2. Prepare a T-account to show the beginning and ending balances and all activity in Retained Earnings (Accumulated Deficit) for 2005.

3. How much in cash dividends did Amazon declare during 2005? Explain your answer.

4. How much treasury stock did Amazon have at December 31, 2005? Explain.

Team Project

Requirements

Obtain the annual reports (or annual report data) of five well-known companies. You can get the reports either from the companies' Web sites, your college library, or by mailing a request directly to the company (allow two weeks for delivery). Or you can visit the Web site for this book (http://www.prenhall.com/horngren) or the SEC EDGAR database, which includes the financial reports of most well-known companies.

1. After selecting five companies, examine their income statements to search for the following items:

    a. Income from continuing operations

    b. Discontinued operations

    c. Extraordinary gains and losses

    d. Net income or net loss

    e. Earnings-per-share data

2. Study the companies' balance sheets to see

    a. What classes of stock each company has issued.

    b. Which item carries a larger balance—the Common Stock account or Paid-In Capital in Excess of Par (also labeled Additional Paid-In Capital).

continued . . .

c. What percentage of each company's total stockholders' equity is made up of retained earnings.

d. Whether the company has treasury stock. If so, how many shares and how much is the cost?

3. Examine each company's statement of stockholders' equity for evidence of
   a. Cash dividends
   b. Stock dividends (Some companies use the term *stock split* to refer to a large stock dividend.)
   c. Treasury stock purchases and sales

4. As directed by your instructor, either write a report or present your findings to your class. You may be unable to understand *everything* you find, but neither can the Wall Street analysts! You will be amazed at how much you have learned.

For Internet exercises, Excel in Practice, and additional online activities, go to the Web site www.prenhall.com/horngren.

Quick Check Answers

1. c   2. c   3. b   4. c   5. a   6. d   7. d   8. a   9. b   10. b

13 Long-Term Liabilities

Learning Objectives

1. Account for bonds payable

2. Measure interest expense by the straight-line amortization method

3. Account for retirement and conversion of bonds payable

4. Report liabilities on the balance sheet

5. Show the advantages and disadvantages of borrowing

n earlier chapters of this book you were adventuresome and operated In Motion T-Shirts while in college. You continued with the business after graduation and expanded to several locations. Suppose you grew In Motion to a good-size company and then sold it at a nice profit. What will you do with the cash you received from selling out?

You've noticed that discount airlines Jet Blue and Virgin Airways have done quite well. So you decide to take the plunge and start an airline. You get a charter, issue stock, and raise $5 million. Air West Airlines is up and running.

Needing more cash you must borrow. This will require Air West to issue long-term notes payable or bonds payable. Virtually all companies—both large and small—have borrowed this way.

In this chapter we show how to account for long-term liabilities—notes payable and bonds payable. The chapter appendix 13A includes some related topics that your instructor may or may not wish to cover.

Notes payable and bonds payable are accounted for similarly. Since we covered notes payable back in Chapter 10, we focus on bonds payable here. Before launching into bonds payable, let's compare bonds with stock, which you learned about in Chapters 11 and 12. The following chart shows how stocks and bonds differ.

Stocks	Bonds
1. Stock represents the *ownership* of a corporation. Each stockholder is an *owner*.	1. Bonds represent a *liability* of the corporation. Each bondholder is a *creditor*.
2. The corporation is *not* obligated to repay the stock.	2. The corporation *must* repay the bonds.
3. The corporation *may* or *may not* pay dividends on the stock. Dividends are *not* an expense.	3. The corporation *must* pay interest on the bonds. Interest is an expense.

Bonds: An Introduction

Large companies such as Blockbuster and American Airlines need large amounts of money to finance operations. They may issue bonds payable to the public. **Bonds payable** are groups of notes payable issued to multiple lenders, called bondholders. By issuing bonds payable, Blockbuster can borrow millions of dollars from thousands of investors. Each investor can buy a selected amount of Blockbuster bonds.

Each bondholder gets a bond certificate, which shows the name of the company that borrowed the money, exactly like a note payable. The certificate states the *principal*, which is the amount the company has borrowed. The bonds' principal amount is also called *maturity value*, or *par value*. The company must then pay each bondholder the principal amount at a specific future date, called the maturity date. In Chapter 10 we saw how to account for short-term notes payable. There's a lot of similarity between the accounting for short-term notes payable and long-term notes payable.

People buy bonds to earn interest. The bond certificate states the interest rate that the company will pay and the dates the interest is due (generally twice a year). Exhibit 13-1 shows a bond certificate issued by Air West Airlines, Inc.

Review these bond fundamentals in Exhibit 13-1.

- **Principal amount** (also called **maturity value**, or **par value**) The amount the borrower must pay back to the bondholders.
- **Maturity date** The date on which the borrower must pay the principal amount to the bondholders.
- **Stated interest rate** The annual rate of interest that the borrower pays the bondholders.

Types of Bonds

There are various types of bonds, including the following.

- **Term bonds** all mature at the same time.
- **Serial bonds** mature in installments at regular intervals. For example, a $500,000, 5-year serial bond may mature in $100,000 annual installments over a 5-year period.

EXHIBIT 13-1 Bond Certificate

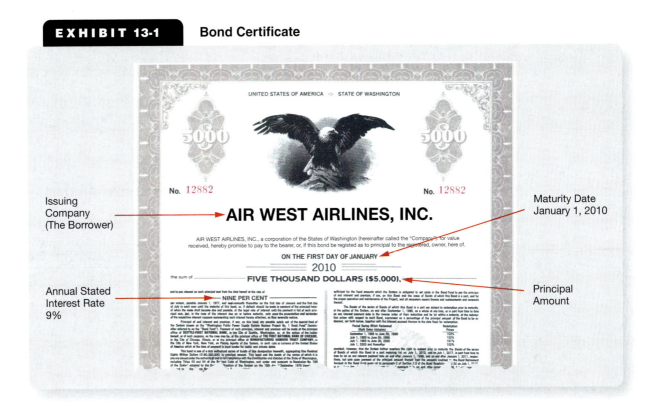

- **Secured bonds** give the bondholder the right to take specified assets of the issuer if the issuer fails to pay principal or interest. A **mortgage** is an example of a secured bond.
- **Debentures** are unsecured bonds backed only by the good faith of the issuer.

Bond Prices

A bond can be issued at any price agreed upon by the issuer and the bondholders. There are three basic categories of bond prices. A bond can be issued at:

- **Maturity (par) value.** Example: A $1,000 bond issued for $1,000. A bond issued at par has no discount or premium.
- **Discount,** a price below maturity (par) value. Example: A $1,000 bond issued for $980. The discount is $20 ($1,000 − $980).
- **Premium,** a price above maturity (par) value. Example: A $1,000 bond issued for $1,015. The premium is $15 ($1,015 − $1,000).

The issue price of a bond does not affect the required payment at maturity. In all cases the company must pay the maturity value of the bonds when they mature.

As a bond approaches maturity, its market price moves toward maturity value. On the maturity date, the market value of a bond exactly equals maturity value because the company pays that amount to retire the bond.

After a bond is issued, investors may buy and sell it through the bond market just as they buy and sell stocks through the stock market. The most famous bond market is the New York Exchange, which lists several thousand bonds.

Bond prices are quoted at a percentage of maturity value. For example,

- A $1,000 bond quoted at 100 is bought or sold for 100% of maturity value ($1,000).
- A $1,000 bond quoted at 101.5 has a price of $1,015 ($1,000 × 1.015).
- A $1,000 bond quoted at 88.375 has a price of $883.75 ($1,000 × .88375).

The issue price of a bond determines the amount of cash the company receives when it issues the bond. In all cases, the company must pay the bonds' maturity value to retire them at maturity.

Exhibit 13-2 shows price information for the bonds of Air West Airlines. On this particular day, 12 of Air West's 9% bonds maturing in 2012 (indicated by 12) were traded. The bonds' highest price on this day was $795 ($1,000 × 0.795). The lowest price of the day was $784.50 ($1,000 × 0.7845). The closing price (last sale of the day) was $795.

EXHIBIT 13-2   **Bond Price Information for Air West Airlines (AirW)**

Bonds	Volume	High	Low	Close
AirW 9% of 12	12	79.5	78.45	79.5

Present Value

Money earns income over time, a fact called the *time value of money*. Appendix 13A covers time value of money in detail, starting on page 679.

Let's see how the time value of money affects bond prices. Assume that a $1,000 bond reaches maturity three years from now and carries no interest. Would you pay $1,000 to purchase this bond? No, because paying $1,000 today to receive $1,000 later yields no income on your investment. How much would you pay today in order to receive $1,000 in three years? The answer is some amount *less* than $1,000. Suppose $750 is a fair price. By investing $750 now to receive $1,000 later, you will earn $250 over the three years. The diagram that follows illustrates the relationship between a bond's price (present value) and its maturity amount (future value).

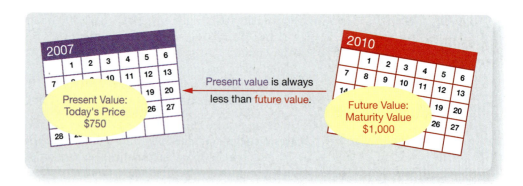

The amount that a person would invest *at the present time* is called the **present value**. The present value is the bond's market price. In our example, $750 is the present value (bond price), and the $1,000 maturity value to be received in three years is the future amount. We show how to compute present value Appendix 13A, page 679.

Bond Interest Rates

Bonds are sold at their market price, which is the bonds' present value. Two interest rates work together to set the price of a bond:

- The **stated interest rate** determines the amount of cash interest the borrower pays each year. The stated interest rate is printed on the bond and *does not change.* For example, Air West Airlines' 9% bonds payable have a stated interest rate of 9% (Exhibit 13-1). Thus, Air West pays $900 of interest annually on each $10,000 bond.
- The **market interest rate** (also known as the **effective interest rate**) is the interest rate that investors demand to earn for loaning their money. The market interest rate *varies* daily. A company may issue bonds with a stated interest rate that differs from the market interest rate.

Air West Airlines may issue its 9% bonds when the market rate has risen to 10%. Will the Air West bonds attract investors in this market? No, because investors can earn 10% on other bonds. Therefore, investors will purchase Air West bonds only at a price less than maturity value. The difference between the lower price and the bonds' maturity value is a *discount.*

Conversely, if the market interest rate is 8%, Air West's 9% bonds will be so attractive that investors will pay more than maturity value for them. The difference between the higher price and maturity value is a *premium.* Exhibit 13-3 shows how the stated interest rate and the market interest rate work together to determine the price of a bond.

EXHIBIT 13-3 Interaction of the Stated Interest Rate and the Market Interest Rate to Determine the Price of a Bond

Example: Bond with a Stated Interest Rate of 9%

Bond's Stated Interest Rate		Market Interest Rate		Issue Price of Bonds Payable
9%	=	9%	→	Maturity value of the bond
9%	<	10%	→	Discount (price below maturity value)
9%	>	8%	→	Premium (price above maturity value)

Issuing Bonds Payable to Borrow Money

The basic journal entry to record the issuance of bonds payable debits Cash and credits Bonds Payable. The company may issue bonds for three different bond prices:

- At *maturity (par)* value
- At a *discount*
- At a *premium*

We begin with the simplest case: issuing bonds payable at maturity (par) value.

Account for bonds payable

Issuing Bonds Payable at Maturity (Par) Value

Air West Airlines has $50,000 of 8% bonds payable that mature in 5 years. Air West issued these bonds at maturity (par) value on January 1, 2008. The issuance entry is:

2008			
Jan. 1	Cash	50,000	
	Bonds Payable		50,000
	Issued bonds.		

Air West, the borrower, makes this one-time journal entry to record the receipt of cash and issuance of bonds payable. Interest payments occur each January 1 and July 1. Air West's first semiannual interest payment is journalized as follows:

2008			
Jan. 1	Interest Expense ($50,000 × 0.08 × 6/12)	2,000	
	Cash		2,000
	Paid semiannual interest.		

Each semiannual interest payment follows this same pattern.

At maturity, Air West will record payment of the bonds as follows:

2013			
Jan. 1	Bonds Payable	50,000	
	Cash		50,000
	Paid off bonds at maturity.		

Now let's see how to issue bonds payable at a discount. This is one of the most common situations.

Issuing Bonds Payable at a Discount

We know that market conditions may force a company such as Air West Airlines to accept a discount price for its bonds. Suppose Air West issues $100,000 of its 9%, five-year bonds when the market interest rate is 9 1/2%. The market price of the bonds drops to 98, which means 98% of par value. Air West receives $98,000 ($100,000 × 0.98) at issuance and makes the following journal entry:

2008			
Jan. 1	Cash ($100,000 × 0.98)	98,000	
	Discount on Bonds Payable	2,000	
	Bonds Payable		100,000
	Issued bonds at a discount.		

After posting, the bond accounts have these balances:

MAIN ACCOUNT	CONTRA ACCOUNT
Bonds Payable	Discount on Bonds Payable
Credit balance 100,000	Debit balance 2,000

Bond carrying amount = $98,000

Discount on Bonds Payable is a contra account to Bonds Payable. Bonds Payable *minus* the discount gives the carrying amount of the bonds. Air West would report these bonds payable as follows immediately after issuance.

Long-term liabilities:		
Bonds payable................................	$100,000	
Less: Discount on bonds payable	(2,000)	$98,000

Interest Expense on Bonds Payable with a Discount

We saw that a bond's stated interest rate may differ from the market interest rate. The market rate was 9 1/2% when Air West issued its 9% bonds. The 1/2% interest-rate difference created the $2,000 discount on the bonds. Investors were willing to pay only $98,000 for a $100,000, 9% bond when they could earn 9 1/2% on other bonds.

Air West borrowed $98,000 but must pay $100,000 when the bonds mature five years later. What happens to the $2,000 discount? The discount is additional interest expense to Air West. The discount raises Air West's interest expense on the bonds to the market interest rate of 9 1/2%. The discount becomes interest expense for Air West through a process called *amortization,* the gradual reduction of an item over time.

Straight-Line Amortization of Bond Discount

We can amortize a bond discount by dividing it into equal amounts for each interest period. This method is called *straight-line amortization.* In our example, the initial discount is $2,000, and there are 10 semiannual interest periods during the bonds' 5-year life.

Therefore 1/10 of the $2,000 bond discount ($200) is amortized each interest period. Air West's first semiannual interest entry is:[1]

2 Measure interest expense by the straight-line amortization method

2008			
July 1	Interest Expense	4,700	
	Cash ($100,000 × 0.09 × 6/12)		4,500
	Discount on Bonds Payable ($2,000/10)		200
	Paid interest and amortized discount.		

Interest expense of $4,700 for each six-month period is the sum of

- The stated interest ($4,500, which is paid in cash)
- *Plus* the amortization of discount ($200).

---

[1]You can record the payment of interest and the amortization of bond discount in two separate entries, as follows:

2008			
July 1	Interest Expense	4,500	
	Cash ($100,000 × 0.09 × 6/12)		4,500
	Paid semiannual interest.		
July 1	Interest Expense	200	
	Discount on Bonds Payable ($2,000/10)		200
	Amortized discount on bonds payable.		

These two entries record the same amount of interest expense ($4,700) as the single entry shown above.

Discount on Bonds Payable has a debit balance. Therefore we credit the Discount account to amortize its balance. Ten amortization entries will decrease the Discount to zero. Then the carrying amount of the bonds payable will be $100,000 at maturity.

Finally, the entry to pay off the bonds at maturity is:

2013				
Jan. 1	Bonds Payable		100,000	
	Cash			100,000
	Paid off bonds at maturity.			

Decision Guidelines

LONG-TERM LIABILITIES—PART A

Air West Airlines has borrowed some money by issuing bonds payable. What type of bonds did Air West issue? How much cash must Air West pay each interest period? How much cash must Air West pay at maturity? The Decision Guidelines address these and other questions.

Decision	Guidelines
a. When will you pay off the bonds?	Types of bonds:
• At maturity? ⟶	• Term bonds
• In installments? ⟶	• Serial bonds
b. Are the bonds secured?	
• Yes ⟶	• Mortgage (secured) bonds
• No ⟶	• Debenture (unsecured) bonds
How are bond prices	
• Quoted? ⟶	• As a percentage of maturity value (Example: A $500,000 bond priced at $510,000 would be quoted at 102 ($510,000 ÷ $500,000 = 1.02)
• Determined? ⟶	• Present value of the future principal amount to pay *plus* present value of the future interest payments (see Appendix 13A)
What are the two interest rates used for bonds? ⟶	• The *stated interest rate* determines the amount of cash interest the borrower pays. This interest rate does *not* change.
	• The *market interest rate* is the rate that investors demand to earn for loaning their money. This interest rate determines the bonds' market price and varies daily.
What causes a bond to be priced at	
• Maturity (par) value? ⟶	• The *stated* interest rate on the bond *equals* the *market* interest rate.
• A discount? ⟶	• The *stated* interest rate on the bond is *less than* the *market* interest rate.
• A premium? ⟶	• The *stated* interest rate on the bond is *greater than* the *market* interest rate.
How to report bonds payable on the balance sheet? ⟶	Maturity (par) value $\begin{cases} -\text{Discount on bonds payable} \\ \quad\quad\text{or} \\ +\text{Premium on bonds payable} \end{cases}$
What is the relationship between interest expense and interest payments when bonds are issued at	
• Maturity (par) value? ⟶	• Interest expense *equals* the interest payment.
• A discount? ⟶	• Interest expense is *greater than* the interest payment.
• A premium? ⟶	• Interest expense is *less than* the interest payment.

Summary Problem 1

West Virginia Power Company has 8% 10-year bonds payable that mature on June 30, 2018. The bonds are issued on June 30, 2008, and West Virginia Power pays interest each June 30 and December 31.

Requirements

1. Will the bonds be issued at par, at a premium, or at a discount if the market interest rate on the date of issuance is 7%? If the market interest rate is 9%?

2. West Virginia Power issued $100,000 of the bonds at 94.
    a. Record issuance of the bonds on June 30, 2008.
    b. Record the payment of interest and amortization of the discount on December 31, 2008. Use the straight-line amortization method.
    c. Compute the bonds' carrying amount at December 31, 2008.
    d. Record the payment of interest and amortization of discount on June 30, 2009.

Solution

Requirement 1

M Market Interest Rate	Bond Price for an 8% Bond
7%	Premium
9%	Discount

Requirement 2

	2008			
a.	June 30	Cash ($100,000 × 0.94)	94,000	
		Discount on Bonds Payable	6,000	
		Bonds Payable		100,000
		Issued bonds at a discount.		
b.	Dec. 31	Interest Expense	4,300	
		Cash ($100,000 × 0.08 × 6/12)		4,000
		Discount on Bonds Payable ($6,000/20)		300
		Paid interest and amortized discount.		
c.		Bond carrying amount at Dec. 31, 2008:		
		$94,300 [$100,000 − ($6,000 − $300)]		
	2009			
d.	June 30	Interest Expense	4,300	
		Cash ($100,000 × 0.08 × 6/12)		4,000
		Discount on Bonds Payable ($6,000/20)		300
		Paid interest and amortized discount.		

Issuing Bonds Payable at a Premium

The issuance of bonds payable at a premium is rare because a premium occurs only when a bond's stated interest rate exceeds the market rate, and companies don't like to pay a stated interest higher than the market rate.

To illustrate a bond premium, let's change the Air West Airlines example. Assume that the market interest rate is 8% when Air West issues its 9%, five-year bonds. These 9% bonds are attractive in an 8% market, and investors will pay a premium to acquire them. Suppose the bonds are priced at 104 (104% of maturity value). In that case, Air West receives $104,000 cash upon issuance. Air West's entry to borrow money and issue these bonds is:

2008			
Jan. 1	Cash ($100,000 × 1.04)	104,000	
	Bonds Payable		100,000
	Premium on Bonds Payable		4,000
	Issued bonds at a premium.		

After posting, the bond accounts have these balances:

MAIN ACCOUNT	**COMPANION ACCOUNT**
Bonds Payable	Premium on Bonds Payable
Credit balance 100,000	Credit balance 4,000

Bond carrying amount $104,000

Bonds Payable and the Premium account each carries a credit balance. The Premium is a companion account to Bonds Payable. Therefore, we add the Premium to Bonds Payable to determine the bond carrying amount. Air West Airlines would report these bonds payable as follows immediately after issuance:

Long-term liabilities:		
Bonds payable	$100,000	
Plus: Premium on bonds payable	4,000	$104,000

Interest Expense on Bonds Payable with a Premium

The 1% difference between the bonds' 9% stated interest rate and the 8% market rate creates the $4,000 premium. Air West borrows $104,000 but must pay back only $100,000 at maturity. The premium is like a saving of interest expense to Air West. The premium cuts Air West's cost of borrowing and reduces interest expense to 8%, the market rate. The amortization of bond premium decreases interest expense over the life of the bonds.

Straight-Line Amortization of Bond Premium

In our example, the beginning premium is $4,000, and there are 10 semiannual interest periods during the bonds' 5-year life. Therefore, 1/10 of the $4,000 ($400) of bond premium is amortized each interest period. Air West's first semiannual interest entry is:[2]

2008			
July 1	Interest Expense	4,100	
	Premium on Bonds Payable ($4,000/10)	400	
	Cash ($100,000 × 0.09 × 6/12)		4,500
	Paid interest and amortized premium.		

Interest expense of $4,100 is:

- The stated interest ($4,500, which is paid in cash)
- *Minus* the amortization of the premium ($400)

At July 1, 2008, immediately after amortizing the bond premium, the bonds have this carrying amount:

$$103,600 \ [\$100,000 + (\$4,000 - \$400)]$$

At December 31, 2008, the bonds' carrying amount will be:

$$103,200 \ [\$100,000 + (\$4,000 - \$400 - \$400)]$$

At maturity on January 1, 2013, the bond premium will have been fully amortized, and the bonds' carrying amount will be $100,000.

Now we move on to some additional bond topics.

Additional Bond Topics

3 Account for retirement and conversion of bonds payable

Companies that issue bonds payable face additional issues, such as:

- Adjusting entries for bonds payable
- Issuance of bonds payable between interest dates
- Retirement of bonds payable
- Convertible bonds payable
- Reporting bonds payable on the balance sheet
- Advantages and disadvantages of issuing bonds versus stock

Adjusting Entries for Bonds Payable

Companies issue bonds payable whenever they need cash. The interest payments seldom occur on December 31, so interest expense must be accrued at year end. The accrual entry should also amortize any bond discount or premium.

---

[2] The payment of interest and the amortization of bond premium can be recorded in separate entries as follows:

2008			
July 1	Interest Expense	4,500	
	Cash ($100,000 × 0.09 × 6/12)		4,500
	Paid semiannual interest.		
July 1	Premium on Bonds Payable ($4,000/10)	400	
	Interest Expense		400
	Amortized premium on bonds payable.		

These two entries record the same amount of interest expense ($4,100) as the single entry shown above.

Suppose Air West Airlines issued $100,000 of 8%, 10-year bonds at a $2,000 discount on October 1, 2009. The interest payments occur on March 31 and September 30 each year. On December 31, Air West accrues interest and amortizes bond discount for three months (October, November, and December) as follows:

2009			
Dec. 31	Interest Expense	2,050	
	Interest Payable ($100,000 × 0.08 × 3/12)		2,000
	Discount on Bonds Payable ($2,000/10 × 3/12)		50
	Accrued interest and amortized discount.		

Interest Payable is credited for three months (October, November, and December). Discount on Bonds Payable must also be amortized for these three months.

The next semiannual interest payment occurs on March 31, 2010, and Air West makes this journal entry:

2010			
Mar. 31	Interest Payable (from Dec. 31)	2,000	
	Interest Expense	2,050	
	Cash ($100,000 × 0.08 × 6/12)		4,000
	Discount on Bonds Payable ($2,000/10 × 3/12)		50
	Paid interest and amortized discount.		

Amortization of a bond premium is similar except that Premium on Bonds Payable is debited.

Issuing Bonds Payable Between Interest Dates

In most of the examples we've seen thus far, Air West Airlines issued bonds payable on an interest date, such as January 1. Corporations can also issue bonds between interest dates. That creates a complication.

Air West Airlines has $100,000 of 8% bonds payable that are dated January 1. That means the interest starts accruing on January 1.

Suppose Air West issues these bonds on April 1. How should we account for the interest for January, February, and March? At issuance on April 1, Air West collects three months' accrued interest from the bondholder and records the issuance of bonds payable as follows:

2008			
April 1	Cash	102,000	
	Bonds Payable		100,000
	Interest Payable ($100,000 × 0.08 × 3/12)		2,000
	Issued bonds two months after the date of the bonds.		

Companies don't split up interest payments. They pay in six-month or annual amounts as stated on the bond certificate.

On the next interest date, Air West will pay six months' interest to whoever owns the bonds at that time. But Air West will have interest expense only for the three months the bonds have been outstanding (April, May, and June). To allocate interest expense to the correct months, Air West makes this entry on July 1 for the customary six-month interest payment:

2008			
July 1	Interest Payable (from April 1)	2,000	
	Interest Expense (for April, May, June)	2,000	
	Cash ($100,000 × 0.08 × 6/12)		4,000
	Paid interest.		

Retirement of Bonds Payable

Normally, companies wait until maturity to pay off, or *retire*, their bonds payable. The basic retirement entry debits Bonds Payable and credits Cash, as we saw earlier. But companies sometimes retire their bonds prior to maturity. The main reason is to relieve the pressure of paying interest.

Some bonds are **callable**, which means the company may *call*, or pay off, the bonds at a specified price. The call price is usually 100 or a few percentage points above par value, perhaps 101 or 102. Callable bonds give the issuer the flexibility to pay off the bonds whenever it is beneficial. An alternative to calling the bonds is to purchase them in the open market at their current market price. Whether the bonds are called or purchased in the open market, the journal entry is the same.

Suppose Air West Airlines has $700,000 of bonds payable outstanding with a remaining discount of $30,000. Lower interest rates have convinced management to pay off these bonds now. These bonds are callable at 100. If the market price of the bonds is 95, will Air West call the bonds at 100 or purchase them in the open market at 95? The market price is lower than the call price, so Air West will pay off the bonds at their market price. Retiring the bonds at 95 results in a gain of $5,000, computed as follows:

Maturity value of bonds being retired	$700,000
Less: Discount	(30,000)
Carrying amount of bonds payable	670,000
Market price ($700,000 × 0.95) paid to retire the bonds	665,000
Gain on retirement of bonds payable	$ 5,000

The following entry records retirement of the bonds, immediately after an interest date:

June 30	Bonds Payable	700,000	
	Discount on Bonds Payable		30,000
	Cash ($700,000 × 0.95)		665,000
	Gain on Retirement of Bonds Payable		5,000
	Retired bonds payable.		

After posting, the bond accounts have zero balances.

Bonds Payable		Discount on Bonds Payable	
Retirement 700,000	Prior	Prior	Retirement 30,000
	balance 700,000	balance 30,000	

The journal entry removes the bonds from the books and records a gain on retirement. Any existing premium would be removed with a debit. If Air West retired only half of these bonds, it would remove only half the discount or premium.

When retiring bonds before maturity, follow these steps:

1. Record partial-period amortization of discount or premium if the retirement date does not fall on an interest date.

2. Write off the portion of Discount or Premium that relates to the bonds being retired.

3. Credit a gain or debit a loss on retirement.

Convertible Bonds Payable

Convertible bonds are popular both with investors and with companies needing to borrow money. **Convertible bonds** may be converted into common stock at the option of the investor. These bonds combine the benefits of interest and principal on the bonds with the opportunity for a gain on the stock. The conversion feature is so attractive that investors accept a lower interest rate than on non-convertible bonds. For example, Amazon.com's convertible bonds payable carry an interest rate of only 4 3/4%. The low interest benefits Amazon.com.

The issuance of convertible bonds payable is recorded like any other debt: Debit Cash and credit Convertible Bonds Payable. Then, if the market price of Amazon's stock rises above the value of the bonds, the bondholders will convert the bonds into stock. The corporation then debits the bond accounts and credits the stock. The carrying amount of the bonds becomes the book value of the newly issued stock. There is no gain or loss.

Assume the Amazon bondholders convert $100,000 of Amazon's bonds payable into 20,000 shares of Amazon's common stock, which has a par value of $0.01 (1 cent) per share. Assume further that the carrying amount of the Amazon bonds is $90,000; thus, there is a bond discount of $10,000. To record the conversion, Amazon would make this journal entry:

May 14	Bonds Payable	100,000	
	Discount on Bonds Payable ($100,000 − $90,000)		10,000
	Common Stock (20,000 × $0.01)		200
	Paid-In Capital in Excess of Par		89,800
	Recorded conversion of bonds payable.		

The entry zeroes out the Bonds Payable account and its related Discount exactly as for a bond retirement. This journal entry transfers the carrying amount of the bonds ($90,000) to stockholders' equity, as follows:

Common Stock	Paid-In Capital in Excess of Par
200	89,800

Total new stockholders' equity = $90,000

Reporting Liabilities on the Balance Sheet

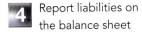
Report liabilities on the balance sheet

Companies report their bonds payable and notes payable among the liabilities on the balance sheet. As we have seen throughout, there are two categories of liabilities, current and long-term.

Serial bonds are payable in installments. The portion payable within one year is a current liability, and the remaining debt is long-term. For example, assume that Toys "Я" Us has $500,000 of bonds payable maturing in $100,000 amounts each year for the next 5 years. The portion payable next year is $100,000. This amount is a current liability, and the remaining $400,000 is a long-term liability. Toys "Я" Us would report the following among its liabilities:

Current liabilities:	
Bonds payable, current	$100,000
Long-term liabilities:	
Bonds payable, long-term	400,000

Notes payable are reported in a similar fashion. We show bonds payable with a discount on page 651 and bonds payable with a premium on page 647.

Advantages and Disadvantages of Issuing Bonds Versus Stock

Borrowing by issuing bonds payable carries a risk: The company may be unable to pay off the bonds. Why then do companies borrow so heavily? Because bonds are a cheaper source of money than stock. Borrowing can help a company increase its earnings per share. Companies thus face this decision: How shall we finance a new project—with bonds or with stock?

Suppose Air West Airlines has net income of $300,000 and 100,000 shares of common stock outstanding before the new project. Air West needs $500,000 for the project and the company is considering two plans:

- Plan 1 is to borrow $500,000 at 10% (issue $500,000 of 10% bonds payable).
- Plan 2 is to issue 50,000 shares of common stock for $500,000.

Air West management believes the new cash can be used to earn income of $200,000 before interest and taxes.

5 Show the advantages and disadvantages of borrowing

Exhibit 13-4 shows the earnings-per-share (EPS) advantage of borrowing.

EXHIBIT 13-4 Earnings-per-Share Advantage of Borrowing Versus Issuing Stock

	Plan 1 Issue $500,000 of 10% Bonds Payable		Plan 2 Issue $500,000 of Common Stock	
Net income before new project		$300,000		$300,000
Expected income on the new project before interest and income tax expenses	$200,000		$200,000	
Less: Interest expense ($500,000 × 0.10)	(50,000)		0	
Project income before income tax	150,000		200,000	
Less: Income tax expense (40%)	(60,000)		(80,000)	
Project net income		90,000		120,000
Net income with new project		$390,000		$420,000
Earnings per share with new project:				
Plan 1 ($390,000/100,000 shares)		$3.90		
Plan 2 ($420,000/150,000 shares)				$2.80

EPS is higher if Air West issues bonds. If all goes well, the company can earn more on the new project ($90,000) than the interest it pays on the bonds ($50,000). Earning more income on borrowed money than the related interest expense is called using **leverage**. It is widely used to increase earnings per share of common stock.

Borrowing can increase EPS, but borrowing has its disadvantages. Debts must be paid during bad years as well as good years. Interest expense may be high enough to eliminate net income and even lead to bankruptcy. This happens to lots of ambitious companies.

Now let's wrap up the chapter with some Decision Guidelines.

Decision Guidelines

LONG-TERM LIABILITIES—PART B

Suppose Air West Airlines needs $50 million to purchase airplanes. Air West issues bonds payable to finance the purchase and now must account for the bonds payable.

The Decision Guidelines outline some of the issues Air West must decide.

Decision

What happens to the bonds' carrying amount when bonds payable are issued at

- Maturity (par) value? ⟶
- A premium? ⟶
- A discount? ⟶

How to account for the retirement of bonds payable?

How to account for the conversion of convertible bonds payable into common stock? (Assume a bond premium.)

What are the advantages of financing operations with

- Stock? ⟶
- Bonds (or notes) payable? ⟶

Guidelines

- Carrying amount *stays* at maturity (par) value.
- Carrying amount *falls* gradually to maturity value.
- Carrying amount *rises* gradually to maturity value.

At maturity date:

Bonds Payable .... Maturity value	
Cash	Maturity value

Before maturity date (assume a discount on the bonds and a gain on retirement):

Bonds Payable .... Maturity value	
Discount on Bonds	
Payable.................	Balance
Cash	Amount Paid
Gain on Retirement	
of Bonds Payable...	Excess

Bonds Payable .... Maturity value	
Premium on Bonds	
Payable....................... Balance	
Common Stock	Par value
Paid-in Capital in	Excess over
Excess of Par	par value

- Creates no liability or interest expense. Less risky to the issuing corporation.
- Results in higher earnings per share—under normal conditions.

Summary Problem 2

Trademark, Inc., has outstanding a $100,000 issue of 6% convertible bonds payable that mature in 2026. Suppose the bonds were dated April 1, 2006, and pay interest each April 1 and October 1.

Requirements

Record the following transactions for Trademark:

a. Issuance of the bonds at 104.8 on April 1, 2006.

b. Payment of interest and amortization of premium on October 1, 2006.

c. Accrual of interest and amortization of premium on December 31, 2006.

d. Payment of interest and amortization of premium on April 1, 2007.

e. Conversion of one-half of the bonds payable into no-par common stock on April 1, 2007.

f. Retirement of one-half of the bonds payable on April 1, 2007. Purchase price to retire the bonds was 102.

Solution

	2006			
a.	April 1	Cash ($100,000 × 1.048)	104,800	
		Bonds Payable		100,000
		Premium on Bonds Payable		4,800
		Issued bonds at a premium.		
b.	Oct. 1	Interest Expense	2,880	
		Premium on Bonds Payable ($4,800/40)	120	
		Cash ($100,000 × 0.06 × 6/12)		3,000
		Paid interest and amortized premium.		
c.	Dec. 31	Interest Expense	1,440	
		Premium on Bonds Payable ($4,800/40 × 1/2)	60	
		Interest Payable ($100,000 × 0.06 × 3/12)		1,500
		Accrued interest and amortized premium.		
	2007			
d.	April 1	Interest Payable (from Dec. 31)	1,500	
		Interest Expense	1,440	
		Premium on Bonds Payable ($4,800/40 × 1/2)	60	
		Cash ($100,000 × 0.06 × 6/12)		3,000
e.	April 1	Bonds Payable ($100,000 × 1/2)	50,000	
		Premium on Bonds Payable		
		[($4,800 − $120 − $60 − $60) × 1/2]	2,280	
		Common Stock		52,280
		Recorded conversion of bonds payable.		
f.	April 1	Bonds Payable ($100,000 × 1/2)	50,000	
		Premium on Bonds Payable		
		[($4,800 − $120 − $60 − $60) × 1/2]	2,280	
		Cash ($50,000 × 1.02)		51,000
		Gain on Retirement of Bonds Payable		1,280
		Retired bonds payable.		

Review Long-Term Liabilities

Accounting Vocabulary

Bond Discount
Excess of a bond's maturity value over its issue price. Also called a **discount (on a bond)**.

Bond Premium
Excess of a bond's issue price over its maturity value. Also called a **premium**.

Bonds Payable
Groups of notes payable issued to multiple lenders called bondholders.

Callable Bonds
Bonds that the issuer may call or pay off at a specified price whenever the issuer wants.

Convertible Bonds
Bonds that may be converted into the common stock of the issuing company at the option of the investor.

Debentures
Unsecured bonds backed only by the good faith of the borrower.

Discount (on a bond)
Excess of a bond's maturity value over its issue price. Also called a **bond discount.**

Effective Interest Rate
Interest rate that investors demand in order to loan their money. Also called the **market interest rate**.

Leverage
Earning more income on borrowed money than the related interest expense, thereby increasing the earnings for the owners of the business.

Market Interest Rate
Interest rate that investors demand in order to loan their money. Also called the **effective interest rate**.

Maturity (par) value
A bond issued at par has no discount on premium.

Mortgage
Borrower's promise to transfer the legal title to certain assets to the lender if the debt is not paid on schedule.

Par Value
Another name for the maturity value of a bond.

Premium
Excess of a bond's issue price over its maturity value. Also called **bond premium.**

Present Value
Amount a person would invest now to receive a greater amount in the future.

Secured Bonds
Bonds that give bondholders the right to take specified assets of the issuer if the issuer fails to pay principal or interest.

Serial Bonds
Bonds that mature in installments over a period of time.

Stated Interest Rate
Interest rate that determines the amount of cash interest the borrower pays and the investor receives each year.

Term Bonds
Bonds that all mature at the same time for a particular lease.

Quick Check

1. Which type of bond is unsecured?
   a. Common bond
   b. Mortgage bond
   c. Serial bond
   d. Debenture bond

2. A $100,000 bond priced at 103.5 can be bought or sold for
   a. $100,000 + interest
   b. $103,500
   c. $3,500
   d. $10,350

3. Which interest rate on a bond determines the amount of the semiannual interest payment?
   a. Market rate
   b. Effective rate
   c. Stated rate
   d. Semiannual rate

4. The final journal entry to record for bonds payable is
   a. Bonds Payable xxx
         Cash xxx
   b. Cash xxx
         Bonds Payable xxx
   c. Interest Expense............................ xxx
         Cash xxx
   d. Discount on Bonds Payable xxx
         Interest Expense xxx

5. Lafferty Corporation's bonds payable carry a stated interest rate of 7%, and the market rate of interest is 8%. The price of the Lafferty bonds will be at
   a. Par value
   b. Maturity value
   c. Premium
   d. Discount

6. Bonds issued at a premium always have
   a. Interest expense equal to the interest payments
   b. Interest expense greater than the interest payments
   c. Interest expense less than the interest payments
   d. None of the above

7. Galena Park Fitness Gym has $500,000 of 10-year bonds payable outstanding. These bonds had a discount of $40,000 at issuance, which was 5 years ago. The company uses the straight-line amortization method. The carrying amount of these bonds payable is
   a. $480,000
   b. $460,000
   c. $500,000
   d. $540,000

8. Nick Spanos Antiques issued its 8%, 10-year bonds payable at a price of $440,000 (maturity value is $500,000). The company uses the straight-line amortization method for the bonds. Interest expense for each year is
   a. $35,200
   b. $46,000
   c. $44,000
   d. $50,000

9. Spice Inc. issued bonds payable on December 31. Spice's bonds were dated July 31. Which statement is true of Spice's journal entry to record issuance of the bonds payable?
   a. Spice must pay one month's accrued interest.
   b. Spice will collect one month's accrued interest in advance.
   c. Spice will collect five months' accrued interest in advance.
   d. Spice will pay five months' interest in advance.

10. Bull & Bear, Inc., retired $100,000 of its bonds payable, paying cash of $103,000. On the retirement date, the bonds payable had a premium of $2,000. The bond retirement created a
    a. Loss of $1,000
    b. Loss of $3,000
    c. Gain of $5,000
    d. Loss of $5,000

    Answers are given after Apply Your Knowledge (p. 678).

Assess Your Progress

Short Exercises

Determining bond prices at par, discount, or premium

S13-1 Determine whether the following bonds payable will be issued at maturity value, at a premium, or at a discount: (pp. 642–643)

a. The market interest rate is 7%. Denver Corp. issues bonds payable with a stated rate of 6 1/2%. (pp. 642–643)

b. Houston, Inc., issued 7% bonds payable when the market rate was 6 3/4%.

c. Cincinnati Corporation issued 8% bonds when the market interest rate was 8%.

d. Miami Company issued bonds payable that pay stated interest of 7%. At issuance, the market interest rate was 8 1/4%.

Pricing bonds

S13-2 Compute the price of the following 7% bonds of Allied Telecom. (pp. 644–645)

a. $100,000 issued at 77.75

b. $100,000 issued at 103.8

c. $100,000 issued at 92.6

d. $100,000 issued at 102.5

Maturity value of a bond

S13-3 For which bond payable in Short Exercise 13-2 will Allied Telecom have to pay the most at maturity? Explain your answer. (pp. 643–644)

Journalizing basic bond payable transactions

S13-4 Hunter Corporation issued a $100,000, 6 1/2%, 10-year bond payable. Journalize the following transactions for Hunter. Include an explanation for each entry.

a. Issuance of the bond payable at par on January 1, 2008. (pp. 645–646)

b. Payment of semiannual cash interest on July 1, 2008. (pp. 645–646)

c. Payment of the bond payable at maturity. (Give the date.) (pp. 645–646)

Determining bonds payable amounts

S13-5 Sonic Drive-Ins borrowed money by issuing $1,000,000 of 6% bonds payable at 96.5.

1. How much cash did Sonic receive when it issued the bonds payable? (pp. 648, 651)

2. How much must Sonic pay back at maturity? (pp. 648, 651)

3. How much cash interest will Sonic pay each six months? (pp. 648, 651)

Bond interest rates

S13-6 A 7%, 10-year bond was issued at a price of 93. Was the market interest rate at the date of issuance closest to 6%, 7%, or 8%? Explain. (pp. 642–643, 646–647)

Issuing bonds payable at a discount; paying interest and amortizing discount by the straight-line method

S13-7 Ogden, Inc., issued a $50,000, 8%, 10-year bond payable at a price of 90 on January 1, 2006. Journalize the following transactions for Ogden. Include an explanation for each entry.

a. Issuance of the bond payable on January 1, 2006. (pp. 646–647)

b. Payment of semiannual interest and amortization of bond discount on July 1, 2006. Ogden uses the straight-line method to amortize bond discount. (pp. 648, 651)

Issuing bonds payable at a premium; paying interest and amortizing premium by the straight-line method

1 2

S13-8 Washington Mutual Insurance Company issued an $80,000, 7%, 10-year bond payable at a price of 110 on January 1, 2009. Journalize the following transactions for Washington. Include an explanation for each entry.

a. Issuance of the bond payable on January 1, 2009. (pp. 652–653)

b. Payment of semiannual interest and amortization of bond premium on July 1, 2009. Washington uses the straight-line method to amortize the premium. (pp. 652–653)

Issuing bonds payable and accruing interest

1 2

S13-9 Onstar Communication issued $100,000 of 6%, 10-year bonds payable on October 1, 2008, at par value. Onstar's accounting year ends on December 31. Journalize the following transactions. Include an explanation for each entry.

a. Issuance of the bonds on October 1, 2008. (pp. 645–646)

b. Accrual of interest expense on December 31, 2008. (pp. 652–653)

c. Payment of the first semiannual interest amount on April 1, 2009. (pp. 652–653)

Issuing bonds payable between interest dates and then paying the interest

1 2

S13-10 Simons Realty issued $250,000 of 6%, 10-year bonds payable at par value on May 1, 2006, four months after the bond's original issue date of January 1, 2006. Journalize the following transactions. Include an explanation for each entry.

a. Issuance of the bonds payable on May 1, 2006. (pp. 652–653)

b. Payment of the first semiannual interest amount on July 1, 2006. (p. 654)

Accounting for the retirement of bonds payable

3

S13-11 On January 1, 2007, Pacifica, Inc., issued $100,000 of 9%, 5-year bonds payable at 104. Pacifica has extra cash and wishes to retire the bonds payable on January 1, 2008, immediately after making the second semiannual interest payment. To retire the bonds, Pacifica pays the market price of 98.

1. What is Pacifica's carrying amount of the bonds payable on the retirement date? (p. 654)

2. How much cash must Pacifica pay to retire the bonds payable? (p. 654)

3. Compute Pacifica's gain or loss on the retirement of the bonds payable. (p. 654)

Accounting for the conversion of bonds payable

3

S13-12 Newmarket Corp. has $1,000,000 of convertible bonds payable outstanding, with a bond premium of $20,000 also on the books. The bondholders have notified Newmarket that they wish to convert the bonds into stock. Specifically, the bonds may be converted into 400,000 shares of Newmarket's $1 par common stock.

1. What is Newmarket's carrying amount of its convertible bonds payable prior to the conversion? (p. 655)

2. Journalize Newmarket's conversion of the bonds payable into common stock. No explanation is required. (p. 655)

Reporting liabilities

S13-13 Master Suites Hotels includes the following selected accounts in its general ledger at December 31, 2008:

Notes payable, long-term	$100,000	Accounts payable	$32,000
Bonds payable	200,000	Discount on bonds payable	6,000
Interest payable (due next year)	1,000		

Prepare the liabilities section of Master Suites' balance sheet at December 31, 2008, to show how the company would report these items. Report a total for current liabilities. (pp. 518, 656–657)

Earnings-per-share effects of financing with bonds versus stock

S13-14 Speegleville Marina needs to raise $1 million to expand. Speegleville's president is considering two plans:
- Plan A: Issue $1,000,000 of 8% bonds payable to borrow the money
- Plan B: Issue 100,000 shares of common stock at $10 per share

Before any new financing, the company expects to earn net income of $300,000, and the company already has 100,000 shares of common stock outstanding. Speegleville believes the expansion will increase income before interest and income tax by $200,000. The income tax rate is 35%.

Prepare an analysis similar to Exhibit 13-4 to determine which plan is likely to result in higher earnings per share. Which financing plan would you recommend? (p. 656–657)

Exercises

Determining whether the bond price will be at par, at a discount, or at a premium

E13-15 Havens Corp. is planning to issue long-term bonds payable to borrow for a major expansion. The chief executive, Richie Havens, asks your advice on some related matters, as follows:

a. At what type of bond price will Havens have total interest expense equal to the cash interest payments? (pp. 645–646)

b. Under which type of bond price will Havens's total interest expense be greater than the cash interest payments? (p. 648)

c. The stated interest rate on the bonds is 7%, and the market interest rate is 8%. What type of bond price can Havens expect for the bonds? (pp. 642–643)

d. Havens could raise the stated interest rate on the bonds to 9% (market rate is 8%). In that case, what type of price can Havens expect for the bonds? (pp. 642–643)

Issuing bonds payable, paying interest, and amortizing discount by the straight-line method

E13-16 On January 1, Deutsch Limited issues 8%, 20-year bonds payable with a maturity value of $100,000. The bonds sell at 97 and pay interest on January 1 and July 1. Deutsch amortizes bond discount by the straight-line method. Record (a) issuance of the bonds on January 1, and (b) the semiannual interest payment and amortization of bond discount on July 1. (pp. 646–651)

Issuing bonds payable, paying and accruing interest

1

E13-17 Pluto Corporation issued $400,000 of 7%, 20-year bonds payable on March 31, 2006. The bonds were issued at 100 and pay interest on March 31 and September 30. Record (a) issuance of the bonds on March 31, 2006, (b) payment of interest on September 30, (c) accrual of interest on December 31, and (d) payment of interest on March 31, 2007. (pp. 645–646)

Bond transactions at par, at a discount, and at a premium

1 **2**

E13-18 Columbus, Inc., issued $50,000 of 10-year, 6% bonds payable on January 1, 2006. Columbus pays interest each January 1 and July 1 and amortizes discount or premium by the straight-line method. The company can issue its bonds payable under various conditions:

a. Issuance at par (maturity) value (pp. 645–646)

b. Issuance at a price of 95 (pp. 645–648)

c. Issuance at a price of 105 (pp. 652–653)

Requirements
1. Journalize Columbus's issuance of the bonds and first semiannual interest payment for each situation. Explanations are not required.
2. Which bond price results in the most interest expense for Columbus? Explain in detail. (pp. 648, 652–653)

Issuing bonds, accruing interest, and paying interest

1

E13-19 Fleetwood Homebuilders issued $200,000 of 6%, 10-year bonds at par on August 31. Fleetwood pays semiannual interest on February 28 and August 31. Journalize for Fleetwood:

a. Issuance of the bonds payable on August 31, 2007. (pp. 645–646)

b. Accrual of interest on December 31, 2007. (pp. 652–653)

c. Payment of semiannual interest on February 28, 2008. (pp. 652–653)

Issuing bonds between interest dates

1

E13-20 Saturn Corporation issued $400,000 of 6% bonds payable on June 30. The bonds were dated April 30, and the semiannual interest dates are April 30 and October 31.

1. How much cash will Saturn receive upon issuance of the bonds on June 30? (pp. 652–653)
2. How much cash interest will Saturn pay on October 31, the first semiannual interest date? (p. 654)

Issuing bonds between interest dates and paying interest

1

E13-21 Lakewood Co. issues $100,000 of 6%, 20-year bonds payable that are dated April 30. Record (a) issuance of bonds at par on May 31 and (b) the next semiannual interest payment on October 31.

Recording retirement of bonds payable

3

E13-22 Virtuoso Transportation issued $600,000 of 8% bonds payable at 97 on October 1, 2010. These bonds are callable at 100 and mature on October 1, 2018. Virtuoso pays interest each April 1 and October 1. On October 1, 2015, when the bonds' market price is 99, Virtuoso retires the bonds in the most economical way available.

continued . . .

Requirement

Record the payment of the interest and amortization of bond discount at October 1, 2015, and the retirement of the bonds on that date. Virtuoso uses the straight-line amortization method.

Recording conversion of bonds payable

E13-23 Worldview Magazine, Inc., issued $700,000 of 15-year, 8 1/2% convertible bonds payable on July 31, 2006, at a price of 98. Each $1,000 maturity amount of the bonds is convertible into 50 shares of $5 par stock. On July 31, 2009, bondholders converted the bonds into common stock.

Requirements

1. What would cause the bondholders to convert their bonds into common stock?
2. Without making journal entries, compute the carrying amount of the bonds payable at July 31, 2009. The company uses the straight-line method to amortize bond discount.
3. All amortization has been recorded properly. Journalize the conversion transaction at July 31, 2009. No explanation is required.

Recording early retirement and conversion of bonds payable

E13-24 Superhero Industries reported the following at September 30:

Long-term liabilities:		
Convertible bonds payable	$200,000	
Less: Discount on bonds payable	(12,000)	$188,000

Requirements

1. Record retirement of half of the bonds on October 1 at the call price of 101.
2. Record conversion of the remainder of the bonds into 10,000 shares of Superhero Industries $1 par common stock on October 1. What would cause the bondholders to convert their bonds into stock?

Reporting liabilities

E13-25 At December 31, MediShare Precision Instruments owes $50,000 on accounts payable, plus salary payable of $10,000 and income tax payable of $8,000. MediShare also has $200,000 of bonds payable that require payment of a $20,000 installment next year and the remainder in later years. The bonds payable require an annual interest payment of $7,000, and MediShare still owes this interest for the current year.

Report MediShare's liabilities on its classified balance sheet. List the current liabilities in descending order (largest first, and so on), and show the total of current liabilities. (pp. 518, 656–657)

Analyzing alternative plans for raising money

E13-26 MC Electronics is considering two plans for raising $1,000,000 to expand operations. Plan A is to issue 9% bonds payable, and plan B is to issue 100,000 shares of common stock. Before any new financing, MC has net income of $300,000 and 100,000 shares of common stock outstanding. Management believes the company can use the new funds to earn additional income of $420,000 before interest and taxes. The income tax rate is 40%.

Requirement

Analyze MC Electronics' situation to determine which plan will result in higher earnings per share. Use Exhibit 13-4 as a guide. (pp. 656–657)

Analyzing bond transactions

E13-27 This (partial and adapted) advertisement appeared in *The Wall Street Journal*.

New Issue

$300,000,000

HEWITT CORPORATION

10.5% Subordinated Debentures due March 31, 2015
interest payable March 31 and September 30

Price 98.50%   **March 31, 2005**

A *subordinated* debenture gives rights to the bondholder that are more restricted than the rights of other bondholders.

Requirements
Answer these questions about Hewitt Corporation's debenture bonds payable:
1. Hewitt issued these bonds payable at their offering price on March 31, 2005. Describe the transaction in detail, indicating who received cash, who paid cash, and how much.
2. Why is the stated interest rate on these bonds so high?
3. Compute Hewitt's annual cash interest payment on the bonds.
4. Compute Hewitt's annual interest expense under the straight-line amortization method.

Analyzing bond transactions

E13-28 Refer to the bond situation of Hewitt Corporation in Exercise 13-27. Hewitt issued the bonds at the advertised price. The company uses the straight-line amortization method and reports financial statements on a calendar-year basis.

Requirements
1. Journalize the following bond transactions of Hewitt Corporation. Explanations are not required.

2005	
Mar. 31	Issuance of the bonds.
Sep. 30	Payment of interest expense and amortization of discount on bonds payable.

continued . . .

2. What is Hewitt's carrying amount of the bonds payable at
   a. September 30, 2005?
   b. March 31, 2006?

Problems (Group A)

Analyzing bonds, recording bonds at par, and reporting on the financial statements

P13-29A Environmental Concerns Limited (ECL) issued $500,000 of 10-year, 6% bonds payable at maturity (par) value on May 1, 2008. The bonds pay interest each April 30 and October 31, and the company ends its accounting year on December 31.

Requirements
1. Fill in the blanks to complete these statements: (pp. 644–645)
   a. ECL's bonds are priced at (express the price as a percentage) _____. (pp. 644–645)
   b. When ECL issued its bonds, the market interest rate was _____%. (pp. 642–643)
   c. The amount of bond discount or premium for ECL to account for is $ _____ because the bonds were issued at _____. (pp. 645–646)
2. Journalize for ECL
   a. Issuance of the bonds payable on May 1, 2008. (pp. 645–646)
   b. Payment of interest on October 31, 2008. (pp. 645–646)
   c. Accrual of interest at December 31, 2008. (pp. 652–653)
   d. Payment of interest on April 30, 2009. (pp. 645–646)

   Explanations are not required.
3. Show what ECL will report on its income statement for 2008 and on its classified balance sheet at December 31, 2008. (pp. 656–657)

Issuing bonds and amortizing discount by the straight-line method

P13-30A On March 1, 2007, Educators Credit Union (ECU) issued 6%, 20-year bonds payable with maturity value of $300,000. The bonds pay interest on February 28 and August 31. ECU amortizes bond premium and discount by the straight-line method.

Requirements
1. If the market interest rate is 5% when ECU issues its bonds, will the bonds be priced at maturity (par) value, at a premium, or at a discount? Explain. (p. 647)
2. If the market interest rate is 7% when ECU issues its bonds, will the bonds be priced at par, at a premium, or at a discount? Explain. (p. 644)
3. The issue price of the bonds is 98. Journalize the following bond transactions:
   a. Issuance of the bonds on March 1, 2007. (pp. 652–653)
   b. Payment of interest and amortization of discount on August 31, 2007. (pp. 652–653)
   c. Accrual of interest and amortization of discount on December 31, 2007. (pp. 652–653)
   d. Payment of interest and amortization of discount on February 28, 2008. (pp. 652–653)

Determining bond price, recording bond transactions by the straight-line amortization method

P13-31A El Conquistador, Inc., finances operations with both bonds and stock. Suppose El Conquistador issued $500,000 of 10-year, 8% bonds payable under various market conditions. Match each market interest rate with the appropriate bond price, as follows. The three possible bond prices are $467,000; $500,000; and $536,000.

Market Interest Rate	Bond Price
7%	?
8%	?
9%	?

El Conquistador pays annual interest each December 31.
After determining the respective bond prices, make the following journal entries for the bond discount situation (explanations are not required):

Dec. 31, 2006	Issuance of the bonds at a discount. (pp. 646–647)
Dec. 31, 2007	Payment of interest and amortization of bond discount by the straight-line method. (pp. 648, 651)
Dec. 31, 2016	Payment of interest and amortization of bond discount by the straight-line method. (pp. 648, 651)
Dec. 31, 2016	Final payment of the bonds payable. (pp. 648, 651)

How much total interest expense will El Conquistador have during the 10-year life of these bonds?

Analyzing a company's long-term debt and journalizing its transactions

P13-32A Captain Billy Whizbang Hamburgers, Inc., issued 6%, 10-year bonds payable at 95 on December 31, 2005. At December 31, 2007, Captain Billy reported the bonds payable as follows:

Long-Term Debt:		
Bonds payable.................	$200,000	
Less: Discount.................	(8,000)	192,000

Captain Billy uses the straight-line amortization method and pays semiannual interest each June 30 and December 31.

Requirements

1. Answer the following questions about Captain Billy Whizbang's bonds payable:
   a. What is the maturity value of the bonds? (pp. 646–647)
   b. What is the carrying amount of the bonds at December 31, 2007? (pp. 646–647)
   c. What is the annual cash interest payment on the bonds? (pp. 648, 651)
   d. How much interest expense should the company record each year? (pp. 648, 651)
2. Record the June 30, 2008, semiannual interest payment and amortization of discount. (pp. 648, 651)
3. What will be the carrying amount of the bonds at December 31, 2008? (pp. 648, 651)

Recording bonds (at par) and reporting bonds payable on the balance sheet—bond issued between interest dates

P13-33A The board of directors of Changing Seasons Health Spa authorizes the issuance of $600,000 of 7%, 10-year bonds payable. The semiannual interest dates are May 31 and November 30. The bonds are issued on July 31, 2008, at par plus accrued interest.

Requirements
1. Journalize the following transactions:
   a. Issuance of the bonds on July 31, 2008.
   b. Payment of interest on November 30, 2008.
   c. Accrual of interest on December 31, 2008.
   d. Payment of interest on May 31, 2009.
2. Report interest payable and bonds payable as they would appear on the Changing Seasons balance sheet at December 31, 2008.

Reporting liabilities on the balance sheet

P13-34A The accounting records of Earthlink Wireless include the following:

Mortgage note payable, long-term	$77,000	Salary payable	$ 9,000
Accounts payable	74,000	Bonds payable, long-term	160,000
Bonds payable,		Premium on bonds payable	
current installment	20,000	(all long-term)	13,000
Interest payable	14,000	Unearned service revenue	3,000
		Common stock, no par	100,000

Requirements
Report these liabilities on the Earthlink Wireless balance sheet, including headings and totals for current liabilities and long-term liabilities. (pp. 518, 646–647, 656–657)

Financing operations with debt or with stock

P13-35A Two businesses are considering how to raise $5 million.

Buchanan Corporation is having its best year since it began operations in 1998. For each of the past 10 years, earnings per share have increased by at least 15%. The outlook for the future is equally bright, with new markets opening up and competitors unable to manufacture products of Buchanan's quality. Buchanan Corporation is planning a large-scale expansion.

Garfield Company has fallen on hard times. Net income has been flat for the last 6 years, with this year falling by 10% from last year's level of profits. Top management has experienced turnover, and the company lacks leadership. To become competitive again, Garfield desperately needs $5 million for expansion.

Requirements
1. As an independent consultant, propose a plan for each company to raise the needed cash. Which company should issue bonds payable? Which company should issue stock? Consider the advantages and the disadvantages of raising money by issuing bonds and by issuing stock, and discuss them in your answer. Use the following memorandum headings to report your plans for the two companies. (pp. 656–657)
   - Plan for Buchanan Corporation to raise $5 million
   - Plan for Garfield Company to raise $5 million

continued . . .

Set up your memo as follows:

```
Date: _____

To: Managements of Buchanan Corporation and Garfield Company

From: (Student Name)

Subject: Plan for each company to raise $5 million
_____

• Plan for Buchanan Corporation to raise $5 million

• Plan for Garfield Company to raise $5 million
```

2. How will what you learned in this problem help you manage a business?

Problems (Group B)

Analyzing bonds, recording bonds at par, and reporting on the financial statements

P13-36B Total Placement Service (TPS) issued $600,000 of 20-year, 7% bonds payable at maturity (par) value on February 1, 2008. The bonds pay interest each January 31 and July 31, and the company ends its accounting year on December 31.

1. Fill in the blanks to complete these statements:
   a. TPS's bonds are priced at (express the price as a percentage) _____. (pp. 644–646)
   b. When TPS issued its bonds, the market interest rate was _____ %. (pp. 642–643)
   c. The amount of bond discount or premium for TPS to account for is $_____ because the bonds were issued at _____. (pp. 645–646)

2. Journalize for TPS
   a. Issuance of the bonds payable on February 1, 2008. (pp. 645–646)
   b. Payment of interest on July 31, 2008. (pp. 645–646)
   c. Accrual of interest at December 31, 2008. (pp. 652–653)
   d. Payment of interest on January 31, 2009. (pp. 645–646)

   Explanations are not required.

3. Show what TPS will report on its income statement for the year ended December 31, 2008, and on its classified balance sheet at December 31, 2008. (pp. 656–657)

Issuing notes payable and amortizing premium by the straight-line method

P13-37B On April 1, 2006, US Ultracom issued 7%, 10-year bonds payable with maturity value of $400,000. The bonds pay interest on March 31 and September 30, and US Ultracom amortizes premium and discount by the straight-line method.

continued . . .

Long-Term Liabilities **673**

Requirements

1. If the market interest rate is 6 1/2% when US Ultracom issues its bonds, will the bonds be priced at maturity (par) value, at a premium, or at a discount? Explain. (pp. 643–644)
2. If the market interest rate is 8% when US Ultracom issues its bonds, will the bonds be priced at par, at a premium, or at a discount? Explain. (pp. 643–644)
3. Assume that the issue price of the bonds is 101. Journalize the following bonds payable transactions:
   a. Issuance of the bonds on April 1, 2006. (pp. 652–653)
   b. Payment of interest and amortization of premium on September 30, 2006. (pp. 652–653)
   c. Accrual of interest and amortization of premium on December 31, 2006. (pp. 652–653)
   d. Payment of interest and amortization of premium on March 31, 2007. (pp. 652–653)

Determining bond price; recording bond transactions by the straight-line amortization method

P13-38B Tristate Recreation Park (TRP) finances operations with both bonds and stock. Suppose TRP issued $200,000 of 10-year, 6% bonds payable under various market conditions. Match each market interest rate with the appropriate bond price, as follows. The three possible bond prices are $216,000; $200,000; and $186,000.

Market Interest Rate	Bond Price
7%	?
6%	?
5%	?

TRP pays annual interest each December 31.

After determining the respective bond prices, make the following journal entries for the bond premium situation (explanations are not required):

Dec. 31, 2008	Issuance of the bonds at a premium. (pp. 652–653)
Dec. 31, 2009	Payment of interest and amortization of bond premium by the straight-line method. (pp. 652–653)
Dec. 31, 2018	Payment of interest and amortization of bond premium by the straight-line method. (pp. 652–653)
Dec. 31, 2018	Final payment of the bonds payable. (pp. 652–653)

How much total interest expense will TRP have during the 10-year life of these bonds?

Analyzing a company's long-term debt and journalizing its transactions

P13-39B Holze Music Co. issued 5%, 10-year bonds payable at 75 on December 31, 2006. At December 31, 2009, Holze reported the bonds payable as follows:

Long-Term Debt:		
Bonds payable...............	$200,000	
Less: Discount...............	(35,000)	$165,000

Holze uses the straight-line amortization method.

continued . . .

Requirements

1. Answer the following questions about Holze's bonds payable:
   a. What is the maturity value of the bonds? (pp. 646–647)
   b. What is the carrying amount of the bonds at December 31, 2009? (pp. 646–647)
   c. What is Holze's annual cash interest payment on the bonds? (pp. 648, 651)
   d. How much interest expense should Holze record each year? (pp. 648, 651)
2. Holze pays annual interest for these bonds each year on December 31. Record the December 31, 2010, annual interest payment and amortization of discount. (pp. 648, 651)
3. What will be the carrying amount of the bonds at December 31, 2010? (pp. 648, 651)

Recording bonds (at par) and reporting bonds payable on the balance sheet—bonds issued between interest dates

P13-40B The board of directors of Beta North America, Inc., authorizes the issuance of $1 million of 9%, 20-year bonds payable. The semiannual interest dates are March 31 and September 30. The bonds are issued on April 30, 2007, at par plus accrued interest.

Requirements

1. Journalize the following transactions:
   a. Issuance of the bonds on April 30, 2007. (pp. 652–653)
   b. Payment of interest on September 30, 2007. (p. 654)
   c. Accrual of interest on December 31, 2007. (pp. 652–653)
   d. Payment of interest on March 31, 2008. (pp. 652–653)
2. Report interest payable and bonds payable as they would appear on the Beta balance sheet at December 31, 2007. (pp. 656–657)

Reporting liabilities on the balance sheet

P13-41B The accounting records of Compass Bookstores, Inc., include the following:

Accounts payable	$ 68,000	Salary payable	$32,000
Mortgage note payable—		Bonds payable, current portion	25,000
long-term	110,000	Discount on all bonds payable	
Interest payable	19,000	(all long-term)	10,000
Bonds payable, long-term	300,000	Income tax payable	16,000
Common stock, no par	155,000		

Requirement

Report these liabilities on Compass Bookstores' balance sheet, including headings and totals for current liabilities and long-term liabilities. (pp. 518, 646–647, 656–657)

Financing operations with debt or with stock

P13-42B Brigadier Homebuilders is embarking on a massive expansion. Plans call for building 100 homes within the next two years. Management estimates that the expansion will cost $15 million. The board of directors is considering obtaining the $15 million through issuing either bonds payable or common stock.

continued . . .

Requirements

1. Write a memo to company management. Discuss the advantages and disadvantages of issuing bonds and of issuing common stock to raise the needed cash. Use the following format for your memo (pp. 656–657):

Date: _____

To: Management of Brigadier Homebuilders

From: (Student Name)

Subject: Advantages and disadvantages of issuing bonds and of issuing stock to raise $15 million for expansion

---

Advantages and disadvantages of issuing bonds:

Advantages and disadvantages of issuing stock:

---

for 24-7 practice, visit www.MyAccountingLab.com

2. How will what you learned in this problem help you manage a business?

Apply Your Knowledge

Decision Cases

Questions about long-term debt

Case 1. The following questions are not related.

1. Duncan Brooks Co. needs to borrow $500,000 to open new stores. Brooks can borrow $500,000 by issuing 5%, 10-year bonds at a price of 96. How much will Brooks actually be borrowing under this arrangement? How much must Brooks pay back at maturity? How will Brooks account for the difference between the amount borrowed and the amount paid back? (pp. 646–647, 648, 651)

2. Brooks prefers to borrow for longer periods when interest rates are low and for shorter periods when interest rates are high. Why is this a good business strategy? (Challenge)

Analyzing alternative ways of raising $4 million

Case 2. Business is going well for Email Designers. The board of directors of this family-owned company believes that Email Designers could earn an additional $1,000,000 income before interest and taxes by expanding into new markets. However, the $4,000,000 the business needs for growth cannot be raised within the family. The directors, who strongly wish to retain family control of the company, must issue securities to outsiders. They are considering three financing plans.

Plan A is to borrow at 6%. Plan B is to issue 100,000 shares of common stock. Plan C is to issue 100,000 shares of nonvoting, $2.50 preferred stock ($2.50 is the annual cash dividend for each share of preferred stock). Email Designers currently has net income of $1,200,000 and 400,000 shares of common stock outstanding. The company's income tax rate is 40%.

Requirements

1. Prepare an analysis similar to Exhibit 13-4 to determine which plan will result in the highest earnings per share of common stock. (pp. 656–657)

2. Recommend one plan to the board of directors. Give your reasons.

Ethical Issue

Axiom Sports Co. owes $5 million on notes payable that will come due for payment in $2.5 million annual installments, starting next year. Cash is scarce, and Axiom management doesn't know where next year's note payment will come from. Axiom has prepared its balance sheet as follows:

Liabilities	
Current:	
Accounts payable	$1,900,000
Salary payable and other accrued liabilities	300,000
Unearned revenue collected in advance	500,000
Income tax payable	200,000
Total current liabilities	2,900,000
Long-term:	
Notes payable	5,000,000

What is wrong with the way Axiom reported its liabilities? Why did Axiom report its liabilities this way? What is unethical about this way of reporting *these* liabilities? Who can be harmed as a result?

Financial Statement Case

Analyzing long-term debt

The Amazon.com balance sheet, income statement (statement of operations), and Note 4 in Appendix A at the end of this book provide details about the company's long-term debt. Use those data to answer the following questions.

Requirements

1. How much did Amazon.com owe on long-term debt at December 31, 2005? How much of this debt was payable in the coming year?

2. Journalize in a single entry Amazon's interest expense for 2005. Amazon paid cash of $105 million for interest.

3. Refer to Note 4 and compute the annual interest on Amazon's 4.75% convertible subordinated notes. Round to the nearest $1 thousand.

Team Project

Each member of the team should select a large corporation and go to its Web site. Surf around until you find the company's balance sheet. Often the appropriate tab is labeled as

- Investor Relations
- About the Company
- Financial Reports
- 10-K Report

From the company's balance sheet scroll down until you find the liabilities.

Requirements

1. List all the company's liabilities—both current and long-term—along with each amount.

2. Read the company's notes to the financial statements and include any details that help you identify the amount of a liability.

3. Compute the company's current ratio and debt ratio. (p. 214)

4. Bring your findings to your team meeting, compare your results with those of your team members, and prepare either a written report or an oral report, as directed by your instructor.

For Internet exercises, Excel in Practice, and additional online activities, go to the Web site www.prenhall.com/horngren.

Quick Check Answers

1. *d*   2. *b*   3. *c*   4. *a*   5. *d*   6. *c*   7. *a*   8. *b*   9. *c*   10. *a*

Appendix 13A

The Time Value of Money: Present Value of a Bond and Effective-Interest Amortization

The term *time value of money* refers to the fact that money earns interest over time. Interest is the cost of using money. To borrowers, interest is the expense of renting money. To lenders, interest is the revenue earned from lending. In this chapter we focus on the borrower, who owes money on the bonds payable.

Present Value

Often a person knows a future amount, such as the maturity value of a bond, and needs to know the bond's present value. The present value of the bond measures its price and tells an investor how much to pay for the bond.

Present Value of 1

Suppose an investment promises you $5,000 at the *end* of one year. How much would you pay *now* to acquire this investment? You would be willing to pay the present value of the $5,000 future amount.

Present value depends on three factors:

1. the amount to be received in the future
2. the time span between your investment and your future receipt
3. the interest rate

Computing a present value is called *discounting* because the present value is *always* less than the future value.

In our example, the future receipt is $5,000. The investment period is one year. Assume that you demand an annual interest rate of 10% on your investment. The following diagram shows that the present value of $5,000 at 10% for one year is $4,545.

Present Value		Future Value
⌐	10%	⌐
Time 0		1 year
$4,545	← Retreat in time (discount) ──	$5,000

You can compute the present value of $5,000 at 10% for one year, as follows:

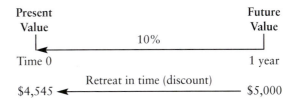

$$\frac{\text{Future value}}{(1 + \text{Interest rate})} = \frac{\$5,000}{1.10} = \$4,545$$

If the $5,000 is to be received two years from now, you will pay only $4,132 for the investment, as follows:

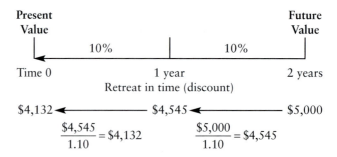

Present-Value Tables

We have shown how to compute a present value. But that computation is burdensome for an investment that spans many years. Present-value tables ease our work. Let's reexamine our examples of present value by using Exhibit 13A-1, Present Value of $1.

EXHIBIT 13A-1 Present Value of $1

Present Value of $1

Period	4%	5%	6%	7%	8%	10%	12%	14%	16%
1	0.962	0.952	0.943	0.935	0.926	0.909	0.893	0.877	0.862
2	0.925	0.907	0.890	0.873	0.857	0.826	0.797	0.769	0.743
3	0.889	0.864	0.840	0.816	0.794	0.751	0.712	0.675	0.641
4	0.855	0.823	0.792	0.763	0.735	0.683	0.636	0.592	0.552
5	0.822	0.784	0.747	0.713	0.681	0.621	0.567	0.519	0.476
6	0.790	0.746	0.705	0.666	0.630	0.564	0.507	0.456	0.410
7	0.760	0.711	0.665	0.623	0.583	0.513	0.452	0.400	0.354
8	0.731	0.677	0.627	0.582	0.540	0.467	0.404	0.351	0.305
9	0.703	0.645	0.592	0.544	0.500	0.424	0.361	0.308	0.263
10	0.676	0.614	0.558	0.508	0.463	0.386	0.322	0.270	0.227
11	0.650	0.585	0.527	0.475	0.429	0.350	0.287	0.237	0.195
12	0.625	0.557	0.497	0.444	0.397	0.319	0.257	0.208	0.168
13	0.601	0.530	0.469	0.415	0.368	0.290	0.229	0.182	0.145
14	0.577	0.505	0.442	0.388	0.340	0.263	0.205	0.160	0.125
15	0.555	0.481	0.417	0.362	0.315	0.239	0.183	0.140	0.108
16	0.534	0.458	0.394	0.339	0.292	0.218	0.163	0.123	0.093
17	0.513	0.436	0.371	0.317	0.270	0.198	0.146	0.108	0.080
18	0.494	0.416	0.350	0.296	0.250	0.180	0.130	0.095	0.069
19	0.475	0.396	0.331	0.277	0.232	0.164	0.116	0.083	0.060
20	0.456	0.377	0.312	0.258	0.215	0.149	0.104	0.073	0.051

For the 10% investment for one year, we find the junction in the 10% column and across from 1 in the Period column. The figure 0.909 is computed as follows: 1/1.10 = 0.909. This work has been done for us and all the present values are given in the table. The heading in Exhibit 13A-1 states $1. To figure present value for $5,000, we multiply $5,000 by 0.909. The result is $4,545, which matches the result we obtained by hand.

For the two-year investment, we read down the 10% column and across the Period 2 row. We multiply 0.826 (computed as 0.909/1.10 = 0.826) by $5,000 and get $4,130, which confirms our earlier computation of $4,132 (the difference is due to rounding in the present-value table). Using the table, we can compute the present value of any single future amount.

Present Value of an Annuity

Let's return to the investment example that provided a single future receipt ($5,000 at the end of two years). Annuity investments provide multiple receipts of an equal amount at fixed intervals.

Consider an investment that promises *annual* cash receipts of $10,000 to be received at the end of each of three years. Assume that you demand a 12% return on your investment. What is the investment's present value? The present value determines how much you would pay today to acquire the investment. The investment spans three periods, and you would pay the sum of three present values. The computation follows.

The present value of this annuity is $24,020. By paying $24,020 today, you will receive $10,000 at the end of each of the three years while earning 12% on your investment.

Year	Annual Cash Receipt	×	Present Value of $1 at 12% (Exhibit 13A-1)	=	Present Value of Annual Cash Receipt
1	$10,000	×	0.893	=	$ 8,930
2	10,000	×	0.797	=	7,970
3	10,000	×	0.712	=	7,120
		Total present value of investment		=	$24,020

The example illustrates repetitive computations of the three future amounts. One way to ease the computational burden is to add the three present values of $1 (0.893 + 0.797 + 0.712) and multiply their sum (2.402) by the annual cash receipt ($10,000) to obtain the present value of the annuity ($10,000 × 2.402 = $24,020).

An easier approach is to use a present value of an annuity table. Exhibit 13A-2 on the next page shows the present value of $1 to be received at the end of each period for a given number of periods. The present value of a three-period annuity at 12% is 2.402 (the junction of the Period 3 row and the 12% column). Thus, $10,000 received annually at the end of each of three years, discounted at 12%, is $24,020 ($10,000 × 2.402), which is the present value.

Present Value of Bonds Payable

The present value of a bond—its market price—is the sum of
- the present value of the principal amount to be received at maturity—a single amount (present value of $1) *plus*
- the present value of the future stated interest amounts—an annuity because it occurs periodically (present value of annuity of $1).

EXHIBIT 13A-2 Present Value of Annuity of $1

Present Value of Annuity of $1

Period	4%	5%	6%	7%	8%	10%	12%	14%	16%
1	0.962	0.952	0.943	0.935	0.926	0.909	0.893	0.877	0.862
2	1.886	1.859	1.833	1.808	1.783	1.736	1.690	1.647	1.605
3	2.775	2.723	2.673	2.624	2.577	2.487	2.402	2.322	2.246
4	3.630	3.546	3.465	3.387	3.312	3.170	3.037	2.914	2.798
5	4.452	4.329	4.212	4.100	3.993	3.791	3.605	3.433	3.274
6	5.242	5.076	4.917	4.767	4.623	4.355	4.111	3.889	3.685
7	6.002	5.786	5.582	5.389	5.206	4.868	4.564	4.288	4.039
8	6.733	6.463	6.210	5.971	5.747	5.335	4.968	4.639	4.344
9	7.435	7.108	6.802	6.515	6.247	5.759	5.328	4.946	4.607
10	8.111	7.722	7.360	7.024	6.710	6.145	5.650	5.216	4.833
11	8.760	8.306	7.887	7.499	7.139	6.495	5.938	5.453	5.029
12	9.385	8.863	8.384	7.943	7.536	6.814	6.194	5.660	5.197
13	9.986	9.394	8.853	8.358	7.904	7.103	6.424	5.842	5.342
14	10.563	9.899	9.295	8.745	8.244	7.367	6.628	6.002	5.468
15	11.118	10.380	9.712	9.108	8.559	7.606	6.811	6.142	5.575
16	11.652	10.838	10.106	9.447	8.851	7.824	6.974	6.265	5.669
17	12.166	11.274	10.477	9.763	9.122	8.022	7.120	6.373	5.749
18	12.659	11.690	10.828	10.059	9.372	8.201	7.250	6.467	5.818
19	13.134	12.085	11.158	10.336	9.604	8.365	7.366	6.550	5.877
20	13.590	12.462	11.470	10.594	9.818	8.514	7.469	6.623	5.929

Discount Price

Let's compute the present value of the 9%, five-year bonds of Air West Airlines. The maturity value of the bonds is $100,000 and they pay 4 1/2% stated interest semi-annually. At issuance, the annual market interest rate is 10% (5% semiannually). Therefore, the market interest rate for each of the 10 semiannual periods is 5%. We use 5% to compute the present value (PV) of the maturity and the present value (PV) of the stated interest. The market price of these bonds is $96,149, as follows:

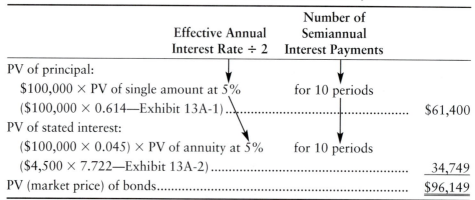

AIR WEST BONDS—DISCOUNT PRICE $96,149

	Effective Annual Interest Rate ÷ 2	Number of Semiannual Interest Payments	
PV of principal:			
$100,000 × PV of single amount at 5%		for 10 periods	
($100,000 × 0.614—Exhibit 13A-1)			$61,400
PV of stated interest:			
($100,000 × 0.045) × PV of annuity at 5%		for 10 periods	
($4,500 × 7.722—Exhibit 13A-2)			34,749
PV (market price) of bonds			$96,149

The market price of the Air West bonds shows a discount because the stated interest rate on the bonds (9%) is less than the market interest rate (10%). We discuss these bonds in more detail in the next section of this appendix.

Premium Price

Let's consider a premium price for the Air West bonds. Now suppose the market interest rate is 8% at issuance (4% for each of the 10 semiannual periods):

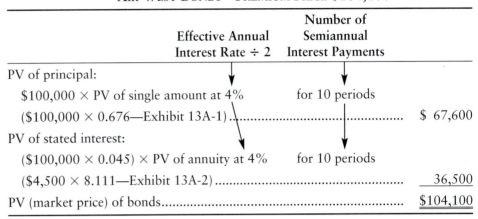

AIR WEST BONDS—PREMIUM PRICE $104,100	
PV of principal:	
$100,000 × PV of single amount at 4% for 10 periods	
($100,000 × 0.676—Exhibit 13A-1)	$ 67,600
PV of stated interest:	
($100,000 × 0.045) × PV of annuity at 4% for 10 periods	
($4,500 × 8.111—Exhibit 13A-2)	36,500
PV (market price) of bonds	$104,100

We discuss accounting for these bonds in the next section.

Effective-Interest Method of Amortization

We began this chapter with straight-line amortization to introduce the concept of amortizing bonds. A more precise way of amortizing bonds is used in practice, and it's called the **effective-interest method**. That method uses the present-value concepts covered in this appendix.

Generally accepted accounting principles require that interest expense be measured using the *effective-interest method* unless the straight-line amounts are similar. In that case, either method is permitted. Total interest expense over the life of the bonds is the same under both methods. We now show how the effective-interest method works.

Effective-Interest Amortization for a Bond Discount

Assume that Air West Airlines issues $100,000 of 9% bonds at a time when the market rate of interest is 10%. These bonds mature in 5 years and pay interest semiannually, so there are 10 semiannual interest payments. As we just saw, the issue price of the bonds is $96,149,[3] and the discount on these bonds is $3,851 ($100,000 − $96,149). Exhibit 13-A3 shows how to measure interest expense by the effective-interest method. (You will need an amortization table to account for bonds by the effective-interest method.)

EXHIBIT 13A-3 Effective-Interest Amortization of a Bond Discount

PANEL A—Bond Data

Maturity value—$100,000
Stated interest rate—9%
Interest paid—4 1/2% semiannually, $4,500 ($100,000 × 0.045)
Market interest rate at time of issue—10% annually, 5% semiannually
Issue price—$96,149 on January 1, 2008

PANEL B—Amortization Table

End of Semiannual Interest Period	A Interest Payment (4 1/2% of maturity value)	B Interest *Expense* (5% of preceding bond carrying amount)	C Discount Amortization (B − A)	D Discount Balance (D − C)	E Bond Carrying Amount ($100,000 − D)
Jan. 1, 2008				$3,851	$ 96,149
July 1	$4,500	$4,807	$307	3,544	96,456
Jan. 1, 2009	4,500	4,823	323	3,221	96,779
July 1	4,500	4,839	339	2,882	97,118
Jan. 1, 2010	4,500	4,856	356	2,526	97,474
July 1	4,500	4,874	374	2,152	97,848
Jan. 1, 2011	4,500	4,892	392	1,760	98,240
July 1	4,500	4,912	412	1,348	98,652
Jan. 1, 2012	4,500	4,933	433	915	99,085
July 1	4,500	4,954	454	461	99,539
Jan. 1, 2013	4,500	4,961*	461	0	100,000

*Adjusted for effect of rounding.

Notes
- Column A The interest payments are constant.
- Column B The interest expense each period is the preceding bond carrying amount multiplied by the market interest rate.
- Column C The excess of interest expense (B) over interest payment (A) is the discount amortization.
- Column D The discount decreases by the amount of amortization for the period (C).
- Column E The bonds' carrying amount increases from $96,149 at issuance to $100,000 at maturity.

The *accounts* debited and credited under the effective-interest method and the straight-line method are the same. Only the *amounts* differ.

---

[3] We compute this present value on page 682.

Exhibit 13-A3 gives the amounts for all the bond transactions of Air West Airlines. Let's begin with issuance of the bonds payable on January 1, 2008, and the first interest payment on July 1. Entries follow, using amounts from the respective lines of Exhibit 13-A3.

2008				
Jan. 1	Cash (column E)		96,149	
	Discount on Bonds Payable (column D)		3,851	
	Bonds Payable (maturity value)			100,000
	Issued bonds at a discount.			

2008				
July 1	Interest Expense (column B)		4,807	
	Discount on Bonds Payable (column C)			307
	Cash (column A)			4,500
	Paid interest and amortized discount.			

Effective-Interest Amortization of a Bond Premium

Air West Airlines may issue its bonds payable at a premium. Assume that Air West issues $100,000 of 5-year, 9% bonds when the market interest rate is 8%. The bonds' issue price is $104,100,[4] and the premium is $4,100.

Exhibit 13-A4 provides the data for all the bond transactions of Air West Airlines. Let's begin with issuance of the bonds on January 1, 2008, and the first interest payment on July 1. These entries follow.

2008				
Jan. 1	Cash (column E)		104,100	
	Bonds Payable (maturity value)			100,000
	Premium on Bonds Payable (column D)			
	Issued bonds at a premium.			4,100

2008				
July 1	Interest Expense (column B)		4,164	
	Premium on Bonds Payable (column C)		336	
	Cash (column A)			4,500
	Paid interest and amortized premium.			

---

[4] Again, we compute the present value of the bonds on page 682.

EXHIBIT 13A-4 | Effective-Interest Amortization of a Bond Premium

PANEL A—Bond Data

Maturity value—$100,000
Stated interest rate—9%
Interest paid—4 1/2% semiannually, $4,500 ($100,000 × 0.045)
Market interest rate at time of issue—8% annually, 4% semiannually
Issue price—$104,100 on January 1, 2008

PANEL B—Amortization Table

End of Semiannual Interest Period	A Interest Payment (4 1/2% of maturity value)	B Interest *Expense* (4% of preceding bond carrying amount)	C Premium Amortization (B − A)	D Premium Balance (D − C)	E Bond Carrying Amount ($100,000 + D)
Jan. 1, 2008				$4,100	$104,100
July 1	$4,500	$4,164	$336	3,764	103,764
Jan. 1, 2009	4,500	4,151	349	3,415	103,415
July 1	4,500	4,137	363	3,052	103,052
Jan. 1, 2010	4,500	4,122	378	2,674	102,674
July 1	4,500	4,107	393	2,281	102,281
Jan. 1, 2011	4,500	4,091	409	1,872	101,872
July 1	4,500	4,075	425	1,447	101,447
Jan. 1, 2012	4,500	4,058	442	1,005	101,005
July 1	4,500	4,040	460	545	100,545
Jan. 1, 2013	4,500	3,955*	545	0	100,000

*Adjusted for effect of rounding.

Notes
- *Column A* The interest payments are constant.
- *Column B* The interest expense each period is the preceding bond carrying amount multiplied by the market interest rate.
- *Column C* The excess of interest payment (A) over interest expense (B) is the premium amortization.
- *Column D* The premium balance decreases by the amount of amortization for the period.
- *Column E* The bonds' carrying amount decreases from $104,100 at issuance to $100,000 at maturity.

Appendix 13A Assignments

Problems

Computing present-value amounts

P13A-1 Exxel, Inc., needs new manufacturing equipment. Two companies can provide similar equipment but under different payment plans:

a. General Electric (GE) offers to let Exxel pay $60,000 each year for five years. The payments include interest at 12% per year. What is the present value of the payments? (pp. 681–683)

continued . . .

      b. Westinghouse will let Exxel make a single payment of $400,000 at the end of five years. This payment includes both principal and interest at 12%. What is the present value of this payment? (pp. 679–680)

      c. Exxel will purchase the equipment that costs the least, as measured by present value. Which equipment should Exxel select? Why? (Challenge)

Computing the present values of bonds

P13A-2 Determine the present value of the following bonds (pp. 652–653):

      a. Ten-year bonds payable with maturity value of $88,000 and stated interest rate of 12%, paid semiannually. The market rate of interest is 12% at issuance.

      b. Same bonds payable as in a, but the market interest rate is 14%.

      c. Same bonds payable as in a, but the market interest rate is 10%.

Recording bond transactions; straight-line amortization

P13A-3 For each bond in Problem 13A-2, journalize issuance of the bond and the first semiannual interest payment. The company amortizes bond premium and discount by the straight-line method. Explanations are not required. (pp. 646–647, 648, 651–653)

Issuing bonds payable and amortizing discount by the effective-interest method

P13A-4 IMAX, Inc., issued $600,000 of 7%, 10-year bonds payable at a price of 90 on March 31, 2008. The market interest rate at the date of issuance was 9%, and the bonds pay interest semiannually.

      1. How much cash did IMAX receive upon issuance of the bonds payable? (p. 684)

      2. Prepare an effective-interest amortization table for the bond discount, through the first two interest payments. Use Exhibit 13-A3 as a guide, and round amounts to the nearest dollar. (p. 684)

      3. Record IMAX's issuance of the bonds on March 31, 2008, and on September 30, 2008, payment of the first semiannual interest amount and amortization of the bond discount. Explanations are not required. (p. 685)

Issuing bonds payable and amortizing premium by the effective-interest method

P13A-5 Jon Spelman Co. issued $200,000 of 8%, 10-year bonds payable at a price of 110 on May 31, 2008. The market interest rate at the date of issuance was 6%, and the Spelman bonds pay interest semiannually.

      1. How much cash did Spelman receive upon issuance of the bonds payable? (p. 685)

      2. Prepare an effective-interest amortization table for the bond premium, through the first two interest payments. Use Exhibit 13-A4 as a guide, and round amounts to the nearest dollar. (p. 685)

      3. Record Spelman's issuance of the bonds on May 31, 2008, and, on November 30, 2008, payment of the first semiannual interest amount and amortization of the bond premium. Explanations are not required. (p. 685)

Effective-interest method for bond discount: recording interest payments and interest expense

P13A-6 Serenity, Inc., is authorized to issue 7%, 10-year bonds payable. On January 2, 2007, when the market interest rate is 8%, the company issues $300,000 of the bonds and receives cash of $279,600. Serenity amortizes bond discount by the effective-interest method. Interest dates are January 2 and July 2.

continued . . .

Requirements

1. Prepare an amortization table for the first two semiannual interest periods. Follow the format of Exhibit 13-A3, page 684.
2. Record issuance of the bonds payable and the first semiannual interest payment on July 2. (p. 684)

Debt payment and discount amortization schedule

P13A-7 Neiderhoffer Corp. issued $500,000 of 8 3/8% (0.08375), five-year bonds payable when the market interest rate was 9 1/2% (0.095). Neiderhoffer pays interest annually at year-end. The issue price of the bonds was $478,402.

Requirement

Create a spreadsheet model to prepare a schedule to measure interest expense on these bonds. Use the effective-interest method of amortization. Round to the nearest dollar, and format your answer as follows. (p. 684)

	A	B	C	D	E	F
1						
2						Bond
3		Interest	Interest	Discount	Discount	Carrying
4	Date	Payment	Expense	Amortization	Balance	Amount
5	1-1-01				$	$478,402
6	12-31-01	$	$	$		
7	12-31-02					
8	12-31-03					
9	12-31-04					
10	12-31-05					
		500000*.08375	+F5*.095	+C6−B6	500000−F5	+F5+D6

Computing a bond's present value, recording its issuance, interest payments, and amortization by the effective-interest method

P13A-8 On December 31, 2008, when the market interest rate is 8%, Willis Realty Co. issues $400,000 of 7.25%, 10-year bonds payable. The bonds pay interest semiannually.

Requirements

1. Determine the present value of the bonds at issuance. (pp. 652–653)
2. Assume that the bonds are issued at the price computed in requirement 1. Prepare an effective-interest method amortization table for the first two semiannual interest periods. (p. 684)
3. Using the amortization table prepared in requirement 2, journalize issuance of the bonds and the first two interest payments. (p. 685)

Comprehensive Problem for Chapters 11 - 13

Apache Motors' Corporate Transactions

Apache Motors' corporate charter authorizes the company to issue 1 million shares of $1 par-value common stock and 200,000 shares of no-par preferred stock. During the first quarter of operations, Apache completed the following selected transactions:

Oct.	1	Issued 50,000 shares of $1-par common stock for cash of $6 per share. (pp. 554–555)
	1	Issued $200,000 of 9%, 10-year bonds payable at 90. (pp. 646–647)
	5	Issued 2,000 shares of no-par preferred stock, receiving cash of $100,000. (pp. 556–557)
Nov.	2	Purchased 11,000 shares of Apache common stock for the treasury at $5 per share. (pp. 602–603)
	19	Experienced a $16,000 extraordinary flood loss of inventory that cost $20,000. Cash received from the insurance company was $4,000. There is no income tax effect from this loss. (pp. 612–613)
Dec.	1	Sold 1,000 shares of the treasury stock for cash of $6.25 per share. (p. 604)
	30	Sold merchandise on account, $700,000. Cost of goods sold was $400,000. Operating expenses totaled $170,000, with $160,000 of this amount paid in cash. Apache uses a perpetual inventory system. (pp. 74–75, 211–212)
	31	Accrued interest and amortized discount (straight-line method) on the bonds payable issued on October 1. (pp. 652–653)
	31	Accrued income tax expense of $35,000. (pp. 569–570)
	31	Closed all revenues, expenses, and losses to Income Summary in a single closing entry. (pp. 549–552)
	31	Declared a quarterly cash dividend of $1.00 per share on the preferred stock. Record date is January 11, with payment scheduled for January 19. (pp. 561–563)

Requirements

1. Record these transactions in the general journal. Explanations are not required.
2. Prepare a multistep income statement, including earnings per share, for the quarter ended December 31. Apache had 40,000 shares of common stock outstanding. (pp. 611–614)

14 The Statement of Cash Flows

Learning Objectives

1. Identify the purposes of the statement of cash flows

2. Distinguish among operating, investing, and financing cash flows

3. Prepare the statement of cash flows by the indirect method

4. Prepare the statement of cash flows by the direct method (Appendix 14A)

Why is cash so important? You can probably answer that question from your own experience: It takes cash to pay the bills. You have some income, you have expenses, and these events create cash receipts and payments.

Businesses, including eBay, work the same way. Net income is a good thing, but eBay needs enough cash to pay the bills and run its operations. Lots of dot.coms have come and gone, but eBay is going strong. One reason is that eBay is cash-rich. In 2004, eBay's operations provided more than $1.3 billion of cash. Having plenty of cash helps eBay fight off competition from Google and others.

This chapter covers cash flows—cash receipts and cash payments. We'll see how to prepare the statement of cash flows, starting with the format used by the vast majority of companies; it's called the *indirect approach*. Chapter Appendix 14A covers the alternate format of the statement of cash flows, the *direct approach*.

The chapter has four distinct sections:

- Introduction: The Statement of Cash Flows
- Preparing the Statement of Cash Flows by the Indirect Method
- Chapter Appendix 14A: Preparing the Statement of Cash Flows by the Direct Method
- Chapter Appendix 14B: Preparing the Statement of Cash Flows Using a Spreadsheet

The introduction applies to both methods. To concentrate on the indirect method, instructors can cover the first two sections. For the direct method, you can cover the introduction and the chapter's Appendix 14A, starting on page 736. The focus company throughout the chapter is Anchor Corporation, which imports auto parts for Jaguars, Porches, and other European cars.

Chapter Appendix 14B shows how to use a spreadsheet to prepare the statement of cash flows. This appendix presents the indirect-method spreadsheet first, and the direct-method spreadsheet last—in the same order that these topics are covered in the chapter.

Introduction: The Statement of Cash Flows

The balance sheet reports financial position, and balance sheets for two periods show whether cash increased or decreased. For example, Anchor Corporation's comparative balance sheet reported the following:

	2008	2007	Increase (Decrease)
Cash..........	$22,000	$42,000	$(20,000)

Anchor's cash decreased by $20,000 during 2008. But the balance sheet doesn't show *why* cash decreased. We need the cash-flow statement for that.

The **statement of cash flows** reports **cash flows**—cash receipts and cash payments. It

- shows where cash came from (receipts) and how cash was spent (payments)
- reports why cash increased or decreased during the period
- covers a span of time and is dated "Year Ended December 31, 2008," same as the income statement

Exhibit 14-1—on the next page—illustrates the relationships among the balance sheet, the income statement, and the statement of cash flows.

How do people use cash-flow information? The statement of cash flows helps

1. **predict future cash flows.** Past cash receipts and payments help predict future cash flows.
2. **evaluate management decisions.** Wise investment decisions help the business prosper. Unwise decisions cause problems. Investors and creditors use cash-flow information to evaluate managers' decisions.
3. **predict ability to pay debts and dividends.** Lenders want to know whether they'll collect on their loans. Stockholders want dividends on their investments. The statement of cash flows helps make these predictions.

1 Identify the purposes of the statement of cash flows

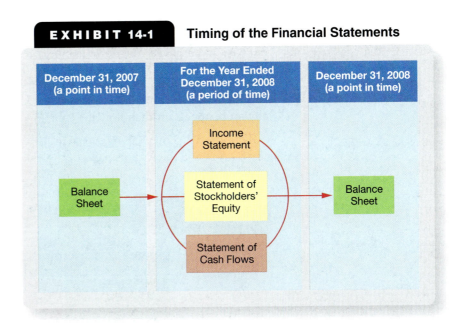

EXHIBIT 14-1 Timing of the Financial Statements

Cash Equivalents

On a statement of cash flows, *Cash* means more than cash on hand and cash in the bank. *Cash* includes **cash equivalents**, which are highly liquid investments that can be converted into cash quickly. Examples of cash equivalents are money-market accounts and investments in U.S. government securities. Throughout this chapter, the term *cash* refers to cash and cash equivalents.

Operating, Investing, and Financing Activities

Distinguish among operating, investing, and financing cash flows

There are three basic types of cash-flow activities:

- Operating activities
- Investing activities
- Financing activities

The statement of cash flows has a section for each category of cash flows. Let's see what each section reports.

Operating Activities

- Create revenues, expenses, gains, and losses
- Affect net income on the income statement
- Affect current assets and current liabilities on the balance sheet
- Are the most important category of cash flows because they reflect the day-to-day operations that determine the future of an organization

Investing Activities

- Increase and decrease long-term assets, such as computers, software, land, buildings, and equipment
- Include purchases and sales of these assets, plus loans to others and collections of loans
- Are next-most important after operating activities

Financing activities

- Increase and decrease long-term liabilities and owners' equity
- Include issuing stock, paying dividends, and buying and selling treasury stock
- Include borrowing money and paying off loans
- Are least important of all the activities because what a company invests in is usually more important than how the company finances the purchase

Exhibit 14-2 shows the relationship between operating, investing, and financing cash flows and the various parts of the balance sheet.

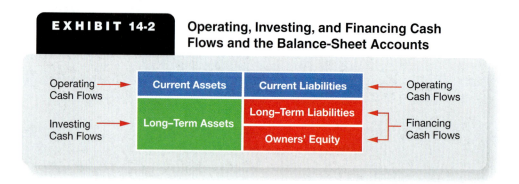

EXHIBIT 14-2 Operating, Investing, and Financing Cash Flows and the Balance-Sheet Accounts

As you can see, operating cash flows affect the current accounts. Investing cash flows affect the long-term assets. Financing cash flows affect long-term liabilities and owners' equity.

Two Formats for Operating Activities

There are two ways to format operating activities on the statement of cash flows:

- **Indirect method**, which reconciles from net income to net cash provided by operating activities
- **Direct method**, which reports all the cash receipts and all the cash payments from operating activities

The indirect and direct methods

- use different computations but produce the same amount of cash flow from operations
- have no effect on investing activities or financing activities

The following illustration shows how to compute cash flows from operating activities by the two methods. All amounts are assumed.

Indirect Method		Direct Method	
Cash flows from operating activities:		Cash flows from operating activities:	
Net income	$300	Collections from customers	$900
Adjustments:		*Deductions:*	
Depreciation, etc.	100	Payments to suppliers, etc.	(500)
Net cash provided by operating activities	$400	Net cash provided by operating activities	$400

Let's begin with the indirect method because 99% of public companies use it. To focus on the direct method, go to chapter Appendix 14A, page 736.

Preparing the Statement of Cash Flows by the Indirect Method

To prepare the statement of cash flows, you need the income statement and both the beginning and the ending balance sheets. Consider Anchor Corporation, an importer of parts for European cars. To prepare the statement of cash flows by the indirect method,

3 Prepare the statement of cash flows by the indirect method

STEP 1 Lay out the statement format as shown in Exhibit 14-3. Steps 2 to 4 will complete the statement of cash flows.

EXHIBIT 14-3 Format of the Statement of Cash Flows: Indirect Method

ANCHOR CORPORATION
Statement of Cash Flows
Year Ended December 31, 2008

Cash flows from operating activities:		
Net income		
Adjustments to reconcile net income to net cash provided by operating activities:		
+ Depreciation / amortization expense		
+ Loss on sale of long-term assets		
− Gain on sale of long-term assets		
− Increases in current assets other than cash		
+ Decreases in current assets other than cash		
+ Increases in current liabilities		
− Decreases in current liabilities		
Net cash provided by operating activities		
± Cash flows from investing activities:		
Sales of long-term assets (investments, land, building, equipment, and so on)		
− Purchases of long-term assets		
Net cash provided by (used for) investing activities		
± Cash flows from financing activities:		
Issuance of stock		
+ Sale of treasury stock		
− Purchase of treasury stock		
+ Issuance of notes or bonds payable (borrowing)		
− Payment of notes or bonds payable		
− Payment of dividends		
Net cash provided by (used for) financing activities		
= Net increase (decrease) in cash during the year		
+ Cash at December 31, 2007		
= Cash at December 31, 2008		

STEP 2 Compute the change in cash from the comparative balance sheet. The change in cash is the "check figure" for the statement of cash flows. Exhibit 14-4 is the comparative balance sheet of Anchor Corporation, where the top line shows that cash decreased by $20,000 during 2008.

696 Chapter 14

EXHIBIT 14-4 Comparative Balance Sheet

ANCHOR CORPORATION
Comparative Balance Sheet
December 31, 2008 and 2007

(In thousands)	2008	2007	Increase (Decrease)	
Assets				
Current:				
Cash	$ 22	$ 42	$ (20)	
Accounts receivable	90	73	17	Operating D
Inventory	143	145	(2)	
Plant assets, net	460	210	250	Investing
Total	$715	$470	$ 245	
Liabilities				
Current:				
Accounts payable	$ 90	$ 50	$ 40	
Accrued liabilities	5	10	(5)	Operating D
Long-term notes payable	160	80	80	Financing
Stockholders' Equity				
Common stock	350	250	100	
Retained earnings	110	80	30	Net income—Operating Otherwise Financing
Total	$715	$470	$ 245	

STEP 3 Take net income, depreciation, and any gains or losses from the income statement. Exhibit 14-5 gives the 2008 income statement of Anchor Corporation, with the relevant items highlighted.

STEP 4 Complete the statement of cash flows, using data from the income statement and the balance sheet. The statement is complete only after you have explained all the year-to-year changes in all the accounts on the balance sheet.

Let's apply these steps to show the operating activities of Anchor Corporation. Exhibit 14-6 gives the operating activities section of the statement of cash flows. All items are highlighted for emphasis. That makes it easy to trace the data from one statement to the other.

Cash Flows from Operating Activities

Operating cash flows begin with net income, taken from the income statement.

A Net Income

The statement of cash flows—indirect method—begins with net income because revenues and expenses, which affect net income, produce cash receipts and cash payments. Revenues bring in cash receipts and expenses must be paid. But the cash flows don't always equal the revenues and the expenses. For example, sales *on account* are revenues that increase net income, but the company hasn't yet collected cash from those sales. Accrued expenses decrease your net income, but you haven't paid cash *if the expenses are accrued*.

To go from net income to cash flow from operations, we must make some adjustments to net income on the statement of cash flows. These additions and subtractions follow net income and are labeled *Adjustments to reconcile net income to net cash provided by operating activities*, as explained on page 698.

The Statement of Cash Flows 697

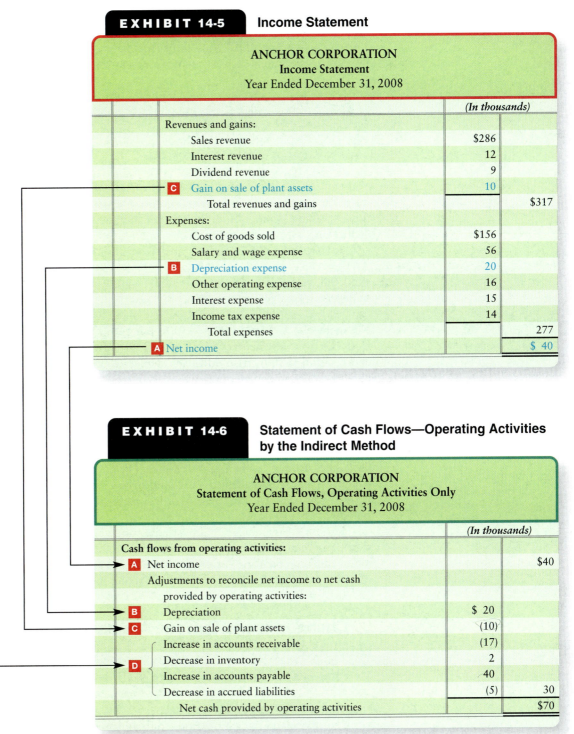

EXHIBIT 14-5 Income Statement

ANCHOR CORPORATION
Income Statement
Year Ended December 31, 2008

(In thousands)

Revenues and gains:		
Sales revenue	$286	
Interest revenue	12	
Dividend revenue	9	
C Gain on sale of plant assets	10	
Total revenues and gains		$317
Expenses:		
Cost of goods sold	$156	
Salary and wage expense	56	
B Depreciation expense	20	
Other operating expense	16	
Interest expense	15	
Income tax expense	14	
Total expenses		277
A Net income		$ 40

EXHIBIT 14-6 Statement of Cash Flows—Operating Activities by the Indirect Method

ANCHOR CORPORATION
Statement of Cash Flows, Operating Activities Only
Year Ended December 31, 2008

(In thousands)

Cash flows from operating activities:		
A Net income		$40
Adjustments to reconcile net income to net cash		
provided by operating activities:		
B Depreciation	$ 20	
C Gain on sale of plant assets	(10)	
Increase in accounts receivable	(17)	
D Decrease in inventory	2	
Increase in accounts payable	40	
Decrease in accrued liabilities	(5)	30
Net cash provided by operating activities		$70

A B C D are explained on pages 696–698 as noted there.

B Depreciation, Depletion, and Amortization Expenses

These expenses are added back to net income to reconcile from net income to cash flow from operations. Let's see why. Depreciation is recorded as follows:

	Depreciation Expense	20,000	
	Accumulated Depreciation		20,000

You can see that depreciation does not affect cash. However, depreciation, like all the other expenses, decreases net income. Therefore, to go from net income to cash flows, we add depreciation back to net income. The add-back cancels the earlier deduction.

Example: Suppose you had only two transactions during the period:

- $1,000 cash sale
- depreciation expense of $300

Net income is $700 ($1,000 − $300). But cash flow from operations is $1,000. To reconcile from net income ($700) to cash flow from operations ($1,000), add back depreciation ($300). Also add back depletion and amortization expenses because they're similar to depreciation.

C Gains and Losses on the Sale of Assets

Sales of long-term assets such as land and buildings are investing activities, and these sales usually create a gain or a loss. The gain or loss is included in net income, which is part of operations. Gains and losses require an adjustment to cash flow from operating activities: The gain or loss must be adjusted out of net income on the statement of cash flows.

Exhibit 14-6 includes an adjustment for a gain (item C). During 2008 Anchor sold equipment, and there was a gain of $8,000 on the sale. The gain must be removed from operating cash flows because the gain itself is not cash. A loss on the sale of plant assets would be added back to net income.

D Changes in the Current Assets and the Current Liabilities

Most current assets and current liabilities result from operating activities. For example,

- accounts receivable result from sales,
- inventory relates to cost of goods sold, and so on.

Changes in the current accounts create adjustments to net income on the cash-flow statement, as follows:

↑ Current assets ⇒ ↓ Cash

1. **An increase in a current asset other than cash causes a decrease in cash.** It takes cash to acquire assets. If Accounts Receivable, Inventory, or Prepaid Expenses increased, cash decreased. Therefore, subtract the increase in the current asset from net income to get cash flow from operations.

↓ Current assets ⇒ ↑ Cash

2. **A decrease in a current asset other than cash causes an increase in cash.** Suppose Anchor's Accounts Receivable decreased by $4,000. What caused the

decrease? Anchor must have collected the Accounts Receivable, and cash increased. Therefore, add decreases in Accounts Receivable and the other current assets to net income.

↓ Current liabilities ⇒ ↓ Cash

3. **A decrease in a current liability causes a decrease in cash.** The payment of a current liability decreases cash. Therefore, we subtract decreases in current liabilities from net income to get cash flow from operations.

↑ Current liabilities ⇒ ↑ Cash

4. **An increase in a current liability causes an increase in cash.** Anchor's Accounts Payable increased. This means that cash was *not* spent to pay the liability, so Anchor has more cash on hand. Thus, an increase in a current liability is *added* to net income.

Evaluating Cash Flows from Operating Activities

During 2008, Anchor Corporation's operations provided net cash flow of $70,000. This amount exceeds net income, as it should because of the add-back of depreciation. However, to fully evaluate a company's cash flows, we must also examine Anchor's investing and financing activities. Let's see how to report investing and financing cash flows, as shown in Exhibit 14-7, which gives Anchor's full-blown statement of cash flows.

EXHIBIT 14-7 Statement of Cash Flows—Indirect Method

ANCHOR CORPORATION
Statement of Cash Flows
Year Ended December 31, 2008

(In thousands)

Cash flows from operating activities:		
A Net income		$ 40
Adjustments to reconcile net income to net cash provided by operating activities:		
Depreciation	$ 20	
Gain on sale of plant assets	(10)	
Increase in accounts receivable	(17)	
Decrease in inventory	2	
Increase in accounts payable	40	
Decrease in accrued liabilities	(5)	30
Net cash provided by operating activities		70
Cash flows from investing activities:		
Acquisition of plant assets	$(310)	
Cash receipt from sale of plant assets	50	
Net cash used for investing activities		(260)
Cash flows from financing activities:		
Cash receipt from issuance of common stock	$ 100	
Cash receipt from issuance of notes payable	90	
Payment of notes payable	(10)	
Payment of dividends	(10)	
Net cash provided by financing activities		170
Net decrease in cash		$(20)
Cash balance, December 31, 2007		42
Cash balance, December 31, 2008		$ 22

Cash Flows from Investing Activities

Investing activities affect long-term assets, such as Plant Assets and Investments. Let's see how to compute the investing cash flows.

Computing Acquisitions and Sales of Plant Assets

Companies keep a separate account for each asset. But for computing investing cash flows, it is helpful to combine all the plant assets into a single Plant Assets account. And we subtract accumulated depreciation from the assets' cost in order to work with a single net figure for plant assets, such as Plant assets, net . . . $460,000. This simplifies the computations.

To illustrate, observe that Anchor Corporation's

- balance sheet reports 2007 plant assets, net of depreciation, of $460,000 at the end of 2008 and $210,000 at the end of 2007 (Exhibit 14-4).
- income statement shows depreciation expense of $20,000 and a $10,000 gain on sale of plant assets (Exhibit 14-5).

Anchor's acquisitions of plant assets during 2008 totaled $310,000 (Exhibit 14-7). Anchor also sold some older plant assets. How much cash did Anchor receive from the sale of plant assets? Cash received from selling plant assets can be computed as follows:

$$\text{Cash receipt} = \text{Book value of plant asset sold} \begin{cases} + \text{Gain} \\ \text{or} \\ - \text{Loss} \end{cases}$$

The book-value information comes from the Plant Assets (Net) account on the balance sheet. The gain or loss comes from the income statement. First, we must compute the book value of plant assets sold, as follows (item to be computed is in color):

Plant Assets (Net)

Beginning balance	+	Acquisitions	−	Depreciation expense	−	Book value of assets sold	=	Ending balance
$210,000	+	$310,000	−	$20,000	−	$40,000	=	$460,000

Now we can compute the cash receipt from the sale as follows (item computed in color):

Cash receipt from sale	=	Book value of assets sold	+	Gain	−	Loss
$50,000	=	$40,000	+	$10,000	−	$0

Trace the cash receipt of $50,000 to the statement of cash flows in Exhibit 14-7.

If the sale resulted in a loss of $5,000, the cash receipt would be $45,000 ($50,000 − $5,000), and the statement of cash flows would report $45,000 as a cash receipt from this investing activity.

The Plant Assets T-account provides another look at the computation of the book value of the assets sold.

Plant Assets (Net)

Beginning balance	210,000	Depreciation	20,000
Acquisitions	310,000	Book value of assets sold	40,000
Ending balance	460,000		

Exhibit 14-8 summarizes the computation of the investing cash flows. Items to be computed are shown in color.

EXHIBIT 14-8 Computing Cash Flows from Investing Activities

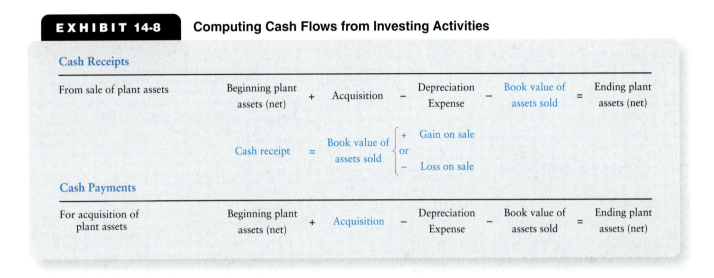

Cash Flows from Financing Activities

Financing activities affect the liability and owners' equity accounts, such as Long-Term Notes Payable, Bonds Payable, Common Stock, and Retained Earnings.

Computing Issuances and Payments of Long-Term Notes Payable

The beginning and ending balances of Notes Payable or Bonds Payable are taken from the balance sheet. If either the amount of new issuances or payments is known, the other amount can be computed. For Anchor Corporation, new issuances of notes payable total $90,000 (Exhibit 14-7). The computation of note payments uses the Long-Term Notes Payable account, with amounts from Anchor Corporation's balance sheet in Exhibit 14-4:

Formula Approach:

Long-Term Notes Payable								
Beginning balance	+	Cash receipt from issuance of notes payable	−	Payment of notes payable	=	Ending balance
$80,000	+	$90,000	−	$10,000	=	$160,000

T-Account Approach:

Long-Term Notes Payable			
		Beginning balance	80,000
Payments	10,000	Issuance of notes payable	90,000
		Ending balance	160,000

Computing Issuances of Stock and Purchases of Treasury Stock

Cash flows for these financing activities can be determined by analyzing the stock accounts. For example, the amount of a new issuance of common stock is determined from Common Stock. Using data from Exhibits 14-4 and 14-7:

Formula Approach:

Common Stock		
Beginning balance +	Cash receipt from issuance of common stock =	Ending balance
$250,000 +	$100,000 =	$350,000

T-Account Approach:

Common Stock	
	Beginning balance 250,000
	Issuance of stock 100,000
	Ending balance 350,000

Apart from the Anchor Corporation example, cash flows affecting Treasury Stock can be analyzed as follows:

Formula Approach:

Treasury Stock (Amounts assumed for illustration only)		
Beginning balance +	Purchase of treasury stock =	Ending balance
$10,000 +	$5,000 =	$15,000

T-Account Approach:

Treasury Stock	
Beginning balance 10,000	
Purchase of treasury stock 5,000	
Ending balance 15,000	

Computing Dividend Payments

The amount of dividend payments can be computed by analyzing Retained Earnings.

Formula Approach:

Retained Earnings			
Beginning balance +	Net income −	Dividends =	Ending balance
$80,000 +	$40,000 −	$10,000 =	$110,000

T-Account Approach:

	Retained Earnings	
	Beginning balance	80,000
Dividends 10,000	Net income	40,000
	Ending balance	110,000

A stock dividend has *no* effect on Cash and is *not* reported on the cash-flow statement. Exhibit 14-9 summarizes the computation of cash flows from financing activities, highlighted in color.

EXHIBIT 14-9 **Computing Cash Flows from Financing Activities**

Cash Receipts

From issuance of notes payable	Beginning notes payable +	Cash receipt from issuance of notes payable −	Payment of notes payable =	Ending notes payable
From issuance of stock	Beginning stock =	Cash receipt from issuance of new stock =		Ending stock

Cash Payments

Of notes payable	Beginning notes payable +	Cash receipt from issuance of notes payable −	Payment of notes payable =	Ending notes payable
To purchase treasury stock	Beginning treasury stock +	Cost of treasury stock purchased =	Ending treasury stock	
Of dividends	Beginning retained earnings +	Net income −	Dividends =	Ending retained earnings

Noncash Investing and Financing Activities

Companies make investments that do not require cash. They also obtain financing other than cash. Our examples thus far have included none of these transactions. Now suppose Anchor Corporation issued common stock of $300,000 to acquire a building. Anchor would record the purchase as follows:

Building	300,000	
Common Stock		300,000

This transaction would not be reported on the cash-flow statement because Anchor paid no cash. But the building and the common stock are important.

The purchase of the building is an investing activity. The issuance of common stock is a financing activity. Taken together, this transaction is a *noncash investing and financing activity*.

Noncash investing and financing activities can be reported in a separate schedule that accompanies the statement of cash flows. Exhibit 14-10 illustrates noncash investing and financing activities (all amounts are assumed). This information follows the cash-flow statement or can be disclosed in a note.

EXHIBIT 14-10 Noncash Investing and Financing Activities (Amounts assumed)

	(Thousands)
Noncash investing and financing activities:	
Acquisition of building by issuing common stock	$300
Acquisition of land by issuing note payable	70
Payment of note payable by issuing common stock	100
Total noncash investing and financing activities	$470

Measuring Cash Adequacy: Free Cash Flow

Throughout we have focused on cash flows from operating, investing, and financing activities. Some investors want to know how much cash a company can "free up" for new opportunities. **Free cash flow** is the amount of cash available from operations after paying for planned investments in long-term assets. Free cash flow can be computed as follows:

$$\text{Free cash flow} = \begin{array}{c}\text{Net cash provided}\\ \text{by operating}\\ \text{activities}\end{array} - \begin{array}{c}\text{Cash payments planned for}\\ \text{investments in plant, equipment,}\\ \text{and other long-term assets}\end{array}$$

PepsiCo, Inc. uses free cash flow to manage its operations. Suppose PepsiCo expects net cash provided by operations of $2.3 billion. Assume PepsiCo plans to spend $1.9 billion to modernize its bottling plants. In this case, PepsiCo's free cash flow would be $0.4 billion ($2.3 billion − $1.9 billion). If a good investment opportunity comes along, PepsiCo should have $0.4 billion to invest in the other company. Shell Oil Company also uses free-cash-flow analysis. A large amount of free cash flow is preferable because it means a lot of cash is available for new investments.

Now let's put into practice what you have learned about the statement of cash flows prepared by the indirect method.

Decision Guidelines

USING CASH-FLOW AND RELATED INFORMATION TO EVALUATE INVESTMENTS

Ann Browning is a private investor. Through the years, she has devised some guidelines for evaluating investments. Here are some of her guidelines.

Question	Financial Statement	What to Look For
Where is most of the company's cash coming from?	Statement of cash flows	Operating activities ⟶ Good sign Investing activities ⟶ Bad sign Financing activities ⟶ Okay sign
Do high sales and profits translate into more cash?	Statement of cash flows	Usually, but cash flows from *operating* activities must be the main source of cash for long-term success.
If sales and profits are low, how is the company generating cash?	Statement of cash flows	If *investing* activities are generating the cash, the business may be in trouble because it is selling off its long-term assets. If *financing* activities are generating the cash, that cannot go on forever. Sooner or later, investors will demand cash flow from operating activities.
Is the cash balance large enough to provide for expansion?	Balance sheet	The cash balance should be growing over time. If not, the company may be in trouble.
Can the business pay its debts?	Income statement	Increasing trend of net income.
	Statement of cash flows	Cash flows from operating activities should be the main source of cash.
	Balance sheet	Current ratio, debt ratio.

Summary Problem

Robins Corporation reported the following income statement and comparative balance sheet for 2009 and 2008, along with transaction data for 2009:

ROBINS CORPORATION
Income Statement
Year Ended December 31, 2009

Sales revenue		$662,000
Cost of goods sold		560,000
Gross profit		102,000
Operating expenses:		
Salary expense	$46,000	
Depreciation expense	10,000	
Rent expense	2,000	
Total operating expenses		58,000
Income from operations		44,000
Other items:		
Loss on sale of equipment		(2,000)
Income before income tax		42,000
Income tax expense		16,000
Net income		$ 26,000

ROBINS CORPORATION
Balance Sheet
December 31, 2009 and 2008

Assets	2009	2008	Liabilities	2009	2008
Current:			Current:		
Cash and equivalents	$ 22,000	$ 3,000	Accounts payable	$ 35,000	$ 26,000
Accounts receivable	22,000	23,000	Accrued liabilities	7,000	9,000
Inventories	35,000	34,000	Income tax payable	10,000	10,000
Total current assets	79,000	60,000	Total current liabilities	52,000	45,000
Equipment, net	126,000	72,000	Bonds payable	84,000	53,000
			Owner's Equity		
			Common stock	52,000	20,000
			Retained earnings	27,000	19,000
			Less: Treasury stock	(10,000)	(5,000)
Total assets	$205,000	$132,000	Total liabilities and equity	$205,000	$132,000

Transaction Data for 2009:

Purchase of equipment	$140,000
Payment of dividends	18,000
Issuance of common stock to retire bonds payable	13,000
Issuance of bonds payable to borrow cash	44,000
Cash receipt from issuance of common stock	19,000
Cash receipt from sale of equipment (book value, $76,000)	74,000
Purchase of treasury stock	5,000

Requirements

Prepare Robins Corporation's statement of cash flows for the year ended December 31, 2009. Format operating cash flows by the indirect method. Follow the four steps outlined below.

STEP 1 Lay out the format of the statement of cash flows.

STEP 2 From the comparative balance sheet, compute the increase in cash during the year, $19,000.

STEP 3 From the income statement, take net income, depreciation, and the loss on sale of equipment to the statement of cash flows.

STEP 4 Complete the statement of cash flows. Account for the year-to-year change in each balance sheet account. Prepare a T-account to show the transaction activity in each long-term balance-sheet account.

Solution

ROBINS CORPORATION
Statement of Cash Flows
Year Ended December 31, 2009

Cash flows from operating activities:			
Net income			$26,000
Adjustments to reconcile net income to net cash			
provided by operating activities:			
	Depreciation	$ 10,000	
	Loss on sale of equipment	2,000	
	Decrease in accounts receivable	1,000	
	Increase in inventories	(1,000)	
	Increase in accounts payable	9,000	
	Decrease in accrued liabilities	(2,000)	19,000
	Net cash provided by operating activities		45,000
Cash flows from investing activities:			
	Purchase of equipment	$(140,000)	
	Sale of equipment	74,000	
	Net cash used for investing activities		(66,000)
Cash flows from financing activities:			
	Issuance of common stock	$ 19,000	
	Payment of dividends	(18,000)	
	Issuance of bonds payable	44,000	
	Purchase of treasury stock	(5,000)	
	Net cash provided by financing activities		40,000
Net increase in cash			$19,000
Cash balance, December 31, 2008			3,000
Cash balance, December 31, 2009			$22,000
Noncash investing and financing activities:			
	Issuance of common stock to retire bonds payable		$13,000
	Total noncash investing and financing activities		$13,000

Relevant T-Accounts:

Equipment, Net	
Bal. 72,000	
140,000	10,000
	76,000
Bal. 126,000	

Bonds Payable	
	Bal. 53,000
13,000	44,000
	Bal. 84,000

Common Stock	
	Bal. 20,000
	13,000
	19,000
	Bal. 52,000

Retained Earnings	
	Bal. 19,000
18,000	26,000
	Bal. 27,000

Treasury Stock	
Bal. 5,000	
5,000	
Bal. 10,000	

Review *The Statement of Cash Flows*

Accounting Vocabulary

Cash Equivalents
Highly liquid short-term investments that can be readily converted into cash.

Cash Flows
Cash receipts and cash payments.

Direct Method
Format of the operating activities section of the statement of cash flows; lists the major categories of operating cash receipts and cash payments.

Financing Activities
Activities that obtain the cash needed to launch and sustain the business; a section of the statement of cash flows.

Free Cash Flow
The amount of cash available from operations after paying for planned investments in plant, equipment, and other long-term assets.

Indirect Method
Format of the operating activities section of the statement of cash flows; starts with net income and reconciles to net cash provided by operating activities.

Investing Activities
Activities that increase or decrease long-term assets; a section of the statement of cash flows.

Operating Activities
Activities that create revenue or expense in the entity's major line of business; a section of the statement of cash flows. Operating activities affect the income statement.

Statement of Cash Flows
Reports cash receipts and cash payments during the period.

Quick Check

1. The main categories of cash-flow activities are
    a. Operating, investing, and financing
    b. Direct and indirect
    c. Noncash investing and financing
    d. Current and long-term

2. The purposes of the cash-flow statement are to
    a. Predict future cash flows
    b. Evaluate management decisions
    c. Determine ability to pay liabilities and dividends
    d. All of the above

3. Operating activities are most closely related to
    a. Current assets and current liabilities
    b. Long-term assets
    c. Long-term liabilities and owners' equity
    d. Dividends and treasury stock

4. Which item does *not* appear on a statement of cash flows prepared by the indirect method?
    a. Net income
    b. Collections from customers
    c. Depreciation
    d. Gain on sale of land

5. Source Today earned net income of $60,000 after deducting depreciation of $4,000 and all other expenses. Current assets decreased by $3,000, and current liabilities increased by $5,000. How much was Source Today's cash provided by operations (indirect method)?
    a. $48,000
    b. $50,000
    c. $72,000
    d. $66,000

6. The Plant Assets account of Star Media shows the following:

Plant Assets, Net

Beg.	100,000	Depr.	30,000
Purchase	400,000	Sale	50,000
End.	420,000		

Star Media sold plant assets at a $10,000 loss. Where on the statement of cash flows should Star Media report the sale of plant assets? How much should Star Media report for the sale?
    a. Investing cash flows—cash receipt of $40,000
    b. Investing cash flows—cash receipt of $50,000
    c. Investing cash flows—cash receipt of $60,000
    d. Financing cash flows—cash receipt of $60,000

7. Round Rock Corp. borrowed $35,000, issued common stock of $10,000, and paid dividends of $25,000. What was Round Rock's net cash provided (used) by financing activities?

   a. $0
   b. $20,000
   c. $(25,000)
   d. $70,000

8. Which item appears on a statement of cash flows prepared by the indirect method?

   a. Payments to suppliers
   b. Payments of income tax
   c. Depreciation
   d. Collections from customers

Appendix 14A: Direct Method

9. Peppertree Copy Center had accounts receivable of $20,000 at the beginning of the year and $50,000 at year-end. Revenue for the year totaled $110,000. How much cash did Peppertree collect from customers?

   a. $180,000
   b. $140,000
   c. $130,000
   d. $80,000

10. Pilot Company had operating expense of $40,000. At the beginning of the year, Pilot owed $8,000 on accrued liabilities. At year-end, accrued liabilities were $4,000. How much cash did Pilot pay for operating expenses?

    a. $32,000
    b. $36,000
    c. $44,000
    d. $45,000

Answers are given after Apply Your Knowledge (p. 735).

Assess Your Progress

Short Exercises

Purposes of the statement of cash flows

S14-1 Describe how the statement of cash flows helps investors and creditors perform each of the following functions (p. 693):
1. Predict future cash flows
2. Evaluate management decisions
3. Predict the ability to make debt payments to lenders and pay dividends to stockholders

Classifying cash-flow items

S14-2 Answer these questions about the statement of cash flows:
a. List the categories of cash flows in order of importance. (pp. 693–694)
b. What is the "check figure" for the statement of cash flows? Where do you get this check figure? (pp. 694–696)
c. What is the first dollar amount to report for the indirect method? (pp. 694–696)

Identifying items for reporting cash flows from operations—indirect method

S14-3 Triumph Corporation is preparing its statement of cash flows by the *indirect* method. Triumph has the following items for you to consider in preparing the statement. Identify each item as an
- Operating activity—addition to net income (O+), or subtraction from net income (O−)
- Investing activity (I)
- Financing activity (F)
- Activity that is not used to prepare the cash-flow statement (N)

Answer by placing the appropriate symbol in the blank space. (pp. 695–696)

_____ a. Increase in accounts payable   _____ g. Depreciation expense
_____ b. Payment of dividends   _____ h. Increase in inventory
_____ c. Decrease in accrued liabilities   _____ i. Decrease in accounts receivable
_____ d. Issuance of common stock
_____ e. Gain on sale of building   _____ j. Purchase of equipment
_____ f. Loss on sale of land

Computing cash flows from operating activities—indirect method

S14-4 DVR Equipment, Inc., reported these data for 2007:

Income Statement	
Net income	$42,000
Depreciation	8,000
Balance sheet	
Increase in Accounts Receivable.......	6,000
Decrease in Accounts Payable	4,000

Compute DVR's net cash provided by operating activities—indirect method. (pp. 696–697)

712   Chapter 14

Computing operating cash flows—indirect method

3

S14-5 (Short Exercise 14-6 is an alternate.) One Way Cellular accountants have assembled the following data for the year ended June 30, 2008.

Cash receipt from sale of land	$30,000	Net income	$60,000
Depreciation expense	15,000	Purchase of equipment	40,000
Payment of dividends	6,000	Decrease in current liabilities	5,000
Cash receipt from issuance of common stock	20,000	Increase in current assets other than cash	12,000

Prepare the *operating* activities section of One Way Cellular's statement of cash flows for the year ended June 30, 2008. One Way uses the *indirect* method for operating cash flows. (pp. 696–697)

Preparing a statement of cash flows—indirect method

3

S14-6 Use the data in Short Exercise 14-5 to prepare One Way Cellular's statement of cash flows for the year ended June 30, 2008. One Way Cellular uses the *indirect* method for operating activities. Use Exhibit 14-7 as a guide, but you may stop after determining the net increase (or decrease) in cash. (pp. 699–700)

Computing investing and financing cash flows

3

S14-7 Sun West Media Corporation had the following income statement and balance sheet for 2009:

SUN WEST MEDIA CORPORATION
Income Statement
Year Ended December 31, 2009

Service revenue	$80,000
Depreciation expense	6,000
Other expenses	54,000
Net income	$20,000

SUN WEST MEDIA CORPORATION
Comparative Balance Sheet
December 31, 2009 and 2008

Assets	2009	2008	Liabilities	2009	2008
Current:			Current:		
Cash	$ 5,000	$ 4,000	Accounts payable	$ 8,000	$ 6,000
Accounts receivable	10,000	6,000	Long-term notes payable	10,000	12,000
Equipment, net	75,000	70,000			
			Owners' Equity		
			Common stock	22,000	20,000
			Retained earnings	50,000	42,000
	$90,000	$80,000		$90,000	$80,000

continued . . .

Compute for Sun West during 2009:

a. Acquisition of equipment. Sun West sold no equipment during the year. (pp. 700–701)

b. Payment of a long-term note payable. During the year Sun West issued a $5,000 note payable. (p. 701)

Preparing the statement of cash flows—indirect method
3

S14-8 Use the Sun West Media Corporation data in Short Exercise S14-7 to prepare Sun West's statement of cash flows—indirect method—for the year ended December 31, 2009. (pp. 699–700)

Computing a cash increase or decrease—indirect method
3

S14-9 JoAnn's Bridal Shops earned net income of $80,000, which included depreciation of $15,000. JoAnn's paid $120,000 for a building and borrowed $60,000 on a long-term note payable. How much did JoAnn's cash balance increase or decrease during the year? (pp. 699–704)

Free cash flow
3

S14-10 Anita Maxwell Company expects the following for 2007:

- Net cash provided by operating activities of $150,000
- Net cash provided by financing activities of $60,000
- Net cash used for investing activities of $80,000 (no sales of long-term assets)

How much free cash flow does Maxwell expect for 2007? (p. 704)

Appendix 14A: Direct Method

Preparing a statement of cash flows—direct method
4

S14-11 Chocolate Inc. began 2007 with cash of $55,000. During the year Chocolate Inc. earned revenue of $600,000 and collected $620,000 from customers. Expenses for the year totaled $420,000, of which Chocolate paid $410,000 in cash to suppliers and employees. Chocolate also paid $140,000 to purchase equipment and a cash dividend of $50,000 to its stockholders during 2007.

Prepare the company's statement of cash flows for the year ended December 31, 2007. Format operating activities by the direct method. (Exhibit 14A-3, p. 738)

Computing operating cash flows—direct method
4

S14-12 (Short Exercise 14-13 is an alternate.) Little People Learning Center (LPLC) has assembled the following data for the year ended June 30, 2005.

Payments to suppliers.................................	$110,000
Purchase of equipment	40,000
Payments to employees.............................	70,000
Payment of note payable	30,000
Payment of dividends	6,000
Cash receipt from issuance of stock............	20,000
Collections from customers.......................	200,000
Cash receipt from sale of land...................	60,000

Prepare the *operating* activities section of LPLC's statement of cash flows for the year ended June 30, 2005. LPLC uses the direct method for operating cash flows. (Exhibit 14A-3, p. 738)

Preparing a statement of cash flows—direct method

S14-13 Use the data in Short Exercise 14-12 to prepare Little People Learning Center's (LPLC) statement of cash flows for the year ended June 30, 2005. LPLC uses the *direct* method for operating activities. Use Exhibit 14A-3, page 738, as a guide, but you may stop after determining the net increase (or decrease) in cash.

Computing operating cash flows—direct method

S14-14 Lagos Toy Company reported the following comparative balance sheet:

LAGOS TOY COMPANY
Comparative Balance Sheet
December 31, 2009 and 2008

Assets	2009	2008	Liabilities	2009	2008
Current:			Current:		
Cash	$ 19,000	$ 16,000	Accounts payable	$ 47,000	$ 42,000
Accounts receivable	54,000	48,000	Salary payable	23,000	21,000
Inventory	80,000	84,000	Accrued liabilities	8,000	11,000
Prepaid expenses	3,000	2,000	Long-term notes payable	66,000	68,000
Long-term investments	75,000	90,000	Stockholders' Equity		
Plant assets, net	225,000	185,000	Common stock	40,000	37,000
			Retained earnings	272,000	246,000
Total	$456,000	$425,000	Total	$456,000	$425,000

Compute for Lagos:

a. Collections from customers during 2009. Sales totaled $140,000. (p. 742)

b. Payments for inventory during 2009. Cost of goods sold was $80,000. (p. 742)

Exercises

Identifying the purposes of the statement of cash flows

E14-15 SmartPages Media Corp. has experienced 10 years of growth in net income. Nevertheless, the business is facing bankruptcy. Creditors are calling all of SmartPages' loans for immediate payment, and the cash is simply not available. Where did SmartPages go wrong? Managers placed too much emphasis on net income and gave too little attention to cash flows.

Requirement
Write a brief memo, in your own words, to explain to the managers of SmartPages Media the purposes of the statement of cash flows. (p. 693)

Identifying activities for the statement of cash flows—indirect method

E14-16 Identify each of the following transactions as
- Operating activity (O)
- Investing activity (I)
- Financing activity (F)
- Noncash investing and financing activity (NIF)
- Transaction that is not reported on the statement of cash flows (N)

continued . . .

For each cash flow, indicate whether the item increases (+) or decreases (−) cash. The *indirect* method is used to report cash flows from operating activities. (pp. 695–696, 703)

_____ a. Loss on sale of land
_____ b. Acquisition of equipment by issuance of note payable
_____ c. Payment of long-term debt
_____ d. Acquisition of building by issuance of common stock
_____ e. Accrual of salary expense
_____ f. Decrease in inventory
_____ g. Increase in prepaid expenses
_____ h. Decrease in accrued liabilities
_____ i. Cash sale of land
_____ j. Issuance of long-term note payable to borrow cash
_____ k. Depreciation
_____ l. Purchase of treasury stock
_____ m. Issuance of common stock
_____ n. Increase in accounts payable
_____ o. Net income
_____ p. Payment of cash dividend

Classifying transactions for the statement of cash flows—indirect method

2

E14-17 Indicate whether each of the following transactions would result in an operating activity, an investing activity, or a financing activity for a statement of cash flows prepared by the *indirect* method and the accompanying schedule of noncash investing and financing activities. (Exhibit 14-3, p. 695; p. 703)

a. Cash	81,000		g. Land	18,000	
Common Stock		81,000	Cash		18,000
b. Treasury Stock	13,000		h. Cash	7,200	
Cash		13,000	Equipment		7,200
c. Cash	60,000		i. Bonds Payable	45,000	
Sales Revenue		60,000	Cash		45,000
d. Land	87,700		j. Building	164,000	
Cash		87,700	Note Payable, Long-Term		164,000
e. Depreciation Expense	9,000		k. Loss on Disposal of Equipment	1,400	
Accumulated Depreciation		9,000	Equipment Net		1,400
f. Dividends Payable	16,500				
Cash		16,500			

Computing cash flows from operating activities—indirect method

3

E14-18 The records of Paramount Color Engraving reveal the following:

Net income	$40,000	Depreciation	$12,000
Sales revenue	9,000	Decrease in current liabilities	20,000
Loss on sale of land	5,000	Increase in current assets	
Acquisition of land	37,000	other than cash	7,000

continued . . .

Requirements

Compute cash flows from operating activities by the indirect method. Use the format of the operating activities section of Exhibit 14-7. Also evaluate the operating cash flow of Paramount Color Engraving. Give the reason for your evaluation. (pp. 693–694, 696–706)

Computing cash flows from operating activities—indirect method

E14-19 The accounting records of DVD Sales, Inc., include these accounts:

Cash		Accounts Receivable	
Mar. 1 5,000		Mar. 1 18,000	
Mar. 31 4,000		Mar. 31 14,000	

Inventory		Accounts Payable	
Mar. 1 19,000			Mar. 1 14,000
Mar. 31 21,000			Mar. 31 19,000

Accumulated Depreciation—Equipment		Retained Earnings	
	Mar. 1 52,000		Mar. 1 64,000
	Depreciation 3,000	Dividend 18,000	Net income 81,000
	Mar. 31 55,000		Mar. 31 127,000

Compute DVD's net cash provided by (used for) operating activities during March. Use the indirect method. (pp. 696–697)

Preparing the statement of cash flows—indirect method

E14-20 The income statement and additional data of Vitamins Plus, Inc., follow:

VITAMINS PLUS, INC.
Income Statement
Year Ended June 30, 2006

Revenues:		
Service revenue		$237,000
Expenses:		
Cost of goods sold	$98,000	
Salary expense	58,000	
Depreciation expense	29,000	
Income tax expense	9,000	194,000
Net income		$ 43,000

Additional data:
a. Acquisition of plant assets is $116,000. Of this amount, $101,000 is paid in cash and $15,000 by signing a note payable.
b. Cash receipt from sale of land totals $24,000. There was no gain or loss.

continued ...

c. Cash receipts from issuance of common stock total $30,000.
d. Payment of note payable is $15,000.
e. Payment of dividends is $11,000.
f. From the balance sheet:

	June 30,	
	2006	2005
Current Assets:		
Cash	$32,000	$20,000
Accounts receivable	43,000	58,000
Inventory	92,000	85,000
Current Liabilities:		
Accounts payable	$35,000	$22,000
Accrued liabilities	13,000	21,000

Requirement

Prepare Vitamins Plus, Inc.'s statement of cash flows for the year ended June 30, 2006, using the indirect method. Include a separate section for noncash investing and financing activities. (pp. 699–700, 703)

E14-21 Compute the following items for the statement of cash flows:

a. Beginning and ending Retained Earnings are $45,000 and $70,000, respectively. Net income for the period is $60,000. How much are cash dividends? (p. 702)

b. Beginning and ending Plant Assets, Net, are $103,000 and $107,000, respectively. Depreciation for the period is $16,000, and acquisitions of new plant assets total $27,000. Plant assets were sold at a $4,000 gain. What was the amount of the cash receipt from the sale? (pp. 701–702)

E14-22 Hawkeye Gymnastics Equipment, Inc., reported the following financial statements for 2006:

HAWKEYE GYMNASTICS EQUIPMENT, INC.
Income Statement
Year Ended December 31, 2006

	(In thousands)
Sales revenue	$710
Cost of goods sold	$340
Depreciation expense	50
Other expenses	200
Total expenses	590
Net income	$120

continued . . .

HAWKEYE GYMNASTICS EQUIPMENT, INC.
Comparative Balance Sheet
December 31, 2006 and 2005

(In thousands) Assets	2006	2005	Liabilities	2006	2005
Current:			Current:		
Cash	$ 19	$ 16	Accounts payable	$ 75	$ 73
Accounts receivable	54	48	Salary payable	1	3
Inventory	83	86	Long-term notes payable	60	68
Long-term investments	90	75	Stockholders' Equity		
Plant assets, net	225	185	Common stock	45	35
			Retained earnings	290	231
Total	$471	$410	Total	$471	$410

Compute the amount of Hawkeye's acquisition of plant assets. Hawkeye sold no plant assets. (pp. 699–701)

Computing financing cash flows
3

E14-23 Use the Hawkeye Gymnastics data in Exercise 14-22 to compute
- a. New borrowing or payment of long-term notes payable, with Hawkeye having only one long-term note payable transaction during the year (pp. 700–701)
- b. Issuance of common stock, with Hawkeye having only one common stock transaction during the year (p. 702)
- c. Payment of cash dividends (p. 702)

Preparing the statement of cash flows—indirect method
3

E14-24 Use the Hawkeye Gymnastics data in Exercises E14-22 and E14-23 to prepare the company's statement of cash flows—indirect method—for the year ended December 31, 2006. Show all amounts in thousands, as in the exercise. (pp. 699–700)

Appendix 14A: Direct Method

Identifying activities for the statement of cash flows—direct method
4

E14-25 Identify each of the following transactions as
- Operating activity (O)
- Investing activity (I)
- Financing activity (F)
- Noncash investing and financing activity (NIF)
- Transaction that is not reported on the statement of cash flows (N)

For each cash flow, indicate whether the item increases (+) or decreases (−) cash. The *direct* method is used for cash flows from operating activities. (pp. 736–737, 739–740)

_____ a. Collection of account receivable

_____ b. Issuance of note payable to borrow cash

_____ c. Depreciation

_____ d. Purchase of treasury stock

_____ e. Issuance of common stock for cash

_____ f. Payment of account payable

continued . . .

The Statement of Cash Flows

_____ g. Issuance of preferred stock for cash
_____ h. Payment of cash dividend
_____ i. Sale of land
_____ j. Acquisition of equipment by issuance of note payable
_____ k. Payment of note payable
_____ l. Acquisition of building by issuance of common stock
_____ m. Purchase of equipment
_____ n. Payment of wages to employees
_____ o. Collection of cash interest
_____ p. Sale of building

Classifying transactions for the statement of cash flows—direct method

E14-26 Indicate where, if at all, each of the following transactions would be reported on a statement of cash flows prepared by the *direct* method and the accompanying schedule of noncash investing and financing activities. (Exhibit 14A-3, p. 738)

a. Land	18,000		g. Salary Expense	4,300	
Cash		18,000	Cash		4,300
b. Cash	7,200		h. Cash	81,000	
Equipment		7,200	Common Stock		81,000
c. Bonds Payable	45,000		i. Treasury Stock	13,000	
Cash		45,000	Cash		13,000
d. Building	164,000		j. Cash	2,000	
Note Payable		164,000	Interest Revenue		2,000
e. Cash	1,400		k. Land	87,700	
Accounts Receivable		1,400	Cash		87,700
f. Dividends Payable	16,500		l. Accounts Payable	8,300	
Cash		16,500	Cash		8,300

Computing cash flows from operating activities—direct method

E14-27 The accounting records of Fuzzy Dice Auto Parts reveal the following:

Payment of salaries and wages	$ 34,000		Net income	$22,000
Depreciation	12,000		Payment of income tax	13,000
Payment of interest	16,000		Collection of dividend revenue	7,000
Payment of dividends	7,000		Payment to suppliers	54,000
Collections from customers	112,000			

Requirement

Compute cash flows from operating activities by the *direct* method. Use the format of the operating activities section of Exhibit 14A-3, page 738.

Identifying items for the statement of cash flows—direct method

E14-28 Selected accounts of Dimension Networks, Inc., show the following:

Accounts Receivable			
Beginning balance	9,000		
Service revenue	40,000	Cash collections	38,000
Ending balance	11,000		

continued ...

Land		
Beginning balance	90,000	
Acquisition	18,000	
Ending balance	108,000	

Long-Term Notes Payable			
		Beginning balance	273,000
Payments	69,000	Issuance for cash	83,000
		Ending balance	287,000

Requirements

For each account, identify the item or items that should appear on a statement of cash flows prepared by the *direct* method. Also state each item's amount and where to report the item. (Exhibit 14A-3, p. 738)

E14-29 The income statement and additional data of Capitol Hill Corporation follow:

Preparing the statement of cash flows—direct method

CAPITOL HILL CORPORATION
Income Statement
Year Ended June 30, 2006

Revenues:		
Sales revenue	$229,000	
Dividend revenue	8,000	$237,000
Expenses:		
Cost of goods sold	$103,000	
Salary expense	45,000	
Depreciation expense	28,000	
Advertising expense	12,000	
Interest expense	2,000	
Income tax expense	9,000	199,000
Net income		$ 38,000

Additional data:
a. Collections from customers are $15,000 more than sales.
b. Dividend revenue, interest expense, and income tax expense equal their cash amounts.
c. Payments to suppliers are the sum of cost of goods sold plus advertising expense.
d. Payments to employees are $1,000 more than salary expense.
e. Acquisition of plant assets is $101,000.
f. Cash receipts from sale of land total $24,000.
g. Cash receipts from issuance of common stock total $30,000.
h. Payment of long-term note payable is $15,000.
i. Payment of dividends is $11,000.
j. Cash balance, June 30, 2005, was $20,000; June 30, 2006, was $27,000.

continued . . .

Requirement

Prepare Capitol Hill Corporation's statement of cash flows for the year ended June 30, 2006. Use the *direct* method. Follow the format given in Exhibit 14A-3, page 738.

Computing amounts for the statement of cash flows—direct method

E14-30 Compute the following items for the statement of cash flows:

a. Beginning and ending Accounts Receivable are $22,000 and $18,000, respectively. Credit sales for the period total $60,000. How much are cash collections from customers? (pp. 740–742)

b. Cost of goods sold is $75,000. Beginning Inventory balance is $25,000, and ending Inventory balance is $21,000. Beginning and ending Accounts Payable are $11,000 and $8,000, respectively. How much are cash payments for inventory? (pp. 740–742)

Computing cash-flow amounts—direct method

E14-31 Elite Mobile Homes reported the following in its financial statements for the year ended December 31, 2007 (adapted, in millions):

	2007	2006
Income Statement		
Net sales	$24,623	$21,207
Cost of sales	18,048	15,466
Depreciation	269	230
Other operating expenses	4,883	4,248
Income tax expense	537	486
Net income	$ 886	$ 777
Balance Sheet		
Cash and equivalents	$ 17	$ 13
Accounts receivable	798	615
Inventories	3,482	2,831
Property and equipment, net	4,345	3,428
Accounts payable	1,547	1,364
Accrued liabilities	938	848
Long-term liabilities	478	464
Common stock	676	446
Retained earnings	4,531	3,788

Determine the following for Elite Mobile Homes during 2007:
a. Collections from customers (pp. 740–742)
b. Payments for inventory (pp. 740–742)
c. Payments of operating expenses (pp. 740–742)
d. Acquisitions of property and equipment (no sales during 2007) (pp. 699–700)
e. Borrowing, with Elite paying no long-term liabilities (pp. 700–702)
f. Cash receipt from issuance of common stock (p. 702)
g. Payment of cash dividends (p. 702)

For computing the operating cash flows, follow the approach outlined in Exhibit 14A-6, page 742.

Problems (Group A)

Using cash-flow information to evaluate performance

P14-32A Top managers of Bernard Associates are reviewing company performance for 2009. The income statement reports a 15% increase in net income, which is outstanding. The balance sheet shows modest increases in assets, liabilities, and stockholders' equity. The assets with the largest increases are plant and equipment because the company is halfway through an expansion program. No other assets and no liabilities are increasing dramatically. A summarized version of the cash-flow statement reports the following:

Net cash provided by operating activities	$310,000
Net cash used for investing activities	(290,000)
Net cash provided by financing activities	80,000
Increase in cash during 2009	$100,000

Requirement
Write a memo giving top managers of Bernard Associates your assessment of 2009 operations and your outlook for the future. Focus on the information content of the cash-flow data. (pp. 694–694)

Preparing an income statement, balance sheet, and statement of cash flows—indirect method

P14-33A American Reserve Rare Coins (ARRC) was formed on January 1, 2006, when ARRC issued its common stock for $200,000. Early in January, ARRC made the following cash payments:

a. For store fixtures, $50,000
b. For inventory, $100,000
c. For rent expense on a store building, $10,000

Later in the year, ARRC purchased inventory on account for $240,000. Before year-end, ARRC paid $140,000 of this account payable.

During 2006, ARRC sold 2,500 units of inventory for $200 each. Before year-end, the company collected 90% of this amount. Cost of goods sold for the year was $300,000, and ending inventory totaled $40,000.

The store employs three people. The combined annual payroll is $90,000, of which ARRC still owes $5,000 at year-end. At the end of the year, ARRC paid income tax of $20,000.

Late in 2006, ARRC declared and paid cash dividends of $40,000.

For equipment, ARRC uses the straight-line depreciation method, over 5 years, with zero residual value.

Requirements
1. Prepare American Reserve's income statement for the year ended December 31, 2006. Use the single-step format, with all revenues listed together and all expenses together. (pp. 272–275, 696–697)
2. Prepare American Reserve's balance sheet at December 31, 2006. (pp. 695–696)
3. Prepare American Reserve's statement of cash flows for the year ended December 31, 2006. Format cash flows from operating activities by the *indirect* method. (pp. 699–700)

Preparing the statement of cash flows—indirect method
2 3

P14-34A Accountants for Datsun, Inc., have assembled the following data for the year ended December 31, 2007:

	December 31,	
	2007	2006
Current Accounts:		
Current assets:		
Cash and cash equivalents	$49,000	$34,000
Accounts receivable	70,100	73,700
Inventories	90,600	86,600
Current liabilities:		
Accounts payable	71,600	67,500
Income tax payable	5,900	6,800

Transaction Data for 2007:

Payment of cash dividends...	$48,000	Depreciation expense	$ 30,200
Issuance of note payable		Purchase of equipment	69,000
to borrow cash	63,000	Acquisition of land by issuing	
Net income	50,500	long-term note payable	118,000
Issuance of common stock		Payment of note payable	47,000
for cash	36,000	Gain on sale of building	3,500

Requirement

Prepare Datsun's statement of cash flows using the *indirect* method to report operating activities. Include an accompanying schedule of non-cash investing and financing activities. (pp. 699–700, 703)

Preparing the statement of cash flows—indirect method
2 3

P14-35A The comparative balance sheet of Fidelity Medical Supply at December 31, 2008, reported the following:

	December 31,	
	2008	2007
Current Assets:		
Cash and cash equivalents	$32,500	$22,500
Accounts receivable	26,600	29,300
Inventories	54,600	53,000
Current Liabilities:		
Accounts payable	$29,100	$28,000
Accrued liabilities	14,300	16,800

Fidelity's transactions during 2008 included the following:

Purchase of building	$104,000	Payment of cash dividends	$17,000
Net income	31,600	Purchase of equipment	55,000
Issuance of common stock		Issuance of long-term note	
for cash	105,000	payable to borrow cash	32,000
Depreciation expense	17,700		

continued ...

Requirements

1. Prepare the statement of cash flows of Fidelity Medical Supply for the year ended December 31, 2008. Use the *indirect* method to report cash flows from operating activities. (pp. 699–700)

2. Evaluate Fidelity's cash flows for the year. Mention all three categories of cash flows and give the reason for your evaluation. (pp. 692–694)

Preparing the statement of cash flows—indirect method

P14-36A The 2008 comparative balance sheet and income statement of Digital Subscriptions, Inc., follow.

Digital Subscriptions had no noncash investing and financing transactions during 2008. During the year, there were no sales of land or equipment, no issuances of notes payable, no retirements of stock, and no treasury stock transactions.

Requirements

1. Prepare the 2008 statement of cash flows, formatting operating activities by the *indirect* method. (pp. 699–700)

2. How will what you learned in this problem help you evaluate an investment? (pp. 692–694)

DIGITAL SUBSCRIPTIONS, INC.
Comparative Balance Sheet

	December 31, 2008	December 31, 2007	Increase (Decrease)
Current assets:			
Cash and cash equivalents	$ 26,700	$ 18,700	$ 8,000
Accounts receivable	46,500	43,100	3,400
Inventories	84,300	89,900	(5,600)
Plant assets:			
Land	35,100	10,000	25,100
Equipment, net	100,900	93,700	7,200
Total assets	$293,500	$255,400	$38,100
Current liabilities:			
Accounts payable	$ 31,100	$ 29,800	$ 1,300
Accrued liabilities	18,100	18,700	(600)
Long-term liabilities:			
Notes payable	55,000	65,000	(10,000)
Stockholders' equity:			
Common stock	131,100	122,300	8,800
Retained earnings	58,200	19,600	38,600
Total liabilities and stockholders' equity	$293,500	$255,400	$38,100

continued . . .

DIGITAL SUBSCRIPTIONS, INC.
Income Statement
Year Ended December 31, 2008

Revenues:		
Sales revenue		$438,000
Interest revenue		11,700
Total revenues		449,700
Expenses:		
Cost of goods sold	$205,200	
Salary expense	76,400	
Depreciation expense	15,300	
Other operating expense	49,700	
Interest expense	24,600	
Income tax expense	16,900	
Total expenses		388,100
Net income		$ 61,600

Appendix 14A: Direct Method

Preparing the statement of cash flows—direct method

P14-37A GSK Inc., accountants have developed the following data from the company's accounting records for the year ended November 30, 2005:
  a. Purchase of plant assets, $100,000
  b. Cash receipt from issuance of notes payable, $44,100
  c. Payments of notes payable, $18,800
  d. Cash receipt from sale of plant assets, $59,700
  e. Cash receipt of dividends, $2,700
  f. Payments to suppliers, $574,500
  g. Interest expense and payments, $37,000
  h. Payments of salaries, $104,000
  i. Income tax expense and payments, $56,000
  j. Depreciation expense, $27,700
  k. Collections from customers, $827,100
  l. Cash receipt from issuance of common stock, $66,900
  m. Payment of cash dividends, $50,500
  n. Cash balance: November 30, 2004–$23,800; November 30, 2005–$83,500

Requirement
Prepare GSK's statement of cash flows for the year ended November 30, 2005. Use the *direct* method for cash flows from operating activities. Follow the format of Exhibit 14A-3, page 738, but do *not* show amounts in thousands.

Preparing an income statement, balance sheet, and statement of cash flows—direct method

P14-38A Use the American Reserve Rare Coins data from Problem 14-33A.

Requirements
1. Prepare American Reserve Rare Coins' income statement for the year ended December 31, 2006. Use the single-step format, with all revenues listed together and all expenses together. (pp. 273–275, 696–697)

continued . . .

2. Prepare American Reserve's balance sheet at December 31, 2006. (pp. 695–696)

3. Prepare American Reserve's statement of cash flows for the year ended December 31, 2006. Format cash flows from operating activities by the *direct* method, as shown in Exhibit 14A-3, page 738.

Preparing the statement of cash flows—direct method

P14-39A Use the Digital Subscriptions, Inc., data from Problem 14-36A.

Requirements
1. Prepare the 2008 statement of cash flows by the *direct* method. Follow the statement format shown in Exhibit 14A-3, page 738.
2. How will what you learned in this problem help you evaluate an investment? (pp. 692–694)

Preparing the statement of cash flows—direct method

P14-40A To prepare the statement of cash flows, accountants for A-Mobile, Inc., you have summarized 2008 activity in the Cash account as follows:

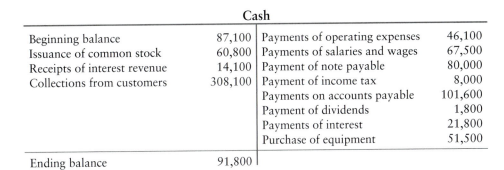

Requirement
Prepare A-Mobile's statement of cash flows for the year ended December 31, 2008, using the *direct* method to report operating activities. Follow the statement format given in Exhibit 14A-3, page 738.

Problems (Group B)

Using cash-flow information to evaluate performance

P14-41B Top managers of Chase Financial Services are reviewing company performance for 2009. The income statement reports a 20% increase in net income over 2008. However, most of the net-income increase resulted from an extraordinary gain on the sale of equipment. The balance sheet shows a large increase in receivables. The cash-flow statement, in summarized form, reports the following:

Net cash used for operating activities	$(80,000)
Net cash provided by investing activities	40,000
Net cash provided by financing activities	50,000
Increase in cash during 2009	$ 10,000

Requirement
Write a memo giving the top managers of Chase Financial Services your assessment of 2009 operations and your outlook for the future. Focus on the information content of the cash-flow data. (pp. 692–694)

Preparing an income statement, balance sheet, and statement of cash flows—indirect method

P14-42B Lucenay Interiors, a furniture store, was formed on January 1, 2008, when Lucenay issued common stock for $400,000. Early in January, Lucenay made the following cash payments:

a. $100,000 for equipment

b. $260,000 for inventory

c. $20,000 for 2008 rent expense on a store building

Later in the year, Lucenay purchased inventory on account. Cost of this inventory was $120,000. Before year-end, Lucenay paid $60,000 of this debt.

During 2008, Lucenay sold 2,000 units of inventory for $200 each. Before year end, Lucenay collected 80% of this amount. Cost of goods sold for the year was $260,000 and at year-end the inventory balance was $120,000.

The store employs a salesperson whose annual pay is $45,000, of which Lucenay owes $4,000 at year-end. At the end of the year, Lucenay paid income tax of $10,000.

Late in 2008, Lucenay paid cash dividends of $11,000.

For equipment, Lucenay uses the straight-line depreciation method, over 5 years, with zero residual value.

Requirements

1. Prepare Lucenay Interiors' income statement for the year ended December 31, 2008. Use the single-step format, with all revenues listed together and all expenses together. (pp. 273–275, 696–697)
2. Prepare Lucenay's balance sheet at December 31, 2008. (pp. 695–696)
3. Prepare Lucenay's statement of cash flows for the year ended December 31, 2008. Format cash flows from operating activities by the *indirect* method. (pp. 699–700)

Preparing the statement of cash flows—indirect method

P14-43B Carlson Corporation accountants have assembled the company's data for the year ended December 31, 2007.

Requirement

Prepare Carlson Corporation's statement of cash flows using the *indirect* method to report operating activities. Include an accompanying schedule of noncash investing and financing activities. (pp. 699–700, 703)

	December 31, 2007	December 31, 2006
Current Accounts:		
Current assets:		
Cash and cash equivalents	$50,000	$22,000
Accounts receivable	69,200	64,200
Inventories	80,000	83,000
Current liabilities:		
Accounts payable	$57,800	$55,800
Income tax payable	14,700	16,700

continued...

Transaction Data for 2007:

Net income	$ 57,000	Purchase of treasury stock	$14,000
Issuance of common stock for cash	41,000	Loss on sale of equipment	11,000
		Payment of cash dividends	18,000
Depreciation expense	21,000	Issuance of long-term note payable to borrow cash	34,000
Purchase of building	160,000		
Retirement of bonds payable by issuing common stock	65,000	Sale of equipment	58,000

Preparing the statement of cash flows—indirect method
2 3

P14-44B The comparative balance sheet of Fitzwater Company at March 31, 2009, reported the following:

	March 31,	
	2009	2008
Current Assets:		
Cash and cash equivalents	$22,200	$15,000
Accounts receivable	14,900	21,700
Inventories	63,200	60,600
Current Liabilities:		
Accounts payable	$30,100	$27,600
Accrued liabilities	10,700	11,100
Income tax payable	8,000	4,700

Fitzwater's transactions during the year ended March 31, 2009, included the following:

Payment of cash dividend	$30,000	Depreciation expense	$17,300
Purchase of equipment	78,700	Purchase of building	47,000
Issuance of note payable to borrow cash	50,000	Net income	75,000
		Issuance of common stock	11,000

Requirements

1. Prepare Fitzwater's statement of cash flows for the year ended March 31, 2009, using the *indirect* method to report cash flows from operating activities. (pp. 699–700)
2. Evaluate Fitzwater's cash flows for the year. Mention all three categories of cash flows and give the reason for your evaluation. (pp. 692–694)

Preparing the statement of cash flows—indirect method
2 3

P14-45B The 2005 comparative balance sheet and income statement of Get Wired, Inc., follow on the next page.

Get Wired, Inc., had no noncash investing and financing transactions during 2005. During the year, there were no sales of land or equipment, no issuances of notes payable, no retirements of stock, and no treasury stock transactions.

continued . . .

GET WIRED, INC.
Comparative Balance Sheet

	December 31, 2005	December 31, 2004	Increase (Decrease)
Current assets:			
Cash and cash equivalents	$ 26,700	$ 15,300	$ 11,400
Accounts receivable	25,300	26,900	(1,600)
Inventories	91,800	79,800	12,000
Plant assets:			
Land	69,000	60,000	9,000
Equipment, net	53,500	49,400	4,100
Total assets	$266,300	$231,400	$34,900
Current liabilities:			
Accounts payable	$ 30,900	$ 35,400	$ (4,500)
Accrued liabilities	30,600	28,600	2,000
Long-term liabilities:			
Notes payable	75,000	100,000	(25,000)
Stockholders' equity:			
Common stock	88,300	64,700	23,600
Retained earnings	41,500	2,700	38,800
Total liabilities and stockholders' equity	$266,300	$231,400	$34,900

GET WIRED, INC.
Income Statement
Year Ended December 31, 2005

Revenues:		
Sales revenue		$213,000
Interest revenue		8,600
Total revenues		221,600
Expenses:		
Cost of goods sold	$70,600	
Salary expense	27,800	
Depreciation expense	4,000	
Other operating expense	10,500	
Interest expense	11,600	
Income tax expense	29,100	
Total expenses		153,600
Net income		$ 68,000

Requirements

1. Prepare the 2005 statement of cash flows, formatting operating activities by the *indirect* method. (pp. 699–700)
2. How will what you learned in this problem help you evaluate an investment? (p. 693)

Preparing the statement of cash flows—direct method

Appendix 14A: Direct Method

P14-46B Accountants for Compass Software have developed the following data from the company's accounting records for the year ended April 30, 2005:

   a. Purchase of plant assets, $59,400
   b. Cash receipt from issuance of common stock, $8,000
   c. Payment of dividends, $48,400
   d. Collection of interest, $4,400
   e. Payments of salaries, $93,000
   f. Cash receipt from sale of plant assets, $22,400
   g. Collections from customers, $605,300
   h. Cash receipt of dividend revenue, $4,100
   i. Payments to suppliers, $370,300
   j. Depreciation expense, $59,900
   k. Cash receipt from issuance of notes payable, $19,600
   l. Payments of notes payable, $50,000
   m. Interest expense and payments, $13,000
   n. Income tax expense and payments, $37,000
   o. Cash balance: April 30, 2004, $39,300; April 30, 2005, $32,000

Requirement

Prepare Compass Software's statement of cash flows for the year ended April 30, 2005. Use the *direct* method for cash flows from operating activities. Follow the format of Exhibit 14A-3, page 738, but do *not* show amounts in thousands.

Preparing an income statement, balance sheet, and statement of cash flows—direct method

P14-47B Use the Lucenay Interiors data from Problem 14-42B.

Requirements

1. Prepare Lucenay Interiors' income statement for the year ended December 31, 2008. Use the single-step format, with all revenues listed together and all expenses together. (pp. 273–275, 696–697)
2. Prepare Lucenay's balance sheet at December 31, 2008. (pp. 695–696)
3. Prepare Lucenay's statement of cash flows for the year ended December 31, 2008. Format cash flows from operating activities by the *direct* method, as shown in Exhibit 14A-3, page 738.

Preparing the statement of cash flows—direct method

P14-48B Use the Get Wired, Inc., data from Problem 14-45B.

Requirements

1. Prepare the 2005 statement of cash flows by the *direct* method. Follow the statement format given in Exhibit 14A-3, page 738.
2. How will what you learned in this problem help you evaluate an investment? (p. 693)

Preparing the statement of cash flows—direct method

P14-49B To prepare the statement of cash flows, accountants for Toll-Free Calling, Inc., have summarized 2008 activity in the Cash account as follows:

Cash

Beginning balance	22,600	Payments on accounts payable	399,100
Receipts of interest	17,100	Payments of dividends	27,200
Collections from customers	673,700	Payments of salaries and wages	143,800
Issuance of common stock	47,300	Payments of interest	26,900
		Purchase of equipment	10,200
		Payments of operating expenses	34,300
		Payment of note payable	67,700
		Payment of income tax	18,900
Ending balance	32,600		

Requirement

Prepare the statement of cash flows of Toll-Free Calling, Inc., for the year ended December 31, 2008, using the *direct* method for operating activities. Follow the statement format given in Exhibit 14A-3, page 738.

for 24/7 practice, visit www.MyAccountingLab.com

Apply Your Knowledge

Decision Cases

Preparing and using the statement of cash flows to evaluate operations

Case 1. The 2008 comparative income statement and the 2008 comparative balance sheet of Golf America, Inc., have just been distributed at a meeting of the company's board of directors. The members of the board of directors raise a fundamental question: Why is the cash balance so low? This question is especially hard to understand because 2008 showed record profits. As the controller of the company, you must answer the question.

GOLF AMERICA, INC.
Comparative Income Statement
Years Ended December 31, 2008 and 2007

(In thousands)	2008	2007
Revenues and gains:		
Sales revenue	$444	$310
Gain on sale of equipment (sale price, $33)	—	18
Total revenues and gains	$444	$328
Expenses and losses:		
Cost of goods sold	$221	$162
Salary expense	48	28
Depreciation expense	46	22
Interest expense	13	20
Amortization expense on patent	11	11
Loss on sale of land (sale price, $61)	—	35
Total expenses and losses	339	278
Net income	$105	$ 50

GOLF AMERICA, INC.
Comparative Balance Sheet
December 31, 2008 and 2007

(In thousands)	2008	2007
Assets		
Cash	$ 25	$ 63
Accounts receivable, net	72	61
Inventories	194	181
Long-term investments	31	0
Property, plant, and equipment, net	125	61
Patents	177	188
Totals	$624	$554
Liabilities and Owners' Equity		
Accounts payable	$ 63	$ 56
Accrued liabilities	12	17
Notes payable, long-term	179	264
Common stock	149	61
Retained earnings	221	156
Totals	$624	$554

continued . . .

Requirements

1. Prepare a statement of cash flows for 2008 in the format that best shows the relationship between net income and operating cash flow. The company sold no plant assets or long-term investments and issued no notes payable during 2008. There were *no* noncash investing and financing transactions during the year. Show all amounts in thousands.

2. Considering net income and the company's cash flows during 2008, was it a good year or a bad year? Give your reasons.

Using cash-flow data to evaluate an investment

Case 2. Showcase Cinemas and Theater by Design are asking you to recommend their stock to your clients. Because Showcase and Theater by Design earn about the same net income and have similar financial positions, your decision depends on their cash-flow statements, summarized as follows:

	Theater by Design		Showcase Cinemas	
Net cash provided by operating activities......................................		$30,000		$70,000
Cash provided by (used for) investing activities:				
Purchase of plant assets	$(20,000)		$(100,000)	
Sale of plant assets....................	40,000	20,000	10,000	(90,000)
Cash provided by (used for) financing activities:				
Issuance of common stock.........	—		30,000	
Paying off long-term debt	(40,000)		—	
Net increase in cash......................		$10,000		$10,000

Based on their cash flows, which company looks better? Give your reasons.

Ethical Issue

Moss Exports is having a bad year. Net income is only $60,000. Also, two important overseas customers are falling behind in their payments to Moss, and Moss's accounts receivable are ballooning. The company desperately needs a loan. The Moss Exports board of directors is considering ways to put the best face on the company's financial statements. Moss's bank closely examines cash flow from operations. Daniel Peavey, Moss's controller, suggests reclassifying as long-term the receivables from the slow-paying clients. He explains to the board that removing the $80,000 rise in accounts receivable from current assets will increase net cash provided by operations. This approach may help Moss get the loan.

Requirements

1. Using only the amounts given, compute net cash provided by operations, both without and with the reclassification of the receivables. Which reporting makes Moss look better?

2. Under what condition would the reclassification of the receivables be ethical? Unethical?

Financial Statement Case

Using the statement of cash flows

Use the Amazon.com statement of cash flows along with the company's other financial statements, all in Appendix A, at the end of this book, to answer the following questions.

Requirements

1. Which method does Amazon use to report net cash flows from *operating* activities? How can you tell?

2. Amazon earned net income during 2005. Did operations *provide* cash or *use* cash during 2005? Give the amount. How did operating cash during 2005 compare with 2004? Be specific, and state the reason for your answer.

3. Suppose Amazon reported net cash flows from operating activities by the direct method. Compute these amounts for the year ended December 31, 2005:
   a. Collections from customers (Other current assets were $15 million at December 31, 2005, and $12 million at December 31, 2004.)
   b. Payments for inventory

4. Evaluate 2005 in terms of net income, cash flows, balance sheet position, and overall results. Be specific.

Team Projects

Project 1. Each member of the team should obtain the annual report of a different company. Select companies in different industries. Evaluate each company's trend of cash flows for the most recent two years. In your evaluation of the companies' cash flows, you may use any other information that is publicly available—for example, the other financial statements (income statement, balance sheet, statement of stockholders' equity, and the related notes) and news stories from magazines and newspapers. Rank the companies' cash flows from best to worst and write a two-page report on your findings.

Project 2. Select a company and obtain its annual report, including all the financial statements. Focus on the statement of cash flows and, in particular, the cash flows from operating activities. Specify whether the company uses the *direct* method or the *indirect* method to report operating cash flows. As necessary, use the other financial statements (income statement, balance sheet, and statement of stockholders' equity) and the notes to prepare the company's cash flows from operating activities by the *other* method.

For Internet exercises, Excel in Practice, and additional online activities, go to the Web site www.prenhall.com/horngren

---

Quick Check Answers

1. a   2. d   3. a   4. b   5. c   6. a   7. b   8. c   9. d   10. c

Appendix 14A

Preparing the Statement of Cash Flows by the Direct Method

The Financial Accounting Standards Board (FASB) prefers the direct method of reporting cash flows from operating activities. The direct method provides clearer information about the sources and uses of cash. But very few companies use the direct method because it takes more computations than the indirect method. Investing and financing cash flows are unaffected by operating cash flows.

 Prepare the statement of cash flows by the direct method

To illustrate the statement of cash flows by the direct method, we will be using Anchor Corporation, a dealer in auto parts for European cars. You can prepare the statement of cash flows by the direct method as follows:

STEP 1 Lay out the format of the statement of cash flows by the direct method, as shown in Exhibit 14A-1.

EXHIBIT 14A-1 Format of the Statement of Cash Flows: Direct Method

ANCHOR CORPORATION
Statement of Cash Flows
Year Ended December 31, 2008

Cash flows from operating activities:
  Receipts:
    Collections from customers
    Interest received
    Dividends received on investments
      Total cash receipts
  Payments:
    To suppliers
    To employees
    For interest and income tax
      Total cash payments
  Net cash provided by operating activities
± Cash flows from investing activities:
  Cash receipts from sales of long-term assets (investments,
    land, building, equipment, and so on)
  − Acquisitions of long-term assets
  Net cash provided by (used for) investing activities
± Cash flows from financing activities:
  Cash receipts from issuance of stock
  + Sale of treasury stock
  − Purchase of treasury stock
  + Cash receipts from issuance of notes or bonds payable (borrowing)
  − Payment of notes or bonds payable
  − Payment of dividends
  Net cash provided by (used for) financing activities
= Net increase (decrease) in cash during the year
  + Cash at December 31, 2007
  = Cash at December 31, 2008

STEP 2 Use the comparative balance sheet to determine the increase or decrease in cash during the period. The change in cash is the "check figure" for the statement of cash flows. Anchor's comparative balance sheet shows that cash decreased by $20,000 during 2008. See Exhibit 14A-2.

EXHIBIT 14A-2 Comparative Balance Sheet (Partial)

ANCHOR CORPORATION
Comparative Balance Sheet (Partial)
December 31, 2008 and 2007

(In thousands)	2008	2007	Increase (Decrease)
Assets			
Current:			
Cash	$22	$42	$(20)

STEP 3 Use the available data to prepare the statement of cash flows. Anchor has assembled the following summary of its 2008 cash transactions.

Operating Activities
1. Collections from customers, $269,000
2. Cash receipt of interest revenue, $12,000
3. Cash receipt of dividend revenue, $9,000
4. Payments to suppliers, $135,000
5. Salary expense and payments, $56,000
6. Interest expense and payments, $15,000
7. Income tax expense and payments, $14,000

Investing Activities
8. Cash payments to acquire plant assets, $310,000
9. Cash receipts from sale of plant assets, $50,000

Financing Activities
10. Cash receipts from issuance of common stock, $100,000
11. Cash receipts from issuance of notes payable, $90,000
12. Payment of note payable, $10,000
13. Payment of cash dividends, $10,000

The statement of cash flows reports only transactions with cash effects. Exhibit 14A-3 gives Anchor Corporation's statement of cash flows for 2008. You should trace each item from the list of transactions to the statement of cash flows in Exhibit 14A-3.

Cash Flows from Operating Activities

Operating cash flows are listed first because they are the most important source of cash. Exhibit 14A-3 shows that Anchor is sound; its operating activities were the largest source of cash receipts, $290,000. Let's examine Anchor's operating cash flows.

Cash Collections from Customers

Cash sales bring in cash immediately; collections of accounts receivable take a little longer. Both are reported as "Collections from customers . . . $269,000" in Exhibit 14A-3.

Cash Receipts of Interest

The income statement reports interest revenue. Only the cash receipts of interest appear on the statement of cash flows—$12,000 in Exhibit 14A-3.

EXHIBIT 14A-3 | **Statement of Cash Flows—Direct Method**

ANCHOR CORPORATION
Statement of Cash Flows
Year Ended December 31, 2008

(In thousands)

Cash flows from operating activities:		
Receipts:		
Collections from customers	$ 269	
Interest received	12	
Dividends received	9	
Total cash receipts		$290
Payments:		
To suppliers	$(135)	
To employees	(56)	
For interest	(15)	
For income tax	(14)	
Total cash payments		(220)
Net cash provided by operating activities		70
Cash flows from investing activities:		
Acquisition of plant assets	$(310)	
Cash receipts from sale of plant assets	50	
Net cash used for investing activities		(260)
Cash flows from financing activities:		
Cash receipts from issuance of common stock	$ 100	
Cash receipts from issuance of notes payable	90	
Payment of note payable	(10)	
Payment of dividends	(10)	
Net cash provided by financing activities		170
Net decrease in cash		$ (20)
Cash balance, December 31, 2007		42
Cash balance, December 31, 2008		$ 22

Now return to "Cash Flows from Operating Activities" on page 737.

Cash Receipts of Dividends

Dividend revenue is reported on the income statement. Cash received from dividends is reported on the statement of cash flows—$9,000 in Exhibit 14A-3.

Payments to Suppliers

Payments to suppliers include all payments for:
- inventory
- operating expenses except employee compensation, interest, and income taxes.

Suppliers are those entities that provide the business with its inventory and essential services. In Exhibit 14A-3, Anchor Corporation reports payments to suppliers of $135,000.

Payments to Employees

This category includes payments for salaries, wages, and other forms of employee compensation. Accrued amounts are not cash flows because they have not yet been paid. The statement of cash flows in Exhibit 14A-3 reports only the cash payments, $56,000.

Payments for Interest Expense and Income Tax Expense

These cash payments are reported separately from the other expenses. For Anchor Corporation, interest ($15,000) and income tax expenses ($14,000) equal their cash payments amounts.

Depreciation, Depletion, and Amortization Expense

These expenses are *not* reported on the statement of cash flows because they do not affect cash.

Cash Flows from Investing Activities

Investing is critical because a company's investments determine its future. Large purchases of plant assets signal expansion. Low levels of investing show that the business is not replenishing assets.

Purchases of Plant Assets and Investments in Other Companies

These cash payments acquire a long-term asset. The first investing activity reported by Anchor Corporation in Exhibit 14A-3 is the purchase of plant assets ($310,000).

Cash Receipts from the Sale of Plant Assets and Investments

These cash receipts are also investing activities. Exhibit 14A-3 reports that Anchor Corporation received $50,000 cash from the sale of plant assets. For the sale of a long-term asset, the statement of cash flows reports only the amount of cash received from the sale—not the gain or loss on the sale value or the book value of the asset sold.

Investors and creditors are critical of a company that sells large amounts of its plant assets. Selling off lots of plant assets may signal an emergency need for cash.

Cash Flows from Financing Activities

Financing refers to how the business obtains money from outside sources. Cash flows from financing activities include the following:

Cash Receipts from Issuance of Stock and Notes Payable

Investors want to know how the entity obtains its financing. Issuing stock and borrowing money are two ways to finance a business. In Exhibit 14A-3, Anchor Corporation issued common stock and received cash of $100,000. Anchor also received cash when it issued notes payable to borrow $90,000.

Payment of Notes Payable and Purchases of Treasury Stock

The payment of notes payable decreases cash, which is the opposite of borrowing. Anchor Corporation reports note payments of $10,000. Other transactions in this category include the purchase and the sale of treasury stock.

Payment of Cash Dividends

The payment of dividends is a financing activity, as shown by Anchor's $10,000 payment in Exhibit 14A-3. A stock dividend has *no* effect on cash and is *not* reported on the cash-flow statement.

Noncash Investing and Financing Activities

Companies make investments that do not require cash. They also obtain financing other than cash. Our examples thus far have included none of these transactions. Now suppose that Anchor Corporation issued common stock of $300,000 to acquire a building. Anchor would record the purchase as follows:

	Building	300,000	
	Common Stock		300,000

The purchase of the building is an investing activity. The issuance of common stock is a financing activity. Taken together, this transaction is a *noncash investing and financing activity*. This transaction would not be reported on the cash-flow statement because Anchor paid no cash. But the building and the common stock are important. Noncash investing and financing activities can be reported in a separate schedule that accompanies the statement of cash flows, as follows (all amounts are assumed). This information follows the cash-flow statement or can be disclosed in a note.

	(Thousands)
Noncash investing and financing activities:	
Acquisition of building by issuing common stock	$300
Acquisition of land by issuing note payable	70
Payment of note payable by issuing common stock	100
Total noncash investing and financing activities	$470

Now let's see how to compute the individual operating cash flows for the direct method.

Computing Operating Cash Flows by the Direct Method

How do we compute the operating cash flows for the direct method? We can use Anchor's income statement (Exhibit 14A-4) and the *changes* in the related balance sheet accounts (Exhibit 14A-5).

Exhibit 14A-6 shows how to compute the operating cash flows under the direct method.

Computing Cash Collections from Customers

Collections can be computed by converting sales revenue (an accrual-basis amount) to the cash basis. Anchor Corporation's income statement (Exhibit 14A-4) reports sales of $286,000. But cash collections are different. Exhibit 14A-5 shows that

EXHIBIT 14A-4 Income Statement

ANCHOR CORPORATION
Income Statement
Year Ended December 31, 2008

(In thousands)

Revenues and gains:		
Sales revenue	$286	
Interest revenue	12	
Dividend revenue	9	
Gain on sale of plant assets	10	
Total revenues and gains		$317
Expenses:		
Cost of goods sold	$156	
Salary and wage expense	56	
Depreciation expense	20	
Other operating expense	16	
Interest expense	15	
Income tax expense	14	
Total expenses		277
Net income		$ 40

EXHIBIT 14A-5 Comparative Balance Sheet

ANCHOR CORPORATION
Comparative Balance Sheet
December 31, 2008 and 2007

(In thousands)	2008	2007	Increase (Decrease)	
Assets				
Current:				
Cash	$ 22	$ 42	$ (20)	
Accounts receivable	90	73	17	} Operating
Inventory	143	145	(2)	
Plant assets, net	460	210	250	} Investing
Total	$715	$470	$245	
Liabilities				
Current:				
Accounts payable	$ 90	$ 50	$ 40	} Operating
Accrued liabilities	5	10	(5)	
Long-term notes payable	160	80	80	
Stockholders' Equity				} Financing
Common stock	350	250	100	
Retained earnings	110	80	30	
Total	$715	$470	$245	

EXHIBIT 14A-6 Direct Method: Computing Cash Flows from Operating Activities

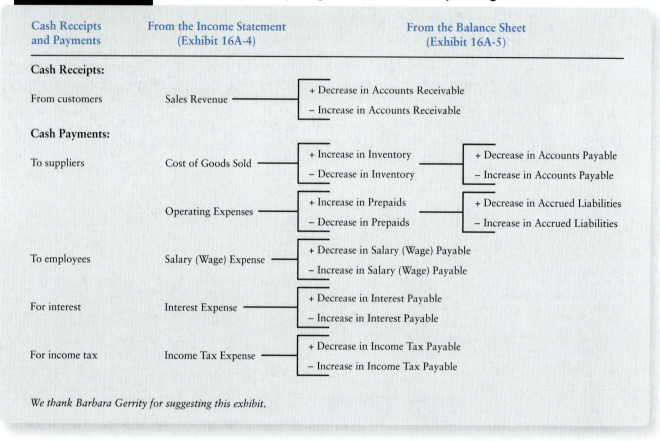

We thank Barbara Gerrity for suggesting this exhibit.

Accounts Receivable increased by $17,000 during the year. Based on those amounts, Cash Collections equal $269,000, as follows:

Collections from Customers = Sales Revenue − Increase in Accounts Receivable

$269,000 = $286,000 − $17,000

Computing Payments to Suppliers

This computation has two parts:

- Payments for inventory
- Payments for operating expenses (other than salaries, wages, interest, and income tax)

Payments for inventory are computed by converting cost of goods sold to the cash basis. We must analyze Cost of Goods Sold from the income statement and Inventory and Accounts Payable from the balance sheet, as follows:

Payments for Inventory = Cost of Goods Sold − Decrease in Inventory − Increase in Accounts Payable

$114,000 = $156,000 − $2,000 − $40,000

Payments for operating expenses use other operating expenses from the income statement and accrued liabilities from the balance sheet. Throughout, all amounts come from Exhibits 14A-4 and 14A-5. Items to be computed are shown in color.

$$\begin{array}{c} \text{Payments for} \\ \text{Operating} \\ \text{Expenses} \end{array} = \begin{array}{c} \text{Other} \\ \text{Operating} \\ \text{Expense} \end{array} + \begin{array}{c} \text{Decrease in} \\ \text{Accrued} \\ \text{Liabilities} \end{array}$$

$$\$21{,}000 = \$16{,}000 + \$5{,}000$$

$$\begin{array}{c} \text{Payments to} \\ \text{Suppliers} \end{array} = \begin{array}{c} \text{Payments for} \\ \text{Inventory} \end{array} + \begin{array}{c} \text{Payments for} \\ \text{Operating} \\ \text{Expenses} \end{array}$$

$$\$135{,}000 = \$114{,}000 + \$21{,}000$$

Computing Payments to Employees and Payments for Interest and Income Tax

Anchor Corporation's payments to employees and payments for interest and income tax were the same as the expenses. In this particular case we can take the expense amounts from the income statement to the statement of cash flows. Normally, however, you must adjust the expense amount for any change in the related liability account, as shown in Exhibit 14A-6.

Computing Investing and Financing Cash Flows

The computations of investing and financing cash flows are given on pages 700–703.

Measuring Cash Adequacy: Free Cash Flow

Throughout we have focused on cash flows from operating, investing, and financing activities. Some investors want to know how much cash a company can "free up" for new opportunities. **Free cash flow** is the amount of cash available from operations after paying for planned investments in long-term assets. Free cash flow can be computed as follows:

$$\text{Free cash flow} = \begin{array}{c} \text{Net cash provided} \\ \text{by operating} \\ \text{activities} \end{array} - \begin{array}{c} \text{Cash payments for planned} \\ \text{investments in plant, equipment,} \\ \text{and other long-term assets} \end{array}$$

PepsiCo, Inc. uses free cash flow to manage its operations. Suppose PepsiCo expects net cash provided by operations of $2.3 billion. Assume PepsiCo plans to spend $1.9 billion to modernize its bottling plants. In this case, PepsiCo's free cash flow would be $0.4 billion ($2.3 billion − $1.9 billion). If a good investment opportunity comes along, PepsiCo should have $0.4 billion to invest in the other company. Shell Oil Company also uses free-cash-flow analysis. A large amount of free cash flow is preferable because it means a lot of cash is available for new investments.

Decision Guidelines

USING CASH-FLOW AND RELATED INFORMATION TO EVALUATE INVESTMENTS

Ann Browning is a private investor. Through the years, she has devised some guidelines for evaluating investments. Here are some of her guidelines.

Question	Financial Statement	What to Look For
Where is most of the company's cash coming from?	Statement of cash flows	Operating activities ⟶ Good sign Investing activities ⟶ Bad sign Financing activities ⟶ Okay sign
Do high sales and profits translate into more cash?	Statement of cash flows	Usually, but cash flows from *operating* activities must be the main source of cash for long-term success.
If sales and profits are low, how is the company generating cash?	Statement of cash flows	If *investing* activities are generating the cash, the business may be in trouble because it is selling off its long-term assets. If *financing* activities are generating the cash, that cannot go on forever. Sooner or later, investors will demand cash flow from operating activities.
Is the cash balance large enough to provide for expansion?	Balance sheet	The cash balance should be growing over time. If not, the company may be in trouble.
Can the business pay its debts?	Income statement	Increasing trend of net income.
	Statement of cash flows	Cash flows from operating activities should be the main source of cash.
	Balance sheet	Current ratio, debt ratio.

Summary Problem

Assume that Berkshire Hathaway is considering buying Granite Shoals Corporation. Granite Shoals reported the following comparative balance sheet and income statement for 2009.

GRANITE SHOALS CORPORATION
Balance Sheet
December 31, 2009 and 2008

	2009	2008	Increase (Decrease)
Cash	$ 19,000	$ 3,000	$16,000
Accounts receivable	22,000	23,000	(1,000)
Inventory	34,000	31,000	3,000
Prepaid expenses	1,000	3,000	(2,000)
Equipment (net)	90,000	79,000	11,000
Intangible assets	9,000	9,000	—
	$175,000	$148,000	$27,000
Accounts payable	$ 14,000	$ 9,000	$ 5,000
Accrued liabilities	16,000	19,000	(3,000)
Income tax payable	14,000	12,000	2,000
Long-term note payable	45,000	50,000	(5,000)
Common stock	31,000	20,000	11,000
Retained earnings	64,000	40,000	24,000
Treasury stock	(9,000)	(2,000)	(7,000)
	$175,000	$148,000	$27,000

GRANITE SHOALS CORPORATION
Income Statement
Year Ended December 31, 2009

Sales revenue	$190,000
Gain on sale of equipment	6,000
Total revenue and gains	196,000
Cost of goods sold	$ 85,000
Depreciation expense	19,000
Other operating expenses	36,000
Total expenses	140,000
Income before income tax	56,000
Income tax expense	18,000
Net income	$ 38,000

Requirements
1. Compute the following cash-flow amounts for 2009.
   a. Collections from customers
   b. Payments for inventory
   c. Payments for other operating expenses
   d. Payment of income tax

e. Acquisition of equipment. Granite Shoals sold equipment that had book value of $15,000.
f. Cash receipt from sale of plant assets
g. Issuance of long-term note payable. Granite Shoals paid off $10,000 of long-term notes payable.
h. Issuance of common stock
i. Payment of dividends
j. Purchase of treasury stock

2. Prepare Granite Shoals Corporation's statement of cash flows (*direct* method) for the year ended December 31, 2009. There were no noncash investing and financing activities. Follow the statement format in Exhibit 14A-3, page 738.

Solution

1. Cash-flow amounts:

   a. Collections from customers = Sales revenue + Decrease in accounts receivables

   $191,000 = $190,000 + $1,000

   b. Payments for inventory = Cost of goods sold + Increase in inventory − Increase in accounts payable

   $83,000 = $85,000 + $3,000 − $5,000

   c. Payments for other operating expenses = Other Operating expenses − Decrease in prepaid expenses + Decrease in accrued liabilities

   $37,000 = $36,000 − $2,000 + $3,000

   d. Payment of income tax = Income tax expense − Increase in income tax payable

   $16,000 = $18,000 − $2,000

   e. Equipment, Net (let X = Acquisitions)

   Beginning + Acquisitions − Depreciation expense − Book value sold = Ending

   $79,000 + X − $19,000 − $15,000 = $90,000

   X = $45,000

   f. Sale of plant assets

   Cash received = Book value of assets sold + Gain on sale

   $21,000 = $15,000 + $6,000

   g. Long-Term Note Payable (let X = Issuance)

   Beginning + Issuance − Payment = Ending

   $50,000 + X − $10,000 = $45,000

   X = $5,000

   h. Common Stock (let X = Issuance)

   Beginning + Issuance = Ending

   $20,000 + X = $31,000

   X = $11,000

i. Retained Earnings (let X = Dividends)

Beginning	+	Net income	−	Dividends	=	Ending
$40,000	+	$38,000	−	X	=	$64,000
				X	=	$14,000

j. Treasury Stock (let X = Purchases)

Beginning	+	Purchases	=	Ending
$2000	+	X	=	$9,000
		X	=	$7,000

2.

GRANITE SHOALS CORPORATION
Statement of Cash Flows
Year Ended December 31, 2009

Cash flows from operating activities:		
Receipts:		
Collections from customers	$191,000	
Payments:		
To suppliers ($83,000 + $37,000)	(120,000)	
For income tax	(16,000)	
Net cash provided by operating activities		$55,000
Cash flows from investing activities:		
Acquisition of plant assets	$ (45,000)	
Sale of plant assets ($15,000 + $6,000)	21,000	
Net cash used for investing activities		(24,000)
Cash flows from financing activities:		
Payment of dividends	$ (14,000)	
Issuance of common stock	11,000	
Payment of note payable	(10,000)	
Purchase of treasury stock	(7,000)	
Issuance of note payable	5,000	
Net cash used for financing activities		(15,000)
Net increase in cash		$16,000
Cash balance, December 31, 2008		3,000
Cash balance, December 31, 2009		$19,000

Assignment materials for the *direct* method include:

- Short Exercises 14-11 through 14-14 on pages 714 and 715.
- Exercises 14-25 through 14-31 on pages 719–722.
- Problems 14-37A through 14-40A on pages 726 and 727.
- Problems 14-46B through 14-49B on pages 731 and 732.

Appendix 14B

Preparing the Statement of Cash Flows Using a Spreadsheet

The body of this chapter discusses the uses of the statement of cash flows in decision making and shows how to prepare the statement using T-accounts. The T-account approach works well as a learning device. In practice, however, most companies face complex situations. In these cases, a spreadsheet can help in preparing the statement of cash flows.

The spreadsheet starts with the beginning balance sheet and concludes with the ending balance sheet. Two middle columns—one for debit amounts and the other for credit amounts—complete the spreadsheet. These columns, labeled Transaction Analysis, hold the data for the statement of cash flows. Accountants can prepare the statement directly from the lower part of the spreadsheet. This appendix is based on the Anchor Corporation data used in the chapter. We begin with the indirect method for operating activities.

Preparing the Spreadsheet—Indirect Method for Operating Activities

The *indirect* method reconciles net income to net cash provided by operating activities. Exhibit 14B-1 is the spreadsheet for preparing the statement of cash flows by the *indirect* method. Panel A shows the transaction analysis, and Panel B gives the statement of cash flows.

Transaction Analysis on the Spreadsheet—Indirect Method

Net income, transaction (a), is the first operating cash inflow. Net income is entered on the spreadsheet (Panel B) as a debit to Net Income under Cash flows from operating activities and as a credit to Retained Earnings. Next come the adjustments to net income, starting with depreciation—transaction (b)—which is debited to Depreciation and credited to Plant Assets, Net. Transaction (c) is the sale of plant assets. The $10,000 gain on the sale is entered as a credit to Gain on Sale of Plant Assets—a subtraction from net income—under operating cash flows. This credit removes the $10,000 gain from operations because the cash proceeds from the sale were $50,000, not $10,000. The $50,000 sale amount is then entered on the spreadsheet under investing activities. Entry (c) is completed by crediting the plant assets' book value of $40,000 to the Plant Assets, Net account.

Entries (d) through (g) reconcile net income to cash flows from operations for increases and decreases in the other current assets and for increases and decreases in the current liabilities. Entry (d) debits Accounts Receivable for its $17,000 increase during the year. This amount is credited to Increase in Accounts Receivable under operating cash flows. Entries (e), (f), and (g) adjust for the other current accounts.

EXHIBIT 14B-1 — Spreadsheet for Statement of Cash Flows—Indirect Method

ANCHOR CORPORATION
Spreadsheet for Statement of Cash Flows (Indirect Method)
Year Ended December 31, 2008

(In thousands)	Balances Dec. 31, 2007	Transaction Analysis Debit		Transaction Analysis Credit		Balances Dec. 31, 2008
PANEL A—Balance-Sheet Accounts						
Cash	42			(m)	20	22
Accounts receivable	73	(d)	17			90
Inventory	145			(e)	2	143
Plant assets, net	210	(h)	310	(b)	20	
				(c)	40	460
Totals	470					715
				(f)		
Accounts payable	50	(g)			40	90
Accrued liabilities	10	(k)	5	(j)		5
Long-term notes payable	80		10	(i)	90	160
Common stock	250	(l)		(a)	100	350
Retained earnings	80		10		40	110
Totals	470		352		352	715
PANEL B—Statement of Cash Flows						
Cash flows from operating activities:						
Net income		(a)	40			
Add (subtract) adjustments:						
Depreciation		(b)	20			
Gain on sale of plant assets				(c)	10	
Increase in accounts receivable				(d)	17	
Decrease in inventory		(e)	2			
Increase in accounts payable		(f)	40			
Decrease in accrued liabilities				(g)	5	
Cash flows from investing activities:						
Acquisition of plant assets				(h)	310	
Cash receipt from sale of plant assets		(c)	50			
Cash flows from financing activities:						
Cash receipts from issuance of common stock		(i)	100			
Cash receipts from issuance of note payable		(j)	90			
Payment of note payable				(k)	10	
Payment of dividends				(l)	10	
			342		362	
Net decrease in cash		(m)	20			
Totals			362		362	

Entries (h) through (l) account for the investing and financing transactions. Entry (h) debits Plant Assets, Net for their purchase and credits Acquisition of plant assets under investing cash flows. Entry (i) debits Cash receipts from issuance of common stock under financing cash flows. The offsetting debit is to Common Stock.

The final item in Exhibit 14B-1 is the Net decrease in cash—transaction (m) on the spreadsheet—a credit to Cash and a debit to Net decrease in cash. To prepare the statement of cash flows, the accountant can rewrite Panel B of the spreadsheet, adding subtotals for the three categories of activities.

Noncash Investing and Financing Activities on the Spreadsheet

Noncash investing and financing activities can be analyzed on the spreadsheet. These transactions include both an investing activity and a financing activity, so they require two spreadsheet entries. Suppose Anchor Corporation purchased a building by issuing common stock of $300,000. Exhibit 14B-2 illustrates the analysis of this transaction. Cash is unaffected. Spreadsheet entry (a) records the purchase of the building, and entry (b) records the issuance of the stock. All amounts are assumed for this illustration.

EXHIBIT 14B-2 Noncash Investing and Financing Activities on the SpreadSheet

ANCHOR CORPORATION
Spreadsheet for Statement of Cash Flows
Year Ended December 31, 2008

	Balances Dec. 31, 2007	Transaction Analysis Debit	Transaction Analysis Credit	Balances Dec. 31, 2008
PANEL A—Balance-Sheet Accounts				
Cash				
Building	600,000	(a)300,000		900,000
Common stock	400,000		(b)300,000	700,000
PANEL B—Statement of Cash Flows				
Noncash investing and financing transactions:				
Purchase of building by issuing common stock		(b)300,000	(a)300,000	

Preparing the Spreadsheet—Direct Method for Operating Activities

The *direct* method separates operating activities into cash receipts and cash payments. Exhibit 14B-3 is the spreadsheet for the preparation of the statement of cash flows by the *direct* method.

EXHIBIT 14B-3 Spreadsheet for Statement of Cash Flows—Direct Method

ANCHOR CORPORATION
Work Sheet for Statement of Cash Flows (Direct Method)
Year Ended December 31, 2008

(In thousands)	Balances Dec. 31, 2007	Transaction Analysis Debit		Transaction Analysis Credit		Balances Dec. 31, 2008
PANEL A—Balance-Sheet Accounts						
Cash	42				20	22
Accounts receivable	73		286	(t)	269	90
Inventory	145	(a)	154	(b)	156	143
Equipment, net	210	(e)	310	(f)	20	
		(n)		(i)	40	460
Totals	470			(o)		715
Accounts payable	50		114		154	90
Accrued liabilities	10	(g)	21	(e)	16	5
Long-term notes payable	80	(m)	10	(j)	90	160
Common stock	250	(r)		(q)	100	350
Retained earnings	80		156	(p)	286	110
		(f)	56	(a)	12	
		(h)	20	(c)	9	
		(i)	16	(d)	10	
		(j)	15	(o)		
		(k)	14			
		(l)	10			
Totals	470	(s)	1,182		1,182	715
PANEL B—Statement of Cash Flows						
Cash flows from operating activities:						
Receipts:						
Collections from customers			269			
Interest received		(b)	12			
Dividends received		(c)	9			
Payments:		(d)				
To suppliers					114	
				(g)	21	
To employees				(m)	56	
For interest				(h)	15	
For income tax				(k)	14	
Cash flows from investing activities:				(l)		
Acquisition of plant assets					310	
Cash receipt from sale of plant assets			50	(n)		
Cash flows from financing activities:		(o)				
Cash receipt from issuance of common stock			100			
Cash receipt from issuance of note payable		(p)	90			
Payment of note payable		(q)			10	
Payment of dividends				(r)	10	
			530	(s)	550	
Net decrease in cash			20			
Totals		(t)	550		550	

Transaction Analysis on the Spreadsheet—Direct Method

For your convenience, we repeat the Anchor Corporation transaction data here.

Operating Activities:
- a. Sales on account, $286,000
- *b. Collections from customers, $269,000
- *c. Cash receipt of interest revenue, $12,000
- *d. Cash receipt of dividend revenue, $9,000
- e. Purchase of inventory on account, $154,000
- f. Cost of goods sold, $156,000
- *g. Payments for inventory on account, $114,000
- *h. Salary expense and payments, $56,000
- i. Depreciation expense, $20,000
- j. Accrual of other operating expense, $16,000
- *k. Interest expense and payments, $15,000
- *l. Income tax expense and payments, $14,000
- *m. Payment of accrued liabilities, $21,000

Investing Activities:
- *n. Cash payments to acquire plant assets, $310,000
- *o. Cash receipt from sale of plant assets, $50,000, including $10,000 gain

Financing Activities:
- *p. Cash receipt from issuance of common stock, $100,000
- *q. Cash receipt from issuance of note payable, $90,000
- *r. Payment of note payable, $10,000
- *s. Declaration and payment of cash dividends, $10,000

*Indicates a cash flow to be reported on the statement of cash flows.

The transaction analysis on the spreadsheet includes all the journal entries. Only balance-sheet accounts are used on the spreadsheet. Therefore, revenues are entered as credits to Retained Earnings, and expenses are entered as debits to Retained Earnings. For example, in transaction (a), sales on account are debited to Accounts Receivable and credited to Retained Earnings. Cash is neither debited nor credited because sales on account do not affect cash. But all transactions should be entered on the spreadsheet to identify all the cash effects of the period's transactions. In transaction (c), the collection of cash for interest revenue is entered by debiting Cash and crediting Retained Earnings.

Entries (n) through (s) account for the investing and financing transactions. Entry (n) debits Equipment, Net for their purchase and credits Acquisition of plant assets under investing cash flows. Entry (p) debits cash receipt from issuance of common stock under financing cash flows. The offsetting credit is to Common stock.

The final item in Exhibit 14B-3 is the Net decrease in cash—transaction (t) on the spreadsheet—a credit to cash and a debit to Net decrease in cash. To prepare the statement of cash flows, you can rewrite Panel B of the spreadsheet, adding subtotals for the three categories of activities.

Appendix 14B Assignments

Problems

Preparing the spreadsheet for the statement of cash flows—indirect method

P14B-1 The 2008 comparative balance sheet and income statement of Alden Group, Inc., follow. Alden had no noncash investing and financing transactions during 2008.

ALDEN GROUP, INC.
Comparative Balance Sheet

	December 31, 2008	December 31, 2007	Increase (Decrease)
Current assets:			
Cash and cash equivalents	$ 13,700	$15,600	$ (1,900)
Accounts receivable	41,500	43,100	(1,600)
Inventories	96,600	93,000	3,600
Plant assets:			
Land	35,100	10,000	25,100
Equipment, net	100,900	93,700	7,200
Total assets	$287,800	$255,400	$32,400
Current liabilities:			
Accounts payable	$ 24,800	$ 26,000	$ (1,200)
Accrued liabilities	24,400	22,500	1,900
Long-term liabilities:			
Notes payable	55,000	65,000	(10,000)
Stockholders' equity:			
Common stock	131,100	122,300	8,800
Retained earnings	52,500	19,600	32,900
Total liabilities and stockholders' equity	$287,800	$255,400	$32,400

ALDEN GROUP, INC.
Income Statement
Year Ended December 31, 2008

Revenues:		
Sales revenue		$438,000
Interest revenue		11,700
Total revenues		449,700
Expenses:		
Cost of goods sold	$205,200	
Salary expense	76,400	
Depreciation expense	15,300	
Other operating expense	49,700	
Interest expense	24,600	
Income tax expense	16,900	
Total expenses		388,100
Net income		$ 61,600

Requirement

Prepare the spreadsheet for the 2008 statement of cash flows. Format cash flows from operating activities by the *indirect* method.

Preparing the spreadsheet for the statement of cash flows—direct method

P14B-2 Using the Alden Group, Inc., data from Problem 14B-1, prepare the spreadsheet for Alden's 2008 statement of cash flows. Format cash flows from operating activities by the *direct* method.

15 Financial Statement Analysis

Learning Objectives

1. Perform a horizontal analysis of financial statements
2. Perform a vertical analysis of financial statements
3. Prepare and use common-size financial statements
4. Compute the standard financial ratios

Google was born in 1998. If it were a person, it would have started elementary school in 2004, and today it would have just about finished the first grade.

If Google were a person, it would graduate from high school in 2016. Given a typical life span, it would expect to be around for almost a century [. . .] In the words of its top two executives, "We're just getting started."

Source: Adapted from Google Inc. 2004 Annual Report, Founder's Letter.

You probably use Google's Internet search engine daily, as many others do. The company is an amazing success story. In fact, on November 17, 2005, Google's stock price topped $400—one of only four companies listed on a major U.S. stock exchange with a stock price that high.

To show you how to analyze financial statements, we'll be using Google Inc. in the first half of this chapter. Then in the second part of the chapter we'll shift over to a different type of company—Palisades Furniture—to round out your introduction to financial statement analysis.

To get started, take a look at Google's comparative income statement, which follows.

GOOGLE INC.
Income Statement (Adapted)
Year Ended December 31,

(In millions)	2004	2003
Revenues (same as Net sales)	$3,189	$1,466
Expenses:		
Cost of revenues (same as Cost of goods sold)	1,458	626
Sales and marketing expense	246	120
General and administrative expense	140	57
Research and development expense	225	91
Other expense	470	225
Income before income tax	650	347
Income tax expense	251	241
Net income	$ 399	$ 106

You can see that 2004 was an incredible year for the company. Net income was over three times the net income of 2003, and Wall Street was very happy.

Investors and creditors can't evaluate a company by examining only one year's data. This is why most financial statements cover at least two periods, like the Google Inc. income statement. In fact, most financial analysis covers trends of three to five years. This chapter shows you how to use some of the analytical tools for charting a company's progress through time.

The graphs in Exhibit 15-1 show some important data about Google's progress. They depict a three-year trend of revenues and research and development (R&D). Revenues (sales) and R&D are important drivers of profits.

EXHIBIT 15-1 Financial Data of Google Inc. (Adapted)

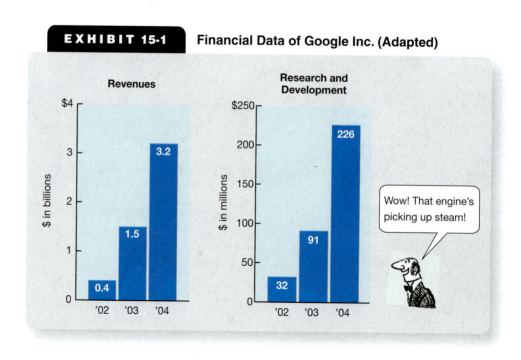

For Google, both revenues and research and development grew dramatically during 2002–2004. These are good signs for the future. But how can we decide what we really think about Google's performance? We need some way to compare a company's performance

- From year to year
- With a competing company, like Yahoo! Inc.
- With the Internet-information industry

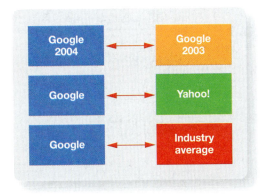

Then we will have a better idea of how to judge Google's present situation and predict what might happen in the near future.

Methods of Analysis

There are two main ways to analyze financial statements.

- Horizontal analysis provides a year-to-year comparison of a company's performance in different periods.
- Another technique, vertical analysis, is the standard way to compare different companies. Let's begin with horizontal analysis.

Horizontal Analysis

 Perform a horizontal analysis of financial statements

Many decisions hinge on whether the numbers—in sales, expenses, and net income—are increasing or decreasing. Have sales and other revenues risen from last year? By how much? Sales may have increased by $20,000, but considered alone, this fact is not very helpful. The *percentage change* in sales over time is more helpful. It is better to know that sales increased by 20% than to know that sales increased by $20,000.

The study of percentage changes in comparative statements is called **horizontal analysis**. Computing a percentage change in comparative statements requires two steps:

1. Compute the dollar amount of the change from the earlier period to the later period.

2. Divide the dollar amount of change by the earlier period amount. We call the earlier period the base period.

Illustration: Google Inc.

Google reports *revenues,* not sales, because Google sells services rather than a product. You can think of revenues and net sales as the same thing. Horizontal analysis is illustrated for Google Inc. as follows (dollar amounts in millions):

	2004	2003	Increase (Decrease) Amount	Percentage
Revenues (same as net sales)..........	$3,189	$1,466	$1,723	117.5%

Sales increased by an incredible 117.5% during 2004, computed as follows:

Step 1 Compute the dollar amount of change in sales from 2003 to 2004:

$$2004 \quad 2003 \quad \text{Increase}$$
$$\$3,189 - \$1,466 = \$1,723$$

Step 2 Divide the dollar amount of change by the base-period amount. This computes the percentage change for the period:

$$\text{Percentage change} = \frac{\text{Dollar amount of change}}{\text{Base-year amount}}$$
$$= \frac{\$1,723}{\$1,466} = 1.175 = 117.5\%$$

Detailed horizontal analyses of Google's financial statements are shown in:

- Exhibit 15-2 Income Statement
- Exhibit 15-3 Balance Sheet

EXHIBIT 15-2 Comparative Income Statement—Horizontal Analysis

GOOGLE INC.
Income Statement (Adapted)
Year Ended December 31, 2004 and 2003

(Dollar amounts in millions)	2004	2003	Increase (Decrease) Amount	Percentage
Revenues	$3,189	$1,466	$1,723	117.5%
Cost of revenues	1,458	626	832	132.9
Gross profit	1,731	840	891	106.1
Operating expenses:				
Sales and marketing expense	246	120	126	105.0
General and administrative expense	140	57	83	145.6
Research and development expense	225	91	134	147.3
Other expense	470	225	245	108.9
Income before income tax	650	347	303	87.3
Income tax expense	251	241	10	4.1
Net income	$ 399	$ 106	$ 293	276.4

EXHIBIT 15-3   Comparative Balance Sheet—Horizontal Analysis

GOOGLE INC.
Balance Sheet (Adapted)
December 31, 2004 and 2003

(Dollar amounts in millions)	2004	2003	Increase (Decrease) Amount	Percentage
Assets				
Current Assets:				
Cash and cash equivalents	$ 427	$149	$ 278	186.6%
Other current assets	2,266	411	1,855	451.3
Total current assets	2,693	560	2,133	380.9
Property, plant and equipment, net	379	188	191	101.6
Intangible assets, net	194	106	88	83.0
Other assets	47	17	30	176.5
Total assets	$3,313	$871	$2,442	280.4
Liabilities				
Current Liabilities:				
Accounts payable	$ 33	$ 46	$ (13)	(28.3)%
Other current liabilities	307	189	118	62.4
Total current liabilities	340	235	105	44.7
Long-term liabilities	44	47	(3)	(6.4)
Total liabilities	384	282	102	36.2
Stockholders' Equity				
Capital stock	1	45	(44)	(97.8)
Retained earnings and other equity	2,928	544	2,384	438.2
Total stockholders' equity	2,929	589	2,340	397.3
Total liabilities and equity	$3,313	$871	$2,442	280.4

Horizontal Analysis of the Income Statement

Google's comparative income statement reveals exceptional growth during 2004. An increase of 100% occurs when an item doubles, so Google's 117.5% increase in revenues means that revenues more than doubled.

The item on Google's income statement with the slowest growth rate is income tax expense. Income taxes increased by 4.1%. On the bottom line, net income grew by an astounding 276.4%. That's real progress!

Horizontal Analysis of the Balance Sheet

Google's comparative balance sheet also shows rapid growth in assets, with total assets increasing by 280.4%. That means total assets almost tripled in one year. Very few companies grow that fast.

Google's liabilities grew more slowly. Total liabilities increased by 36.2%, and Accounts Payable actually decreased, as indicated by the liability figures in parentheses. Here's how to compute the percentage decrease in Google's Accounts Payable:

STEP 1   Increase
(Decrease)   2004   2003
$(13)   = $33   − $46

STEP 2   Percentage Change = Dollar amount of change / Base-year amount

(28.3)% = $(13) / $46

Trend Percentages

Trend percentages are a form of horizontal analysis. Trends indicate the direction a business is taking. How have sales changed over a five-year period? What trend does net income show? These questions can be answered by trend percentages over a period, such as three to five years.

Trend percentages are computed by selecting a base year. The base-year amounts are set equal to 100%. The amounts for each following year are expressed as a percentage of the base amount. To compute trend percentages, divide each item for following years by the base-year amount.

Trend % = Any year $ / Base year $

Google Inc.'s total revenues were $19 million in 2000 and rose to $3,189 million in 2004. The company's trend of revenues is so dramatic that percentages in the thousands are hard to interpret.

To illustrate trend analysis, we use a more representative company, Caterpillar Inc., which is famous for its CAT earthmoving machinery. Caterpillar's trend of net sales during 2000–2004 follows, with dollars in millions. The base year is 2000, so that year's percentage is set equal to 100.

(in millions)	2004	2003	2002	2001	2000
Net sales..................	$30,251	$22,763	$20,152	$20,450	$20,175
Trend percentages......	150%	113%	99.9%	101%	100%

We want trend percentages for the five-year period 2000 through 2004. Trend percentages are computed by dividing each year's amount by the 2000 amount.

Net sales increased a little in 2001 and took a dip in 2002. The rate of growth increased in 2003 and took off in 2004.

You can perform a trend analysis on any item you consider important. Trend analysis is widely used to predict the future.

Vertical Analysis

 Perform a vertical analysis of financial statements

As we have seen, horizontal analysis and trend percentages highlight changes in an item over time. But no single technique gives a complete picture of a business, so we also need vertical analysis.

Vertical analysis of a financial statement shows the relationship of each item to its base amount, which is the 100% figure. Every other item on the statement is then reported as a percentage of that base. For an income statement, net sales is the base. Suppose under normal conditions a company's gross profit is 50% of revenues. A drop to 40% may cause the company to suffer a loss. Investors view a large decline in gross profit with alarm.

Illustration: Google Inc.

Exhibit 15-4 shows the vertical analysis of Google's income statement. In this case,

$$\text{Vertical analysis \%} = \frac{\text{Each income-statement item}}{\text{Revenues (net sales)}}$$

EXHIBIT 15-4 Comparative Income Statement—Vertical Analysis

GOOGLE INC.
Income Statement (Adapted)
Year Ended December 31, 2004

(Dollar amounts in millions)	Amount	Percent of Total
Revenues	$3,189	100.0%
Cost of revenues	1,458	45.7
Gross profit	1,731	54.3
Operating expenses:		
Sales and marketing expense	246	7.7
General and administrative expense	140	4.4
Research and development expense	225	7.1
Other expense	470	14.7
Income before income tax	650	20.4
Income tax expense	251	7.9
Net income	$ 399	12.5%

For Google, the vertical-analysis percentage for cost of revenues is 45.7% ($1,458/$3,189 = 0.457). On the bottom line, Google's net income is 12.5% of revenues. That is very good.

Exhibit 15-5 shows the vertical analysis of Google's balance sheet. The base amount (100%) is total assets.

The vertical analysis of Google's balance sheet reveals several interesting things.

- Current assets make up 81.3% of total assets. For most companies this percentage is closer to 30%.
- Property, plant, and equipment make up only 11.4% of total assets. This percentage is low because of the nature of Google's business. Google's Web-based operations don't require lots of buildings and equipment.
- Total liabilities are only 11.6% of total assets, and stockholders' equity makes up 88.4% of total assets. Most of Google's equity is additional paid-in capital and retained earnings—signs of a strong company.

How Do We Compare One Company with Another?

3 Prepare and use common-size financial statements

Horizontal analysis and vertical analysis provide lots of useful data about a company. As we have seen, Google's percentages depict a very successful company. But the Google data apply only to one business.

To compare Google Inc. to another company we can use a common-size statement. A **common-size statement** reports only percentages—the same percentages

EXHIBIT 15-5 Comparative Balance Sheet—Vertical Analysis

GOOGLE INC.
Balance Sheet (Adapted)
December 31, 2004

(Dollar amount in millions)	Amount	Percent of Total
Assets		
Current Assets:		
Cash and cash equivalents	$ 427	12.9%
Other current assets	2,266	68.4
Total current assets	2,693	81.3
Property, plant, and equipment, net	379	11.4
Intangible assets, net	194	5.9
Other assets	47	1.4
Total assets	$3,313	100.0%
Liabilities		
Current Liabilities:		
Accounts payable	$ 33	1.0%
Other current liabilities	307	9.3
Total current liabilities	340	10.3
Long-term liabilities	44	1.3
Total liabilities	384	11.6
Stockholders' Equity		
Common stock	1	0.0
Retained earnings and other equity	2,928	88.4
Total stockholders' equity	2,929	88.4
Total liabilities and equity	$3,313	100.0%

that appear in a vertical analysis. For example, Google's common-size income statement comes directly from the percentages in Exhibit 15-4.

We can use a common-size income statement to compare Google Inc. and Yahoo! Inc. on profitability. Google and Yahoo! compete in the Internet service industry. Which company earns a higher percentage of revenues as profits for its shareholders? Exhibit 15-6 gives both companies' common-size income statements for 2004.

Exhibit 15-6 shows that Yahoo! Inc. is more profitable than Google. Yahoo!'s gross profit percentage is 63.7%, compared to Google's 54.3%. And, most importantly, Yahoo!'s percentage of net income to revenues is 23.5%. That means almost one-fourth of Yahoo!'s revenues ends up as profits for the company's stockholders.

Benchmarking

Benchmarking is the practice of comparing a company with other leading companies. There are two main types of benchmarks in financial statement analysis.

EXHIBIT 15-6 — Common-Size Income Statement Google versus Yahoo!

GOOGLE INC.
Common-Size Income Statement
Google Versus YAHOO!

	Google Inc.	Yahoo! Inc.
Revenues	100.0%	100.0%
Cost of revenues	45.7	36.3
Gross profit	54.3	63.7
Sales and marketing expense	7.7	21.8
General and administrative expense	4.4	7.3
Research and development expense	7.1	10.3
Other expense (income)	14.7	(11.5)
Income before income tax	20.4	35.8
Income tax expense	7.9	12.3
Net income	12.5%	23.5%

Benchmarking Against a Key Competitor

Exhibit 15-6 uses a key competitor, Yahoo! Inc., to measure Google's profitability. The two companies compete in the same industry, so Yahoo! serves as an ideal benchmark for Google. The graphs in Exhibit 15-7 highlight the profitability difference between Google and Yahoo!. Focus on the segment of the graphs showing net income. Yahoo! is clearly more profitable than Google.

EXHIBIT 15-7 — Graphical Analysis of Common-Size Income Statement Google Versus Yahoo!

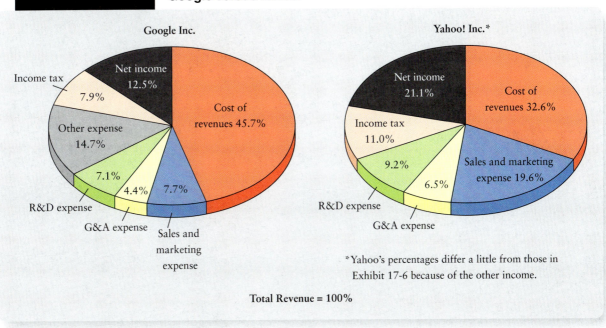

*Yahoo's percentages differ a little from those in Exhibit 17-6 because of the other income.

Total Revenue = 100%

Benchmarking Against the Industry Average

The industry average can also serve as a useful benchmark for evaluating a company. An industry comparison would show how Google is performing alongside the average for its industry. *Annual Statement Studies,* published by The Risk Management Association, provides common-size statements for most industries. To compare Google Inc. to the industry average, simply insert the industry-average common-size income statement in place of Yahoo! Inc. as shown in Exhibit 15-6.

Now let's put your learning to practice. Work the summary problem, which reviews the concepts from the first half of this chapter.

Summary Problem 1

Perform a horizontal analysis and a vertical analysis of the comparative income statement of Kimball Corporation, which makes iPod labels. State whether 2008 was a good year or a bad year, and give your reasons.

KIMBALL CORPORATION
Comparative Income Statement
Years Ended December 31, 2008 and 2007

	2008	2007
Net sales	$275,000	$225,000
Expenses:		
Cost of goods sold	$194,000	$165,000
Engineering, selling, and administrative expenses	54,000	48,000
Interest expense	5,000	5,000
Income tax expense	9,000	3,000
Other expense (income)	1,000	(1,000)
Total expenses	263,000	220,000
Net income	$ 12,000	$ 5,000

Solution

KIMBALL CORPORATION
Horizontal Analysis of Comparative Income Statement
Years Ended December 31, 2008 and 2007

			Increase (Decrease)	
	2008	2007	Amount	Percent
Net sales	$275,000	$225,000	$50,000	22.2%
Expenses:				
Cost of goods sold	$194,000	$165,000	$29,000	17.6
Engineering, selling, and administrative expenses	54,000	48,000	6,000	12.5
Interest expense	5,000	5,000	—	—
Income tax expense	9,000	3,000	6,000	200.0
Other expense (income)	1,000	(1,000)	2,000	—*
Total expenses	263,000	220,000	43,000	19.5
Net income	$ 12,000	$ 5,000	$ 7,000	140.0%

*Percentage changes are typically not computed for shifts from a negative to a positive amount, and vice versa.

The horizontal analysis shows that total revenues increased 22.2%. Total expenses increased by 19.5%, and net income rose by 140%.

KIMBALL CORPORATION
Vertical Analysis of Comparative Income Statement
Years Ended December 31, 2008 and 2007

	2008 Amount	2008 Percent	2007 Amount	2007 Percent
Net sales	$275,000	100.0%	$225,000	100.0%
Expenses:				
Cost of goods sold	$194,000	70.5	$165,000	73.3
Engineering, selling, and administrative expenses	54,000	19.6	48,000	21.3
Interest expense	5,000	1.8	5,000	2.2
Income tax expense	9,000	3.3	3,000	1.4**
Other expense (income)	1,000	0.4	(1,000)	(0.4)
Total expenses	263,000	95.6	220,000	97.8
Net income	$ 12,000	4.4%	$ 5,000	2.2%

**Number rounded up.

The vertical analysis shows decreases in the percentages of net sales consumed by:

- cost of goods sold (from 73.3% to 70.5%)
- engineering, selling, and administrative expenses (from 21.3% to 19.6%).

These two items are Kimball's largest dollar expenses, so their percentage decreases are important.

2008 net income rose to 4.4% of sales, compared with 2.2% the preceding year. The analysis shows that 2008 was significantly better than 2007.

Using Ratios to Make Decisions

Online financial databases, such as Lexis/Nexis and the Dow Jones News Retrieval Service, provide data on thousands of companies. Suppose you want to compare some companies' recent earnings histories. You might have the computer compare companies' returns on stockholders' equity. The computer could then give you the names of the 20 companies with the highest return on equity. You can use any ratio that is relevant to a particular decision.

The ratios we discuss in this chapter may be classified as follows:

1. Measuring ability to pay current liabilities
2. Measuring ability to sell inventory and collect receivables
3. Measuring ability to pay long-term debt
4. Measuring profitability
5. Analyzing stock as an investment

Measuring Ability to Pay Current Liabilities

Compute the standard financial ratios

Working capital is defined as:

$$\text{Working capital} = \text{Current assets} - \text{Current liabilities}$$

Working capital measures the ability to meet short-term obligations with current assets. Two decision tools based on working-capital data are the *current ratio* and the *acid-test ratio*.

Current Ratio

The most widely used ratio is the **current ratio,** which is current assets divided by current liabilities. The current ratio measures ability to pay current liabilities with current assets.

Exhibit 15-8 gives the comparative income statement and balance sheet of Palisades Furniture Co., which we'll be using in the remainder of this chapter.

The current ratios of Palisades Furniture at December 31, 2008 and 2007, follow, along with the average for the retail furniture industry:

		Palisades' Current Ratio		Industry
	Formula	2008	2007	Average
Current ratio =	$\dfrac{\text{Current assets}}{\text{Current liabilities}}$	$\dfrac{\$262{,}000}{\$142{,}000} = 1.85$	$\dfrac{\$236{,}000}{\$126{,}000} = 1.87$	1.50

A high current ratio indicates that the business has sufficient current assets to maintain normal business operations. Compare Palisades Furniture's current ratio of 1.85 with the industry average of 1.50 and with the current ratios of some well-known companies:

Company	Current Ratio
Walgreen Co	1.90
Amazon.com	1.57
FedEx	1.05

continued after exhibit on page 769 . . .

EXHIBIT 15-8 Comparative Financial Statements

PALISADES FURNITURE CO.
Comparative Income Statement
Years Ended December 31, 2008 and 2007

	2008	2007
Net sales	$858,000	$803,000
Cost of goods sold	513,000	509,000
Gross profit	345,000	294,000
Operating expenses:		
Selling expenses	126,000	114,000
General expenses	118,000	123,000
Total operating expenses	244,000	237,000
Income from operations	101,000	57,000
Interest revenue	4,000	—
Interest (expense)	(24,000)	(14,000)
Income before income taxes	81,000	43,000
Income tax expense	33,000	17,000
Net income	$ 48,000	$ 26,000

PALISADES FURNITURE CO.
Comparative Balance Sheet
December 31, 2008 and 2007

	2008	2007
Assets		
Current Assets:		
Cash	$ 29,000	$ 32,000
Accounts receivable, net	114,000	85,000
Inventories	113,000	111,000
Prepaid expenses	6,000	8,000
Total current assets	262,000	236,000
Long-term investments	18,000	9,000
Property, plant, and equipment, net	507,000	399,000
Total assets	$787,000	$644,000
Liabilities		
Current Liabilities:		
Notes payable	$ 42,000	$ 27,000
Accounts payable	73,000	68,000
Accrued liabilities	27,000	31,000
Total current liabilities	142,000	126,000
Long-term notes payable	289,000	198,000
Total liabilities	431,000	324,000
Stockholders' Equity		
Common stock, no par	186,000	186,000
Retained earnings	170,000	134,000
Total stockholders' equity	356,000	320,000
Total liabilities and equity	$787,000	$644,000

What is an acceptable current ratio? The answer depends on the industry. The norm for companies in most industries is around 1.50, as reported by The Risk Management Association. Palisades Furniture's current ratio of 1.85 is strong. In most industries, a current ratio of 2.0 is very strong.

Acid-Test Ratio

The **acid-test** (or **quick**) **ratio** tells us whether the entity could pay all its current liabilities if they came due immediately. That is, could the company pass this *acid test?*

To compute the acid-test ratio, we add cash, short-term investments, and net current receivables (accounts and notes receivable, net of allowances) and divide this sum by current liabilities. Inventory and prepaid expenses are *not* included in the acid test because they are the least-liquid current assets. Palisades Furniture's acid-test ratios for 2008 and 2007 follow.

	Formula	Palisades' Acid-Test Ratio 2008	Palisades' Acid-Test Ratio 2007	Industry Average
Acid-test ratio =	$\dfrac{\text{Cash + Short-term investments + Net current receivables}}{\text{Current liabilities}}$	$\dfrac{\$29{,}000 + \$0 + \$114{,}000}{\$142{,}000} = 1.01$	$\dfrac{\$32{,}000 + \$0 + \$85{,}000}{\$126{,}000} = 0.93$	0.40

The company's acid-test ratio improved during 2008 and is significantly better than the industry average. Palisades' 1.01 acid-test ratio also compares favorably with the acid-test values of some well-known companies.

Company	Acid-Test Ratio
Procter & Gamble....................	0.49
Wal-Mart Stores, Inc...............	0.15
General Motors, Inc................	0.91

The norm for the acid-test ratio ranges from 0.20 for shoe retailers to 1.00 for manufacturers of equipment, as reported by The Risk Management Association. An acid-test ratio of 0.90 to 1.00 is acceptable in most industries.

Measuring Ability to Sell Inventory and Collect Receivables

The ability to sell inventory and collect receivables is fundamental to business. In this section, we discuss three ratios that measure the company's ability to sell inventory and collect receivables.

Inventory Turnover

Inventory turnover measures the number of times a company sells its average level of inventory during a year. A high rate of turnover indicates ease in selling inventory; a low rate indicates difficulty. A value of 6 means that the company sold its average level of inventory six times—every two months—during the year.

To compute inventory turnover, we divide cost of goods sold by the average inventory for the period. We use the cost of goods sold—not sales—because both cost of goods sold and inventory are stated *at cost*. Sales at *retail* are not comparable with inventory at *cost*.

Palisades Furniture's inventory turnover for 2008 is:

Formula	Palisades' Inventory Turnover	Industry Average
Inventory turnover = $\dfrac{\text{Cost of goods sold}}{\text{Average inventory}}$	$\dfrac{\$513{,}000}{\$112{,}000} = 4.6$	3.4

Cost of goods sold comes from the income statement (Exhibit 15-8). Average inventory is figured by averaging the beginning inventory ($111,000) and ending inventory ($113,000). (See the balance sheet, Exhibit 15-8.)

Inventory turnover varies widely with the nature of the business. For example, Google has no inventory turnover because the company carries no inventory. Most manufacturers of farm machinery have an inventory turnover close to three times a year. In contrast, companies that remove natural gas from the ground hold their inventory for a very short period of time and have an average turnover of 30. Palisades Furniture's turnover of 4.6 times a year is high for its industry, which has an average turnover of 3.4 times per year.

Accounts Receivable Turnover

Accounts receivable turnover measures the ability to collect cash from credit customers. The higher the ratio, the faster the cash collections. But a receivable turnover that's too high may indicate that credit is too tight, causing the loss of sales to good customers.

To compute accounts receivable turnover, divide net credit sales by average net accounts receivable. Palisades Furniture's accounts receivable turnover ratio for 2008 is computed as follows:

Formula	Palisades' Accounts Receivable Turnover	Industry Average
Accounts receivable turnover = $\dfrac{\text{Net credit sales}}{\text{Average net accounts receivable}}$	$\dfrac{\$858{,}000}{\$99{,}500} = 8.6$	51.0

Average net accounts receivable is figured by adding the beginning accounts receivable balance ($85,000) and the ending balance ($114,000), then dividing by 2: [($85,000 + $114,000)/2 = $99,500].

Palisades' receivable turnover of 8.6 times per year is much slower than the industry average. Why the difference? Palisades is a hometown store that sells to local people who pay their accounts over time. Many furniture stores sell their receivables to other companies called *factors*. That keeps receivables low and receivable turnover high. Palisades Furniture follows a different strategy.

Days' Sales in Receivables

The **days'-sales-in-receivables** ratio also measures the ability to collect receivables. Days' sales in receivables tell us how many days' sales remain in Accounts Receivable. To compute the ratio, we can follow a logical two-step process:

First, divide net sales by 365 days to figure average sales for one day.

Second, divide this average day's sales amount into average net accounts receivable.

The data to compute this ratio for Palisades Furniture, Inc., for 2008 are taken from the income statement and the balance sheet (Exhibit 15-8):

Formula	Palisades' Days' Sales in Accounts Receivable	Industry Average
Days' Sales in *average* Accounts Receivable:		
1. One day's sales $= \dfrac{\text{Net sales}}{365 \text{ days}}$	$\dfrac{\$858,000}{365 \text{ days}} = \$2,351$	
2. Days' sales in average accounts receivable $= \dfrac{\text{Average net accounts receivable}}{\text{One day's sales}}$	$\dfrac{\$99,500}{\$2,351} = 42 \text{ days}$	7 days

Average accounts receivable of $99,500 = ($85,000 + $114,000)/2.

Palisades' ratio tells us that 42 average days' sales remain in accounts receivable and need to be collected. Palisades' days'-sales-in-receivables ratio is much higher (worse) than the industry average because Palisades collects its own receivables. Palisades Furniture remains competitive because of its personal relationship with customers. Without their good paying habits, the company's cash flow would suffer.

Measuring Ability to Pay Long-Term Debt

The ratios discussed so far yield insight into current assets and current liabilities. They help us measure ability to sell inventory, collect receivables, and pay current liabilities. Most businesses also have long-term debt. Two key indicators of a business's ability to pay long-term liabilities are the *debt ratio* and the *times-interest-earned ratio*.

Debt Ratio

A loan officer at Metro Bank is evaluating loan applications from two companies. Both companies have asked to borrow $500,000 and have agreed to repay the loan over a 5-year period. The first firm already owes $600,000 to another bank. The second owes only $100,000. Other things equal, you are more likely to lend money to Company 2 because that company owes less than Company 1.

This relationship between total liabilities and total assets—called the **debt ratio**—shows the proportion of assets financed with debt. If the debt ratio is 1, then all the assets are financed with debt. A debt ratio of 0.50 means that debt finances half the assets; the owners of the business have financed the other half. The higher the debt ratio, the higher the company's financial risk.

The debt ratios for Palisades Furniture at the ends of 2008 and 2007 follow.

Formula	Palisades' Debt Ratio 2008	Palisades' Debt Ratio 2007	Industry Average
Debt ratio $= \dfrac{\text{Total liabilities}}{\text{Total assets}}$	$\dfrac{\$431,000}{\$787,000} = 0.55$	$\dfrac{\$324,000}{\$644,000} = 0.50$	0.64

Palisades Furniture's debt ratio of 0.55 is not very high. The Risk Management Association reports that the average debt ratio for most companies ranges from 0.57 to 0.67, with relatively little variation from company to company. Palisades' debt ratio indicates a fairly low-risk position compared with the industry average debt ratio of 0.64.

Times-Interest-Earned Ratio

The debt ratio says nothing about ability to pay interest expense. Analysts use the **times-interest-earned-ratio** to relate income to interest expense. This ratio is also called the **interest-coverage ratio**. It measures the number of times operating income can cover interest expense. A high interest-coverage ratio indicates ease in paying interest expense; a low ratio suggests difficulty.

To compute this ratio, we divide income from operations (operating income) by interest expense. Calculation of Palisades' times-interest-earned ratio follows.

Formula	Palisades' Times-Interest-Earned Ratio 2008	2007	Industry Average
Times-interest-earned ratio = $\dfrac{\text{Income from operations}}{\text{Interest expense}}$	$\dfrac{\$101,000}{\$24,000} = 4.21$	$\dfrac{\$57,000}{\$14,000} = 4.07$	2.80

The company's times-interest-earned ratio of around 4.00 is significantly better than the average for furniture retailers. The norm for U.S. business, as reported by The Risk Management Association, falls in the range of 2.0 to 3.0. Based on its debt ratio and its times-interest-earned ratio, Palisades Furniture appears to have little difficulty *servicing its debt*, that is, paying liabilities.

Measuring Profitability

The fundamental goal of business is to earn a profit. Ratios that measure profitability are reported in the business press and discussed on *Money Line*. We examine four profitability measures.

Rate of Return on Net Sales

In business, the term *return* is used broadly as a measure of profitability. Consider a ratio called the **rate of return on net sales**, or simply **return on sales**. (The word *net* is usually omitted for convenience, even though net sales is used to compute the ratio.) This ratio shows the percentage of each sales dollar earned as net income. Palisades Furniture's rate of return on sales follows.

Formula	Palisades' Rate of Return on Sales 2008	2007	Industry Average
Rate of return on sales = $\dfrac{\text{Net income}}{\text{Net sales}}$	$\dfrac{\$48,000}{\$858,000} = 0.056$	$\dfrac{\$26,000}{\$803,000} = 0.032$	0.008

Companies strive for a high rate of return on sales. The higher the rate of return, the more sales dollars end up as profit. The increase in Palisades Furniture's return on sales is significant and identifies the company as more successful than the average furniture store. Compare Palisades' rate of return on sales to the rates of return for some leading companies in other industries:

Company	Rate of Return on Sales
Google Inc.	0.125
Texas Instruments	0.045
Walgreen	0.036

Rate of Return on Total Assets

The **rate of return on total assets**, or simply **return on assets**, measures success in using assets to earn a profit. Two groups finance a company's assets.

- Creditors have loaned money to the company, and they earn interest.
- Shareholders have invested in stock, and their return is net income.

The sum of interest expense and net income is thus the return to the two groups that have financed the company's assets. Computation of the return-on-assets ratio for Palisades Furniture follows.

Formula	Palisades' 2008 Rate of Return on Total Assets	Industry Average
Rate of return on assets = $\dfrac{\text{Net income} + \text{Interest expense}}{\text{Average total assets}}$	$\dfrac{\$48,000 + \$24,000}{\$715,500} = 0.101$	0.078

Average total assets is the average of beginning and ending total assets from the comparative balance sheet: ($644,000 + $787,000)/2 = $715,500. Compare Palisades Furniture's rate of return on assets with the rates of some other companies:

Company	Rate of Return on Assets
Amazon.com	0.256
FedEx	0.056
Procter & Gamble	0.136

Rate of Return on Common Stockholders' Equity

A popular measure of profitability is **rate of return on common stockholders' equity**, often shortened to **return on equity**. This ratio shows the relationship between net income and common stockholders' equity—how much income is earned for each $1 invested by the common shareholders.

To compute this ratio, we first subtract preferred dividends from net income to get net income available to the common stockholders. Then divide net income available to common stockholders by average common equity during the year. Common equity is total stockholders' equity minus preferred equity. The 2008 rate of return on common stockholders' equity for Palisades Furniture follows.

Formula	Palisades' 2008 Rate of Return on Common Stockholders' Equity	Industry Average
Rate of return on common stockholders' equity = $\dfrac{\text{Net income} - \text{Preferred dividends}}{\text{Average common stockholders' equity}}$	$\dfrac{\$48,000 - \$0}{\$338,000} = 0.142$	0.121

Average equity is the average of the beginning and ending balances [($356,000 + $320,000)/2 = $338,000].

Palisades' return on equity (0.142) is higher than its return on assets (0.101). This difference results from borrowing at one rate—say, 8%—and investing the money to earn a higher rate, such as the firm's 14.2% return on equity. This practice is called **trading on the equity**, or using **leverage**. It is directly related to the debt ratio. The higher the debt ratio, the higher the leverage. Companies that finance operations with debt are said to *leverage* their positions.

During good times, leverage increases profitability. But leverage can have a negative impact on profitability. Therefore, leverage is a double-edged sword, increasing profits during good times but compounding losses during bad times. Compare Palisades Furniture's return on equity with the rates of some leading companies.

Company	Rate of Return on Common Equity
Walgreen	0.176
Procter & Gamble	0.410
FedEx	0.109

Palisades Furniture is not as profitable as these leading companies. A return on equity of 15% to 20% year after year is considered good in most industries.

Earnings per Share of Common Stock

Earnings per share of common stock, or simply **earnings per share** (**EPS**), is perhaps the most widely quoted of all financial statistics. EPS is the only ratio that must appear on the face of the income statement. EPS is the amount of net income earned for each share of the company's outstanding *common* stock. Recall that:

$$\text{Outstanding stock} = \text{Issued stock} - \text{Treasury stock}$$

Earnings per share is computed by dividing net income available to common stockholders by the number of common shares outstanding during the year. Preferred dividends are subtracted from net income because the preferred stockholders have a prior claim to dividends. Palisades Furniture has no preferred stock outstanding and no preferred dividends.

The firm's EPS for 2008 and 2007 follow (Palisades had 10,000 shares of common stock outstanding throughout 2007 and 2008).

Formula	Palisades' Earnings per Share	
	2008	2007
Earnings per share of common stock = $\dfrac{\text{Net income} - \text{Preferred dividends}}{\text{Number of shares of common stock outstanding}}$	$\dfrac{\$48{,}000 - \$0}{10{,}000} = \$4.80$	$\dfrac{\$26{,}000 - \$0}{10{,}000} = \$2.60$

Palisades Furniture's EPS increased 85%. Its stockholders should not expect this big a boost in EPS every year. Most companies strive to increase EPS by 10% to 15% annually, and leading companies do so. But even the most successful companies have an occasional bad year.

Analyzing Stock Investments

Investors purchase stock to earn a return on their investment. This return consists of two parts: (1) gains (or losses) from selling the stock at a price above or below purchase price and (2) dividends. The ratios we examine in this section help analysts evaluate stock investments.

Price/Earnings Ratio

The **price/earnings ratio** is the ratio of the market price of a share of common stock to the company's earnings per share. It shows the market price of $1 of earnings. This ratio, abbreviated P/E, appears in *The Wall Street Journal* stock listings.

Calculations for the P/E ratios of Palisades Furniture Co. follow. The market price of its common stock was $60 at the end of 2008 and $35 at the end of 2007.

These prices can be obtained from a financial publication, a stockbroker, or the company's Web site.

	Palisades' Price/Earnings Ratio	
Formula	2008	2007
P/E ratio = $\dfrac{\text{Market price per share of common stock}}{\text{Earnings per share}}$	$\dfrac{\$60.00}{\$4.80} = 12.5$	$\dfrac{\$35.00}{\$2.60} = 13.5$

Palisades Furniture's P/E ratio of 12.5 means that the company's stock is selling at 12.5 times earnings. The decline from the 2007 P/E ratio of 13.5 is no cause for alarm because the market price of the stock is not under Palisades Furniture's control. Net income is more controllable, and net income increased during 2008.

Dividend Yield

Dividend yield is the ratio of dividends per share to the stock's market price per share. This ratio measures the percentage of a stock's market value that is returned annually as dividends. *Preferred* stockholders, who invest primarily to receive dividends, pay special attention to dividend yield.

Palisades Furniture paid annual cash dividends of $1.20 per share of common stock in 2008 and $1.00 in 2007, and market prices of the company's common stock were $60 in 2008 and $35 in 2007. The firm's dividend yields on common stock follow.

	Dividend Yield on Palisades' Common Stock	
Formula	2008	2007
Dividend yield on common stock* = $\dfrac{\text{Dividend per share of common stock}}{\text{Market price per share of common stock}}$	$\dfrac{\$1.20}{\$60.00} = .020$	$\dfrac{\$1.00}{\$35.00} = .029$

*Dividend yields may also be calculated for preferred stock.

An investor who buys Palisades Furniture common stock for $60 can expect to receive 2% of the investment annually in the form of cash dividends.

Book Value per Share of Common Stock

Book value per share of common stock is common equity divided by the number of common shares outstanding. Common equity equals total stockholders' equity less preferred equity. Palisades Furniture has no preferred stock outstanding. Its book-value-per-share-of-common-stock ratios follow (10,000 shares of common stock were outstanding).

	Book Value per Share of Palisades' Common Stock	
Formula	2008	2007
Book value per share of common stock = $\dfrac{\text{Total stockholders' equity} - \text{Preferred equity}}{\text{Number of shares of common stock outstanding}}$	$\dfrac{\$356{,}000 - \$0}{10{,}000} = \$35.60$	$\dfrac{\$320{,}000 - \$0}{10{,}000} = \$32.00$

Many experts argue that book value is not useful for investment analysis. It bears no relationship to market value and provides little information beyond stockholders' equity reported on the balance sheet. But some investors base their investment decisions on book value. For example, some investors rank stocks on the basis of the ratio of market price to book value. To these investors, the lower the ratio, the more attractive the stock.

Red Flags in Financial Statement Analysis

Analysts look for *red flags* that may signal financial trouble. Recent accounting scandals highlight the importance of these red flags. The following conditions may reveal that the company is too risky.

- **Movement of Sales, Inventory, and Receivables.** Sales, receivables, and inventory generally move together. Increased sales lead to higher receivables and require more inventory to meet demand. Strange movements among sales, inventory, and receivables make the financial statements look suspect.
- **Earnings Problems.** Has net income decreased significantly for several years in a row? Has income turned into a loss? Most companies cannot survive consecutive loss years.
- **Decreased Cash Flow.** Cash flow validates net income. Is cash flow from operations consistently lower than net income? If so, the company is in trouble. Are the sales of plant assets a major source of cash? If so, the company may face a cash shortage.
- **Too Much Debt.** How does the company's debt ratio compare to that of major competitors? If the debt ratio is too high, the company may be unable to pay its debts.
- **Inability to Collect Receivables.** Are days' sales in receivables growing faster than for competitors? A cash shortage may be looming.
- **Buildup of Inventories.** Is inventory turnover too slow? If so, the company may be unable to sell goods, or it may be overstating inventory.

Do any of these red flags apply to Google Inc.? No, Google's financial statements depict a strong and growing company. Will Google continue to grow at its present breakneck pace? Stay tuned. Time will tell.

The Decision Guidelines summarize the most widely used ratios.

Decision Guidelines

USING RATIOS IN FINANCIAL STATEMENT ANALYSIS

Mike and Roberta Robinson operate a financial-services firm. They manage other people's money and do most of their own financial-statement analysis. How do they measure companies' ability to pay bills, sell inventory, collect receivables, and so on? They use the standard ratios discussed in this chapter.

Ratio	Computation	Information Provided
Measuring ability to pay current liabilities:		
1. Current ratio	$\dfrac{\text{Current assets}}{\text{Current liabilities}}$	Measures ability to pay current liabilities with current assets
2. Acid-test (quick) ratio	$\dfrac{\text{Cash} + \text{Short-term investments} + \text{Net current receivables}}{\text{Current liabilities}}$	Shows ability to pay all current liabilities if they came due immediately
Measuring ability to sell inventory and collect receivables:		
3. Inventory turnover	$\dfrac{\text{Cost of goods sold}}{\text{Average inventory}}$	Indicates salability of inventory—the number of times a company sells its average inventory during a year
4. Accounts receivable turnover	$\dfrac{\text{Net credit sales}}{\text{Average net accounts receivable}}$	Measures ability to collect cash from customers
5. Days' sales in receivables	$\dfrac{\text{Average net accounts receivable}}{\text{One day's sales}}$	Shows how many days' sales remain in Accounts Receivable—how many days it takes to collect the average level of receivables
Measuring ability to pay long-term debt:		
6. Debt ratio	$\dfrac{\text{Total liabilities}}{\text{Total assets}}$	Indicates percentage of assets financed with debt
7. Times-interest-earned ratio	$\dfrac{\text{Income from operations}}{\text{Interest expense}}$	Measures the number of times operating income can cover interest expense
Measuring profitability:		
8. Rate of return on net sales	$\dfrac{\text{Net income}}{\text{Net sales}}$	Shows the percentage of each sales dollar earned as net income
9. Rate of return on total assets	$\dfrac{\text{Net income} + \text{Interest expense}}{\text{Average total assets}}$	Measures how profitably a company uses its assets
10. Rate of return on common stockholders' equity	$\dfrac{\text{Net income} - \text{Preferred dividends}}{\text{Average common stockholders' equity}}$	Gauges how much income is earned for each dollar invested by the common shareholders
11. Earnings per share of common stock	$\dfrac{\text{Net income} - \text{Preferred dividends}}{\text{Number of shares of common stock outstanding}}$	Gives the amount of net income earned for each share of the company's common stock

continued...

Ratio	Computation	Information Provided
Analyzing stock as an investment:		
12. Price/earnings ratio	$$\frac{\text{Market price per share of common stock}}{\text{Earnings per share}}$$	Indicates the market price of $1 of earnings
13. Dividend yield	$$\frac{\text{Annual dividend per share of common (or preferred) stock}}{\text{Market price per share of common (or preferred) stock}}$$	Shows the percentage of a stock's market value returned as dividends to stockholders each year
14. Book value per share of common stock	$$\frac{\text{Total stockholders' equity} - \text{Preferred equity}}{\text{Number of shares of common stock outstanding}}$$	Indicates the recorded accounting amount for each share of common stock outstanding

Summary Problem 2

JAVA INC.
Five-Year Selected Financial Data (adapted)
Years Ended January 31,

Operating Results*	2007	2006	2005	2004
Net sales	$13,848	$13,673	$11,635	$ 9,054
Cost of goods sold	9,704	8,599	6,775	5,318
Interest expense	109	75	45	46
Income from operations	338	1,455	1,817	1,333
Net income (net loss)	(8)	877	1,127	824
Cash dividends	76	75	76	77
Financial Position				
Merchandise inventory	1,677	1,904	1,462	1,056
Total assets	7,591	7,012	5,189	3,963
Current ratio	1.48:1	0.95:1	1.25:1	1.20:1
Stockholders' equity	3,010	2,928	2,630	1,574
Average number of shares of common stock outstanding (in thousands)	860	879	895	576

*Dollar amounts are in thousands.

Requirements

Compute the following ratios for 2005 through 2007, and evaluate Java's operating results. Are operating results strong or weak? Did they improve or deteriorate during this period? Your analysis will reveal a clear trend.

1. Gross profit percentage
2. Net income as a percentage of sales
3. Earnings per share
4. Inventory turnover
5. Times-interest-earned ratio
6. Rate of return on stockholders' equity

Solution

	2007	2006	2005
1. Gross profit percentage	$\dfrac{\$13{,}848 - \$9{,}704}{\$13{,}848} = 29.9\%$	$\dfrac{\$13{,}673 - \$8{,}599}{\$13{,}673} = 37.1\%$	$\dfrac{\$11{,}635 - \$6{,}775}{\$11{,}635} = 41.8\%$
2. Net income as a percentage of sales	$\dfrac{\$(8)}{\$13{,}848} = (.06\%)$	$\dfrac{\$877}{\$13{,}673} = 6.4\%$	$\dfrac{\$1{,}127}{\$11{,}635} = 9.7\%$
3. Earnings per share	$\dfrac{\$(8)}{860} = \$(0.01)$	$\dfrac{\$877}{879} = \$1.00$	$\dfrac{\$1{,}127}{895} = \$1.26$
4. Inventory turnover	$\dfrac{\$9{,}704}{(\$1{,}677 + \$1{,}904)/2} = 5.4$ times	$\dfrac{\$8{,}599}{(\$1{,}904 + \$1{,}462)/2} = 5.1$ times	$\dfrac{\$6{,}775}{(\$1{,}462 + \$1{,}056)/2} = 5.4$ times
5. Times-interest-earned ratio	$\dfrac{\$338}{\$109} = 3.1$ times	$\dfrac{\$1{,}455}{\$75} = 19.4$ times	$\dfrac{\$1{,}817}{\$45} = 40.4$ times
6. Rate of return on stockholders' equity	$\dfrac{\$(8)}{(\$3{,}010 + \$2{,}928)/2} = (0.3\%)$	$\dfrac{\$877}{(\$2{,}928 + \$2{,}630)/2} = 31.6\%$	$\dfrac{\$1{,}127}{(\$2{,}630 + \$1{,}574)/2} = 53.6\%$

Evaluation: During this period, Java's operating results deteriorated on all these measures except inventory turnover. The gross profit percentage is down sharply, as are the times-interest-earned ratio and return on equity. From these data it is clear that Java could sell its coffee, but not at the markups the company enjoyed in the past. The final result, in 2007, was a net loss for the year.

Review Financial Statement Analysis

Accounting Vocabulary

Account Receivable Turnover
Measure a company's ability to collect cash from credit customers. To compute accounts receivable turnover, divide net credit sales by average net accounts receivable.

Acid-Test Ratio
Ratio of the sum of cash plus short-term investments plus net current receivables to total current liabilities. Tells whether the entity can pay all its current liabilities if they come due immediately. Also called the **quick ratio**.

Benchmarking
The practice of comparing a company with other companies that are leaders.

Book Value per Share of Common Stock
Common stockholders' equity divided by the number of shares of common stock outstanding. The recorded amount for each share of common stock outstanding.

Collection Period
Ratio of average net accounts receivable to one day's sale. Indicates how many days' sales remain in Accounts Receivable awaiting collection. Also called the **days' sales in receivables**.

Common-Size Treatment
A financial statement that reports only percentages (no dollar amounts).

Current Ratio
Current assets divided by current liabilities. Measures ability to pay current liabilities with current assets.

Days' Sales in Receivables
Ratio of average net accounts receivable to one day's sale. Indicates how many days' sales remain in Accounts Receivable awaiting collection. Also called the **collection period**.

Debt Ratio
Ratio of total liabilities to total assets. Shows the proportion of a company's assets that is financed with debt.

Dividend Yield
Ratio of dividends per share of stock to the stock's market price per share. Tells the percentage of a stock's market value that the company returns to stockholders annually as dividends.

Earnings per Share (EPS)
Amount of a company's net income for each share of its outstanding common stock.

Horizontal Analysis
Study of percentage changes in comparative financial statements.

Interest-Coverage Ratio
Ratio of income from operations to interest expense. Measure the number of times that operating income can cover interest expense. Also called the **times-interest earned ratio**.

Inventory Turnover
Ratio of cost of goods sold to average inventory. Indicates how rapidly inventory is sold.

Leverage
Earning more income on borrowed money than the related interest expense, thereby increasing the earnings for the owners of the business. Also called **trading on equity**.

Price/Earnings Ratio
Ratio of the market price of a share of common stock to the company's earnings per share. Measures the value that the stock market places on $1 of a company's earnings.

Quick Ratio
Ratio of the sum of cash plus short-term investments plus net current receivables to total current liabilities. Tells whether the entity can pay all its current liabilities if they come due immediately. Also called the **acid-test ratio**.

Rate of Return on Common Stockholders' Equity
Net income minus preferred dividends, divided by average common stockholders' equity. A measure of profitability. Also called **return on equity**.

Rate of Return on Net Sales
Ratio of net income to net sales. A measure of profitability. Also called **return on sales**.

Rate of Return on Total Assets
Net income plus interest expense, divided by average total assets. This ratio measures a company's success in using its assets to earn income for the persons who finance the business. Also called **return on assets**.

Return on Assets
Net income plus interest expense, divided by average total assets. This ratio measure a company's success in using its assets to earn income for the persons who finance the business. Also called **rate of return on total assets**.

Return on Equity
Net income minus preferred dividends, divided by average common stockholders' equity. A measure of profitability. Also called **rate of return on common stockholders' equity**.

Return on Sales
Ratio of net income to net sales. A measure of profitability. Also called **rate of return on net sales**.

Times-Interest-Earned Ratio
Ratio of income from operations to interest expense. Measures the number of times that operating income can cover interest expense. Also called the **interest-coverage ratio**.

Trading on Equity
Earning more income on borrowed money than the related interest expense, thereby increasing the earnings for the owners of the business. Also called **leverage**.

Trend Percentages
A form of horizontal analysis in which percentages are computed by selecting a base year as 100% and expressing amounts for following years as a percentage of the base amount.

Vertical Analysis
Analysis of a financial statement that reveals the relationship of each statement item to a specified base, which is the 100% figure.

Working Capital
Current assets minus current liabilities; measures a business's ability to meet its short-term obligations with its current assets.

Quick Check

Liberty Corporation reported these figures:

	2007	2006		2007
Cash and equivalents	$ 2,345	$ 1,934	Sales	$19,564
Receivables	2,097	1,882	Cost of sales	7,105
Inventory	1,294	1,055	Operating expenses	7,001
Prepaid expenses	1,616	2,300	Operating income	5,458
Total current assets	7,352	7,171	Interest expense	199
Other assets	17,149	15,246	Other expense	2,209
Total assets	$24,501	$22,417	Net income	$ 3,050
Total current liabilities	$ 7,341	$ 8,429		
Long-term liabilities	5,360	2,622		
Common equity	11,800	11,366		
Total liabilities and equity	$24,501	$22,417		

1. Horizontal analysis of Liberty's balance sheet for 2007 would report
   a. Cash as 9.6% of total assets
   b. 21% increase in Cash
   c. Current ratio of 1.00
   d. Inventory turnover of 6 times

2. Vertical analysis of Liberty's balance sheet for 2007 would report
   a. 21% increase in Cash
   b. Current ratio of 1.00
   c. Cash as 9.6% of total assets
   d. Inventory turnover of 6 times

3. A common-size income statement for Liberty would report (amounts rounded)
   a. Net income of 16%
   b. Cost of sales at 36%
   c. Sales of 100%
   d. All the above

4. Which statement best describes Liberty's acid-test ratio?
   a. Less than 1
   b. Equal to 1
   c. Greater than 1
   d. None of the above

5. Liberty's inventory turnover during 2007 was
   a. 6 times
   b. 7 times
   c. 8 times
   d. Not determinable from the data given

6. During 2005, Liberty's days' sales in receivables ratio was
    a. 39 days
    b. 37 days
    c. 35 days
    d. 30 days

7. Which measure expresses Liberty's times-interest-earned ratio?
    a. 15 times
    b. 27 times
    c. 20 times
    d. 51.8%

8. Liberty's return on common stockholders' equity can be described as
    a. Weak
    b. Normal
    c. Average
    d. Strong

9. The company has 2,500 shares of common stock outstanding. What is Liberty's earnings per share?
    a. 2.04
    b. 3.6 times
    c. $1.22
    d. $3.05

10. Liberty's stock has traded recently around $44 per share. Use your answer to question 9 to measure the company's price/earnings ratio.
    a. 36
    b. 44
    c. 1.00
    d. 69

Answers are given after Apply Your Knowledge (p. 803).

Assess Your Progress

Short Exercises

Horizontal analysis of revenues and gross profit

S15-1 Micatin Corp. reported the following on its comparative income statement:

(in millions)	2006	2005	2004
Revenue	$9,993	$9,489	$8,995
Cost of sales	5,905	5,785	5,404

Perform a horizontal analysis of revenues and gross profit—both in dollar amounts and in percentages—for 2006 and 2005. (p. 757)

Trend analysis of revenues and net income

S15-2 Micatin Corp. reported the following revenues and net income amounts:

(in millions)	2006	2005	2004	2003
Revenues	$9,993	$9,489	$8,995	$8,777
Net income	634	590	579	451

1. Show Micatin's trend percentages for revenues and net income. Use 2003 as the base year, and round to the nearest percent.
2. Which measure increased faster during 2004–2006? (p. 760)

Vertical analysis of assets

S15-3 TriState Optical Company reported the following amounts on its balance sheet at December 31, 2006:

	2006
Cash and receivables	$ 48,000
Inventory	38,000
Property, plant, and equipment, net	96,000
Total assets	$182,000

Perform a vertical analysis of TriState assets at the end of 2006. (p. 760)

Common-size income statements of two companies

S15-4 Compare Sanchez, Inc., and Alioto Corp. by converting their income statements to common size.

	Sanchez	Alioto
Net sales	$9,489	$19,536
Cost of goods sold	5,785	14,101
Other expense	3,114	4,497
Net income	$ 590	$ 938

continued...

Which company earns more net income? Which company's net income is a higher percentage of its net sales? (pp. 761–762).

S15-5 though S15-9 use the following data for Short Exercises S15-5 through S15-9. Lowe's Companies, the home-improvement-store chain, reported these summarized figures (in billions):

LOWE'S COMPANIES
Income Statement (Adapted)
Year Ended January 30, 20X4

Net sales	$30.8
Cost of goods sold	21.2
Interest expense	.2
All other expenses	7.5
Net income	$ 1.9

LOWE'S COMPANIES
Balance Sheet (Adapted)
January 31,

	20X4	20X3		20X4	20X3
Cash	$ 1.4	$ 0.8	Total current liabilities	$ 4.4	$ 3.6
Short-term investments	0.2	0.3	Long-term liabilities	4.3	4.2
Accounts receivable	0.1	0.2	Total liabilities	8.7	7.8
Inventory	4.6	4.0			
Other current assets	0.4	0.3	Common stock	2.6	2.4
Total current assets	6.7	5.6	Retained earnings	7.7	5.9
All other assets	12.3	10.5	Total equity	10.3	8.3
Total assets	$19.0	$16.1	Total liabilities and equity	$19.0	$16.1

Evaluating a company's current ratio

S15-5 Use the foregoing Lowe's Companies data.
1. Compute Lowe's current ratio at December 31, 20X4 and 20X3. (p. 767)
2. Did Lowe's current ratio improve, deteriorate, or hold steady during 2006? (p. 767)

Computing inventory turnover and days' sales in receivables

S15-6 Use the foregoing Lowe's Companies data to compute the following (amounts in billions):
a. The rate of inventory turnover for 20X4. (pp. 769–770)
b. Days' sales in average receivables during 20X4. Round dollar amounts to three decimal places. (p. 770)

Measuring ability to pay liabilities

S15-7 Use the foregoing financial statements of Lowe's Companies.
1. Compute the debt ratio at December 31, 20X4. (p. 771)
2. Is Lowe's ability to pay its liabilities strong or weak? Explain your reasoning. (p. 771)

Measuring profitability

S15-8 Use the foregoing financial statements of Lowe's Companies to compute these profitability measures for 20X4.
  a. Rate of return on net sales. (p. 772)
  b. Rate of return on total assets. Interest expense for 20X4 was $0.2 billion. (p. 773)
  c. Rate of return on common stockholders' equity. (p. 773)
  Are these rates of return strong or weak? Explain. (pp. 773–774)

Computing EPS and the price/earnings ratio

S15-9 Use the foregoing financial statements of Lowe's Companies, plus the following items (in billions):

Number of shares of common stock outstanding	0.8

1. Compute earnings per share (EPS) for Lowe's. Round to the nearest cent. (p. 774)
2. Compute Lowe's price/earnings ratio. The price of a share of Lowe's stock is $66.50. (pp. 774–775)

Using ratio data to reconstruct an income statement

S15-10 A skeleton of Heirloom Mills' income statement appears as follows (amounts in thousands):

INCOME STATEMENT

Net sales	$7,200
Cost of goods sold	(a)
Selling and administrative expenses	1,710
Interest expense	(b)
Other expenses	150
Income before taxes	1,000
Income tax expense	(c)
Net income	$ (d)

Use the following ratio data to complete Heirloom Mills' income statement: (pp. 768, 770, 772)
  a. Inventory turnover was 5.5 (beginning inventory was $790; ending inventory was $750).
  b. Rate of return on sales is 0.095.

Using ratio data to reconstruct a balance sheet

S15-11 A skeleton of Heirloom Mills' balance sheet appears as follows (amounts in thousands):

BALANCE SHEET

Cash	$ 50	Total current liabilities	$2,100
Receivables	(a)	Long-term note payable	(e)
Inventories	750		
Prepaid expenses	(b)	Other long-term liabilities	820
Total current assets	(c)		
Plant assets, net	(d)	Stockholders' equity	2,400
Other assets	2,150	Total liabilities and	
Total assets	$6,800	equity	$ (f)

continued ...

Financial Statement Analysis

Use the following ratio data to complete Heirloom Mills' balance sheet: (pp. 767, 769)

a. Current ratio is 0.70.

b. Acid-test ratio is 0.30.

Exercises

Computing year-to-year changes in working capital

E15-12 Compute the dollar amount of change and the percentage of change in Media Enterprises' working capital each year during 2008 and 2009. Is this trend favorable or unfavorable?

	2009	2008	2007
Total current assets	$330,000	$300,000	$280,000
Total current liabilities	160,000	150,000	140,000

Horizontal analysis of an income statement

E15-13 Prepare a horizontal analysis of the following comparative income statement of Enchanted Designs, Inc. Round percentage changes to the nearest one-tenth percent (three decimal places) (pp. 758–759):

ENCHANTED DESIGNS
Comparative Income Statement
Years Ended December 31, 2007 and 2006

	2007	2006
Net sales revenue	$430,000	$373,000
Expenses:		
Cost of goods sold	$202,000	$188,000
Selling and general expenses	98,000	93,000
Other expense	7,000	4,000
Total expenses	307,000	285,000
Net income	$123,000	$ 88,000

Why did net income increase by a higher percentage than net sales revenue during 2007? (pp. 758–759)

Computing trend percentages

E15-14 Compute trend percentages for Thousand Oaks Realty's net revenue and net income for the following 5-year period, using 2004 as the base year. Round to the nearest full percent. (p. 760)

(in thousands)	2008	2007	2006	2005	2004
Net revenue	$1,318	$1,187	$1,106	$1,009	$1,043
Net income	122	114	83	71	85

Which grew faster during the period, net revenue or net income?

Vertical analysis of a balance sheet

E15-15 Alpha Graphics, Inc., has requested that you perform a vertical analysis of its balance sheet. (p. 762)

ALPHA GRAPHICS, INC.
Balance Sheet
December 31, 2006

Assets	
Total current assets	$ 42,000
Property, plant, and equipment, net	207,000
Other assets	35,000
Total assets	$284,000
Liabilities	
Total current liabilities	$ 48,000
Long-term debt	108,000
Total liabilities	156,000
Stockholders' Equity	
Total stockholders' equity	128,000
Total liabilities and stockholders' equity	$284,000

Preparing a common-size income statement

E15-16 Prepare a comparative common-size income statement for Enchanted Designs, Inc., using the 2007 and 2006 data of Exercise 15-13 and rounding percentages to one-tenth percent (three decimal places). To an investor, how does 2007 compare with 2006? Explain your reasoning. (pp. 761–762)

Computing four key ratios

E15-17 The financial statements of Nature's Health Foods include the following items:

	Current Year	Preceding Year
Balance sheet:		
Cash	$ 17,000	$ 22,000
Short-term investments	11,000	26,000
Net receivables	54,000	73,000
Inventory	77,000	71,000
Prepaid expenses	16,000	8,000
Total current assets	$175,000	$200,000
Total current liabilities	$131,000	$ 91,000
Income statement:		
Net credit sales	$464,000	
Cost of goods sold	317,000	

Requirements
Compute the following ratios for the current year:
a. Current ratio (p. 767)
b. Acid-test ratio (p. 769)
c. Inventory turnover (pp. 769–770)
d. Days' sales in average receivables (pp. 770–771)

Analyzing the ability to pay current liabilities

E15-18 Big Bend Picture Frames has asked you to determine whether the company's ability to pay current liabilities and total liabilities improved or deteriorated during 2007. To answer this question, compute these ratios for 2007 and 2006:

a. Current ratio (p. 767)
b. Acid-test ratio (p. 769)
c. Debt ratio (p. 771)
d. Times-interest-earned ratio (p. 772)

Summarize the results of your analysis in a written report.

	2007	2006
Cash	$ 61,000	$ 47,000
Short-term investments	28,000	—
Net receivables	122,000	116,000
Inventory	237,000	272,000
Total assets	560,000	490,000
Total current liabilities	275,000	202,000
Long-term note payable	40,000	52,000
Income from operations	165,000	158,000
Interest expense	48,000	39,000

Analyzing profitability

E15-19 Compute four ratios that measure the ability to earn profits for Bonaparte, Inc., whose comparative income statement follows. 2004 data are given as needed. (pp. 772–774):

BONAPARTE
Comparative Income Statement
Years Ended December 31, 2006 and 2005

Dollars in Thousands	2006	2005	2004
Net sales	$174,000	$158,000	
Cost of goods sold	$ 93,000	$ 86,000	
Selling and general expenses	46,000	41,000	
Interest expense	9,000	10,000	
Income tax expense	10,000	9,000	
Net income	$ 16,000	$ 12,000	
Additional data:			
Total assets	$204,000	$191,000	$171,000
Common stockholders' equity	$ 96,000	$ 89,000	$ 79,000
Preferred dividends	$ 3,000	$ 3,000	$ 0
Common shares outstanding during the year	20,000	20,000	18,000

Did the company's operating performance improve or deteriorate during 2006? (pp. 772–774)

Evaluating a stock as an investment

E15-20 Evaluate the common stock of Shamrock State Bank as an investment. Specifically, use the three stock ratios to determine whether the common stock has increased or decreased in attractiveness during the past year. (pp. 774–775)

	2008	2007
Net income	$ 60,000	$ 52,000
Dividends—common	20,000	20,000
Dividends—preferred	12,000	12,000
Total stockholders' equity at year-end (includes 80,000 shares of common stock)	780,000	600,000
Preferred stock, 6%	200,000	200,000
Market price per share of common stock	$16.50	$13

Using ratio data to reconstruct a company's balance sheet

E15-21 The following data (dollar amounts in millions) are adapted from the financial statements of Super Saver Stores, Inc.

Total current assets	$10,500
Accumulated depreciation	$ 2,000
Total liabilities	$15,000
Preferred stock	$ 0
Debt ratio	60%
Current ratio	1.50

Requirement

Complete Super Saver's condensed balance sheet. (pp. 768, 770)

Current assets		$?
Property, plant, and equipment	$?	
Less Accumulated depreciation	(?)	?
Total assets		$?
Current liabilities		$?
Long-term liabilities		?
Stockholders' equity		?
Total liabilities and stockholders' equity		$?

Problems (Group A)

Trend percentages, return on common equity, and comparison with the industry

P15-22A Net sales revenue, net income, and common stockholders' equity for Shawnee Mission Corporation, a manufacturer of contact lenses, follow for a four-year period.

(in thousands)	2008	2007	2006	2005
Net sales revenue	$761	$704	$641	$662
Net income	60	40	36	48
Ending common stockholders' equity	366	354	330	296

continued . . .

Financial Statement Analysis   **791**

Common-size statements, analysis of profitability, and financial position, and comparison with the industry

2 **3** **4**

Requirements

1. Compute trend percentages for each item for 2006 through 2008. Use 2005 as the base year, and round to the nearest whole percent. (p. 760)
2. Compute the rate of return on common stockholders' equity for 2006 through 2008, rounding to three decimal places. (p. 773)

P15-23A Todd Department Stores' chief executive officer (CEO) has asked you to compare the company's profit performance and financial position with the average for the industry. The CEO has given you the company's income statement and balance sheet, as well as the industry average data for retailers.

TODD DEPARTMENT STORES, INC.
Income Statement Compared with Industry Average
Year Ended December 31, 2006

	Todd	Industry Average
Net sales	$781,000	100.0%
Cost of goods sold	528,000	65.8
Gross profit	253,000	34.2
Operating expenses	163,000	19.7
Operating income	90,000	14.5
Other expenses	5,000	0.4
Net income	$ 85,000	14.1%

TODD DEPARTMENT STORES, INC.
Balance Sheet Compared with Industry Average
December 31, 2006

	Todd	Industry Average
Current assets	$305,000	70.9%
Fixed assets, net	119,000	23.6
Intangible assets, net	4,000	0.8
Other assets	22,000	4.7
Total assets	$450,000	100.0%
Current liabilities	$207,000	48.1%
Long-term liabilities	102,000	16.6
Stockholders' equity	141,000	35.3
Total liabilities and stockholders's equity	$450,000	100.0%

Requirements

1. Prepare a common-size income statement and balance sheet for Todd. The first column of each statement should present Todd's

continued...

—common-size statement, and the second column, the industry averages. (pp. 761–763)

2. For the profitability analysis, compute Todd's (a) ratio of gross profit to net sales, (b) ratio of operating income to net sales, and (c) ratio of net income to net sales. Compare these figures with the industry averages. Is Todd's profit performance better or worse than the industry average? (pp. 762, 764, 771)

3. For the analysis of financial position, compute Todd's (a) ratio of current assets to total assets and (b) ratio of stockholders' equity to total assets. Compare these ratios with the industry averages. Is Todd's financial position better or worse than the industry averages? (pp. 761–762, 764)

Effects of business transactions on selected ratios

P15-24A Financial statement data of Yankee Traveler Magazine include the following items (dollars in thousands):

Cash	$ 22,000
Accounts receivable, net	82,000
Inventories	149,000
Total assets	637,000
Short-term notes payable	49,000
Accounts payable	103,000
Accrued liabilities	38,000
Long-term liabilities	191,000
Net income	71,000
Common shares outstanding	50,000

Requirements

1. Compute Yankee Traveler's current ratio (p. 767), debt ratio (p. 771), and earnings per share (p. 774). Round all ratios to two decimal places, and use the following format for your answer:

Transaction	Current Ratio	Debt Ratio	Earnings per Share

2. Compute the three ratios after evaluating the effect of each transaction that follows. Consider each transaction *separately*.

   a. Purchased inventory on account, $46,000.
   b. Borrowed $125,000 on a long-term note payable.
   c. Issued 5,000 shares of common stock, receiving cash of $120,000.
   d. Received cash on account, $19,000.

Format your answer as follows:

Transaction	Current Ratio	Debt Ratio	Earnings per Share
a.			

Using ratios to evaluate a stock investment

P15-25A Comparative financial-statement data of Weinstein, Inc., follow.

WEINSTEIN, INC.
Comparative Income Statement
Years Ended December 31, 2009 and 2008

	2009	2008
Net sales	$462,000	$427,000
Cost of goods sold	240,000	218,000
Gross profit	222,000	209,000
Operating expenses	136,000	134,000
Income from operations	86,000	75,000
Interest expense	11,000	12,000
Income before income tax	75,000	63,000
Income tax expense	25,000	27,000
Net income	$ 50,000	$ 36,000

WEINSTEIN, INC.
Comparative Balance Sheet
December 31, 2009 and 2008

	2009	2008	2007*
Current assets:			
Cash	$ 96,000	$ 97,000	
Current receivables, net	112,000	116,000	$103,000
Inventories	147,000	162,000	207,000
Prepaid expenses	16,000	7,000	
Total current assets	371,000	382,000	
Property, plant, and equipment, net	214,000	178,000	
Total assets	$585,000	$560,000	598,000
Total current liabilities	$226,000	$243,000	
Long-term liabilities	119,000	97,000	
Total liabilities	345,000	340,000	
Preferred stock, 6%	100,000	100,000	
Common stockholders' equity, no par	140,000	120,000	90,000
Total liabilities and stockholders' equity	$585,000	$560,000	

*Selected 2007 amounts.

Other Information:
1. Market price of Weinstein's common stock: $49 at December 31, 2009, and $32.50 at December 31, 2008.
2. Common shares outstanding: 10,000 during 2009 and 9,000 during 2008.
3. All sales on credit.

Requirements
1. Compute the following ratios for 2009 and 2008:
   a. Current ratio (p. 767)
   b. Times-interest-earned ratio (pp. 771–772)
   c. Inventory turnover (pp. 769–770)

continued . . .

d. Return on common stockholders' equity (p. 773)

e. Earnings per share of common stock (p. 774)

f. Price/earnings ratio (pp. 774–775)

2. Decide (a) whether Weinstein's ability to pay debts and to sell inventory improved or deteriorated during 2009 and (b) whether the investment attractiveness of its common stock appears to have increased or decreased.

Using ratios to decide between two stock investments

4 5

P15-26A Assume that you are purchasing an investment and have decided to invest in a company in the digital phone business. You have narrowed the choice to Singular Corp. and Very Zone, Inc., and have assembled the following data:

Selected income-statement data for the current year:

	Singular	Very Zone
Net sales (all on credit)	$421,000	$497,000
Cost of goods sold	209,000	258,000
Interest expense	—	19,000
Net income	50,000	72,000

Selected balance-sheet data at the *beginning* of the current year:

	Singular	Very Zone
Current receivables, net	$ 40,000	$ 48,000
Inventories	83,000	88,000
Total assets	259,000	270,000
Common stock, $1 par (10,000 shares)	10,000	
$1 par (15,000 shares)		15,000

Selected balance-sheet and market-price data at the *end* of the current year:

	Singular	Very Zone
Current assets:		
Cash	$ 26,000	$ 19,000
Short-term investments	40,000	18,000
Current receivables, net	38,000	46,000
Inventories	67,000	100,000
Prepaid expenses	2,000	3,000
Total current assets	173,000	186,000
Total assets	265,000	328,000
Total current liabilities	100,000	98,000
Total liabilities	100,000	131,000
Common stock, $1 par (10,000 shares)	10,000	
$1 par (15,000 shares)		15,000
Total stockholders' equity	157,000	197,000
Market price per share of common stock	$ 80	$ 86.40

continued ...

Your strategy is to invest in companies that have low price/earnings ratios but appear to be in good shape financially. Assume that you have analyzed all other factors and that your decision depends on the results of ratio analysis.

Requirements

Compute the following ratios for both companies for the current year, and decide which company's stock better fits your investment strategy.

a. Acid-test ratio (p. 769)
b. Inventory turnover (pp. 769–770)
c. Days' sales in average receivables (pp. 770–771)
d. Debt ratio (p. 771)
e. Earnings per share of common stock (p. 774)
f. Price/earnings ratio (pp. 774–775)

Analyzing two companies based on their ratios

P15-27A Take the role of an investment analyst at Prudential Bache. It is your job to recommend investments for your clients. The only information you have are some ratio values for two companies in the pharmaceuticals industry.

Ratio	Healthtime Inc.	Mocek Corp.
Return on equity (pp. 771–772)	21.5%	32.3%
Return on assets (p. 770)	16.4%	17.1%
Days' sales in receivables (pp. 761–762)	42	36
Inventory turnover (pp. 761–762)	8	6
Gross profit percentage (pp. 772–774)	51%	53%
Net income as a percentage of sales (pp. 772–774)	8.3%	7.2%
Times-interest-earned (pp. 772–774)	9	16

Write a report to Prudential Bache's investment committee. Recommend one company's stock over the other. State the reasons for your recommendation.

Problems (Group B)

Trend percentages, return on sales, and comparison with the industry

P15-28B Net sales, net income, and total assets for Azbell Electronics for a four-year period follow.

(in thousands)	2008	2007	2006	2005
Net sales	$307	$313	$266	$281
Net income	9	21	11	18
Total assets	266	254	209	197

continued . . .

796 Chapter 15

Requirements

1. Compute trend percentages for each item for 2006 through 2008. Use 2005 as the base year and round to the nearest whole percentage. (p. 760)
2. Compute the rate of return on net sales for 2006 through 2008, rounding to three decimal places. (p. 772)

Common-size statements, analysis of profitability, and financial position, and comparison with the industry

P15-29B Top managers of Crescent City Music Company have asked your help in comparing the company's profit performance and financial position with the average for the industry. The accountant has given you the company's income statement and balance sheet and also the following data for the industry:

CRESCENT CITY MUSIC COMPANY
Income Statement Compared with Industry Average
Year Ended December 31, 2008

	Crescent City	Industry Average
Net sales	$957,000	100.0%
Cost of goods sold	613,000	65.9
Gross profit	344,000	34.1
Operating expenses	204,000	28.1
Operating income	140,000	6.0
Other expenses	10,000	0.4
Net income	$130,000	5.6%

CRESCENT CITY MUSIC COMPANY
Balance Sheet Compared with Industry Average
December 31, 2008

	Crescent City	Industry Average
Current assets	$486,000	74.4%
Fixed assets, net	117,000	20.0
Intangible assets, net	24,000	0.6
Other assets	3,000	5.0
Total assets	$630,000	100.0%
Current liabilities	$246,000	45.6%
Long-term liabilities	136,000	19.0
Stockholders' equity	248,000	35.4
Total liabilities and stockholders' equity	$630,000	100.0%

continued ...

Requirements

1. Prepare a common-size income statement and balance sheet for Crescent City Music Company. The first column of each statement should present Crescent City's common-size statement, and the second column should show the industry averages. (pp. 761–762)
2. For the profitability analysis, compute Crescent City's (a) ratio of gross profit to net sales, (b) ratio of operating income to net sales, and (c) ratio of net income to net sales. Compare these figures with the industry averages. Is Crescent City's profit performance better or worse than the average for the industry? (pp. 761, 764)
3. For the analysis of financial position, compute Crescent City's (a) ratios of current assets and current liabilities to total assets and (b) ratio of stockholders' equity to total assets. Compare these ratios with the industry averages. Is Crescent City's financial position better or worse than average for the industry? (pp. 761, 764)

Effects of business transactions on selected ratios

[4]

P15-30B Financial statement data on I70 RV Park include the following:

Cash	$ 47,000	Accounts payable	$ 96,000
Accounts receivable, net	123,000	Accrued liabilities	50,000
Inventories	189,000	Long-term liabilities	224,000
Total assets	833,000	Net income	110,000
Short-term notes payable	72,000	Common shares outstanding	20,000

Requirements

1. Compute I70 RV Park's current ratio (p. 767), debt ratio (p. 771), and earnings per share (p. 774). Round all ratios to two decimal places, and use the following format for your answer:

Transaction Letter	Current Ratio	Debt Ratio	Earnings per Share

2. Compute the three ratios after evaluating the effect of each transaction that follows. Consider each transaction *separately*.
   a. Borrowed $27,000 on a long-term note payable.
   b. Issued 10,000 shares of common stock, receiving cash of $108,000.
   c. Purchased inventory of $48,000 on account.
   d. Received cash on account, $6,000.

Format your answer as follows:

Transaction	Current Ratio	Debt Ratio	Earnings per Share
a.			

Using ratios to evaluate a stock investment

P15-31B Comparative financial statement data of Banfield DVDs, Inc., follow:

BANFIELD DVDs, INC.
Comparative Income Statement
Years Ended December 31, 2006 and 2005

	2006	2005
Net sales	$667,000	$599,000
Cost of goods sold	378,000	283,000
Gross profit	289,000	316,000
Operating expenses	129,000	147,000
Income from operations	160,000	169,000
Interest expense	37,000	51,000
Income before income tax	123,000	118,000
Income tax expense	34,000	53,000
Net income	$ 89,000	$ 65,000

BANFIELD DVDs INC.
Comparative Balance Sheet
December 31, 2006 and 2005

	2006	2005	2004*
Current assets:			
Cash	$ 37,000	$ 40,000	
Current receivables, net	208,000	151,000	$138,000
Inventories	298,000	286,000	184,000
Prepaid expenses	5,000	20,000	
Total current assets	548,000	497,000	
Property, plant, and equipment, net	287,000	276,000	
Total assets	$835,000	$773,000	707,000
Total current liabilities	$286,000	$267,000	
Long-term liabilities	245,000	235,000	
Total liabilities	531,000	502,000	
Preferred stock, 4%	50,000	50,000	
Common stockholders' equity, no par	308,000	221,000	198,000
Total liabilities and stockholders' equity	$889,000	$773,000	

*Selected 2004 amounts.

Other Information:
1. Market price of Banfield's common stock: $92.80 at December 31, 2006, and $67.50 at December 31, 2005.
2. Common shares outstanding: 15,000 during 2006 and 14,000 during 2005.
3. All sales on credit.

Requirements
1. Compute the following ratios for 2006 and 2005:
   a. Current ratio (p. 767)
   b. Times-interest-earned ratio (p. 772)

continued . . .

c. Inventory turnover (pp. 769–770)
d. Return on common stockholders' equity (p. 773)
e. Earnings per share of common stock (p. 774)
f. Price/earnings ratio (pp. 774–775)

Decide whether (a) Banfield's ability to pay its debts and to sell inventory improved or deteriorated during 2006 and (b) the investment attractiveness of its common stock appears to have increased or decreased.

Using ratios to decide between two stock investments

P15-32B Assume that you are considering purchasing stock in a company in the music industry. You have narrowed the choice to Minnesota Music Makers (MMM), and Carolina Sound and have assembled the following data:

Selected income-statement data for the current year:

	MMM	Carolina
Net sales (all on credit)	$603,000	$519,000
Cost of goods sold	484,000	387,000
Interest expense	—	8,000
Net income	75,000	38,000

Selected balance-sheet and market-price data at the *end* of the current year:

	MMM	Carolina
Current assets:		
Cash	$ 45,000	$ 39,000
Short-term investments	76,000	13,000
Current receivables, net	99,000	164,000
Inventories	211,000	183,000
Prepaid expenses	19,000	15,000
Total current assets	450,000	414,000
Total assets	974,000	938,000
Total current liabilities	306,000	338,000
Total liabilities	667,000	691,000
Common stock, $1 par (150,000 shares)	150,000	
$5 par (20,000 shares)		100,000
Total stockholders' equity	307,000	247,000
Market price per share of common stock	$ 8	$ 41.80

Selected balance-sheet data at the *beginning* of the current year:

	MMM	Carolina
Current receivables, net	$102,000	$193,000
Inventories	209,000	197,000
Total assets	842,000	909,000
Common stock, $1 par (150,000 shares)	150,000	
$5 par (20,000 shares)		100,000

continued . . .

Your strategy is to invest in companies that have low price/earnings ratios but appear to be in good shape financially. Assume that you have analyzed all other factors and that your decision depends on the results of ratio analysis.

Requirements

Compute the following ratios for both companies for the current year and decide which company's stock better fits your investment strategy.

a. Acid-test ratio (p. 769)
b. Inventory turnover (pp. 769–770)
c. Days' sales in average receivables (pp. 770–771)
d. Debt ratio (p. 771)
e. Earnings per share of common stock (p. 774)
f. Price/earnings ratio (pp. 774–775)

Analyzing two companies based on their ratios

P15-33B Take the role of an investment analyst at A. G. Edwards. It is your job to recommend investments for your client. The only information you have are the ratio values for two companies in the graphics software industry.

Ratio	Hourglass Software Company	PC Tech, Inc.
Return on equity (p. 773)	36%	29%
Return on assets (p. 773)	21%	20%
Days' sales in receivables (p. 771)	43	51
Inventory turnover (pp. 769–770)	8	9
Gross profit percentage (p. 761)	71%	62%
Net income as a percent of sales (p. 761)	14%	16%
Times-interest earned (p. 772)	18	12

Write a report to the A. G. Edwards investment committee. Recommend one company's stock over the other. State the reasons for your recommendation.

for 24/7 practice, visit www.MyAccountingLab.com

Apply Your Knowledge

Decision Cases

Assessing the effects of transactions on a company

Case 1. General Motors, Inc., and Ford Motor Company both had a bad year in 2005; the companies' auto units suffered net losses. The loss pushed some return measures into the negative column, and the companies' ratios deteriorated. Assume top management of GM and Ford are pondering ways to improve their ratios. In particular, management is considering the following transactions:

1. Borrow $100 million on long-term debt.
2. Purchase treasury stock for $500 million cash.
3. Expense one-fourth of the goodwill carried on the books.
4. Create a new auto-design division at a cash cost of $300 million.
5. Purchase patents from DaimlerChrysler, paying $20 million cash.

Requirements

Top management wants to know the effects of these transactions (increase, decrease, or no effect) on the following ratios:

a. Current ratio (p. 767)

b. Debt ratio (p. 772)

c. Return on equity (pp. 773–774)

Understanding the components of accounting ratios

Case 2. Lance Berkman is the controller of Saturn, a dance club whose year-end is December 31. Berkman prepares checks for suppliers in December and posts them to the appropriate accounts in that month. However, he holds on to the checks and mails them to the suppliers in January. What financial ratio(s) are most affected by the action? What is Berkman's purpose in undertaking this activity? (Challenge)

Ethical Issue

Betsy Ross Flag Company's long-term debt agreements make certain demands on the business. For example, Ross may not purchase treasury stock in excess of the balance of retained earnings. Also, long-term debt may not exceed stockholders' equity, and the current ratio may not fall below 1.50. If Ross fails to meet any of these requirements, the company's lenders have the authority to take over management of the company.

Changes in consumer demand have made it hard for Ross to attract customers. Current liabilities have mounted faster than current assets, causing the current ratio to fall to 1.47. Before releasing financial statements, Ross management is scrambling to improve the current ratio. The controller points out that an investment can be classified as either long-term or short-term, depending on management's intention. By deciding to convert an investment to cash within one year, Ross can classify the investment as short-term—a current asset. On the controller's recommendation, Ross's board of directors votes to reclassify long-term investments as short-term.

Requirements

1. What effect will reclassifying the investments have on the current ratio? Is Ross's true financial position stronger as a result of reclassifying the investments?

2. Shortly after the financial statements are released, sales improve; so, too, does the current ratio. As a result, Ross management decides not to sell the investments it had reclassified as short-term. Accordingly, the company reclassifies the investments as long-term. Has management behaved unethically? Give the reasoning underlying your answer.

Financial Statement Case

Analyzing a balance sheet and measuring profitability

Amazon.com's financial statements in Appendix A at the end of this book reveal some interesting relationships. Answer these questions about Amazon.com:

1. What is most unusual about the balance sheet?

2. Compute trend percentages for net sales and net income. Use 2003 as the base year. Which trend percentage looks strange? Explain your answer.

3. Compute inventory turnover for 2005 and 2004. The inventory balance at December 31, 2003, was $294 million. Do the trend of net income from 2004 to 2005 and the change in the rate of inventory turnover tell the same story or a different story? Explain your answer.

Team Projects

Project 1. Select an industry you are interested in, and use the leading company in that industry as the benchmark. Then select two other companies in the same industry. For each category of ratios in the Decision Guidelines on pp. 777–778, compute all the ratios for the three companies. Write a two-page report that compares the two companies with the benchmark company.

Project 2. Select a company and obtain its financial statements. Convert the income statement and the balance sheet to common size, and compare the company you selected to the industry average. The Risk Management Association's *Annual Statement Studies*, Dun & Bradstreet's *Industry Norms & Key Business Ratios*, and Prentice Hall's *Almanac of Business and Industrial Financial Ratios*, by Leo Troy, publish common-size statements for most industries.

For Internet exercises, Excel in Practice, and additional online activities, go to the Web site www.prenhall.com/horngren.

Quick Check Answers

1. *b*   2. *c*   3. *d*   4. *a*   5. *a*   6. *b*   7. *b*   8. *d*   9. *c*   10. *a*

Comprehensive Problem for Chapters 14 and 15

Analyzing a Company for Its Investment Potential

In its annual report, WRS Athletic Supply includes the following five-year financial summary. Analyze the company's financial summary for the fiscal years 2001 through 2005 to decide whether to invest in the common stock of WRS.

WRS ATHLETIC SUPPLY, INC.
5-Year Financial Summary (Partial; adapted)

(Dollar Amounts in Thousands Except per Share Data)	2005	2004	2003	2002	2001	2000
Net sales	$244,524	$217,799	$191,329	$165,013	$137,634	
Net sales increase	12%	14%	16%	20%	17%	
Domestic comparative store sales increase	5%	6%	5%	8%	9%	
Other income—net	2,001	1,873	1,787	1,615	1,391	
Cost of sales	191,838	171,562	150,255	129,664	108,725	
Operating, selling, and general and administrative expenses	41,043	36,173	31,550	27,040	22,363	
Interest costs:						
Debt	1,063	1,357	1,383	1,045	803	
Interest income	(138)	(171)	(188)	(204)	(189)	
Income tax expense	4,487	3,897	3,692	3,338	2,740	
Net income	8,039	6,671	6,295	5,377	4,430	
Per share of common stock:						
Net income	1.81	1.49	1.41	1.21	0.99	
Dividends	0.30	0.28	0.24	0.20	0.16	
Financial Position						
Current assets	$ 30,483	$ 27,878	$ 26,555	$ 24,356	$ 21,132	
Inventories at LIFO cost	24,891	22,614	21,442	19,793	17,076	$16,497
Net property, plant, and equipment	51,904	45,750	40,934	35,969	25,973	
Total assets	94,685	83,527	78,130	70,349	49,996	
Current liabilities	32,617	27,282	28,949	25,803	16,762	
Long-term debt	19,608	18,732	15,655	16,674	9,607	
Shareholders' equity	39,337	35,102	31,343	25,834	21,112	
Financial Ratios						
Current ratio	0.9	1.0	0.9	0.9	1.3	
Return on assets	9.2%	8.5%	8.7%	9.5%	9.6%	
Return on shareholders' equity	21.6%	20.1%	22.0%	22.9%	22.4%	

Include the following sections in your analysis, and fully explain your final decision.

1. Trend analysis for net sales and net income (use 2001 as the base year)
2. Profitability analysis
3. Measuring ability to sell inventory (WRS uses the LIFO method)
4. Measuring ability to pay debts
5. Measuring dividends

16 Introduction to Management Accounting

Learning Objectives

1. Distinguish management accounting from financial accounting

2. Identify trends in the business environment and the role of management accountability

3. Classify costs and prepare an income statement for a service company

4. Classify costs and prepare an income statement for a merchandising company

5. Classify costs and prepare an income statement for a manufacturing company

6. Use reasonable standards to make ethical judgments

You got a 40% discount on your new Regal sport boat, and you're relaxing after a day on the lake. As you sit there, you wonder how Regal was able to sell the boat at such a low price. Management accounting information helped Regal design the boat to maximize performance while holding down costs. Managing costs helps a company sell the right product for the right price.

Chapters 1 through 15 of this book laid your foundation in the building blocks of accounting:

- Accounts in the ledger for accumulating information
- Journals for recording transactions
- Financial statements for reporting operating results, financial position, and cash flows

What you've learned so far is called *financial accounting* because its main products are the financial statements.

This chapter shifts the focus to the accounting tools that managers use to run a business. As you can imagine, it's called *management accounting*. If you've ever dreamed of having your own business, you'll find management accounting fascinating.

As a college student, one of the authors of this book learned some of these tools in an accounting class. He then applied them to his father's laundry business. Dad quickly learned that some parts of the business weren't earning enough profit. The result? Dad closed a location, saved some energy, and kept the same level of income. Hopefully, you'll find management accounting equally helpful.

Before launching into how managers use accounting, let's see some of the groups to whom managers must answer. We call these groups the stakeholders of the company because each group has a stake in the business.

Management Accountability

Accountability is responsibility for one's actions. **Management accountability** is the manager's responsibility to the various stakeholders of the company. Many different stakeholders have an interest in an organization, as shown in Exhibit 16-1. Keep in mind that managers are merely the employees of the owners.

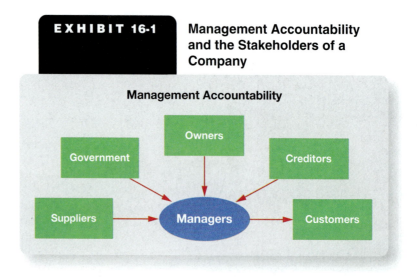

EXHIBIT 16-1 Management Accountability and the Stakeholders of a Company

Exhibit 16-2 shows the links between management and the various stakeholders of a company. The exhibit is organized by the three main categories of cash-flow activities: operating, investing, and financing. For each activity we list the stakeholders and what they provide to the organization. The far-right column then shows how managers are accountable to the stakeholders.

EXHIBIT 16-2 | Management Accountability to Stakeholders

Stakeholders	Provide and	Management is accountable for
Operating activities		
Suppliers	Products and services	Using the goods and services to earn a profit
Employees	Time and expertise	Providing a safe and productive work environment
Customers	Cash	Providing products and services for a reasonable price
Investing activities		
Suppliers	Long-term assets (equipment, buildings, land)	Purchasing the most productive assets
Financing activities		
Owners	Cash or other assets	Providing a return on the owners' investment
Creditors	Cash	Repaying principal and interest
Actions that affect society		
Governments	Permission to operate	Obeying laws and paying taxes
Communities	Human and physical resources	Providing jobs and operating in an ethical manner to support the community

To earn the stakeholders' trust, managers provide information about their decisions and the results of those decisions. Thus, management accountability requires two forms of accounting:

- Financial accounting for *external* reporting
- Management accounting for *internal* planning and control

This chapter launches your study of management accounting.

Distinguish management accounting from financial accounting

Financial accounting provides financial statements that report results of operations, financial position, and cash flows both to managers and to external stakeholders: owners, creditors, suppliers, customers, the government, and society. Financial accounting satisfies management's accountability to:

- Owners and creditors for their investment decisions
- Regulatory agencies, such as the Securities Exchange Commission, the Federal Trade Commission, and the Internal Revenue Service
- Customers and society to ensure that the company acts responsibly

The financial statements that you studied in chapters 1 through 15 report on the company as a whole.

Management accounting provides information to help managers plan and control operations as they lead the business. This includes managing the company's plant, equipment, and human resources. Management accounting often requires forward-looking information because of the futuristic nature of business decisions.

Managers are responsible to external stakeholders, so they must plan and control operations carefully.

- **Planning** means choosing goals and deciding how to achieve them. For example, a common goal is to increase operating income (profits). To achieve this goal, managers may raise selling prices or advertise more in the hope of increasing sales. The **budget** is a quantitative expression of the plan that managers use to coordinate the business's activities. The budget shows the expected financial impact of decisions and helps identify the resources needed to achieve goals.
- **Controlling** means implementing the plans and evaluating operations by comparing actual results to the budget. For example, managers can compare actual costs to budgeted costs to evaluate their performance. If actual costs fall below budgeted costs, that is good news. But if actual costs exceed the budget, managers may need to make changes. Cost data help managers make these types of decisions.

Exhibit 16-3 highlights the differences between management accounting and financial accounting. Both management accounting and financial accounting use the accrual basis of accounting. But management accounting is required to meet no external reporting requirements, such as generally accepted accounting principles. Therefore, managers have more leeway in preparing management accounting reports, as you can see in points 1 through 4 of the exhibit.

Managers tailor their management accounting system to help them make wise decisions. Managers weigh the *benefits* of the system (better information leads to higher profits) against the *costs* to develop and run the system. Weighing the costs against benefits is called **cost/benefit analysis**. To remain in service, a management accounting system's benefits must exceed its costs.

EXHIBIT 16-3 Management Accounting Versus Financial Accounting

	Management Accounting	Financial Accounting
1. Primary users	Internal—the company's managers	External—investors, creditors, and government authorities
2. Purpose of information	Help managers plan and control operations	Help investors and creditors make investment and credit decisions
3. Focus and time dimension of the information	Relevance of the information and focus on the future—example: 2009 budget prepared in 2008	Relevance and reliability of the information and focus on the past—example: 2009 actual performance reported in 2010
4. Type of report	Internal reports are restricted only by cost/benefit analysis; no audit required	Financial statements are restricted by GAAP and audited by independent CPAs
5. Scope of information	Detailed reports on parts of the company (products, departments, territories), often on a daily or weekly basis	Summary reports primarily on the company as a whole, usually on a quarterly or annual basis
6. Behavioral	Concern about how reports will affect employee behavior	Concern about adequacy of disclosures; behavioral implications are secondary

Point 5 indicates that management accounting provides more detailed and timely information than does financial accounting. On a day-to-day basis, managers identify ways to cut costs, set prices, and evaluate employee performance. Company Intranets and handheld computers provide this information with the click of a mouse.

Point 6 reminds us that management accounting reports affect people's behavior. "You get what you measure," so employees perform well on the parts of their jobs that the accounting system measures. For example, if a manufacturing company evaluates a plant manager based only on costs, the manager may use cheaper materials or hire less experienced workers. These actions will cut costs, but they can hurt profits if product quality drops and sales fall as a result. Therefore, managers must consider how their decisions will motivate company employees.

Today's Business Environment

Today's business environment affects everyone. Managers of both large corporations and mom-and-pop businesses must consider recent trends, such as the following.

2 Identify trends in the business environment and the role of management accountability.

- **Shift Toward a Service Economy** Service companies provide health-care, communication, banking, and other important benefits to society. FedEx, Google, and Citibank don't sell products; they sell their services. In the last century, many developed economies shifted their focus from manufacturing to service, and now service companies employ more than 55% of the workforce. The U.S. Census Bureau expects services, such as technology and health care, to grow especially fast.
- **Global Competition** To be competitive, many companies are moving operations to other countries to be closer to new markets. Other companies are partnering with foreign companies to meet local needs. For example, Ford, General Motors, and DaimlerChrysler all built plants in Brazil to feed Brazil's car-hungry middle class.
- **Time-Based Competition** The Internet, electronic commerce (e-commerce), and express delivery speed the pace of business. Customers who instant message around the world won't wait two weeks to receive DVDs purchased on Amazon.com. Time is the new competitive turf for world-class business. To compete, companies have developed the following:

    Advanced Information Systems Many companies use **enterprise resource planning (ERP) systems** to integrate all their worldwide functions, departments, and data. ERP systems help to streamline operations, and that enables companies to respond quickly to changes in the marketplace.

    E-Commerce Companies use the Internet in everyday operations of selling and customer service. For example, a sales clerk can sell to thousands of customers around the world by providing every product the company offers 24–7.

    Just-in-time Management Inventory held too long becomes obsolete. Storing goods takes space that costs money. The just-in-time philosophy helps managers cut costs by speeding the transformation of raw materials into finished products. **Just-in-time (JIT)** means producing *just in time* to satisfy needs. Ideally, suppliers deliver materials for today's production in exactly the right quantities *just in time* to begin production, and finished units are completed *just in time* for delivery to customers.

- **Total Quality Management** Companies must deliver high-quality goods and services to stay alive. **Total quality management (TQM)** is a philosophy designed to provide customers with superior products and services. Companies achieve this goal by continuously improving quality and reducing or eliminating defects and waste. In TQM, each business function sets higher and higher goals. With TQM, General Motors was able to cut warranty cost from $1,600 to $1,000 per vehicle.

Now let's see how different types of companies use management accounting.

- Service companies
- Merchandising companies
- Manufacturing companies

Service Companies, Merchandising Companies, and Manufacturing Companies

3 Classify costs and prepare an income statement for a service company

In this section we compare and contrast the accounting by three different types of businesses. We begin with service companies.

Service companies, such as eBay (online auction), H&R Block (tax-return preparation), and Randstad (temporary personnel services), sell services. As with other types of businesses, service companies seek to provide three things:

- Quality services
- At a reasonable price
- In a timely manner

Management is accountable to owners to generate a profit and provide a reasonable return on the owner's investment in the company.

Service companies have the simplest accounting. Service companies carry no inventories of products for sale. All of their costs are period costs. **Period costs** are those costs that are incurred and expensed in the same accounting period.

To illustrate the differences in accounting for service companies, merchandisers, and manufacturers, we use three separate companies:

- Service — Joe's Delivery Service delivers for Maria's Birthday Cakes.
- Merchandising — Maria's Birthday Cakes buys the cakes—ready for delivery—from Roberto's Bakery.
- Manufacturing — Roberto's Bakery makes the cakes for sale to Maria's.

We now take you through the accounting for these three businesses. Let's look first at Joe's Delivery Service. Joe Baca's college friend, Maria Schenk, started a business that delivers birthday cakes and a birthday card to college students. Maria's customers are the students' parents. For a small price, she delivers a cake and a birthday card, including the parents' signatures, to their student on his or her birthday. Maria pays Joe to deliver the cakes from her business to the student dorm rooms.

Here is the income statement for Joe's Delivery Service for the year ended December 31, 2009.

EXHIBIT 16-4 Income Statement for a Service Company

JOE'S DELIVERY SERVICE
Income Statement
Year Ended December 31, 2009

Service revenue	$ 36,000	100%
Expenses:		
Salary expense	15,000	42%
Fuel expense	3,000	8%
Depreciation expense—truck	6,000	17%
	24,000	67%
Operating income	$ 12,000	33%

The delivery service has no inventory, so Joe's income statement has no Cost of Goods Sold. The largest expense is for the salaries of drivers who deliver the birthday cakes. Salary expense eats up 42% of Joe's revenue. Joe's Delivery Service had a 33% profit margin for 2009.

Service companies need to know which services are most profitable, and that means evaluating both revenues and costs. Knowing the cost per service helps managers set the price of each service and then to calculate operating income. In 2009, Joe delivered 12,000 cakes. What is the cost per cake delivered? Use the following formula to calculate the unit cost for a service:

$$\text{Unit cost per service} = \text{Total service costs} \div \text{Total number of services provided}$$
$$= \$24{,}000 \div 12{,}000 \text{ cakes delivered} = \$2 \text{ per cake delivered}$$

Merchandising Companies

4 Classify costs and prepare an income statement for a merchandising company

Merchandising companies, such as Amazon.com, Wal-Mart, and Footlocker, resell products they buy from suppliers. Merchandisers keep an inventory of products, and managers are accountable for the purchasing, storage, and sale of the products.

In contrast with service companies, merchandisers' income statements report Cost of Goods Sold as the major expense. The cost-of-goods-sold section of the income statement shows the flow of the product costs through the inventory. These product costs are **inventoriable product costs** because the products are held in inventory until sold. For *external reporting*, Generally Accepted Accounting Principles (GAAP) require companies to treat inventoriable product costs as an asset until the product is sold, at which time the costs are expensed.

Merchandising companies' inventoriable product costs include *only* the goods' purchase cost plus freight in. The activity in the Inventory account provides the information for the cost-of-goods-sold section of the income statement as shown in the following formula:

Beginning Inventory + Purchases + Freight In − Ending Inventory = Cost of Goods Sold

To highlight the roles of beginning inventory, purchases, and ending inventory, we use the periodic inventory system. However, the concepts in this chapter apply equally to companies that use perpetual inventory systems.

In management accounting we distinguish inventoriable product costs from period costs. **Period costs** are those operating costs that are expensed in the period in which they are incurred. Therefore, period costs are the expenses that are not part of inventoriable product cost.

Let's continue with Maria Schenk's business. Exhibit 16-5 shows the income statement of Maria's Birthday Cakes for the year ended December 31, 2009.

The beginning inventory of cakes cost $300, which is the cost of the cakes still on hand at December 31, 2008. During 2009, Maria purchased additional cakes from Roberto's Bakery. The total cost to purchase and receive the cakes was $72,100. At the end of 2009, Maria's ending inventory included cakes costing $400. Of the $72,400 available for sale, the cost of cakes sold in 2009 was $72,000. Other operating expenses include the $36,000 paid to Joe's Delivery Service. This amount agrees to the service revenue shown on the income statement for Joe's Delivery Service (page 812).

Notice that cost of goods sold is 40% of sales. Managers watch the gross profit % (60% for Maria's) to make sure it doesn't change too much. A large decrease in the gross profit percentage may indicate that the company has a problem with inventory theft or shrinkage (waste). The company's profit margin is 21% for the year ended December 31, 2009.

EXHIBIT 16-5 | Income Statement for a Merchandising Company

MARIA'S BIRTHDAY CAKES
Income Statement
Year Ended December 31, 2009

Sales revenue		$180,000	100%
Cost of goods sold:			
Beginning inventory	$ 300		
Purchases and freight in	72,100		
Cost of goods available for sale	72,400		
Ending inventory	(400)		
Cost of goods sold		72,000	40%
Gross profit		108,000	60%
Operating expenses:			
Delivery expense	$36,000		20%
Advertising expense	18,000		10
Salary expense	10,000		6
Rent expense	6,000		3
Total operating expenses		70,000	39
Operating income		$ 38,000	21%

Merchandising companies need to know which products are most profitable. Knowing the unit cost per product helps managers set selling prices. During the year Maria sold 12,000 cakes. What is the cost of each cake she sold? Use the following formula to calculate the unit cost per cake:

Unit cost per cake = Total cost of goods sold ÷ Total number of cakes sold
                = $72,000 ÷ 12,000 = $6 per cake

Now practice what you've learned by solving Summary Problem 1.

Summary Problem 1

Jackson, Inc., a retail distributor of futons, provided the following information for 2009:

Merchandise inventory, January 1	$ 20,000
Merchandise inventory, December 31	30,000
Selling expense	50,000
Delivery expense	18,000
Purchases of futons	265,000
Rent expense	15,000
Utilities expense	3,000
Freight in	15,000
Administrative expense	64,000
Sales revenue	500,000
Units sold during the year	2,500 futons

Requirements
1. Calculate cost of goods sold. What is the cost per futon sold?
2. Calculate the total period costs.
3. Prepare Jackson, Inc.'s income statement for the year ended December 31, 2009. What is the gross profit percentage? The profit margin percentage?

Solution

1. Cost of goods sold = Beginning inventory + Purchases + Freight-in − Ending inventory
   $270,000 = $20,000 + $265,000 + $15,000 − $30,000

   The cost per futon sold = Cost of goods sold ÷ number of futons sold
   $108 = $270,000 ÷ 2,500 futons

2. Total period costs include all expenses not included in inventory:

Selling expense	$ 50,000
Delivery expense	18,000
Rent expense	15,000
Utilities expense	3,000
Administrative expense	64,000
Total period costs	$150,000

3. Income Statement

JACKSON, INC.
Income Statement
Year Ended December 31, 2009

Sales revenue		$500,000	100%
Cost of goods sold:			
Merchandise inventory, January 1	$ 20,000		
Purchases and freight in ($265,000 + $15,000)	280,000		
Cost of goods available for sale	300,000		
Merchandise inventory, December 31	30,000		
Cost of goods sold		270,000	54%
Gross profit		230,000	46%
Operating expenses:			
Administrative expense	$ 64,000		
Selling expense	50,000		
Delivery expense	18,000		
Rent expense	15,000		
Utilities expense	3,000	150,000	30%
Operating income		$ 80,000	16%

Gross profit % = $230,000 / $500,000 = 46%

Profit margin % = $80,000 / $500,000 = 16%

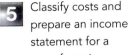

5 Classify costs and prepare an income statement for a manufacturing company

Manufacturing Companies

Manufacturing companies use labor, equipment, supplies, and facilities to convert raw materials into finished products. Managers in manufacturing companies must use these resources to create a product that customers want. They are responsible for generating profits and maintaining positive cash flows.

In contrast with service and merchandising companies, manufacturing companies have a broad range of production activities. That requires tracking costs in three kinds of inventory:

1. **Materials inventory:** *Raw materials used in making a product.* For example, a baker's raw materials include flour, sugar, and eggs. Materials to manufacture a boat include fiberglass, plywood, wiring, glass, and upholstery fabric.

2. **Work in process inventory:** *Goods that are in the manufacturing process but not yet complete.* Some production activities have transformed the raw materials, but the product is not yet ready for sale. A baker's work in process inventory includes dough ready for cooking. A boat manufacturer's work in process could include a hull without an engine or seats.

3. **Finished goods inventory:** *Completed goods that have not yet been sold.* Finished goods are the products that the manufacturer sells to a merchandiser (or to other customers).

Inventoriable Product Costs

The completed product in finished goods inventory is an **inventoriable product cost**. The inventoriable product cost includes three components of manufacturing costs:

- Direct materials
- Direct labor
- Manufacturing overhead

Direct materials and direct labor are examples of direct costs. A **direct cost** is a cost that can be directly traced to a cost object, such as a product. A **cost object** is anything for which managers want a separate measurement of cost. Managers may want to know the cost of a product or a department, a sales territory, or an activity. Costs that cannot be traced directly to a cost object are **indirect costs**. In manufacturing companies, product costs include direct costs (direct materials and direct labor) and indirect costs (manufacturing overhead).

- **Direct materials** become a physical part of the finished product. The cost of direct materials (purchase cost plus freight in) can be traced directly to the finished product.
- **Direct labor** is the labor of employees who convert materials into the company's products. The cost of direct labor can be traced *directly* to the finished products.
- **Manufacturing overhead** includes all manufacturing costs other than direct materials and direct labor. These costs are created by all of the supporting production activities, including storing materials, setting up machines, and cleaning the work areas. These activities incur costs of indirect materials, indirect labor, repair and maintenance, utilities, rent, insurance, property taxes, and depreciation on manufacturing plant buildings and equipment. Manufacturing overhead is also called **factory overhead** or **indirect manufacturing cost**.

Exhibit 16-6 summarizes a manufacturer's inventoriable product costs.

> **EXHIBIT 16-6** Manufacturer's Inventoriable Product Costs

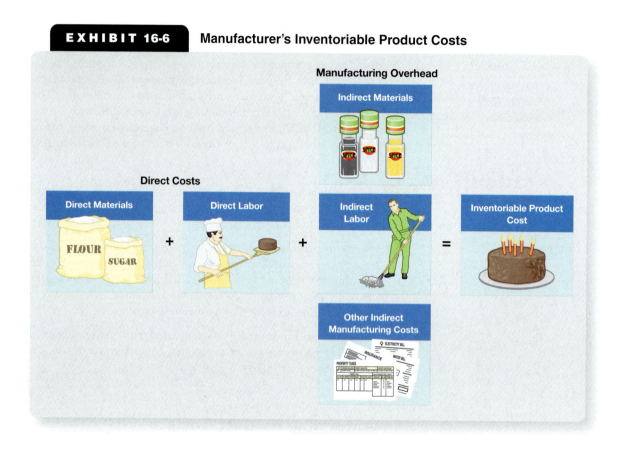

A Closer Look at Manufacturing Overhead

- *Manufacturing overhead includes only those indirect costs that are related to the manufacturing operation.* Insurance and depreciation on the *manufacturing plant's* building and equipment are indirect manufacturing costs, so they are part of manufacturing overhead. In contrast, depreciation on *delivery trucks* is not part of manufacturing overhead. Instead, depreciation on delivery trucks is a cost of moving the product to the customer. Its cost is delivery expense (a period cost), not an inventoriable product cost. Similarly, the cost of auto insurance for the sales force is marketing expense (a period cost), not manufacturing overhead.
- *Manufacturing overhead includes indirect materials and indirect labor.* The spices used in cakes become physical parts of the finished product. But these costs are minor compared with flour and sugar for the cake. Since those low-priced materials' costs can't conveniently be traced to a particular cake, these costs are called **indirect materials** and become part of manufacturing overhead.

  Like indirect materials, **indirect labor** is difficult to trace to specific products so it is part of manufacturing overhead. Examples include the pay of forklift operators, janitors, and plant managers.

Now let's look at the income statement for Roberto's Bakery for the year ended December 31, 2009, given in Exhibit 16-7. Roberto's only customer is Maria Schenk, who buys the birthday cakes and then delivers them to students.

Roberto's cost of goods sold represents 61% of his sales revenue. This is the inventoriable product cost of the goods that Roberto sold to Maria's Birthday Cakes. Roberto's balance sheet at December 31, 2009, reports the inventoriable product costs of the finished birthday cakes that are still on hand at the end of that year. The cost of the ending inventory ($600) will become the beginning inventory of

EXHIBIT 16-7 | Income Statement for a Manufacturing Company

ROBERTO'S BAKERY
Income Statement
Year Ended December 31, 2009

Sales revenue		$60,000	100%
Cost of goods sold:			
Beginning finished goods inventory	$ 300		
Cost of goods manufactured*	36,900		
Cost of goods available for sale	37,200		
Ending finished goods inventory	(600)		
Cost of goods sold		36,600	61%
Gross profit		23,400	39%
Operating expenses:			
Salary expense	$ 3,000		
Depreciation expense	400	3,400	6%
Operating income		$20,000	33%

*From the Schedule of Cost of Goods Manufactured in Exhibit 16-10.

next year and will then be included as part of the Cost of Goods Sold on Roberto's income statement next year. The operating expenses, which represent 6% of sales revenue, are period costs.

Exhibit 16-8 summarizes the differences between inventoriable product costs and period costs for service, merchandising, and manufacturing companies.

EXHIBIT 16-8 | Inventoriable Product Costs and Period Costs for Service, Merchandising, and Manufacturing Companies

Type of Company	Inventoriable Product Costs—Initially an asset (Inventory), and expensed (Cost of Goods Sold) when the inventory is sold	Period Costs—Expensed in the period incurred; never considered an asset
Service company	None	Salaries, depreciation, utilities, insurance, property taxes, advertising expenses
Merchandising company	Purchases plus freight in	Salaries, depreciation, utilities, insurance, property taxes, advertising, delivery expenses
Manufacturing company	Direct materials, direct labor, and manufacturing overhead (including indirect materials; indirect labor; depreciation on the manufacturing plant and equipment; plant insurance, utilities, and property taxes)	Delivery expense; depreciation expense, utilities, insurance, and property taxes on executive headquarters (separate from the manufacturing plant); advertising; CEO's salary

Let's compare Roberto's income statement in Exhibit 16-7 with Maria's income statement in Exhibit 16-5. The only difference is that the merchandiser (Maria) uses *purchases* in computing cost of goods sold, while the manufacturer (Roberto's) uses the *cost of goods manufactured*. Notice that the term **cost of goods manufactured** is in the past tense. It is the manufacturing cost of the goods that Roberto's *completed during 2009*. Here's the difference between a manufacturer and a merchandiser:

- The manufacturer *made* the product that it later sold.
- The merchandiser *purchased* a pre-manufactured product that was complete and ready for sale.

CALCULATING THE COST OF GOODS MANUFACTURED The cost of goods manufactured summarizes the activities and the costs that take place in a manufacturing plant over the period. Let's begin by reviewing these activities. Exhibit 16-9 reminds us that the manufacturer starts by buying materials. Then the manufacturer uses direct labor and manufacturing plant and equipment (overhead) to transform these materials into work in process inventory. When inventory is completed, it becomes finished goods inventory. These are all inventoriable product costs because they are related to the inventory production process.

EXHIBIT 16-9 Manufacturing Company: Inventoriable Product Costs and Period Costs

Balance Sheet

Inventoriable Product Costs:
- Purchases of Materials plus Freight in → Materials Inventory
- Direct labor
- Manufacturing Overhead*

Materials Inventory → Work in Process Inventory → Finished Goods Inventory

Income Statement

Sales Revenue
minus
when sales occur → Cost of Goods Sold (an expense)
equals Gross Profit
minus

Operating Expenses (Period Costs):
- R&D Expense
- Sales Salary Expense
- Depreciation Expense on Salespersons' Cars
- Delivery Expense
- Warranty Expense

equals Operating Income

*Examples: Indirect labor, plant supplies, plant insurance, and depreciation. When insurance and depreciation relate to manufacturing, they are inventoriable; when they relate to nonmanufacturing functions, they are operating expenses (period costs).

Finished goods are the only category of inventory that's ready to sell. The cost of the finished goods that the manufacturer sells becomes its cost of goods sold on the income statement. Costs the manufacturer incurs in nonmanufacturing activities, such as sales salaries, are operating expenses—period costs—that are expensed in the period incurred. Exhibit 16-9 shows that these operating costs are deducted from gross profit to compute operating income.

You now have a clear understanding of the flow of activities and costs in the plant, and you're ready to figure the cost of goods manufactured. Exhibit 16-10 shows how Roberto's computes its cost of goods manufactured. This is the cost of the 12,300 cakes that Roberto *finished* during 2009.

Cost of goods manufactured summarizes the activities and related costs incurred to produce inventory during the year. As of December 31, 2008, Roberto had spent a

EXHIBIT 16-10 | Schedule of Cost of Goods Manufactured

ROBERTO'S BAKERY
Schedule of Cost of Goods Manufactured
Year Ended December 31, 2009

Beginning work in process inventory			$ 800
Add: Direct materials used			
Beginning materials inventory	$ 150		
Purchases of direct materials plus freight in	10,800		
Available for use	10,950		
Ending materials inventory	(50)		
Direct materials used		$10,900	
Direct labor		12,100	
Manufacturing overhead:			
Indirect materials	$3,600		
Indirect labor	3,000		
Depreciation—plant and equipment	6,000		
Plant utilities, insurance, and property taxes	600		
		13,200	
Total manufacturing costs incurred during year			36,200
Total manufacturing costs to account for			37,000
Less: Ending work in process inventory			(100)
Costs of goods manufactured			$36,900

total of $800 to partially complete the cakes still being made. This 2008 ending work in process inventory became the beginning work in process inventory for 2009.

Exhibit 16-10 shows that during the year, Roberto's Bakery used $10,900 of direct materials, $12,100 of direct labor, and $13,200 of manufacturing overhead.

Total manufacturing costs incurred during the year are the sum of these three amounts:

TOTAL MANUFACTURING COSTS	
Direct materials used	$10,900
Direct labor	12,100
Manufacturing overhead	13,200
Total manufacturing costs incurred...........	$36,200

Adding total manufacturing cost ($36,200) to the beginning Work in Process Inventory of $800 gives the total manufacturing cost to account for, $37,000. At December 31, 2009, unfinished cakes costing only $100 remained in Work in Process (WIP) Inventory. The bakery finished 12,300 cakes and sent them to Finished Goods (FG) Inventory. Cost of goods manufactured for the year was $36,900. Here's the computation of cost of goods manufactured:

Beginning + Direct materials + Direct labor + Manufacturing − Ending = Cost of goods
WIP   used   overhead   WIP   manufactured

$800   + $10,900   + $12,100   + $13,200   − $100   = $36,900

FLOW OF COSTS THROUGH THE INVENTORY ACCOUNTS Exhibit 16-11 diagrams the flow of costs through Roberto's inventory accounts. The format is the same for all three stages:

- Direct materials
- Work in process
- Finished goods

The final amount at each stage flows into the next stage. Take time to see how the schedule of cost of goods manufactured in Exhibit 16-11 uses the flows of the direct materials and work in process stages. Then examine the income statement for Maria's Birthday Cakes in Exhibit 16-5. Maria, the merchandiser, uses only a single Inventory account.

EXHIBIT 16-11   Flow of Costs Through a Manufacturer's Inventory Accounts

Direct Materials Inventory		Work in Process Inventory		Finished Goods Inventory	
Beginning inventory	$ 150	Beginning inventory	$ 800	Beginning inventory	$ 300
+ Purchases and freight in	10,800	+ Direct materials used	$10,900	+ Cost of goods manufactured	36,900
		+ Direct labor	12,100		
		+ Manufacturing overhead	13,200		
		Total manufacturing costs incurred during the year	36,200		
= Direct materials available for use	10,950	= Total manufacturing costs to account for	37,000	= Cost of goods available for sale	37,200
− Ending inventory	(50)	− Ending inventory	(100)	− Ending inventory	(600)
= Direct materials used	$10,900	= Cost of goods manufactured	$36,900	= Cost of goods sold	$36,600

Source: The authors are indebted to Judith Cassidy for this presentation.

Calculating Unit Product Cost

Manufacturing companies need to know which products are most profitable. Knowing the unit product cost helps managers decide on the prices to charge for each product. They can then measure operating income and determine the cost of finished goods inventory. Roberto produced 12,300 cakes during 2009. What did it cost Roberto to make each cake?

Unit product cost = Cost of goods manufactured ÷ Total units produced
= $36,900 ÷ 12,300 cakes = $3 per cake

During 2009, Roberto sold 12,200 cakes, and he knows each cake cost $3 to produce. With this information Roberto can compute his cost of goods sold as a manager would, as follows:

$$\text{Cost of goods sold} = \text{Number of units sold} \times \text{Unit product cost}$$
$$= 12,200 \times \$3 = \$36,600$$

Ethical Standards

 Use reasonable standards to make ethical judgments

The WorldCom and Enron scandals underscore that ethical behavior is a critical component of quality. Unfortunately, the ethical path is not always clear. You may want to act ethically and do the right thing, but the consequences can make it difficult to decide what to do. Consider the following examples:

- Sarah Baker is examining the expense reports of her staff, who counted inventory at Top-Flight's warehouses in Arizona. She discovers that Mike Flinders has claimed travel expenses of $1,000 for hotel bills. Flinders could not show the paid receipts. Another staff member, who also claimed $1,000, did attach hotel receipts. When asked about the receipt, Mike admits that he stayed with an old friend, not in the hotel, but he believes he deserves the money he saved. After all, the company would have paid his hotel bill.
- As the accountant of Casey Computer Co., you are aware of Casey's weak financial condition. Casey is close to signing a lucrative contract that should ensure its future. To do so, the controller states that the company *must* report a profit this year. He suggests: "Two customers have placed orders that are to be shipped in early January. Ask production to fill and ship those orders on December 31, so we can record them in this year's sales."

These situations pose ethical challenges for a manager. The Institute of Management Accountants (IMA) has developed standards to help management accountants meet the ethical challenge. The IMA standards remind us that society expects professional accountants to exhibit the highest level of ethical behavior. An excerpt from the *Standards of Ethical Conduct for Management Accountants* appears in Exhibit 16-12. These standards require management accountants to:

- Maintain their professional competence
- Preserve the confidentiality of the information they handle
- Act with integrity and objectivity

EXHIBIT 16-12   **IMA Standards of Ethical Conduct for Management Accountants (excerpt)**

Management accountants have an obligation to maintain the highest standards of ethical conduct. These standards include the following:

Competence
- Maintain professional competence by ongoing development of knowledge and skills
- Perform professional duties in accordance with relevant laws, regulations, and technical standards

Confidentiality
- Refrain from disclosing confidential information acquired in the course of work except when authorized, unless legally obligated to do so

Integrity
- Avoid actual or apparent conflicts of interest and advise all appropriate parties of any potential conflict
- Refuse any gift, favor, or hospitality that would influence or would appear to influence actions
- Communicate unfavorable as well as favorable information and professional judgments or opinions

Objectivity
- Communicate information fairly and objectively

Source: Adapted from Institute of Management Accountants, *Standards of Ethical Conduct for Management Accountants* (Montvale, N.J.).

To resolve ethical dilemmas, the IMA also suggests discussing ethical situations with your immediate supervisor, or with an objective adviser.

Let's return to the two ethical dilemmas. By asking to be reimbursed for hotel expenses he did not incur, Mike Flinders violated the IMA's integrity standards (conflict of interest in which he tried to enrich himself at the company's expense). Because Sarah Baker discovered the inflated expense report, she would not be fulfilling her ethical responsibilities (integrity and objectivity) if she allowed the reimbursement and did not take disciplinary action.

The second dilemma, in which the controller asked you to accelerate the shipments, is less clear-cut. You should discuss the available alternatives and their consequences with others. Many people believe that following the controller's suggestion to manipulate the company's income would violate the standards of competence, integrity, and objectivity. Others would argue that because Casy Computer already has the customer order, shipping the goods and recording the sale in December is still ethical behavior. If you refuse to ship the goods in December and you simply resign without attempting to find an alternative solution, you might only hurt yourself and your family.

Decision Guidelines

BUILDING BLOCKS OF MANAGEMENT ACCOUNTING

Hewlett-Packard (HP) engages in *manufacturing* when it assembles its computers, *merchandising* when it sells them on its Web site, and support *services* such as start-up and implementation services. HP had to make the following decisions in designing its management accounting system to provide managers with the information they need to run the manufacturing, merchandising, and service operations efficiently and effectively.

Decision	Guidelines
What information should management accountants provide? What is the primary focus of management accounting?	Management accounting provides information that helps managers make better decisions; it has a • Focus on *relevance* to business decisions • *Future* orientation
How do you decide on a company's management accounting system, which is not regulated by GAAP?	Use cost/benefit analysis: Design the management accounting system so that benefits (from helping managers make wise decisions) outweigh the costs of the system.

How do you distinguish among service, merchandising, and manufacturing companies? How do their balance sheets differ?	*Service companies:*
	• Provide customers with intangible services
	• Have no inventories on the balance sheet
	
	Merchandising companies:
	• Resell tangible products purchased ready-made from suppliers
	• Have only one category of inventory
	
	Manufacturing companies:
	• Use labor, plant, and equipment to transform raw materials into new finished products
	• Have three categories of inventory:
	    Materials inventory
	    Work in process inventory
	    Finished goods inventory

How do you compute cost of goods sold?	• *Service companies:* No cost of goods sold, because they don't sell tangible goods
	• *Merchandising companies:*
	    Beginning *merchandise* inventory
	    + Purchases and freight in
	    − Ending *merchandise* inventory
	    = Cost of goods sold
	• *Manufacturing companies:*
	    Beginning *finished goods* inventory
	    + Cost of goods manufactured
	    − Ending *finished goods* inventory
	    = Cost of goods sold

Decision	Guidelines
How do you compute the cost of goods manufactured for a manufacturer?	Beginning *work in process* inventory + Current period manufacturing costs (direct materials used + direct labor + manufacturing overhead) − Ending *work in process* inventory = Cost of goods manufactured
Which costs are initially treated as assets for external reporting? When are these costs expensed?	*Inventoriable product costs* are initially treated as assets (Inventory); these costs are expensed (as Cost of Goods Sold) when the products are sold.
What costs are inventoriable under GAAP?	• *Service companies:* No inventoriable product costs • *Merchandising companies:* Purchases and freight in • *Manufacturing companies:* Direct materials used, direct labor, and manufacturing overhead
Which costs are never inventoriable product costs?	Period costs. These are never assets. They're always expenses.

Summary Problem 2

Requirements

1. For a manufacturing company, identify the following as either an inventoriable product cost or a period cost:
    a. Depreciation on plant equipment
    b. Depreciation on salespersons' automobiles
    c. Insurance on plant building
    d. Marketing manager's salary
    e. Raw materials
    f. Manufacturing overhead
    g. Electricity bill for home office
    h. Production employee wages

2. Show how to compute cost of goods manufactured. Use the following amounts: direct materials used ($24,000); direct labor ($9,000); manufacturing overhead ($17,000); beginning work in process inventory ($5,000); and ending work in process inventory ($4,000).

Solution

1. Inventoriable product cost: a, c, e, f, h
   Period cost: b, d, g

2. Cost of goods manufactured:

Beginning work in process inventory................................		$ 5,000
Add: Direct materials used...................................	$24,000	
Direct labor..	9,000	
Manufacturing overhead............................	17,000	
Total manufacturing costs incurred during the period ..		50,000
Total manufacturing costs to account for............................		55,000
Less: Ending work in process inventory		(4,000)
Cost of goods manufactured		$51,000

Review Introduction to Management Accounting

Accounting Vocabulary

Controlling
Implementing plans and evaluating the results of business operations by comparing the actual results to the budget.

Cost/Benefit Analysis
Weighing costs against benefits to help make decisions.

Cost Object
Anything for which managers want a separate measurement of cost.

Cost of Goods Manufactured
The manufacturing or plant-related costs of the goods that finished the production process this period.

Direct Cost
A cost that can be traced to a cost object.

Direct Labor
The compensation of employees who physically convert materials into finished products.

Direct Materials
Materials that become a physical part of a finished product and whose costs are traceable to the finished product.

Enterprise Resource Planning (ERP)
Software systems that can integrate all of a company's worldwide functions, departments, and data into a single system.

Factory Overhead
All manufacturing costs other than direct materials and direct labor. Also called **manufacturing overhead** or **indirect manufacturing costs**.

Finished Goods Inventory
Completed goods that have not yet been sold.

Indirect Cost
A cost that cannot be traced to a cost object.

Indirect Labor
Labor costs that are difficult to trace to specific products.

Indirect Manufacturing Cost
All manufacturing costs other than direct materials and direct labor. Also called **factory overhead** or **manufacturing overhead**.

Indirect Materials
Materials whose costs cannot conveniently be directly traced to particular finished products.

Inventoriable Product Costs
All costs of a product that GAAP requires companies to treat as an asset for external financial reporting. These costs are not expensed until the product is sold.

Just-in-Time (JIT)
A system in which a company produces just in time to satisfy needs. Suppliers deliver materials just in time to begin production and finished units are completed just in time for delivery to the customer.

Management Accountability
The manager's fiduciary responsibility to manage the resources of an organization.

Management Accounting
The branch of accounting that focuses on information for internal decision makers of a business.

Manufacturing Company
A company that uses labor, plant, and equipment to convert raw materials into new finished products.

Manufacturing Overhead
All manufacturing costs other than direct materials and direct labor. Also called **factory overhead** or **indirect manufacturing costs**.

Materials Inventory
Raw materials for use in manufacturing.

Merchandising Company
A company that resells products previously bought from suppliers.

Period Costs
Operating costs that are expensed in the period in which they are incurred.

Planning
Choosing goals and deciding how to achieve them.

Service Company
A company that sells intangible services, rather than tangible products.

Total Manufacturing Costs
Costs that include direct materials, direct labor, and manufacturing overhead.

Total Quality Management (TQM)
A philosophy of delighting customers by providing them with superior products and services. Requires improving quality and eliminating defects and waste throughout the value chain.

Work in Process Inventory
Goods that are partway through the manufacturing process but not yet complete.

Quick Check

1. Which is *not* a characteristic of management accounting information?
   a. Emphasizes the external financial statements
   b. Focuses on the future
   c. Provides detailed information about individual parts of the company
   d. Emphasizes relevance

2. World-class businesses must compete based on time. To compete effectively many companies have developed
   a. Enterprise resource planning
   b. Cost standards
   c. Just-in-time management
   d. All of the above

3. Today's business environment is characterized by
   a. Shift toward a service economy
   b. Global competition
   c. Time-based competition
   d. All of the above

4. Which account does PepsiCo, but not FedEx (a service company) have?
   a. Advertising expense
   b. Cost of goods sold
   c. Salary payable
   d. Retained earnings

5. Which is a direct cost of manufacturing a sportboat?
   a. Cost of boat engine
   b. Depreciation on plant and equipment
   c. Salary of engineer who rearranges plant layout
   d. Cost of customer hotline

6. Which of the following is *not* part of manufacturing overhead for producing a computer?
   a. Insurance on plant and equipment
   b. Manufacturing plant property taxes
   c. Depreciation on delivery trucks
   d. Manufacturing plant utilities

7. In computing cost of goods sold, which of the following is the manufacturer's counterpart to the merchandiser's purchases?
   a. Direct materials used
   b. Cost of goods manufactured
   c. Total manufacturing costs to account for
   d. Total manufacturing costs incurred during the period

Questions 8 and 9 use the data that follow. Suppose a bakery reports this information (in thousands of dollars):

Beginning materials inventory	$ 6
Ending materials inventory	5
Beginning work in process inventory	2
Ending work in process inventory	1
Beginning finished goods inventory	3
Ending finished goods inventory	5
Direct labor	30
Purchases of direct materials	100
Manufacturing overhead	20

8. If the cost of direct materials used is $101, what is cost of goods manufactured?
    a. $152
    b. $151
    c. $150
    d. $149

9. If the cost of goods manufactured is $152, what is cost of goods sold?
    a. $154
    b. $153
    c. $152
    d. $150

10. A management accountant who avoids conflicts of interest meets the ethical standard of
    a. Objectivity
    b. Confidentiality
    c. Competence
    d. Integrity

Answers are given after Apply Your Knowledge (p. 849).

Assess Your Progress

Short Exercises

Business trends terminology

S16-1 Match the term with the definition below. (pp. 828–829)

a. ERP
b. Just-in-time (JIT)
c. E-commerce
d. Total quality management

_____ 1. A philosophy of delighting customers by providing them with superior products and services. Requires improving quality and eliminating defects and waste.

_____ 2. Use of the Internet for such business functions as sales and customer service. Enables companies to reach thousands of customers around the world.

_____ 3. Software systems that integrate all of a company's worldwide functions, departments, and data into a single system.

_____ 4. A system in which a company produces just in time to satisfy needs. Suppliers deliver materials just in time to begin production, and finished units are completed just in time for delivery to customers.

Management accountability and the stakeholders

S16-2 Management has the responsibility to manage the resources of an organization in a responsible manner. For each of the following management responsibilities, indicate the primary stakeholder group to whom management is responsible. In the space provided, write the letter corresponding to the appropriate stakeholder group. (pp. 808–810).

_____ 1. Providing high-quality, reliable products/services for a reasonable price in a timely manner

_____ 2. Paying taxes in a timely manner

_____ 3. Providing a safe, productive work environment

_____ 4. Generating a profit

_____ 5. Repaying principal plus interest in a timely manner

a. Owners
b. Creditors
c. Suppliers
d. Employees
e. Customers
f. Government
g. Community

Management accounting vs. financial accounting

S16-3 For each of the following, indicate whether the statement relates to management accounting (MA) or financial accounting (FA): (pp. 809–810)

_____ 1. Helps investors make investment decisions

_____ 2. Provides detailed reports on parts of the company

_____ 3. Helps in planning and controlling operations

_____ 4. Reports can influence employee behavior

continued . . .

_____ 5. Reports must following Generally Accepted Accounting Principles (GAAP)

_____ 6. Reports audited annually by independent certified public accountants

Calculating income and cost per unit for a service organization

S16-4 Duncan and Noble provides hair cutting services in the local community. In August, Carol Duncan, the owner, incurred the following operating costs to cut the hair of 200 clients:

Hair supplies expense....................	$ 700
Building rent expense	1,100
Utilities	150
Depreciation on equipment	50

Duncan and Noble earned $5,000 in revenues from haircuts for the month of August. What is the net operating income for the month? What is the cost of one haircut? (pp. 811–813)

Computing cost of goods sold

S16-5 The Glass Doctor, a retail merchandiser of auto windshields, has the following information.

Web site maintenance	$ 7,000
Delivery expenses	1,000
Freight in	3,000
Purchases.................................	40,000
Ending inventory	5,000
Revenues	60,000
Marketing expenses.................	10,000
Beginning inventory................	8,000

Compute The Glass Doctor's cost of goods sold. (pp. 813–814)

Computing cost of goods sold

S16-6 Compute the missing amounts.

	Company A	Company B
Sales..	$100,000	(d)
Cost of goods sold		
Beginning inventory.............................	(a)	$ 30,000
Purchases and freight in........................	59,000	(e)
Cost of goods available for sale	(b)	90,000
Ending inventory	2,000	2,000
Cost of goods sold................................	60,000	(f)
Gross margin...	$ 40,000	$112,000
Selling and administrative expenses.........	(c)	85,000
Operating income....................................	$ 12,000	(g)

Match type of company with product and period costs

S16-7 For each of the following costs, indicate if the cost would be found on the income statement of a service company (S), a merchandising company (Mer), and/or a manufacturing company (Man). Some costs can be found on the income statements of more than one type of company. (pp. 811–822)

<u>S, Mer, Man</u> Example: Advertising costs

_____ 1. Cost of goods manufactured
_____ 2. The CEO's salary
_____ 3. Cost of goods sold
_____ 4. Building rent expense
_____ 5. Customer service expense

Computing direct materials used

S16-8 You are a new accounting intern at Cookies By Design. Your boss gives you the following information:

Purchases of direct materials	$6,500
Freight in	200
Property taxes	1,000
Ending inventory of direct materials	1,500
Beginning inventory of direct materials	4,000

Compute direct materials used. (p. 815)

Distinguishing between direct and indirect costs

S16-9 Consider Hallmark Cards' manufacturing plant. Match one of the following terms with each example of a manufacturing cost given below:

1. Direct materials
2. Direct labor
3. Indirect materials
4. Indirect labor
5. Other manufacturing overhead

Examples of manufacturing costs: (p. 818)

_____ a. Artists' wages
_____ b. Wages of warehouse workers
_____ c. Paper
_____ d. Depreciation on equipment
_____ e. Manufacturing plant manager's salary
_____ f. Property taxes on manufacturing plant
_____ g. Glue for envelopes

Computing manufacturing overhead

S16-10 Polo Company manufactures sunglasses. Suppose the company's March records include the following items.

Glue for frames	$ 250	Company president's salary	$25,000
Depreciation expense on company cars used by sales force	3,000	Plant foreman's salary	4,000
		Plant janitor's wages	1,000
Plant depreciation expense	7,000	Oil for manufacturing equipment	50
Interest expense	2,000	Lenses	50,000

continued ...

List the items and amounts that are manufacturing overhead costs. Calculate Polo's total manufacturing overhead cost in March. (pp. 821–822)

Compute cost of goods manufactured

S16-11 Max-Fli Golf Company had the following inventory data for the year ended December 31, 2008:

Direct materials used	$12,000
Manufacturing overhead	18,000
Work in process inventory:	
Beginning	7,000
Ending	5,000
Direct labor	9,000
Finished goods inventory	10,000

Compute Max-Fli's cost of goods manufactured for 2008. (pp. 821–822)

Inventoriable product costs vs. period costs

S16-12 Classify each of a paper manufacturer's costs as an inventoriable product cost or a period cost: (pp. 815–821)

a. Salaries of scientists studying ways to speed forest growth
b. Cost of computer software to track inventory
c. Cost of electricity at a paper mill
d. Salaries of the company's top executives
e. Cost of chemicals to treat paper
f. Cost of TV ads
g. Depreciation on the gypsum board plant
h. Cost of lumber to be cut into boards
i. Life insurance on CEO

Ethical decisions

S16-13 The Institute of Management Accountants' *Standards of Ethical Conduct for Management Accountants* (Exhibit 16-12, page 823) require management accountants to meet standards regarding:

- Competence
- Confidentiality
- Integrity
- Objectivity

Consider the following situations. Which guidelines are violated in each situation? (pp. 823–824)

a. You tell your brother that your company will report earnings significantly above financial analysts' estimates.
b. You see that others take home office supplies for personal use. As an intern, you do the same thing, assuming that this is a "perk."
c. At a conference on e-commerce, you skip the afternoon session and go sightseeing.
d. You failed to read the detailed specifications of a new general ledger package that you asked your company to purchase. After it is

continued . . .

installed, you are surprised that it is incompatible with some of your company's older accounting software.

e. You do not provide top management with the detailed job descriptions they requested because you fear they may use this information to cut a position from your department.

Exercises

Understanding today's business environment

E16-14 Complete the following statements with one of the terms listed here.

E-commerce	Just-in-time (JIT) manufacturing
Enterprise Resource Planning (ERP)	Total quality management (TQM)

a. _____ is a management philosophy that focuses on producing products as needed by the customer.
b. The goal of _____ is to please customers by providing them with superior products and services by eliminating defects and waste.
c. _____ can integrate all of a company's worldwide functions, departments, and data.
d. Firms adopt _____ to conduct business on the Internet.

Management vs. financial accounting and managers' use of information

E16-15 Complete the following statements with one of the terms listed here. You may use a term more than once, and some terms may not be used at all. (p. 809)

Budget	Creditors	Managers	Planning
Controlling	Financial accounting	Management accounting	Shareholders

a. Companies must follow GAAP in their _____ systems.
b. Financial accounting develops reports for external parties, such as _____ and _____.
c. When managers compare the company's actual results to the plan, they are performing the _____ role of management.
d. _____ are decision makers inside a company.
e. _____ provides information on a company's past performance.
f. _____ systems are not restricted by GAAP but are chosen by comparing the costs versus the benefits of the system.
g. Choosing goals and the means to achieve them is the _____ function of management.

Calculating income and cost per unit for a service company

E16-16 Fido Grooming provides grooming services in the local community. In July, John Conway, owner, incurred the following operating costs to groom 600 dogs:

Wages..	$4,800
Grooming supplies expense.............	1,200
Building rent expense......................	1,000
Utilities	250
Depreciation on equipment.............	100

continued ...

Fido Grooming earned $15,000 in revenues from grooming for the month of July.

Requirement

What is Fido's net operating income for July? What is the cost to groom one dog? (pp. 812–813)

Preparing an income statement and computing the unit cost for a service company

E16-17 Gloria's Grooming is a competitor of Fido Grooming. Gloria Stanley, owner, incurred the following operating costs to groom 2,000 dogs for the first quarter of 2009 (January, February, and March):

Wages	$16,000
Grooming supplies expense	4,000
Building rent expense	2,500
Utilities	1,000
Depreciation on furniture and equipment	500

Gloria's Grooming earned $45,000 in revenues for the first quarter of 2009.

Requirements

1. Prepare an income statement for the first quarter of 2009. Compute the ratio of operating expense to total revenue and operating income to total revenue. (pp. 812–813)
2. Compute Gloria's unit cost to groom one dog. (pp. 813–814)

Preparing an income statement and computing the unit cost for a merchandising company

E16-18 Kingston Brush Company sells standard hair brushes. The following information summarizes Kingston's operating activities for 2009:

Selling and administrative expenses	$ 45,000
Purchases	63,000
Sales revenue	125,000
Merchandise inventory, January 1, 2009	7,000
Merchandise inventory, December 31, 2009	5,000

Requirements

1. Prepare an income statement for 2009. Compute the ratio of operating expense to total revenue and operating income to total revenue. (pp. 813–814)
2. Kingston sold 5,800 brushes in 2009. Compute the unit cost for one brush. (pp. 813–814)

Service, merchandising, and manufacturing companies and their inventories

E16-19 Complete the following statements with one of the terms listed here. You may use a term more than once, and some terms may not be used at all. (pp. 812–817)

Finished goods inventory	Merchandise inventory	Service companies
Manufacturing companies	Merchandising companies	Work in process inventory
Materials inventory		

continued . . .

Introduction to Management Accounting **837**

a. _____ produce their own inventory.
b. _____ typically have a single category of inventory.
c. _____ do not have tangible products intended for sale.
d. _____ resell products they previously purchased ready-made from suppliers.
e. _____ use their workforce and equipment to transform raw materials into new finished products.
f. Swaim, a company based in North Carolina, makes furniture. Partially completed sofas are _____. Completed sofas that remain unsold in the warehouse are _____. Fabric and wood are _____.
g. For Kellogg's, corn, cardboard boxes, and waxed-paper liners are classified as _____.

Cost terminology

3 4 5

E16-20 Match one of the following terms with each definition below. (pp. 817–818)

a. Direct labor
b. Direct materials
c. Indirect labor
d. Indirect materials
e. Inventoriable product costs
f. Manufacturing overhead
g. Period costs

_____ 1. Operating costs that are expensed in the period in which they are incurred.
_____ 2. Materials that become a physical part of a finished product and whose costs are traceable to the finished product.
_____ 3. All manufacturing costs other than direct materials and direct labor.
_____ 4. Labor costs that are difficult to trace to specific products.
_____ 5. Materials whose costs cannot conveniently be directly traced to particular finished products.
_____ 6. Product costs included in inventory, as required by GAAP.
_____ 7. The compensation of employees who physically convert materials into the company's products; labor costs that are directly traceable to finished products.

Computing cost of goods manufactured

E16-21 Compute the missing amounts. (pp. 820–821)

	Company X	Company Y	Company Z
Beginning work in process inventory....	(a)	$40,000	$2,000
Direct materials used...........................	$14,000	35,000	(g)
Direct labor...	10,000	20,000	1,000
Manufacturing overhead.....................	(b)	10,000	500
Total manufacturing costs incurred during year.......................................	44,000	(d)	(h)
Total manufacturing costs to account for..	$54,000	(e)	$6,500
Less: Ending work in process inventory..	(c)	25,000	2,500
Costs of goods manufactured.............	$50,000	(f)	(i)

Preparing a statement of cost of goods manufactured

E16-22 Snyder Corp., a lamp manufacturer, provided the following information for the year ended December 31, 2008.

Inventories:	Beginning	Ending
Materials	$ 50,000	$ 25,000
Work in process	100,000	65,000
Finished goods	40,000	43,000

Other information:

Depreciation: plant building and equipment	$ 15,000	Repairs and maintenance—plant	$ 5,000
Materials purchases	155,000	Indirect labor	30,000
Insurance on plant	20,000	Direct labor	120,000
Sales salaries expense	48,000	Administrative expenses	52,000

Requirements
1. Prepare a schedule of cost of goods manufactured. (pp. 820–821)
2. What is the unit product cost if Snyder manufactured 3,000 lamps for the year? (p. 822)

Flow of costs through a manufacturer's inventory accounts

E16-23 Compute cost of goods manufactured and cost of goods sold from the following amounts: (p. 822)

	Beginning of Year	End of Year
Direct materials inventory	$22,000	$26,000
Work in process inventory	38,000	30,000
Finished goods inventory	18,000	23,000
Purchases of direct materials		75,000
Direct labor		82,000
Manufacturing overhead		39,000

Ethical decisions

E16-24 Mary Gonzales is the controller at Automax, a car dealership. Cory Loftus recently has been hired as bookkeeper. Cory wanted to attend a class on Excel spreadsheets, so Mary temporarily took over Cory's duties, including overseeing a fund for topping-off a car's gas before a test drive. Mary found a shortage in this fund and confronted Cory when he returned to work. Cory admitted that he occasionally uses this fund to pay for his own gas. Mary estimated that the amount involved is close to $300.

Requirements (pp. 823–824)
1. What should Mary Gonzales do?
2. Would you change your answer to the previous question if Mary Gonzales was the one recently hired as controller and Cory Loftus was a well-liked longtime employee who indicated that he always eventually repaid the fund?

Introduction to Management Accounting

Problems (Group A)

Calculating income and cost per unit for a service company

P16-25A The Tree Doctors provide tree-spraying services in the company's home county. Fergus McNabb, owner, incurred the following operating costs for the month of May 2008:

Salaries and wages	$8,000
Chemicals	4,500
Depreciation on buildings and equipment	700
Depreciation on truck	300
Supplies expense	500
Gasoline and utilities	1,000

The Tree Doctors earned $20,000 in revenues for the month of May by spraying trees totaling 30,000 feet in height.

Requirements
1. Prepare an income statement for the month of May. Compute the ratio of total operating expense to total revenue and operating income to total revenue. (p. 813)
2. Compute the unit operating cost of spraying one foot of tree height. (pp. 813–814)

Preparing an income statement for a merchandising company

P16-26A In 2007 Clyde Blackstock opened Clyde's Pets, a small retail shop selling pet supplies. On December 31, 2007, Clyde's accounting records showed the following:

Inventory on December 31, 2007	$10,250
Inventory on January 1, 2007	15,000
Sales revenue	54,000
Utilities for shop	3,000
Rent for shop	4,000
Sales commissions	2,250
Purchases of merchandise	27,000

Requirement
Prepare an income statement for Clyde's Pets, a merchandiser, for the year ended December 31, 2007. (pp. 812–813)

Preparing cost of goods manufactured schedule and income statement for a manufacturing company

P16-27A Clyde's Pets succeeded so well that Clyde decided to manufacture his own brand of chewing bone—Denim Bones. At the end of December 2009, his accounting records showed the following:

Inventories:	Beginning	Ending
Materials	$13,500	$ 9,000
Work in process	0	1,250
Finished goods	0	5,700

continued . . .

Other information:

Direct material purchases	$ 31,000	Utilities for plant	$ 4,500
Plant janitorial services	1,250	Rent on plant	9,000
Sales salaries expense	5,000	Customer service hotline expense	1,000
Delivery expense	1,500	Direct labor	18,000
Sales revenue	105,000		

Requirements

1. Prepare a schedule of cost of goods manufactured for Denim Bones for the year ended December 31, 2009. (pp. 820–821)
2. Prepare an income statement for Denim Bones for the year ended December 31, 2009. (p. 819)
3. How does the format of the income statement for Denim Bones differ from the income statement of Clyde's Pets? (pp. 813, 819)
4. Denim Bones manufactured 17,500 units of its product in 2009. Compute the company's unit product cost for the year. (p. 819)

Preparing financial statements for a manufacturer

5

P16-28A Certain item descriptions and amounts are missing from the monthly schedule of cost of goods manufactured and the income statement of Tinto Manufacturing Company. Fill in the missing items. (pp. 820–821)

_____ MANUFACTURING COMPANY

_____

_____ June 30, 2010

Beginning _____			$ 21,000
Direct _____:			
Beginning materials inventory	$ X		
Purchase of materials	51,000		
_____	78,000		
Ending materials inventory	(23,000)		
Direct _____		$ X	
Direct _____		X	
Manufacturing overhead		40,000	
Total _____ costs _____			166,000
Total _____ costs _____			X
Ending _____			(25,000)
_____			$ X
Sales revenue		$ X	
Cost of goods sold:			
Beginning _____	$115,000		
_____	X		
Cost of goods _____	X		
Ending _____	X		
Cost of goods sold		209,000	
Gross profit		254,000	
_____ expenses:			
Marketing expense	99,000		
Administrative expense	X	154,000	
_____ income		$ X	

Flow of costs through a manufacturer's inventory accounts

P16-29A Bass Shoe Company makes loafers. During the most recent year, Bass incurred total manufacturing costs of $21.4 M. Of this amount, $3.0 M was direct materials used and $13.8 M was direct labor. Beginning balances for the year were Direct Materials Inventory, $.7 M; Work in Process Inventory, $.9 M; and Finished Goods Inventory, $.4 M. At the end of the year, inventory accounts showed these amounts:

	Materials	Direct Labor	Manufacturing Overhead
Direct Materials Inventory........	$.6M	$ —0—	$ —0—
Work in Process Inventory........	.4M	.45M	.15M
Finished Goods Inventory.........	.1M	.15M	.05M

Requirements

Refer to Exhibit 16-11, p. 822. Compute:

1. Bass Shoe Company's cost of goods manufactured for the year.
2. Bass's cost of goods sold for the year.
3. The cost of materials purchased during the year.

Making ethical decisions

P16-30A Lee Reinhardt is the new controller for Night Software, Inc., which develops and sells education software. Shortly before the December 31 fiscal year-end, Richard Oliver, the company president, asks Reinhardt how things look for the year-end numbers. He is not happy to learn that earnings growth may be below 15% for the first time in the company's five-year history. Oliver explains that financial analysts have again predicted a 15% earnings growth for the company and that he does not intend to disappoint them. He suggests that Reinhardt talk to the assistant controller, who can explain how the previous controller dealt with such situations. The assistant controller suggests the following strategies:

a. Persuade suppliers to postpone billing until January 1.

b. Record as sales certain software awaiting sale that is held in a public warehouse.

c. Delay the year-end closing a few days into January of the next year, so that some of next year's sales are included as this year's sales.

d. Reduce the allowance for bad debts (and bad debts expense), given the company's continued strong performance.

e. Postpone routine monthly maintenance expenditures from December to January.

Which of these suggested strategies are inconsistent with IMA standards? What should Reinhardt do if Oliver insists that she follow all of these suggestions? (pp. 823–824)

Problems (Group B)

Calculating income and cost per unit for a service company

P16-31B The Dent Fixer repairs small dents and dings in the doors and other body panels of automobiles. Grant Edwards, owner, incurred the following operating costs in the month of October 2008.

continued . . .

Salary	$4,000
Depreciation on truck	250
Supplies expense	150
Gasoline	250
Utilities	650

The Dent Fixer earned $8,000 in revenue for the month of October, when Edwards repaired 160 automobiles.

Requirements
1. Prepare an income statement for the month of October. Compute the ratio of total operating expense to total revenue and operating income to total revenue. (p. 813)
2. Compute the unit operating cost per automobile repaired. (p. 814)

Preparing an income statement for a merchandising company

P16-32B On January 1, 2008, Lindsey Owens opened Picture Perfect, a small retail store that sells picture frames, crafts, and art. On December 31, 2008, her accounting records showed the following:

Store rent	$7,000	Sales revenue	$90,000
Sales salaries	4,500	Store utilities	1,950
Freight in	600	Purchases of merchandise	36,000
Inventory on December 31, 2008	9,600	Inventory on January 1, 2008	12,000
Advertising expense	2,300		

Requirement
Prepare an income statement for Picture Perfect, a merchandiser, for the year ended December 31, 2008. (p. 813)

Preparing cost of goods manufactured schedule and income statement for a manufacturing company

P16-33B Picture Perfect succeeded so well that Lindsey Owens decided to manufacture her own special brand of picture frames, to be called Always. At the end of December 2009, her accounting records showed the following:

Inventories:	Beginning	Ending
Materials	$ 13,000	$ 8,000
Work in process	0	2,000
Finished goods	0	3,000

Other information:			
Direct material purchases	$ 32,000	Rent on plant	$11,000
Plant janitorial services	750	Customer warranty refunds	1,500
Sales commissions	4,000	Depreciation expense on delivery truck	2,500
Administrative expenses	7,000		
Sales revenue	128,000	Depreciation expense on plant equipment	3,250
Utilities for plant	1,000	Direct labor	20,000

continued...

Requirements

1. Prepare a schedule of cost of goods manufactured for Always Manufacturing, for the year ended December 31, 2009. (pp. 820–821)
2. Prepare an income statement for Always Manufacturing, for the year ended December 31, 2009. (p. 819)
3. How does the format of the income statement for Always Manufacturing differ from the income statement of Picture Perfect? (pp. 813, 819)
4. Always Manufacturing made 1,300 picture frames in 2009. Compute the company's unit product cost for the year. (pp. 813, 819)

Preparing financial statements for a manufacturer

P16-34B Certain item descriptions and amounts are missing from the monthly schedule of cost of goods manufactured and income statement of Lima Manufacturing Company. Fill in the missing items.

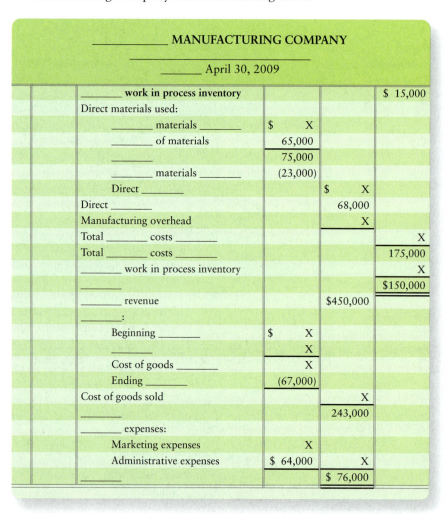

Flow of costs through a manufacturer's inventory accounts

P16-35B Wrangler Company makes casual jeans. During the most recent year, Wrangler incurred direct labor cost of $60 M and manufacturing overhead of $75M. The company purchased direct materials of $25.7M. Beginning balances for the year were Direct Materials Inventory, $3.4M;

continued...

work in Process Inventory, $3.8M; and Finished Goods Inventory, $7.4M. At year-end, inventory accounts showed these amounts:

	Materials	Direct Labor	Manufacturing Overhead
Direct Materials Inventory........	$ .9M	$ —0—	$ —0—
Work in Process Inventory........	1.5M	2.0M	2.5M
Finished Goods Inventory.........	2.4M	3.2M	4.0M

Requirements
Refer to Exhibit 16-11, p. 822. Compute:
1. Wrangler Company's cost of direct materials used for the year.
2. Wrangler's cost of goods manufactured for the year.
3. The company's cost of goods sold for the year.

Making ethical decisions

P16-36B Tom Williams is the new controller for Vance Design, a designer and manufacturer of sportswear. Shortly before the December 31 fiscal year-end, Tenisha Roberts (the company president) asks Tom how things look for the year-end numbers. Tenisha is not happy to learn that earnings growth may be below 10% for the first time in the company's five-year history. Tenisha explains that financial analysts have again predicted a 12% earnings growth for the company and that she does not intend to disappoint them. She suggests that Tom talk to the assistant controller, who can explain how the previous controller dealt with this type of situation. The assistant controller suggests the following strategies:

a. Postpone planned advertising expenditures from December to January.

b. Do not record sales returns and allowances because they are individually immaterial.

c. Persuade retail customers to accelerate January orders to December.

d. Reduce the allowance for bad debts, given the company's continued strong performance.

e. Vance Design ships finished goods to public warehouses across the country for temporary storage, until it receives firm orders from customers. As Vance Design receives orders, it directs the warehouse to ship the goods to the nearby customer. The assistant controller suggests recording goods sent to the public warehouses as sales.

Which of these suggested strategies are inconsistent with IMA standards? What should Tom Williams do if Tenisha Roberts insists that he follow all of these suggestions? (pp. 823–824)

Apply Your Knowledge

Decision Cases

Case 1. PowerSwitch, Inc., designs and manufactures switches used in telecommunications. Serious flooding throughout North Carolina affected PowerSwitch's facilities. Inventory was completely ruined, and the company's computer system, including all accounting records, was destroyed.

Before the disaster recovery specialists clean the buildings, Stephen Plum, the company controller, is anxious to salvage whatever records he can to support an insurance claim for the destroyed inventory. He is standing in what is left of the accounting department with Paul Lopez, the cost accountant.

"I didn't know mud could smell so bad," Paul says. "What should I be looking for?"

"Don't worry about beginning inventory numbers," responds Stephen, "we'll get them from last year's annual report. We need first-quarter cost data."

"I was working on the first-quarter results just before the storm hit," Paul says. "Look, my report's still in my desk drawer. All I can make out is that for the first quarter, material purchases were $476,000 and direct labor, manufacturing overhead, and total manufacturing costs to account for were $505,000, $245,000, and $1,425,000, respectively. Wait, and cost of goods available for sale was $1,340,000."

"Great," says Stephen. "I remember that sales for the period were approximately $1.7 million. Given our gross profit of 30%, that's all you should need."

Paul is not sure about that, but decides to see what he can do with this information. The beginning inventory numbers are

- Direct materials, $113,000

- Work in process, $229,000

- Finished goods, $154,000

He remembers a schedule he learned in college that may help him get started.

Requirements

1. Exhibit 16-11 (p. 822) resembles the schedule Paul has in mind. Use it to determine the ending inventories of direct materials, work in process, and finished goods.

2. Draft an insurance claim letter for the controller, seeking reimbursement for the flood damage to inventory. PowerSwitch's insurance representative is Gary Ogleby, at Industrial Insurance Co., 1122 Main Street, Hartford, CT 06268.

The policy number is #3454340-23. PowerSwitch's address is 5 Research Triangle Way, Raleigh, NC 27698.

Case 2. The IMA's *Standards of Ethical Conduct for Management Accountants* can be applied to more than just management accounting. They are also relevant to college students. Explain at least one situation that shows how each IMA standard in Exhibit 16-12 (p. 823) is relevant to your experiences as a student. For example, the ethical standard of competence would suggest not cutting classes!

Ethical Issue

Hector Valencia recently resigned his position as controller for Shamalay Automotive, a small, struggling foreign car dealer in Austin, Texas. Hector has just started a new job as controller for Mueller Imports, a much larger dealer for the same car manufacturer. Demand for this particular make of car is exploding, and the manufacturer cannot produce enough to satisfy demand. The manufacturer's regional sales managers are each given a certain number of cars. Each sales manager then decides how to divide the cars among the independently owned dealerships in the region. Because most dealerships can sell every car they receive, the key is getting a large number of cars from the manufacturer's regional sales manager.

Hector's former employer, Shamalay Automotive, received only about 25 cars a month. Consequently, the dealership was not very profitable.

Hector is surprised to learn that his new employer, Mueller Imports, receives over 200 cars a month. Hector soon gets another surprise. Every couple of months, a local jeweler bills the dealer $5,000 for "miscellaneous services." Franz Mueller, the owner of the dealership, personally approves payment of these invoices, noting that each invoice is a "selling expense." From casual conversations with a salesperson, Hector learns that Mueller frequently gives Rolex watches to the manufacturer's regional sales manager and other sales executives. Before talking to anyone about this, Hector decides to work through his ethical dilemma using the framework from Chapter 7. Put yourself in Hector's place and complete the framework.

1. What is the ethical issue?
2. What are my options?
3. What are the possible consequences?
4. What shall I do?

Team Project

Search the Internet for a nearby company that also has a Web page. Arrange an interview with a management accountant, a controller, or other accounting/finance officer of the company. Before you conduct the interview, answer the following questions:

1. Is this a service, merchandising, or manufacturing company? What is its primary product or service?

2. Is the primary purpose of the company's Web site to provide information about the company and its products, to sell online, or to provide financial information for investors?

3. Are parts of the company's Web site restricted so that you need password authorization to enter? What appears to be the purpose of limiting access?

4. Does the Web site provide an e-mail link for contacting the company?

At the interview, begin by clarifying your answers to questions 1 through 4, and ask the following additional questions:

5. If the company sells over the Web, what benefits has the company derived? Did the company perform a cost-benefit analysis before deciding to begin Web sales?

Or

If the company does not sell over the Web, why not? Has the company performed a cost/benefit analysis and decided not to sell over the Web?

6. What is the biggest cost of operating the Web site?

7. Does the company make any purchases over the Internet? What percentage?

8. How has e-commerce affected the company's management accounting system? Have the management accountant's responsibilities become more or less complex? More or less interesting?

9. Does the company use Web-based accounting applications, such as accounts receivable or accounts payable?

10. Does the company use an ERP system? If so, do managers view the system as a success? What have been the benefits? The costs?

For Internet Exercises, Excel in Practice, and additional online activities, go to the Web site www.prenhall.com/horngren

Quick Check Answers

1. *a* 2. *c* 3. *d* 4. *b* 5. *a* 6. *c* 7. *b* 8. *a* 9. *d* 10. *d*

17 Job Order Costing

Learning Objectives

1. Distinguish between job order costing and process costing
2. Record materials and labor in a job order costing system
3. Record overhead in a job order costing system
4. Record completion and sales of finished goods and the adjustment for under- or overallocated overhead
5. Calculate unit costs for a service company

Many schools use fundraising events to finance extracurricular events. Let's say that you are responsible for an enchilada dinner to finance a band trip. You have to decide how many dinners you expect to sell, what price to charge, and the ingredients needed. Knowing the cost to prepare an enchilada dinner is important. You want to set a price low enough to draw a crowd and high enough to generate a profit.

This chapter shows how to measure cost in situations similar to the enchilada dinner. This type of cost accounting system is called job order costing because production is arranged by the job. Chapter 18 then covers the other main type of costing system—called process costing.

Businesses face the same situation. They must draw a crowd—sell enough goods and services to earn a profit. So, regardless of the type of business you own or manage, you need to know how much it costs to produce your product or service. This applies whether you plan a career in marketing, engineering, or finance.

Marketing managers must consider their unit product cost in order to set the selling price high enough to cover costs. Engineers study the materials, labor, and overhead that go into a product to pinpoint ways to cut costs. Production managers then decide whether it is more profitable to make the product or to *outsource* it (buy from an outside supplier). The finance department arranges financing for the venture.

You can see that it's important for managers in all areas to know how much it costs to make a product. This chapter and the next shows you how to figure these costs.

How Much Does It Cost to Make a Product? Two Approaches

1 Distinguish between job order costing and process costing

Cost accounting systems accumulate cost information so that managers can measure how much it costs to produce each unit of merchandise. For example, Intel must know how much each processor costs to produce. FedEx knows its cost of flying each pound of freight one mile. These unit costs help managers

- Set selling prices that will lead to profits
- Compute cost of goods sold for the income statement
- Compute the cost of inventory for the balance sheet

If a manager knows the cost to produce each product, then the manager can plan and control the cost of resources needed to create the product and deliver it to the customer. A cost accounting system assigns these costs to the company's product or service.

JOB ORDER COSTING Some companies manufacture batches of unique products or specialized services. A **job order costing** system accumulates costs for each batch, or job. Law firms, music studios, health-care providers, building contractors, and furniture manufacturers are examples of companies that use job order costing systems. For example, Dell makes personal computers based on customer orders (see the "Customize" button on Dell's Web site).

PROCESS COSTING Other companies, such as Procter & Gamble and PepsiCo, produce identical units through a series of production steps or processes. A **process costing** system accumulates the costs of each process needed to complete the product. Chevron Texaco and Kraft Foods are examples of companies that use process costing systems.

Both job order and process costing systems:

- Accumulate the costs incurred to make the product
- Assign costs to the products

Accountants use **cost tracing** to assign directly traceable costs, such as direct materials and direct labor, to the product. They use a less precise technique—**cost allocation**—to assign manufacturing overhead and other indirect costs to the product. Let's see how a job order costing system works for a manufacturing company.

Job Order Costing for Manufacturing Products

How Job Costs Flow Through the Accounts: An Overview

The job order costing system tracks costs as raw materials move from the storeroom to the production floor to finished products. Exhibit 17-1 diagrams the flow of costs through a job order costing system. Let's consider how a manufacturer, Seasons Greeting Cards, uses job order costing. For Seasons Greeting, each customer order is a separate job. Seasons Greeting uses a **job cost record** to accumulate the costs of each job's:

- Direct materials
- Direct labor
- Manufacturing overhead

The company starts the job cost record when work begins on the job. As Seasons Greeting incurs costs, the company adds costs to the job cost record. For jobs started but not yet finished, the job cost records show the Work in Process Inventory. When Seasons Greeting finishes a job, the company totals the costs and transfers costs from Work in Process Inventory to Finished Goods Inventory.

When the job's units are sold, the costing system moves the costs from Finished Goods Inventory to Cost of Goods Sold. Exhibit 17-1 summarizes this sequence.

2 Record materials and labor in a job order costing system

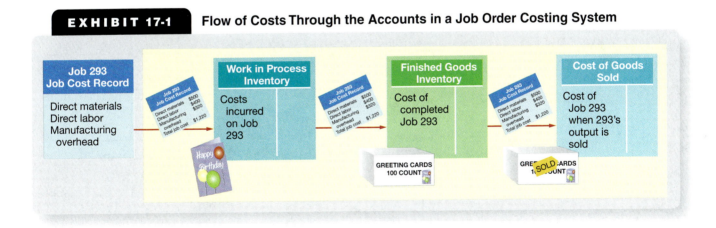

EXHIBIT 17-1 Flow of Costs Through the Accounts in a Job Order Costing System

Job Order Costing: Accounting for Materials and Labor

Accounting for Materials

PURCHASING MATERIALS On January 1, 2009, Seasons Greeting had these inventory balances:

Materials Inventory	Work in Process Inventory	Finished Goods Inventory
4,000	7,000	9,000

During the year, Seasons Greeting purchased paper for $22,000 on account. We record the purchase of materials as follows:

(1) Materials Inventory	22,000	
Accounts Payable		22,000

Materials Inventory

4,000	
22,000	

Materials Inventory is a general ledger account. Seasons Greeting also uses a subsidiary ledger for materials. The subsidiary materials ledger includes a separate record for each type of material, as shown in Exhibit 17-2. The balance of the Materials Inventory account in the general ledger should always equal the sum of the balances in the subsidiary materials ledger.

EXHIBIT 17-2 Subsidiary Materials Ledger Record

SUBSIDIARY MATERIALS LEDGER RECORD — *Seasons Greeting*

Item No. B–220   Description: Paper

Date	Received			Used				Balance		
	Units	Cost	Total Cost	Mat. Req. No.	Units	Cost	Total Cost	Units	Cost	Total Cost
2009										
7-20								20	$14	$280
7-23	20	$14	$280					40	14	560
7-24				334	10	$14	$140	30	14	420

USING MATERIALS Seasons Greeting works on many jobs during the year. In 2009 the company used materials costing $21,000, including paper ($18,000) and ink ($3,000). The paper can be traced to the job, so the paper is a *direct material*. Direct material costs go directly into the Work in Process Inventory account.

By contrast, the cost of ink is difficult to trace to a specific job, so ink is an *indirect material*. The cost of indirect material is recorded first as Manufacturing Overhead. The following journal entry then records the use of materials in production.

(2) Work in Process Inventory (for direct materials)	18,000	
Manufacturing Overhead (for indirect materials)	3,000	
Materials Inventory		21,000

We can summarize the flow of materials costs through the T-accounts as follows:

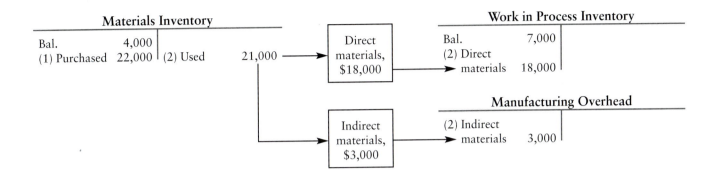

For both direct materials and indirect materials, the production team completes a document called a **materials requisition** to request the transfer of materials to the production floor. Exhibit 17-3 shows Seasons Greeting's materials requisition for the 10 units of paper needed to make 1,000 greeting cards for Job 16.

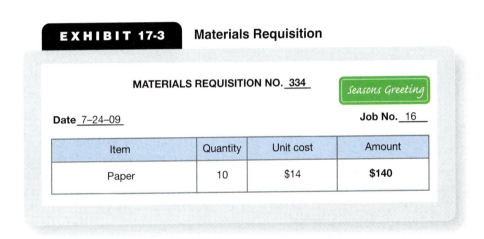

EXHIBIT 17-3 Materials Requisition

Exhibit 17-4 is a job cost record. It assigns the cost of the direct material (paper) to Job 16. Follow the $140 cost of the paper from the materials inventory record (Exhibit 17-2), to the materials requisition (Exhibit 17-3), and to the job cost record in Exhibit 17-4. Notice that all the dollar amounts in these exhibits show Seasons Greeting's *costs*—not the prices at which Seasons Greeting sells its products. Let's see how to account for labor costs.

Accounting for Labor

Seasons Greeting incurred labor costs of $24,000 during 2009. We record manufacturing wages as follows:

(3) Manufacturing Wages	24,000	
Wages Payable		24,000

EXHIBIT 17-4 Direct Materials on Job Cost Record

JOB COST RECORD — Seasons Greeting

Job No. 16
Customer Name and Address: Macy's New York City
Job Description: 1,000 Birthday Greeting Cards

Date Promised	7-31	Date Started	7-24	Date Completed		
	Direct Materials		Direct Labor		Manufacturing Overhead Allocated	
Date	Requisition Numbers	Amount	Labor Time Record Numbers	Amount	Date	Rate	Amount
7-24	334	$140					
					Overall Cost Summary		
					Direct Materials.......$		
					Direct Labor.............		
					Manufacturing Overhead Allocated........		
Totals					Total Job Cost.......$		

This entry includes the costs of both direct labor and indirect labor.

Each employee completes a labor time record for each job he or she works on. The **labor time record** in Exhibit 17-5 identifies the employee (Jay Barlow), the amount of time he spent on Job 16 (5 hours), and the labor cost charged to the job ($60 = 5 hours × $12 per hour).

EXHIBIT 17-5 Labor Time Record

Seasons Greeting totals the labor time records for each job. Exhibit 17-6 shows how Seasons Greeting adds the direct labor cost to the job cost record. The "Labor

EXHIBIT 17-6 Direct Labor on Job Cost Record

JOB COST RECORD — Seasons Greeting

Job No. 16
Customer Name and Address Macy's New York City
Job Description 1,000 Birthday Greeting Cards

Date Promised	7-31	Date Started	7-24	Date Completed		
	Direct Materials		Direct Labor		Manufacturing Overhead Allocated	
Date	Requisition Numbers	Amount	Labor Time Record Numbers	Amount	Date	Rate	Amount
7-24	334	$140	236, 251, 258	$200			
					Overall Cost Summary		
					Direct Materials..........$		
					Direct Labor................		
					Manufacturing Overhead Allocated............		
Totals					Total Job Cost..........$		

Time Record Numbers" show that on July 24, three employees worked on Job 16. Labor time record 251 is Jay Barlow's, from Exhibit 17-5. Labor time records 236 and 258 (not shown) indicate that two other employees also worked on Job 16. The job cost record shows that Seasons Greeting assigned Job 16 a total of $200 of direct labor costs for the three employees' work.

During 2009 Seasons Greeting incurred $20,000 for direct labor and $4,000 for indirect labor (overhead). These amounts include the labor costs for Job 16 that we've been working with plus all the company's other jobs as well.

Seasons Greeting's accounting for labor cost requires the company to:

- Assign labor cost to individual jobs, as we saw for Jay Barlow's work on Job 16
- Transfer labor cost out of the Manufacturing Wages account and into Work in Process Inventory (for direct labor) and into Manufacturing Overhead (for indirect labor)

The following journal entry zeroes out the Manufacturing Wages account and shifts the labor cost to Work in Process and the Overhead account.

(4)	Work in Process Inventory (for direct labor)	20,000	
	Manufacturing Overhead (for indirect labor)	4,000	
	Manufacturing Wages		24,000

This entry brings the balance in Manufacturing Wages to zero. Its transferred balance is now divided between Work in Process Inventory ($20,000 of direct labor) and Manufacturing Overhead ($4,000 of indirect labor), as shown in the following T-accounts:

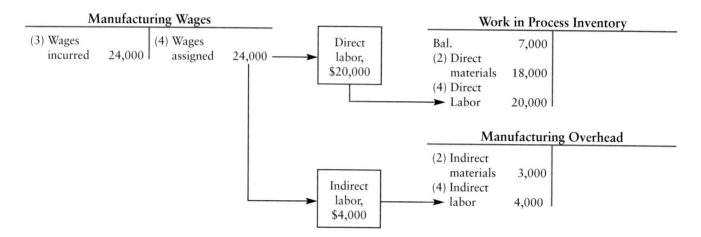

Many companies have automated these accounting procedures.

Study the Decision Guidelines to summarize the first half of the chapter. Then work the summary problem that follows.

Decision Guidelines

JOB ORDER COSTING:
TRACING DIRECT MATERIALS AND DIRECT LABOR

Seasons Greeting Cards uses a job order costing system that assigns manufacturing costs to each individual job for greeting cards. These guidelines explain some of the decisions Seasons made in designing its system.

Decision	Guidelines
Should we use job costing or process costing?	Use *job order costing* when the company produces unique products (custom greeting cards) in small batches (usually a "batch" contains a set of seasonal cards). Use *process costing* when the company produces identical products in large batches, often in a continuous flow.
How to record:	
• Purchase and use of materials?	*Purchase of materials:* Materials Inventory　　　　　　　　　　　　　XX 　　Accounts Payable (or Cash)　　　　　　　　　　XX *Use of materials:* Work in Process Inventory (direct materials)　　XX Manufacturing Overhead (indirect materials)　　XX 　　Materials Inventory　　　　　　　　　　　　　XX
• Incurrence and assignment of labor to jobs?	*Incurrence of labor cost:* Manufacturing Wages　　　　　　　　　　　　XX 　　Wages Payable (or Cash)　　　　　　　　　　XX *Assignment of labor cost to jobs:* Work in Process Inventory (direct labor)　　　XX Manufacturing Overhead (indirect labor)　　　XX 　　Manufacturing Wages　　　　　　　　　　　　XX

Summary Problem 1

Tom Baker manufactures custom teakwood patio furniture. Suppose Baker has the following transactions:

a. **Purchased raw materials on account, $135,000.**

b. **Materials costing $130,000 were requisitioned (used) for production. Of this total, $30,000 were indirect materials.**

c. **Labor time records show that direct labor of $22,000 and indirect labor of $5,000 were incurred (but not yet paid).**

d. **Assigned labor cost to work in process and manufacturing overhead.**

Requirement

Prepare journal entries for each transaction. Then explain each journal entry in terms of what got increased and what got decreased.

Solution

a.

Materials Inventory	135,000	
Accounts Payable		135,000

When materials are purchased on account:

- Debit (increase) Materials Inventory for the *cost* of the materials purchased.
- Credit (increase) Accounts Payable to record the liability for the cost of the materials.

b.

Work in Process Inventory	100,000	
Manufacturing Overhead	30,000	
Materials Inventory		130,000

When materials are requisitioned (used) in production, we record the movement of materials out of materials inventory and into production, as follows:

- Debit (increase) Work in Process Inventory for the cost of the *direct* materials (in this case, $100,000—the $130,000 total materials requisitioned less the $30,000 indirect materials).
- Debit (increase) Manufacturing Overhead for the cost of the *indirect* materials.
- Credit (decrease) Materials Inventory for the cost of both direct materials and indirect materials moved out of the materials storage area and into production.

c.

Manufacturing Wages ($22,000 + $5,000)	27,000	
Wages Payable		27,000

To record total labor costs actually incurred,

- Debit (increase) Manufacturing Wages.
- Credit (increase) Wages Payable to record the liability for wages incurred, but not paid.

d.

Work in Process Inventory	22,000	
Manufacturing Overhead	5,000	
Manufacturing Wages		27,000

To assign the labor costs,

- Debit (increase) Work in Process Inventory for the cost of the *direct* labor.
- Debit (increase) Manufacturing Overhead for the cost of the *indirect* labor.
- Credit (decrease) Manufacturing Wages to zero out its balance.

Job Order Costing: Allocating Manufacturing Overhead

 Record overhead in a job order costing system

All manufacturing overhead costs are *accumulated* as debits to a single general ledger account—Manufacturing Overhead. We have already assigned the costs of indirect materials (entry 2, bottom of page 854) and indirect labor (entry 4, bottom of page 857) to manufacturing overhead. In addition to indirect materials and indirect labor, Seasons Greeting incurred the following overhead costs:

- Depreciation on plant and equipment, $7,000
- Plant utilities, $4,000
- Plant insurance, $1,000
- Property taxes on the plant, $2,000

Entries 5 through 8 record these manufacturing overhead costs. The account titles in parentheses indicate the specific records that were debited in the overhead subsidiary ledger.

(5) Manufacturing Overhead (Depreciation—Plant and Equipment)	7,000	
Accumulated Depreciation—Plant and Equipment		7,000
(6) Manufacturing Overhead (Plant Utilities)	4,000	
Cash		4,000
(7) Manufacturing Overhead (Plant Insurance)	1,000	
Prepaid Insurance—Plant		1,000
(8) Manufacturing Overhead (Property Taxes—Plant)	2,000	
Property Taxes Payable		2,000

The actual manufacturing overhead costs (such as indirect materials, indirect labor, plus depreciation, utilities, insurance, and property taxes on the plant) are debited to Manufacturing Overhead as they occur throughout the year. By the end of the year, the Manufacturing Overhead account has accumulated all the actual overhead costs as debits:

Manufacturing Overhead

(2) Indirect materials	3,000
(4) Indirect labor	4,000
(5) Depreciation—plant and equipment	7,000
(6) Plant utilities	4,000
(7) Plant insurance	1,000
(8) Property taxes—plant	2,000
Total overhead cost	21,000

Now you have seen how Seasons Greeting *accumulates* overhead costs in the accounting records. But how does Seasons Greeting *assign* overhead costs to individual jobs? As you can see, overhead includes a variety of costs that Seasons Greeting cannot trace to individual jobs. For example, it is impossible to say how much of the cost of plant utilities is related to Job 16. Yet manufacturing overhead costs are as essential as direct materials and direct labor, so Seasons Greeting must find some way to assign overhead costs to specific jobs. Otherwise, each job would not bear its fair share of total cost. Seasons Greeting may then set unrealistic prices for some of its greeting cards and wind up losing money on some of its hard-earned sales.

Allocating Manufacturing Overhead to Jobs

Companies perform two steps in allocating manufacturing overhead:

1. **Compute the predetermined overhead rate.** The **predetermined manufacturing overhead rate** (sometimes called the **budgeted overhead rate**) is computed as follows:

$$\text{Predetermined manufacturing overhead rate} = \frac{\text{Total estimated manufacturing overhead costs}}{\text{Total estimated quantity of the manufacturing overhead allocation base}}$$

The most accurate allocation can be made only when total overhead cost is known—and that's at the end of the year. But managers can't wait that long for product cost information. So the predetermined overhead rate is calculated before the year begins. Then throughout the year, companies use this predetermined rate to allocate overhead cost to individual jobs. The predetermined overhead rate is based on two factors:

- Total *estimated* manufacturing overhead costs for the year
- Total *estimated* quantity of the manufacturing overhead allocation base

The key to assigning indirect manufacturing costs to jobs is to identify a workable manufacturing overhead allocation base. The **allocation base** is a common denominator that links overhead costs to the products. Ideally, the allocation base is the primary cost driver of manufacturing overhead. As the phrase implies, a **cost driver** is the primary factor that causes a cost. Traditionally manufacturing companies have used:

- Direct labor hours (for labor-intensive production environments)
- Direct labor cost (for labor-intensive production environments)
- Machine hours (for machine-intensive production environments)

For simplicity, we'll assume Seasons Greeting uses only one allocation base to assign manufacturing overhead to jobs. Later in the textbook, Chapter 19 relaxes this assumption. There, we'll see how companies use a method called *activity-based costing* to identify different allocation bases that link indirect costs with specific jobs more precisely. First, however, we need to develop a solid understanding of the simpler system that we describe here.

2. **Allocate manufacturing overhead costs to jobs as the company makes its products.** Allocate manufacturing overhead cost to jobs as follows:

$$\text{Allocated manufacturing overhead cost} = \text{Predetermined manufacturing overhead rate (from Step 1)} \times \text{Actual quantity of the allocation base used by each job}$$

As we have seen, Seasons Greeting traces direct costs directly to each job. Now let's see how it allocates overhead cost to jobs. Recall that indirect manufacturing costs include plant depreciation, utilities, insurance, and property taxes, plus indirect materials and indirect labor.

1. Seasons Greeting uses direct labor cost as the allocation base. In 2008, Seasons Greeting estimated that total overhead costs for 2009 would be $20,000 and direct labor cost would total $25,000. Using this information, we can compute the predetermined manufacturing overhead rate as follows:

$$\text{Predetermined manufacturing overhead rate} = \frac{\text{Total estimated manufacturing overhead costs}}{\text{Total estimated quantity of the manufacturing overhead allocation base}} = \frac{\text{Total estimated manufacturing overhead costs}}{\text{Total estimated direct labor cost}}$$

$$= \frac{\$20,000}{\$25,000} = 0.80, \text{ or } 80\%$$

As jobs are completed in 2009, Seasons Greeting will allocate $0.80 of overhead cost for each $1 of labor cost incurred for the job ($0.80 = 80% × $1). Seasons Greeting uses the same predetermined overhead rate (80% of direct labor cost) to allocate manufacturing overhead to all jobs worked on throughout the year. Now back to Job 16.

2. The total direct labor cost for Job 16 is $200 and the predetermined overhead allocation rate is 80% of direct labor cost. Therefore, Seasons Greeting allocates $160 ($200 × 0.80) of manufacturing overhead to Job 16.

The completed job cost record for the Macy's order (Exhibit 17-7) shows that Job 16 cost Seasons Greeting a total of $500: $140 for direct materials, $200 for direct labor, and $160 of allocated manufacturing overhead. Job 16 produced 1,000 greeting cards, so Seasons Greeting's cost per greeting card is $0.50 ($500 ÷ 1,000).

EXHIBIT 17-7 **Manufacturing Overhead on Job Cost Record**

JOB COST RECORD

Seasons Greeting

Job No. 16
Customer Name and Address Macy's New York City
Job Description 1,000 Birthday Greeting Cards

Date Promised	7–31	Date Started	7–24	Date Completed		7–29
	Direct Materials		Direct Labor		Manufacturing Overhead Allocated	
Date	Requisition Numbers	Amount	Labor Time Record Numbers	Amount	Date	Rate	Amount
7–24	334	$140	236, 251, 258	$200	7–29	80% of Direct Labor Cost	$160
					Overall Cost Summary		
					Direct Materials $140		
					Direct Labor....................200		
					Manufacturing Overhead Allocated 160		
Totals		$140		$200	Total Job Cost.............$500		

Seasons Greeting worked on many jobs, including Job 16, during 2009. The company allocated manufacturing overhead to each of these jobs. Seasons Greeting's direct labor cost for 2009 was $20,000, and total overhead allocated to all jobs is 80% of the $20,000 direct labor cost, or $16,000. The journal entry to allocate manufacturing overhead cost to Work in Process Inventory is

	(9) Work in Process Inventory	16,000	
	Manufacturing Overhead		16,000

The flow of manufacturing overhead through the T-accounts follows:

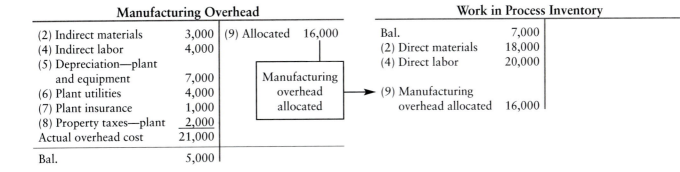

After allocation, a $5,000 debit balance remains in the Manufacturing Overhead account. This means that Seasons Greeting's actual overhead costs ($21,000) exceed the overhead allocated to Work in Process Inventory ($16,000). We say that Seasons Greeting's Manufacturing Overhead is *underallocated*. We'll show how to correct this problem later in the chapter.

Accounting for Completion and Sale of Finished Goods and Adjusting Manufacturing Overhead

Now you know how to accumulate and assign the cost of direct materials, direct labor, and overhead to jobs. To complete the process, we must:

- Account for the completion and sale of finished goods
- Adjust manufacturing overhead at the end of the period

Accounting for the Completion and Sale of Finished Goods

4 Record completion and sales of finished goods and the adjustment for under- or overallocated overhead

Study Exhibit 17-1 on page 853 to review the flow of costs as a job goes from work in process to finished goods to cost of goods sold. Seasons Greeting reported the following inventory balances one year ago, back on December 31, 2008:

Materials Inventory...................	$4,000
Work in Process Inventory...........	7,000
Finished Goods Inventory...........	9,000

The following transactions occurred in 2009:

Cost of goods manufactured	$55,000
Sales on account	85,000
Cost of goods sold	54,000

The $55,000 cost of goods manufactured is the cost of the jobs Seasons Greeting completed during 2009. The cost of goods manufactured goes from Work in Process Inventory to Finished Goods Inventory as completed products move into the finished goods storage area. Seasons Greeting records goods completed in 2009 as follows:

(10) Finished Goods Inventory	55,000	
Work in Process Inventory		55,000

As the greeting cards are sold, Seasons Greeting records sales revenue and accounts receivable, as follows:

(11) Accounts Receivable	85,000	
Sales Revenue		85,000

The goods have been shipped to customers, so Seasons Greeting must also decrease the Finished Goods Inventory account and increase Cost of Goods Sold with the following journal entry:

(11) Cost of Goods Sold	54,000	
Finished Goods Inventory		54,000

The key T-accounts for Seasons Greeting's manufacturing costs now show

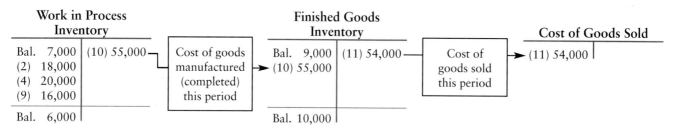

Some jobs are completed, and their costs are transferred out to Finished Goods Inventory ($54,000). We end the period with other jobs started but not finished ($6,000 ending balance of Work in Process Inventory) and jobs completed and not sold ($10,000 ending balance of Finished Goods Inventory).

Adjusting Underallocated or Overallocated Manufacturing Overhead at the End of the Period

During the year, Seasons Greeting:

- Debits Manufacturing Overhead for actual overhead costs
- Credits Manufacturing Overhead for amounts allocated to Work in Process Inventory

The total debits to the Manufacturing Overhead Account rarely equal the total credits. Why? Because Seasons Greeting allocates overhead to jobs using a *predetermined* allocation rate that's based on estimates. The predetermined allocation rate represents the *expected* relation between overhead costs and the allocation base. In our example, the $5,000 debit balance of Manufacturing Overhead shown at the top of page 865 is called **underallocated overhead** because the manufacturing overhead allocated to Work in Process Inventory is *less* than actual overhead cost. (**Overallocated overhead** has a credit balance.)

Accountants adjust underallocated and overallocated overhead at year-end, when closing the Manufacturing Overhead account. When overhead is underallocated, as in our example, a credit to Manufacturing Overhead is needed to bring the account balance to zero. What account should we debit?

Because Seasons Greeting *undercosted* jobs during the year, the correction should increase (debit) Cost of Goods Sold:

(12)	Cost of Goods Sold	5,000	
	Manufacturing Overhead		5,000

The Manufacturing Overhead balance is now zero and Cost of Goods Sold is up to date.

Manufacturing Overhead			
Actual	21,000	Allocated	16,000
		Closed	5,000

Cost of Goods Sold	
54,000	
5,000	
59,000	

Exhibit 17-8 summarizes the accounting for manufacturing overhead:
- Before the period
- During the period
- At the end of the period

EXHIBIT 17-8 — Summary of Accounting for Manufacturing Overhead

Before the Period

$$\text{Compute predetermined manufacturing overhead rate} = \frac{\text{Total estimated manufacturing overhead cost}}{\text{Total estimated quantity of allocation base}}$$

During the Period

$$\text{Allocate the overhead} = \text{Actual quantity of the manufacturing overhead allocation base} \times \text{Predetermined manufacturing overhead rate}$$

At the End of the Period

Close the Manufacturing Overhead account:

Jobs are undercosted — If actual > allocated → **Underallocated** manufacturing overhead
Need to *increase* Cost of Goods Sold, as follows:

Cost of Goods Sold	XXX	
Manufacturing Overhead		XXX

Jobs are overcosted — If allocated > actual → **Overallocated** manufacturing overhead
Need to *reduce* Cost of Goods Sold, as follows:

Manufacturing Overhead	XXX	
Cost of Goods sold		XXX

Overview of Job Order Costing in a Manufacturing Company

Exhibit 17-9 provides an overview of Seasons Greeting's job order costing system. Each entry is keyed to 1 of the 12 transactions described on page 869. Study this exhibit carefully.

Now review the flow of costs through Seasons Greeting's general ledger accounts (amounts in thousands):

- Material and labor costs are split between (a) direct costs (traced directly to specific jobs in Work in Process Inventory) and (b) indirect costs (accumulated in Manufacturing Overhead and then allocated to Work in Process Inventory).
- The Work in Process Inventory account summarizes all transactions that occurred on the floor of the manufacturing plant.
- The $55 credit to Work in Process Inventory (debit to Finished Goods Inventory) is the cost of goods manufactured. This is the cost of goods completed and ready for sale, which is the manufacturer's counterpart to merchandise purchases.
- At the end of the period Seasons Greeting closed the $5,000 underallocated Manufacturing Overhead to Cost of Goods Sold.

Job Order Costing in a Service Company

5 Calculate unit costs for a service company

As we have seen, service firms have no inventory. These firms incur only noninventoriable costs. But their managers still need to know the costs of different jobs in order to set prices for their services, as follows (amounts assumed):

Cost of Job 19	$6,000
Add standard markup of 50% ($6,000 × .50).........	3,000
Sale price of Job 19..	$9,000

A merchandising company can set the selling price of its products this same way.

We now illustrate how service firms assign costs to jobs. The law firm of Walsh Associates considers each client a separate job. Walsh's most significant cost is direct labor—attorney time spent on clients' cases. How do service firms trace direct labor to individual jobs?

Suppose Walsh's accounting system is not automated. Walsh employees can fill out a weekly **time record**. Software tallies the total time spent on each job. Attorney Lois Fox's time record in Exhibit 17-10 shows that she devoted 14 hours to client 367 during the week of June 10, 2009.

Fox's salary and benefits total $100,000 per year. Assuming a 40-hour workweek and 50 workweeks in each year, Fox has 2,000 available work hours per year (50 weeks × 40 hours per week). Fox's hourly pay rate is

$$\text{Hourly rate to the employer} = \frac{\$100{,}000 \text{ per year}}{2{,}000 \text{ hours per year}} = \$50 \text{ per hour}$$

Fox worked 14 hours for client 367, so the direct labor cost traced to client 367 is 14 hours × $50 per hour = $700.

For automated services like Web-site design, employees enter the client number when they start on the client's job. Software records the time elapsed until the employee signs off that job.

Job Order Costing 869

EXHIBIT 17-9 Job Costing—Flow of Costs Through Seasons Greeting's Accounts (amounts in thousands)

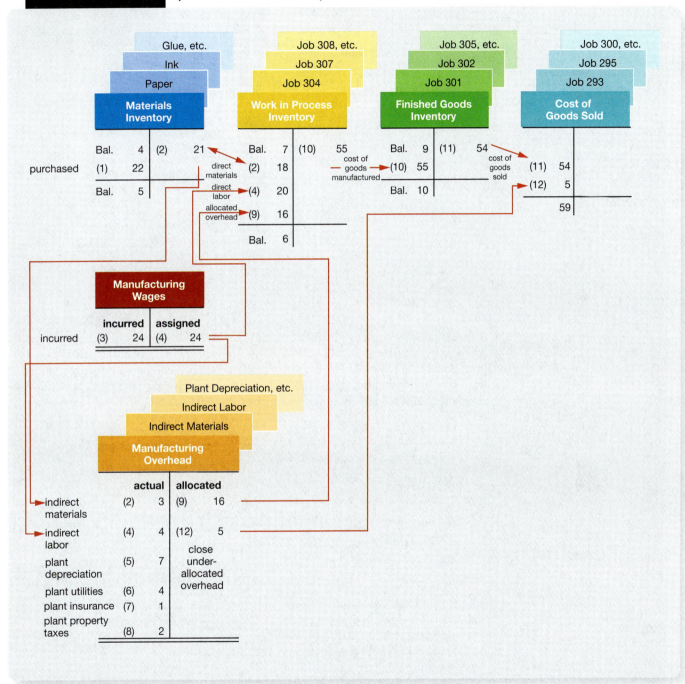

EXHIBIT 17-10 Employee Time Record

Barnett Associates
Name: Lois Fox

Employee Time Record
Week of 6/10/09

Weekly Summary

Client #	Total hours
367	14
415	13
520	13

	M	T	W	Th	F
8:00 – 8:30	367	520	415	367	415
8:30 – 9:00					
9:00 – 9:30					
9:30 – 10:00					
10:00 – 10:30				367	
10:30 – 11:00					
11:00 – 11:30	520				
11:30 – 12:00	520				
12:00 – 1:00					
1:00 – 1:30	520	367	415	520	415
1:30 – 2:00					
2:00 – 2:30					
2:30 – 3:00					
3:00 – 3:30					
3:30 – 4:00					
4:00 – 4:30				367	
4:30 – 5:00					

Founding partner John Walsh wants to know the total cost of serving each client, not just the direct labor cost. Walsh Associates also allocates indirect costs to individual jobs (clients). The law firm develops a predetermined indirect cost allocation rate, following the same approach that Seasons Greeting used on page 863. In December 2008, Walsh estimates that the following indirect costs will be incurred in 2009:

Office rent	$200,000
Office support staff	70,000
Maintaining and updating law library for case research	25,000
Advertisements in the yellow pages	3,000
Sponsorship of the symphony	2,000
Total indirect costs	$300,000

Walsh uses direct labor hours as the allocation base, because direct labor hours are the main driver of indirect costs. He estimates that Walsh attorneys will work 10,000 direct labor hours in 2009.

STEP 1. **Compute the predetermined indirect cost allocation rate.**

$$\frac{\text{Predetermined indirect cost}}{\text{allocation rate}} = \frac{\$300{,}000 \text{ expected indirect costs}}{10{,}000 \text{ expected direct labor hours}}$$

$$= \$30 \text{ per direct labor hour}$$

STEP 2. **Allocate indirect costs to jobs by multiplying the predetermined indirect cost rate (Step 1) by the actual quantity of the allocation base used by each job.** Client 367 required 14 direct labor hours, so the indirect costs are allocated as follows:

$$14 \text{ direct labor hours} \times \$30/\text{hour} = \$420$$

To summarize, the total costs assigned to client 367 are

Direct labor: 14 hours × $50/hour	$ 700
Indirect costs: 14 hours × $30/hour	420
Total costs	$1,120

You have now learned how to use a job order cost system and assign costs to jobs. Review the Decision Guidelines to solidify your understanding.

Decision Guidelines

JOB ORDER COSTING

Companies using a job order costing system treat each job separately. Here are some of the decisions that a company makes when designing its job order costing system:

Decision	Guidelines
Are utilities, insurance, property taxes, and depreciation • Manufacturing overhead? • Or operating expenses?	These costs are part of manufacturing overhead *only* if they are incurred in the manufacturing plant. If unrelated to manufacturing, they are operating expenses. For example, if related to the research lab, they are R&D expenses. If related to executive headquarters, they are administrative expenses. If related to distribution centers, they are selling expenses. These are all operating expenses, not manufacturing overhead.

How to record *actual* manufacturing overhead costs?	Manufacturing Overhead XXX
	    Accumulated Depreciation—
	       Plant and Equipment XX
	    Prepaid Insurance—Plant & Equip. XX
	    Utilities Payable (or Cash) XX
	       and so on XX

How to compute a predetermined manufacturing overhead rate?	$$\frac{\text{Total estimated manufacturing overhead cost}}{\text{Total estimated quantity of allocation base}}$$
How to record allocation of manufacturing overhead?	Work in Process Inventory XX Manufacturing Overhead XX
What is the *amount* of the allocated manufacturing overhead?	Actual quantity of the manufacturing overhead allocation base × Predetermined manufacturing overhead rate

How to close Manufacturing Overhead at the end of the period?	Close directly to Cost of Goods Sold, as follows:
	For *underallocated* overhead:
	Cost of Goods Sold XX
	    Manufacturing Overhead XX
	For *overallocated* overhead:
	Manufacturing Overhead XX
	    Cost of Goods sold XX

When providing services, how to trace employees' direct labor to individual jobs?	Either automated software directly captures the amount of time employees spend on a client's job, or employees fill out a time record.
Why allocate noninventoriable costs to jobs?	Managers need total product costs for internal decisions (such as setting selling prices).

Summary Problem 2

Skippy Scooters manufactures motor scooters. The company has automated production, so it allocates manufacturing overhead based on machine hours. Skippy expects to incur $240,000 of manufacturing overhead costs and to use 4,000 machine hours during 2009.

At the end of 2008, Skippy reported the following inventories:

Materials Inventory..........................	$20,000
Work in Process Inventory	17,000
Finished Goods Inventory	11,000

During January 2009, Skippy actually used 300 machine hours and recorded the following transactions:

a. Purchased materials on account, $31,000.

b. Used direct materials, $39,000.

c. Manufacturing wages incurred totaled $40,000.

d. Manufacturing labor was 90% direct labor and 10% indirect labor.

e. Used indirect materials, $3,000.

f. Incurred other manufacturing overhead, $13,000 (credit Accounts Payable).

g. Allocated manufacturing overhead for January 2009.

h. Cost of completed motor scooters, $100,000.

i. Sold motor scooters on account, $175,000; cost of motor scooters sold, $95,000.

Requirements

1. Compute Skippy's predetermined manufacturing overhead rate for 2009.

2. Record the transactions in the general journal.

3. Enter the beginning balances and then post the transactions to the following accounts:

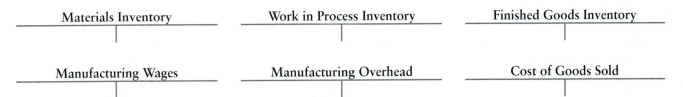

Materials Inventory   Work in Process Inventory   Finished Goods Inventory

Manufacturing Wages   Manufacturing Overhead   Cost of Goods Sold

4. Close the ending balance of Manufacturing Overhead. Post your entry to the T-accounts.

5. What are the ending balances in the three inventory accounts and in Cost of Goods Sold?

Solution

Requirement 1

$$\text{Predetermined manufacturing overhead rate} = \frac{\text{Total estimated manufacturing overhead cost}}{\text{Total estimated quantity of allocation base}}$$

$$= \frac{\$240{,}000}{4{,}000 \text{ machine hours}}$$

$$= \$60/\text{machine hour}$$

Requirement 2
Journal entries:

a.	Materials Inventory		31,000	
	Accounts Payable			31,000
b.	Work in Process Inventory		39,000	
	Materials Inventory			39,000
c.	Manufacturing Wages		40,000	
	Wages Payable			40,000
d.	Work in Process Inventory ($40,000 × 0.90)		36,000	
	Manufacturing Overhead ($40,000 × 0.10)		4,000	
	Manufacturing Wages			40,000
e.	Manufacturing Overhead		3,000	
	Materials Inventory			3,000
f.	Manufacturing Overhead		13,000	
	Accounts Payable			13,000
g.	Work in Process Inventory (300 × $60)		18,000	
	Manufacturing Overhead			18,000
h.	Finished Goods Inventory		100,000	
	Work in Process Inventory			100,000
i.	Accounts Receivable		175,000	
	Sales Revenue			175,000
j.	Costs of Goods Sold		95,000	
	Finished Goods Inventory			95,000

Requirement 3
Post the transactions:

Materials Inventory			
Bal.	20,000	(b)	39,000
(a)	31,000	(e)	3,000
Bal.	9,000		

Work in Process Inventory			
Bal.	17,000	(h)	100,000
(b)	39,000		
(d)	36,000		
(g)	18,000		
Bal.	10,000		

Finished Goods Inventory			
Bal.	11,000	(j)	95,000
(h)	100,000		
Bal.	16,000		

Manufacturing Wages			
(c)	40,000	(d)	40,000

Manufacturing Overhead			
(d)	4,000	(g)	18,000
(e)	3,000		
(f)	13,000		
Bal.	2,000		

Cost of Goods Sold			
(j)	95,000		

Requirement 4
Close Manufacturing Overhead:

Cost of Goods Sold		2,000	
Manufacturing Overhead			2,000

Manufacturing Overhead			
(d)	4,000	(g)	18,000
(e)	3,000		2,000
(f)	13,000		

Cost of Goods Sold			
(j)	95,000		
	2,000		
Bal.	97,000		

Requirement 5
Ending Balances:

Materials Inventory (from Requirement 3)	$ 9,000
Work in Process Inventory (from Requirement 3)	10,000
Finished Goods Inventory (from Requirement 3)	16,000
Cost of Goods Sold (from Requirement 4)	97,000

Review *Job Order Costing*

Accounting Vocabulary

Allocation Base
A common denominator that links indirect costs to cost objects. Ideally, the allocation base is the primary cost driver of the indirect costs.

Cost Allocation
Assigning indirect costs (such as manufacturing overhead) to cost objects (such as jobs or production processes).

Cost Driver
The primary factor that causes a cost.

Cost Tracing
Assigning direct costs (such as direct materials and direct labor) to cost objects (such as jobs or production processes) that used those costs.

Job Cost Record
Document that accumulates the direct materials, direct labor, and manufacturing overhead costs assigned to an individual job.

Job Order Costing
A system that accumulates costs for each job. Law firms, music studios, health-care providers, mail-order catalog companies, building contractors, and custom furniture manufacturers are examples of companies that use job order costing systems.

Labor Time Record
Identifies the employee, the amount of time spent on a particular job, and the labor cost charged to the job; a record used to assign direct labor cost to specific jobs.

Materials Requisition
Request for the transfer of materials to the production floor, prepared by the production team.

Overallocated (manufacturing) Overhead
The manufacturing overhead allocated to Work in Progress Inventory is more than the amount of manufacturing overhead costs actually incurred.

Predetermined Manufacturing Overhead Rate
Estimated manufacturing overhead cost per unit of the allocation base, computed at the beginning of the year.

Process Costing
System for assigning costs to large numbers of identical units that usually proceed in a continuous fashion through a series of uniform productions steps or processes.

Time Record
Source document used to trace direct labor to specific jobs.

Underallocated (manufacturing) Overhead
The manufacturing overhead allocated to Work in Progress Inventory is less than the amount of manufacturing overhead costs actually incurred.

Quick Check

1. Would an advertising agency use job or process costing? What about a paper mill?
   a. Advertising agency—job order costing
      Paper mill—job order costing
   b. Advertising agency—process costing
      Paper mill—job order costing
   c. Advertising agency—job order costing
      Paper mill—process costing
   d. Advertising agency—process costing
      Paper mill—process costing

2. When a manufacturing company *uses* direct materials, it *traces* the cost by debiting:
   a. Materials Inventory
   b. Direct Materials
   c. Work in Process Inventory
   d. Manufacturing Overhead

3. When a manufacturing company *uses* indirect materials, it *assigns* the cost by debiting:
   a. Materials Inventory
   b. Manufacturing Overhead
   c. Indirect Materials
   d. Work in Process Inventory

4. When a manufacturing company *uses* direct labor, it *traces* the cost by debiting:
   a. Work in Process Inventory
   b. Manufacturing Wages
   c. Manufacturing Overhead
   d. Direct Labor

Questions 5, 6, 7, and 8 are based on the following information about Dell Corporation's manufacturing of computers. Assume Dell
- Allocates manufacturing overhead based on machine hours.
- Budgeted 10 million machine hours and $90 million of manufacturing overhead costs.
- Actually used 12 million machine hours and incurred the following actual costs (in millions):

Indirect labor	$10
Depreciation on plant	47
Machinery repair	15
Direct labor	75
Plant supplies	5
Plant utilities	8
Advertising	35
Sales commissions	25

5. What is Dell's predetermined manufacturing overhead rate?
   a. $0.11/machine hour
   b. $0.13/machine hour
   c. $7.50/machine hour
   d. $9.00/machine hour

6. What is Dell's actual manufacturing overhead cost?
   a. $220
   b. $160
   c. $120
   d. $85

7. How much manufacturing overhead would Dell allocate?
   a. $108
   b. $90
   c. $85
   d. $220

8. What entry would Dell make to close the manufacturing overhead account?

a.	Manufacturing Overhead	5	
	Costs of Goods Sold		5
b.	Cost of Goods Sold	5	
	Manufacturing Overhead		5
c.	Manufacturing Overhead	23	
	Costs of Goods Sold		23
d.	Cost of Goods Sold	23	
	Manufacturing Overhead		23

9. Dell's management can use product cost information to:
   a. Set prices of its products
   b. Decide which products to emphasize
   c. Identify ways to cut production costs
   d. All of the above

10. For which of the following reasons would John Walsh, owner of the Walsh Associates law firm, want to know the total costs of a job (serving a particular client)?
    a. For inventory valuation
    b. To determine the fees to charge clients
    c. For external reporting
    d. For all of the above

Answers are given after Apply Your Knowledge (p. 899).

Assess Your Progress

Short Exercises

Distinguishing between job costing and process costing

S17-1 Would the following companies use job order costing or process costing? (pp. 852–853)

    A manufacturer of plywood

    A manufacturer of wakeboards

    A manufacturer of luxury yachts

    A professional services firm

    A landscape contractor

Flow of costs in job order costing

S17-2 For a manufacturer that uses job order costing, show the order of the cost flow through the following accounts, starting with the purchase of materials in the Materials Inventory (1). (p. 853)

    __1__ a. Materials Inventory

    _____ b. Finished Goods Inventory

    _____ c. Cost of Goods Sold

    _____ d. Work in Process Inventory

Accounting for materials

S17-3 PackRite manufactures backpacks. Its plant records include the following materials-related transactions:

Purchases of canvas (on account)	$70,000
Purchases of thread (on account)	1,000
Material requisitions:	
Canvas	63,000
Thread	300

What journal entries record these transactions? Post these transactions to the Materials Inventory account. If the company had $35,000 of Materials Inventory at the beginning of the period, what is the ending balance of Materials Inventory? (pp. 853–855).

Accounting for materials

S17-4 Use the following T-accounts to determine direct materials used and indirect materials used. (pp. 853–855)

Materials Inventory				Work in Process Inventory			
Bal.	15			Bal.	30		
Purchases	230	X		Direct materials	Y	Cost of goods manufactured	630
Bal.	25			Direct labor	300		
				Manufacturing overhead	150		
				Bal.	50		

Job Order Costing

Accounting for labor

S17-5 Seattle Crystal reports the following labor-related transactions at its plant in Seattle, Washington.

Plant janitor's wages	600
Furnace operator's wages	900
Glass blowers' wages	75,000

Record the journal entries for the incurrence and assignment of these wages. (pp. 855–858)

Accounting for overhead

S17-6 Teak Outdoor Furniture manufactures wood patio furniture. The company reports the following costs for June 2008. What is the balance in the Manufacturing Overhead account? (p. 862)

Wood	$230,000
Nails, glue, and stain	21,000
Depreciation on saws	5,000
Indirect manufacturing labor	40,000
Depreciation on delivery truck	2,200
Assembly-line workers' wages	56,000

Allocating overhead

S17-7 Job 303 includes direct materials cost of $500 and direct labor costs of $400. If the manufacturing overhead allocation rate is 70% of direct labor cost, what is the total cost assigned to Job 303? (pp. 863–864)

Accounting for materials, labor, overhead, and completed goods

S17-8 Boston Enterprises produces LCD touch screen products. The company reports the following information at December 31, 2008. Boston began operations on January 30, 2008.

Materials Inventory		Work in Process Inventory		Finished Goods Inventory		Manufacturing Wages		Manufacturing Overhead	
52,000	33,000	30,000	125,000	125,000	110,000	72,000	72,000	3,000	54,000
		60,000						12,000	
		54,000						37,000	

1. What is the cost of direct materials used? The cost of indirect materials used?
2. What is the cost of direct labor? The cost of indirect labor?
3. What is the cost of goods manufactured?
4. What is cost of goods sold (before adjusting for any under- or overallocated manufacturing overhead)? (pp. 865–866)

Allocating overhead

S17-9 Refer to S17-8.

1. What is the actual manufacturing overhead of Boston Enterprises? Allocated manufacturing overhead? (pp. 866–867)
2. Is manufacturing overhead underallocated or overallocated? By how much? (pp. 866–867)

Under/overallocated overhead

S17-10 The T-account showing the manufacturing overhead activity for Brian Corp. for 2007 is as follows:

Manufacturing Overhead	
200,000	210,000

1. What is the actual manufacturing overhead? Allocated manufacturing overhead? (p. 866)
2. What is the predetermined manufacturing overhead rate as a percentage of direct labor cost, if actual direct labor costs were $168,000? (p. 853)
3. Is manufacturing overhead underallocated or overallocated? By how much? (pp. 866–867)
4. Is Cost of Goods Sold too high or too low? (pp. 866–867)

Closing out under/overallocated overhead

S17-11 Refer to S17-10. Make the journal entry to close out Brian Corp.'s Manufacturing Overhead account. (pp. 866–867)

Job order costing in a service company

S17-12 Sautter Advertising pays Thomas Tibbs $110,000 per year. Tibbs works 2,000 hours per year.

1. What is the hourly cost to Sautter Advertising of employing Tibbs? (pp. 869–871)
2. What direct labor cost would be traced to client 507 if Tibbs works 14 hours to prepare client 507's magazine ad? (pp. 868–871)

Job order costing in a service company

S17-13 Refer to S17-12. Assume that Sautter's advertising agents are expected to work a total of 12,000 direct labor hours in 2009. Sautter's estimated total indirect costs are $240,000.

1. What is Sautter's indirect cost allocation rate? (pp. 868–871)
2. What indirect costs will be allocated to client 507 if Tibbs works 14 hours to prepare the magazine ad? (pp. 868–871)

Exercises

Distinguishing job order and process costing

E17-14 Complete the following statements with the term job order costing or process costing. (pp. 852–853)

a. _____ is used by companies that produce small quantities of many different products.
b. Georgia-Pacific pulverizes wood into pulp to manufacture cardboard. The company uses a _____ system.
c. To record costs of maintaining thousands of identical mortgage files, financial institutions like Money Tree use a _____ system.
d. Companies that produce large numbers of identical products use _____ systems for product costing.
e. The computer repair service that visits your home and repairs your computer uses a _____ system.

Accounting for job costs

E17-15 Thrifty Trailers' job cost records yielded the following information:

Job No.	Date Started	Date Finished	Date Sold	Total Cost of Job at March 31
1	February 21	March 16	March 17	$ 3,000
2	February 29	March 21	March 26	13,000
3	March 3	April 11	April 13	6,000
4	March 7	March 29	April 1	4,000

Requirements

Using the dates above to identify the status of each job, compute Thrifty's cost of (a) Work in Process Inventory at March 31, (b) Finished Goods Inventory at March 31, and (c) Cost of Goods Sold for March. (pp. 865–866)

Job order costing journal entries

E17-16 Record the following transactions in Sloan's Seats' general journal. (pp. 873–875)

a. Incurred and paid Web site expenses, $3,500.
b. Incurred and paid manufacturing wages, $15,000.
c. Purchased materials on account, $14,000.
d. Used in production: direct materials, $6,000; indirect materials, $4,000.
e. Assigned $15,000 of manufacturing labor to jobs, 60% of which was direct labor and 40% of which was indirect labor.
f. Recorded manufacturing overhead: depreciation on plant, $13,000; plant insurance, $1,000; plant property tax, $4,000 (credit Property Tax Payable).
g. Allocated manufacturing overhead to jobs, 200% of direct labor costs.
h. Completed production, $30,000.
i. Sold inventory on account, $20,000; cost of goods sold, $10,000.

Identifying job order costing journal entries

E17-17 Describe the lettered transactions in the following manufacturing accounts: (pp. 873–875)

Materials Inventory	
(a)	(b)

Work in Process Inventory	
(b)	(g)
(d)	
(f)	

Finished Goods Inventory	
(g)	(h)

Manufacturing Wages	
(c)	(d)

Manufacturing Overhead	
(b)	(f)
(d)	(i)
(e)	

Cost of Goods Sold	
(h)	
(i)	

Using the Work in Process Inventory account

E17-18 September production generated the following activity in Rohr Chassis Company's Work in Process Inventory account:

Work in Process Inventory	
September 1 Bal.	20,000
Direct materials used	30,000
Direct labor assigned to jobs	32,000
Manufacturing overhead allocated to jobs	16,000

continued...

Completed production, not yet recorded, consists of Jobs 142 and 143, with total costs of $40,000 and $38,000, respectively.

Requirements
1. Compute the cost of work in process at September 30. (pp. 873–875)
2. Prepare the journal entry for production completed in September. (pp. 865–866)
3. Prepare the journal entry to record the sale (on credit) of Job 143 for $45,000. Also make the cost-of-goods-sold entry. (pp. 873–875)
4. What is the gross profit on Job 143? What other costs must this gross profit cover?

Allocating manufacturing overhead

E17-19 Selected cost data for Classic Poster Co. are as follows:

Estimated manufacturing overhead cost for the year	$100,000
Estimated direct labor cost for the year	80,000
Actual manufacturing overhead cost for the year	83,000
Actual direct labor cost for the year	64,000

Requirements
1. Compute the predetermined manufacturing overhead rate per direct labor dollar. (p. 863)
2. Prepare the journal entry to allocate overhead cost for the year. (p. 864)
3. Use a T-account to determine the amount of underallocated or overallocated manufacturing overhead. (pp. 866–867)
4. Prepare the journal entry to close the balance of the Manufacturing Overhead account. (pp. 866–867)

Allocating manufacturing overhead

E17-20 Alba Foundry uses a predetermined manufacturing overhead rate to allocate overhead to individual jobs, based on the machine hours required. At the beginning of 2009, the company expected to incur the following:

Manufacturing overhead costs	$ 600,000
Direct labor cost	1,500,000
Machine hours	60,000

At the end of 2009, the company had actually incurred:

Direct labor cost	$1,210,000
Depreciation on manufacturing property, plant, and equipment	480,000
Property taxes on plant	20,000
Sales salaries	25,000
Delivery drivers' wages	15,000
Plant janitors' wages	10,000
Machine hours	55,000 hours

continued...

Requirements

1. Compute Alba's predetermined manufacturing overhead rate. (p. 863)
2. Record the summary journal entry for allocating manufacturing overhead. (p. 864)
3. Post the manufacturing overhead transactions to the Manufacturing Overhead T-account. Is manufacturing overhead underallocated or overallocated? By how much? (pp. 866–867)
4. Close the Manufacturing Overhead account to Cost of Goods Sold. Does your entry increase or decrease cost of goods sold? (pp. 866–867)

Allocating manufacturing overhead

E17-21 Refer to the data in E17-20. Alba's accountant found an error in her 2009 cost records. Depreciation on manufacturing property, plant, and equipment was actually $530,000, not the $480,000 she originally reported.

Unadjusted balances at the end of 2009 include:

Finished Goods Inventory	$130,000
Cost of Goods Sold	600,000

Requirements

1. Use a T-account to determine whether manufacturing overhead is underallocated or overallocated, and by how much. (pp. 866–867)
2. Record the entry to close out the underallocated or overallocated manufacturing overhead. (pp. 866–867)
3. What is the adjusted ending balance of Cost of Goods Sold? (pp. 866–867)

Job order costing in a service company

E17-22 Martin Realtors, a real estate consulting firm, specializes in advising companies on potential new plant sites. The company uses a job order costing system with a predetermined indirect cost allocation rate, computed as a percentage of direct labor costs.

At the beginning of 2009, managing partner Ken Martin prepared the following budget for the year:

Direct labor hours (professionals)	17,000 hours
Direct labor costs (professionals)	$2,550,000
Office rent	300,000
Support staff salaries	900,000
Utilities	330,000

Lieberman Manufacturing, Inc., is inviting several consultants to bid for work. Ken Martin estimates that this job will require about 220 direct labor hours.

Requirements

1. Compute Martin Realtors' (a) hourly direct labor cost rate and (b) indirect cost allocation rate. (pp. 868–871)

continued...

2. Compute the predicted cost of the Lieberman Manufacturing job. (pp. 868–871)

3. If Martin wants to earn a profit that equals 50% of the job's cost, how much should he bid for the Lieberman Manufacturing job? (pp. 868–871)

Allocating manufacturing overhead

E17-23 The manufacturing records for Kool Kayaks at the end of the 2008 fiscal year show the following information about manufacturing overhead:

Overhead allocated to production	$405,000
Actual manufacturing overhead costs	$430,250
Overhead allocation rate for the year	$40 per machine hour

Requirements

1. How many machine hours did Kool Kayaks use in 2008? (p. 864)
2. Was manufacturing overhead over- or underallocated for the year? By how much? (pp. 866–867)
3. Record the entry to close out the over- or underallocated overhead. (pp. 866–867)

Problems (Group A)

Analyzing job cost data

P17-24A Hartley Manufacturing makes carrying cases for portable electronic devices. Its job order costing records yield the following information:

Job No.	Date Started	Date Finished	Sold	Total Cost of Job at November 30	Total Manufacturing Costs Added in December
1	11/3	11/12	11/13	$1,500	
2	11/3	11/30	12/1	2,000	
3	11/17	12/24	12/27	300	$ 700
4	11/29	12/29	1/3	500	1,600
5	12/8	12/12	12/14		750
6	12/23	1/6	1/9		500

Requirements

1. Using the dates above to identify the status of each job, compute Hartley's account balances at November 30 for Work in Process Inventory, Finished Goods Inventory, and Cost of Goods Sold. Compute account balances at December 31 for Work in Process Inventory, Finished Goods Inventory, and Cost of Goods Sold. (pp. 865–866)
2. Record summary journal entries for the transfer of completed units from work in process to finished goods for November and December. (pp. 865–866)
3. Record the sale of Job 3 for $1,500. (pp. 865–866)
4. What is the gross profit for Job 3? What other costs must this gross profit cover?

Accounting for construction transactions

P17-25A Steinborn Construction, Inc., is a home builder in New Mexico. Steinborn uses a job order costing system in which each house is a job. Because it constructs houses, the company uses accounts titled Construction Wages and Construction Overhead. The following events occurred during August:

a. Purchased materials on account, $480,000.

b. Incurred construction wages of $220,000. Requisitioned direct materials and used direct labor in construction:

	Direct Materials	Direct Labor
House 402	$58,000	$42,000
House 403	69,000	33,000
House 404	68,000	50,000
House 405	85,000	53,000

c. Depreciation of construction equipment, $6,400.

d. Other construction overhead costs incurred on houses 402 through 405:

Indirect labor...	$42,000
Equipment rentals paid in cash	37,000
Worker liability insurance expired	7,000

e. Allocated overhead to jobs at the predetermined overhead rate of 40% of direct labor cost.

f. Houses completed: 402, 404.

g. House sold: 404 for $200,000.

Requirements

1. Record the events in the general journal. (p. 864)
2. Open T-accounts for Work in Process Inventory and Finished Goods Inventory. Post the appropriate entries to these accounts, identifying each entry by letter. Determine the ending account balances, assuming that the beginning balances were zero. (pp. 873–875)
3. Add the costs of the unfinished houses, and show that this total amount equals the ending balance in the Work in Process Inventory account. (p. 864)
4. Add the cost of the completed house that has not yet been sold, and show that this equals the ending balance in Finished Goods Inventory. (p. 864)
5. Compute gross profit on the house that was sold. What costs must gross profit cover for Steinborn Construction?

Preparing and using a job cost record

P17-26A Yu Technology Co. manufactures CDs and DVDs for computer software and entertainment companies. Yu uses job order costing and has a perpetual inventory system.

continued...

On November 2, Yu began production of 5,000 DVDs, Job 423, for Cheetah Pictures for $1.10 each. Yu promised to deliver the DVDs to Cheetah by November 5. Yu incurred the following costs:

Date	Labor Time Record No.	Description	Amount
11-2	655	10 hours @ $20	$200
11-3	656	20 hours @ $15	300

Date	Materials Requisition No.	Description	Amount
11-2	63	31 lbs. polycarbonate plastic @ $11	$341
11-2	64	25 lbs. acrylic plastic @ $28	700
11-3	74	3 lbs. refined aluminum @ $48	144

Yu Technology allocates manufacturing overhead to jobs based on the relation between estimated overhead ($540,000) and estimated direct labor costs ($450,000). Job 423 was completed and shipped on November 3.

Requirements
1. Prepare a job cost record similar to Exhibit 17-7 for Job 423. Calculate the predetermined overhead rate, then apply manufacturing overhead to the job. (pp. 863–864)
2. Journalize in summary form the requisition of direct materials and the assignment of direct labor and manufacturing overhead to Job 423. (pp. 853–854, 855–856, 865–866)
3. Journalize completion of the job and the sale of the 5,000 DVDs. (pp. 865–866)

Accounting for manufacturing overhead
3 4

P17-27A Weiters Woods manufactures jewelry boxes. The primary materials (wood, brass, and glass) and direct labor are traced directly to the products. Manufacturing overhead costs are allocated based on machine hours. Data for 2008 follow:

	Budget	Actual
Machine hours	28,000 hours	32,800 hours
Maintenance labor (repairs to equipment)	12,000	22,500
Plant supervisor's salary	42,000	44,000
Screws, nails, and glue	23,000	41,000
Plant utilities	48,000	90,850
Freight out	35,000	44,500
Depreciation on plant and equipment	85,000	81,000
Advertising expenses	40,000	55,000

Requirements
1. Compute the predetermined manufacturing overhead rate. (p. 863)
2. Post actual and allocated manufacturing overhead to the Manufacturing Overhead T-account. (pp. 865–866)

continued...

3. Close the under- or overallocated overhead to Cost of Goods Sold. (pp. 866–867)
4. The predetermined manufacturing overhead rate usually turns out to be inaccurate. Why don't accountants just use the actual manufacturing overhead rate? (p. 863)

Comprehensive accounting for manufacturing transactions

P17-28A Lonyx Telecommunications produces components for telecommunication systems. Initially the company manufactured the parts for its own networks, but it gradually began selling them to other companies as well. Lonyx's trial balance on April 1 follows.

LONYX TELECOMMUNICATIONS
Trial Balance
April 1, 2009

Account Title	Balance Debit	Balance Credit
Cash	$ 18,000	
Accounts receivable	170,000	
Inventories:		
Materials	5,300	
Work in process	41,300	
Finished goods	21,300	
Plant assets	250,000	
Accumulated depreciation		$ 68,000
Accounts payable		129,000
Wages payable		2,800
Common stock		140,000
Retained earnings		166,100
Sales revenue		—
Cost of goods sold	—	
Manufacturing wages	—	
Manufacturing overhead	—	
Marketing and general expenses	—	
	$505,900	$505,900

April 1 balances in the subsidiary ledgers were:
- Materials ledger: glass substrate, $4,800; indirect materials, $500.
- Work in process ledger: Job 120, $41,300.
- Finished goods ledger: fiber optic cable, $9,300; laser diodes, $12,000.

April transactions are summarized as follows:
a. Collections on account, $149,000.
b. Marketing and general expenses incurred and paid, $25,000.
c. Payments on account, $38,000.
d. Materials purchased on credit: glass substrate, $24,500; indirect materials, $4,600.

continued...

e. Materials used in production (requisitioned):
   - Job 120: glass substrate, $750.
   - Job 121: glass substrate, $7,800.
   - Indirect materials, $2,000.
f. Manufacturing wages incurred during April, $38,000, of which $36,000 was paid. Wages payable at March 31 were paid during April, $2,800.
g. Labor time records for the month: Job 120, $4,000; Job 121, $18,000; indirect labor, $16,000.
h. Depreciation on plant and equipment, $2,400.
i. Manufacturing overhead was allocated at the predetermined rate of 70% of direct labor cost.
j. Jobs completed during the month: Job 120, 400 fiber optic cables at total cost of $48,850.
k. Credit sales on account: all of Job 120 for $110,000.
l. Closed the Manufacturing Overhead account to Cost of Goods Sold.

Requirements

1. Open T-accounts for the general ledger, the materials ledger, the work in process ledger, and the finished goods ledger. Insert each account balance as given, and use the reference *Bal.* (pp. 873–875)
2. Record the April transactions directly in the accounts, using the letters as references. Lonyx uses a perpetual inventory system. (pp. 873–875)
3. Prepare a trial balance at April 30.
4. Use the Work in Process T-account to prepare a schedule of cost of goods manufactured for the month of April. (You may want to review Exhibit 16-10.)
5. Prepare an income statement for the month of April. To calculate cost of goods sold, you may want to review Exhibit 16-7. (*Hint:* In transaction l you closed any under/overallocated manufacturing overhead to Cost of Goods Sold. In the income statement, show this correction as an adjustment to Cost of Goods Sold. If manufacturing overhead is underallocated, the adjustment will increase Cost of Goods Sold. If overhead is overallocated, the adjustment will decrease Cost of Goods Sold.)

Job order costing in a service company

P17-29A Bluebird Design, Inc., is a Web site design and consulting firm. The firm uses a job order costing system, in which each client is a different job. Bluebird Design traces direct labor, licensing costs, and travel costs directly to each job. It allocates indirect costs to jobs based on a predetermined indirect cost allocation rate, computed as a percentage of direct labor costs.

At the beginning of 2009, managing partner Judi Jacquin prepared the following budget:

Direct labor hours (professional)............	6,250 hours
Direct labor costs (professional).............	$1,000,000
Support staff salaries...............................	120,000
Computer leases......................................	45,000
Office supplies...	25,000
Office rent...	60,000

continued...

In November 2009, Bluebird Design served several clients. Records for two clients appear here:

	Food Coop	Mesilla Chocolates
Direct labor hours	750 hours	50 hours
Licensing costs	$ 2,000	$150
Travel costs	14,000	—

Requirements

1. Compute Bluebird Design's predetermined indirect cost allocation rate for 2009. (pp. 868–871)
2. Compute the total cost of each job. (pp. 868–871)
3. If Jacquin wants to earn profits equal to 20% of sales revenue, how much (what fee) should she charge each of these two clients? (pp. 868–871)
4. Why does Bluebird Design assign costs to jobs? (pp. 868–871)

Problems (Group B)

Analyzing job cost data

P17-30B EnginePro, Inc., reconditions engines. Its job order costing records yield the following information. EnginePro uses a perpetual inventory system.

Job No.	Date Started	Date Finished	Sold	Total Cost of Job at March 31	Total Manufacturing Costs Added in April
1	2/26	3/7	3/9	$1,400	
2	2/3	3/12	3/13	1,600	
3	3/29	3/31	4/3	1,300	
4	3/31	4/1	4/1	500	$ 400
5	4/8	4/12	4/14		700
6	4/23	5/6	5/9		1,200

Requirements

1. Using the dates above to identify the status of each job, compute EnginePro's account balances at March 31 for Work in Process Inventory, Finished Goods Inventory, and Cost of Goods Sold. Compute account balances at April 30 for Work in Process Inventory, Finished Goods Inventory, and Cost of Goods Sold. (pp. 865–866)
2. Make summary journal entries to record the transfer of completed jobs from Work in Process to Finished Goods for March and April. (pp. 865–866)
3. Record the sale of Job 5 for $1,600. (pp. 865–866)
4. Compute the gross profit for Job 5. What costs must the gross profit cover?

Accounting for manufacturing transactions

P17-31B Vacation Homes manufactures prefabricated chalets in Utah. The company uses a job order costing system in which each chalet is a job. The following events occurred during May.

a. Purchased materials on account, $405,000.
b. Incurred manufacturing wages of $112,000. Requisitioned direct materials and used direct labor in manufacturing:

	Direct Materials	Direct Labor
Chalet 20	$41,000	$15,000
Chalet 21	56,000	29,000
Chalet 22	62,000	19,000
Chalet 23	66,000	21,000

c. Depreciation of manufacturing equipment, $20,000.
d. Other overhead costs incurred on chalets 20 through 23:

Indirect labor..	$28,000
Equipment rentals paid in cash............	10,400
Plant insurance expired........................	6,000

e. Allocated overhead to jobs at the predetermined rate of 60% of direct labor cost.
f. Chalets completed: 20, 22, and 23.
g. Chalets sold: 20 for $99,000; 23 for $141,900.

Requirements
1. Record the preceding events in the general journal. (p. 874)
2. Open T-accounts for Work in Process Inventory and Finished Goods Inventory. Post the appropriate entries to these accounts, identifying each entry by letter. Determine the ending account balances, assuming that the beginning balances were zero. (pp. 855–856)
3. Add the costs of the unfinished chalet, and show that this equals the ending balance in Work in Process Inventory. (p. 866)
4. Add the cost of the completed chalet that has not yet been sold, and show that this equals the ending balance in Finished Goods Inventory. (p. 864)
5. Compute the gross profit on each chalet that was sold. What costs must the gross profit cover for Vacation Homes?

Preparing and using a job cost record

P17-32B Alamo Co. manufactures tires for all-terrain vehicles. Alamo uses job order costing and has a perpetual inventory system.

On June 22, 2008, Alamo received an order for 100 TX tires from ATV Corporation at a price of $55 each. The job, assigned number 300, was promised for July 10. After purchasing the materials, Alamo began production on June 30 and incurred the following costs in completing the order:

Date	Labor Time Record No.	Description	Amount
6/30	1896	12.5 hours @ $20	$250
7/3	1904	30 hours @ $19	570

continued...

Date	Materials Requisition No.	Description	Amount
6/30	437	60 lbs. rubber @ $12	$ 720
7/2	439	40 meters polyester fabric @ $12.50	500
7/3	501	100 meters steel cord @ $10	1,000

Alamo allocates manufacturing overhead to jobs on the basis of the relation between estimated overhead ($400,000) and estimated direct labor cost ($250,000). Job 300 was completed on July 3 and shipped to ATV on July 5.

Requirements

1. Prepare a job cost record similar to Exhibit 17-7 for Job 300. Calculate the predetermined overhead rate, then apply manufacturing overhead to the job. (pp. 863–864)
2. Journalize in summary form the requisition of direct materials and the assignment of direct labor and manufacturing overhead to Job 300. (pp. 853–854, 855–856, 865–866)
3. Journalize completion of the job and sale of the tires. (pp. 865–866)

Accounting for manufacturing overhead
3 **4**

P17-33B Regal Company produces hospital uniforms. The company allocates manufacturing overhead based on the machine hours each job uses. Regal reports the following cost data for 2009:

	Budget	Actual
Machine hours	7,000 hours	6,500 hours
Indirect materials	50,000	52,000
Depreciation on trucks used to deliver uniforms to customers	14,000	12,000
Depreciation on plant and equipment	65,000	67,000
Indirect manufacturing labor	40,000	43,000
Customer service hotline	19,000	21,000
Plant utilities	27,000	20,000

Requirements

1. Compute the predetermined manufacturing overhead rate. (p. 863)
2. Post actual and allocated manufacturing overhead to the Manufacturing Overhead T-account. (pp. 865–866)
3. Close the under- or overallocated overhead to Cost of Goods Sold. (pp. 866–867)
4. How can managers use accounting information to help control manufacturing overhead costs? (pp. 873–874)

Comprehensive accounting for manufacturing transactions

P17-34B WireComm manufactures specialized components used in wireless communication. Initially, the company manufactured the components for its own use, but it gradually began selling them to other wireless companies as well. The trial balance of WireComm's manufacturing operations on January 1, 2009, is as follows:

WIRECOMM—MANUFACTURING OPERATIONS
Trial Balance
January 1, 2009

Account Title	Balance Debit	Balance Credit
Cash	$147,000	
Accounts receivable	88,000	
Inventories:		
Materials	17,000	
Work in process	44,000	
Finished goods	61,000	
Plant assets	353,000	
Accumulated depreciation		$157,000
Accounts payable		84,000
Wages payable		5,500
Common stock		225,000
Retained earnings		238,500
Sales revenues		—
Cost of goods sold	—	
Manufacturing wages	—	
Manufacturing overhead	—	
Marketing and general expenses	—	
	$710,000	$710,000

January 1 balances in the subsidiary ledgers were:
- Materials ledger: electronic parts, $15,300; indirect materials, $1,700.
- Work in process ledger: Job 90, $44,000.
- Finished goods ledger: transmitters, $38,000; power supplies, $23,000.

January transactions are summarized as follows:
a. Payments on account, $81,000.
b. Marketing and general expenses incurred and paid, $22,000.
c. Collections on account, $195,000.
d. Materials purchased on credit: electronic parts, $49,000; indirect materials, $6,000.
e. Materials used in production (requisitioned):
- Job 90: electronic parts, $4,000.
- Job 91: electronic parts, $38,000.
- Indirect materials, $7,000.

continued . . .

f. Manufacturing wages incurred during January, $56,000, of which $50,500 was paid. Wages payable at December 31 were paid during January, $5,500.

g. Labor time records for the month: Job 90, $6,000; Job 91, $28,000; indirect labor, $22,000.

h. Depreciation on manufacturing plant and equipment, $7,500.

i. Manufacturing overhead was allocated at the predetermined rate of 120% of direct labor cost.

j. Jobs completed during the month: Job 90, 1,000 transmitters, at total cost of $61,200.

k. Credit sales on account: all of Job 90 for $125,000.

l. Close the Manufacturing Overhead account to Cost of Goods Sold.

Requirements

1. Open T-accounts for the general ledger, the materials ledger, the work in process ledger, and the finished goods ledger. Insert each account balance as given, and use the reference *Bal.* (pp. 873–875)

2. Record the January transactions directly in the accounts, using the letters as references. WireComm uses a perpetual inventory system. (pp. 873–875)

3. Prepare a trial balance at January 31.

4. Use the Work in Process T-account to prepare a schedule of cost of goods manufactured for the month of January. (You may want to review Exhibit 16-10.)

5. Prepare an income statement for the month of January. To calculate cost of goods sold, you may want to review Exhibit 16-7. (*Hint:* In transaction l, you closed any under/overallocated manufacturing overhead to Cost of Goods Sold. In the income statement, show this correction as an adjustment to Cost of Goods Sold. If manufacturing overhead is underallocated, the adjustment will increase Cost of Goods Sold. If overhead is overallocated, the adjustment will decrease Cost of Goods Sold.)

Job order costing in a service company

P17-35B Simms Advertising is an Internet advertising agency. The firm uses a job order costing system in which each client is a different job. Simms Advertising traces direct labor, software licensing costs, and travel costs directly to each job. The company allocates indirect costs to jobs based on a predetermined indirect cost allocation rate, computed as a percentage of direct labor costs.

At the beginning of 2008, managing partner Stacy Simms prepared the following budget:

Direct labor hours (professional)	16,000 hours
Direct labor costs (professional)	$1,600,000
Support staff salaries	350,000
Rent and utilities	150,000
Supplies	15,000
Leased computer hardware	285,000

continued...

In January 2008, Simms Advertising served several clients. Records for two clients appear here:

	VacationPlan.com	Port Arthur Golf Resort
Direct labor hours...................	450 hours	30 hours
Software licensing costs............	$1,500	$300
Travel costs.............................	9,000	—

Requirements

1. Compute Simms Advertising's predetermined indirect cost allocation rate for 2008. (pp. 868–871)
2. Compute the total cost of each job. (pp. 868–871)
3. If Simms Advertising wants to earn profits equal to 30% of sales revenue, how much (what fee) should it charge each of these two clients? (pp. 868–871)
4. Why does Simms Advertising assign costs to jobs? (pp. 868–871)

for 24/7 practice, visit www.MyAccountingLab.com

Apply Your Knowledge

Decision Cases

Costing and pricing identical products

Case 1. Hiebert Chocolate Ltd. is located in Memphis. The company prepares gift boxes of chocolates for private parties and corporate promotions. Each order contains a selection of chocolates determined by the customer, and the box is designed to the customer's specifications. Accordingly, Hiebert uses a job order costing system and allocates manufacturing overhead based on direct labor cost.

One of Hiebert's largest customers is the Goforth and Leos law firm. This organization sends chocolates to its clients each Christmas and also provides them to employees at the firm's gatherings. The law firm's managing partner, Bob Goforth, placed the client gift order in September for 500 boxes of cream-filled dark chocolates. But Goforth and Leos did not place its December staff-party order until the last week of November. This order was for an additional 100 boxes of chocolates identical to the ones to be distributed to clients.

Hiebert budgeted the cost per box for the original 500-box order as follows:

Chocolate, filling, wrappers, box..	$14.00
Employee time to fill and wrap the box (10 min.)	2.00
Manufacturing overhead	1.00
Total manufacturing cost...	$17.00

Ben Hiebert, president of Hiebert Chocolate Ltd., priced the order at $20 per box.

In the past few months, Hiebert has experienced price increases for both dark chocolate and direct labor. All other costs have remained the same. Hiebert budgeted the cost per box for the second order as:

Chocolate, filling, wrappers, box..	$15.00
Employee time to fill and wrap the box (10 min.)	2.20
Manufacturing overhead	1.10
Total manufacturing cost...	$18.30

1. Do you agree with the cost analysis for the second order? Explain your answer. (pp. 853–854, 864–866)

2. Should the two orders be accounted for as one job or two in Hiebert's system? (pp. 853–854)

3. What sale price per box should Ben Hiebert set for the second order? What are the advantages and disadvantages of this price?

Accounting for manufacturing overhead

Case 2. Nature's Own manufactures organic fruit preserves sold primarily through health food stores and on the Web. The company closes for two weeks each December to enable employees to spend time with their families over the holiday season. Nature's Own's manufacturing overhead is mostly straight-line depreciation on its plant and air-conditioning costs for keeping the berries cool during the sum-

896 Chapter 17

mer months. The company uses direct labor hours as the manufacturing overhead allocation base. President Cynthia Ortega has just approved new accounting software and is telling Controller Jack Strong about her decision.

"I think this new software will be great," Ortega says. "It will save you time in preparing all those reports."

"Yes, and having so much more information just a click away will help us make better decisions and help control costs," replies Strong. "We need to consider how we can use the new system to improve our business practices."

"And I know just where to start," says Ortega. "You complain each year about having to predict the weather months in advance for estimating air-conditioning costs and direct labor hours for the denominator of the predetermined manufacturing overhead rate, when professional meteorologists can't even get tomorrow's forecast right! I think we should calculate the predetermined overhead rate on a monthly basis."

Controller Strong is not so sure this is a good idea.

Requirements

1. What are the advantages and disadvantages of Ortega's proposal?

2. Should Nature's Own compute its predetermined manufacturing overhead rate on an annual basis or monthly basis? Explain. (p. 863)

Ethical Issue

Ethics

Farley, Inc. is a contract manufacturer that produces customized computer components for several well-known computer-assembly companies. Farley's latest contract with CompWest.com calls for Farley to deliver sound cards that simulate surround sound from two speakers. Farley spent several hundred thousand dollars to design the sound card to meet CompWest.com's specifications.

Farley's president, Bryon Wilson, has stipulated a pricing policy that requires the bid price for a new job to be based on Farley's estimated costs to design, manufacture, distribute, and provide customer service for the job, plus a profit margin. Upon reviewing the contract figures, Farley's controller, Paul York, was startled to find that the cost estimates developed by Farley's cost accountant, Tony Hayes, for the CompWest.com bid were based on only the manufacturing costs. York is upset with Hayes. He is not sure what to do next.

Requirements

1. How did using manufacturing cost only rather than all costs associated with the CompWest.com job affect the amount of Farley's bid for the job?

2. Identify the parties involved in Paul York's ethical dilemma. What are his alternatives? How would each party be affected by each alternative? What should York do next?

Team Project

Major airlines like American, Delta, and Continental are struggling to meet the challenges of budget carriers such as Southwest and JetBlue. Suppose Delta CFO

continued . . .

Comparing job costs across airlines, evaluating strategic alternatives

M. Michele Burns has just returned from a meeting on strategies for responding to competition from budget carriers. The vice president of operations suggested doing nothing: "We just need to wait until these new airlines run out of money. They cannot be making money with their low fares." In contrast, the vice president of marketing, not wanting to lose market share, suggests cutting Delta's fares to match the competition. "If JetBlue charges only $75 for that flight from New York, so must we!" Others, including CFO Burns, emphasized the potential for cutting costs. Another possibility is starting a new budget airline within Delta. CEO Leo Mullin cut the meeting short, and directed Burns to "get some hard data."

As a start, Burns decides to collect cost and revenue data for a typical Delta flight, and then compare it to the data for a competitor. Assume she prepares the following schedule:

	Delta	JetBlue
Route: New York to Tampa	Flight 1247	Flight 53
Distance	1,000 miles	1,000 miles
Seats per plane	142	162
One-way ticket price	$80–$621*	$75
Food and beverage	Meal	Snack

*The highest price is first class airfare

Excluding food and beverage, Burns estimates that the cost per available seat mile is 8.4 cents for Delta, compared to 5.3 cents for JetBlue. (That is, the cost of flying a seat for one mile—whether or not the seat is occupied—is 8.4 cents for Delta, and 5.3 cents for JetBlue.) Assume the average cost of food and beverage is $5 per passenger for snacks and $10 for a meal.

Split your team into two groups. Group 1 should prepare its response to Requirement 1 and group 2 should prepare its response to Requirement 2 before the entire team meets to consider Requirements 3 and 4.

Requirements

1. Use the data to determine for Delta:
   a. the total cost of Flight 1247, assuming a full plane (100% load factor)
   b. the revenue generated by Flight 1247, assuming a 100% load factor and average revenue per one-way ticket of $102
   c. the profit per Flight 1247, given the responses to a. and b.

2. Use the data to determine for JetBlue:
   a. the total cost of Flight 53, assuming a full plane (100% load factor)
   b. the revenue generated by Flight 53, assuming a 100% load factor
   c. the profit per Flight 53, given the responses to a. and b.

3. Based on the responses to Requirements 1 and 2, carefully evaluate each of the four alternative strategies discussed in Delta's executive meeting.

continued...

4. The analysis in this project is based on several simplifying assumptions. As a team, brainstorm factors that your quantitative evaluation does not include, but that may affect a comparison of Delta's operations to budget carriers.

For Internet exercises, Excel in Practice, and additional online activities, go to the Web site www.prenhall.com/horngren.

Quick Check Answers

1. c 2. c 3. b 4. a 5. d 6. d 7. a 8. c 9. d 10. b

18 Process Costing

Learning Objectives

1 Distinguish between process costing and job order costing

2 Compute equivalent units

3 Use process costing to assign costs to units completed and to units in ending work in process inventory

4 Use the weighted-average method to assign costs to units completed and to units in ending work in process inventory in a second department

What's your favorite crayon color? Purple heart? Caribbean green? Electric lime? Or maybe Laser lemon? Have you ever wondered how they make these crayons? Every day Crayola makes 12 million crayons through five different processes:

- Mixing wax and pigment
- Molding and cooling
- Inspecting
- Labeling
- Packaging

Binney and Smith, the owner of Crayola, needs to know how much it costs to make each batch. That helps Binney and Smith set selling prices and measure profits. The company can also control costs if it knows how the processes are operating. The company uses accounting information to answer these questions.

Crayola mass-produces crayons in a sequence of processes. The company accumulates costs for each *process*. Then Crayola spreads these costs over the processes used to make crayons. This is easier than trying to keep track of the cost of each crayon, especially when the company manufactures 12 million crayons every day!

Let's start by contrasting the two basic types of costing systems:

- Job order costing
- Process costing

Process Costing: An Overview

Two Basic Costing Systems: Job Order Costing and Process Costing

1 Distinguish between process costing and job order costing

We saw in Chapter 17 that companies like Dell Computer, Boeing, and PricewaterhouseCoopers, the CPA firm, use job order costing to determine the cost of their custom goods and services. Companies like Seasons Greeting, a manufacturer of handmade greeting cards, create a job order for each customer. In contrast, Shell Oil, Crayola, and Sony use a series of steps (called *processes*) to make large quantities of similar products. Shell, Crayola, and Sony typically use *process costing* systems.

To introduce process costing, we will look at the crayon manufacturing process. Let's combine Crayola's manufacturing into three processes: Mixing, Molding, and Packaging. Crayola accumulates the costs of each process. The company then assigns these costs to the crayons passing through that process.

Suppose Crayola's production costs incurred to make 10,000 crayons and the costs per crayon are:

	Total Costs	Cost per Crayon
Mixing	$200	$0.02
Molding	100	0.01
Packaging	300	0.03
Total cost	$600	$0.06

The total cost to produce 10,000 crayons is the sum of the costs incurred for the three processes. The cost per crayon is the total cost divided by the number of crayons, or $600/10,000 = $.06 per crayon.

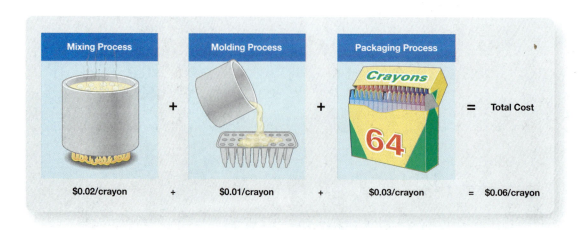

Crayola Company uses the cost per unit of each process to:

- Control costs. The company can find ways to cut the costs where actual process costs are more than planned process costs.
- Set selling prices. The company wants the selling price to cover the costs of making the crayons and also to earn a profit.
- Calculate the ending inventory of crayons for the balance sheet and the cost of goods sold for the income statement.

At any moment, some crayons are in the mixing process, some are in the molding process, and others are in the packaging department. Computing the crayons' cost becomes more complicated when some of the units are still in process. In this chapter, you will learn how to use process costing to calculate the cost of homogeneous products, such as crayons, gasoline, and breakfast cereal.

How Does the Flow of Costs Differ Between Job and Process Costing?

Exhibit 18-1 compares cost flows in:

- A job order costing system for Dell Computer
- A process costing system for Crayola

Panel A shows that Dell's job order costing system has a single Work in Process Inventory control account. Keep in mind that the Work in Process Inventory account in the general ledger is supported by an individual subsidiary cost record for each job (for example, each custom-built computer). The job order system assigns direct materials, direct labor, and manufacturing overhead to individual jobs, as discussed in Chapter 17.

In contrast, Crayola uses a series of *manufacturing processes* to produce crayons. Exhibit 18-2 shows the following:

- Mixing process: Crayola uses labor and heated tanks to mix wax and pigments.
- Molding process: Crayola uses labor and crayon molds to shape the crayons.
- Packaging process: Crayola uses labor, roller presses, cardboard containers, and labels to package crayons.

Exhibit 18-1, Panel B summarizes the flow of costs through this process costing system. Study the exhibit carefully, focusing on the following key points.

1. Each process (Mixing, Molding, and Packaging) is a separate department and each department has its own Work in Process Inventory account.
2. Direct materials, direct labor, and manufacturing overhead are assigned to Work in Process Inventory for each process, as shown in these T-accounts:

	Work in Process Inventory Mixing	Work in Process Inventory Molding	Work in Process Inventory Packaging
Direct materials	Wax & Pigment	None	Boxes & Labels
Direct labor	Mixing operators' wages	Molding operators' wages	Packaging operators' wages
Manufacturing overhead	Depreciation of mixing tanks	Depreciation of molds	Depreciation of roller presses

continued on page 905 . . .

904 Chapter 18

EXHIBIT 18-1 Comparison of Job Order Costing and Process Costing

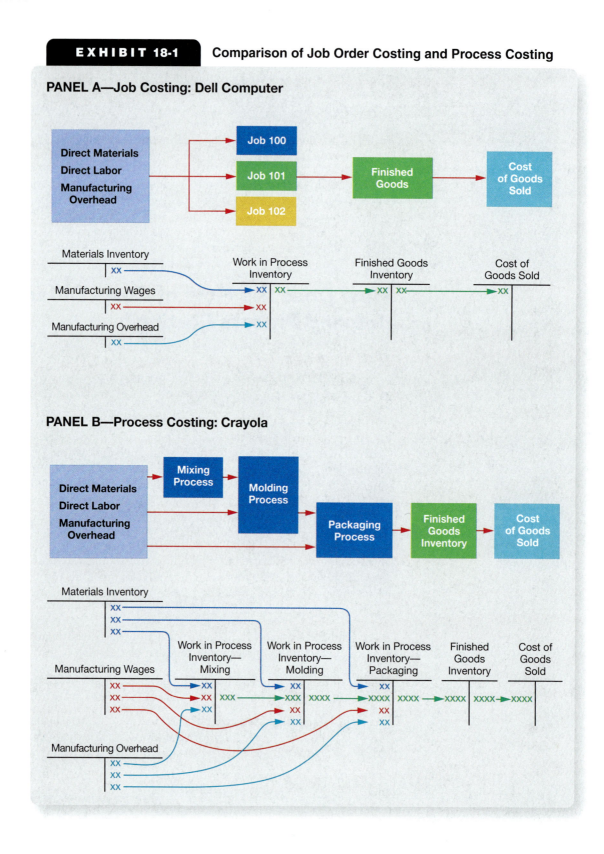

EXHIBIT 18-2 | Flow of Costs in Production of Crayons

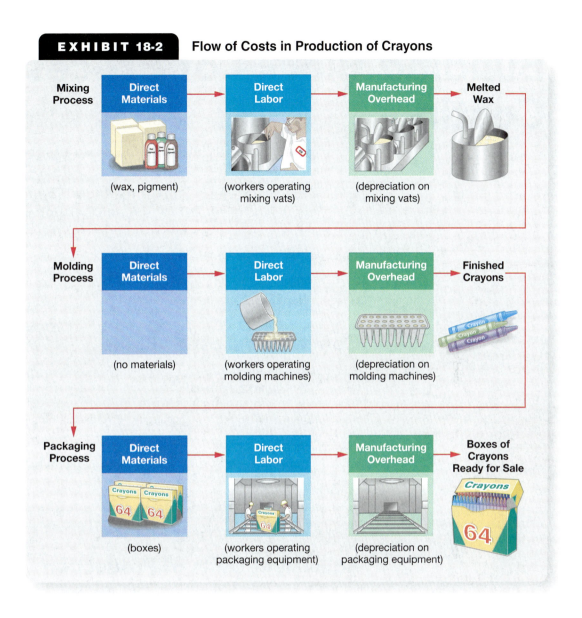

3. When the Mixing Department's process is complete, the wax moves out of mixing and into the Molding Department. The Mixing Department's cost is also transferred out of Work in Process Inventory—Mixing into Work in Process Inventory—Molding.

4. When the Molding Department's process is complete, the finished crayons move from molding into the Packaging Department. The cost of the crayons flows out of Work in Process Inventory—Molding into Work in Process Inventory—Packaging.

5. When production is complete, the boxes of crayons go into finished goods storage. The combined costs from all departments then flow into Finished Goods Inventory. In process costing, *costs flow into Finished Goods Inventory only from the Work in Process Inventory account of the **last** manufacturing process.*

Building Blocks of Process Costing

Process costing is more complex than job costing. For example, Panel B of Exhibit 18-1 shows that we need to determine an amount of the total costs incurred in the Mixing Department to be assigned to:

- The wax that was transferred out of the Mixing Department
- The ending inventory in the Mixing Department

To do this, we use two building blocks of process costing:

- Conversion costs
- Equivalent units of production

Conversion Costs

Chapter 16 introduced three kinds of manufacturing costs: direct materials, direct labor, and manufacturing overhead. Companies like Hewlett Packard and Harley-Davidson use automated production processes. For many companies direct labor is a small part of total manufacturing costs. Such companies often use only two categories:

- Direct materials
- **Conversion costs** (direct labor plus manufacturing overhead)

Combining direct labor and manufacturing overhead in a single category simplifies the accounting. We call this category *conversion costs* because it is the cost (direct labor plus manufacturing overhead) to *convert* raw materials into finished products.

Equivalent Units of Production

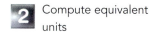

Compute equivalent units

Completing most products takes time, so the Crayola Company may have work in process inventories for crayons that are partially completed. Accountants have developed the concept of equivalent units to measure the amount of work done during a period. **Equivalent units** express the amount of work done during a period in terms of fully complete units of output. Assume Crayola's production plant has 10,000 crayons in ending work in process inventory. Each crayon is 80% complete. If conversion costs are incurred evenly throughout the process, then getting 10,000 crayons 80% of the way through production takes about the same amount of work as completing 8,000 crayons (10,000 × 80%). Thus, ending work in process inventory has 8,000 equivalent units.

Here's how to compute equivalent units for costs that are incurred evenly throughout the production process, using our 80% example:

Number of partially complete units	×	Percentage of process completed	=	Number of equivalent units
10,000	×	80%	=	8,000

Use this formula when costs are incurred evenly throughout production. This is usually true for conversion costs (direct labor and manufacturing overhead). However, direct materials are often added at a particular point in the process. For example, Crayola's wax is added at the beginning of production, and packaging materials are added at the end. How many equivalent units of wax, conversion costs, and packaging materials are in the ending inventory of 10,000 crayons?

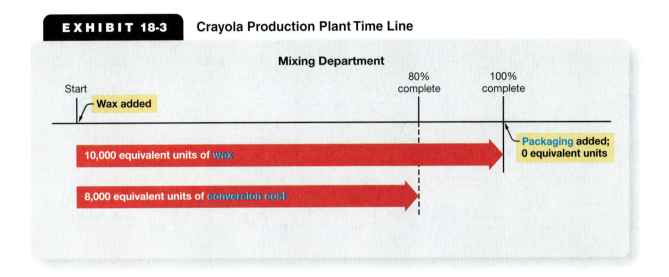

EXHIBIT 18-3 Crayola Production Plant Time Line

Look at the time line in Exhibit 18-3. The 10,000 crayons in ending work in process inventory have:

- 10,000 equivalent units of wax (10,000 × 100% have the wax material)
- 0 equivalent units of packaging materials (The crayons have not been packaged yet.)
- 8,000 equivalent units of conversion costs (10,000 × 80% complete in conversion costs)

This example illustrates an important point:

> We must compute separate equivalent units for:
> - Materials
> - Conversion costs

Process Costing in the First Department with No Beginning Inventory

 Use process costing to assign costs to units completed and to units in ending work in process inventory

To illustrate process costing, we will use Puzzle Me, a company that recycles calendars into jigsaw puzzles. Exhibit 18-4 illustrates the two major production processes:

- The Assembly Department applies the glue to cardboard and then presses a calendar page onto the cardboard.
- The Cutting Department cuts the calendar board into puzzle pieces and packages the puzzles in a box. The box is then moved to finished goods storage.

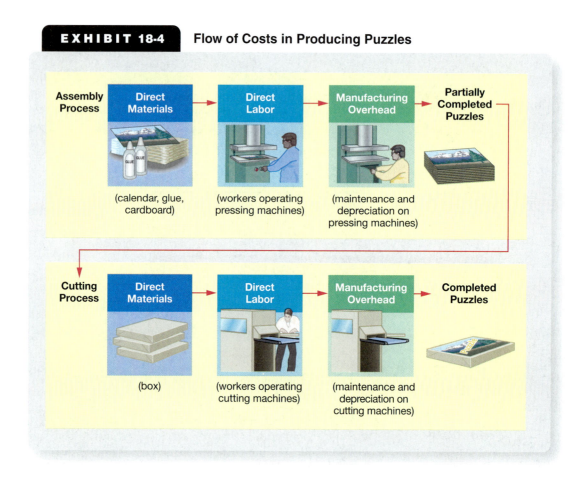

EXHIBIT 18-4 Flow of Costs in Producing Puzzles

The production process uses materials, machines, and human resources in both departments, as shown in the two Work in Process Inventory accounts:

Where Costs Are Added in the Manufacture of Calendars

	Work in Process Inventory Assembly	Work in Process Inventory Cutting
Direct materials	Calendar, cardboard, glue	Package
Direct labor	Assembly/pressing operators' wages	Cutting/packaging operators' wages
Manufacturing overhead	Depreciation on pressing machine	Depreciation on cutting/packaging machine
	Machine maintenance	Machine maintenance
	Supervisor salary	Supervisor salary

Now, let's see how Puzzle Me uses process costing to measure its cost to produce puzzles. During July, the Assembly Department incurred the following costs to make 50,000 puzzle boards:

Direct materials...............................		$140,000
Conversion costs:		
Direct labor	$20,000	
Manufacturing overhead	48,000	
Total conversion costs................		68,000
Costs to account for		$208,000

The accounting period ends before all of the puzzle boards are made. Therefore, the Assembly Department must allocate some of its costs to

- 40,000 puzzle boards completed and transferred to the Cutting Department
- 10,000 puzzle boards still in the Assembly Department at the end of the accounting period

Suppose at the end of July the Assembly Department still has 10,000 puzzle boards that are only 25% complete. We split the $208,000 cost between

- 40,000 completed puzzle boards that have been transferred to the Cutting Department
- 10,000 partially completed puzzle boards remaining in the Assembly Department's work in process inventory on July 31

Process costing can be performed in four steps:

- Step 1: Summarize the flow of physical units.
- Step 2: Compute output in terms of equivalent units.
- Step 3: Compute the cost per equivalent unit.
- Step 4: Assign costs to units completed and to units still in ending work in process inventory.

Step 1: Summarize the Flow of Physical Units

Let's assume that Puzzle Me has no work in process on July 1. During July, Puzzle Me started 50,000 puzzle boards. It is helpful to separate the "units to account for" from the "units accounted for."

- "Units to account for" include the number of puzzle boards still in process at the beginning of July plus the number of puzzle boards started during July. We want to know the costs incurred during the accounting period to manufacture these puzzle boards.
- "Units accounted for" shows what happened to the puzzle boards in process during July. We want to take the July costs incurred in each department and allocate them to the puzzle boards completed and to the puzzle boards still in process at the end of July.

We use the following formula:

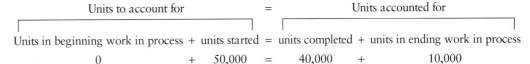

Units in beginning work in process	+	units started	=	units completed	+	units in ending work in process
0	+	50,000	=	40,000	+	10,000

Of the 50,000 puzzle boards started by the Assembly Department in July, 40,000 were completed and transferred out to the Cutting Department. The remaining 10,000 are only partially completed. These partially complete units are the Assembly Department's ending work in process inventory on July 31. The following T-account shows the physical flow of production in units.

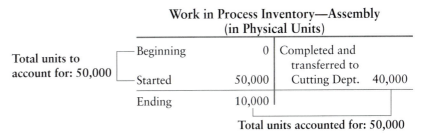

The remaining steps will help us assign the costs of direct materials, direct labor, and manufacturing overhead to production. We need to assign these three product cost elements to each puzzle so that we can compute the cost of

- Puzzles that have passed through the Assembly Department during July
- Puzzle boards still in the Assembly Department production process at the end of July

Step 2: Compute Output in Terms of Equivalent Units

The Assembly Department time line in Exhibit 18-5 shows that all direct materials are added at the beginning of the process. In contrast, conversion costs are incurred evenly throughout the process. This is because labor and overhead production activities occur daily. Thus, we must compute equivalent units separately for:

- Direct materials
- Conversion costs

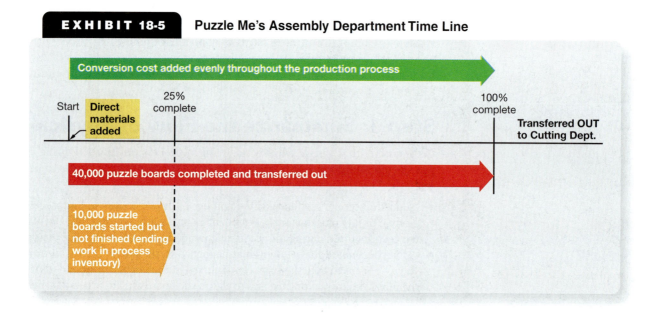

EXHIBIT 18-5 Puzzle Me's Assembly Department Time Line

The Assembly Department worked on 50,000 puzzle boards during July. As Exhibit 18-5 shows, 40,000 puzzles boards are now complete for both materials and conversion costs. Another 10,000 puzzle boards are only 25% complete. How many equivalent units did Assembly produce during July?

EQUIVALENT UNITS FOR MATERIALS Equivalent units for materials total 50,000 because all the direct materials have been added to all 50,000 units worked on during July.

$$\text{Equivalent units for materials} = 40,000 + 10,000 = 50,000$$

EQUIVALENT UNITS FOR CONVERSION COSTS Equivalent units for conversion costs total 42,500. Conversion costs are complete for the 40,000 puzzle boards completed and transferred out. But only 25% of the conversion work has been done on the 10,000 puzzle boards in ending work in process inventory. Therefore, ending inventory represents only 2,500 equivalent units for conversion costs.

$$\text{Equivalent units for conversion costs} = 40,000 + 10,000(.25) = 42,500$$

Exhibit 18-6 summarizes steps 1 and 2.

EXHIBIT 18-6 — Step 1: Summarize the Flow of Physical Units; Step 2: Compute Output in Terms of Equivalent Units

PUZZLE ME ASSEMBLY DEPARTMENT
Month Ended July 31, 2008

Flow of Production	Step 1 Flow of Physical Units	Step 2: Equivalent Units — Direct Materials	Step 2: Equivalent Units — Conversion Costs
Units to account for:			
Beginning work in process, June 30	—		
Started in production during July	50,000		
Total physical units to account for	50,000		
Units accounted for:			
Completed and transferred out during July	40,000	40,000	40,000
Ending work in process, July 31	10,000	10,000	2,500*
Total physical units accounted for	50,000		
Equivalent units		50,000	42,500

*10,000 units each 25% complete = 2,500 equivalent units

Step 3: Compute the Cost per Equivalent Unit

The cost per equivalent unit requires information about total costs and equivalent units. The computations are

$$\text{Cost per equivalent unit for direct materials} = \frac{\text{Total direct materials cost}}{\text{Equivalent units of materials}}$$

$$\text{Cost per equivalent unit for conversion costs} = \frac{\text{Total conversion cost}}{\text{Equivalent units for conversion}}$$

Exhibit 18-7 summarizes the total costs to account for in the Assembly Department (cost data are from the bottom of page 908).

EXHIBIT 18-7 — Summary of Total Costs to Account For

PUZZLE ME ASSEMBLY DEPARTMENT
Work in Process Inventory—Assembly
Month Ended July 31, 2008

	Physical Units	Dollars		Physical Units	Dollars
Beginning inventory, June 30	0	$ 0	Transferred out	40,000	$?
Production started:	50,000				
Direct materials		140,000			
Conversion costs:					
Direct labor		20,000			
Manufacturing overhead		48,000			
Total to account for	50,000	$208,000			
			Ending inventory	10,000	$?

The Assembly Department has 50,000 physical units and $208,000 of costs to account for. Our next task is to split these costs between:

- 40,000 puzzle boards transferred out to the Cutting Department
- 10,000 partially complete puzzle boards that remain in the Assembly Department's ending work in process inventory

In Exhibit 18-6, we computed equivalent units for direct materials (50,000) and conversion costs (42,500). Because the equivalent units differ, we must compute a separate cost per unit for direct materials and for conversion costs. Exhibit 18-7 shows that the direct materials costs are $140,000. Conversion costs are $68,000, which is the sum of direct labor ($20,000) and manufacturing overhead ($48,000).

The cost per equivalent unit of material is $2.80, and the cost per equivalent unit of conversion cost is $1.60, as shown in Exhibit 18-8.

EXHIBIT 18-8 Step 3: Compute the Cost per Equivalent Unit

PUZZLE ME ASSEMBLY DEPARTMENT
Month Ended July 31, 2008

	Direct Materials	Conversion Costs
Beginning work in process, June 30	$ 0	$ 0
Costs added during July (from Exhibit 18-7)	$140,000	$ 68,000
Divide by equivalent units (from Exhibit 18-6)	÷ 50,000	÷ 42,500
Cost per equivalent unit	$ 2.80	$ 1.60

Step 4: Assign Costs to Units Completed and to Units in Ending Work in Process Inventory

We must determine how much of the $208,000 total costs to be accounted for by the Assembly Department should be assigned to:

- 40,000 completed puzzle boards that have been transferred out to the Cutting Department
- 10,000 partially completed puzzle boards remaining in the Assembly Department's ending work in process inventory

Exhibit 18-9 shows how to assign costs.

The total cost of completed puzzle boards for the Assembly Department is 40,000 × ($2.80 + $1.60) = $176,000, as shown in Exhibit 18-9. The cost of the 10,000 partially completed puzzle boards in ending work in process inventory is $32,000, which is the sum of direct material costs ($28,000) and conversion costs ($4,000).

Exhibit 18-9 has accomplished our goal of splitting the $208,000 total cost between:

The 40,000 puzzles completed and transferred out to the Cutting Department	$176,000
The 10,000 puzzles remaining in the Assembly Department's ending work in process inventory on July 31 ($28,000 + $4,000)......	32,000
Total costs of the Assembly Department...	$208,000

EXHIBIT 18-9 — Step 4: Assign Costs to Units Completed and to Units in Ending Work in Process Inventory

PUZZLE ME ASSEMBLY DEPARTMENT
Month Ended July 31, 2008

	Direct Materials	Conversion Costs		Total
Completed and transferred out (40,000)	[40,000 × ($2.80 + $1.60)]		=	$176,000
Ending work in process inventory (10,000):				
Direct materials	[10,000 × $2.80]		=	28,000
Conversion costs		[2,500 × $1.60]	=	4,000
Total cost of ending inventory				32,000
Total costs accounted for				$208,000

Journal entries to record July production in the Assembly Department follow (data from Exhibit 18-7):

Work in Process Inventory—Assembly	208,000	
Materials Inventory		140,000
Manufacturing Wages		20,000
Manufacturing Overhead		48,000
To assign materials, labor, and overhead cost to Assembly.		

The entry to transfer the cost of the 40,000 completed puzzles out of the Assembly Department and into the Cutting Department follows (data from Exhibit 18-9):

Work in Process Inventory—Cutting	176,000	
Work in Process Inventory—Assembly		176,000
To transfer costs from Assembly to Cutting.		

After these entries are posted, the Work in Process Inventory—Assembly account appears as follows:

Work in Process Inventory—Assembly

Balance, June 30	—	Transferred to Cutting 176,000	
Direct materials	140,000		
Direct labor	20,000		
Manufacturing overhead	48,000		
Balance, July 31	32,000		

Decision Guidelines

PROCESS COSTING—FIRST PROCESS (NO BEGINNING INVENTORY)

Here are some of the key decisions Puzzle Me made in setting up its process costing system.

Decision	Guidelines
How do costs flow from Work in Process Inventory to Finished Goods Inventory in Puzzle Me's process costing system?	In Puzzle Me's process costing system, costs flow from: Work in Process Inventory — Assembly ↓ Work in Process Inventory — Cutting ↓ Finished Goods Inventory Costs flow from one Work in Process Inventory account to the next until they flow into Finished Goods Inventory.
How many Work in Process Inventory accounts does Puzzle Me's process costing system have?	Puzzle Me uses a separate Work in Process Inventory account for each process, Assembly and Cutting.
How do we account for partially completed products?	Use equivalent units.
	Puzzle Me computes equivalent units separately for materials and conversion costs because materials are added at a particular point in the production process, but conversion costs are added evenly throughout the process.
How are equivalent units computed?	Puzzle Me's *conversion costs* are incurred evenly throughout the production process, so the equivalent units are computed as follows: $$\text{Equivalent units} = \text{Number of partially complete units} \times \text{Percentage of process completed}$$ Puzzle Me's equivalent units for *materials* are computed as follows: • If materials are added to physical units at the beginning of the process, then equivalent units of materials = total of physical units worked on. • If materials are added at the end of the process, then equivalent units of materials = 0.
How is the cost per equivalent unit computed?	Divide the cost by the number of equivalent units.
How are the costs of the Assembly process split between • Puzzles completed and transferred out? • Partially complete puzzles in ending work in process inventory?	Multiply the cost per equivalent unit by • Number of equivalent units of work completed and transferred out • Number of equivalent units of work in the ending work in process inventory

Summary Problem 1

Use the four steps of process costing to identify the missing amounts X for the cost of units completed and transferred out and Y for the cost of ending work in process in the following report prepared by Santa Fe Paints for September.

MIXING DEPARTMENT
Month Ended September 30, 2008

	Physical Units	Total Costs
Beginning work in process, August 31	—	$ —
Started in production during September	18,000	38,000*
Total to account for	18,000	$38,000
Completed and transferred to Finishing Department during September	14,000	$ X
Ending work in process, September 30 (25% complete as to direct materials, 50% complete as to conversion cost)	4,000	Y
Total accounted for	18,000	$38,000

*Includes direct materials of $6,000 and conversion costs of $32,000.

Solution

STEP 1 Summarize the flow of physical units.

STEP 2 Compute output in terms of equivalent units.

MIXING DEPARTMENT
Month Ended September 30, 2008

Flow of Production	Step 1 Flow of Physical Units	Step 2: Equivalent Units Direct Materials	Step 2: Equivalent Units Conversion Costs
Units to account for:			
Beginning work in process, August 31	—		
Started in production during September	18,000		
Total physical units to account for	18,000		
Units accounted for:			
Completed and transferred out in September	14,000	14,000	14,000
Ending work in process, September 30	4,000	1,000*	2,000*
Total physical units accounted for	18,000		
Equivalent units		15,000	16,000

*Direct materials: 4,000 units each 25% complete = 1,000 equivalent units
Conversion costs: 4,000 units each 50% complete = 2,000 equivalent units

STEP 3 Compute the cost per equivalent unit.

Summary of total costs to account for. This supports the computation of cost per equivalent unit.

MIXING DEPARTMENT
Month Ended September 30, 2008

	Direct Materials	Conversion Costs	Total
Beginning work in process, August 31	$ 0	$ 0	$ 0
Costs added during September	6,000	32,000	38,000
Total costs to account for	$6,000	$32,000	$38,000

MIXING DEPARTMENT
Month Ended September 30, 2008

	Direct Materials	Conversion Costs
Beginning work in process, August 31	$ —	$ —
Costs added during September	$6,000	$32,000
Divide by equivalent units	÷15,000	÷16,000
Cost per equivalent unit	$ 0.40	$ 2.00

STEP 4 Assign costs to units completed and to units in ending work in process inventory.

MIXING DEPARTMENT
Month Ended September 30, 2008

	Direct Materials	Conversion Costs	Total
X: Units completed and transferred out (14,000)	[14,000 × ($0.40 + $2.00)]		= $33,600
Units in ending work in process inventory (4,000)			
Direct materials	[1,000 × $0.40]		= $ 400
Conversion costs		[2,000 × $2.00]	= 4,000
Y: Total costs of ending work in process inventory			4,400
Total costs accounted for			$38,000

Process Costing in a Second Department

Use the weighted-average method to assign costs to units completed and to units in ending work in process inventory in a second department

Most products require a series of processing steps. In this section, we consider a second department—Puzzle Me's Cutting Department—to complete the picture of process costing.

The Cutting Department receives the puzzle boards and cuts the board into puzzle pieces before inserting the pieces into the boxes at the end of the process. Exhibit 18-10 shows the following:

- Glued puzzle boards are transferred in from the Assembly Department at the beginning of the Cutting Department's process.
- The Cutting Department's conversion costs are added evenly throughout the process.
- The Cutting Department's direct materials (box) are added at the end of the process.

Keep in mind that *direct materials* in the Cutting Department refers to the boxes added *in that department* and not to the materials (calendars, cardboard, and glue) added in the Assembly Department. Likewise, *conversion costs* in the Cutting Department refers to the direct labor and manufacturing overhead costs incurred only in the Cutting Department.

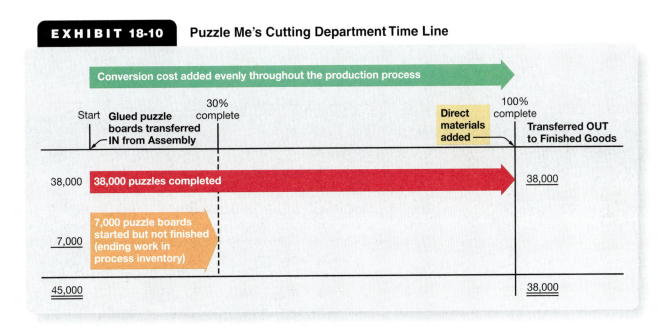

EXHIBIT 18-10 Puzzle Me's Cutting Department Time Line

The Weighted-Average Process Costing Method

As you saw in earlier chapters, companies may use different inventory methods. For manufacturing companies, two methods are commonly used for process costing:

- Weighted-average
- FIFO (first-in, first-out)

The difference in the two methods involves the treatment of the costs of beginning inventory. Here we illustrate the weighted-average method of accounting for process costs because it is easier and the differences between the two methods' results are usually insignificant. The appendix to this chapter covers the FIFO method.

Exhibit 18-11 lists July information for Puzzle Me's Cutting Department. Study this information carefully. We'll be using these data in the remainder of the chapter.

EXHIBIT 18-11   Puzzle Me's Cutting Department Data for July

Units:		
Beginning work in process, June 30 (0% complete as to direct materials, 60% complete as to conversion costs)		5,000 puzzle boards
Transferred in from Assembly Department during July (Exhibit 18-6)		40,000 puzzle boards
Completed and transferred out to Finished Goods Inventory during July		38,000 puzzles
Ending work in process, July 31 (0% complete as to direct materials, 30% complete as to conversion work)		7,000 puzzles
Costs:		
Beginning work in process, June 30 (transferred-in costs, $22,000; conversion costs, $1,200)		$ 23,200
Transferred in from Assembly Department during July (from Exhibit 18-9)		$176,000
Direct materials added during July in Cutting Department		$ 19,000
Conversion costs added during July in Cutting Department:		
Direct labor	$ 3,840	
Manufacturing overhead	11,000	$ 14,840

Remember that work in process inventory at the close of business on June 30 is both:

- Ending inventory for June
- Beginning inventory for July

Exhibit 18-11 shows that Puzzle Me's Cutting Department started the July period with 5,000 puzzle boards partially completed through work done in the Cutting Department in June. During July, the Cutting Department started work on 40,000 additional puzzle boards that were received from the Assembly Department.

The weighted-average method combines the Cutting Department's:

- Work done last month—in June—to start the Cutting process on the 5,000 puzzle boards that were in beginning work in process inventory
- Work done in July to complete the 5,000 puzzle boards in beginning inventory and to work on the 40,000 additional puzzle boards that were transferred in from the Assembly Department during July

Thus, the **weighted-average process costing method** determines the average cost of all the Cutting Department's equivalent units of work on these 45,000 puzzle boards (5,000 beginning work in process inventory + 40,000 transferred in).

Just as we did for the Assembly Department, our goal is to split the total cost in the Cutting Department between:

- 38,000 puzzles that the Cutting Department completed and transferred out to finished goods inventory
- 7,000 partially completed puzzles remaining in the Cutting Department's ending work in process inventory at the end of July

We use the same four-step costing procedure that we used for the Assembly Department.

Steps 1 and 2: Summarize the Flow of Physical Units and Compute Output in Terms of Equivalent Units

Summarize the Flow of Physical Units

Using the following formula, let's account for July production, as follows:

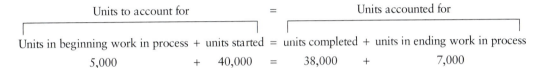

We must account for these 45,000 units (beginning inventory of 5,000 plus 40,000 started). Exhibit 18-12 shows that of the 45,000 units to account for, Puzzle Me completed and transferred out 38,000 units. That left 7,000 units as ending work in process in the Cutting Department on July 31. The following T-account illustrates the physical flow in units for the Cutting Department.

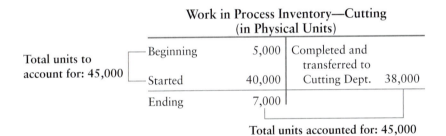

Steps 2 and 3 will help us determine the costs of these units.

Compute Equivalent Units

Exhibit 18-12 computes the Cutting Department's equivalent units of work. Under the weighted-average method, Puzzle Me computes the equivalent units for the total work done to date. This includes all the work done in the current period (July), plus the work done last period (June) on the beginning work in process inventory.

We can see in Exhibit 18-12 that the total equivalent units with respect to:

- Transferred-in costs include all 45,000 units because they are complete with respect to work done in the Assembly Department.
- Direct materials include only the 38,000 finished puzzles because Cutting Department materials are added at the end.
- Conversion costs include the 38,000 finished puzzles plus the 2,100 puzzles (7,000 puzzle boards × 30%) that are still in process at the end of the month. Conversion work occurs evenly throughout the cutting process.

The Cutting Department has three categories of equivalent units:

- Equivalent Units for Transferred-In Costs: The equivalent units for transferred-in costs will always be 100% of the units to account for, because these units must be 100% complete on previous work before coming to the Cutting Department.

EXHIBIT 18-12 — Step 1: Summarize the Flow of Physical Units; Step 2: Compute Output in Terms of Equivalent Units

PUZZLE ME CUTTING DEPARTMENT
Month Ended July 31, 2008

	Step 1	Step 2: Equivalent Units		
Flow of Production	Flow of Physical Units	Transferred In	Direct Materials	Conversion Costs
Units to account for:				
Beginning work in process, June 30	5,000			
Transferred in during July	40,000			
Total physical units to account for	45,000			
Units accounted for:				
Completed and transferred out during July	38,000	38,000	38,000*	38,000*
Ending work in process, July 31	7,000	7,000	—†	2,100†
Total physical units accounted for	45,000			
Equivalent units		45,000	38,000	40,100

In the Cutting Department:
*Units completed and transferred out
    Direct materials: 38,000 units each 100% completed = 38,000 equivalent units
    Conversion costs: 38,000 units each 100% completed = 38,000 equivalent units
†Ending inventory
    Direct materials: 7,000 units each 0% completed = 0 equivalent units
    Conversion costs: 7,000 units each 30% completed = 2,100 equivalent units

- Equivalent Units for Direct Materials: The equivalent units of materials include only the units transferred out because these are the only units ready to be placed in a box for transfer to the Finished Goods Inventory.
- Equivalent Units for Conversion Costs: The computation of equivalent units for conversion costs is similar to our computation of equivalent units in the Assembly Department. Equivalent units include 100% of the units transferred out and 30% of the units in the Cutting Department's ending work in process inventory.

Step 3: Summarize Total Costs to Account For and Compute the Cost per Equivalent Unit

Exhibit 18-13 accumulates the Cutting Department's total costs to account for. In addition to direct material and conversion costs, the Cutting Department must account for transferred-in costs. **Transferred-in costs** are those costs that were incurred in a previous process (the Assembly Department, in the Puzzle Me example) and brought into a later process (the Cutting Department) as part of the product's cost.

Exhibit 18-13 shows that the Cutting Department's total cost to account for ($233,040) is the sum of:

- The cost incurred in June to start the Cutting process on the 5,000 puzzles in Cutting's beginning work in process inventory ($23,200)
- The costs added to Work in Process Inventory—Cutting during July ($209,840 = $176,000 transferred in from the Assembly Department + $19,000 direct materials incurred in the Cutting Department + $14,840 conversion costs incurred in the Cutting Department)

EXHIBIT 18-13 — Step 3: Compute the Cost per Equivalent Unit

PUZZLE ME CUTTING DEPARTMENT
Month Ended July 31, 2008

	Transferred In	Direct Materials	Conversion Costs	Total
Beginning work in process, June 30 (from Exhibit 18-11)	$ 22,000	$ —	$ 1,200	$ 23,200
Costs added during July (from Exhibit 18-11)	176,000	19,000	14,840	209,840
Total costs	$198,000	$ 19,000	$ 16,040	
Divide by equivalent units (from Exhibit 18-12)	÷ 45,000	÷ 38,000	÷ 40,100	
Cost per equivalent unit	$ 4.40	$ 0.50	$ 0.40	
Total costs to account for				$233,040

Exhibit 18-13 also shows the cost per equivalent unit. For each cost category, we divide total cost by the number of equivalent units. Perform this computation for all cost categories: transferred-in costs, direct materials, and conversion costs. In this illustration the total cost per equivalent unit is $5.30 ($4.40 + $0.50 + $0.40).

Step 4: Assign Total Costs to Units Completed and to Units in Ending Work in Process Inventory

Exhibit 18-14 shows how Puzzle Me assigns the total Cutting Department costs ($233,040, from Exhibit 18-13) to

- Units completed and transferred out to finished goods inventory ($201,400)
- Units remaining in the Cutting Department's ending work in process inventory ($31,640)

We use the same approach as we used for the Assembly Department in Exhibit 18-9. Multiply the number of equivalent units from step 2 (Exhibit 18-12) by the cost per equivalent unit from step 3 (Exhibit 18-13).

EXHIBIT 18-14 — Step 4: Assign Total Costs to Completed Units and to Units in Ending Work in Process Inventory

PUZZLE ME CUTTING DEPARTMENT
Month Ended July 31, 2008

	Transferred In	Direct Materials	Conversion Costs	Total
Units completed and transferred out to Finished goods inventory		[38,000 × ($4.40 + $0.50 + $0.40)]		= $201,400
Ending work in process, July 31:				
Transferred-in costs	[7,000 × $4.40]			= 30,800
Direct materials		—		—
Conversion costs			[2,100 × $0.40]	= 840
Total ending work in process, July 31				31,640
Total costs accounted for				$233,040

Exhibit 18-15 shows how Exhibit 18-14 assigns the Cutting Department's costs.

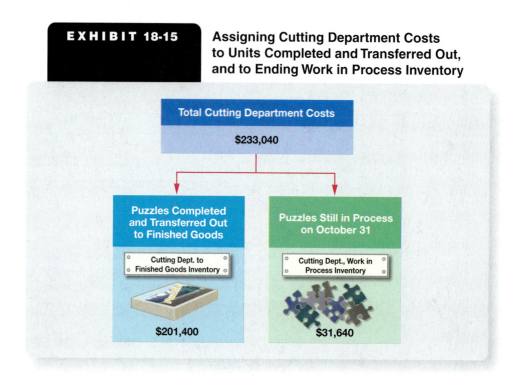

The Cutting Department's journal entries are similar to those of the Assembly Department. First, recall the entry previously made to transfer the cost of puzzle boards into the Cutting Department (page 913):

	Work in Process Inventory—Cutting	176,000	
	Work in Process Inventory—Assembly		176,000
	To transfer costs from Assembly to Cutting.		

The following entry records the Cutting Department other costs during July (data from Exhibit 18-11):

	Work in Process Inventory—Cutting	33,840	
	Materials Inventory		19,000
	Manufacturing Wages		3,840
	Manufacturing Overhead		11,000
	To assign materials and conversion costs to the		
	Cutting Department.		

The entry to transfer the cost of completed puzzles out of the Cutting Department and into Finished Goods Inventory is based on the dollar amount in Exhibit 18-14:

	Finished Goods Inventory	201,400	
	Work in Process Inventory—Cutting		201,400
	To transfer costs from Cutting to Finished Goods.		

After posting, the key accounts appear as follows:

Work in Process Inventory—Assembly

(Exhibit 18-7)		(Exhibit 18-9)	
Balance, June 30	—	Transferred to Cutting	176,000
Direct materials	140,000		
Direct labor	20,000		
Manufacturing overhead	48,000		
Balance, July 31	32,000		

Work in Process Inventory—Cutting

(Exhibit 18-11)		(Exhibit 18-14)	
Balance, June 30	23,200	Transferred to Finished	
Transferred in from Assembly	176,000	Goods Inventory	201,400
Direct materials	19,000		
Direct labor	3,840		
Manufacturing overhead	11,000		
Balance, July 31	31,640		

Finished Goods Inventory

Balance, June 30			
Transferred in from Cutting	201,400		

How Managers Use a Production Cost Report

As we saw in Chapter 17, accountants prepare cost reports to help production managers evaluate the efficiency of their manufacturing operations. Both job order and process costing are similar in that they:

- *Accumulate* costs as the product moves through production
- *Assign* costs to the units (such as gallons of gasoline or number of crayons) passing through that process

The difference between job order costing and process costing lies in the way costs are accumulated. Job order costing uses a *job cost sheet* and process costing uses a *production cost report*.

The **production cost report** in Exhibit 18-16 summarizes Puzzle Me's Cutting Department operations during July. The report combines the costs to account for and the cost per equivalent unit (Exhibit 18-13). It shows how those costs were assigned to the puzzles completed and transferred out of the Cutting Department ($201,400) and to ending work in process inventory ($31,640).

How do managers use the production cost report?

- Controlling cost: Puzzle Me uses product cost data to reduce costs. For materials the company may need to change suppliers or a certain component. Labor may need different employee job requirements. New production equipment may help save on labor cost.
- Evaluating performance: Managers are often rewarded based on how well they meet the budget. Puzzle Me compares the actual direct materials and conversion costs with expected amounts. If actual unit costs are too high, managers look for ways to cut. If actual costs are less than expected, the Cutting Department's managers may receive a pay raise.
- Pricing products: Puzzle Me must set its selling price high enough to cover the manufacturing cost of each puzzle ($5.30 = $4.40 + $0.50 + $0.40 in Exhibit 18-13) plus marketing and distribution costs.

EXHIBIT 18-16 | Production Cost Report (Weighted-Average)

PUZZLE ME CUTTING DEPARTMENT
Production Cost Report (Weighted-Average Method)
Month Ended July 31, 2008

	Transferred In	Direct Materials	Conversion Costs	Total
Costs to account for:				
Beginning work in process, June 30	$ 22,000	$ —	$ 1,200	$ 23,200
Costs added during July	176,000	19,000	14,840	209,840
Total costs to account for	$198,000	$19,000	$16,040	$233,040
Costs accounted for:				
Equivalent units	÷ 45,000	÷ 38,000	÷ 40,100	
Cost per equivalent unit	$ 0.40	$ 0.50	$ 0.40	
Assignment of total costs:				
Units completed during July	[38,000 × ($4.40 + $ 0.50 + $ 0.40)]			$201,400
Ending work in process, July 31				
Transferred-in costs	[7,000 × $4.40]			30,800
Direct materials		—		—
Conversion costs			[2,100 × $ 0.40]	840
Total ending work in process, July 31				31,640
Total costs accounted for				$233,040

- Identifying the most profitable products: Selling price and cost data help managers figure out which products are most profitable. They can then promote the most profitable products.
- Preparing the financial statements: Finally, the production cost report aids financial reporting. It provides inventory data for the balance sheet and cost of goods sold for the income statement.

Decision Guidelines

PROCESS COSTING—SECOND PROCESS

Process costing is more complicated in second (or later) department because of units and costs transferred in from previous departments. Let's use Puzzle Me's Cutting Department to review some of the key process costing decisions that arise in a second (or later) process that has beginning inventory.

Decision	Guidelines
At what point in the Cutting process are transferred-in costs (from the Assembly process) incurred?	Transferred-in costs are incurred at the *beginning* of the Cutting process. The puzzles must be completely assembled before cutting begins.
How do we compute equivalent units using the weighted-average method?	Weighted-average equivalent units equal • All work done on units completed and transferred out this period (whether work was done this period or last period), plus • Work done to *start* the ending inventory
What checks and balances does the four-step process costing procedure provide?	The four-step procedure provides two important checks: 1. The units to account for (beginning inventory + units started or transferred in) must equal the units accounted for (units completed and transferred out + units in ending inventory). 2. The total costs to account for (cost of beginning inventory + costs incurred in the current period) must equal the costs accounted for (cost of units completed and transferred out + cost of ending work in process inventory).
What is the main goal of the Cutting Department's process costing?	The main goal is to split total costs between • Puzzles completed and transferred out to finished goods inventory • Puzzles that remain in the Cutting Department's ending work in process inventory
For what kinds of decisions do Puzzle Me's managers use the Cutting Department's production cost report?	Managers use the cost per equivalent unit for (1) Controlling cost (2) Evaluating performance (3) Pricing products (4) Identifying the financial statements (5) Preparing the financial statements

Summary Problem 2

This problem extends Summary Problem 1 to a second department, Finishing. During September, Santa Fe Paints reports the following in its Finishing Department:

FINISHING DEPARTMENT DATA FOR SEPTEMBER 2008

Units:

Beginning work in process, August 31 (20% complete as to direct materials, 70% complete as to conversion work)............	4,000 units
Transferred in from Mixing Department during September.........	14,000 units
Completed and transferred out to Finished Goods Inventory during September..	15,000 units
Ending work in process, September 30 (30% complete as to direct materials, 80% complete as to conversion work).......	3,000 units

Costs:

Work in process, August 31 (transferred-in costs, $11,400; direct materials costs, $1,000; conversion costs, $1,800).........	$14,200
Transferred in from Mixing Department during September (bottom of page 916)...	33,600
Finishing direct materials added during September.....................	5,360
Finishing conversion costs added during September	24,300

Requirement

Assign the Finishing Department's September total costs to units completed and to units in ending work in process inventory, using the weighted-average method.

Hint: Don't confuse the Finishing Department with finished goods inventory. The Finishing Department is Santa Fe Paint's second process. The paint does not become part of finished goods inventory until Santa Fe has completed the second process, which is the Finishing Department.

Solution

STEPS 1 AND 2 Summarize the flow of physical units; compute output in terms of equivalent units.

FINISHING DEPARTMENT
Month Ended September 30, 2008

	Step 1	Step 2: Equivalent Units		
Flow of Production	Flow of Physical Units	Transferred In	Direct Materials	Conversion Costs
Units to account for:				
Beginning work in process, August 31	4,000			
Transferred in from Mixing during September	14,000			
Total physical units to account for	18,000			
Units accounted for:				
Completed and transferred out during September	15,000	15,000	15,000	15,000
Ending work in process, September 30	3,000	3,000	900*	2,400*
Total physical units accounted for	18,000			
Equivalent units		18,000	15,900	17,400

*Ending inventory
  Direct materials: 3,000 units each 30% completed = 900 equivalent units
  Conversion costs: 3,000 units each 80% completed = 2,400 equivalent units

STEP 3 Summarize total costs to account for; compute the cost per equivalent unit.

FINISHING DEPARTMENT
Month Ended September 30, 2008

	Transferred In	Direct Materials	Conversion Costs	Total
Beginning work in process, August 31	$11,400	$1,000	$1,800	$14,200
Costs added during September	33,600	5,360	24,300	63,260
Total costs	$45,000	$6,360	26,100	
Divide by equivalent units	÷18,000	÷15,900	÷17,400	
Cost per equivalent unit	$2.50	$0.40	$1.50	
Total costs to account for				$77,460

STEP 4 Assign costs to units completed and to units in ending work in process inventory.

FINISHING DEPARTMENT
Month Ended September 30, 2008

	Transferred In	Direct Materials	Conversion Costs	Total
Units completed and transferred out to				
Finished Goods Inventory		[15,000 × $2.50 + $0.40 + $1.50)]		$66,000
Ending work in process, September 30:				
Transferred-in costs	[3,000 × $2.50]			7,500
Direct materials		[900 × $0.40]		360
Conversion costs			[2,400 × $1.50]	3,600
Total ending work in process, September 30				11,460
Total costs accounted for				$77,460

Review Process Costing

Accounting Vocabulary

Conversion Costs
Direct labor plus manufacturing overhead.

Equivalent Units
Express the amount of work done during a period in terms of fully complete units of output.

Production Cost Report
Summarizes a processing department's operations for a period.

Transferred-in Costs
Costs incurred in a previous process that are carried forward as part of the product's cost when it moves to the next process.

Weighted-Average Process Costing Method
A process costing method that costs all equivalent units of work with a weighted average of the previous period's and the current period's cost per equivalent unit.

Quick Check

1. Which of these companies would use process costing?
   a. Saatchi & Saatchi advertising firm
   b. Accenture management consultants
   c. Pace Foods, producer of Pace picante sauce
   d. Amazon.com

2. Which of the following statements describes Puzzle Me's process costing system? (p. 908)
   a. Direct materials and direct labor are traced to each specific order.
   b. Costs flow through a sequence of Work in Process Inventory accounts and then into Finished Goods Inventory from the final Work in Process Inventory account.
   c. Costs flow directly from a single Work in Process Inventory account to Finished Goods Inventory.
   d. The subsidiary Work in Process Inventory accounts consist of separate records for each individual order, detailing the materials, labor, and overhead assigned to that order.

   Use the following data to answer questions 3 through 7. Suppose Chupa Chups, a candy manufacturer, uses a mixing process that adds sugar at the beginning and flavorings 75% of the way through the mixing process. Conversion costs are incurred evenly throughout the mixing process, and mixing had no beginning inventory. The company started making 10,000 lollipops, completed mixing for 8,000 lollipops, and in ending work in process inventory has 2,000 lollipops that are 60% through the mixing process.

3. Compute the equivalent units of *sugar* used.
   a. 8,000
   b. 8,700
   c. 9,200
   d. 10,000

4. How many equivalent units of *flavorings* did Chupa Chups use?
   a. 8,000
   b. 8,700
   c. 9,200
   d. 10,000

5. What are the equivalent units of *conversion costs*?
   a. 8,000
   b. 8,700
   c. 9,200
   d. 10,000

6. If the cost per equivalent unit is $0.50 for sugar, $1.00 for flavorings, and $0.40 for conversion costs, what is the cost assigned to the Mixing Department's *ending work in process inventory*?
   a. $1,480
   b. $1,800
   c. $2,520
   d. $3,800

7. Suppose Chupa Chup's second process, Shaping, starts out with 3,000 lollipops in its beginning work in process inventory. During the month 8,000 units came to Shaping from Mixing. At the end of the period Shaping has 1,500 lollipops 70% through the process. Compute the number of equivalent units of *transferred-in* costs that the Shaping process will use to compute its cost per equivalent unit.

    a. 6,500
    b. 8,000
    c. 9,500
    d. 11,000

8. The cost of the Shaping Department's beginning work in process inventory included $20 of transferred-in cost. Transferred-in costs of Shaping added $200. Use the equivalent units for transferred-in costs that you computed for question 7 to determine Shaping's cost per equivalent unit for transferred-in costs.

    a. $0.02
    b. $0.12
    c. $0.20
    d. $2.00

9. In general, transferred-in costs include:

    a. Costs incurred in the previous period
    b. Costs incurred in all prior processes
    c. Costs incurred in only the previous process
    d. Costs incurred in all prior periods

10. A production cost report shows

    a. Costs to account for
    b. Cost of units completed
    c. Cost of ending work in process inventory
    d. All the above

    Answers are given after Apply Your Knowledge (p. 949).

Assess Your Progress

Short Exercises

Distinguishing between the flow of costs in job order costing and process costing

S18-1 Use Exhibit 18-1 to help you describe, in your own words, the major difference in the flow of costs between a job order costing system and a process costing system. (pp. 903–905)

Comparison of job order costing and process costing

S18-2 Indicate whether each of the following statements is true or false. (pp. 863–865)

_____ 1. Job order costing accumulates the costs of each process.
_____ 2. Companies that manufacture cell phones use process costing.
_____ 3. After the product moves through the final stage of the manufacturing process, its cost moves to finished goods inventory.
_____ 4. Production reports summarize the costs of each job completed in a job order costing system.

Calculate conversion costs

S18-3 Florida Orange manufactures orange juice. Last month's total manufacturing costs for the Saratoga operation included:

Direct materials	$400,000
Direct labor	35,000
Manufacturing overhead	125,000

What was the conversion cost for Florida Orange's Saratoga operation last month? (pp. 906–907)

Compute equivalent units

S18-4 LG manufactures cell phones. The conversion costs to produce cell phones for November are added evenly throughout the process in the assembly department. For each of the following separate assumptions, calculate the equivalent units of conversion costs in the ending work in process inventory for the assembly department:

1. 12,000 cell phones were 80% complete (pp. 906–907)
2. 22,000 cell phones were 20% complete (pp. 906–907)

Compute equivalent units

S18-5 FritoLay makes potato chips. At the end of the month, the ending work in process included 6,000 units in the Mixing Department. All materials are added at the beginning of the mixing process. What are the equivalent units of direct materials cost in ending work in process for the Mixing Department? (pp. 906–907)

Calculate conversion costs and unit cost

S18-6 China Spring produces premium bottled water. China Spring purchases artesian water, stores the water in large tanks, and then runs the water through two processes: filtration and bottling.

During February, the filtration process incurred the following costs in processing 200,000 liters:

Wages of workers operating the filtration equipment	$ 23,950
Manufacturing overhead allocated to filtration	24,050
Water	120,000

continued...

China Spring had no beginning inventory in the Filtration Department in February.

1. Compute the February conversion costs in the Filtration Department. (pp. 906–907)
2. The Filtration Department completely processed 200,000 liters in February. What was the filtration cost per liter? (pp. 911–912)

Drawing a time line; computing equivalent units

S18-7 Refer to S18-6. At China Spring, water is added at the beginning of the filtration process. Conversion costs are added evenly throughout the process. Now assume that in February, 150,000 liters were completed and transferred out of the Filtration Department into the Bottling Department. The 50,000 units remaining in Filtration's ending work in process inventory were 80% of the way through the filtration process. Recall that China Spring has no beginning inventories.

1. Draw a time line for the filtration process. (pp. 910–911)
2. Compute the equivalent units of direct materials and conversion costs for the Filtration Department. (p. 911)

Computing equivalent units

S18-8 The Mixing Department of Healthy Foods had 40,000 units to account for in October. Of the 40,000 units, 30,000 units were completed and transferred to the next department, and 10,000 units were 30% complete. All of the materials are added at the beginning of the process. Conversion costs are added equally throughout the process. Compute the total equivalent units of direct materials and conversion costs. (p. 911)

Computing the cost per equivalent unit

S18-9 Refer to S18-8. The Mixing Department of Healthy Foods has 40,000 equivalent units of materials and 33,000 equivalent units of conversion costs for October. The direct materials costs are $30,000 and the conversion costs are $16,500. Compute the cost per equivalent unit for direct materials and for conversion costs. (pp. 912–913)

Computing cost of units transferred out and units in ending work in process

S18-10 Refer to S18-8 and S18-9. Healthy Foods' costs per equivalent unit are $0.75 for direct materials and $0.50 for conversion costs. Calculate the cost of (1) the 30,000 units completed and transferred out and (2) the 10,000 units, 30% complete, in the ending work in process inventory. (pp. 912–913)

Compute the physical flow

S18-11 The Baking Department at Rainbow Bakery had no loaves in beginning inventory, started 15,000 loaves of bread, and completed 10,000 loaves during January.

Requirements
1. What are the total loaves to account for? (pp. 910–911)
2. How many loaves are in ending Baking Department work in process inventory on January 31? (pp. 910–911)
3. What are the total loaves accounted for? (pp. 910–911)

Compute the physical flow

S18-12 The Baking Department at Rainbow Baker had a beginning work in process inventory of 6,000 cakes, completed 10,000 cakes, and had 5,000 cakes in ending work in process inventory in February.

Requirements
1. How many cakes were started in February? (pp. 910–911)
2. What are the total cakes to account for? (pp. 910–911)
3. What are the total cakes accounted for? (pp. 910–911)

Compute the physical flow

S18-13 Calculate the missing items for each of the following flows of physical units. (pp. 910–911)

Units to account for:	Dept. A	Dept. 33	Dept. Z17
Beginning work in process	100	(3)	50
Started in production during month	250	105	(7)
Total physical units to account for	350	170	(6)
Units accounted for:			
Completed and transferred out during month	(2)	120	120
Ending work in process	120	(4)	30
Total physical units accounted for	(1)	170	(5)

Exercises

Diagramming flows through a process costing system

E18-14 Pule produces kitchen cabinets in a two-stage process of milling and assembling. Direct materials are added in the Milling Department. Direct labor and overhead are incurred in both departments. The company's general ledger includes the following accounts:

Cost of Goods Sold	Materials Inventory
Manufacturing Wages	Finished Goods Inventory
Work in Process Inventory—Milling	Manufacturing Overhead
Work in Process Inventory—Assembling	

Outline the flow of costs through the company's accounts, including a brief description of each flow. Include a T-account for each account title given. (pp. 863–865)

Journalizing process costing transactions

E18-15 Record the following process costing transactions in the general journal: (pp. 921–923)

a. Requisition of direct materials by the Milling Department, $4,000.

b. Assignment of conversion costs to the Assembling Department:

> Direct labor, $4,700
> Manufacturing overhead, $2,900

c. Cost of goods completed and transferred out of Milling and into Assembling, $10,250.

d. Cost of goods completed and transferred out of the Assembling Department into Finished Goods Inventory, $15,600.

Drawing a time line, computing equivalent units, and assigning cost to completed units and ending work in process; no beginning inventory or cost transferred in

E18-16 Paint My World prepares and packages paint products. Paint My World has two departments: (1) Blending and (2) Packaging. Direct materials are added at the beginning of the blending process (dyes) and at the end of the packaging process (cans). Conversion costs are added evenly throughout each process. Data from the month of May for the Blending Department are as follows:

continued . . .

Gallons:	
Beginning work in process inventory	0
Started production	8,000 gallons
Completed and transferred out to Packaging in May	6,000 gallons
Ending work in process inventory (30% of the way through blending process)	2,000 gallons
Costs:	
Beginning work in process inventory	$ 0
Costs added during May:	
Direct materials	4,800
Direct labor	800
Manufacturing overhead	2,170
Total costs added during May	$ 7,770

Requirements
1. Draw a time line for the Blending Department. (pp. 911–912)
2. Use the time line to help you compute the Blending Department's equivalent units for direct materials and for conversion costs. (p. 911)
3. Compute the total costs of the units (gallons)
   a. Completed and transferred out to the Packaging Department (pp. 912–913)
   b. In the Blending Department ending work in process inventory (pp. 912–913)

Preparing journal entries and posting to work in process T-account

E18-17 Refer to E18-16.

Requirements
1. Present the journal entries to record the assignment of direct materials and direct labor and the allocation of manufacturing overhead to the Blending Department. Also, give the journal entry to record the costs of the gallons completed and transferred out to the Packaging Department. (pp. 912–913)
2. Post the journal entries to the Work in Process Inventory—Blending T-account. What is the ending balance? (p. 913)
3. What is the average cost per gallon transferred out of Blending into Packaging? Why would Paint My World's managers want to know this cost?

Computing equivalent units; assigning cost to goods completed and ending work in process inventory; first department, no beginning inventory

E18-18 The following information was taken from the ledger of Riley Co. Ending inventory is 60% complete as to direct materials but 30% complete as to conversion work.

WORK IN PROCESS—FORMING

	Physical Units	Dollars		Physical Units	Dollars
Beginning inventory, June 30	-0-	$ -0-	Transferred to Finishing	72,000	$?
Production started:	80,000				
Direct materials		$215,040			
Conversion costs		148,800			
Ending Inventory, July 31	8,000	?			

continued . . .

Requirements

1. Compute the equivalent units for direct materials and conversion costs. (p. 911)
2. Compute the cost per equivalent unit. (pp. 912–913)
3. Assign the costs to units completed and transferred out and ending work in process inventory. (pp. 912–913)

Computing equivalent units; assigning cost to goods completed and ending work in process inventory; first department, no beginning inventory

E18-19 The Assembly Department of Audio Manufacturers began June with no work in process inventory. During the month, production that cost $41,200 (direct materials, $9,100, and conversion costs, $32,100) was started on 23,000 units. The Assembly Department completed and transferred to the Testing Department a total of 15,000 units. The ending work in process inventory was 40% complete as to direct materials and 80% complete as to conversion work.

Requirements

1. Compute the equivalent units for direct materials and conversion costs. (p. 911)
2. Compute the cost per equivalent unit. (pp. 912–913)
3. Assign the costs to units completed and transferred out and ending work in process inventory. (pp. 912–913)
4. Record the journal entry for the costs transferred out of Assembly into Testing. (p. 913)
5. Post all the transactions in the Work in Process Inventory—Assembly Department T-account. What is the ending balance? (p. 913)

Drawing a time line; computing equivalent units; assigning costs to completed units and ending work in process; no beginning inventory or cost transferred in

E18-20 Anderson Winery in Napa Valley, California, has two departments: Fermenting and Packaging. Direct materials are added at the beginning of the fermenting process (grapes) and at the end of the packaging process (bottles). Conversion costs are added evenly throughout each process. Data from the month of March for the Fermenting Department are as follows:

Gallons:	
Beginning work in process inventory	0
Started production	8,000 gallons
Completed and transferred out to Packaging in March	6,550 gallons
Ending work in process inventory (80% of the way through the fermenting process)	1,450 gallons
Costs:	
Beginning work in process inventory	$ 0
Costs added during March:	
Direct materials	10,400
Direct labor	2,400
Manufacturing overhead	4,539
Total costs added during March	$17,339

continued . . .

Requirements

1. Draw a time line for the Fermenting Department. (pp. 911–912)
2. Use the time line to help you compute the equivalent units for direct materials and for conversion costs. (p. 911)
3. Compute the total costs of the units (gallons)
    a. Completed and transferred out to the Packaging Department (pp. 912–913)
    b. In the Fermenting Department ending work in process inventory (pp. 912–913)

Preparing journal entries and posting to work in process T-account

E18-21 Refer to E18-20.

Requirements

1. Present the journal entries to record the assignment of direct materials and direct labor and the allocation of manufacturing overhead to the Fermenting Department. Also give the journal entry to record the cost of the gallons completed and transferred out to the Packaging Department. (pp. 912–913)
2. Post the journal entries to the Work in Process Inventory—Fermenting T-account. What is the ending balance? (p. 913)
3. What is the average cost per gallon transferred out of Fermenting into Packaging? Why would Anderson Winery's managers want to know this cost?

Computing equivalent units, two departments; weighted-average method

E18-22 Selected production and cost data of Kristi's Divinity Co. follow for May 2008.

	Flow of Physical Units	
Flow of Production	Mixing Department	Heating Department
Units to account for:		
Beginning work in process, April 30	20,000	6,000
Started during May	70,000	
Transferred in during May		80,000
Total physical units to account for	90,000	86,000
Units accounted for:		
Completed and transferred out during May	80,000	74,000
Ending work in process, May 31	10,000	12,000
Total physical units accounted for	90,000	86,000

On May 31, the Mixing Department ending work in process inventory was 70% complete as to materials and 20% complete as to conversion costs. The Heating Department ending work in process inventory was 65% complete as to materials and 55% complete as to conversion costs. Kristi's uses weighted-average costing.

continued . . .

Process Costing **937**

Requirements

1. Compute the equivalent units for direct materials and for conversion costs for the Mixing Department. (p. 911)
2. Compute the equivalent units for transferred-in costs, direct materials, and conversion costs for the Heating Department. (pp. 919–920)

Drawing a time line; computing equivalent units; computing cost per equivalent unit; assigning costs; journalizing; second department, weighted-average method

E18-23 Clear Spring Company produces premium bottled water. In the second department, the Bottling Department, conversion costs are incurred evenly throughout the bottling process, but packaging materials are not added until the end of the process. Costs in beginning work in process inventory include transferred in costs of $1,760, direct labor of $600, and manufacturing overhead of $520. February data for the Bottling Department follow:

CLEAR SPRING COMPANY
Work in Process Inventory—Bottling
Month Ended February 28, 2009

	Physical Units	Dollars		Physical Units	Dollars
Beginning inventory, January 31 (40% complete)	8,000	$ 2,880	Transferred out	154,000	$?
Production started:					
Transferred in	160,000	136,000			
Direct materials		30,800			
Conversion costs:					
Direct labor		33,726			
Manufacturing overhead		22,484			
Total to account for	168,000	$225,890			
Ending inventory, February 28 (70% complete)	14,000	$?			

Requirements

1. Draw a time line. (pp. 917–920)
2. Compute the Bottling Department equivalent units for the month of February. Use the weighted-average method. (pp. 919–920)
3. Compute the cost per equivalent unit for February. (pp. 920–921)
4. Assign the costs to units completed and transferred out and to ending inventory. (p. 921)
5. Prepare the journal entry to record the cost of units completed and transferred out. (p. 923)
6. Post all transactions to the Work in Process Inventory—Bottling Department T-account. What is the ending balance? (p. 923)

Problems (Group A)

Computing equivalent units and assigning costs to completed units and ending work in process; no beginning inventory or cost transferred in

P18-24A Dee Electronics makes CD players in three processes: assembly, programming, and packaging. Direct materials are added at the beginning of the assembly process. Conversion costs are incurred evenly throughout the process. The Assembly Department had no work in process on May 30. In mid-June, Dee Electronics started production on 100,000 CD players. Of this number, 76,400 CD players were assembled during June and transferred out to the Programming Department. The June 30 work in process in the Assembly Department was 40% of the way through the assembly process. Direct materials costing $375,000 were placed in production in Assembly during June, and direct labor of $157,248 and manufacturing overhead of $100,272 were assigned to that department.

Requirements

1. Draw a time line for the Assembly Department. (pp. 910–911)
2. Use the time line to help you compute the number of equivalent units (p. 911) and the cost per equivalent unit in the Assembly Department for June. (pp. 912–913)
3. Assign total costs in the Assembly Department to (a) units completed and transferred to Programming during June and (b) units still in process at June 30. (pp. 912–913)
4. Prepare a T-account for Work in Process Inventory—Assembly to show its activity during June, including the June 30 balance. (p. 913)

Computing equivalent units; assigning costs to completed units and ending work in process; journalizing transactions; no beginning inventory or cost of goods transferred in

P18-25A Reed Paper Co. produces the paper used by wallpaper manufacturers. Reed's four-stage process includes mixing, cooking, rolling, and cutting. During August, the Mixing Department started and completed mixing for 4,500 rolls of paper. The department started but did not finish the mixing for an additional 500 rolls, which were 20% complete with respect to both direct materials and conversion work at the end of August. Direct materials and conversion costs are incurred evenly throughout the mixing process. The Mixing Department incurred the following costs during August:

Work in Process Inventory—Mixing	
Balance, Aug. 1	0
Direct materials	5,520
Direct labor	580
Manufacturing overhead	5,860

Requirements

1. Draw a time line for the Mixing Department. (pp. 910–911)
2. Use the time line to help you compute the number of equivalent units and the cost per equivalent unit in the Mixing Department for August. (pp. 911–912)

continued...

3. Show that the sum of (a) cost of goods transferred out of the Mixing Department and (b) ending Work in Process Inventory—Mixing equals the total cost accumulated in the department during August. (pp. 912–913)

4. Journalize all transactions affecting the company's mixing process during August, including those already posted. (pp. 912–913)

Computing equivalent units and assigning costs to completed units and ending WIP inventory; two materials, added at different points; no beginning inventory or cost transferred in

P18-26A Hall's Exteriors produces exterior siding for homes. The Preparation Department begins with wood, which is chopped into small bits. At the end of the process, an adhesive is added. Then the wood/adhesive mixture goes on to the Compression Department, where the wood is compressed into sheets. Conversion costs are added evenly throughout the preparation process. January data for the Preparation Department are as follows (in millions):

Sheets		Costs	
Beginning work in process inventory	0 sheets	Beginning work in process inventory	$ 0
Started production	3,000 sheets	Costs added during January:	
Completed and transferred out to Compression in January	1,950 sheets	Wood	2,700
		Adhesives	1,365
Ending work in process inventory (40% of the way through the preparation process)	1,050 sheets	Direct labor	629
		Manufacturing overhead	2,452
		Total costs	7,146

Requirements

1. Draw a time line for the Preparation Department. (pp. 910–911)
2. Use the time line to help you compute the equivalent units for direct materials and for conversion costs. (*Hint:* Each direct material added at a different point in the production process requires its own equivalent-unit computation.) (p. 911)
3. Compute the total costs of the units (sheets)
   a. Completed and transferred out to the Compression Department (pp. 912–913)
   b. In the Preparation Department's ending work in process inventory (pp. 912–913)
4. Prepare the journal entry to record the cost of the sheets completed and transferred out to the Compression Department. (p. 913)
5. Post the journal entries to the Work in Process Inventory—Preparation T-account. What is the ending balance? (p. 913)

Computing equivalent units for a second department with beginning inventory; preparing a production cost report and recording transactions on the basis of the report's information; weighted-average method

P18-27A Casey Carpet manufactures broadloom carpet in seven processes: spinning, dyeing, plying, spooling, tufting, latexing, and shearing. In the Dyeing Department, direct materials (dye) are added at the beginning of the process. Conversion costs are incurred evenly throughout the process. Casey uses weighted-average process costing. Information for March 2007 follows:

continued . . .

Units:	
Beginning work in process	75 rolls
Transferred in from Spinning Department during March	560 rolls
Completed during March	500 rolls
Ending work in process (80% complete as to conversion work)	135 rolls
Costs:	
Beginning work in process (transferred-in costs, $4,400; materials cost, $1,575; conversion costs, $5,199)	$11,174
Transferred in from Spinning Department during March	21,000
Materials costs added during March	11,760
Conversion costs added during March (manufacturing wages, $8,445; manufacturing overhead, $43,508)	51,953

Requirements

1. Prepare a time line for Casey's Dyeing Department. (pp. 917–918)
2. Use the time line to help you compute the equivalent units, cost per equivalent unit, and total costs to account for in Casey's Dyeing Department for March. (pp. 920–923)
3. Prepare the March production cost report for Casey's Dyeing Department. (pp. 923–924)
4. Journalize all transactions affecting Casey's Dyeing Department during March, including the entries that have already been posted. (pp. 921–923)

Computing equivalent units for a second department with beginning inventory; assigning costs to completed units and ending work in process; weighted-average method

P18-28A SeaWorthy uses three processes to manufacture lifts for personal watercraft: forming a lift's parts from galvanized steel, assembling the lift, and testing the completed lifts. The lifts are transferred to finished goods before shipment to marinas across the country.

SeaWorthy's Testing Department requires no direct materials. Conversion costs are incurred evenly throughout the testing process. Other information follows:

Units:	
Beginning work in process	2,000 units
Transferred in from the Assembling Department during the period	7,000 units
Completed during the period	4,000 units
Ending work in process (40% complete as to conversion work)	5,000 units
Costs:	
Beginning work in process (transferred-in costs, $93,000; conversion costs, $18,000)	$111,000
Transferred in from the Assembling Department during the period	672,000
Conversion costs added during the period	54,000

continued . . .

The cost transferred into Finished Goods Inventory is the cost of the lifts transferred out of the Testing Department. SeaWorthy uses weighted-average process costing.

Requirements

1. Draw a time line for the Testing Department. (pp. 917–918)
2. Use the time line to compute the number of equivalent units of work performed by the Testing Department during the period. (pp. 919–920)
3. Compute SeaWorthy's transferred-in and conversion costs per equivalent unit. Use the unit costs to assign total costs to (a) units completed and transferred out of Testing and (b) units in Testing's ending work in process inventory. (pp. 920–921)
4. Compute the cost per unit for lifts completed and transferred out to Finished Goods Inventory. Why would management be interested in this cost? (p. 921)

Problems (Group B)

Computing equivalent units and assigning costs to completed units and ending work in process; no beginning inventory or cost transferred in

P18-29B Great Lips produces women's lipstick, which is manufactured in a single processing department. Direct materials are added at the beginning of the process, and conversion costs are incurred evenly throughout the process. No lipstick was in process on September 30. Great Lips started production on 20,400 lipstick tubes during October 2008. Completed production for October totaled 15,200 units. The October 31 work in process was 75% of the way through the production process. Direct materials costing $4,080 were placed in production during October, and direct labor of $3,315 and manufacturing overhead of $2,415 were assigned to the process.

Requirements

1. Draw a time line for Great Lips. (pp. 910–911)
2. Use the time line to help you compute the number of equivalent units (p. 910) and the cost per equivalent unit for October. (pp. 912–913)
3. Assign total costs to (a) units completed and transferred to finished goods and (b) units still in process at October 31. (pp. 912–913)
4. Prepare a T-account for Work in Process Inventory to show activity during October, including the October 31 balance. (p. 913)

Computing equivalent units; assigning costs to completed units and ending work in process; journalizing transactions; no beginning inventory or cost of goods transferred in

P18-30B The Great Southern Furniture Company produces dining tables in a three-stage process: cutting, assembly, and staining. Direct materials (lumber) are added at the beginning of the cutting process, and conversion costs are incurred evenly throughout the process. September 2009 activity in the Cutting Department included cutting 11,000 meters of lumber, which were transferred to the Assembly Department. Also, work began on 1,000 meters of lumber, which on September 30 were 70% of the way through the cutting process.

continued . . .

942 Chapter 18

Costs incurred in the Cutting Department during September are summarized as follows:

Work in Process Inventory—Cutting

Balance, Sept. 1	0
Direct materials	1,860,000
Direct labor	139,100
Manufacturing overhead	165,100

Requirements

1. Draw a time line for the Cutting Department. (pp. 910–911)
2. Use the time line to help you compute the number of equivalent units and the cost per equivalent unit in the Cutting Department for September. (pp. 911–912)
3. Show that the sum of (a) cost of goods transferred out of the Cutting Department and (b) ending Work in Process Inventory—Cutting equals the total cost accumulated in the department during September. (pp. 912–913)
4. Journalize all transactions affecting the company's cutting process during September, including those already posted. (pp. 912–913)

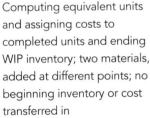

Computing equivalent units and assigning costs to completed units and ending WIP inventory; two materials, added at different points; no beginning inventory or cost transferred in

P18-31B Jolly Giant produces canned Italian green beans. The green beans move through three departments: (1) Mixing, (2) Retort (sterilization), and (3) Packing. In the Mixing Department, green beans are added at the beginning of the process, the mixture is partly cooked, then chopped red peppers are added at the end of the process. Conversion costs are added evenly throughout the mixing process. April 2008 data from the Mixing Department are as follows:

Gallons		Costs	
Beginning work in process inventory	0 gallons	Beginning work in process inventory	$ 0
Started production	15,000 gallons	Costs added during April:	
Completed and transferred out to		Green beans	16,500
Retort in April	12,900 gallons	Red peppers	11,610
		Conversion costs (direct labor, $11,108; manufacturing	
Ending work in process inventory (60% of the way through the mixing process)	2,100 gallons	overhead, $17,212)	28,320
		Total costs	$56,430

Requirements

1. Draw a time line for the Mixing Department. (pp. 910–911)
2. Use the time line to help you compute the equivalent units. (*Hint*: Each direct material added at a different point in the production process requires its own equivalent-unit computation.) (p. 911)

continued . . .

3. Compute the total costs of the units (gallons)
   a. Completed and transferred out to the Retort Department (pp. 912–913)
   b. In the Mixing Department's ending work in process inventory (pp. 912–913)
4. Prepare the journal entry to record the cost of the gallons completed and transferred out to the Retort Department. (p. 913)
5. Post the transactions to the Work in Process Inventory—Mixing T-account. What is the ending balance? (p. 913)
6. What is the primary purpose of the work required in steps 1 through 3?

Computing equivalent units for a second department with beginning inventory; preparing a production cost report and recording transactions on the basis of the report's information; weighted-average method

P18-32B Chrome Accessories manufactures chrome bumpers for classic cars in a two-stage process that includes molding and plating. The direct materials (chrome) are added at the end of the plating process. Conversion costs are incurred evenly throughout the process. Chrome Accessories uses weighted-average process costing. At March 31, 2009, before recording the transfer of cost to Finished Goods Inventory, Chrome Accessories' records included the following data for the Plating Department:

Units:	
Beginning work in process	600 bumpers
Transferred in from the Molding Department during March	3,000 bumpers
Completed during March	2,200 bumpers
Ending work in process (50% complete as to conversion work)	1,400 bumpers
Costs:	
Beginning work in process (transferred-in cost, $18,000; conversion costs, $12,480)	$30,480
Transferred in from the Molding Department during March	36,000
Materials cost added during March	24,200
Conversion costs added during March (manufacturing wages, $21,732; manufacturing overhead, $38,288)	60,020

Requirements
1. Draw a time line for the Plating Department. (pp. 917–919)
2. Use the time line to help you compute the equivalent units, cost per equivalent unit, and total costs to account for in the Plating Department for March. (pp. 920–923)
3. Prepare the March production cost report for the Plating Department. (pp. 923–924)
4. Journalize all transactions affecting the Plating Department during March, including the entries that have already been posted. (pp. 921–923)

P18-33B Goldman Company uses three departments to produce handles for kitchen cabinets. Forming the handles requires mixing the raw materials, molding, and drying.

continued . . .

Computing equivalent units for a second department with beginning inventory; assigning costs to completed units and ending work in process; weighted-average method

Goldman's Drying Department requires no direct materials. Conversion costs are incurred evenly throughout the drying process. Other information follows:

Units:	
Beginning work in process	7,000 units
Transferred in from the Molding Department during the period	28,000 units
Completed during the period	16,000 units
Ending work in process (20% complete as to conversion work)	19,000 units
Costs:	
Beginning work in process (transferred-in cost, $140; conversion cost, $231)	$ 371
Transferred in from the Molding Department during the period	4,760
Conversion costs added during the period	2,937

After the drying process, the handles are packaged for shipment to retail outlets. Goldman uses weighted-average process costing.

Requirements

1. Draw a time line of the Drying Department's process for the period. (pp. 917–919)
2. Use the time line to compute the number of equivalent units of work performed by the Drying Department during the period. (pp. 919–920)
3. Compute Goldman's transferred-in and conversion costs per equivalent unit. Use the unit costs to assign total costs to (a) units completed and transferred to the assembly operation and (b) units in the Drying Department's ending work in process inventory. (pp. 920–921)

Apply Your Knowledge

Decision Case

Billy Davidson operates Billy's Worm Farm in Mississippi. Davidson raises worms for fishing. He sells a box of 20 worms for $12.60 per box. Davidson has invested $400,000 in the worm farm. He had hoped to earn a 24% annual rate of return (net income divided by total assets), which works out to a 2% monthly return on his investment. After looking at the farm's bank balance, Davidson fears he is not achieving this return. To evaluate the farm's performance, he prepared the following process-costing reports. The finished goods inventory is zero because the worms ship out as soon as they reach the required size. Monthly operating expenses total $2,000 (in addition to the costs below).

BILLY'S WORM FARM
Brooding Department
Month Ended June 30, 2007

Flow of Production	Flow of Physical Units	Equivalent Units		
		Transferred In	Direct Materials	Conversion Costs
Units to account for:				
Beginning work in process inventory	9,000			
Transferred in during June	21,000			
Total units to account for	30,000			
Units accounted for:				
Completed and shipped out during June	20,000	20,000	20,000	20,000
Ending work in process, June 30	10,000	10,000	6,000	3,600
Total physical units accounted for	30,000			
Equivalent units		30,000	26,000	23,600

BILLY'S WORM FARM
Brooding Department
Production Cost Report (Weighted-Average Method)
Month Ended June 30, 2007

	Transferred In	Direct Materials	Conversion Costs	Total
Units costs:				
Beginning work in process, May 31	$21,000	$ 39,940	$ 5,020	$ 65,960
Costs added during June	46,200	152,460	56,340	255,000
Total costs to account for	$67,200	$192,400	$61,360	$320,960
Divide by equivalent units	÷30,000	÷26,000	÷23,600	
Cost per equivalent unit	$ 2.24	$ 7.40	$ 2.60	
Assignment of total cost:				
Units completed and shipped out during June	[20,000 × ($2.24 + $7.40 + $2.60)]			$244,800
Ending work in process, June 30:				
Transferred-in costs	[10,000 × $2.24]			22,400
Direct materials		[6,000 × $7.40]		44,400
Conversion costs			[3,600 × $2.60]	9,360
Total ending work in progress, June 30				76,160
Total cost accounted for				$320,960

Requirements
Billy Davidson has the following questions about the farm's performance during June.

1. What is the cost per box of worms sold? (*Hint:* This is the unit cost of the boxes completed and shipped out of brooding.) (p. 921)

2. What is the gross profit per box?

3. How much operating income did Billy's Worm Farm make in June?

4. What is the return on Davidson's investment of $400,000 for the month of June? (Compute this as June's operating income divided by Davidson's $400,000 investment, expressed as a percentage.)

5. What monthly operating income would provide a 2% monthly rate of return? What price per box would Billy's Worm Farm have had to charge in June to achieve a 2% monthly rate of return?

Ethical Issue

Rick Pines and Joe Lopez are the plant managers for High Mountain Lumber's particle board division. High Mountain Lumber has adopted a just-in-time management philosophy. Each plant combines wood chips with chemical adhesives to produce particle board to order, and all production is sold as soon as it is completed. Laura Green is High Mountain Lumber's regional controller. All of High Mountain Lumber's plants and divisions send Green their production and cost information. While reviewing the numbers of the two particle board plants, she is surprised to find that both plants estimate their ending work in process inventories at 75% complete, which is higher than usual. Green calls Lopez, whom she has known for some time. He admits that to ensure their division would meet its profit goal and that both he and Pines would make their bonus (which is based on division profit), they agreed to inflate the percentage completion. Lopez explains, "Determining the percent complete always requires judgment. Whatever the percent complete, we'll finish the work in process inventory first thing next year."

Requirements
1. How would inflating the percentage completion of ending work in process inventory help Pines and Lopez get their bonus?

2. The particle board division is the largest of High Mountain Lumber's divisions. If Green does not correct the percentage completion of this year's ending work in process inventory, how will the misstatement affect High Mountain Lumber's financial statements?

3. Evaluate Lopez's justification, including the effect, if any, on next year's financial statements.

4. Address the following: What is the ethical issue? What are the options? What are the potential consequences? What should Green do?

Team Project

Idaho Food Processors processes potatoes into french fries. Production requires two processes: cutting and cooking. Direct materials are added at the beginning of the cutting process (potatoes) and at the end of the cooking process (boxes). Conversion costs are incurred evenly throughout each process. Idaho uses the weighted-average method of process costing.

Assume that McDonald's offers Idaho $0.40 per pound to supply restaurants in the Far East. If Idaho accepts McDonald's offer, the cost (per equivalent unit) that Idaho will incur to fill the McDonald's order equals the April cost per equivalent unit. M. A. Keltner, manager of the cooking process, must prepare a report recommending whether Idaho should accept the offer. Keltner gathers the following information from April's cooking operations:

IDAHO FOOD PROCESSORS
Cooking Department
April 2008 Activity and Costs

Beginning work in process inventory	12,000 pounds
Raw shoestring fries transferred in during April	129,000 pounds
French fries completed and transferred out	130,000 pounds
Ending work in process inventory (30% of way through process)	11,000 pounds
Conversion costs *within* the Cooking Dept. to start the 12,000 pounds of beginning work in process inventory in March	$ 576
Costs added during April:	
Direct materials	9,100
Conversion costs	15,420

Rita Mendez manages the cutting process. She reports the following data for her department's April operations.

IDAHO FOOD PROCESSORS
Cutting ~~Cooking~~ Department
April 2008 Activity and Costs

Beginning work in process inventory	21,000 pounds
Potatoes started in April	121,000 pounds
Raw shoestring fries completed and transferred out	129,000 pounds
Ending work in process inventory (60% of way through process)	13,000 pounds
Costs to start the 21,000 pounds of beginning work in process inventory in March ($1,260 for direct materials; $840 for conversion costs)	$ 2,100
Costs added during April:	
Direct materials	7,260
Conversion costs	12,840

Split your team into two groups. Each group should meet separately before a meeting of the entire team.

Requirements

1. The first group takes the role of M.A. Keltner, manager of the cooking production process. Before meeting with the entire team, determine the maximum transferred-in cost per pound of raw shoestring fries the Cooking Department can incur from the Cutting Department if Idaho is to make a profit on the McDonald's order. (*Hint:* You may find it helpful to prepare a time line as a guide to your analysis.) (pp. 917–923)

2. The second group takes the role of Rita Mendez, manager of the cutting process. Before meeting with the entire team, determine the April cost per pound of raw shoestring fries in the cutting process. (*Hint:* You may find it helpful to prepare a time line as a guide to your analysis.)

3. After each group meets, the entire team should meet to decide whether Idaho should accept or reject McDonald's offer.

For Internet Exercises, Excel in Practice, and additional online activities, go to the Web site www.prenhall.com/horngren.

Quick Check Answers

1. c 2. b 3. d 4. a 5. c 6. a 7. d 8. a 9. b 10. d

Appendix 18A

The FIFO Process Costing Method

The cost per equivalent unit often changes over time. In the second half of the chapter, we used the weighted-average process costing method in Puzzle Me's Cutting Department. The weighted-average method values both beginning inventory and current production at the same cost per equivalent unit. That cost is a weighted average of last period's and this period's costs.

In contrast, the **first-in, first-out (FIFO) method** of process costing values each equivalent unit of work at the cost per equivalent unit in effect during the period the work is done. Therefore, FIFO requires us to keep the beginning inventory units and costs (which were incurred *last period*) completely separate from current-period production and costs.[1]

Let's see how Puzzle Me could use FIFO process costing in its Cutting Department. Consider a batch of puzzles transferred out of the Assembly Department and into Cutting at the end of June. These puzzles did not make it completely through the Cutting Department during June, so the puzzles are in the Cutting Department's ending (work in process) inventory at the end of June. The puzzles are not completed until July. Under FIFO, when these puzzles are completed in July, the total Cutting Department cost of these puzzles is the sum of

- June's equivalent units of Cutting's work on these puzzles, costed at June's cost per equivalent unit, *plus*
- July's equivalent units of Cutting's work on these puzzles, costed at July's cost per equivalent unit

Steps 1 and 2: Summarize the Flow of Physical Units and Compute Output in Terms of Equivalent Units

SUMMARIZE THE FLOW OF PHYSICAL UNITS Exhibit 18A gives the July data for Puzzle Me's Cutting Department.

---

[1] The FIFO and weighted-average process costing methods differ only in how they treat beginning inventory. Because Puzzle Me's first department, Assembly, had no beginning work in process inventory, we did not need to specify which method that department used.

EXHIBIT 18A-1 | Puzzle Me's Cutting Department Time Line (FIFO)

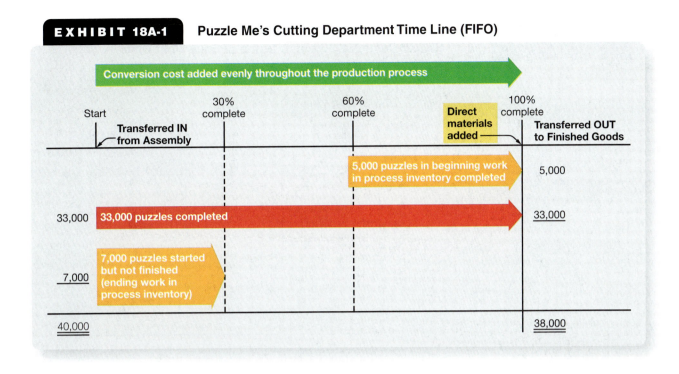

The time line in Exhibit 18A-1 shows that glued puzzles are transferred in from Assembly at the beginning of Cutting's process, but Cutting's direct materials (boxes) are not added until the end of the process.

The FIFO time line that diagrams the Cutting Department's flow of physical units (step 1) is more complex than the weighted-average time line in Exhibit 18-10. Why? Because FIFO costs each equivalent unit of work at the cost per equivalent unit in effect at the time the work was done. Under FIFO, we must separate the work done last period (June) from the work done this period (July). Exhibit 18A-1 identifies work that Cutting performed during *July*.

Start with the 38,000 puzzles completed and transferred out of the Cutting Department and into finished goods inventory during July. The time line in Exhibit 18A-1 shows that these include:

- 5,000 puzzles that were the Cutting Department's beginning work in process inventory. These puzzles were *completed* (but not started) in July.
- 33,000 puzzles that Cutting both *started* and *completed* during July. This number is computed as:

38,000	puzzles completed and transferred out of the Cutting Department in July
(5,000)	puzzles completed from Cutting's beginning inventory
33,000	puzzles *started and completed during July*

The time line also shows that the 40,000 puzzles *transferred into* Cutting from Assembly during July also fall into two categories: (1) 33,000 puzzles *started and completed* in the Cutting Department during July, plus (2) 7,000 puzzles *started* in Cutting but not completed in July.

Exhibit 18A-2 summarizes the flow of physical units diagrammed in the time line. The Cutting Department starts July with 5,000 puzzles in beginning inventory and begins work on 40,000 more transferred in from Assembly during the month.

EXHIBIT 18A-2   **FIFO, Step 1: Summarize the Flow of Physical Units;
Step 2: Compute Output in Terms of Equivalent Units**

PUZZLE ME CUTTING DEPARTMENT
Month Ended July 31, 2008

	Step 1	Step 2: Equivalent Units		
Flow of Production	Flow of Physical Units	Transferred In	Direct Materials	Conversion Costs
Units to account for:				
Beginning work in process, June 30	5,000			
Transferred in during July	40,000			
Total physical units to account for	45,000			
Units accounted for:				
Completed and transferred out during July:				
From beginning work in process inventory	5,000	—	5,000*	2,000*
Started and completed during July				
(38,000 – 5,000)	33,000	33,000	33,000	33,000
Ending work in process, July 31	7,000	7,000	—†	2,100†
Total physical units accounted for	45,000			
Equivalent units		40,000	38,000	37,100

During July in the Cutting Department:
*Finish beginning inventory
    Direct materials: 5,000 units each 100% completed = 5,000 equivalent units
    Conversion costs: 5,000 units each 40% completed = 2,000 equivalent units
†Start ending inventory
    Direct materials: 7,000 units each 0% completed = 0 equivalent units
    Conversion costs: 7,000 units each 30% completed = 2,100 equivalent units

Cutting thus must account for 45,000 puzzles (5,000 + 40,000). Where did these 45,000 puzzles go? Exhibit 18A-2 shows that 38,000 were completed and transferred out to finished goods inventory (the 5,000 from beginning inventory + 33,000 started and completed during July). The remaining 7,000 puzzles are still in the Cutting Department's ending inventory.

COMPUTE EQUIVALENT UNITS The Cutting Department has three categories of equivalent units. In addition to direct materials (boxes) and conversion costs added in the Cutting Department, Puzzle Me must also compute equivalent units for the glued puzzles that are *transferred in* from the Assembly Department. (All second and later departments must account for units (and costs) transferred in from preceding departments.) Exhibit 18A-1 shows that these transferred-in costs (from Assembly) act like costs that are added at the very beginning of the Cutting process.

To figure out how many equivalent units of work the Cutting Department completed *during July,* look at the time line in Exhibit 18A-1 and add the number of equivalent units of work performed to:

- *Complete* the 5,000 puzzles in beginning inventory that were started in June,
- *Start and complete* an additional 33,000 puzzles, and
- *Start* (but not complete) the 7,000 puzzles that make up the department's work in process inventory at the end of July.

Repeat these computations for each of the three cost categories.

EQUIVALENT UNITS TRANSFERRED IN Keep in mind that our goal is to figure the number of equivalent units of work performed *during July*. Also recall that transferred-in costs (from Assembly) act like costs that are added at the very beginning of the Cutting process. The time line in Exhibit 18A-1 shows that the 5,000 units in Cutting's beginning inventory were *not* transferred in from Assembly *this* month.

Look at the time line again—it shows that the 33,000 puzzles Cutting started and completed during July and the 7,000 puzzles in Cutting's ending inventory *were* transferred in during July. Exhibit 18A-2 shows that the total transferred-in equivalent units during July is 40,000 (33,000 + 7,000).

EQUIVALENT UNITS OF DIRECT MATERIALS The time line in Exhibit 18A-1 shows that the Cutting Department's direct materials (boxes) are not added until the end of the process. Exhibit 18A-1 shows that during July the 5,000 units in beginning inventory were completed, so they reached the end of the production process, where the boxes are added. The 33,000 units started and completed also reached the end of the process. However, ending inventory has not yet reached the point where workers insert boxes. Thus, Exhibit 18A-2 shows that Cutting added 5,000 + 33,000 = 38,000 equivalent units of materials (boxes) during July.

EQUIVALENT UNITS OF CONVERSION COSTS The time line shows that beginning inventory was 60% complete at the beginning of July. To complete these units during July, these 5,000 puzzles from the Cutting Department's beginning inventory went through the final 40% of the Cutting process. This yields 5,000 × 0.40 = 2,000 equivalent units of conversion work during July. The 33,000 puzzles started and completed during July went through the entire process during July. The 7,000 puzzles in ending inventory that were *started* in Cutting during July made it 30% of the way through the process by July 31. Cutting performed 7,000 × 0.30 = 2,100 equivalent units of conversion work on this ending inventory during July. Thus, Exhibit 18A-2 shows that the total conversion work performed in Cutting during July includes:

2,000	units to *complete* the beginning inventory (5,000 × (100% − 60%))
33,000	units from puzzles started *and* completed during July (33,000 × 100%)
2,100	units to *start* the ending inventory (7,000 × 30% complete)
37,100	total equivalent units of conversion costs during July

Step 3: Summarize Total Costs to Account for and Compute the Cost per Equivalent Unit

Exhibit 18A-3 accumulates the Cutting Department's July costs from Exhibit 18-11. *Under FIFO, the July cost per equivalent unit equals the costs incurred in July divided by the equivalent units of work performed in July.* The $24,000 cost of the beginning inventory is kept separate and is not included in the cost per equivalent unit for work done in July. Why? Because Cutting incurred this $24,000 in *June* to start the 5,000 puzzles in process on July 1.

EXHIBIT 18A-3 | FIFO, Steps 3 and 4: Summarize Total Costs to Account for and Compute the Cost per Equivalent Unit

PUZZLE ME CUTTING DEPARTMENT
Month Ended July 31, 2008

	Transferred In	Direct Materials	Conversion Costs	Total
Beginning work in process, June 30 (Exhibit 18-11)				$ 23,200
Costs added during July (Exhibit 18-11)	$176,000	$19,000	$14,840	209,840
Divide by equivalent units (Exhibit 18A-2)	÷40,000	÷38,000	÷37,100	
Cost per equivalent unit	$4.40	$0.50	$0.40	
Total costs to account for				$233,040

Step 4: Assign Total Costs to Units Completed and to Units in Ending Work in Process Inventory

Exhibit 18A-4 shows that the Cutting Department uses the same approach as we have used previously to assign its total cost ($233,040 from Exhibit 18A-3) to:

- Units completed and transferred out to Finished Goods Inventory
- Units still in Cutting's ending work in process inventory

Multiply the number of equivalent units from step 2 (Exhibit 18A-2) by the cost per equivalent unit from step 4 (Exhibit 18A-3).

Exhibit 18A-4 shows that when computing the cost of puzzles completed and transferred out of Cutting, we must remember to include the costs of the beginning inventory:

- $23,200 of Cutting Department beginning inventory costs (incurred in June)
- $3,300 of costs to complete that beginning inventory in July [(5,000 equivalent units of materials added × $0.50) + (2,000 equivalent units of conversion costs added × $0.40)]

The entry to transfer the cost of completed puzzles out of the Cutting Department and into Finished Goods Inventory is based on the dollar amount computed in Exhibit 18A-4:

	Finished Goods Inventory		201,400	
	Work in Process Inventory—Cutting			201,400

EXHIBIT 18A-4 — FIFO, Step 5: Assign Total Costs to Units Completed and to Units in Ending Work in Process Inventory

PUZZLE ME CUTTING DEPARTMENT
Month Ended July 31, 2008

	Transferred In	Direct Materials	Conversion Costs	Total
Units completed and transferred out to				
Finished Goods Inventory:				
From beginning work in process, June 30				$ 23,200
Costs added during July:				
Direct materials		[5,000 × $0.50]		2,500
Conversion costs			[2,000 × $0.40]	800
Total completed from beginning inventory				26,500
Units started and completed during July		[33,000 × ($4.40 + $0.50 + $0.40)]		174,900
Total costs transferred out				$201,400
Ending work in process, July 31:				
Transferred-in costs	[7,000 × $4.40]			30,800
Direct materials		—		—
Conversion costs			[2,100 × $0.40]	840
Total ending work in process, July 31				31,640
Total costs accounted for				$233,040

Many companies combine Exhibits 18A-3 and 18A-4 to form a FIFO-based production cost report. (This report is the FIFO-based counterpart to the weighted-average-based production cost report in Exhibit 18-16.)

Appendix 18A Assignments

Short Exercises

Drawing a time line; computing equivalent units; FIFO method

S18A-34 Refer to the Clear Spring bottling process in E18-23.

1. Draw a time line for the Bottling Department under FIFO process costing. Your time line should be similar to Exhibit 18A-1. (p. 951)
2. Use the time line to help you compute the Bottling Department's equivalent units using the FIFO method. (p. 952)

Computing costs per equivalent unit; FIFO method

S18A-35 Refer to E18-23 and S18A-34. Compute the costs per equivalent unit using FIFO.

Assigning costs; FIFO method

S18A-36 Use the information about Clear Spring's Bottling Department in E18-23, S18A-34, and S18A-35 to assign the costs to units completed and transferred out and to ending inventory under FIFO.

Appendix Exercise

Computing equivalent units; FIFO method

E18A-37 Donnie's Frozen Pizzas uses FIFO process costing. Selected production and cost data follow for April 2009.

	Flow of Physical Units	
Flow of Production	Mixing Department	Heating Department
Units to account for:		
Beginning work in process, March 31	20,000	6,000
Transferred in during April	70,000	80,000
Total physical units to account for	90,000	86,000
Units accounted for:		
Completed and transferred out during April		
From beginning work in process inventory	20,000	6,000
Started and completed during April	60,000	70,000
Ending work in process, April 30	10,000	10,000
Total physical units accounted for	90,000	86,000

Requirements

1. a. On March 31, the Mixing Department beginning work in process inventory was 60% complete as to materials and 75% complete as to conversion costs. This means that for the beginning inventory _____% of the materials and _____% of the conversion costs were added during April.

    b. On April 30, the Mixing Department ending work in process inventory was 70% complete as to materials and 20% complete as to conversion costs. This means that for the ending inventory _____% of the materials and _____% of the conversion costs were added during April.

    c. On March 31, the Cooking Department beginning work in process inventory was 60% complete as to materials and 80% complete as to conversion costs. This means that for the beginning inventory _____% of the materials and _____% of the conversion costs were added during April.

    d. On April 30, the Cooking Department ending work in process inventory was 65% complete as to materials and 55% complete as to conversion costs. This means that for the ending inventory _____% of the materials and _____% of the conversion costs were added during April.

2. Use the information in the Flow of Physical Units table and the information in Requirement 1 to compute the equivalent units for transferred-in costs, direct materials, and conversion costs for both the Mixing and the Cooking Departments.

Appendix Problems

P18A-38 Viva, Inc., manufactures tire tubes in a two-stage process that includes assembly and sealing. The Sealing Department tests the tubes and adds a puncture-resistant coating to each tube to prevent air leaks.

Drawing a time line; computing equivalent units; assigning costs; journalizing; FIFO method

The direct materials (coating) are added at the end of the sealing process. Conversion costs are incurred evenly throughout the process. Work in process of the Sealing Department on February 28, 2008, consisted of 700 tubes that were 30% of the way through the production process. During March, 3,600 tubes were transferred in from the Assembly Department. The Sealing Department transferred 3,100 tubes to Finished Goods Inventory in March, and 1,200 were still in process on March 31. This ending inventory was 50% of the way through the sealing process. Viva uses FIFO process costing.

At March 31, before recording the transfer of costs from the Sealing Department to Finished Goods Inventory, the Viva general ledger included the following account:

Work in Process Inventory—Sealing

Balance, Feb. 28	28,100
Transferred in from Assembly	36,000
Direct materials	24,800
Direct labor	25,340
Manufacturing overhead	33,990

Requirements

1. Draw a time line for the Sealing Department. (p. 951)
2. Use the time line to help you compute (a) the equivalent units, (b) cost per equivalent unit, and (c) total costs to account for in the Sealing Department for March. (pp. 952–953)
3. Assign total Sealing Department costs to (a) goods transferred out of the Sealing Department and (b) Work in Process Inventory—Sealing on March 31. (p. 954)
4. Journalize all transactions affecting the Sealing Department during March, including the entries that have already been posted. (pp. 921, 923)

Computing equivalent units for a second department with beginning inventory; assigning costs; FIFO method

P18A-39 Work P18-33B, using the FIFO method. The Drying Department beginning work in process of 7,000 units is 30% complete as to conversion costs. Round equivalent unit costs to three decimal places.

19 Activity-Based Costing and Other Cost Management Tools

Learning Objectives

1. Develop activity-based costs (ABC)
2. Use activity-based management (ABM) to achieve target costs
3. Describe a just-in-time (JIT) production system, and record its transactions
4. Use the four types of quality costs to make decisions

David Larimer, Matt Sewell, and Brian Jobe are college friends who share an apartment. They split the following monthly costs equally:

Rent and utilities	$570
Cable TV	50
High-speed Internet access	40
Groceries	240
Total monthly costs	$900

Each roommate's share is $300 ($900/3).

Things go smoothly the first few months. But then David calls a meeting. "Since I started having dinner at Amy's, I shouldn't have to pay a full share for the groceries." Matt then pipes in: "I'm so busy surfing the Net that I never have time to watch TV. I don't want to pay for the cable TV any more. And Brian, since your friend Jennifer eats here most evenings, you should pay a double share of the grocery bill." Brian retorts, "Matt, then you should pay for the Internet access, since you're the only one around here who uses it!"

What happened? The friends originally shared the costs equally. But they are not participating equally in eating, watching TV, and surfing the Net. Splitting these costs equally isn't the best arrangement.

The roommates could better match their costs with the people who participate in each activity. This means splitting cable TV between David and Brian,

letting Matt pay for Internet access, and allocating the grocery bill 1/3 to Matt and 2/3 to Brian. Exhibit 19-1 compares the results of this refined system with the original system.

EXHIBIT 19-1 More-Refined Versus Less-Refined Cost Allocation System

	David	Matt	Brian
More-refined cost allocation system:			
Rent and utilities	$190	$190	$190
Cable TV	25	—	25
High-speed Internet access	—	40	—
Groceries	—	80	160
Total costs allocated	$215	$310	$375
Original cost allocation system	$300	$300	$300
Difference	$ (85)	$ 10	$ 75

No wonder David called the meeting! The original system cost him $300 a month, but under the refined system David pays only $215. ■

Fedex, PepsiCo, and Intel face situations like this every day. What's the best way to allocate our costs to the things we do? The stakes are high—friendships for David, Matt, and Brian and profits and losses for companies.

Refining Cost Systems

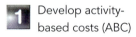
Develop activity-based costs (ABC)

Sharpening the Focus: Assigning Costs Based on the Activities That Caused the Costs

Let's illustrate cost refinement by looking at Dell, the computer company. In today's competitive market, Dell needs to know what it costs to make a laptop. The cost information helps Dell set a selling price to cover costs and provide a profit. To remain competitive with Gateway and HP, Dell must hold costs down.

We've seen that direct costs (materials and labor) are easy to assign to products. But indirect costs (utilities, supervisor salaries, and plant depreciation) are another story. It's the indirect costs—and they are significant—that cause the headaches. One way to manage costs is to refine the way indirect costs are allocated. Exhibit 19-2 provides an example. The first column of Exhibit 19-2 starts with Dell's production function—making the computers. Production is where most companies begin refining their cost systems.

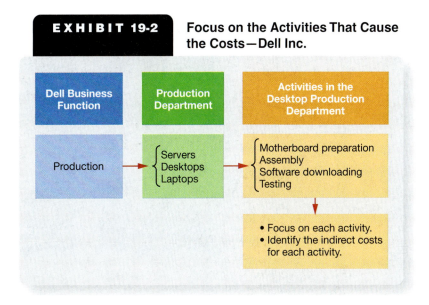

EXHIBIT 19-2 Focus on the Activities That Cause the Costs—Dell Inc.

Before business got so competitive, managers could limit their focus to a broad business function such as production, and use a single plantwide rate to allocate manufacturing overhead cost to their inventory.

But today's environment calls for more refined cost accounting. Managers need better data to set prices and identify the most profitable products. They drill down to focus on the costs incurred by each activity within the production function, as shown in the lower right of Exhibit 19-2. This has led to a better way to allocate indirect cost to production, and it's called activity-based costing.

Activity-Based Costing

Activity-based costing (ABC) focuses on *activities*. The costs of those activities become the building blocks for measuring the costs of products and services. Companies like Dell, Coca-Cola, and American Express use ABC.

Each activity has its own (usually unique) cost driver. For example, Dell allocates indirect assembly costs to computers based on the number of times a worker touches the computer as it moves through assembly. Computers that require more touches cost more to manufacture. Exhibit 19-3 shows some representative activities and cost drivers for Dell.

Developing an Activity-Based Costing System

The main difference between ABC and traditional systems is that ABC uses a separate allocation rate for each activity. ABC requires four steps, as outlined in Exhibit 19-4.

The first step in developing an activity-based costing system is to identify the activities. Analyzing all the activities required for a product or service forces managers to think about how each activity might be improved—or whether it's necessary at all.

EXHIBIT 19-3 Activities and Cost Drivers

EXHIBIT 19-4 Activity-Based Costing in Four Easy Steps

ABC Step	Application
1. Identify each activity and estimate its total indirect cost.	Activity Customer service Estimated total indirect cost per year $60,000
2. Identify the cost driver for each activity and estimate the total quantity of each drivers allocation base.	Cost driver for customer service Phone calls Estimated total number of customer-service phone calls each year 40,000
3. Compute the cost allocation rate for each activity. $\text{Cost allocation rate} = \dfrac{\text{Estimated total indirect cost}}{\text{Estimated total quantity of the allocation base}}$	$\text{Cost allocation rate} = \dfrac{\$60,000}{40,000 \text{ calls}} = \$1.50 \text{ per call}$
4. Allocate indirect costs to the cost object—in this case, all the customer-service calls during April. $\text{Allocated activity cost} = \text{Cost allocation rate} \times \text{Actual quantity of the allocation base}$	Cost of customer service for April = $1.50 per call × 3,000 calls during April = $4,500

Traditional Versus Activity-Based Costing Systems: Fischer Chemical Company

To illustrate an ABC system, we use Fischer Chemical Company. Fischer produces hundreds of different chemicals, including mass quantities of "commodity" chemicals for large companies such as Xerox and Goodyear, and small quantities of "specialty" chemicals for others.

We begin with a traditional cost system to show its weakness. The ABC system that follows is clearly superior.

A Traditional Cost System

Fischer Chemical's cost system allocates all manufacturing overhead the traditional way—based on a single allocation rate: 200% of direct labor cost. Fischer's controller, Martha Wise, gathered data for two of the company's products:

- Aldehyde—a *commodity* chemical used in a wide range of plastics
- Phenylephrine hydrochloride (PH)—a *specialty* chemical (A single customer uses PH in blood-pressure medications.)

Based on Fischer's traditional cost system, Wise computed each product's gross profit as shown in Exhibit 19-5.

EXHIBIT 19-5 Fischer's Traditional Cost System—Manufacturing Cost and Gross Profit

	Aldehyde	PH
Sale price per pound	$12.00	$70.00
Less: Manufacturing cost per pound:		
Direct materials	5.00	14.00
Direct labor	1.00	12.00
Manufacturing overhead		
(at 200% of direct labor cost)	2.00	24.00
Total manufacturing cost per pound	8.00	50.00
Gross profit per pound	$4.00	$20.00

The gross profit for the PH chemical is $20 per pound—5 times as high as the gross profit for the aldehyde ($4). Fischer CEO Randy Smith is surprised that PH appears so much more profitable. He asks Wise to check this out. Wise confirms that the gross profit per pound is 5 times as high for PH. Smith wonders whether Fischer should produce more PH chemicals.

Smith

Based on recent activity, here's how Fischer Chemicals allocated overhead cost to each pound of product:

Aldehyde (7,500 pounds @ $2 per pound)	$15,000
PH (5 pounds @ $24 per pound)	$ 120

Key Point: Because direct labor cost is the single allocation base for all products, Fischer allocates far more total overhead cost to aldehyde than to PH. This costing is accurate only if direct labor really is the overhead cost driver, and only if aldehyde really does cause more overhead than PH.

CEO Smith calls a meeting with production foreman Steve Pronai and controller Wise. Smith is perplexed: The accounting numbers show that PH is much more profitable (on a per-pound basis) than aldehyde. He expected aldehyde to be more efficient because it's produced in a few large batches. By contrast, PH is produced in many small batches.

Wise fears that the problem could be Fischer's cost accounting system. Wise suggests that foreman Pronai work with her to develop a pilot ABC system. Exhibit 19-6 compares the traditional single-allocation-base system (Panel A) to the new ABC system that Wise's team developed (Panel B).

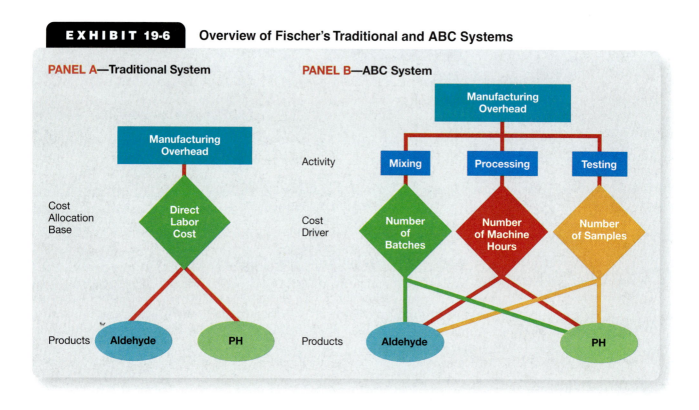

EXHIBIT 19-6 Overview of Fischer's Traditional and ABC Systems

Activity-Based Cost System

Panel B of Exhibit 19-6 shows that Fischer's ABC team identifies three activities: mixing, processing, and testing. Each activity has its own cost driver. But exactly how does ABC work? The ABC team develops the new system by following the four steps described in Exhibit 19-4.

Let's see how an ABC system works, with a focus on the mixing activity. Exhibit 19-7 develops Fischer's ABC system. Follow the details of each step. Make sure you understand exactly how each ABC step applies to Fischer's mixing process.

Controller Wise then uses the ABC costs allocated to aldehyde and to PH (from Exhibit 19-7) to recompute manufacturing overhead costs, as shown in Exhibit 19-8. For each product, Wise adds the total costs of mixing, processing, and testing. She then divides each product's total manufacturing overhead cost by the number of pounds produced to get the overhead cost per pound.

EXHIBIT 19-7 Fischer's ABC System

Step 1: Identify activities and estimate their total indirect costs.

Controller Wise's team identifies all the manufacturing activities. Focus on Mixing.

Foreman Pronai estimates total Mixing cost at $600,000.

Step 2: Identify the cost driver for each activity. Then estimate the total quantity of each driver's allocation base.

The allocation base for each activity should be its cost driver. The number of batches drive Mixing costs.

Wise and Pronai estimate the Mixing Department will produce 4,000 batches.

Step 3: Compute the allocation rate for each activity.

Wise computes the allocation rate for Mixing as follows:

$$\text{Cost allocation rate} = \frac{\$600,000}{4,000 \text{ batches}} = \$150 \text{ per batch}$$

Step 4: Allocate indirect costs to the cost object—batches of chemicals in this case.

Wise allocates Mixing costs as follows:

Aldehyde: 60 batches × $150 per batch = $9,000
PH: 1 batch × $150 per batch = $ 150

Activity-based costs are more accurate because ABC considers the resources each product actually uses. Focus on the bottom line of Exhibit 19-8. Manufacturing overhead cost of:

- Aldehyde is $1.68 per pound, which is less than the $2.00 cost under the old system (shown in color in Exhibit 19-5).
- PH is $110 per pound, which far exceeds the $24 cost under the old system (shown in color in Exhibit 19-5).

EXHIBIT 19-8 Fischer's Manufacturing Overhead Costs Under ABC

Manufacturing Overhead Costs	Aldehyde	PH
Mixing (from Exhibit 19-7)	$ 9,000	$150
Processing (amounts assumed)	1,600	170
Testing (amounts assumed)	2,000	230
Total manufacturing overhead cost	$12,600	$550
Divide by number of pounds (bottom of page 963)	÷ 7,500 lb	÷ 5 lb
Manufacturing overhead cost per pound	$ 1.68/lb	$110/lb

Now that we know the indirect costs of aldehyde and PH under ABC, let's see how Fischer's managers *use* the ABC cost information to make better decisions.

Activity-Based Management: Using ABC for Decision Making

> **2** Use activity-based management (ABM) to achieve target costs

Activity-based management (ABM) uses activity-based costs to make decisions that increase profits while meeting customer needs. We show how Fischer can use ABC in two kinds of decisions:

1. Pricing and product mix
2. Cost cutting

Pricing and Product Mix Decisions

Controller Wise now knows the ABC manufacturing overhead cost per pound (Exhibit 19-8). To determine which products are the most profitable, she recomputes each product's total manufacturing cost and gross profit. Panel A of Exhibit 19-9 shows that the total manufacturing cost per pound of aldehyde is $7.68 under the ABC system. Contrast this with the $8.00 cost per pound under Fischer's traditional cost system, as shown in Panel B. More important, the ABC data in Panel A show that PH costs $130 per pound, rather than the $50 per pound indicated by the old system (Panel B). Fischer has been losing $60 on each pound of PH—and this is *before* R&D, marketing, and distribution expenses! It seems that PH chemicals are dragging the company down.

EXHIBIT 19-9 Comparison of Fischer's Manufacturing Product Costs Under ABC and Traditional Systems

PANEL A—Total Manufacturing Cost and Gross Profit Under ABC

	Aldehyde	PH
Sale price per pound	$12.00	$ 70.00
Less: Manufacturing cost per pound:		
Direct materials	$ 5.00	$ 15.00
Direct labor	1.00	5.00
Manufacturing overhead (from Exhibit 19-8)	1.68	110.00
Total manufacturing cost	7.68	130.00
Gross profit (loss) per pound	$ 4.32	$(60.00)

PANEL B—Total Manufacturing Cost and Gross Profit Under the Traditional Cost System (Exhibit 19-5)

	Aldehyde	PH
Sale price per pound	$12.00	$70.00
Less: Manufacturing cost per pound	8.00	50.00
Gross profit per pound	$ 4.00	$20.00

This illustration shows that ABC is often the best way to measure the cost of manufacturing a product. ABC therefore helps businesses set the selling prices of their products. The selling price must cover *all* costs—both manufacturing costs and operating expenses—plus provide a profit.

As you'll see in the next section, Fischer may be able to use ABC to cut costs. If Fischer can't cut costs enough to earn a profit on PH, then Fischer may have to raise the sale price. If customers won't pay more, Fischer may have to drop PH. *This is the exact opposite of the strategy suggested by cost data from the traditional system. That system favored PH.*

Cutting Costs

Most companies adopt ABC to get better product costs for pricing and product-mix decisions. But they often benefit more by cutting costs. ABC and value engineering can work together. **Value engineering** means reevaluating activities to reduce costs. It requires these cross-functional teams:

- Marketers to identify customer needs
- Engineers to design more efficient products
- Accountants to estimate costs

Why are managers turning to value engineering? Because it gets results. Companies like General Motors and Carrier Corporation are following Japanese automakers Toyota and Nissan and setting sale prices based on **target prices**—what customers are willing to pay for the product or service. Exhibit 19-10 provides an example. Study each column separately.

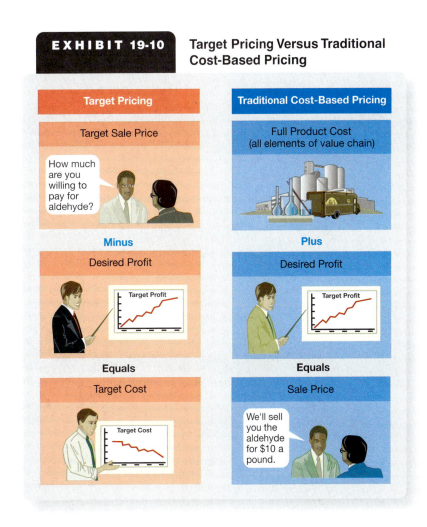

EXHIBIT 19-10 Target Pricing Versus Traditional Cost-Based Pricing

Instead of starting with product cost and then adding a profit to determine the sale price (right column of the exhibit), target pricing (left column) does just the opposite. Target pricing starts with the price that customers are willing to pay and then subtracts the company's desired profit to determine the **target cost**. Then the company works backward to develop the product at the target cost. The target cost is a goal the company must shoot for.

Let's return to our Fischer Chemical illustration. The ABC analysis in Exhibit 19-9, Panel A, prompts CEO Smith to push aldehyde because it appears that PH is losing money. The marketing department says the selling price of aldehyde is likely to fall to $9.50 per pound. Smith wants to earn a profit equal to 20% of the sale price.

What is Fischer's target full-product cost per pound of aldehyde? Here's the computation:

Target sale price per pound of aldehyde	$9.50
– Desired profit ($9.50 × 20%)	(1.90)
= Target cost per pound of aldehyde	$7.60

Does Fischer's current full-product cost meet this target? Let's see.

Current total manufacturing cost per pound of aldehyde (Exhibit 19-9)	$7.68
Nonmanufacturing costs (operating expenses)	0.50
Current full-product cost per pound of aldehyde	$8.18

Fischer's current cost does not meet the target cost.

Because Fischer's current full-product cost ($8.18) exceeds the target cost of $7.60, Smith assembles a value-engineering team to identify ways to cut costs. The team analyzes each production activity. For each activity, the team considers how to

- Cut costs given Fischer's current production process
- Redesign the production process to further cut costs

Of the team's several proposals, Smith decides to

Redesign Mixing to reduce the mixing cost per batch. Group raw materials that are used together to reduce the time required to assemble the materials for mixing. Estimated cost saving is $160,000, and the number of batches remains unchanged at 4,000.

Will this change allow Fischer to reach the target cost? Exhibit 19-11 shows how controller Wise recomputes the cost of Mixing based on the value-engineering study.

EXHIBIT 19-11 Recomputing Activity Costs After a Value-Engineering Study

		Manufacturing Overhead			Total Cost
		Mixing	Processing	Testing	
Estimated total indirect costs of activity:					
Mixing ($600,000 − $160,000)		$440,000			
Estimated total quantity of each allocation base		4,000 batches			
Compute the cost allocation rate for each activity:					
(Divide estimated indirect cost by estimated		$440,000	Amounts	Amounts	
quantity of the allocation base)		÷ 4,000 batches	assumed	assumed	
Cost allocation rate for each activity		=$110.00/batch			
Actual quantity of each allocation base used by aldehyde:					
Mixing	×	60 batches			
Allocate the costs to aldehyde:					
Mixing (60 batches × $110.00)	=	$6,600	+ $1,400	+ $1,100	= $9,100

Exhibit 19-11 shows that value engineering cuts total manufacturing overhead cost of aldehyde to $9,100 from $12,600 (in Exhibit 19-8). Spread over 7,500 pounds of aldehyde, overhead costs $1.21 per pound ($9,100 ÷ 7,500). Now Wise totals the revised cost estimates for aldehyde:

Direct materials (from Exhibit 19-9)................	$5.00
Direct labor (from Exhibit 19-9)......................	1.00
Manufacturing overhead..................................	1.21
Total manufacturing cost of aldehyde..............	$7.21

Cost of $7.21 is quite an improvement from the prior manufacturing cost of $7.68 per pound (Exhibit 19-9, Panel A). Value engineering worked. Now Fischer can meet the $7.60 target cost.

Decision Guidelines

ACTIVITY-BASED COSTING

Several years ago Dell refined its cost system. Starting with an Excel spreadsheet, Dell developed a simple ABC system to focus on its 10 most critical activities. Here are some of the decisions Dell faced as it began refining its cost system.

Decision	Guidelines
How to develop an ABC system?	1. Identify each activity and estimate its total indirect costs. 2. Identify the cost driver for each activity. Then estimate the total quantity of each driver's allocation base. 3. Compute the cost allocation rate for each activity. 4. Allocate indirect costs to the cost object.
How to compute a cost allocation rate for an activity?	$$\frac{\text{Estimated total indirect cost of the activity}}{\text{Estimated total quantity of the allocation base}}$$
How to allocate an activity's cost to the cost object?	$$\begin{array}{c}\text{Cost allocation rate} \\ \text{for the activity}\end{array} \times \begin{array}{c}\text{Actual quantity of the allocation} \\ \text{base used by the cost object}\end{array}$$
For what kinds of decisions do managers use ABC?	Managers use ABC data to decide on • Pricing and product mix • Cost cutting
How to set target costs?	Target sale price (based on market research) − Desired profit = Target cost
How to achieve target costs?	Use value engineering to cut costs by improving product design and production processes.
What are the main benefits of ABC?	• More accurate product cost information. • More detailed information on the costs of activities and their cost drivers helps managers control costs.

Summary Problem 1

Indianapolis Auto Parts (IAP) has a Seat Manufacturing Department that uses activity-based costing. IAP's system has the following features:

Activity	Allocation Base	Cost Allocation Rate
Purchasing	Number of purchase orders	$50.00 per purchase order
Assembling	Number of parts	$0.50 per part
Packaging	Number of finished seats	$1.00 per finished seat

Each auto seat has 20 parts. Direct materials cost per seat is $11. Suppose Ford has asked IAP for a bid on 50,000 built-in baby seats that would be installed as an option on some Ford SUVs. IAP will use a total of 200 purchase orders if Ford accepts IAP's bid.

Requirements

1. Compute the total cost IAP will incur to (a) purchase the needed materials and then (b) assemble and (c) package 50,000 baby seats. Also compute the average cost per seat.

2. For bidding, IAP adds a 30% markup to total cost. What total price will IAP bid for the entire Ford order?

3. Suppose that instead of an ABC system, IAP has a traditional product costing system that allocates all costs other than direct materials at the rate of $65 per direct labor hour. The baby-seat order will require 10,000 direct labor hours. What price will IAP bid using this system's total cost?

4. Use your answers to Requirements 2 and 3 to explain how ABC can help IAP make a better decision about the bid price to offer Ford.

Solution

Requirement 1
Total Cost of Order and Average Cost per Seat:

Direct materials, 50,000 × $11.00	$ 550,000
Activity costs:	
Purchasing, 200 × $50.00	10,000
Assembling, 50,000 × 20 × $0.50	500,000
Packaging, 50,000 × $1.00	50,000
Total cost of order	$1,110,000
Divide by number of seats	÷ 50,000
Average cost per seat	$ 22.20

Requirement 2
Bid Price (ABC System):

Bid price ($1,110,000 × 130%)	$1,443,000

Requirement 3
Bid Price (Traditional System):

	Direct materials, 50,000 × $11.00	$ 550,000
	Other product costs, 10,000 × $65	650,000
	Total cost of order	$1,200,000
	Bid price ($1,200,000 × 130%)	$1,560,000

Requirement 4
IAP's bid would be $117,000 higher using the traditional system than using ABC ($1,560,000 − $1,443,000). Assuming the ABC system more accurately captures the costs caused by the order, the traditional system overcosts the order. This leads to a higher bid price and reduces IAP's chance of winning the bid. The ABC system can increase IAP's chance of getting the order by bidding a lower price.

Just-in-Time (JIT) Systems

Competition is fierce, especially in manufacturing and technology-related services. Chinese and Indian companies are producing high-quality goods at very low costs. As we saw in the discussion of activity-based costing, there's a never-ending quest to cut costs.

The cost of buying, storing, and moving inventory can be significant for Home Depot, Toyota, and Dell. To lower inventory costs, many companies use a just-in-time (JIT) system.

> **3** Describe a just-in-time production system, and record its transactions

Companies with **JIT systems** buy materials and complete finished goods *just in time* for delivery to customers. Production is completed in self-contained work cells as shown in Exhibit 19-12. Each cell includes the machinery and labor resources to manufacture a product. Employees work in a team and are empowered to complete the work without supervision. Workers complete a small batch of units and are responsible for inspecting for quality throughout the process. As the completed product moves out of the work cell, the suppliers deliver more materials just in time to keep production moving along.

By contrast, traditional production systems separate manufacturing into various processing departments that focus on a single activity. Work in process moves from one department to another, and that wastes time.

Under JIT, a customer's order—customer demand—triggers manufacturing. The sales order "pulls" materials, labor, and overhead into production. This "demand–pull" system extends back to the suppliers of materials. Suppliers make frequent deliveries of defect-free materials *just in time* for production. Purchasing only what customers demand reduces inventory. Less inventory frees floor space for more productive use. Thus, JIT systems help to reduce waste. Exhibit 19-12 shows a traditional production system in Panel B. The traditional system requires more inventory, more workers, and usually costs more to operate than a JIT system.

Companies like Toyota, Carrier, and Dell credit JIT for saving them millions. But JIT systems are not without problems. With no inventory buffers, JIT users lose sales when they can't get materials on time, or when poor-quality materials arrive just in time. There's no way to make up for lost time. As a result, many JIT companies still maintain small inventories of critical materials.

Just-in-Time Costing

JIT costing leads many companies to simplify their accounting. **Just-in-time costing**, sometimes called **backflush costing**, seems to work backwards. JIT costing starts with output that has been completed and then assigns manufacturing costs to units sold and to inventories. There are three major differences between JIT costing and traditional standard costing as shown in Exhibit 19-13.

1. JIT systems do not track the cost of products from raw materials inventory to work in process inventory to finished goods inventory. Instead, JIT costing waits until the units are completed to record the cost of production.

2. JIT systems combine raw materials and work in process inventories into a single account called Raw and In-Process Inventory.

3. Under the JIT philosophy, workers perform many tasks. Most companies using JIT combine labor and manufacturing overhead costs into a single account called Conversion Costs. Conversion Costs is a temporary account

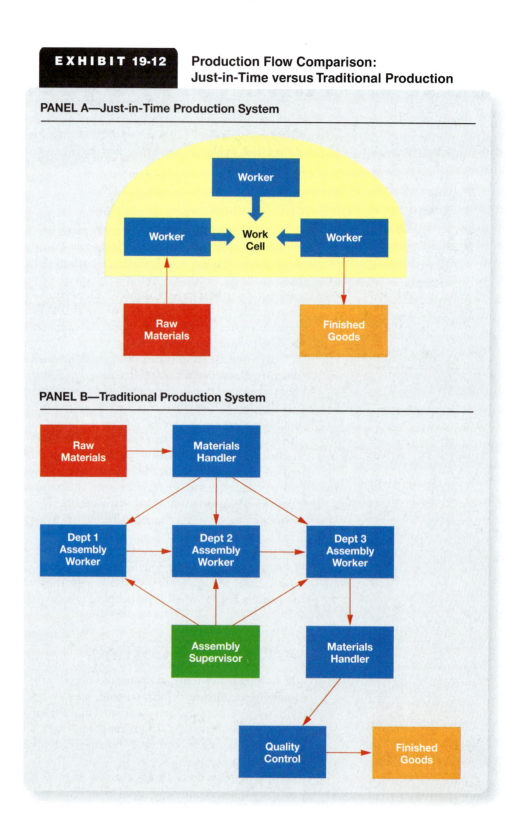

EXHIBIT 19-12 Production Flow Comparison: Just-in-Time versus Traditional Production

that works just like the Manufacturing Overhead account. Actual conversion costs accumulate as debits in the Conversion Cost account. This account is credited when conversion costs are allocated to completed units. Accountants close any under- or overallocated conversion costs to Cost of Goods Sold at the end of the year, just like they do for under- or overallocated manufacturing overhead.

EXHIBIT 19-13 | Comparison of Traditional and Just-in-Time Costing

	Traditional	Just-in-Time
Recording production activity	Build the costs of products as they move from raw materials into work in process and on to finished goods inventory	Record the costs of products when units are completed
Inventory accounts	Materials Inventory Work in Process Inventory Finished Goods Inventory	Raw and In-Process Inventory Finished Goods Inventory
Manufacturing costs	Direct Materials Direct Labor Manufacturing Overhead	Direct Materials Conversion Costs

Now, back to JIT Costing on page 973.

JIT Costing Illustrated: Mintel Company

To illustrate JIT costing, consider Mintel Company, which converts silicon wafers into integrated circuits for computers. Mintel has only one direct material cost: silicon wafers. This cost is recorded in the Raw and In-Process Inventory account. All other manufacturing costs, including labor, various materials, and overhead, are indirect costs of converting the "raw" silicon wafers into finished goods (integrated circuits). All these indirect costs are collected in the "Conversion Costs" account.

JIT does not use a separate Work in Process Inventory account. Instead, it uses only two inventory accounts:

- Raw and In-Process Inventory, which combines direct materials with work in process
- Finished Goods Inventory

At July 31, Mintel had $100,000 of beginning Raw and In-Process Inventory and $900,000 of beginning Finished Goods Inventory. During August, Mintel uses JIT costing to record the following transactions.

1. Mintel purchased $3,020,000 of direct materials (silicon wafers) on account.

1.	Raw and In-Process Inventory	3,020,000	
	Accounts Payable		3,020,000
	Purchased direct materials on account.		

2. Mintel spent $18,540,000 on labor and overhead.

2.	Conversion Costs	18,540,000	
	Wages Payable, Accumulated Depreciation, etc.		18,540,000
	Incurred conversion costs.		

3. Mintel completed 3,000,000 circuits that it moved to finished goods. The standard cost of each circuit is $7 ($1 direct materials + $6 conversion cost). The debit (increase) to Finished Goods Inventory is standard cost of $21,000,000

(3,000,000 completed circuits × $7). There is no work in process inventory in JIT costing, so Mintel credits:
- Raw and In-Process Inventory for the silicon wafers, $3,000,000 (3,000,000 completed circuits × $1 standard raw material cost per circuit)
- Conversion Costs for the labor and other indirect costs allocated to the finished circuits, $18,000,000 (3,000,000 completed circuits × $6 standard conversion cost per circuit)

3.	Finished Goods Inventory (3,000,000 × $7)	21,000,000	
	Raw and In-Process Inventory (3,000,000 × $1)		3,000,000
	Conversion Costs (3,000,000 × $6)		18,000,000
	Completed production.		

This is the essence of JIT costing. The system does not track costs as the circuits move through manufacturing. Instead, *completion* of the circuits triggers the accounting system to go back and pull costs from Raw and In-Process Inventory and to allocate conversion costs to the finished products.

4. Mintel sold 2,900,000 circuits (2,900,000 circuits × cost of $7 per circuit = $20,300,000). The cost of goods sold entry is:

4.	Cost of Goods Sold	20,300,000	
	Finished Goods Inventory		20,300,000
	Cost of sales.		

Exhibit 19-14 shows Mintel's relevant accounts. Combining raw materials with work in process to form the single Raw and In-Process Inventory account eliminates detail.

EXHIBIT 19-14 Mintel's JIT Costing Accounts

Raw and In-Process Inventory
- Direct Materials Purchased →
- Bal. 100,000
- (1) 3,020,000 | (3) 3,000,000
- Bal. 120,000

Actual Conversion Cost →
Conversion Costs
- (2) 18,540,000 | (3) 18,000,000
- (5) 540,000

Finished Goods Inventory
- Bal. 900,000
- (3) 21,000,000 | (4) 20,300,000
- Bal. 1,600,000

Cost of Goods Sold
- (4) 20,300,000
- (5) 540,000
- Bal. 20,840,000

5. You can see from Exhibit 19-14 that conversion costs are underallocated by $540,000 (actual cost of: $18,540,000 − applied cost of $18,000,000). Under- and overallocated conversion costs are treated just like under- and over-

allocated manufacturing overhead and closed to Cost of Goods Sold, as follows for Mintel:

5.	Cost of Goods Sold	540,000	
	Conversion Costs		540,000
	Closed conversion costs account.		

In the final analysis, cost of goods sold for August is $20,840,000, as shown in the T-account on page 976.

Continuous Improvement and the Management of Quality

Use the four types of quality costs to make decisions

Companies using just-in-time production systems strive for high-quality production. Poor-quality materials or defective products shut down production, and that runs counter to the JIT philosophy.

To meet this challenge, many companies adopt *total quality management (TQM)*. The goal of TQM is to provide customers with superior products and services. Each business function monitors its activities to improve quality and eliminate defects and waste. Continuous improvement is the goal. Take a break, or miss a beat, and a Chinese manufacturer will put you out of business.

Well-designed products reduce inspections, rework, and warranty claims. Investing in research and development (R&D) can generate savings in marketing and customer service. World-class companies like Toyota and Dell *design* and *build* quality into their products rather than having to *inspect* and *repair* later. Let's see how they achieve the goal of high quality.

The Four Types of Quality Costs

The four types of quality-related costs include:

1. **Prevention costs** *avoid* poor-quality goods or services.
2. **Appraisal costs** *detect* poor-quality goods or services.
3. **Internal failure costs** avoid poor-quality goods or services *before* delivery to customers.
4. **External failure costs** occur when the company *delivers poor-quality goods or services* to customers and then has to make things right with the customer.

Exhibit 19-15 gives examples of the four types of quality costs. Most prevention costs occur in the R&D stage of the value chain. In contrast, most appraisal and internal failure costs occur in production. External failure occurs in customer service or, worse, they result from lost sales due to an unhappy customer. Prevention is much cheaper than external failure. One expert estimates that 8¢ spent on prevention saves $1 in failure costs.

EXHIBIT 19-15 | Four Types of Quality Costs

Prevention Costs	Appraisal Costs
Training personnel	Inspection at various stages of production
Improved materials	Inspection of final products or services
Preventive maintenance	Product testing

Internal Failure Costs	External Failure Costs
Production loss caused by downtime	Lost profits due to unhappy customers
Rework	Warranty costs
Rejected product units	Service costs at customer sites
	Sales returns due to product defects

Deciding Whether to Adopt a New Quality Program

Let's revisit Fischer Chemical Company. CEO Randy Smith is considering spending the following on a new quality program to:

Inspect raw materials	$100,000
Reengineer to improve product quality	750,000
Inspect finished goods	150,000
Preventive maintenance of equipment	100,000

Fischer expects this quality program to reduce costs by the following amounts:

Avoid lost profits due to unhappy customers	$800,000
Fewer sales returns	50,000
Decrease the cost of rework	250,000
Lower warranty costs	100,000

Smith asks controller Wise to

1. Classify each cost into one of the four categories (prevention, appraisal, internal failure, external failure). Total the estimated cost for each category.

2. Recommend whether Fischer should undertake the quality program. Wise uses Exhibit 19-16 to compare the costs to:
    - Undertake the quality program, or
    - Do not undertake the quality program.

> **EXHIBIT 19-16** Analysis of Fischer's Proposed Quality Program

Undertake the Quality Program		Do Not Undertake the Quality Program	
Prevention		**Internal Failure**	
Reengineer to improve product quality	$ 750,000	Cost of rework	$ 250,000
Preventive maintenance of equipment	100,000	Total internal failure costs	$ 250,000
Total prevention costs	$ 850,000		
		External Failure	
		Lost profits due to unhappy customers	$ 800,000
Appraisal		Sales returns	50,000
Inspect raw materials	$ 100,000	Warranty costs	100,000
Inspect finished goods	150,000	Total external failure costs	$ 950,000
Total appraisal costs	$ 250,000	Total costs of not undertaking the	
Total costs of the quality program	$1,100,000	quality program	$1,200,000

Decision: Undertake the Quality Program and Save $100,000.

These estimates suggest that Fischer would save $100,000 ($1,200,000 − $1,100,000) by undertaking the quality program.

Quality costs can be hard to measure. For example, it's very hard to measure external failure costs. Lost profits due to unhappy customers do not appear in the accounting records! Therefore, total quality management uses lots of nonfinancial measures such as the number of customer complaints and the volume of incoming customer-service phone calls.

Decision Guidelines

JUST-IN-TIME AND QUALITY COSTS

Dell Computer is famous for using just-in-time production and total quality management. Dell's managers made the following decisions.

Decision

How to change from traditional production to JIT?

Guidelines

Traditional	JIT
Similar machines grouped together	Production cells
Larger batches	Smaller batches
Higher inventories	Lower inventories
Each worker does a few tasks	Each worker does a wide range of tasks
Many suppliers	Fewer, but well-coordinated suppliers

How does costing work under JIT?

Under JIT costing,

1. Raw materials and work in process are combined into a single Raw and In-Process Inventory account.
2. Labor and overhead are combined into a Conversion Cost account.
3. Summary journal entries are recorded *after* units are completed.

What are the four types of quality costs?

Prevention
Appraisal
Internal failure
External failure

How to manage the four types of quality costs?

Invest up front in prevention and appraisal to reduce internal and external failure costs.

Summary Problem 2

Flores Company manufactures cell phones and uses JIT costing. The standard unit cost is $30: $20 direct materials and $10 conversion costs. Direct materials purchased on account during June totaled $2,500,000. Actual conversion costs totaled $1,100,000. Flores completed 100,000 cell phones in June and sold 98,000.

Requirements

1. Journalize these transactions.
2. Were conversion costs under- or overallocated? Explain your answer and then make the entry to close the Conversion Costs account.
3. How much cost of goods sold did Flores have in June?

Solutions

Requirement 1

Raw and In-Process Inventory		2,500,000	
Accounts Payable			2,500,000
Conversion Costs		1,100,000	
Wages Payable, Accumulated Depreciation, etc.			1,000,000
Finished Goods Inventory		3,000,000	
Raw and In-Process Inventory (100,000 × $20)			2,000,000
Conversion Costs (100,000 × $10)			1,000,000
Cost of Goods Sold (98,000 × $30)		2,940,000	
Finished Goods Inventory			2,940,000

Requirement 2

Conversion costs were underallocated. Actual costs ($1,100,000) exceeded the cost allocated to inventory ($1,000,000).			
Cost of Goods Sold		100,000	
Conversion Costs			100,000

Requirement 3
COGS = $3,040,000 ($2,940,000 + $100,000)

Review

Activity-Based Costing and Other Cost Management Tools

Accounting Vocabulary

Activity-Based Costing (ABC)
Focuses on activities as the fundamental cost objects. The costs of those activities become building blocks for compiling the indirect costs of products, services, and customers.

Activity-Based Management (ABM)
Using activity-based cost information to make decisions that increase profits while satisfying customers needs.

Appraisal Costs
Costs incurred to detect poor-quality goods or services.

Backflush Costing
A standard costing system that starts with output completed and then assigns manufacturing costs to units sold and to inventories. Also called **just-in-time costing**.

External Failure Costs
Costs incurred when the company does not detect poor-quality goods or services until after delivery to customers.

Internal Failure Costs
Costs incurred when the company detects and corrects poor-quality goods or services before delivery to customers.

Just-in-Time (JIT) Costing
A standard costing system that starts with output completed and then assigns manufacturing costs to units sold and to inventories. Also called **backflush costing**.

Prevention Costs
Costs incurred to avoid poor-quality goods or services.

Target Cost
Allowable cost to develop, produce, and deliver the product or service. Equals target price minus desired profit.

Target Price
What customers are willing to pay for the product or service.

Value Engineering
Reevaluating activities to reduce costs while satisfying customer needs.

Quick Check

1. Which statement is *false*?
   a. ABC focuses on indirect costs.
   b. Information technology makes it feasible for most companies to adopt ABC.
   c. An ABC system is more refined than one that uses a companywide overhead rate.
   d. ABC is primarily for manufacturing companies.

Use the following for questions 2 through 4. Two of Dell's production activities are *kitting* (assembling the raw materials needed for each computer in one kit) and *boxing* the completed products for shipment to customers. Assume that Dell spends $5 million a month on kitting and $10 million a month on boxing. Dell allocates

- Kitting costs based on the number of parts used in the computer
- Boxing costs based on the cubic feet of space the computer requires

Suppose Dell estimates it will use 500 million parts a month and ship products with a total volume of 20 million cubic feet.

Assume that each desktop computer requires 100 parts and has a volume of 5 cubic feet.

2. What is the activity cost allocation rate for:

	Kitting	Boxing
a.	$0.0125/part	$0.25/cubic foot
b.	$0.01/part	$0.50/cubic foot
c.	$0.25/part	$0.20/cubic foot
d.	$160/part	$2/cubic foot

3. What are the kitting and boxing costs assigned to one desktop computer?

	Kitting	Boxing
a.	$0.9375	$3.50
b.	$0.625	$2.00
c.	$1.25	$1.25
d.	$1.00	$2.50

4. Dell contracts with its suppliers to pre-kit certain component parts before delivering them to Dell. Assume this saves $1.5 million of the kitting cost and reduces the total number of parts by 400 million (because Dell considers each pre-kit as one part). If a desktop now uses 80 parts, what is the new kitting cost assigned to one desktop?
   a. $2.80
   b. $0.70
   c. $0.9375
   d. $1.00

5. Dell can use ABC information for what decisions?
   a. Pricing
   b. Cost cutting
   c. Product mix
   d. All of the above

6. Which of the following is true for Dell, the computer company?
   a. Most of Dell's costs are for direct materials and direct labor. Indirect costs are a small proportion of total costs.
   b. Dell uses only a few activities, so a companywide overhead allocation rate would serve Dell quite well.
   c. ABC helps Dell keep costs low and remain competitive.
   d. All the above are true.

7. Dell enjoys many benefits from using JIT. Which is *not* a benefit of adopting JIT?
   a. Ability to continue production despite disruptions in deliveries of raw materials
   b. More space available for production
   c. Ability to respond quickly to changes in customer demand
   d. Lower inventory carrying costs

8. Which account is *not* used in JIT costing?
   a. Work in process inventory
   b. Conversion costs
   c. Raw and in-process inventory
   d. Finished goods inventory

9. The cost of lost future sales after a customer finds a defect in a product is which type of quality cost?
   a. Internal failure cost
   b. External failure cost
   c. Appraisal cost
   d. Prevention cost

10. Dell's spending on testing its computers before shipment to customers is which type of quality cost?
    a. Prevention cost
    b. Appraisal cost
    c. External failure cost
    d. None of the above

    Answers are given after Apply Your Knowledge (p. 1005).

Assess Your Progress

Short Exercises

Activity-based costing

S19-1 Activity-based costing requires four steps. Rank the following steps in the order they would be completed. Number the first step as "1" until you have ranked all four steps. (p. 962)

_____ a. Compute the cost allocation rate for each activity
_____ b. Identify the cost driver for each activity and estimate the total quantity of each driver's allocation base
_____ c. Allocate indirect costs to the cost object
_____ d. Identify each activity and estimate its total indirect cost

Calculating costs using ABC

S19-2 Bubba and Roscoe are college friends planning a skiing trip to Aspen before the new year. They estimated the following costs for the trip:

	Estimated Costs	Cost Driver	Activity Allocation	
			Bubba	Roscoe
Food	$ 500	Pounds of food eaten	20	30
Skiing	300	# of lift tickets	3	0
Lodging	300	# of nights	2	2
	$1,100			

1. Bubba suggests that the costs be shared equally. Calculate the amount each person would pay. (p. 960)
2. Roscoe doesn't like the idea because he plans to stay in the room rather than ski. Roscoe suggests that each type of cost be allocated to each person based on the cost driver listed above. Using the activity allocation for each person, calculate the amount that each person would pay based on his own consumption of the activity. (p. 960)

Computing indirect manufacturing costs per unit

S19-3 Daily Corp. is considering the use of activity-based costing. The following information is provided for the production of two product lines:

Activity	Cost	Cost Driver
Setup	$100,000	Number of setups
Machine maintenance	50,000	Machine hours
Total indirect manufacturing costs	$150,000	

	Product A	Product B	Total
Direct labor hours	6,000	4,000	10,000
Number of setups	30	70	100
Number of machine hours	1,250	3,750	5,000

Daily plans to produce 200 units of Product A and 200 units of Product B.

Compute the ABC indirect manufacturing cost per unit for each product. (pp. 965–966)

Computing indirect manufacturing costs per unit

S19-4 The following information is provided for the Astro Antenna Corp., which manufactures two products: low-gain antennas, and high-gain antennas for use in remote areas.

Activity	Cost	Cost Driver
Setup	$50,000	Number of setups
Machine maintenance	30,000	Machine hours
Total indirect costs	$80,000	

	Lo-Gain	Hi-Gain	Total
Direct labor hours	1,500	2,500	4,000
Number of setups	20	20	40
Number of machine hours	1,800	1,200	3,000

Astro plans to produce 100 Lo-Gain antennas and 200 Hi-Gain antennas.
1. Compute the ABC indirect manufacturing cost per unit for each product. (pp. 965–966)
2. Compute the indirect manufacturing cost per unit using direct labor hours from the single-allocation-base system. (p. 963)

Using ABC to compute product costs per unit

S19-5 Weekly Corp. makes two products: C and D. The following data have been summarized:

	Product C	Product D
Direct materials cost per unit	$700	$1,800
Direct labor cost per unit	300	200
Indirect manufacturing cost per unit	?	?

Indirect manufacturing cost information includes:

		Allocation Base Units	
Activity	Allocation Rate	Product C	Product D
Setup	$1,200	30	70
Machine maintenance	$ 10	1,250	3,750

The company plans to manufacture 200 units of each product.
   Calculate the product cost per unit for Products C and D using activity-based costing. (pp. 965–966)

Using ABC to make decisions

S19-6 Johnstone Corp. manufactures mid-fi and hi-fi stereo receivers. The following data have been summarized:

	Mid-Fi	Hi-Fi
Direct materials cost per unit	$800	$1,000
Direct labor cost per unit	200	300
Indirect manufacturing cost per unit	?	?

continued . . .

Indirect manufacturing cost information includes:

Activity	Allocation Rate	Allocation Base Units	
		Mid-Fi	Hi-Fi
Setup	$1,200	20	20
Inspections	$ 600	40	10
Machine maintenance	$ 10	1,800	1,200

The company plans to manufacture 100 units of the mid-fi receivers and 200 units of the hi-fi receivers.

Calculate the product cost per unit for both products using activity-based costing. (pp. 965–966)

Allocating indirect costs and computing income

S19-7 Alamo, Inc., is a technology consulting firm focused on Web site development and integration of Internet business applications. The president of the company expects to incur $706,000 of indirect costs this year, and she expects her firm to work 5,000 direct labor hours. Alamo's systems consultants earn $350 per hour. Clients are billed at 150% of direct labor cost. Last month Alamo's consultants spent 100 hours on Crockett's engagement.

1. Compute Alamo's indirect cost allocation rate per direct labor hour. (p. 965)
2. Compute the total cost assigned to the Crockett engagement. (p. 965)
3. Compute the operating income from the Crockett engagement. (p. 965)

Computing ABC allocation rates

S19-8 Refer to Short Exercise S19-7. The president of Alamo, Inc. suspects that her allocation of indirect costs could be giving misleading results, so she decides to develop an ABC system. She identifies three activities: documentation preparation, information technology support, and training. The president figures that documentation costs are driven by the number of pages, information technology support costs are driven by the number of software applications used, and training costs are most closely associated with the number of direct labor hours worked. Estimates of the costs and quantities of the allocation bases follow:

Activity	Estimated Cost	Allocation Base	Estimated Quantity of Allocation Base
Documentation preparation	$100,000	Pages	3,125 pages
Information technology support	156,000	Applications used	780 applications
Training	450,000	Direct labor hours	5,000 hours
Total indirect costs	$706,000		

Compute the cost allocation rate for each activity. (p. 965)

Using ABC to allocate costs and compute profit

S19-9 Refer to Short Exercises S19-7 and S19-8. Suppose Alamo's direct labor rate was $350 per hour, the documentation cost was $32 per page, the information technology support cost was $100 per application, and training costs were $90 per direct labor hour. The Crockett engagement used the following resources last month:

Cost Driver	Crockett
Direct labor hours	100
Pages	300
Applications used	78

1. Compute the cost assigned to the Crockett engagement, using the ABC system. (pp. 965–966)
2. Compute the operating income from the Crockett engagement, using the ABC system. (p. 966)

Just-in-time characteristics

S19-10 Indicate whether each of the following is characteristic of a JIT production system or a traditional production system. (pp. 973–977)

a. Products produced in large batches.
b. Large stocks of finished goods protect against lost sales if customer demand is higher than expected.
c. Suppliers make frequent deliveries of small quantities of raw materials.
d. Long setup times.
e. Employees do a variety of jobs, including maintenance and setups as well as operating machines.
f. Machines are grouped into self-contained production cells or production lines.
g. Machines are grouped according to function. For example, all cutting machines are located in one area.
h. Suppliers can access the company's intranet.
i. The final operation in the production sequence "pulls" parts from the preceding operation.
j. Each employee is responsible for inspecting his or her own work.
k. Management works with suppliers to ensure defect-free raw materials.

Recording JIT costing journal entries

S19-11 Xeno Products uses a JIT system to manufacture trading pins for the 2008 Olympic Games in China. The standard cost per pin is $2 for raw materials and $3 for conversion costs. Last month Xeno recorded the following data:

Number of pins completed	4,000 pins	Raw material purchases	$ 9,000
Number of pins sold	3,500 pins	Conversion costs	$13,000

Use JIT costing to prepare journal entries for the month, including the entry to close the Conversion Costs account. (pp. 975–976)

Matching cost-of-quality examples to categories

S19-12 Harry, Inc., manufactures motor scooters. For each of the following examples of quality costs, indicate the quality cost category it represents. (p. 977)

P Prevention costs   IF Internal failure costs
A Appraisal costs   EF External failure costs

_____ 1. Preventive maintenance on machinery

_____ 2. Direct materials, direct labor, and manufacturing overhead costs incurred to rework a defective scooter that is detected in-house through inspection

_____ 3. Lost profits from lost sales if company's reputation was hurt because customers previously purchased a poor-quality scooter

_____ 4. Costs of inspecting raw materials, such as chassis and wheels

_____ 5. Working with suppliers to achieve on-time delivery of defect-free raw materials.

_____ 6. Cost of warranty repairs on a scooter that malfunctions at customer's location

_____ 7. Costs of testing durability of vinyl

_____ 8. Cost to re-inspect reworked scooters

Exercises

Product costing in an activity-based costing system

E19-13 Frederick, Inc., uses activity-based costing to account for its chrome bumper manufacturing process. Company managers have identified four manufacturing activities: materials handling, machine setup, insertion of parts, and finishing. The budgeted activity costs for 2009 and their allocation bases are as follows:

Activity	Total Budgeted Cost	Allocation Base
Materials handling	$ 9,000	Number of parts
Machine setup	3,400	Number of setups
Insertion of parts	48,000	Number of parts
Finishing	80,000	Finishing direct labor hours
Total	$140,400	

Frederick, Inc., expects to produce 1,000 chrome bumpers during the year. The bumpers are expected to use 3,000 parts, require 10 setups, and consume 2,000 hours of finishing time.

Requirements
1. Compute the cost allocation rate for each activity. (p. 965)
2. Compute the indirect manufacturing cost of each bumper. (p. 965)

Product costing in an activity-based costing system

E19-14 Turbo Champs Corp. uses activity-based costing to account for its 4-wheeler manufacturing process. Company managers have identified three supporting manufacturing activities: inspection, machine setup, and machine

continued . . .

maintenance. The budgeted activity costs for 2008 and their allocation bases are as follows:

Activity	Total Budgeted Cost	Allocation Base
Inspection	$ 6,000	Number of inspections
Machine setup	24,000	Number of setups
Machine maintenance	2,000	Maintenance hours
Total	$32,000	

Turbo Champs expects to produce 10 custom-built 4-wheelers for the year. The 4-wheelers are expected to require 30 inspections, 20 setups, and 100 maintenance hours.

Requirements
1. Compute the cost allocation rate for each activity. (p. 965)
2. Compute the indirect manufacturing cost of each 4-wheeler. (p. 965)

Product costing in an activity-based costing system

E19-15 Eason Company manufactures wheel rims. The controller budgeted the following ABC allocation rates for 2009:

Activity	Allocation Base	Cost Allocation Rate
Materials handling	Number of parts	$ 3.00 per part
Machine setup	Number of setups	300.00 per setup
Insertion of parts	Number of parts	24.00 per part
Finishing	Finishing direct labor hours	50.00 per hour

The number of parts is now a feasible allocation base because Eason recently purchased bar coding technology. Eason produces two wheel rim models: standard and deluxe. Budgeted data for 2009 are as follows:

	Standard	Deluxe
Parts per rim	4.0	6.0
Setups per 1,000 rims	15.0	15.0
Finishing direct labor hours per rim	1.0	2.5
Total direct labor hours per rim	2.0	3.0

The company's managers expect to produce 1,000 units of each model during the year.

Requirements
1. Compute the total budgeted indirect manufacturing cost for 2009. (p. 965)
2. Compute the ABC indirect manufacturing cost per unit of each model. Carry each cost to the nearest cent. (p. 965)
3. Prior to 2009, Eason used a direct labor hour single-allocation-base system. Compute the (single) allocation rate based on direct labor hours for 2009. Use this rate to determine the indirect manufacturing cost per wheel rim for each model, to the nearest cent. (p. 965)

Using activity-based costing to make decisions

E19-16 Refer to Exercise E19-15. For 2010, Eason's managers have decided to use the same indirect manufacturing costs per wheel rim that they computed in 2009. In addition to the unit indirect manufacturing costs, the following data are budgeted for the company's standard and deluxe models for 2010:

	Standard	Deluxe
Sale price	$300.00	$440.00
Direct materials	30.00	46.00
Direct labor	45.00	50.00

Because of limited machine-hour capacity, Eason can produce *either* 2,000 standard rims *or* 2,000 deluxe rims.

Requirements
1. If Eason's managers rely on the ABC unit cost data computed in E19-15, which model will they produce? Carry each cost to the nearest cent. (All nonmanufacturing costs are the same for both models.) (p. 966)
2. If the managers rely on the single-allocation-base cost data, which model will they produce? (p. 966)
3. Which course of action will yield more income for Eason?

Activity-based management and target cost

E19-17 Refer to Exercises E19-15 and E19-16. Controller Matthew Barnhill is surprised by the increase in cost of the deluxe model under ABC. Market research shows that for the deluxe rim to provide a reasonable profit, Eason will have to meet a target manufacturing cost of $350 per rim. A value engineering study by Eason's employees suggests that modifications to the finishing process could cut finishing cost from $50 to $40 per hour and reduce the finishing direct labor hours per deluxe rim from 2.5 hours to 2 hours. Direct materials would remain unchanged at $46 per rim, as would direct labor at $50 per rim. The materials handling, machine setup, and insertion of parts activity costs also would remain the same. Would implementing the value engineering recommendation enable Eason to achieve its target cost for the deluxe rim? (pp. 967–968)

Using activity-based costing to make decisions

E19-18 Daisy Dog Collars uses activity-based costing. Daisy's system has the following features:

Activity	Allocation Base	Cost Allocation Rate
Purchasing	Number of purchase orders	$60.00 per purchase order
Assembling	Number of parts	0.40 per part
Packaging	Number of finished collars	0.20 per collar

Each collar has 3 parts; direct materials cost per collar is $8. Suppose PetSmart has asked for a bid on 30,000 dog collars. Daisy will issue a total of 100 purchase orders if PetSmart accepts Daisy's bid.

continued . . .

Requirements

1. Compute the total cost Daisy will incur to purchase the needed materials and then assemble and package 30,000 dog collars. Also compute the cost per collar. (p. 965)
2. For bidding, Daisy adds a 30% markup to total cost. What total price will the company bid for the entire PetSmart order? (p. 966)
3. Suppose that instead of an ABC system, Daisy has a traditional product costing system that allocates all costs other than direct materials at the rate of $9.50 per direct labor hour. The dog collar order will require 10,000 direct labor hours. What total price will Daisy bid using this system's total cost? (p. 966)
4. Use your answers to Requirements 2 and 3 to explain how ABC can help Daisy make a better decision about the bid price it will offer PetSmart. (p. 966)

Recording manufacturing costs in a JIT costing system

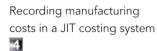

E19-19 Luxor, Inc., produces universal remote controls. Luxor uses a JIT costing system. One of the company's products has a standard direct materials cost of $8 per unit and a standard conversion cost of $32 per unit.

During January 2007, Luxor produced 500 units and sold 480. It purchased $4,400 of direct materials and incurred actual conversion costs totaling $15,280.

Requirements

1. Prepare summary journal entries for January. (pp. 975–976)
2. The January 1, 2007, balance of the Raw and In-Process Inventory account was $80. Use a T-account to find the January 31 balance. (p. 976)
3. Use a T-account to determine whether conversion cost is over- or underallocated for the month. By how much? Give the journal entry to close the Conversion Costs account. (p. 976)

Recording manufacturing costs in a JIT costing system

E19-20 Cameron produces electronic calculators. Suppose Cameron's standard cost per calculator is $24 for materials and $64 for conversion costs. The following data apply to July production:

Materials purchased	$ 6,500
Conversion costs incurred	$14,840
Number of cameras completed	200 cameras
Number of cameras sold	196 cameras

Cameron uses JIT costing.

Requirements

1. Prepare summary journal entries for July, including the entry to close the Conversion Costs account. (pp. 975–976)
2. The beginning balance of Finished Goods Inventory was $1,000. Use a T-account to find the ending balance of Finished Goods Inventory. (p. 976)

Classifying quality costs

E19-21 Millan & Co. makes electronic components. Mike Millan, the president, recently instructed vice president Steve Bensen to develop a total quality control program. "If we don't at least match the quality improvements our competitors are making," he told Bensen, "we'll soon be out of business." Bensen began by listing various "costs of quality" that Millan incurs. The first six items that came to mind were:

a. Costs incurred by Millan customer representatives traveling to customer sites to repair defective products

b. Lost profits from lost sales due to reputation for less-than-perfect products

c. Costs of inspecting components in one of Millan's production processes

d. Salaries of engineers who are designing components to withstand electrical overloads

e. Costs of reworking defective components after discovery by company inspectors

f. Costs of electronic components returned by customers

Requirements

Classify each item as a prevention cost, an appraisal cost, an internal failure cost, or an external failure cost. (p. 977)

Classifying quality costs and using these costs to make decisions

E19-22 Clason, Inc., manufactures door panels. Suppose Clason is considering spending the following amounts on a new total quality management (TQM) program:

Strength-testing one item from each batch of panels	$70,000
Training employees in TQM	30,000
Training suppliers in TQM	40,000
Identifying preferred suppliers who commit to on-time delivery of perfect-quality materials	60,000

Clason expects the new program would save costs through the following:

Avoid lost profits from lost sales due to disappointed customers	$90,000
Avoid rework and spoilage	60,000
Avoid inspection of raw materials	50,000
Avoid warranty costs	15,000

Requirements

1. Classify each item as a prevention cost, an appraisal cost, an internal failure cost, or an external failure cost. (p. 977)
2. Should Clason implement the new quality program? Give your reason. (p. 978)

Classifying quality costs and using these costs to make decisions

E19-23 Keaton manufactures high-quality speakers. Suppose Keaton is considering spending the following amounts on a new quality program:

Additional 20 minutes of testing for each speaker	$ 600,000
Negotiating with and training suppliers to obtain higher-quality materials and on-time delivery	400,000
Redesigning the speakers to make them easier to manufacture	1,400,000

Keaton expects this quality program to save costs, as follows:

Reduce warranty repair costs	$200,000
Avoid inspection of raw materials	500,000
Avoid rework because of fewer defective units	750,000

It also expects this program to avoid lost profits from:

Lost sales due to disappointed customers	$850,000
Lost production time due to rework	300,000

Requirements

1. Classify each of these costs into one of the four categories of quality costs (prevention, appraisal, internal failure, external failure). (p. 977)
2. Should Keaton implement the quality program? Give your reasons. (p. 978)

Problems (Group A)

Product costing in an ABC system

P19-24A The Niehbur Manufacturing Company in Hondo, Texas, assembles and tests electronic components used in handheld video phones. Consider the following data regarding component T24:

Direct materials cost	$81.00
Activity costs allocated	?
Manufacturing product cost	?

The activities required to build the component follow.

Activity	Allocation Base	Cost Allocated to Each Unit
Start station	Number of raw component chassis	2 × $ 1.30 = $ 2.60
Dip insertion	Number of dip insertions	? × $ 0.40 = 12.00
Manual insertion	Number of manual insertions	12 × $ 0.80 = ?
Wave solder	Number of components soldered	1 × $ 1.60 = 1.60
Backload	Number of backload insertions	7 × $? = 4.20
Test	Testing hours	0.40 × $80.00 = ?
Defect analysis	Defect analysis hours	0.10 × $? = 5.00
Total		$?

continued . . .

Requirements

1. Fill in the blanks in both the opening schedule and the list of activities. (p. 965)
2. How is labor cost assigned to products under this ABC product costing system?
3. Why might managers favor this ABC system instead of Niehbur's older system, which allocated all conversion costs on the basis of direct labor? (pp. 965–966)

Product costing in an ABC system

P19-25A Lawton, Inc., manufactures bookcases and uses an activity-based costing system. Lawton's activity areas and related data follow.

Activity	Budgeted Cost of Activity	Allocation Base	Cost Allocation Rate
Materials handling	$ 200,000	Number of parts	$ 0.80
Assembling	3,000,000	Direct labor hours	15.00
Finishing	160,000	Number of finished units	3.90

Lawton produced two styles of bookcases in April: the standard bookcase and an unfinished bookcase, which has fewer parts and requires no finishing. The totals for quantities, direct materials costs, and other data follow.

Product	Total Units Produced	Total Direct Materials Costs	Total Number of Parts	Total Assembling Direct Labor Hours
Standard bookcase	3,000	$29,300	80,000	3,000
Unfinished bookcase	3,600	28,800	84,000	2,000

Requirements

1. Compute the manufacturing product cost per unit of each type of bookcase. (pp. 965–966)
2. Suppose that premanufacturing activities, such as product design, were assigned to the standard bookcases at $4 each and to the unfinished bookcases at $3 each. Similar analyses were conducted of postmanufacturing activities such as distribution, marketing, and customer service. The postmanufacturing costs were $20 per standard bookcase and $15 per unfinished bookcase. Compute the full product costs per unit. (p. 969)
3. Which product costs are reported in the external financial statements? Which costs are used for management decision making? Explain the difference.
4. What price should Lawton's managers set for unfinished bookcases to earn a unit profit of $16? (p. 966)

Comparing costs from ABC and single-rate systems

P19-26A Hampton Pharmaceuticals manufactures an over-the-counter allergy medication. The company sells both large commercial containers of 1,000 capsules to health-care facilities and travel packs of 20 capsules to shops in airports, train stations, and hotels. The following information has been developed to determine if an activity-based costing system would be beneficial:

Activity	Estimated Indirect Activity Costs	Allocation Base	Estimated Quantity of Allocation Base
Materials handling	$ 95,000	Kilos	19,000 kilos
Packaging	200,000	Machine hours	2,000 hours
Quality assurance	112,500	Samples	1,875 samples
Total indirect costs	$407,500		

Other production information includes:

	Commercial Containers	Travel Packs
Units produced	2,000 containers	40,000 packs
Weight in kilos	8,000	6,000
Machine hours	1,200	400
Number of samples	200	300

Requirements
1. Compute the cost allocation rate for each activity. (p. 965)
2. Use the activity-based cost allocation rates to compute the activity costs per unit of the commercial containers and the travel packs. (*Hint*: First compute the total activity costs allocated to each product line, and then compute the cost per unit.) (pp. 965–966)
3. Hampton's original single-allocation-base costing system allocated indirect costs to products at $150 per machine hour. Compute the total indirect costs allocated to the commercial containers and to the travel packs under the original system. Then compute the indirect cost per unit for each product. (p. 963)
4. Compare the activity-based costs per unit to the costs from the single-allocation-base system. How have the unit costs changed? Explain why the costs changed as they did. (pp. 965–966)

Recording manufacturing costs for a JIT costing system

P19-27A High Range produces fleece jackets. The company uses JIT costing for its JIT production system.

High Range has two inventory accounts: Raw and In-Process Inventory and Finished Goods Inventory. On February 1, 2009, the account balances were Raw and In-Process Inventory, $6,000; Finished Goods Inventory, $1,000.

continued ...

The standard cost of a jacket is $40—$15 direct materials plus $25 conversion costs. Data for February's activity follow.

Number of jackets completed	18,000	Direct materials purchased	$265,000
Number of jackets sold	17,600	Conversion costs incurred	551,000

Requirements

1. What are the major features of a JIT production system such as that of High Range? (pp. 973–977)
2. Prepare summary journal entries for February. Under- or over-allocated conversion costs are closed to Cost of Goods Sold monthly. (pp. 975–976)
3. Use a T-account to determine the February 28, 2009, balance of Raw and In-Process Inventory. (p. 976)

Analyzing costs of quality

P19-28A Roxi, Inc., is using a costs-of-quality approach to evaluate design engineering efforts for a new wakeboard. Roxi's senior managers expect the engineering work to reduce appraisal, internal failure, and external failure activities. The predicted reductions in activities over the 2-year life of the wakeboards follow. Also shown are the cost allocation rates for each activity.

Activity	Predicted Reduction in Activity Units	Activity Cost Allocation Rate per Unit
Inspection of incoming materials........	400	$ 40
Inspection of work in process.............	400	20
Number of defective units discovered in-house	1,100	50
Number of defective units discovered by customers	300	70
Lost sales to dissatisfied customers.....	100	100

Requirements

1. Calculate the predicted quality cost savings from the design engineering work. (p. 978)
2. Roxi spent $106,000 on design engineering for the new wakeboard. What is the net benefit of this "preventive" quality activity? (p. 978)
3. What major difficulty would Roxi's managers have in implementing this costs-of-quality approach? What alternative approach could they use to measure quality improvement? (pp. 978–979)

Problems (Group B)

Product costing in an ABC system

P19-29B Abram Technology's Assembly Department, which assembles and tests digital processors, reports the following data regarding processor G27:

Direct materials cost		$56.00
Activity costs allocated		?
Manufacturing product cost		$?

The activities required to build the processors are as follows:

Activity	Allocation Base	Cost Allocated to Each Board
Start station	Number of processor boards	1 × $ 0.90 = $0.90
Dip insertion	Number of dip insertions	20 × $ 0.25 = ?
Manual insertion	Number of manual insertions	5 × $? = 2.00
Wave solder	Number of processor boards soldered	1 × $ 6.80 = 6.80
Backload	Number of backload insertions	? × $ 0.70 = 2.80
Test	Testing hours	0.15 × $90.00 = ?
Defect analysis	Defect analysis hours	0.16 × $? = 8.00
Total		$?

Requirements

1. Fill in the blanks in both the opening schedule and the list of activities. (p. 965)
2. How is labor cost assigned to products under this ABC product costing system?
3. Why might managers favor this ABC system instead of Abram's older system that allocated all conversion costs on the basis of direct labor? (pp. 965–966)

Product costing in an ABC system

P19-30B Woodway Furniture manufactures computer desks. The company uses activity-based costing. Its activities and related data follow.

Activity	Budgeted Cost of Activity	Allocation Base	Cost Allocation Rate
Materials handling	$ 300,000	Number of parts	$ 0.60
Assembling	2,500,000	Direct labor hours	15.00
Painting	170,000	Number of painted desks	5.00

continued . . .

998   Chapter 19

Woodway produced two styles of desks in April: the standard desk and an unpainted desk. Data for each follow:

Product	Total Units Produced	Total Direct Materials Costs	Total Number of Parts	Total Assembling Direct Labor Hours
Standard desk	6,000	$102,000	120,000	6,000
Unpainted desk	1,500	22,500	30,000	900

Requirements

1. Compute the per-unit manufacturing product cost of standard desks and unpainted desks. (pp. 965–966)
2. Premanufacturing activities, such as product design, were assigned to the standard desks at $5 each and to the unpainted desks at $3 each. Similar analyses were conducted of postmanufacturing activities such as distribution, marketing, and customer service. The post-manufacturing costs were $25 per standard desk and $22 per unpainted desk. Compute the full product costs per desk. (p. 969)
3. Which product costs are reported in the external financial statements? Which costs are used for management decision making? Explain the difference.
4. What price should Woodway's managers set for standard desks to earn a $42.00 profit per desk? (p. 966)

Comparing costs from ABC and single-rate systems

P19-31B Wallace, Inc., develops software for Internet applications. The market is very competitive. Wallace offers a wide variety of different software—from simple programs that enable new users to create personal Web pages (called Personal-Page), to complex commercial search engines (called Hi-Secure). The company's managers know they need accurate product-cost data. They have developed the following information to determine if an activity-based costing system would be beneficial.

Activity	Estimated Indirect Activity Costs	Allocation Base	Estimated Quantity of Allocation Base
Applications development	$ 800,000	New applications	4 new applications
Content production	1,200,000	Lines of code	12 million lines
Testing	288,000	Testing hours	1,800 testing hours
Total indirect costs	$2,288,000		

Other production information for Personal-Page and Hi-Secure includes:

	Personal-Page	Hi-Secure
Units produced	20,000	10
Number of new applications	1	1
Lines of code	500,000	7,500,000
Hours of testing	100	600

continued . . .

Requirements

1. Compute the cost allocation rate for each activity. Carry each cost to the nearest cent. (p. 965)
2. Use the activity-based cost allocation rates to compute the activity costs per unit of Personal-Page and Hi-Secure. (*Hint:* First compute the total activity costs allocated to each product line, and then compute the cost per unit.) (pp. 965–966)
3. Wallace's original single-allocation-base costing system allocated indirect costs to products at $50 per programmer hour. Personal-Page requires 10,000 programmer hours; Hi-Secure requires 15,000 programmer hours. Compute the total indirect costs allocated to Personal-Page and Hi-Secure under the original system. Then compute the indirect cost per unit for each product. (p. 963)
4. Compare the activity-based costs per unit to the costs from the single-allocation-base system. How have the unit costs changed? Explain why the costs changed as they did. (pp. 965–966)

Recording manufacturing costs for a JIT costing system

3

P19-32B Timekeepers produces sports watches. The company has a JIT production system and uses JIT costing.

Timekeepers has two inventory accounts: Raw and In-Process Inventory and Finished Goods Inventory. On August 1, 2007, the account balances were Raw and In-Process Inventory, $12,000; Finished Goods Inventory, $2,000.

Timekeepers's standard cost per watch is $50: $30 direct materials plus $20 conversion costs. The following data pertain to August manufacturing and sales:

Number of watches completed	9,000 watches	Raw materials purchased	$300,000
Number of watches sold	8,800 watches	Conversion costs incurred	$100,000

Requirements

1. What are the major features of a JIT production system such as that of Timekeepers? (pp. 975–976)
2. Prepare summary journal entries for August. Under- and overallocated conversion costs are closed to Cost of Goods Sold at the end of each month. (pp. 975–976)
3. Use a T-account to determine the August 31, 2007, balance of Raw and In-Process Inventory. (p. 976)

Analyzing costs of quality

4

P19-33B Largo Toys is using a costs-of-quality approach to evaluate design engineering efforts for a new toy robot. The company's senior managers expect the engineering work to reduce appraisal, internal failure, and external failure activities. The predicted reductions in activities over the 2-year life of the toy robot follow. Also shown are the cost allocation rates for each activity.

continued . . .

Activity	Predicted Reduction in Activity Units	Activity Cost Allocation Rate Per Unit
Inspection of incoming materials	300	$20
Inspection of finished goods	300	30
Number of defective units discovered in-house	3,200	15
Number of defective units discovered by customers	900	40
Lost sales to dissatisfied customers	300	60

Requirements

1. Calculate the predicted quality cost savings from the design engineering work. (p. 978)
2. Largo Toys spent $60,000 on design engineering for the new toy robot. What is the net benefit of this "preventive" quality activity? (p. 978)
3. What major difficulty would Largo Toys' managers have in implementing this costs-of-quality approach? What alternative approach could they use to measure quality improvement? (pp. 978–979)

for 24/7 practice, visit www.MyAccountingLab.com

Apply Your Knowledge

Decision Cases

Comparing costs from ABC and single-rate systems; activity-based management

Case 1. Harris Systems specializes in servers for workgroup, e-commerce, and ERP applications. The company's original job costing system has two direct cost categories: direct materials and direct labor. Overhead is allocated to jobs at the single rate of $22 per direct labor hour.

A task force headed by Harris's CFO recently designed an ABC system with four activities. The ABC system retains the current system's two direct cost categories. Thus, it budgets only overhead costs for each activity. Pertinent data follow.

Activity	Allocation Base	Cost Allocation Rate
Materials handling	Number of parts	$ 0.85
Machine setup	Number of setups	500.00
Assembling	Assembling hours	80.00
Shipping	Number of shipments	1,500.00

Harris Systems has been awarded two new contracts, which will be produced as Job A and Job B. Budget data relating to the contracts follow.

	Job A	Job B
Number of parts	15,000	2,000
Number of setups	6	4
Number of assembling hours	1,500	200
Number of shipments	1	1
Total direct labor hours	8,000	600
Number of output units	100	10
Direct materials cost	$220,000	$30,000
Direct labor cost	$160,000	$12,000

Requirements

1. Compute the product cost per unit for each job, using the original costing system (with two direct cost categories and a single overhead allocation rate). (p. 963)

2. Suppose Harris Systems adopts the ABC system. Compute the product cost per unit for each job using ABC. (pp. 965–966)

3. Which costing system more accurately assigns to jobs the costs of the resources consumed to produce them? Explain. (p. 964)

4. A dependable company has offered to produce both jobs for Harris for $5,400 per output unit. Harris may outsource (buy from the outside company) either Job A only, Job B only, or both jobs. Which course of action will Harris's managers take if they base their decision on (a) the original system? (b) ABC system costs? Which course of action will yield more income? Explain.

Use activity-based management to achieve target costs

Case 2. To remain competitive, Harris Systems' management believes the company must produce Job B–type servers (from Decision Case 1) at a target cost of $5,400. Harris Systems has just joined a B2B e-market site that management believes will enable the firm to cut direct materials costs by 10%. Harris's management also believes that a value-engineering team can reduce assembly time.

Compute the assembling cost savings per Job B–type server required to meet the $5,400 target cost. (*Hint:* Begin by calculating the direct materials, direct labor, and allocated activity costs per server.) (p. 969)

Ethical Issue

Cassidy Manning is assistant controller at LeMar Packaging, Inc., a manufacturer of cardboard boxes and other packaging materials. Manning has just returned from a packaging industry conference on activity-based costing. She realizes that ABC may help LeMar meet its goal of reducing costs by 5% over each of the next three years.

LeMar Packaging's Order Department is a likely candidate for ABC. While orders are entered into a computer that updates the accounting records, clerks manually check customers' credit history and hand-deliver orders to shipping. This process occurs whether the sales order is for a dozen specialty boxes worth $80, or 10,000 basic boxes worth $8,000.

Manning believes that identifying the cost of processing a sales order would justify (1) further computerization of the order process and (2) changing the way the company processes small orders. However, the significant cost savings would arise from elimination of two positions in the Order Department. The company's sales order clerks have been with the company many years. Manning is uncomfortable with the prospect of proposing a change that will likely result in terminating these employees.

Requirements

Use the IMA's ethical standards to consider Manning's responsibility when cost savings come at the expense of employees' jobs.

Team Project

Bronson Shrimp Farms, in Alabama, has a Processing Department that processes raw shrimp into two products:

- Headless shrimp
- Peeled and deveined shrimp

Bronson recently submitted bids for two orders: (1) headless shrimp for a cruise line and (2) peeled and deveined shrimp for a restaurant chain. Bronson won the first bid, but lost the second. The production and sales managers are upset. They believe that Bronson's state-of-the-art equipment should have given the company an edge in the peeled and deveined market. Consequently, production managers are starting to keep their own sets of product cost records.

Bronson is reexamining both its production process and its costing system. The existing costing system has been in place since 1991. It allocates all indirect costs based on direct labor hours. Bronson is considering adopting activity-based costing. Controller Heather Barefield and a team of production managers performed a preliminary study. The team identified six activities, with the following (department-wide) estimated indirect costs and cost drivers for 2008:

Activity	Estimated Total Cost of Activity	Allocation Base
Redesign of production process (costs of changing process and equipment)...............	$ 5,000	Number of design changes
Production scheduling (production scheduler's salary)...	6,000	Number of batches
Chilling (depreciation on refrigerators)...............................	1,500	Weight (in pounds)
Processing (utilities and depreciation on equipment).........	20,675	Number of cuts
Packaging (indirect labor and depreciation on equipment).........	1,425	Cubic feet of surface exposed
Order filling (order-takers' and shipping clerks' wages)................	7,000	Number of orders
Total indirect costs for the entire department.................................	$41,600	

The raw shrimp are chilled and then cut. For headless shrimp, employees remove the heads, then rinse the shrimp. For peeled and deveined shrimp, the headless shrimp are further processed—the shells are removed and the backs are slit for deveining. Both headless shrimp and peeled and deveined shrimp are packaged in foam trays and covered with shrink wrap. Order-filling personnel assemble orders of headless shrimp as well as peeled and deveined shrimp.

Barefield estimates that Bronson will produce 10,000 packages of headless shrimp and 50,000 packages of peeled and deveined shrimp in 2008. The two products incur the following costs per package:

	Costs per Package	
	Headless Shrimp	Peeled and Deveined Shrimp
Shrimp......................	$3.50	$4.50
Foam trays.................	$0.05	$0.05
Shrink wrap...............	$0.05	$0.02
Number of cuts..........	12 cuts	48 cuts
Cubic feet of exposed surface....	1 cubic foot	0.75 cubic foot
Weight (in pounds)	2.5 pounds	1 pound
Direct labor hours.....................	0.01 hour	0.05 hour

Bronson pays direct laborers $20 per hour. Barefield estimates that each product line also will require the following *total* resources:

	Headless Shrimp			Peeled and Deveined Shrimp		
Design changes	1 change	}	for all	4 changes	}	for all
Batches	40 batches		10,000	20 batches		50,000
Sales orders	90 orders		packages	110 orders		packages

Requirements

Form groups of four students. All group members should work together to develop the group's answers to the three requirements.

(Carry all computations to at least four decimal places.)

1. Using the original costing system with the single indirect cost allocation base (direct labor hours), compute the total budgeted cost per package for the headless shrimp and then for the peeled and deveined shrimp. (*Hint:* First, compute the indirect cost allocation rate—that is, the predetermined overhead rate. Then, compute the total budgeted cost per package for each product.) (p. 963)

2. Use activity-based costing to recompute the total budgeted cost per package for the headless shrimp and then for the peeled and deveined shrimp. (*Hint:* First, calculate the budgeted cost allocation rate for each activity. Then, calculate the total indirect costs of (a) the entire headless shrimp product line and (b) the entire peeled and deveined shrimp product line. Next, compute the indirect cost per package of each product. Finally, calculate the total cost per package of each product.) (pp. 965–966)

3. Write a memo to Bronson CEO Gary Pololu explaining the results of the ABC study. Compare the costs reported by the ABC system with the costs reported by the original system. Point out whether the ABC system shifted costs toward headless shrimp or toward peeled and deveined shrimp, and explain why. Finally, explain whether Pololu should feel more comfortable making decisions using cost data from the original system or from the new ABC system.

For Internet Exercises, Excel in Practice, and additional online activities, go to the Web site www.prenhall.com/horngren.

Quick Check Answers

1. *d* 2. *b* 3. *d* 4. *a* 5. *d* 6. *c* 7. *a* 8. *a* 9. *b* 10. *b*

20 Cost-Volume-Profit Analysis

Learning Objectives

1. Identify how changes in volume affect costs

2. Use CVP analysis to compute breakeven points

3. Use CVP analysis for profit planning, and graph the CVP relations

4. Use CVP methods to perform sensitivity analyses

5. Calculate the breakeven point for multiple product lines or services

Remember when you were 15 and ready to drive? Before you received your license, you needed training and practice. Many of us took driving courses to prepare for the driving tests. Do you think driving schools are profitable? How many students do they need to cover the costs of a training facility, instructors, and a fleet of cars? What happens to income if the business adds a new Honda to its fleet?

This chapter will look at cost behavior and you will learn how cost-volume-profit (CVP) analysis is used to manage a business. **Cost-volume-profit (CVP) analysis** expresses the relationships among costs, volume, and profit or loss. It's a wonderful management tool and easy to understand. You can take this material home and apply it to your family's business—immediately!

Cost Behavior

Some costs increase as the volume of activity increases. Other costs are not affected by volume changes. Managers need to know how a business's costs are affected by changes in its volume of activity. Let's look at the three different types of **costs.**

- Variable costs
- Fixed costs
- Mixed costs

Variable Costs

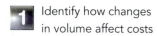
Identify how changes in volume affect costs

Total variable costs change in direct proportion to changes in the volume of activity. For our purposes, an activity is a business action that affects costs. Those activities include selling, producing, driving, and calling. These activities can be measured by units sold, units produced, miles driven, and the number of phone calls placed. So variable costs are those costs that increase or decrease in total as the volume of activity increases or decreases.

For example, Mi Tierra Driving School offers classroom and driving instruction. For each student taking driving lessons, the school spends $15 per month for gasoline. Mi Tierra can provide driving lessons for 15 to 30 students. To calculate total variable costs Ms. Lopez, the office manager, would show:

Number of Students per Month	Gasoline Cost per Student	Total Gasoline Cost per Month
15	$15	$225
20	$15	$300
30	$15	$450

As you can see, the total variable cost of gasoline increases as the number of students increases. But the gasoline cost per student does not change. Exhibit 20-1 graphs total variable costs for gasoline as the number of students increase from 0 to 30.

If there are no students, Mi Tierra incurs no gasoline costs, so the total variable cost line begins at the bottom left corner. This point is called the *origin,* and it represents zero volume and zero cost. The *slope* of the variable cost line is the change in gasoline cost (on the vertical axis) divided by the change in the number of students (on the horizontal axis). The slope of the graph equals the variable cost per unit. In Exhibit 20-1, the slope of the variable cost line is $15 because the driving school spends $15 on gas for each student.

If the driving school signs 15 students for the month, it will spend a total of $225 (15 students × $15 each) for gasoline. Follow this total variable cost line to the right to see that doubling the number of students to 30 likewise doubles the total variable cost to $450 (30 × $15 = $450). Exhibit 20-1 shows how the *total variable cost* of gasoline varies with the number of students. *But note that the per-person cost remains constant* at $15 per student.

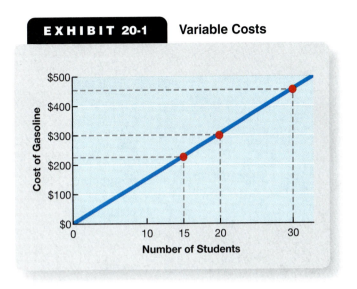

EXHIBIT 20-1 Variable Costs

Remember this important fact about **variable costs**:

> Total variable costs fluctuate with changes in volume, but the variable cost per unit remains constant.

Fixed Costs

In contrast, **total fixed costs** are costs that do not change over wide ranges of volume. Mi Tierra's fixed costs include depreciation on the cars, as well as the salaries of the driving instructors. Mi Tierra has these fixed costs regardless of the number of students—15, 20, or 30.

Suppose Mi Tierra incurs $12,000 of fixed costs each month, and the number of students enrolled is between 15 and 30 students. Exhibit 20-2 graphs total fixed costs as a flat line that intersects the cost axis at $12,000, because Mi Tierra will incur the same $12,000 of fixed costs regardless of the number of students.

Total fixed cost doesn't change, as shown in Exhibit 20-2. But the *fixed cost per student* depends on the number of students. If Mi Tierra teaches 15 students, the fixed cost per student is $800 ($12,000 ÷ 15 students). If the number of students doubles to 30, the fixed cost per student is cut in half to $400 ($12,000 ÷ 30 students).

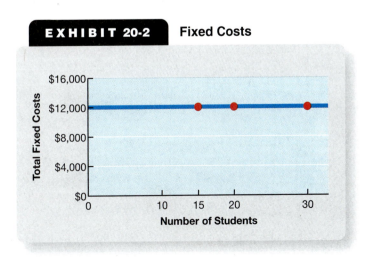

EXHIBIT 20-2 Fixed Costs

Thus, the fixed cost per student is *inversely* proportional to the number of students, as shown here.

Total Fixed Costs	Number of Students	Fixed Cost per Student
$12,000	15	$800
$12,000	20	$600
$12,000	30	$400

Remember this important fact about **fixed costs**:

> Total fixed costs remain constant,
> but fixed cost per unit is inversely proportional to volume.

Mixed Costs

Costs that have both variable and fixed components are called **mixed costs**. For example, Mi Tierra's cell-phone company may charge $10 a month to provide the service and $0.15 for each minute you talk. If you talk for 100 minutes, the company will bill you $25 [$10 + (100 × $0.15)].

Exhibit 20-3 shows how you can separate your cell-phone bill into fixed and variable components. The $10 monthly charge is a fixed cost because it is the same no matter how many minutes you use the cell phone. The $0.15-per-minute charge is a variable cost that increases in direct proportion to the number of minutes you talk. If you talk for 100 minutes, your total variable cost is $15 (100 × $0.15). If you double your talking to 200 minutes, total variable cost also doubles to $30 (200 × $0.15), and your total bill rises to $40 ($10 + $30).

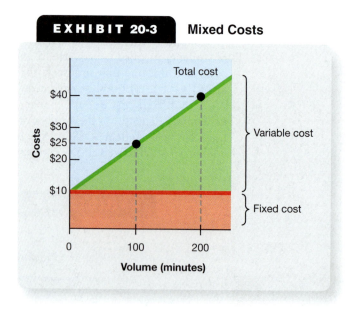

EXHIBIT 20-3   Mixed Costs

High-Low Method to Separate Fixed Cost from Variable Cost

An easy method to separate mixed costs into variable and fixed components is the **high-low method**. This method requires you to identify the highest and lowest levels of activity over a period of time. Using this information, you complete three steps:

STEP 1. Calculate the variable cost per unit.

Variable cost per unit = Change in total cost ÷ Change in volume of activity

STEP 2. Calculate total fixed costs.

Total fixed cost = Total mixed cost − Total variable cost

STEP 3. Create and use an equation to show the behavior of a mixed cost.

Total mixed cost = (Variable cost per unit × number of units) + Total fixed costs

Let's revisit the Mi Tierra Driving School illustration. A summary of Mi Tierra's auto maintenance costs for the past year shows these costs for each quarter:

	Student Driving Hours	Total Maintenance Cost	
1st Quarter	360	$1,720	
2nd Quarter	415	1,830	
3rd Quarter	480	1,960	← Highest Volume and Cost
4th Quarter	240	1,480	← Lowest Volume and Cost

The highest volume is 480 student-driving hours in the 3rd quarter of the year, and the lowest volume is 240 student-driving hours. We can use the high-low method to identify Mi Tierra's fixed and variable costs of auto maintenance.

STEP 1. Calculate the variable cost per unit.

Variable cost per unit = Change in total cost ÷ Change in volume of activity
= ($1,960 − $1,480) ÷ (480 hours − 240 hours)
= $480 ÷ 240 hours
= $2 per student-driving hour

STEP 2. Calculate total fixed costs.

Total fixed cost = Total mixed cost − Total variable cost
= $1,960 − ($2 × 480)
= $1,960 − $960
= $1,000

This example uses the highest cost and volume to calculate total fixed costs, but you can use any volume and calculate the same $1,000 total fixed cost.

STEP 3. Create and use an equation to show the behavior of a mixed cost.

Total mixed cost = (Variable cost per unit × number of units) + Total fixed costs
Total car maintenance cost = $2 per student-driver hour + $1,000

Using this equation, the estimated car maintenance cost for 400 student-driver hours would be:

$$(\$2 \times 400 \text{ student-driver hours}) + \$1,000 = \$1,800$$

This method provides a rough estimate of fixed and variable costs for cost-volume-profit analysis. The high and low volumes become the relevant range, which we discuss in the next section. Managers find the high-low method to be quick and easy, but regression analysis provides the most accurate estimates and is discussed in cost accounting textbooks.

Relevant Range

The **relevant range** is the band of volume where total fixed costs remain constant and the variable cost *per unit* remains constant. To estimate costs, managers need to know the relevant range. Why? Because:

- Total "fixed" costs can differ from one relevant range to another
- The variable cost *per unit* can differ in various relevant ranges

Exhibit 20-4 shows fixed costs for Mi Tierra Driving School over three different relevant ranges. If the school expects to offer 15,000 student-driving hours next year, the relevant range is between 10,000 and 20,000 student-driving hours, and managers budget fixed costs of $80,000.

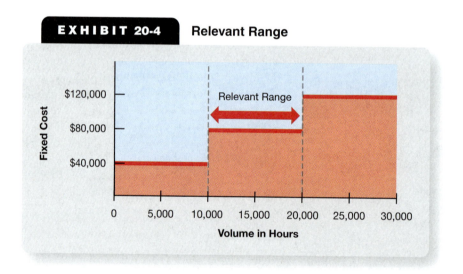

EXHIBIT 20-4 Relevant Range

To offer 22,000 student-driving hours, Mi Tierra will have to expand the school. This will increase total fixed costs for added rent cost. Exhibit 20-4 shows that total fixed costs increase to $120,000 as the relevant range shifts to this higher band of volume. Conversely, if Mi Tierra expects to offer only 8,000 student-driving hours, the school will budget only $40,000 of fixed costs. Managers will have to lay off employees or take other actions to cut fixed costs.

Variable cost per unit can also change outside the relevant range. For example, Mi Tierra Driving School may get a quantity discount for training materials if it can provide more than 20,000 student-driving hours.

We have now covered the basics of CVP analysis. Let's apply CVP analysis to answer some interesting management questions.

Basic CVP Analysis: What Must We Sell to Break Even?

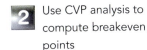

Use CVP analysis to compute breakeven points

Kim Chan is considering starting an e-tail business to sell art posters on the Internet. Chan plans to be a "virtual retailer" and carry no inventory. Chan's software will total customer orders each day and automatically order posters from a wholesaler. Chan buys only what she needs to fulfill yesterday's sales orders. Here are Chan's basic CVP data:

Selling price per poster	$ 35
Variable cost per poster	$ 21
Fixed costs for server leasing, software, and office rental	$7,000

Chan faces several important questions:

- How many posters must Chan sell to break even?
- What will profits be if sales double?
- How will changes in selling price, variable costs, or fixed costs affect profits?

Before getting started, let's review the assumptions required for CVP analysis to be accurate.

Assumptions

CVP analysis assumes that:

1. Managers can classify each cost as either variable or fixed.
2. The only factor that affects costs is change in volume. Fixed costs don't change.

Chan's business meets these assumptions.

1. The $21 purchase cost for each poster is a variable cost. Thus, Chan's *total variable cost* increases directly with the number of posters she sells (an extra $21 in cost for each poster sold). The $7,000 monthly server, software, and office rentals are fixed costs and don't change regardless of the number of posters she sells.
2. Sales volume is the only factor that affects Chan's costs.

Most business conditions don't perfectly meet these assumptions, so managers regard CVP analysis as approximate, not exact.

How Much Must Chan Sell to Break Even? Three Approaches

Virtually all businesses want to know their breakeven point. The **breakeven point** is the sales level at which operating income is zero: Total revenues equal total costs. Sales below the breakeven point result in a loss. Sales above breakeven provide a profit. Chan needs to know how many posters she must sell to break even, and that will help her plan her profits.

There are several ways to figure the breakeven point, including the

- Income statement approach
- Contribution margin approach

We start with the income statement approach because it is the easiest method to remember. You are already familiar with the income statement.

The Income Statement Approach

Start by expressing income in equation form:

$$\text{Sales revenue} - \underbrace{\text{Total costs}}_{\text{Sales revenue} - \text{Variable costs} - \text{Fixed costs}} = \text{Operating income}$$

Sales revenue equals the unit sale price ($35 per poster in this case) multiplied by the number of units (posters) sold. Variable costs equal variable cost per unit ($21 in this case) times the number of units sold. Chan's fixed costs total $7,000. At the breakeven point, operating income is zero. We use this information to solve the income statement equation for the number of posters Chan must sell to break even.

SALES REVENUE	−	VARIABLE COSTS	−	FIXED COSTS	=	OPERATING INCOME
$\left(\begin{array}{c}\text{Sale price}\\ \text{per unit}\end{array} \times \text{Units sold}\right)$	−	$\left(\begin{array}{c}\text{Variable cost}\\ \text{per unit}\end{array} \times \text{Units sold}\right)$	−	Fixed costs	=	Operating income
($35 × Units sold)	−	($21 × Units sold)	−	$7,000	=	$0
($35	−	$21) × Units sold	−	$7,000	=	$0
		$14 × Units sold			=	$7,000
		Units sold			=	$7,000/$14
		Breakeven sales in units			=	500 posters

Kim Chan must sell 500 posters to break even. Her breakeven sales level in dollars is $17,500 (500 posters × $35).

Be sure to check your calculations. "Prove" the breakeven point by substituting the breakeven number of units into the income statement. Then check to ensure that this level of sales results in zero profit.

$$\text{Proof:} \quad (\$35 \times 500) - (\$21 \times 500) - \$7,000 = \$0$$
$$\$17,500 - \$10,500 - \$7,000 = \$0$$

The Contribution Margin Approach: A Shortcut

This shortcut method of computing the breakeven point uses Chan's contribution margin. **Contribution margin** is sales revenue minus variable costs. It is called the *contribution margin* because the excess of sales revenue over variable costs contributes to covering fixed costs and then to providing operating income. We can refer to contribution margin on a total basis or on a per-unit basis, as follows:

Total contribution margin = Total sales revenue − Total variable costs
Contribution margin per unit = Sales revenue per unit − Variable cost per unit

The **contribution margin income statement** shows costs by cost behavior—variable costs and fixed costs—and highlights the contribution margin. The format shows:

$$\begin{aligned} &\text{Sales revenue} \\ &- \text{Variable costs} \\ &= \text{Contribution margin} \\ &- \text{Fixed costs} \\ &= \text{Operating income} \end{aligned}$$

Now let's rearrange the income statement and use the contribution margin to develop a shortcut method for finding the number of posters Chan must sell to break even.

$$\text{Sales revenue} - \text{Variable costs} - \text{Fixed costs} = \text{Operating income}$$

$$\left(\frac{\text{Sale price}}{\text{per unit}} \times \text{Units sold}\right) - \left(\frac{\text{Variable cost}}{\text{per unit}} \times \text{Units sold}\right) - \text{Fixed costs} = \text{Operating income}$$

$$\left(\frac{\text{Sale price}}{\text{per unit}} - \frac{\text{Variable cost}}{\text{per unit}}\right) \times \text{Units sold} = \text{Fixed costs} + \text{Operating income}$$

$$\underbrace{\text{Contribution margin per unit}} \times \text{Units sold} = \text{Fixed costs} + \text{Operating income}$$

Dividing both sides of the equation by contribution margin per unit yields the cost-volume-profit equation:

$$\text{Units sold} = \frac{\text{Fixed costs} + \text{Operating income}}{\text{Contribution margin per unit}}$$

Kim Chan can use this contribution margin approach to find her breakeven point. Her fixed costs total $7,000. Operating income is zero at breakeven. Her contribution margin per poster is $14 ($35 sale price − $21 variable cost). Chan's breakeven computation is:

$$\text{BREAKEVEN SALES IN UNITS} = \frac{\$7,000}{\$14}$$

$$= \textcolor{blue}{500 \text{ posters}}$$

Why does this shortcut method work? Each poster Chan sells provides $14 of contribution margin. To break even, Chan must generate enough contribution margin to cover $7,000 of fixed costs. At the rate of $14 per poster, Chan must sell 500 posters ($7,000/$14) to cover her fixed costs. You can see that the contribution margin approach simply rearranges the income statement equation, so the breakeven point is the same under both methods.

To "prove" the breakeven point, you can also use the contribution margin income statement format:

Proof:

Sales revenue ($35 × 500 posters)	$17,500
Less: Variable costs ($21 × 500 posters)	(10,500)
Contribution margin ($14 × 500 posters)	7,000
Less: Fixed costs	(7,000)
Operating income	$ 0

Using the Contribution Margin Ratio to Compute the Breakeven Point in Sales Dollars

Companies can use the contribution margin ratio to compute their breakeven point in terms of *sales dollars*. The **contribution margin ratio** is the ratio of contribution margin to sales revenue. For Kim Chan's poster business, we have:

$$\text{Contribution margin ratio} = \frac{\text{Contribution margin}}{\text{Sales revenue}} = \frac{\$14}{\$35} = 40\%$$

The 40% contribution margin ratio means that each dollar of sales revenue contributes $0.40 toward fixed costs and profit, as shown in Exhibit 20-5.

EXHIBIT 20-5 Breakdown of $1 of Revenue into Variable Costs and Contribution Margin

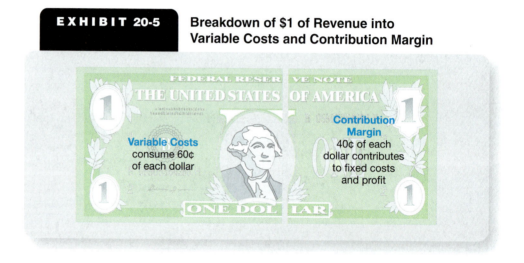

The contribution margin *ratio* approach differs from the shortcut contribution margin approach we've just seen in only one way: Here we use the contribution margin *ratio* rather than the dollar amount of the contribution margin:

$$\text{BREAKEVEN SALES IN DOLLARS} = \frac{\text{Fixed costs}}{\text{Contribution margin ratio}}$$

Using this ratio formula, Kim Chan's breakeven point in sales dollars is

$$\text{BREAKEVEN SALES IN DOLLARS} = \frac{\$7,000}{0.40}$$
$$= \$17,500$$

This is the same breakeven sales revenue as shown in the proof at the bottom of page 1015.

Why does the contribution margin ratio formula work? Each dollar of Kim Chan's sales contributes 40% of each dollar of sales to fixed costs and profit. To break even, she must generate enough contribution margin at the rate of 40% of sales to cover the $7,000 fixed costs ($7,000 ÷ 0.40 = $17,500).

Now, we've seen how companies use *contribution margin* to estimate breakeven points in CVP analysis. But managers use the contribution margin for other purposes too, such as motivating the sales force. Salespeople who know the contribution margin of each product can generate more profit by emphasizing high-margin products. This is why many companies base sales commissions on the contribution margins produced by sales rather than on sales revenue alone.

Using CVP to Plan Profits

3 Use CVP analysis for profit planning, and graph the CVP relations

For established products and services, managers are more interested in the sales level needed to earn a target profit than in the breakeven point. Managers of new business ventures are also interested in the profits they can expect to earn. For example, now that Kim Chan knows she must sell 500 posters to break even, she wants to know how many more posters she must sell to earn a monthly operating profit of $4,900.

How Much Must Chan Sell to Earn a Profit?

What is the only difference from our prior analysis? Here, Chan wants to know how many posters she must sell to earn a $4,900 profit. We can use the income statement approach or the shortcut contribution margin approach to find the answer. Let's start with the income statement approach.

SALES REVENUE − VARIABLE COSTS − FIXED COSTS = OPERATING INCOME

($35 × Units sold) − ($21 × Units sold) − $7,000 = $4,900

($35 − $21) × Units sold − $7,000 = $4,900

$14 × Units sold = $11,900

Units sold = $11,900/$14

Units sold = 850 posters

Proof:

($35 × 850) − ($21 × 850) − $7,000 = $4,900

$29,750 − $17,850 − $7,000 = $4,900

This analysis shows that Chan must sell 850 posters each month to earn an operating profit of $4,900. This is 850 − 500 = 350 more posters than the breakeven sales level (500 posters).

The proof shows that Chan needs sales revenues of $29,750 to earn a profit of $4,900. Alternatively, we can compute the dollar sales necessary to earn a $4,900 profit directly, using the contribution margin ratio form of the CVP formula:

$$\text{TARGET SALES IN DOLLARS} = \frac{\text{Fixed costs} + \text{Operating income}}{\text{Contribution margin ratio}}$$

$$= \frac{\$7,000 + \$4,900}{0.40}$$

$$= \frac{\$11,900}{0.40}$$

$$= \$29,750$$

Graphing Cost-Volume-Profit Relations

Kim Chan can graph the CVP relations for her proposed business. A graph provides a picture that shows how changes in the levels of sales will affect profits. As in the variable-, fixed-, and mixed-cost graphs of Exhibits 20-1, 2, and 3, Chan shows the volume of units (posters) on the horizontal axis and dollars on the vertical axis.

Then she follows four steps to graph the CVP relations for her business, as illustrated in Exhibit 20-6.

STEP 1 Choose a sales volume, such as 1,000 posters. Plot the point for total sales revenue at that volume: 1,000 posters × $35 per poster = sales of $35,000. Draw the *sales revenue line* from the origin (0) through the $35,000 point. Why start at the origin? If Chan sells no posters, there's no revenue.

STEP 2 Draw the *fixed cost line*, a horizontal line that intersects the dollars axis at $7,000. The fixed cost line is flat because fixed costs are the same ($7,000) no matter how many posters Chan sells.

STEP 3 Draw the *total cost line*. Total cost is the sum of variable cost plus fixed cost. Thus, total cost is *mixed*. So the total cost line follows the form of the mixed cost line in Exhibit 20-3. Begin by computing variable cost at the chosen sales volume: 1,000 posters × $21 per poster = variable cost of $21,000. Add variable cost to fixed cost: $21,000 + $7,000 = $28,000. Plot the total cost point ($28,000) for 1,000 units. Then draw a line through this point from the $7,000 fixed cost intercept on the dollars vertical axis. This is the *total cost line*. The total cost line starts at the fixed cost line because even if Chan sells no posters, she still incurs the $7,000 fixed cost.

STEP 4 Identify the *breakeven point* and the areas of operating income and loss. The breakeven point is where the sales revenue line intersects the total cost line. This is where revenue exactly equals total costs—at 500 posters, or $17,500 in sales.

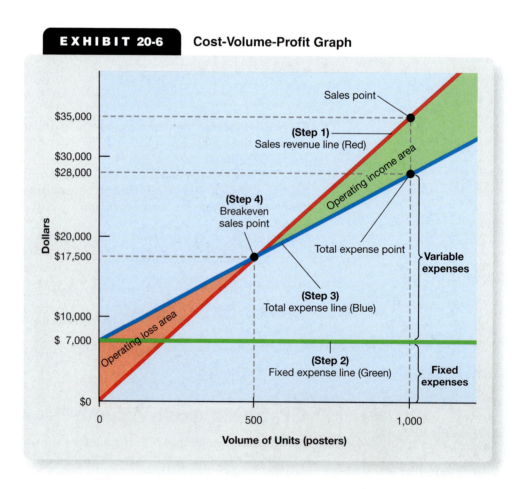

EXHIBIT 20-6 Cost-Volume-Profit Graph

Mark the *operating income* and the *operating loss* areas on the graph. To the left of the breakeven point, total costs exceed sales revenue—leading to an operating loss, indicated by the red zone.

To the right of the breakeven point, the business earns a profit because sales revenue exceeds total cost, as shown by the green zone.

Why bother with a graph? Why not just use the income statement approach or the shortcut contribution margin approach? Graphs like Exhibit 20-6 help managers quickly estimate the profit or loss earned at different levels of sales. The income statement and contribution margin approaches indicate income or loss for only a single sales amount.

Summary Problem 1

Happy Feet buys hiking socks for $6 a pair and sells them for $10. Management budgets monthly fixed costs of $10,000 for sales volumes between 0 and 12,000 pairs.

Requirements

1. Use both the income statement approach and the shortcut contribution margin approach to compute the company's monthly breakeven sales in units.

2. Use the contribution margin ratio approach to compute the breakeven point in sales dollars.

3. Compute the monthly sales level (in units) required to earn a target operating income of $6,000. Use either the income statement approach or the shortcut contribution margin approach.

4. Prepare a graph of Happy Feet's CVP relationships, similar to Exhibit 20-6. Draw the sales revenue line, the fixed cost line, and the total cost line. Label the axes, the breakeven point, the operating income area, and the operating loss area.

Solution

Requirement 1
Income statement approach:

$$\text{Sales revenue} - \text{Variable costs} - \text{Fixed costs} = \text{Operating income}$$

$$\left(\text{Sale price per unit} \times \text{Units sold}\right) - \left(\text{Variable cost per unit} \times \text{Units sold}\right) - \text{Fixed costs} = \text{Operating income}$$

$$(\$10 \times \text{Units sold}) - (\$6 \times \text{Units sold}) - \$10{,}000 = \$0$$

$$(\$10 - \$6) \times \text{Units sold} = \$10{,}000$$

$$\$4 \times \text{Units sold} = \$10{,}000$$

$$\text{Units sold} = \$10{,}000 \div \$4$$

$$\text{Breakeven sales in units} = 2{,}500 \text{ units}$$

Shortcut contribution margin approach:

$$\text{Units sold} = \frac{\text{Fixed costs} + \text{Operating income}}{\text{Contribution margin per unit}}$$

$$\text{Breakeven sales in units} = \frac{\$10{,}000 + \$0}{\$10 - \$6}$$

$$= \frac{\$10{,}000}{\$4}$$

$$= 2{,}500 \text{ units}$$

Requirement 2

$$\text{Breakeven sales in dollars} = \frac{\text{Fixed costs} + \text{Operating income}}{\text{Contribution margin ratio}}$$

$$= \frac{\$10{,}000 + \$0}{0.40^*}$$

$$= \$25{,}000$$

$$^*\text{Contribution margin ratio} = \frac{\text{Contribution margin per unit}}{\text{Sale price per unit}} = \frac{\$4}{\$10} = 0.40$$

Requirement 3
Income statement equation approach:

$$\text{Sales revenue} - \text{Variable costs} - \text{Fixed costs} = \text{Operating income}$$

$$\left(\begin{array}{c}\text{Sale price} \\ \text{per unit}\end{array} \times \begin{array}{c}\text{Units} \\ \text{sold}\end{array}\right) - \left(\begin{array}{c}\text{Variable} \\ \text{cost per unit}\end{array} \times \begin{array}{c}\text{Units} \\ \text{sold}\end{array}\right) - \text{Fixed costs} = \text{Operating income}$$

$$(\$10 \times \text{Units sold}) - (\$6 \times \text{Units sold}) - \$10,000 = \$6,000$$
$$(\$10 - \$6) \times \text{Units sold} = \$10,000 + \$6,000$$
$$\$4 \times \text{Units sold} = \$16,000$$
$$\text{Units sold} = \$16,000 \div \$4$$
$$\text{Units sold} = 4,000 \text{ units}$$

Shortcut contribution margin approach:

$$\text{Units sold} = \frac{\text{Fixed costs} + \text{Operating income}}{\text{Contribution margin per unit}}$$
$$= \frac{\$10,000 + \$6,000}{(\$10 - \$6)}$$
$$= \frac{\$16,000}{\$4}$$
$$= 4,000 \text{ units}$$

Requirement 4

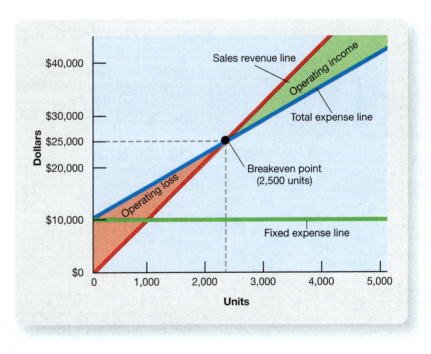

Using CVP for Sensitivity Analysis

Managers often want to predict how changes in sale price, costs, or volume affect their profits. Managers can use CVP relationships to conduct sensitivity analysis. **Sensitivity analysis** is a "what if" technique that asks what results are likely if selling price or costs change, or if an underlying assumption changes. Let's see how Kim Chan can use CVP analysis to estimate the effects of some changes in her business environment.

Changing the Selling Price

Competition in the art poster business is so fierce that Kim Chan believes she must cut the selling price to $31 per poster to maintain her market share. Suppose Chan's variable costs remain $21 per poster and her fixed costs stay at $7,000. How will the lower sale price affect her breakeven point?

Using the income statement approach:

SALES REVENUE − VARIABLE COSTS − FIXED COSTS = OPERATING INCOME

($31 × Units sold) − ($21 × Units sold) − $7,000 = $0

($31 − $21) × Units sold − $7,000 = $0

$10 × Units sold = $7,000

Units sold = $7,000/$10

Units sold = 700 posters

Proof:

Sales revenue (700 × $31)	$21,700
Less: Variable costs (700 × $21)	(14,700)
Contribution margin (700 × $10)	7,000
Less: Fixed costs	(7,000)
Operating income	$ 0

With the original $35 sale price, Chan's breakeven point was 500 posters (page 1015). With the new lower sale price of $31 per poster, her breakeven point increases to 700 posters. The lower sale price means that each poster contributes less toward fixed costs, so Chan must sell 200 more posters to break even.

Changing Variable Costs

Return to Kim Chan's original data on page 1013. Chan's supplier raises his prices, which increases her purchase cost for each poster to $28 (instead of the original $21). Chan can't pass this increase on to her customers, so she holds her sale price at the original $35 per poster. Her fixed costs remain at $7,000. How many posters must Chan sell to break even after her supplier raises his prices?

Using the income statement approach:

SALES REVENUE	− VARIABLE COSTS	− FIXED COSTS	= OPERATING INCOME
($35 × Units sold)	− ($28 × Units sold)	− $7,000	= $0
($35 − $28) × Units sold		− $7,000	= $0
$7 × Units sold			= $7,000

Breakeven units sold = $7,000/$7

Breakeven units sold = 1,000 posters

Higher variable costs per poster reduce Chan's per-unit contribution margin from $14 per poster to $7 per poster. As a result, Chan must sell more posters to break even—1,000 rather than the original 500 posters. This analysis shows why managers are particularly concerned with controlling costs during an economic downturn. Increases in cost raise the breakeven point, and a higher breakeven point can lead to problems if demand falls due to a recession.

Of course, a decrease in variable costs would have the opposite effect. Lower variable costs increase the contribution margin on each poster and, therefore, lower the breakeven point.

Changing Fixed Costs

Return to Kim Chan's original data on page 1013. Kim is considering spending an additional $3,500 on Web site banner ads. This would increase her fixed costs from $7,000 to $10,500. If she sells the posters at the original price of $35 each and her variable costs remain at $21 per poster, what is her new breakeven point?

Using the income statement approach:

SALES REVENUE	− VARIABLE COSTS	− FIXED COSTS	= OPERATING INCOME
($35 × Units sold)	− ($21 × Units sold)	− $10,500	= $0
($35 − $21) × Units sold		− $10,500	= $0
$14 × Units sold			= $10,500

Breakeven units sold = $10,500/$14

Breakeven units sold = 750 posters

Higher fixed costs increase the total contribution margin required to break even. In this case, increasing the fixed costs from $7,000 to $10,500 increases the breakeven point to 750 posters (from the original 500 posters).

Managers usually prefer a lower breakeven point to a higher one. But don't overemphasize this one aspect of CVP analysis. Even though investing in the Web banner ads increases Chan's breakeven point, Chan should pay the extra $3,500 if that would increase both her sales and profits.

Exhibit 20-7 on the next page shows how all of these changes affect the contribution margin and breakeven.

Margin of Safety

The **margin of safety** is the excess of expected sales over breakeven sales. The margin of safety is therefore the "cushion" or drop in sales that the company can absorb without incurring a loss.

The higher the margin of safety ⇒ The greater the cushion against loss ⇒ The less risky the business plan

EXHIBIT 20-7 How Changes in Selling Price, Variable Costs, and Fixed Costs Affect the Contribution Margin per Unit and the Breakeven Point

Cause	Effect	Result
Change	Contribution Margin per Unit	Breakeven Point
Selling Price per Unit Increases	Increases	Decreases
Selling Price per Unit Decreases	Decreases	Increases
Variable Cost per Unit Increases	Decreases	Increases
Variable Cost per Unit Decreases	Increases	Decreases
Total Fixed Cost Increases	Is not affected	Increases
Total Fixed Cost Decreases	Is not affected	Decreases

Managers use the margin of safety to evaluate the risk of both their current operations and their plans for the future. Let's apply the margin of safety to Kim Chan's poster business.

Kim Chan's original breakeven point was 500 posters. Suppose Chan expects to sell 900 posters. Her margin of safety is:

MARGIN OF SAFETY IN UNITS = EXPECTED SALES IN UNITS − BREAKEVEN SALES IN UNITS

$$= 900 \text{ posters} - 500 \text{ posters}$$
$$= 400 \text{ posters}$$

MARGIN OF SAFETY IN DOLLARS = MARGIN OF SAFETY IN UNITS × SALE PRICE PER UNIT

$$= 400 \text{ posters} \times \$35$$
$$= \$14,000$$

Sales can drop by 400 posters, or $14,000, before Chan incurs a loss. This margin of safety (400 posters) is 44.4% of expected sales (900 posters). That's a comfortable margin of safety.

Information Technology and Sensitivity Analysis

Information technology allows managers to perform lots of sensitivity analyses before launching a new product or shutting down a plant. Excel spreadsheets are useful for sensitivity analyses like those we just did for Kim Chan. Spreadsheets can show how one change (or several changes simultaneously) affects operations. Managers can plot basic CVP data to show profit-planning graphs similar to Exhibit 20-6.

Large companies use enterprise resource planning software—SAP, Oracle, and Peoplesoft—for their CVP analysis. For example, after Sears stores lock their doors at 9:00 P.M., records for each individual transaction flow into a massive database. From a Diehard battery sold in California to a Trader Bay polo shirt sold in New Hampshire, the system compiles an average of 1.5 million transactions a day. With the click of a mouse, managers can conduct breakeven or profit planning analysis on any product they choose.

Effect of Sales Mix on CVP Analysis

5 Calculate the breakeven point for multiple product lines or services

Most companies sell more than one product. Selling price and variable costs differ for each product, so each product line makes a different contribution to profits. The same CVP formulas we used earlier apply to a company with multiple products.

To calculate breakeven for each product line, we must compute the *weighted-average contribution margin* of all the company's products. The sales mix provides the weights. **Sales mix** is the combination of products that make up total sales. For example, Fat Cat Furniture sold 6,000 cat beds and 4,000 scratching posts during the past year. The sales mix of 6,000 beds and 4,000 posts creates a ratio of 3:2 or a percentage of 60% for the beds and 40% for the posts. For every 3 cat beds, Fat Cat expects to sell 2 scratching posts, so Fat Cat expects 3/5 of the sales to be cat beds and 2/5 to be scratching posts.

Fat Cat's total fixed costs are $40,000. The cat bed's unit selling price is $44 and variable costs per bed are $24. The scratching post's unit selling price is $100 and variable cost per post is $30. To compute breakeven sales in units for both product lines, Fat Cat completes three steps.

STEP 1. Calculate the weighted-average contribution margin per unit, as follows:

	Cat Beds	Scratching Posts	Total
Sale price per unit	$44	$100	
Deduct: Variable cost per unit	(24)	(30)	
Contribution margin per unit	$20	$ 70	
Sales mix in units	× 3	× 2	5
Contribution margin	$60	$140	$200
Weighted-average contribution margin per unit ($200/5)			$ 40

STEP 2. Calculate the breakeven point in units for the "package" of products:

$$\text{BREAKEVEN SALES IN TOTAL UNITS} = \frac{\text{Fixed costs} + \text{Operating income}}{\text{Weighted-average contribution margin per unit}}$$

$$= \frac{\$40{,}000 + \$0}{\$40}$$

$$= 1{,}000 \text{ items}$$

STEP 3. Calculate the breakeven point in units for each product line. Multiply the "package" breakeven point in units by each product line's proportion of the sales mix.

Breakeven sales of cat beds (1,000 × 3/5)	600 cat beds
Breakeven sales of scratching posts (1,000 × 2/5)	400 scratching posts

In this example the calculations yield round numbers. When the calculations don't yield round numbers, round your answer up to the next whole number.

The overall breakeven point in sales dollars is $66,400:

600 cat beds at $44 selling price each	$26,400
400 scratching posts at $100 selling price each	40,000
Total revenues	$66,400

We can prove this breakeven point by preparing a contribution margin income statement:

	Cat Beds	Scratching Posts	Total
Sales revenue:			
Cat beds (600 × $44)	$26,400		
Scratching posts (400 × $100)		$40,000	$66,400
Variable costs:			
Cat beds (600 × $24)	14,400		
Scratching posts (400 × $30)		12,000	26,400
Contribution margin	$12,000	$28,000	$40,000
Fixed costs			(40,000)
Operating income			$ 0

If the sales mix changes, then Fat Cat can repeat this analysis using new sales mix information to find the breakeven points for each product line.

In addition to finding the breakeven point, Fat Cat can also estimate the sales needed to generate a certain level of operating profit. Suppose Fat Cat would like to earn operating income of $20,000. How many units of each product must Fat Cat now sell?

$$\text{BREAKEVEN SALES IN TOTAL UNITS} = \frac{\text{Fixed costs} + \text{Operating income}}{\text{Weighted-average contribution margin per unit}}$$

$$= \frac{\$40,000 + \$20,000}{\$40}$$

$$= 1,500 \text{ items}$$

Breakeven sales of cat beds (1,500 × 3/5)	900 cat beds
Breakeven sales of scratching posts (1,500 × 2/5)	600 scratching posts

We can prove this planned profit level by preparing a contribution margin income statement:

	Cat Beds	Scratching Posts	Total
Sales revenue:			
Cat beds (900 × $44)	$39,600		
Scratching posts (600 × $100)		$60,000	$99,600
Variable costs:			
Cat beds (900 × $24)	21,600		
Scratching posts (600 × $30)		18,000	39,600
Contribution margin	$18,000	$42,000	$60,000
Fixed costs			(40,000)
Operating income			$20,000

You have learned how to use CVP analysis as a managerial tool. Review the CVP Analysis Decision Guidelines to make sure you understand these basic concepts.

Decision Guidelines

COST-VOLUME-PROFIT ANALYSIS

As a manager, you will find CVP very useful. Here are some questions you will ask, and guidelines for answering them.

Decision	Guidelines
How do changes in volume of activity affect	
• total costs?	Total *variable* costs → Change in proportion to changes in volume (number of products or services sold)
	Total *fixed* costs → No change
• cost per unit?	Variable cost per unit → No change
	Fixed cost per unit:
	• Decreases when volume rises (Fixed costs are spread over *more* units)
	• Increases when volume drops (Fixed costs are spread over *fewer* units)

How do I calculate the sales needed to break even or earn a target operating income

• in units?

Income Statement Method:

$$\text{Sales revenue} - \text{Variable costs} - \text{Fixed costs} = \text{Operating income}$$

$$\left(\begin{array}{c}\text{Sale price} \\ \text{per unit}\end{array} \times \begin{array}{c}\text{Units} \\ \text{sold}\end{array}\right) - \left(\begin{array}{c}\text{Variable cost} \\ \text{per unit}\end{array} \times \begin{array}{c}\text{Units} \\ \text{sold}\end{array}\right) - \text{Fixed costs} = \text{Operating income}$$

$$\left(\begin{array}{c}\text{Sale price} \\ \text{per unit}\end{array} - \begin{array}{c}\text{Variable cost} \\ \text{per unit}\end{array}\right) \times \begin{array}{c}\text{Units} \\ \text{sold}\end{array} = \text{Fixed costs} + \text{Operating income}$$

$$\underbrace{}$$

$$\text{Contribution margin per unit} \times \begin{array}{c}\text{Units} \\ \text{sold}\end{array} = \text{Fixed costs} + \text{Operating income}$$

$$\begin{array}{c}\text{Units} \\ \text{sold}\end{array} = \frac{\text{Fixed costs} + \text{Operating income}}{\text{Contribution margin per unit}}$$

Shortcut Contribution Margin Method:

$$\frac{\text{Fixed costs} + \text{Operating income}}{\text{Contribution margin per unit}}$$

• in dollars?

Shortcut Contribution Margin Ratio Method:

$$\frac{\text{Fixed costs} + \text{Operating income}}{\text{Contribution margin ratio}}$$

How will changes in sale price or variable or fixed costs, affect the breakeven point?

Cause	Effect	Result
Change	Contribution Margin per Unit	Breakeven Point
Selling Price per Unit Increases	Increases	Decreases
Selling Price per Unit Decreases	Decreases	Increases
Variable Cost per Unit Increases	Decreases	Increases
Variable Cost per Unit Decreases	Increases	Decreases
Total Fixed Cost Increases	Is not affected	Increases
Total Fixed Cost Decreases	Is not affected	Decreases

Decision	Guidelines
How do I use CVP analysis to measure risk?	Margin of safety = Expected sales − Breakeven sales
How do I calculate my breakeven point when I sell more than one product or service?	**Step 1.** Compute the weighted-averaged contribution margin per unit as on page 1025. **Step 2.** Calculate the breakeven point in units for the "package" of products. **Step 3.** Calculate breakeven point in units for each product line. Multiply the "package" breakeven point in units by each product line's proportion of the sales mix.

Summary Problem 2

Happy Feet buys hiking socks for $6 a pair and sells them for $10. Management budgets monthly fixed costs of $12,000 for sales volumes between 0 and 12,000 pairs.

Requirements
Consider each of the following questions separately by using the foregoing information each time.

1. Calculate the breakeven point in units.
2. Happy Feet reduces its selling price from $10 a pair to $8 a pair. Calculate the new breakeven point in units.
3. Happy Feet finds a new supplier for the socks. Variable costs will decrease by $1 a pair. Calculate the new breakeven point in units.
4. Happy Feet plans to advertise in hiking magazines. The advertising campaign will increase total fixed costs by $2,000 per month. Calculate the new breakeven point in units.
5. In addition to selling hiking socks, Happy Feet would like to start selling sports socks. Happy Feet expects to sell 1 pair of hiking socks for every 3 pair of sports socks. Happy Feet will buy the sports socks for $4 a pair and sell them for $8 a pair. Total fixed costs will stay at $12,000 per month. Calculate the breakeven point in units for both hiking socks and sports socks.

Solution

Requirement 1

$$\text{Units sold} = \frac{\text{Fixed costs}}{\text{Contribution margin per unit}}$$

$$\text{Breakeven sales in units} = \frac{\$12,000}{\$10-\$6}$$

$$= \frac{\$12,000}{\$4}$$

$$= 3,000 \text{ units}$$

Requirement 2

$$\text{Units sold} = \frac{\text{Fixed costs}}{\text{Contribution margin per unit}}$$

$$\text{Breakeven sales in units} = \frac{\$12,000}{\$8-\$6}$$

$$= \frac{\$12,000}{\$2}$$

$$= 6,000 \text{ units}$$

Requirement 3

$$\text{Units sold} = \frac{\text{Fixed costs}}{\text{Contribution margin per unit}}$$

$$\text{Breakeven sales in units} = \frac{\$12,000}{\$10-\$5}$$

$$= \frac{\$12,000}{\$5}$$

$$= 2,400 \text{ units}$$

Requirement 4

$$\text{Units sold} = \frac{\text{Fixed costs}}{\text{Contribution margin per unit}}$$

$$\text{Breakeven sales in units} = \frac{\$14,000}{\$10 - \$6}$$

$$= \frac{\$14,000}{\$4}$$

$$= 3,500 \text{ units}$$

Requirement 5

STEP 1 Calculate the Weighted-Average Contribution Margin:

	Hiking	Sports	
Sales price per unit	$ 10.00	$ 8.00	
Variable expenses per unit	6.00	4.00	
Contribution margin per unit	$ 4.00	$ 4.00	
Sales mix in units	× 1	× 3	4
Contribution margin per unit	$ 4.00	$ 12.00	$ 16.00
Weighted-average CM ($16/4)			$ 4.00

STEP 2 Calculate breakeven point for "package" of products:

$$\text{BREAKEVEN SALES IN UNITS} = \frac{\text{Fixed costs}}{\text{Contribution margin per unit}}$$

$$= \frac{\$12,000}{\$4}$$

$$= 3,000 \text{ units}$$

STEP 3 Calculate breakeven point for each product line:

Number of hiking socks (3,000 × (1/4))	750
Number of sport socks (3,000 × (3/4))	2,250

Review *Cost-Volume-Profit Analysis*

Accounting Vocabulary

Absorption Costing
The costing method that assigns both variable and fixed manufacturing costs to products.

Breakeven Point
The sales level at which operating income is zero: Total revenues equal total expenses.

Contribution Margin
Sales revenue minus variable expenses.

Contribution Margin Income Statement
Income statement that groups costs by behavior—variable costs or fixed costs—and highlights the contribution margin.

Contribution Margin Ratio
Ratio of contribution margin to sales revenue.

Cost Behavior
Describes how costs change as volume changes.

Cost-Volume-Profit (CVP) Analysis
Expresses the relationships among costs, volume, and profit or loss.

Fixed Costs
Costs that tend to remain the same in amount, regardless of variations in level of activity.

High-Low Method
A method used to separate mixed costs into variable and fixed components, using the highest and lowest total cost.

Margin of Safety
Excess of expected sales over breakeven sales. Drop in sales a company can absorb without incurring an operating loss.

Mixed Costs
Costs that have both variable and fixed components.

Relevant Range
The band of volume where total fixed costs remain constant and the variable cost per unit remains constant.

Sales Mix
Combination of products that make up total sales.

Sensitivity Analysis
A "what if" technique that asks what results will be if actual prices or costs change, or if an underlying assumption changes.

Total Fixed Costs
Costs that do not change in total despite wide changes in volume.

Total Variable Costs
Costs that change in total in direct proportion to changes in volume.

Variable Costing
The costing method that assigns only variable manufacturing costs to products.

Quick Check

1. For Mi Tierra's Driving School, straight-line depreciation on the cars is:
   a. Variable cost
   b. Fixed cost
   c. Mixed cost
   d. None of the above

2. Assume Telluride Railway is considering hiring a reservations agency to handle passenger reservations. The agency would charge a flat fee of $10,000 per month, plus $1 per passenger reservation. What is the total reservation cost if 100,000 passengers take the trip next month?
   a. $1.10
   b. $10,000
   c. $100,000
   d. $110,000

3. If Telluride Railway's fixed costs total $50,000 per month, the variable cost per passenger is $10, and tickets sell for $60, what is the breakeven point in units?
   a. 1,000 passengers
   b. 833 passengers
   c. 714 passengers
   d. 100 passengers

4. Suppose Telluride Railway's total revenues are $3 million, its variable costs are $1.8 million, and its fixed costs are $0.6 million. Compute the breakeven point in dollars.
   a. $1.2 million
   b. $1.5 million
   c. $2.0 million
   d. $2.5 million

5. If Telluride Railway's fixed costs total $50,000 per month, the variable cost per passenger is $36, and tickets sell for $60, how much revenue must the Railway have to earn $100,000 in operating income per month?
   a. $60,000
   b. $150,000
   c. $250,000
   d. $375,000

6. On a CVP graph, the total cost line intersects the vertical (dollars) axis at:
   a. The level of the fixed costs
   b. The level of the variable costs
   c. The breakeven point
   d. The origin

7. If a company increases its selling price per unit for Product A, then the new breakeven point will
   a. Increase
   b. Decrease
   c. Remain the same

8. If a company increases its fixed costs for Product B, then the contribution margin per unit will
   a. Increase
   b. Decrease
   c. Remain the same

9. Telluride Railway had the following revenue over the past 5 years:

2003	$ 600,000
2004	700,000
2005	900,000
2006	800,000
2007	1,000,000

   To predict revenues for 2008, Telluride uses the average for the past 5 years. The company's breakeven revenue is $800,000 per year. What is Telluride's margin of safety?
   a. $0
   b. $50,000
   c. $100,000
   d. $110,000

10. Telluride Railway sells half of its tickets for the regular price of $60. The other half go to senior citizens and children for the discounted price of $40. Variable cost per passenger is $10 for both groups, and fixed costs total $50,000 per month. What is Telluride's breakeven point in total passengers? regular passengers? discount passengers?
    a. 600/300/300
    b. 1,000/500/500
    c. 1,250/625/625
    d. 1,500/750/750

    Answers are given after Apply Your Knowledge (p. 1048).

Assess Your Progress

Short Exercises

Variable and fixed costs

S20-1 Chicago Acoustics builds innovative loudspeakers for music and home theater. Identify the following costs as variable or fixed. Indicate V for variable costs and F for fixed costs. (pp. 1008–1010)

- __F__ 1. Depreciation on routers used to cut wood enclosures
- __V__ 2. Wood for speaker enclosures
- __F__ 3. Patents on crossover relays
- __V__ 4. Crossover relays
- __V__ 5. Grill cloth
- __V__ 6. Glue
- __F__ 7. Quality inspector's salary

Variable and fixed costs

S20-2 Sally's DayCare has been in operation for several years. She needs your help to classify the following as variable costs or fixed costs. Indicate V for variable costs and F for fixed costs. (pp. 1008–1010)

- __F__ 1. Building rent
- __F__ 2. Toys
- __F__ 3. Playground equipment
- __V__ 4. Afternoon snacks
- __F__ 5. Sally's salary
- __F__ 6. Wages of after school employees
- __V__ 7. Drawing paper
- __F__ 8. Tables and chairs

Mixed costs

S20-3 Suppose Global-Link offers an international calling plan that charges $5.00 per month plus $0.35 per minute for calls outside the United States. (pp. 1010–1012)

1. Under this plan, what is your monthly international long-distance cost if you call Europe for
   a. 20 minutes?
   b. 40 minutes?
   c. 80 minutes?
2. Draw a graph illustrating your total cost under this plan. Label the axes, and show your costs at 20, 40, and 80 minutes.

Mixed costs

S20-4 Mike owns a machine shop. In reviewing his utility bill for the last 12 months he found that his highest bill ($2,400) occurred in August when his machines worked 1,000 machine hours. His lowest utility bill of $2,200 occurred in December when his machines worked 500 machine hours. Calculate (1) the variable rate per machine hour and (2) Mike's total fixed utility cost. (pp. 1010–1012)

Computing breakeven point in sales units

S20-5 Playtime Park competes with DisneyWorld by providing a variety of rides. Playtime sells tickets at $60 per person as a one-day entrance fee. Variable costs are $20 per person, and fixed costs are $275,000 per month. Compute the number of tickets Playtime must sell to break even. Perform a numerical proof to show that your answer is correct. (pp. 1013–1017)

Computing breakeven point in sales dollars

S20-6 Refer to Short Exercise S20-5.
1. Compute Playtime Park's contribution margin ratio. Carry your computation to five decimal places. (p. 1016)
2. Use the contribution margin ratio CVP formula to determine the sales revenue Playtime Park needs to break even. (p. 1016)

Sensitivity analysis of changing sale price and variable costs on breakeven point

S20-7 Refer to Short Exercise S20-5.
1. Suppose Playtime Park cuts its ticket price from $60 to $50 to increase the number of tickets sold. Compute the new breakeven point in tickets and in sales dollars. Carry your computations to five decimal places. (p. 1016)
2. Ignore the information in part 1 above. Instead, assume that Playtime Park reduces the variable cost from $20 to $15 per ticket. Compute the new breakeven point in tickets and in dollars. Carry your computations to five decimal places. (p. 1016)

Sensitivity analysis of changing fixed cost on breakeven point

S20-8 Refer to Short Exercise S20-5. Suppose Playtime Park reduces fixed costs from $275,000 per month to $200,000 per month. Compute the new breakeven point in tickets and in sales dollars. (pp. 1014, 1016)

Computing margin of safety

S20-9 Refer to Short Exercise S20-5. If Playtime Park expects to sell 7,000 tickets, compute the margin of safety in tickets and in sales dollars. (pp. 1014, 1016)

Computing contribution margin, breakeven point, and units to achieve operating income

S20-10 Complete the calculations using the information provided for each scenario. (pp. 1014–1016)

	A	B	C
Number of units	1,000	3,000	8,000
Sale price per unit	$ 10	$ 16	$ 30
Variable costs per unit	6	8	21
Total fixed costs	50,000	21,000	180,000
Target operating income	50,000	70,000	90,000
Calculate:			
Contribution margin per unit	_____	_____	_____
Contribution margin ratio	_____	_____	_____
Breakeven point in units	_____	_____	_____
Breakeven point in sales dollars	_____	_____	_____
Units to achieve target operating income	_____	_____	_____

Calculating weighted-average contribution margin

S20-11 WetNWild Swim Park sells individual and family tickets, which include a meal, 3 beverages, and unlimited use of the swimming pools. WetNWild has the following ticket prices and variable costs for 2008:

	Individual	Family
Sale price per ticket..................	$25	$75
Variable cost per ticket	15	60

WetNWild expects to sell 1 individual ticket for every 3 family tickets. Compute the weighted-average contribution margin per ticket. (p. 1026)

Calculating breakeven point for two product lines

5

S20-12 Refer to Short Exercise S20-11. For 2009, WetNWild expects a sales mix of 2 individual tickets for every 3 family tickets. In this mix, the weighted-average contribution margin per ticket is $13. WetNWild's total fixed costs are $39,000. Calculate

1. The total number of tickets WetNWild must sell to break even. (p. 1026)
2. The number of individual tickets and the number of family tickets the company must sell to break even. (p. 1026)

Exercises

CVP definitions

1

E20-13 Match the term with the definition.

a. Breakeven
b. Contribution margin
c. Cost behavior
d. Margin of safety
e. Relevant range
f. Sales mix
g. Fixed costs
h. Variable costs

_____ 1. Costs that do not change in total despite wide changes in volume (pp. 1009–1010)
_____ 2. The sales level at which operating income is zero: total revenues equal total costs (p. 1013)
_____ 3. Drop in sales a company can absorb without incurring an operating loss (pp. 1023–1024)
_____ 4. Combination of products that make up total sales (p. 1025)
_____ 5. Sales revenue minus variable costs (p. 1014)
_____ 6. Describes how costs change as volume changes (p. 1008)
_____ 7. Costs that change in total in direct proportion to changes in volume (p. 1008)
_____ 8. The band of volume where total fixed costs remain constant and the variable cost *per unit* remains constant (p. 1012)

Variable and fixed costs

1

E20-14 LubeNGo provides several services, including oil changes. LubeNGo operates in a building with space for the service work and a waiting room for customers. Classify each of the following as a variable cost (V) or a fixed cost (F). (pp. 1008–1010)

_____ 1. Oil filter
_____ 2. Building rent
_____ 3. Oil
_____ 4. Wages of maintenance worker
_____ 5. Television
_____ 6. Manager's salary
_____ 7. Cash register
_____ 8. Equipment

Graphing cost-volume-profit relationships

E20-15 Graph these cost behavior patterns over a relevant range of 0–10,000 units:
  a. Variable costs of $8 per unit (p. 1008)
  b. Mixed costs made up of fixed costs of $20,000 and variable costs of $3 per unit (p. 1010)
  c. Fixed costs of $15,000 (pp. 1009–1010)

Mixed costs; the high-low method

E20-16 The manager of Quik Car Inspection reviewed his monthly operating costs for the past year. His costs ranged from $4,000 for 1,000 inspections to $3,600 for 600 inspections.

Requirements
1. Calculate the variable cost per inspection. (p. 1011)
2. Calculate the total fixed costs. (p. 1011)
3. Write the equation and calculate the operating costs for 900 inspections. (pp. 1011–1012)

Preparing contribution margin income statements and calculating breakeven sales

E20-17 For its top managers, Aussie Travel formats its income statement as follows:

AUSSIE TRAVEL
Contribution Margin Income Statement
Three Months Ended March 31, 2007

Sales revenue	$312,500
Variable costs	125,000
Contribution margin	187,500
Fixed costs	170,000
Operating income	$ 17,500

Aussie's relevant range is between sales of $250,000 and $360,000.

Requirements
1. Calculate the contribution margin ratio. (p. 1016)
2. Prepare two contribution margin income statements: one at the $250,000 level and one at the $360,000 level. (*Hint:* The proportion of each sales dollar that goes toward variable costs is constant within the relevant range. The proportion of each sales dollar that goes toward contribution margin also is constant within the relevant range.) (pp. 1015–1016)
3. Compute breakeven sales in dollars. (p. 1016)

Computing breakeven sales by the contribution margin approach

E20-18 Hang Ten Co. produces sports socks. The company has fixed costs of $85,000 and variable costs of $0.85 per package. Each package sells for $1.70.

Requirements
1. Compute the contribution margin per package and the contribution margin ratio. (pp. 1014–1016)
2. Find the breakeven point in units and in dollars, using the contribution margin approach. (pp. 1014–1016)

Computing a change in breakeven sales

E20-19 Owner Shan Lo is considering franchising her Noodles restaurant concept. She believes people will pay $5 for a large bowl of noodles. Variable costs are $1.50 per bowl. Lo estimates monthly fixed costs for a franchise at $8,400.

Requirements
1. Use the contribution margin ratio approach to find a franchise's breakeven sales in dollars. (p. 1016)
2. Lo believes most locations could generate $25,000 in monthly sales. Is franchising a good idea for Lo if franchisees want a minimum monthly operating income of $8,750? (p. 1017)

Computing breakeven sales and operating income or loss under different conditions

E20-20 Gordon's Steel Parts produces parts for the automobile industry. The company has monthly fixed costs of $640,000 and a contribution margin of 80% of revenues.

Requirements
1. Compute Gordon's monthly breakeven sales in dollars. Use the contribution margin ratio approach. (p. 1016)
2. Use contribution margin income statements to compute Gordon's monthly operating income or operating loss if revenues are $500,000 and if they are $1,000,000. (p. 1014)
3. Do the results in Requirement 2 make sense given the breakeven sales you computed in Requirement 1? Explain.

Analyzing a cost-volume-profit graph

E20-21 Zac Hill is considering starting a Web-based educational business, e-Prep MBA. He plans to offer a short-course review of accounting for students entering MBA programs. The materials would be available on a password-protected Web site; students would complete the course through self-study. Hill would have to grade the course assignments, but most of the work is in developing the course materials, setting up the site, and marketing. Unfortunately, Hill's hard drive crashed before he finished his financial analysis. However, he did recover the following partial CVP chart:

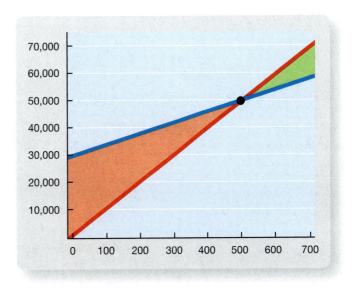

continued . . .

Requirements

1. Label each axis, the sales revenue line, the total costs line, the fixed costs, the operating income area, and the breakeven point. (p. 1018)
2. If Hill attracts 400 students to take the course, will the venture be profitable? (p. 1018)
3. What are the breakeven sales in students and dollars? (pp. 1014–1016)

Impact on breakeven point if sale price, variable costs, and fixed costs change

E20-22 Mi Tierra Driving School charges $200 per student to prepare and administer written and driving tests. Variable costs of $120 per student include trainers' wages, study materials, and gasoline. Annual fixed costs of $50,000 include the training facility and fleet of cars. For each of the following independent situations, calculate the contribution margin per unit and the breakeven point in units:

1. Breakeven point with no change in information. (p. 1014)
2. Decrease sale price to $180 per student. (p. 1022)
3. Decrease variable costs to $110 per student. (pp. 1022–1023)
4. Decrease fixed costs to $40,000. (p. 1023)

Compare the impact of changes in the sale price, variable costs, and fixed costs on the contribution margin per unit and the breakeven point in units.

Computing breakeven and the margin of safety

E20-23 Robbie's Repair Shop has a monthly target operating income of $12,000. Variable costs are 70% of sales, and monthly fixed costs are $9,000.

Requirements

1. Compute the monthly margin of safety in dollars if the shop achieves its income goal. (pp. 1023–1024)
2. Express Robbie's margin of safety as a percentage of target sales.

Calculating breakeven point for two product lines

E20-24 Scotty's Scooters plans to sell a standard scooter for $54 and a chrome scooter for $78. Scotty purchases the standard scooter for $36 and the chrome scooter for $50. Scotty expects to sell two standard scooters for every three chrome scooters. His monthly fixed costs are $12,000. How many of each type of scooter must Scotty sell each month to break even? To earn $6,600? (pp. 1014–1017)

Problems (Group A)

Contribution margin; sensitivity analysis; margin of safety

P20-25A Fox Club Clothiers is managed as traditionally as the button-down shirts that have made it famous. Arch Fox founded the business in 1972 and has directed operations "by the seat of his pants" ever since. Approaching retirement, he must turn over the business to his son, Ralph. Recently Arch and Ralph had this conversation:

Ralph: Dad, I am convinced that we can increase sales by advertising. I think we can spend $600 monthly on advertising and increase monthly sales by $6,000. With our contribution margin, operating income should increase by $3,000.

Arch: You know how I feel about advertising. We've never needed it in the past. Why now?

continued ...

Ralph: Two new shops have opened near us this year, and those guys are getting lots of business. I've noticed our profit margin slipping as the year has unfolded. Our margin of safety is at its lowest point ever.

Arch: Profit margin I understand, but what is the contribution margin that you mentioned? And what is this "margin of safety"?

Requirement
Explain for Arch Fox the contribution margin approach to decision making. Show how Ralph Fox computed the $3,000. (Advertising is a fixed cost.) Also, describe what Ralph means by margin of safety, and explain why the business's situation is critical. (pp. 1014–1015, 1023)

Calculating cost-volume-profit elements

P20-26A The budgets of four companies yield the following information:

	Company			
	North	East	South	West
Target sales	$703,000	$ (4)	$600,000	$ (10)
Variable costs	(1)	150,000	280,000	156,000
Fixed costs	(2)	123,000	138,000	(11)
Operating income (loss)	$ 27,200	$ (5)	$ (7)	$ 35,000
Units sold	190,000	10,000	(8)	(12)
Contribution margin per unit	$ 1.48	$ (6)	$ 100	$ 12
Contribution margin ratio	(3)	0.20	(9)	.20

Fill in the blanks for each company. Which company has the lowest breakeven point in sales dollars? What causes the low breakeven point? (pp. 1014–1017)

BE sales and sales to earn a target operating income; contribution margin income statement

P20-27A British Productions performs London shows. The average show sells 1,000 tickets at $60 per ticket. There are 120 shows a year. The average show has a cast of 60, each earning an average of $320 per show. The cast is paid after each show. The other variable cost is program-printing cost of $8 per guest. Annual fixed costs total $459,200.

Requirements
1. Compute revenue and variable costs for each show. (pp. 1008–1009)
2. Use the income statement equation approach to compute the number of shows British Productions must perform each year to break even. (p. 1014)
3. Use the contribution margin approach to compute the number of shows needed each year to earn a profit of $4,264,000. Is this profit goal realistic? Give your reason. (pp. 1014–1015)
4. Prepare British Productions' contribution margin income statement for 120 shows for 2007. Report only two categories of costs: variable and fixed. (pp. 1014–1016)

Analyzing CVP relationships

P20-28A Kincaid company sells flags with team logos. Kincaid has fixed costs of $639,600 per year plus variable costs of $4.20 per flag. Each flag sells for $12.00.

Requirements

1. Use the income statement equation approach to compute the number of flags Kincaid must sell each year to break even. (p. 1014)
2. Use the contribution margin ratio CVP formula to compute the dollar sales Kincaid needs to earn $32,500 in operating income for 2007. (p. 1016)
3. Prepare Kincaid's contribution margin income statement for the year ended December 31, 2007, for sales of 70,000 flags. Cost of goods sold is 60% of variable costs. Operating costs make up the rest of variable costs and all of fixed costs. (pp. 1015–1016)
4. The company is considering an expansion that will increase fixed costs by 20% and variable costs by 30 cents per flag. Compute the new breakeven point in units and in dollars. Should Kincaid undertake the expansion? Give your reason. (pp. 1022–1023)

Computing breakeven sales and sales needed to earn a target operating income; graphing CVP relationships; sensitivity analysis

P20-29A Big Time Investment Group is opening an office in Dallas. Fixed monthly costs are office rent ($8,100), depreciation on office furniture ($1,700), utilities ($2,000), special telephone lines ($1,000), a connection with an online brokerage service ($2,000), and the salary of a financial planner ($4,800). Variable costs include payments to the financial planner (9% of revenue), advertising (12% of revenue), supplies and postage (4% of revenue), and usage fees for the telephone lines and computerized brokerage service (5% of revenue).

Requirements

1. Use the contribution margin ratio CVP formula to compute Big Time's breakeven revenue in dollars. If the average trade leads to $700 in revenue for Big Time, how many trades must be made to break even? (pp. 1014–1015)
2. Use the income statement equation approach to compute the dollar revenues needed to earn a target monthly operating income of $9,800. (p. 1014)
3. Graph Big Time's CVP relationships. Assume that an average trade leads to $700 in revenue for Big Time. Show the breakeven point, the sales revenue line, the fixed cost line, the total cost line, the operating loss area, the operating income area, and the sales in units (trades) and dollars when monthly operating income of $9,800 is earned. The graph should range from 0 to 80 units. (pp. 1017–1023)
4. Suppose that the average revenue Big Time earns increases to $800 per trade. Compute the new breakeven point in trades. How does this affect the breakeven point? (p. 1022)

Calculating breakeven point for two product lines; margin of safety

P20-30A The contribution margin income statement of Krazy Kustard Donuts for March 2008 follows:

KRAZY KUSTARD DONUTS
Contribution Margin Income Statement
For the Month of March 2008

Sales revenue			$128,000
Variable costs:			
Costs of goods sold		$32,560	
Marketing costs		17,280	
General and administrative cost		5,402	55,242
Contribution margin			72,758
Fixed costs:			
Marketing cost		38,880	
General and administrative cost		4,320	43,200
Operating income			$ 29,558

Krazy Kustard sells 2 dozen plain donuts for every dozen custard-filled donuts. A dozen plain donuts sells for $6, with a variable cost of $2 per dozen. A dozen custard-filled donuts sells for $7, with a variable cost of $4.20 per dozen.

Requirements

1. Determine Krazy Kustard's monthly breakeven point in dozens of plain donuts and custard-filled donuts. Prove your answer by preparing a summary contribution margin income statement at the breakeven level of sales. Show only two categories of costs: variable and fixed. (pp. 1025–1027)
2. Compute Krazy Kustard's margin of safety in dollars for March 2008. (p. 1014)
3. If Krazy Kustard can increase monthly sales volume by 10%, what will operating income be? (The sales mix remains unchanged.) (p. 1017)

Problems (Group B)

Variable costs; fixed costs; BEP

P20-31B Saffron Restaurant Supply is opening early next year. The owner is considering two plans for paying her employees. Plan 1 calls for paying employees straight salaries. Under plan 2, Saffron would pay employees low salaries but give them a big part of their pay in commissions on sales. Discuss the effects of the two plans on variable costs, fixed costs, breakeven sales, and likely profits for a new business in the start-up stage. Indicate which plan you favor for Saffron.

Calculating cost-volume-profit elements

P20-32B The budgets of four companies yield the following information:

		Company			
		J	K	L	M
Target sales		$810,000	$300,000	$190,000	$ (10)
Variable costs		270,000	(4)	(7)	260,000
Fixed costs		(1)	56,000	100,000	(11)
Operating income (loss)		$ 66,000	$ (5)	$ (8)	$ 80,000
Units sold		(2)	40,000	12,000	16,000
Contribution margin per unit		$ 6	$ (6)	$ 9.50	$ 40
Contribution margin ratio		(3)	0.40	(9)	(12)

Fill in the blanks for each company. Which company has the lowest breakeven point in sales dollars? What causes the low breakeven point? (pp. 1014–1017)

BE sales and sales to earn a target operating income; contribution margin income statement

P20-33B Broadway Shows is a traveling production company that coordinates New York Broadway productions each year. The average show sells 800 tickets at $50 per ticket. There are 100 shows each year. Each show has a cast of 40, each actor earning an average of $260 per show. The cast is paid after each show. The other variable cost is program printing cost of $6 per guest. Annual fixed costs total $892,800.

Requirements
1. Compute revenue and variable costs for each show. (p. 1008)
2. Use the income statement equation approach to compute the number of shows needed annually to break even. (p. 1014)
3. Use the contribution margin approach to compute the number of shows needed annually to earn a profit of $1,438,400. Is this goal realistic? Give your reason. (p. 1014)
4. Prepare the contribution margin income statement for 100 shows performed in 2008. Report only two categories of costs: variable and fixed. (pp. 1015–1016)

Analyzing CVP relationships

P20-34B Go Spirit imprints calendars with college names. The company has fixed costs of $1,104,000 each month plus variable costs of $3.60 per carton of calendars. Go Spirit sells each carton of calendars for $10.50.

Requirements
1. Use the income statement equation approach to compute the number of cartons of calendars Go Spirit must sell each month to break even. (p. 1014)
2. Use the contribution margin ratio CVP formula to compute the dollar amount of monthly sales Go Spirit needs to earn $285,000 in operating income. (Round the contribution margin ratio to 2 decimal places.) (p. 1016)
3. Prepare Go Spirit's contribution margin income statement for June 2009 for sales of 450,000 cartons of calendars. Cost of goods sold is

continued . . .

70% of variable costs. Operating costs make up the rest of the variable costs and all of the fixed costs. (pp. 1015–1016)

4. The company is considering an expansion that will increase fixed costs by 40% and variable costs by one-fourth. Compute the new breakeven point in units and in dollars. How would this expansion affect Go Spirit's risk? Should Go Spirit expand? (pp. 1022–1023)

Computing breakeven sales and sales needed to earn a target operating income; graphing CVP relationships; sensitivity analysis

P20-35B Retirement Investors is opening an office in Denver. Fixed monthly costs are office rent ($2,500), depreciation on office furniture ($260), utilities ($380), special telephone lines ($500), a connection with an online brokerage service ($640), and the salary of a financial planner ($3,400). Variable costs include payments to the financial planner (10% of revenue), advertising (5% of revenue), supplies and postage (2% of revenue), and usage fees for the telephone lines and computerized brokerage service (3% of revenue).

Requirements

1. Use the contribution margin ratio CVP formula to compute the investment firm's breakeven revenue in dollars. If the average trade yields $400 in revenue for Retirement Investors, how many trades must be made to break even? (p. 1016)

2. Use the income statement equation approach to compute dollar revenues needed to earn monthly operating income of $3,840. (p. 1014)

3. Graph Retirement Investors' CVP relationships. Assume that an average trade yields $400 in revenue for the firm. Show the breakeven point, the sales revenue line, the fixed cost line, the total cost line, the operating loss area, the operating income area, and the sales in units (trades) and dollars when monthly operating income of $3,840 is earned. The graph should range from 0 to 40 units. (pp. 1017–1019)

4. Suppose that the average revenue Retirement Investors earns decreases to $320 per trade. How does this affect the breakeven point in number of trades? (p. 1016)

Calculating breakeven point for two product lines; margin of safety

P20-36B The contribution margin income statement of Cosmo Coffee for February 2009 follows:

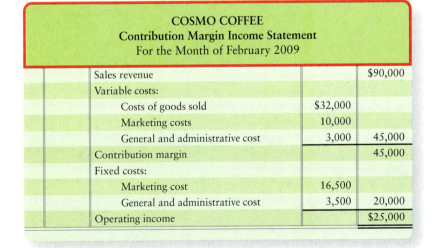

COSMO COFFEE			
Contribution Margin Income Statement			
For the Month of February 2009			
Sales revenue			$90,000
Variable costs:			
Costs of goods sold		$32,000	
Marketing costs		10,000	
General and administrative cost		3,000	45,000
Contribution margin			45,000
Fixed costs:			
Marketing cost		16,500	
General and administrative cost		3,500	20,000
Operating income			$25,000

continued . . .

Cosmo Coffee sells three small coffees for every large coffee. A small coffee sells for $2, with a variable cost of $1. A large coffee sells for $4, with a variable cost of $2.

Requirements

1. Determine Cosmo Coffee's monthly breakeven point in the numbers of small coffees and large coffees. Prove your answer by preparing a summary contribution margin income statement at the breakeven level of sales. Show only two categories of costs: variable and fixed. (pp. 1025–1026)
2. Compute Cosmo Coffee's margin of safety in dollars for February 2009. (p. 1014)
3. If Cosmo Coffee can increase monthly sales volume by 10%, what will operating income be? (The sales mix remains unchanged.) (pp. 1016–1017, 1025)

for 24/7 practice, visit www.MyAccountingLab.com

Apply Your Knowledge

Decision Cases

Case 1. Steve and Linda Hom live in Bartlesville, Oklahoma. Two years ago, they visited Thailand. Linda, a professional chef, was impressed with the cooking methods and the spices used in the Thai food. Bartlesville does not have a Thai restaurant, and the Homs are contemplating opening one. Linda would supervise the cooking, and Steve would leave his current job to be the maitre d'. The restaurant would serve dinner Tuesday through Saturday.

Steve has noticed a restaurant for lease. The restaurant has seven tables, each of which can seat four. Tables can be moved together for a large party. Linda is planning two seatings per evening, and the restaurant will be open 50 weeks per year.

The Homs have drawn up the following estimates:

Average revenue, including beverages and dessert	$ 45 per meal
Average cost of food	$ 15 per meal
Chef's and dishwasher's salaries	$ 61,200 per *year*
Rent (premises, equipment)	$4,000 per month
Cleaning (linen and premises)	$ 800 per month
Replacement of dishes, cutlery, glasses	$ 300 per month
Utilities, advertising, telephone	$2,300 per month

Requirements

Compute the *annual* breakeven number of meals and sales revenue for the restaurant. Also compute the number of meals and the amount of sales revenue needed to earn operating income of $75,600 for the year. How many meals must the Homs serve each night to earn their target income of $75,600? Should the couple open the restaurant?

Ethical Issue

You have just begun your summer internship at Omni Instruments. The company supplies sterilized surgical instruments for physicians. To expand sales, Omni is considering paying a commission to its sales force. The controller, Matthew Barnhill, asks you to compute (1) the new breakeven sales figure and (2) the operating profit if sales increase 15% under the new sales commission plan. He thinks you can handle this task because you learned CVP analysis in your accounting class.

You spend the next day collecting information from the accounting records, performing the analysis, and writing a memo to explain the results. The company president is pleased with your memo. You report that the new sales commission plan will lead to a significant increase in operating income and only a small increase in breakeven sales.

The following week, you realize that you made an error in the CVP analysis. You overlooked the sales personnel's $2,800 monthly salaries and you did not include this fixed marketing cost in your computations. You are not sure what to do. If you tell Matthew Barnhill of your mistake, he will have to tell the president. In this case, you are afraid Omni might not offer you permanent employment after your internship.

Requirements

1. How would your error affect breakeven sales and operating income under the proposed sales commission plan? Could this cause the president to reject the sales commission proposal?

2. Consider your ethical responsibilities. Is there a difference between (a) initially making an error and (b) subsequently failing to inform the controller?

3. Suppose you tell Matthew Barnhill of the error in your analysis. Why might the consequences not be as bad as you fear? Should Barnhill take any responsibility for your error? What could Barnhill have done differently?

4. After considering all the factors, should you inform Barnhill or simply keep quiet?

For Internet Exercises, Excel in Practice, and additional online activities, go to the Web site, www.prenhall.com/horngren.

Quick Check Answers

1. *b* 2. *d* 3. *a* 4. *b* 5. *d* 6. *a* 7. *b* 8. *c* 9. *a* 10. *c*

Appendix 20A

Variable Costing and Absorption Costing

Up to this point, we've focused on the income statements that companies report to the public under GAAP. GAAP requires that we assign both variable and fixed manufacturing costs to products. This approach is called **absorption costing** because products absorb both fixed and variable manufacturing costs. Supporters of absorption costing argue that companies cannot produce products without incurring fixed costs, so these costs are an important part of product costs. Financial accountants usually prefer absorption costing.

The alternate method is called variable costing. **Variable costing** assigns only variable manufacturing costs to products. Fixed costs are considered *period costs* and are *expensed immediately* because the company incurs these fixed costs whether or not it produces any products or services. In variable costing, fixed costs are not product costs. Management accountants often prefer variable costing for their planning and control decisions.

The key difference between absorption costing and variable costing is that:

- Absorption costing considers fixed manufacturing costs as inventoriable product costs
- Variable costing considers fixed manufacturing costs as period costs (expenses)

All other costs are treated the same way under both absorption and variable costing:

- Variable manufacturing costs are inventoriable products costs.
- All nonmanufacturing costs—both fixed and variable—are period costs and are expensed immediately when incurred.

Exhibit 20A-1 summarizes the difference between variable and absorption costing, with the differences shown in color.

EXHIBIT 20A-1 Differences Between Absorption Costing and Variable Costing

Type of Cost	Absorption Costing	Variable Costing
Product Costs (Capitalized as Inventory until expensed as Cost of Goods Sold)	Direct materials Direct labor Variable manufacturing overhead Fixed manufacturing overhead	Direct materials Direct labor Variable manufacturing overhead
Period Costs (Expensed in period incurred)	Variable nonmanufacturing costs Fixed nonmanufacturing costs	Fixed manufacturing overhead Variable nonmanufacturing costs Fixed nonmanufacturing costs
Income Statement Format	Conventional income statement, as in Chapters 1–17	Contribution margin income statement

Applying Variable Costing Versus Absorption Costing: Limonade

To see how absorption costing and variable costing differ, let's consider the following example. Limonade incurs the following costs for its powdered sports beverage mix in March 2009.

Direct materials cost per case	$ 8.00
Direct labor cost per case	$ 3.00
Variable manufacturing overhead cost per case	$ 2.00
Total fixed manufacturing overhead costs	$50,000
Total fixed selling and administrative costs	$25,000
Cases of powdered mix produced	10,000
Cases of powdered mix sold	8,000
Sale price per case of powdered mix	$ 25

There were no beginning inventories, so Limonade has 2,000 cases of powdered mix in ending inventory (10,000 cases produced − 8,000 cases sold).

What is Limonade's inventoriable product cost per case under absorption costing and variable costing?

	Absorption Costing	Variable Costing
Direct materials	$ 8.00	$ 8.00
Direct labor	3.00	3.00
Variable manufacturing overhead	2.00	2.00
Fixed manufacturing overhead ($50,000/10,000 cases)	5.00	
Total cost per case	$18.00	$13.00

The only difference between absorption and variable costing is that fixed manufacturing overhead is a product cost under absorption costing, but a period cost under variable costing. This is why the cost per case is $5 higher under absorption (total cost of $18) than under variable costing ($13).

Exhibit 20A-2 shows the income statements using absorption costing and variable costing. The exhibit also shows the calculation for ending inventory at March 31, 2009.

Absorption costing income is higher because of the differing treatments of fixed manufacturing cost. Look at the two ending inventory amounts:

- $36,000 under absorption costing
- $26,000 under variable costing

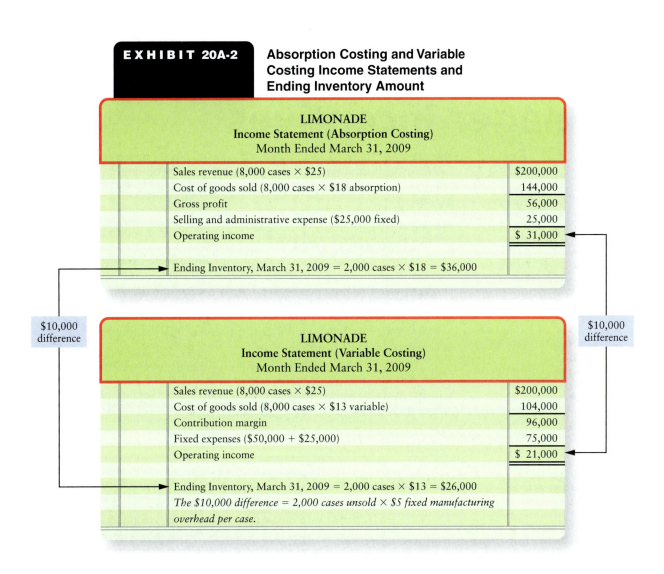

EXHIBIT 20A-2 Absorption Costing and Variable Costing Income Statements and Ending Inventory Amount

This $10,000 difference results because ending inventory under absorption costing holds $10,000 of fixed manufacturing cost that got expensed under variable costing, as follows:

Units of ending finished goods inventory		Fixed manufacturing cost per unit		Difference in ending inventory
2,000	×	$5	=	$10,000

PRODUCTION EXCEEDS SALES Limonade produced 10,000 units and sold only 8,000 units, leaving 2,000 units in ending inventory. Whenever production exceeds sales, as for Limonade, absorption costing will produce more reported income.

SALES EXCEED PRODUCTION Companies sometimes sell more units of inventory than they produced that period. How can they do that? By drawing down inventories built up in prior periods. In these situations, inventory quantities decrease, and fixed costs in the earlier inventory get expensed under variable costing. That leads to the opposite result: Variable costing will produce more reported income whenever sales exceed production.

Absorption Costing and Manager Incentives

Suppose the Limonade manager receives a bonus based on absorption costing income. Will the manager increase or decrease production? The manager knows that absorption costing assigns each case of Limonade $5 of fixed manufacturing overhead.

- For every case that is produced but not sold, absorption costing "hides" $5 of fixed overhead in ending inventory (an asset).
- The more cases added to inventory, the more fixed overhead is "hidden" in ending inventory at the end of the month.
- The more fixed overhead in ending inventory, the smaller the cost of goods sold and the higher the operating income.

To maximize the bonus under absorption costing, the manager may increase production to build up inventory.

This incentive directly conflicts with the just-in-time philosophy, which emphasizes minimal inventory levels. Companies that have adopted just-in-time should either (1) evaluate their managers based on variable costing income or (2) use strict controls to prevent inventory buildup.

Short Exercises

Variable costing income statement

S20A-37 Limonade produced 11,000 cases of powdered drink mix and sold 10,000 cases in April 2009. The sale price was $25, variable costs were $10 per case ($8 manufacturing and $2 selling and administrative), and total fixed costs were $75,000 ($55,000 manufacturing and $20,000 selling and administrative). The company had no beginning inventory. Prepare the April income statement using variable costing. (p. 1051)

Absorption costing income statement; reconciling incomes

S20A-38 Refer to Short Exercise S20A-37.
1. Prepare the April income statement under absorption costing. (p. 1051)
2. Is absorption costing income higher or lower than variable costing income? Explain why. (p. 1051)

Exercise

Variable and absorption costing; reconciling incomes

E20A-39 The 2008 data that follow pertain to Seams Company, a manufacturer of swimming goggles. (Seams had no beginning inventories in January 2008.)

Sale price	$35	Fixed manufacturing overhead	$2,000,000
Variable manufacturing cost per unit	15	Fixed operating costs	300,000
		Number of goggles produced	200,000
Sales commission cost per unit	5	Number of goggles sold	185,000

continued ...

Requirements

1. Prepare both conventional (absorption costing) and contribution margin (variable costing) income statements for Seams for the year ended December 31, 2008. (p. 1051)
2. Which statement shows the higher operating income? Why? (p. 1051)
3. Seams' marketing vice president believes a new sales promotion that costs $150,000 would increase sales to 200,000 goggles. Should the company go ahead with the promotion? Give your reason. (p. 1051)

Problems

Variable and absorption costing; reconciling incomes; production exceeds sales

P20A-40 Gia's Foods produces frozen meals, which it sells for $8 each. The company computes a new monthly fixed manufacturing overhead rate based on the planned number of meals to be produced that month. All costs and production levels are exactly as planned. The following data are from Gia's Foods' first month in business.

	January 2007
Sales	1,000 meals
Production	1,400 meals
Variable manufacturing cost per meal	$ 4
Sales commission cost per meal	$ 1
Total fixed manufacturing overhead	$700
Total fixed marketing and administrative costs	$600

Requirements

1. Compute the product cost per meal produced under absorption costing and under variable costing. (p. 1050)
2. Prepare income statements for January 2007 using
    a. Absorption costing (p. 1051)
    b. Variable costing (p. 1051)
3. Is operating income higher under absorption costing or variable costing in January? (p. 1051)

Variable and absorption costing; reconciling incomes; sales exceed production

P20A-41 Video King manufactures video games, which it sells for $40 each. The company uses a fixed manufacturing overhead rate of $4 per game. All costs and production levels are exactly as planned. The following data are from Video King's first two months in business during 2008:

	October	November
Sales	2,000 units	3,000 units
Production	2,500 units	2,500 units
Variable manufacturing cost per game	$ 15	$ 15
Sales commission per game	$ 8	$ 8
Total fixed manufacturing overhead	$10,000	$10,000
Total fixed marketing and administrative costs	$ 9,000	$ 9,000

continued . . .

Requirements

1. Compute the product cost per game produced under absorption costing and under variable costing. (p. 1050)
2. Prepare monthly income statements for November, using
    a. Absorption costing (p. 1051)
    b. Variable costing (p. 1051)
3. Is operating income higher under absorption costing or variable costing in November? Explain the pattern of differences in operating income based on absorption costing versus variable costing. (p. 1051)

Team Project

FASTPACK Manufacturing produces filament packaging tape. In 2007, FASTPACK produced and sold 15 million rolls of tape. The company has recently expanded its capacity, so it now can produce up to 30 million rolls per year. FASTPACK's accounting records show the following results from 2007:

Sale price per roll	$ 3.00
Variable manufacturing costs per roll	$ 2.00
Variable marketing and administrative costs per roll	$ 0.50
Total fixed manufacturing overhead costs	$8,400,000
Total fixed marketing and administrative costs	$1,100,000
Sales	15 million rolls
Production	15 million rolls

There were no beginning or ending inventories in 2007.

In January 2008, FASTPACK hired a new president, Kevin McDaniel. McDaniel has a one-year contract that specifies he will be paid 10% of FASTPACK's 2008 absorption costing operating income, instead of a salary. In 2008, McDaniel must make two major decisions:

- Should FASTPACK undertake a major advertising campaign? This campaign would raise sales to 24 million rolls. This is the maximum level of sales FASTPACK can expect to make in the near future. The ad campaign would add an additional $2.3 million in fixed marketing and administrative costs. Without the campaign, sales will be 15 million rolls.

- How many rolls of tape will FASTPACK produce?

At the end of the year, FASTPACK Manufacturing's Board of Directors will evaluate McDaniel's performance and decide whether to offer him a contract for the following year.

Requirements

Within your group, form two subgroups. The first subgroup assumes the role of Kevin McDaniel, FASTPACK Manufacturing's new president. The second subgroup assumes the role of FASTPACK Manufacturing's Board of Directors. McDaniel will meet with the Board of Directors shortly after the end of 2008 to decide whether he

continued . . .

will remain at FASTPACK. Most of your effort should be devoted to advance preparation for this meeting. Each subgroup should meet separately to prepare for the meeting between the Board and McDaniel. [*Hint:* Keep computations (other than per-unit amounts) in millions.]

Kevin McDaniel should:

1. Compute FASTPACK Manufacturing's 2007 operating income.

2. Decide whether to adopt the advertising campaign. Prepare a memo to the Board of Directors explaining this decision. Give this memo to the Board of Directors as soon as possible (before the joint meeting).

3. Assume FASTPACK adopts the advertising campaign. Decide how many rolls of tape to produce in 2008.

4. Given your response to Requirement 3, prepare an absorption costing income statement for the year ended December 31, 2008, ending with operating income before bonus. Then compute your bonus separately. The variable cost per unit and the total fixed costs (with the exception of the advertising campaign) remain the same as in 2007. Give this income statement and your bonus computation to the Board of Directors as soon as possible (before your meeting with the Board).

5. Decide whether you wish to remain at FASTPACK for another year. You currently have an offer from another company. The contract with the other company is identical to the one you currently have with FASTPACK—you will be paid 10% of absorption costing operating income instead of a salary.

The Board of Directors should:

1. Compute FASTPACK's 2007 operating income.

2. Determine whether FASTPACK should adopt the advertising campaign.

3. Determine how many rolls of tape FASTPACK should produce in 2008.

4. Evaluate McDaniel's performance, based on his decisions and the information he provided the Board. (*Hint:* You may want to prepare a variable costing income statement.)

5. Evaluate the contract's bonus provision. Are you satisfied with this provision? If so, explain why. If not, recommend how it should be changed.

After McDaniel has given the Board his memo and income statement, and after the Board has had a chance to evaluate McDaniel's performance, McDaniel and the Board should meet. The purpose of the meeting is to decide whether it is in their mutual interest for McDaniel to remain with FASTPACK, and if so, the terms of the contract FASTPACK will offer McDaniel.

21 Short-Term Business Decisions

Learning Objectives

1. Describe and identify information relevant to business decisions

2. Make special order and pricing decisions

3. Make dropping a product and product-mix decisions

4. Make outsourcing and sell as is or process further decisions

Most major airlines, including Delta, outsource work. In 2002, Delta announced plans to save over $15 million a year by outsourcing its reservation work to call centers in the Philippines and India. In 2005, Delta revealed plans to cut maintenance costs 34% a year by outsourcing much of its airplane maintenance to Miami- and Canadian-based firms. But why would Delta outsource so much of its work? Primarily to cut costs. Most of the major airlines are experiencing financial difficulties due to rising fuel costs and tight competition so they need to find ways to cut costs. One way is through outsourcing. Companies can save 20% or more by outsourcing call center work to English-speaking workers in developing countries.

Outsourcing also enables companies to concentrate on their core competencies—the operating activities in which they are experts. When companies focus on just their core competencies, they often outsource the activities that do not give them a competitive advantage. For example, heavy maintenance of

aircraft, which can take two to three weeks per plane, requires specialized expertise. This expertise is provided by members of the outside airline maintenance industry, which performs over half of all airline maintenance. Delta's strategy is to focus on its core competency—flying passengers—and outsource other operating activities, such as reservations and airplane maintenance, to companies who excel at those activities.

In the last chapter, we saw how managers use cost behavior to determine the company's break even point and to estimate the sales volume needed to achieve target profits. In this chapter, we'll see how managers use their knowledge of cost behavior to make six special business decisions, such as whether or not to outsource operating activities. The decisions we'll discuss in this chapter pertain to short periods of time so managers do not need to worry about the time value of money. In other words, they do not need to compute the present value of the revenues and expenses relating to the decision. In Chapter 22 we will discuss longer-term decisions (such as plant expansions) in which the time value of money becomes important. Before we look at the six business decisions in detail, let's consider a manager's decision-making process and the information managers need to evaluate their options.

How Managers Make Decisions

Exhibit 21-1 illustrates how managers make decisions among alternative courses of action. Management accountants help with the third step: gathering and analyzing *relevant information* to compare alternatives.

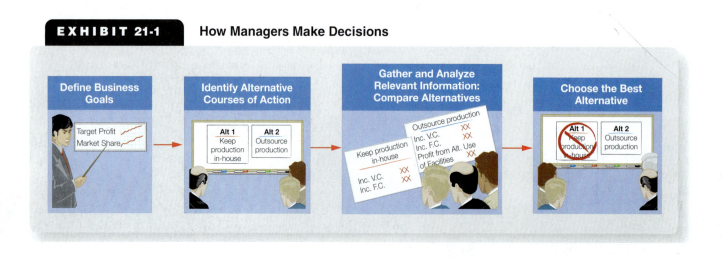

EXHIBIT 21-1 How Managers Make Decisions

Relevant Information

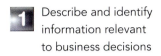 Describe and identify information relevant to business decisions

When managers make decisions, they focus on costs and revenues that are relevant to the decisions. Exhibit 21-2 shows that **relevant information** is:

1. expected *future* data that
2. *differs* among alternatives.

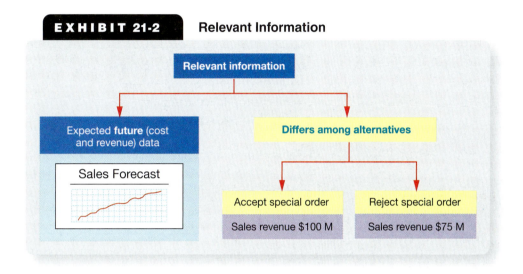

EXHIBIT 21-2 Relevant Information

Recall our discussion of relevant costs in Chapter 16. In deciding whether to purchase a Toyota Corolla or Nissan Sentra, the cost of the car, the sales tax, and the insurance premium are relevant to the decision because these costs

- are incurred in the *future* (after you decide to buy the car), and
- *differ between alternatives* (each car has a different invoice price, sales tax, and insurance premium).

These costs are *relevant* because they can affect your decision of which car to purchase.

Irrelevant costs are costs that *do not* affect your decision. For example, because the Corolla and Sentra both have similar fuel efficiency and maintenance ratings, we do not expect the car operating costs to differ between alternatives. Because these costs do not differ, they do not affect your decision. In other words, they are *irrelevant* to the decision. Similarly, the cost of a campus parking sticker is also irrelevant because the sticker costs the same whether you buy the Sentra or the Corolla.

Sunk costs are also irrelevant to your decision. Sunk costs are costs that were incurred in the *past* and cannot be changed regardless of which future action is taken. Perhaps you want to trade in your current truck when you buy your new car. The amount you paid for the truck—which you bought for $15,000 a year ago—is a sunk cost. In fact, it doesn't matter at all whether you paid $15,000 or $50,000—it's still a sunk cost. No decision made *now* can alter the past. You already bought the truck so *the price you paid for it is a sunk cost*. All you can do *now* is keep the truck, trade it in, or sell it for the best price you can get, even if that price is substantially less than what you originally paid for the truck.

What *is* relevant is what you can get for your truck in the future. Suppose that the Nissan dealership offers you $8,000 for your truck. The Toyota dealership offers you $10,000. Because the amounts differ and the transaction will take place in the future, the trade-in cost is relevant to your decision.

The same principle applies to all situations—*only relevant data affect decisions.* Let's consider another application of this general principle.

Suppose Pendleton Woolen Mills is deciding whether to use pure wool or a wool blend in a new line of sweaters. Assume Pendleton Woolen Mills predicts the following costs under the two alternatives:

	Expected Materials and Labor Cost per Sweater		
	Wool	Wool Blend	Cost Difference
Direct materials................	$10	$6	$4
Direct labor....................	2	2	0
Total cost of direct materials and direct labor........	$12	$8	$4

The cost of direct materials is relevant because this cost differs between alternatives (the wool costs $4 more than the wool blend). The labor cost is irrelevant because that cost is the same for both.

Stop & Think

You are considering replacing your Pentium IV computer with the latest model. Is the $1,200 you spent (in 2005) on the Pentium relevant to your decision about buying the new model?

Answer: The $1,200 cost of your Pentium is irrelevant. The $1,200 is a *sunk* cost that you incurred in the past so it is the same whether or not you buy the new computer.

Relevant Nonfinancial Information

Nonfinancial, or qualitative factors, also play a role in managers' decisions. For example, closing manufacturing plants and laying off employees can seriously hurt employee morale. Outsourcing can reduce control over delivery time or product quality. Offering discounted prices to select customers can upset regular customers and tempt them to take their business elsewhere. Managers must always fully consider the likely quantitative *and* qualitative effects of their decisions.

Managers who ignore qualitative factors can make serious mistakes. For example, the City of Nottingham, England, spent $1.6 million on 215 solar-powered parking meters after seeing how well the parking meters worked in countries along the Mediterranean Sea. However, they did not consider that British skies are typically overcast. The result? The meters didn't always work because of the lack of sunlight. The city *lost* money because people ended up parking free! Relevant qualitative information has the same characteristics as relevant financial information: The qualitative factor occurs in the *future* and it *differs* between alternatives. The amount of *future* sunshine required *differed* between alternatives: The mechanical meters didn't require any sunshine, but the solar-powered meters needed a lot of sunshine.

Keys to Making Short-Term Special Decisions

Our approach to making short-term special decisions is called the *relevant information approach*, or the *incremental analysis approach*. Instead of looking at the company's *entire* income statement under each decision alternative, we'll just look at how operating income would *change or differ* under each alternative. Using this approach, we'll leave out irrelevant information—the costs and revenues that won't differ between alternatives.

We'll consider six kinds of decisions in this chapter:

1. Special sales orders
2. Pricing
3. Dropping products, departments, and territories
4. Product mix
5. Outsourcing (make or buy)
6. Selling as is or processing further

As you study these decisions, keep in mind the two keys in analyzing short-term special business decisions shown in Exhibit 21-3:

1. **Focus on relevant revenues, costs, and profits.** Irrelevant information only clouds the picture and creates information overload. That's why we'll use the incremental analysis approach.

2. **Use a contribution margin approach that separates variable costs from fixed costs.** Because fixed costs and variable costs behave differently, they must be analyzed separately. Traditional (absorption costing) income statements, which blend fixed and variable costs together, can mislead managers. Contribution margin income statements, which isolate costs by behavior (variable or fixed), help managers gather the cost-behavior information they need. Keep in mind that unit manufacturing costs are mixed costs, too, so they can also mislead managers. If you use unit manufacturing costs in your analysis, be sure to first separate the cost's fixed and variable components.

We'll use these two keys in each decision.

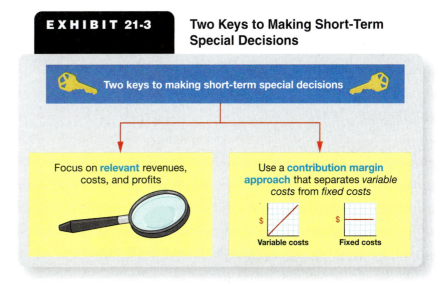

EXHIBIT 21-3 Two Keys to Making Short-Term Special Decisions

Special Sales Order and Regular Pricing Decisions

2 Make special order and pricing decisions

We'll start our discussion on the six business decisions by looking at special sales order decisions and regular pricing decisions. In the past, managers did not consider pricing to be a short-term decision. However, product life cycles are shrinking in most industries. Companies often sell products for only a few months before replacing them with an updated model. The clothing and technology industries have always had short life cycles. Even auto and housing styles change frequently. Pricing has become a shorter-term decision than it was in the past.

Let's examine a special sales order in detail, and then we will discuss regular pricing decisions.

When to Accept a Special Sales Order

A special order occurs when a customer requests a one-time order at a *reduced* sale price. Before agreeing to the special deal, management must consider the questions shown in Exhibit 21-4.

EXHIBIT 21-4   **Special Order Considerations**

- Do we have excess capacity available to fill this order?
- Will the reduced sales price be high enough to cover the *incremental* costs of filling the order (the variable costs and any additional fixed costs)?
- Will the special order affect regular sales in the long run?

First, managers must consider available capacity. If the company is already making as many units as possible and selling them all at its *regular* sales price, it wouldn't make sense to fill a special order at a *reduced* sales price. Why sell for *less* than the current sales price? Therefore, available excess capacity is almost a necessity for accepting a special order. This is true for service firms (law firms, hair salons, and so forth) as well as manufacturers.

Second, managers need to consider whether the special reduced sales price is high enough to cover the incremental costs of filling the order. The special price *must* exceed the variable costs of filling the order or the company will lose money on the deal. In other words, the special order must provide a positive contribution margin. Next, the company must consider fixed costs. If the company has excess capacity, fixed costs probably won't be affected by producing more units (or delivering more service). However, in some cases, management may have to incur some other fixed cost to fill the special order. If so, they'll need to consider whether the special sales price is high enough to generate a positive contribution margin *and* cover the additional fixed costs.

Finally, managers need to consider whether the special order will affect regular sales in the long run. Will regular customers find out about the special order and demand a lower price or take their business elsewhere? Will the special order customer come back *again and again*, asking for the same reduced price? Will the special order price start a price war with competitors? Managers should determine that the answers to these questions are "no" or consider how customers will respond. Managers may decide that any profit from the special sales order is not worth these risks.

Let's consider a special sales order example. Suppose ACDelco sells oil filters for $3.20 each. Assume that a mail-order company has offered ACDelco $35,000 for 20,000 oil filters, or $1.75 per filter ($35,000 ÷ 20,000 = $1.75). This sale:

- Will use manufacturing capacity that would otherwise be idle
- Will not change fixed costs
- Will not require any variable *nonmanufacturing* expenses (because no extra marketing costs are incurred with this special order)
- Will not affect regular sales

We have addressed every consideration except one: Is the special sales price high enough to cover the variable *manufacturing* costs associated with the order? Let's first take a look at the *wrong* way and then the *right* way to figure out the answer to this question.

Suppose ACDelco made and sold 250,000 oil filters before considering the special order. Using the traditional (absorption costing) income statement on the left-hand side of Exhibit 21-5, the manufacturing cost per unit is $2.00 ($500,000 ÷ 250,000). A manager who does not examine these numbers carefully may believe that ACDelco should *not* accept the special order at a sale price of $1.75 because each oil filter costs $2.00 to manufacture. But appearances can be deceiving! Remember that the unit manufacturing cost of a product ($2.00) is a *mixed* cost, containing both fixed and variable cost components. To correctly answer our question, we need to find only the *variable* portion of the manufacturing unit cost.

EXHIBIT 21-5 Traditional (Absorption Costing) Format and Contribution Margin Format Income Statements

INCOME STATEMENT
(at a production and sales level of 250,000 units)
Year Ended December 31, 2007

Traditional (Absorption Costing) Format			Contribution Margin Format			
Sales revenue		$800,000	Sales revenue			$800,000
Less cost of goods sold		(500,000)	Less variable expenses:			
Gross profit		300,000	Manufacturing		$(300,000)	
Less marketing and administrative expenses		(200,000)	Marketing and administrative		(75,000)	(375,000)
			Contribution margin			425,000
			Less fixed expenses:			
			Manufacturing		$(200,000)	
			Marketing and administrative		(125,000)	(325,000)
Operating income		$100,000	Operating income			$100,000

The right-hand side of Exhibit 21-5 shows the contribution margin income statement that separates variable expenses from fixed expenses. The contribution margin income statement allows us to see that the *variable* manufacturing cost per unit is only $1.20 ($300,000 ÷ 250,000). The special sales price of $1.75 is *higher* than the variable manufacturing cost of $1.20. Therefore, the special order will provide a positive contribution margin of $0.55 per unit ($1.75 − $1.20). Since the special order is for 20,000 units, ACDelco's total contribution margin should increase by $11,000 (20,000 units × $0.55 per unit) if it accepts this order.

Using an incremental analysis approach, ACDelco compares the additional revenues from the special order with the incremental expenses to see if the special order will contribute to profits. Exhibit 21-6 shows that the special sales order will increase revenue by $35,000 (20,000 × $1.75), but will also increase variable manufacturing cost by $24,000 (20,000 × $1.20). As a result, ACDelco's contribution margin will increase by $11,000, as previously anticipated. The other costs seen in Exhibit 21-5 are irrelevant. Variable marketing and administrative expenses will be the same whether or not ACDelco accepts the special order, because ACDelco made no special efforts to get this sale. Fixed manufacturing expenses won't change because ACDelco has enough idle capacity to produce 20,000 extra oil filters without requiring additional facilities. Fixed marketing and administrative expenses won't be affected by this special order either. Because there are no additional fixed costs, the total increase in contribution margin flows directly to operating income. As a result, the special sales order will increase operating income by $11,000.

EXHIBIT 21-6 | Incremental Analysis of Special Sales Order

Expected increase in revenues—sale of 20,000 oil filters × $1.75 each	$ 35,000
Expected increase in expenses—variable manufacturing costs:	
20,000 oil filters × $1.20 each	(24,000)
Expected increase in operating income	$ 11,000

Notice that the analysis follows the two keys to making short-term special business decisions discussed earlier: (1) Focus on relevant data (revenues and costs that *will change* if ACDelco accepts the special order) and (2) use of a contribution margin approach that separates variable costs from fixed costs.

To summarize, for special sales orders, the decision rule is:

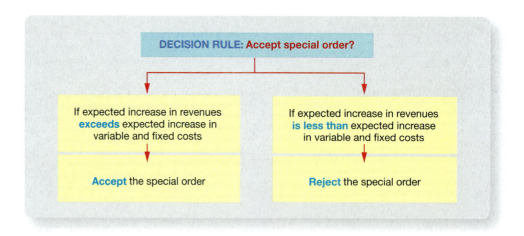

Stop & Think

The absorption costing income statement on the left-hand side of Exhibit 21-5 shows that the total cost of manufacturing 250,000 filters is $500,000. What is the flaw in reasoning that ACDelco should accept special orders only if the sale price exceeds $2.00 each?

Answer: The flaw in this analysis arises from treating a fixed cost as though it changes in total like a variable cost does. Manufacturing one extra oil filter will only cost $1.20—the variable manufacturing cost. Fixed expenses are irrelevant because ACDelco will incur $200,000 of fixed manufacturing overhead expenses whether or not the company accepts the special order. Producing 20,000 more oil filters will not increase *total* fixed expenses so manufacturing costs increase at the rate of $1.20 per unit, not $2.00 per unit.

How to Set Regular Prices

In the special order decision, ACDelco decided to sell a limited quantity of oil filters for $1.75 each, even though the normal price was $3.20 per unit. But how did ACDelco decide to set its regular price at $3.20 per filter? Exhibit 21-7 shows that managers start with three basic questions when setting regular prices for their products or services.

EXHIBIT 21-7 | Regular Pricing Considerations

- What is our target profit?
- How much will customers pay?
- Are we a price-taker or a price-setter for this product?

The answers to these questions are often complex and ever-changing. Stockholders expect the company to achieve certain profits. Economic conditions, historical company earnings, industry risk, competition, and new business developments all affect the level of profit that stockholders' expect. Stockholders usually tie their profit expectations to the amount of assets invested in the company. For example, stockholders may expect a 10% annual return on their investment. A company's stock price tends to decline if it does not meet target profits, so managers must keep costs low while generating enough revenue to meet target profits.

This leads to the second question: How much will customers pay? Managers cannot set prices above what customers are willing to pay or sales will decline. The amount customers will pay depends on the competition, the product's uniqueness, the effectiveness of marketing campaigns, general economic conditions, and so forth.

To address the third pricing question, imagine a continuum with price-takers at one end and price-setters at the other end. A company's products and services fall somewhere along this continuum, shown in Exhibit 21-8. Companies are price-takers when they have little or no control over the prices of their products or services. This occurs when their products and services are *not* unique or when competition is intense. Examples include food commodities (milk and corn), natural resources (oil and lumber), and generic consumer products and services (paper towels, dry cleaning, and banking).

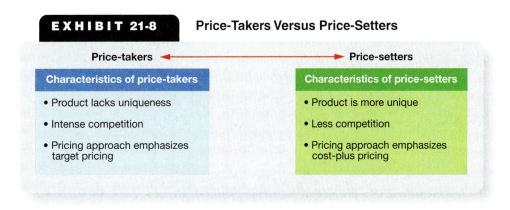

EXHIBIT 21-8 | Price-Takers Versus Price-Setters

Companies are price-setters when they have more control over pricing—in other words, they can "set" the price to some extent. Companies are price-setters when their products are unique, which results in less competition. Unique products, such as original art and jewelry, specially manufactured machinery, patented perfume scents, and custom-made furniture, can command higher prices.

Obviously, managers would rather be price-setters than price-takers. To gain more control over pricing, companies try to differentiate their products. They want to make their products unique, in terms of features, service, or quality, or at least make you *think* their product is unique or somehow better—companies achieve this differentiation through their advertising efforts. Consider Nike's tennis shoes,

Starbucks' coffee, Hallmark's wrapping paper, Nexus's shampoo, Tylenol's acetaminophen, General Mills' cereal, Capital One's credit cards, Shell's gas, Abercrombie and Fitch's jeans—the list goes on and on. Are these products really better or significantly different from their lower-priced competitors? Possibly. If these companies can make customers believe that this is true so, they've gained more control over their pricing because customers are willing to pay *more* for their product or service. The downside? These companies must charge higher prices or sell more just to cover their advertising costs.

A company's approach to pricing depends on whether its product or service is on the price-taking or price-setting side of the spectrum. Price-takers emphasize a target-pricing approach. Price-setters emphasize a cost-plus pricing approach. Keep in mind that many products fall somewhere along the continuum. Therefore, managers tend to use both approaches to some extent. We'll now discuss each approach in turn.

Target Pricing

When a company is a price-taker, it emphasizes a target pricing approach to pricing. Target pricing starts with the market price of the product (the price customers are willing to pay) and then subtracts the company's desired profit to determine the product's **target full cost**—the *full* cost to develop, produce, and deliver the product or service.

> Revenue at market price
> Less: Desired profit
> Target full cost

In this relationship, the market price is "taken." Recall from Chapter 16 that a product's *full* cost contains all elements from the value chain—both inventoriable costs and period costs. It also includes both fixed and variable costs. If the product's current cost is higher than the target cost, the company must find ways to reduce costs or it will not meet its profit goals. Managers often use ABC costing along with value engineering (as discussed in Chapter 19) to find ways to cut costs. Let's look at an example of target pricing.

Let's assume that oil filters are a commodity, and that the current market price is $3.00 per filter (not the $3.20 sales price assumed in the earlier ACDelco example). Because the oil filters are a commodity, ACDelco will emphasize a target-pricing approach. Let's assume ACDelco's stockholders expect a 10% annual return on the company's assets. If the company has $1,000,000 of assets, the desired profit is $100,000 ($1,000,000 × 10%). Exhibit 21-9 calculates the target full cost at the current sales volume (250,000 units). Once we know the target full cost, we can analyze the fixed and variable cost components separately.

EXHIBIT 21-9 Calculating Target Full Cost

	Calculations	Total
Revenue at market price	250,000 units × $3.00 price =	$750,000
Less: Desired profit	10% × $1,000,000 of assets	(100,000)
Target full cost		$650,000

Can ACDelco make and sell 250,000 oil filters at a full cost of $650,000? We know from ACDelco's contribution margin income statement (Exhibit 21-5) that the company's variable costs are $1.50 per unit ($375,000 ÷ 250,000 units). This variable cost per unit includes both manufacturing costs ($1.20 per unit) and marketing and administrative costs ($0.30 per unit). We also know the company incurs $325,000 in fixed costs in its current relevant range. Again, some fixed cost stems from manufacturing and some from marketing and administrative activities. *In setting regular sales prices, companies must cover **all** of their costs—whether inventoriable or period, fixed or variable.*

Making and selling 250,000 filters currently costs the company $700,000 [(250,000 units × $1.50 variable cost per unit) + $325,000 of fixed costs], which is more than the target full cost ($650,000). So, what are ACDelco's options?

1. Accept a lower profit (an operating income of $50,000, which is a 5% return, not the 10% target return)
2. Reduce fixed costs
3. Reduce variable costs
4. Use other strategies. For example, ACDelco could attempt to increase sales volume. Recall that the company has excess capacity so making and selling more units would only affect variable costs. The company could also consider changing or adding to its product mix. Finally, it could attempt to differentiate its oil filters from the competition to gain more control over sales prices.

Let's look at some of these options. ACDelco may first try to cut fixed costs. As shown in Exhibit 21-10, the company would have to reduce fixed costs to $275,000 to meet its target profit level.

EXHIBIT 21-10 Calculating Target Fixed Cost

	Calculations	Total
Target full cost		$650,000
Less: Current variable costs	250,000 units × $1.50	(375,000)
Target fixed cost		$275,000

If the company can't reduce its fixed costs by $50,000 ($325,000 current fixed costs − $275,000 target fixed costs), it would have to lower its variable cost to $1.30 per unit, as shown in Exhibit 21-11.

EXHIBIT 21-11 Calculating Target Unit Variable Cost

	Total
Target full cost	$650,000
Less: Current fixed costs	(325,000)
Target total variable costs	$325,000
Divided by number of units	÷ 250,000
Target variable cost per unit	$ 1.30

If ACDelco can't reduce variable costs to that level either, could it meet its target profit through a combination of lowering both fixed costs and variable costs?

Stop & Think

Suppose ACDelco can reduce its current fixed costs but only by $25,000. If it wants to meet its target profit, by how much will it have to reduce the variable cost of each unit? Assume sales volume remains at 250,000 units.

Answer: Companies typically try to cut both fixed and variable costs. Because ACDelco can only cut its fixed costs by $25,000, to meet its target profit, it would have to cut its variable costs as well:

	Total
Target full cost	$650,000
Less: Reduced fixed costs ($325,000 − $25,000)	(300,000)
Target total variable costs	$350,000
Divided by number of units	÷250,000
Target variable cost per unit	$1.40

In addition to lowering its fixed costs by $25,000, the company must reduce its variable costs by $0.10 per unit ($1.50 − $1.40) to meet its target profit at the existing volume of sales.

Another strategy would be to increase sales. ACDelco's managers can use CVP analysis, as you learned in Chapter 20, to figure out how many oil filters the company would have to sell to achieve its target profit. How could the company increase demand for the oil filters? Perhaps it could reach new markets or advertise. How much would advertising cost—and how many extra oil filters would the company have to sell to cover the cost of advertising? These are only some of the questions managers must ask. As you can see, managers don't have an easy task when the current cost exceeds the target full cost. Sometimes companies just can't compete given the current market price. If that's the case, they may have no other choice than to exit the market for that product.

Cost-Plus Pricing

When a company is a price-setter, it emphasizes a cost-plus approach to pricing. This pricing approach is essentially the *opposite* of the target-pricing approach. Cost-plus pricing starts with the company's full costs (as a given) and *adds* its desired profit to determine a cost-plus price.

> Full cost
> Plus: Desired profit
> Cost-plus price

When the product is unique, the company has more control over pricing. The company still needs to make sure that the cost-plus price is not higher than what customers are willing to pay. Let's go back to our original ACDelco example. This time, let's say the oil filters benefit from brand recognition so the company has some control over the price it charges for its filters. Exhibit 21-12 takes a cost-plus pricing approach, assuming the current level of sales:

If the current market price for generic oil filters is $3.00, as we assumed earlier, can ACDelco sell its brand-name filters for $3.20 apiece? The answer depends on how well the company has been able to differentiate its product or brand name. The company may use focus groups or marketing surveys to find out how customers would respond to its cost-plus price. The company may find out that its cost-plus

EXHIBIT 21-12 — Calculating Cost-Plus Price

	Calculations	Total
Current variable costs	250,000 units × $1.50 per unit =	$375,000
Plus: Current fixed costs		+ 325,000
Full product cost		$700,000
Plus: Desired profit	10% × $1,000,000 of assets	+ 100,000
Target revenue		$800,000
Divided by number of units		÷ 250,000
Cost-plus price per unit		$ 3.20

price is too high, or it may find that it could set the price even higher without jeopardizing sales.

Stop & Think

Which costing systems (job costing or process costing) do you think price-setters and price-takers typically use?

Answer: Companies tend to be price-setters when their products are unique. Unique products are produced as single items or in small batches. Therefore, these companies use job costing to determine the product's cost. However, companies are price-takers when their products are high-volume commodities. Process costing better suits this type of product.

Notice how pricing decisions used our two keys to decision making: (1) focus on relevant information and (2) use a contribution margin approach that separates variable costs from fixed costs. In pricing decisions, all cost information is relevant because the company must cover *all* costs along the value chain before it can generate a profit. However, we still needed to consider variable costs and fixed costs separately because they behave differently at different volumes.

Our pricing decision rule is:

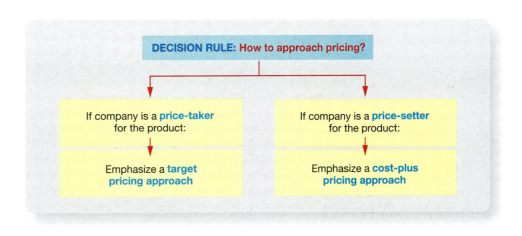

Decision Guidelines

RELEVANT INFORMATION FOR BUSINESS DECISIONS

Nike makes special order and regular pricing decisions. Even though it sells mass-produced tennis shoes and sport clothing, Nike has differentiated its products with advertising. Nike's managers consider both quantitative and qualitative factors as they make pricing decisions. Here are key guidelines Nike's managers follow in making their decisions.

Decision	Guideline
What information is relevant to a short-term special business decision?	Relevant data: 1. Are expected *future* data 2. *Differ* between alternatives
What are two key guidelines in making short-term special business decisions?	1. Focus on *relevant* data 2. Use a *contribution margin* approach that separates variable costs from fixed costs
Should Nike accept a lower sale price than the regular price for a large order from a customer in São Paulo, Brazil?	If the revenue from the order exceeds the extra variable and fixed costs incurred to fill the order, then accepting the order will increase operating income.
What should Nike consider in setting its regular product prices?	Nike considers: 1. The profit stockholders expect it to make 2. The price customers will pay 3. Whether it is a price-setter or a price-taker
What approach should Nike take to pricing?	Nike has differentiated its products by advertising. Thus, Nike tends to be a price-setter. Nike's managers can emphasize a cost-plus approach to pricing.
What approach should discount shoe stores, such as Payless Shoes, take to pricing?	Payless Shoes sells generic shoes (no-name brands) at low prices. Payless is a price-taker so managers use a target-pricing approach to pricing.

Summary Problem 1

Szigety Industries makes tennis balls. Szigety Industries' only plant can produce up to 2.5 million cans of balls per year. Current production is 2 million cans. Annual manufacturing, selling, and administrative fixed costs total $700,000. The variable cost of making and selling each can of balls is $1.00. Stockholders expect a 12% annual return on the company's $3 million of assets.

Requirements

1. What is Szigety's current full cost of making and selling 2 million cans of tennis balls? What is the current full *unit* cost of each can of tennis balls?
2. Assume Szigety is a price-taker, and the current market price is $1.45 per can of balls (this is the price at which manufacturers sell to retailers). What is the *target* full cost of producing and selling 2 million cans of balls? Given Szigety Industries' current costs, will the company reach stockholders' profit goals?
3. If Szigety cannot change its fixed costs, what is the target variable cost per can of balls?
4. Suppose Szigety could spend an extra $100,000 on advertising to differentiate its product so that it could be a price-setter. Assuming the original volume and costs, plus the $100,000 of new advertising costs, what cost-plus price will Szigety want to charge for a can of balls?
5. Nike has just asked Szigety to supply them with 400,000 cans of balls at a special order price of $1.20 per can. Nike wants Szigety to package the balls under the Nike label (Szigety will imprint the Nike logo on each ball and can). Szigety will have to spend $10,000 to change the packaging machinery. Assuming the original volume and costs, should Szigety Industries accept this special order? (Unlike the chapter problem, assume Szigety will incur variable selling costs as well as variable manufacturing costs related to this order)

Solutions

Requirement 1
The full unit cost is:

Fixed costs	$700,000
Plus: Total variable costs (2 million cans × $1.00 per unit)	+ 2,000,000
Total full costs	$2,700,000
Divided by number of cans	÷ 2,000,000
Full cost per can	$1.35

Requirement 2
The target full cost is:

	Calculations	Total
Revenue at market price	2,000,000 units × $1.45 price =	$2,900,000
Less: Desired profit	12% × $3,000,000 of assets	(360,000)
Target *full* cost		$2,540,000

Szigety's current total full costs ($2,700,000 from Requirement 1) are $160,000 higher than the target full cost ($2,540,000). If Szigety can't reduce costs, it won't be able to meet stockholders' profit expectations.

Requirement 3
Assuming Szigety cannot reduce its fixed costs, the target variable cost per can is:

	Total
Target *full* cost (from Requirement 2)	$2,540,000
Less: Fixed costs	(700,000)
Target total variable cost	$1,840,000
Divided by number of units	÷2,000,000
Target variable cost per unit	$0.92

Since Szigety cannot reduce its fixed costs, it needs to reduce variable costs by $0.08 per can ($1.00 − $0.92) to meet its profit goals. This would require an 8% cost reduction, which may not be possible.

Requirement 4
If Szigety can differentiate its tennis balls, it will gain more control over pricing. The company's new cost-plus price would be:

Current total costs (from Requirement 1)	$2,700,000
Plus: Additional cost of advertising	+100,000
Plus: Desired profit (from Requirement 2)	+360,000
Target revenue	$3,160,000
Divided by number of units	÷2,000,000
Cost-plus price per unit	$1.58

Szigety must study the market to determine whether retailers would pay $1.58 per can of balls.

Requirement 5
Nike's special order price ($1.20) is less than the current full cost of each can of balls ($1.35 from Requirement 1). However, this should not influence management's decision. Szigety could fill Nike's special order using existing excess capacity. Szigety takes an incremental analysis approach to its decision: comparing the extra revenue with the incremental costs of accepting the order. Variable costs will increase if Szigety accepts the order so the variable costs are relevant. Only the *additional* fixed costs of changing the packaging machine ($10,000) are relevant since all other fixed costs will remain unchanged.

Revenue from special order (400,000 × $1.20 per unit)	$480,000
Less: Variable cost of special order (400,000 × $1.00)	(400,000)
Contribution margin from special order	$ 80,000
Less: Additional fixed costs of special order	(10,000)
Operating income provided by special order	$ 70,000

Szigety should accept the special order because it will increase operating income by $70,000. However, Szigety also needs to consider whether its regular customers will find out about the special price and demand lower prices too.

Other Short-Term Special Business Decisions

In the second part of the chapter, we'll look at other short-term business decisions that managers face, including:

- When to drop a product, department, or territory
- Which products to emphasize
- When to outsource
- When to sell as is or process further

When to Drop Products, Departments, or Territories

3 Make dropping a product and product-mix decisions

Managers must often decide whether to drop products, departments, or territories that are not as profitable as desired. Newell Rubbermaid—maker of Sharpie markers, Graco strollers, and Rubbermaid plastics—recently dropped some of its European products lines. Home Depot closed some of its Expo Stores. Kroger food stores replaced some in-store movie rental departments with health food departments. How do managers make these decisions? Exhibit 21-13 shows some questions managers must consider when deciding whether to drop a product line, department, or territory.

EXHIBIT 21-13 Considerations for Dropping Products, Departments, or Territories

- Does the product provide a positive contribution margin?
- Will fixed costs continue to exist, even if we drop the product?
- Are there any direct fixed costs that can be avoided if we drop the product?
- Will dropping the product affect sales of the company's other products?
- What could we do with the freed capacity?

Once again, we follow the two key guidelines for special business decisions: (1) focus on relevant data and (2) use a contribution margin approach. The relevant financial data are still the changes in revenues and expenses, but now we are considering a *decrease* in volume rather than an *increase*, as we did in the special sales order decision. In the following example, we will consider how managers decide to drop a product. Managers would use the same process in deciding whether to drop a department or territory.

Earlier, we assumed that ACDelco offered only one product—oil filters. Now let's assume it makes and sells air cleaners too. Exhibit 21-14 shows the company's contribution margin income statement by product line. Because the air cleaner product line has an operating *loss* of $19,074, management is considering dropping the line.

The first question management should ask is "Does the product provide a positive contribution margin?" If the product line has a negative contribution margin, then the product is not even covering its variable costs. Therefore, the company should drop the product line. However, if the product line has a positive contribution margin, then it is *helping* to cover at least some of the company's fixed costs. In ACDelco's case, the air cleaners provide a $5,000 positive contribution margin. ACDelco's managers now need to consider fixed costs.

EXHIBIT 21-14 — Contribution Margin Income Statements by Product Line

	Total (270,000 units)	Product Line Oil Filters (250,000 units)	Product Line Air Cleaners (20,000 units)
Sales revenue	$835,000	$800,000	$ 35,000
Less: Variable expenses	(405,000)	(375,000)	(30,000)
Contribution margin	430,000	425,000	5,000
Less: Fixed expenses:			
Manufacturing	(200,000)	(185,185)*	(14,815)†
Marketing and administrative	(125,000)	(115,741)†	(9,259)†
Total fixed expenses	(325,000)	(300,926)	(24,074)
Operating income (loss)	$105,000	$124,074	$(19,074)

* $200,000 ÷ 270,000 units = $0.74074 per unit; 250,000 units × $0.74074 = $185,185; 20,000 units × $0.74074 = $14,815
† $125,000 ÷ 270,000 units = $0.462963 per unit; 250,000 units × $0.462963 = $115,741; 20,000 units × $0.462963 = $9,259

Suppose ACDelco allocates fixed expenses between product lines in proportion to the number of units sold. Dividing the fixed manufacturing expense of $200,000 by 270,000 total units (oil filters, 250,000; air cleaners, 20,000) yields a fixed manufacturing cost of $0.74074 per unit. Allocating this unit cost to the 250,000 oil filters assigns fixed manufacturing cost of $185,185 to this product, as shown in Exhibit 21-14. The same procedure allocates $14,815 to the 20,000 air cleaners. Fixed marketing and administrative expenses are allocated in the same manner.

It is important to note that this allocation method is arbitrary. ACDelco could allocate fixed costs in many different ways, and each way would have allocated a different amount of fixed costs to each product line. Therefore, allocated fixed costs are *irrelevant* because they are arbitrary in amount. What is relevant is:

1. Will the fixed costs continue to exist *even if* the product line is dropped?
2. Are there any *direct* fixed costs of the air cleaners that can be avoided if the product line is dropped?

Fixed Costs Continue to Exist and Will Not Change

Fixed costs that will continue to exist even after a product is dropped are often called unavoidable fixed costs. Unavoidable fixed costs are *irrelevant* to the decision because they *will not change* if the company drops the product line—they will be incurred either way. Let's assume that all of ACDelco's fixed costs ($325,000) will continue to exist even if the company drops the air cleaners. Perhaps ACDelco makes the air cleaners in the same plant using the same machinery as the oil filters. If this is the case, only the contribution margin the air cleaners provide is relevant. If ACDelco drops the air cleaners, it will lose the $5,000 contribution margin.

The incremental analysis shown in Exhibit 21-15 verifies the loss. If ACDelco drops the air cleaners, revenue will decrease by $35,000, but variable expenses will decrease by only $30,000, resulting in a net $5,000 decrease in operating income. Because fixed costs are unaffected, they aren't included in the analysis. This analysis suggests that management should *not* drop air cleaners.

Direct Fixed Costs That Can Be Avoided

Even though ACDelco allocates its fixed costs between product lines, some of the fixed costs might *belong* only to the air cleaner product line. These would be direct

EXHIBIT 21-15   **Incremental Analysis for Dropping a Product When Fixed Costs Will *Not* Change**

Expected decrease in revenues:	
Sale of air cleaners (20,000 × $1.75)	$35,000
Expected decrease in expenses:	
Variable manufacturing expenses (20,000 × $1.50)	30,000
Expected *decrease* in operating income	$ (5,000)

fixed costs of the air cleaners.[1] For example, suppose ACDelco employs a part-time foreman to oversee *just* the air cleaner product line. The foreman's $13,000 salary is a direct fixed cost that ACDelco can *avoid* if it stops producing air cleaners. Avoidable fixed costs, such as the foreman's salary, *are relevant* to the decision because they would change (go away) if the product line is dropped.

Exhibit 21-16 shows that in this situation, operating income will *increase* by $8,000 if ACDelco drops air cleaners. Why? Because revenues will decline by $35,000 but expenses will decline even more—by $43,000. The result is a net increase to operating income of $8,000. This analysis suggests that management should drop air cleaners.

EXHIBIT 21-16   **Incremental Analysis for Dropping a Product When Direct Fixed Costs Can be Avoided**

Expected decrease in revenues:		
Sale of air cleaners (20,000 × $1.75)		$35,000
Expected decrease in expenses:		
Variable manufacturing expenses (20,000 × $1.50)	$30,000	
Fixed expenses—foreman's salary	13,000	
Expected decrease in total expenses		43,000
Expected *increase* in operating income		$ 8,000

Other Considerations

Management must also consider whether dropping the product line, department, or territory would hurt other sales. In the examples given so far, we assumed that dropping the air cleaners would not affect oil filter sales. However, think about a grocery store. Even if the produce department is not profitable, would managers drop it? Probably not, because if they did, they would lose customers who want one-stop shopping. In such situations, managers must also include the loss of contribution margin from *other* departments affected by the change when deciding whether or not to drop a department.

Management should also consider what they could do with freed capacity. In the ACDelco example, we assumed that it produces both oil filters and air cleaners using the same manufacturing equipment. If ACDelco drops the air cleaners, could it make and sell another product using the freed machine hours? Managers should

---

[1] To aid in decision making, companies should separate direct fixed costs from indirect fixed costs on their contribution margin income statements. Companies should *trace direct fixed costs* to the appropriate product line and only *allocate indirect fixed costs* among product lines. As in the ACDelco example, companies do not always make this distinction on the income statement.

consider whether using the machinery to produce a different product would be more profitable than using the machinery to produce air cleaners.

Stop & Think

Assume all of ACDelco's *current* fixed costs are unavoidable. If the company drops air cleaners, they could make spark plugs with the freed capacity. The company expects spark plugs would provide $50,000 of sales, incur $30,000 of variable costs, and incur $10,000 of new direct fixed costs. Should ACDelco drop the air cleaners and use the freed capacity to make spark plugs?

Answer: If all fixed costs are unavoidable, we saw that ACDelco would lose $5,000 of contribution margin if it dropped air cleaners. ACDelco should compare this loss with the expected gain from producing and selling spark plugs with the freed capacity:

Sales of spark plugs	$50,000
Less: Variable costs of spark plugs	(30,000)
Less: Direct fixed costs of spark plugs	(10,000)
Operating income gained from spark plugs	$10,000

The gain from producing spark plugs ($10,000) outweighs the loss from dropping air cleaners ($5,000). This suggests that management should replace air cleaner production with spark plug production.

Special decisions should take into account all costs affected by the choice of action. Managers must ask: What total costs—variable and fixed—will change? As Exhibits 21-15 and 21-16 show, the key to deciding whether to drop products, departments, or territories is to compare the lost revenue against the costs that can be saved and to consider what would be done with the freed capacity. The decision rule is:

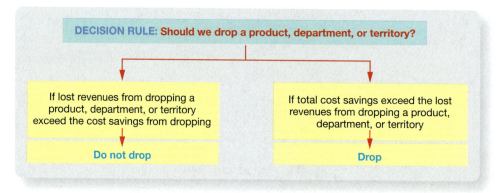

Product Mix: Which Product to Emphasize?

Companies do not have unlimited resources. **Constraints** that restrict production or sale of a product vary from company to company. For a manufacturer like Dell, the production constraint may be labor hours, machine hours, or available materials. For a merchandiser like Wal-Mart, the primary constraint is cubic feet of display space. Other companies are constrained by sales demand. Competition may be stiff, and so the company may be able to sell only a limited number of units. In such cases, the company produces only as much as it can sell. However, if a company can sell all the units it can produce, which products should it emphasize? For which items should production be increased? Companies facing constraints consider the questions shown in Exhibit 21-17.

Consider Chazz, a manufacturer of shirts and jeans. The company can sell all the shirts and jeans it produces, but it only has 2,000 machine hours of capacity.

EXHIBIT 21-17 Product Mix Considerations

- What constraint(s) stops us from making (or displaying) all the units we can sell?
- Which products offer the highest contribution margin per unit of the constraint?
- Would emphasizing one product over another affect fixed costs?

The company uses the same machines to produce both jeans and shirts. In this case, machine hours is the constraint. Note that this is a short-term decision because in the long run, Chazz could expand its production facilities to meet sales demand, if it made financial sense to do so. The following data suggest that shirts are more profitable than jeans:

	Per Unit	
	Shirts	**Jeans**
Sale price...	$30	$60
Less: Variable expenses.............................	(12)	(48)
Contribution margin	$18	$12
Contribution margin ratio:		
Shirts—$18 ÷ $30	60%	
Jeans—$12 ÷ $60		20%

However, an important piece of information is missing—the time it takes to make each product. Let's assume Chazz can produce either 20 pairs of jeans *or* 10 shirts per machine hour. *The company will incur the same fixed costs either way so fixed costs are irrelevant.* Which product should it emphasize?

To maximize profits when fixed costs are irrelevant, follow the decision rule:

DECISION RULE: Which product to emphasize?

Emphasize the product with the **highest contribution margin per unit of the constraint.**

Because *machine hours* is the constraint, Chazz needs to figure out which product has the *highest contribution margin per machine hour*. Exhibit 21-18 determines the contribution margin per machine hour for each product.

EXHIBIT 21-18 Product Mix—Which Product to Emphasize

	Shirts	Jeans
(1) Units that can be produced each machine hour	10	20
(2) Contribution margin per unit	× $18	× $12
Contribution margin per machine hour (1) × (2)	$180	$240
Available capacity—number of machine hours	× 2,000	× 2,000
Total contribution margin at full capacity	$360,000	$480,000

Jeans have a higher contribution margin per machine hour ($240 = 20 pairs of jeans per hour × $12 per pair) than shirts ($180 = 10 shirts per hour × $18 per shirt). Chazz will earn more profit by producing jeans. Why? Because even though jeans have a lower contribution margin *per unit*, Chazz can make twice as many jeans as shirts in the available machine hours. Exhibit 21-18 also proves that Chazz earns more total profit by making jeans. Multiplying the contribution margin per machine hour by the available number of machine hours shows that Chazz can earn $480,000 of contribution margin by producing jeans, but only $360,000 by producing shirts.

To maximize profit, Chazz should make 40,000 jeans (2,000 machine hours × 20 jeans per hour) and zero shirts. Why zero shirts? Because for every machine hour spent making shirts, Chazz would *give up* $60 of contribution margin ($240 per hour for jeans versus $180 per hour for shirts).

We made two assumptions here: (1) Chazz's sales of other products, if any, won't be hurt by this decision and (2) Chazz can sell as many jeans as it can produce. Let's challenge these assumptions. First, How could making only jeans hurt sales of other products. Using other production equipment, Chazz also makes ties and knit sweaters that coordinate with their shirts. Tie and sweater sales might fall if Chazz no longer offers coordinating shirts.

Let's challenge our second assumption. A new competitor has decreased the demand for Chazz's jeans. Now the company can only sell 30,000 pairs of jeans. Chazz should only make as many jeans as it can sell, and use the remaining machine hours to produce shirts. Let's see how this constraint in sales demand changes profitability.

Recall from Exhibit 21-18 that Chazz will make $480,000 of contribution margin from using all 2,000 machine hours to produce jeans. However, if Chazz only makes 30,000 jeans, it will only use 1,500 machine hours (30,000 machine hours ÷ 20 jeans per machine hour). That leaves 500 machine hours available for making shirts. Chazz's new contribution margin will be:

	Shirts	Jeans	Total
Contribution margin per machine hour (from Exhibit 21-18)	$ 180	$ 240	
Machine hours devoted to product	× 500	× 1,500	2,000
Total contribution margin at full capacity	$90,000	$360,000	$450,000

Because of the change in product mix, Chazz's total contribution margin will fall from $480,000 to $450,000, a $30,000 decline. Chazz had to give up $60 of contribution margin per machine hour ($240 − $180) on the 500 hours it spent producing shirts rather than jeans. However, Chazz had no choice—the company would have incurred an *actual loss* from producing jeans that it could not sell. If Chazz had produced 40,000 jeans but only sold 30,000, the company would have spent $480,000 to make the unsold pants (10,000 jeans × $48 variable cost per pair of jeans), yet received no sales revenue from them.

What about fixed costs? In most cases, changing the product mix emphasis in the short run will not affect fixed costs so fixed costs are irrelevant. However, it is possible that fixed costs could differ by emphasizing a different product mix. What if Chazz had a month-to-month lease on a zipper machine used only for making jeans? If Chazz only made shirts, it could *avoid* the lease cost. However, if Chazz makes any jeans, it needs the machine. In this case, the fixed costs become relevant because they differ between alternative product mixes (shirts only *versus* jeans only or jeans and shirts).

Notice that the analysis again follows the two guidelines for special business decisions: (1) focus on relevant data (only those revenues and costs that differ) and (2) use a contribution margin approach, which separates variable from fixed costs.

Stop & Think

Would Chazz's product mix decision change if it had a $20,000 cancelable lease on a zipper machine needed only for jean production? Assume Chazz can sell as many units as it makes.

Answer: We would compare the profitability as follows:

	Shirts	Jeans
Total contribution margin at full capacity (from Exhibit 21-18)	$360,000	$480,000
Less: Avoidable fixed costs	-0-	(20,000)
Net benefit	$360,000	$460,000

Even considering the zipper machine lease, producing jeans is more profitable than producing shirts. Chazz would prefer producing jeans over shirts, unless demand for jeans drops so low that the net benefit from jeans is less than $360,000 (the benefit gained from solely producing shirts).

When to Outsource

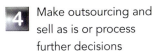

4 Make outsourcing and sell as is or process further decisions

Delta outsources much of its reservation work and airplane maintenance. IBM outsources most of its desktop production of personal computers. Make-or-buy decisions are often called **outsourcing** decisions because managers must decide whether to buy a component product or service or produce it in-house. The heart of these decisions is *how best to use available resources*.

Let's see how managers make outsourcing decisions. DefTone, a manufacturer of music CDs, is deciding whether to make the paper liners for the CD jewel boxes in-house or whether to outsource them to Mūz-Art, a company that specializes in producing paper liners. DefTone's cost to produce 250,000 liners is:

	Total Cost (250,000 liners)
Direct materials	$ 40,000
Direct labor	20,000
Variable manufacturing overhead	15,000
Fixed manufacturing overhead	50,000
Total manufacturing cost	$125,000
Number of liners	÷250,000
Cost per liner	$0.50

Mūz-Art offers to sell DefTone the liners for $0.37 each. Should DefTone make the liners or buy them from Mūz-Art? DefTone's $0.50 cost per unit to make the liner is $0.13 higher than the cost of buying it from Mūz-Art. It appears that DefTone should outsource the liners. But the correct answer is not so simple. Why? Because manufacturing unit costs contain both fixed and variable components. In deciding whether or not to outsource, managers must assess fixed and variable costs separately. Exhibit 21-19 shows some of the questions management must consider when deciding whether or not to outsource.

Let's see how these considerations apply to DefTone. By purchasing the liners, DefTone can avoid all variable manufacturing costs—$40,000 of direct materials,

EXHIBIT 21-19 Outsourcing Considerations

- How do our variable costs compare to the outsourcing cost?
- Are any fixed costs avoidable if we outsource?
- What could we do with the freed capacity?

$20,000 of direct labor, and $15,000 of variable manufacturing overhead. In total, the company will save $75,000 in variable manufacturing costs, or $0.30 per liner ($75,000 ÷ 250,000 liners). However, DefTone will have to pay the variable outsourcing price of $0.37 per unit, or $92,500 for the 250,000 liners. Based only on variable costs, the lower cost alternative is to manufacture the liners in-house. However, managers must still consider fixed costs.

Assume first, that DefTone cannot avoid any of the fixed costs by outsourcing. In this case, the company's fixed costs are irrelevant to the decision because DefTone would continue to incur $50,000 of fixed costs either way (the fixed costs don't differ between alternatives). DefTone should continue to make its own liners because the variable cost of outsourcing the liners ($92,500) exceeds the variable cost of making the liners ($75,000).

However, what if DefTone can avoid some fixed costs by outsourcing the liners? Let's assume that management can reduce fixed overhead cost by $10,000 by outsourcing the liners, so DefTone will still incur $40,000 of fixed overhead ($50,000 − $10,000) even if they outsource the liners. In this case, fixed costs become relevant to the decision because they differ between alternatives. Exhibit 21-20 shows the differences in costs between the make and buy alternatives under this scenario.

EXHIBIT 21-20 Incremental Analysis for Outsourcing Decision

Liner Costs	Make Liners	Buy Liners	Difference
Variable costs:			
Direct materials	$ 40,000	—	$40,000
Direct labor	20,000	—	20,000
Variable overhead	15,000	—	15,000
Purchase cost from Mūz-Art			
(250,000 × $0.37)	—	$ 92,500	(92,500)
Fixed overhead	50,000	40,000	10,000
Total cost of liners	$125,000	$132,500	$ (7,500)

Exhibit 21-20 shows that it would still cost DefTone less to make the liners than to buy them from Mūz-Art, even with the $10,000 reduction in fixed costs. The net savings from making 250,000 liners is $7,500.

Exhibit 21-20 also shows that outsourcing decisions follow our two key guidelines for special business decisions: (1) Focus on relevant data (differences in costs in this case) and (2) use a contribution margin approach that separates variable costs from fixed costs.

Note how the unit cost—which does *not* separate costs according to behavior—can be deceiving. If DefTone's managers made their decision by comparing the total manufacturing cost per liner ($0.50) to the outsourcing unit cost per liner ($0.37), they would have incorrectly decided to outsource. Recall the manufacturing unit cost ($0.50) contains both fixed and variable components, whereas the outsourcing cost ($0.37) is strictly variable. To make the correct decision, DefTone had to separate the two cost components and analyze them separately.

Our decision rule for outsourcing is:

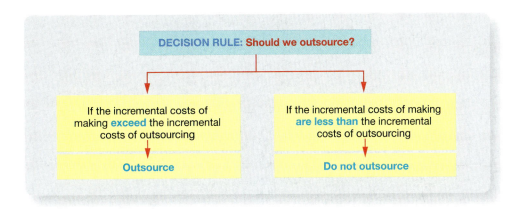

Stop & Think

Assuming that DefTone could save $10,000 in fixed costs by outsourcing, what is the most they would be willing to pay per liner to outsource production of 250,000 liners?

Answer: To answer this question, we must first find the outsourcing price at which DefTone would be *indifferent* between making the liners and outsourcing the liners. DefTone would be indifferent if the total costs were the *same* either way:

$$\text{Costs if making liners} = \text{Costs if outsourcing liners}$$
$$\text{Variable manufacturing costs} + \text{Fixed costs} = \text{Variable outsourcing price} + \text{Fixed costs}$$
$$(250{,}000 \text{ units} \times \$0.30 \text{ per unit}) + \$50{,}000 = (250{,}000 \times \text{outsourcing price per unit}) + \$40{,}000$$
$$\$75{,}000 + \$50{,}000 - \$40{,}000 = (250{,}000 \times \text{outsourcing price per unit})$$
$$\$85{,}000 = (250{,}000 \times \text{outsourcing price per unit})$$
$$\$85{,}000 \div 250{,}000 = \text{outsourcing price per unit}$$
$$\$0.34 = \text{outsourcing price per unit}$$

DefTone would be indifferent between making and outsourcing the liners if the outsourcing price was $0.34 per unit. At that price, DefTone would incur the same cost to manufacture or outsource the liners. DefTone would save money only if the outsourcing price is less than $0.34 per unit. Therefore, the most DefTone would pay to outsource is $0.33 per liner. As shown below, at $0.33 per liner, DefTone would save $2,500 from outsourcing:

Liner Costs	Make Liners	Buy Liners	Difference
Variable costs	$ 75,000 (250,000 units × $0.30 per unit)	$ 82,500 (250,000 × $0.33 per unit)	($7,500)
Plus: Fixed costs	50,000	40,000	10,000
Total costs	$125,000	$122,500	$2,500

We haven't considered what DefTone could do with the freed capacity it would have if it decided to outsource the liners. The analysis in Exhibit 21-20 assumes there is no other use for the production facilities if DefTone buys the liners from Mūz-Art.

But suppose DefTone has an opportunity to use its freed-up facilities to make more CDs, which have an expected profit of $18,000. Now, DefTone must consider its **opportunity cost**—the benefit forgone by not choosing an alternative course of action. In this case, DefTone's opportunity cost of making the liners is the $18,000 profit it forgoes if it does not free its production facilities to make the additional CDs.

Let's see how DefTone's managers decide among three alternatives:

1. Use the facilities to make the liners.
2. Buy the liners and leave facilities idle (continue to assume $10,000 of avoidable fixed costs from outsourcing liners).
3. Buy the liners and use facilities to make more CDs (continue to assume $10,000 of avoidable fixed costs from outsourcing liners).

The alternative with the lowest *net* cost is the best use of DefTone's facilities. Exhibit 21-21 compares the three alternatives.

EXHIBIT 21-21 Best Use of Facilities, Given Opportunity Costs

	Make Liners	Buy Liners — Facilities Idle	Buy Liners — Make Additional CDs
Expected cost of 250,000 liners (from Exhibit 21-20)	$125,000	$132,500	$132,500
Expected *profit* from additional CDs	—	—	(18,000)
Expected net cost of obtaining 250,000 liners	$125,000	$132,500	$114,500

DefTone should buy the liners from Mūz-Art and use the vacated facilities to make more CDs. If DefTone makes the liners, or if it buys the liners from Mūz-Art but leaves its production facilities idle, it will forgo the opportunity to earn $18,000.

Stop & Think

How will the $18,000 opportunity cost change the *maximum* amount DefTone is willing to pay to outsource each liner?

Answer: DefTone will now be willing to pay *more* to outsource its liners. In essence, the company is willing to pay for the opportunity to make more CDs.

DefTone's managers should consider qualitative factors as well as revenue and cost differences in making their final decision. For example, DefTone managers may believe they can better control quality by making the liners themselves. This argues for making the liners.

Outsourcing decisions are increasingly important in today's globally wired economy. In the past, make-or-buy decisions often ended up as "make" because coordination, information exchange, and paperwork problems made buying from suppliers too inconvenient. Now, companies can use the Internet to tap into information systems of suppliers and customers located around the world. Paperwork vanishes, and information required to satisfy the strictest JIT delivery schedule is available in real time. As a result, companies are focusing on their core competencies and outsourcing more functions.

Sell As Is or Process Further?

At what point in processing should a company sell its product? Many companies, especially in the food processing and natural resource industries, face this business decision. Companies in these industries process a raw material (milk, corn, livestock, crude oil, lumber, and so forth) to a point before it is saleable. For example, Kraft pasteurizes raw milk before it is saleable. Kraft must then decide whether it should sell the pasteurized milk "as is," or process it further into other dairy products (reduced-fat milk, butter, sour cream, cottage cheese, yogurt, blocks of cheese, shredded cheese, and so forth). Managers consider the questions shown in Exhibit 21-22 when deciding whether to sell as is or process further.

EXHIBIT 21-22 Sell As Is or Process Further Considerations

- How much revenue will we receive if we sell the product as is?
- How much revenue will we receive if we sell the product *after* processing it further?
- How much will it cost to process the product further?

Let's look at one of Chevron's sell as is or process further decisions. Suppose Chevron spent $125,000 to process crude oil into 50,000 gallons of regular gasoline, as shown in Exhibit 21-23. After processing crude oil into regular gasoline, should Chevron sell the regular gas as is or should it spend more to process the gasoline into premium grade? In making the decision, Chevron's managers consider the following relevant information:

EXHIBIT 21-23 Sell As Is or Process Further Decision

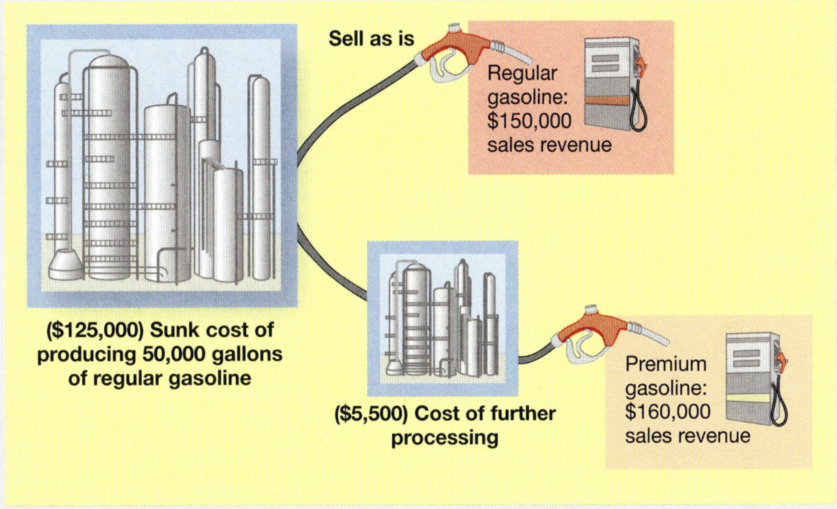

- Chevron could sell regular gasoline for $3.00 per gallon, for a total of $150,000 (50,000 × $3.00).
- Chevron could sell premium gasoline for $3.20 per gallon, for a total of $160,000 (50,000 × $3.20).
- Chevron would have to spend $0.11 per gallon, or $5,500 (50,000 gallons × $0.11) to further process regular gasoline into premium-grade gas.

Notice Chevron's managers do *not* consider the $125,000 spent on processing crude oil into regular gasoline. Why? It is a sunk cost. Recall from our previous discussion that a sunk cost is a past cost that cannot be changed regardless of which future action the company takes. Chevron has incurred $125,000—regardless of whether it sells the regular gasoline as is or processes it further into premium gasoline. Therefore, the cost is *not* relevant to the decision.

By analyzing only the relevant costs in Exhibit 21-24, managers see that they can increase profit by $4,500 if they convert the regular gasoline into premium gasoline. The $10,000 extra revenue ($160,000 − $150,000) outweighs the incremental $5,500 cost of the extra processing.

EXHIBIT 21-24 Incremental Analysis for Sell As Is or Process Further Decision

	Sell As Is	Process Further	Difference
Expected revenue from selling 50,000 gallons of regular gasoline at $3.00 per gallon	$150,000		
Expected revenue from selling 50,000 gallons of premium gasoline at $3.20 per gallon		$160,000	$10,000
Additional costs of $0.11 per gallon to convert 50,000 gallons of regular gasoline into premium gasoline		(5,500)	(5,500)
Total net revenue	$150,000	$154,500	$ 4,500

Thus, the decision rule is:

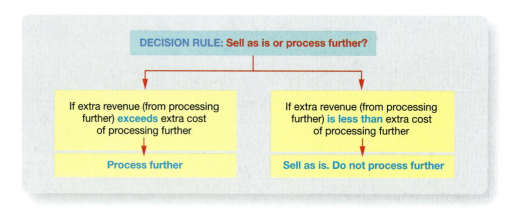

Recall that our keys to decision making include (1) focusing on relevant information and (2) using a contribution margin approach that separates variable costs from fixed costs. The analysis in Exhibit 21-24 includes only those *future* costs and revenues that *differ* between alternatives. We assumed Chevron already has the equipment and labor necessary to convert regular gasoline into premium grade gasoline. Because fixed costs would not differ between alternatives, they were irrelevant. However, if Chevron has to acquire equipment, or hire employees to convert the gasoline into premium grade gasoline, the extra fixed costs would be relevant. Once again, we see that fixed costs are only relevant if they *differ* between alternatives.

Stop & Think

Suppose one of Chevron's customers wants to buy the 50,000 gallons, but in the form of regular gasoline, not premium gasoline. The customer is willing to pay more than $3.00 a gallon for the regular gasoline. What is the minimum price Chevron should charge?

Answer: Exhibit 21-24 shows that if Chevron does not process the gasoline into premium grade, it would give up $154,500 of net revenue ($160,000 revenues given up − $5,500 further processing cost not incurred). To obtain at least the same income from selling the gasoline as regular grade, Chevron must sell the regular gasoline for at least $3.09 per gallon ($154,500 ÷ 50,000 gallons of regular gasoline). At $3.09 per gallon, Chevron would be indifferent between the two alternatives. If the customer offers to pay more than $3.09 per gallon, Chevron will be better off selling regular gasoline to this customer. If the customer offers less than $3.09, Chevron will be better off further processing the gasoline into premium grade gasoline.

Decision Guidelines

SHORT-TERM SPECIAL BUSINESS DECISIONS

Amazon.com has confronted most of the special business decisions we've covered. Here are the key guidelines Amazon.com's managers follow in making their decisions.

Decision	Guideline
Should Amazon.com drop its electronics product line?	If the cost savings exceed the lost revenues from dropping the electronics product line, then dropping will increase operating income.
Given limited warehouse space, which products should Amazon.com focus on selling?	Amazon.com should focus on selling the products with the highest contribution margin per unit of the constraint, which is cubic feet of warehouse space.
Should Amazon.com outsource its warehousing operations?	If the incremental costs of operating its own warehouses exceed the costs of outsourcing, then outsourcing will increase operating income.
How should Amazon decide whether to sell a product as is or process further?	Process further only if the extra sales revenue (from processing further) exceeds the extra costs of additional processing.

Summary Problem 2

Requirements

1. Aziz produces standard and deluxe sunglasses:

	Per Pair	
	Standard	Deluxe
Sale price...	$20	$30
Variable expenses	16	21

The company has 15,000 machine hours available. In one machine hour, Aziz can produce either 70 pairs of the standard model or 30 pairs of the deluxe model. Which model should Aziz emphasize?

2. Just Do It! incurs the following costs for 20,000 pairs of its high-tech hiking socks:

Direct materials	$ 20,000
Direct labor	80,000
Variable manufacturing overhead	40,000
Fixed manufacturing overhead	80,000
Total manufacturing cost..	$220,000
Cost per pair ($220,000 ÷ 20,000)	$ 11

Another manufacturer has offered to sell Just Do It! similar socks for $10 a pair, a total purchase cost of $200,000. If Just Do It! outsources *and* leaves its plant idle, it can save $50,000 of fixed overhead cost. Or, the company can use the released facilities to make other products that will contribute $70,000 to profits. In this case, the company will not be able to avoid any fixed costs. Identify and analyze the alternatives. What is the best course of action?

Solutions

Requirement 1

	Style of Sunglasses	
	Standard	Deluxe
Sale price per pair..	$ 20	$ 30
Variable expense per pair	(16)	(21)
Contribution margin per pair	$ 4	$ 9
Units produced each machine hour................	× 70	× 30
Contribution margin per machine hour.........	$ 280	$ 270
Capacity—number of machine hours	× 15,000	× 15,000
Total contribution margin at full capacity	$4,200,000	$4,050,000

Decision: Emphasize the standard model because it has the higher contribution margin per unit of the constraint—machine hours—resulting in a higher contribution margin for the company.

Requirement 2

	Make Socks	Buy Socks — Facilities Idle	Buy Socks — Make Other Products
Relevant costs:			
Direct materials	$ 20,000	—	—
Direct labor	80,000	—	—
Variable overhead	40,000	—	—
Fixed overhead	80,000	$ 30,000	$ 80,000
Purchase cost from outsider (20,000 × $10)	—	200,000	200,000
Total cost of obtaining socks	220,000	230,000	280,000
Profit from other products	—	—	(70,000)
Net cost of obtaining 20,000 pairs of socks	$220,000	$230,000	$210,000

Decision: Just Do It! should buy the socks from the outside supplier and use the released facilities to make other products.

Review

Accounting Vocabulary

Constraint
A factor that restricts production or sale of a product.

Opportunity Cost
The benefit forgone by not choosing an alternative course of action.

Outsourcing
A make-or-buy decision: Managers decide whether to buy a component product or service or produce it in-house.

Relevant Information
Expected *future* data that *differs* among alternatives.

Sunk Cost
A past cost that cannot be changed regardless of which future action is taken.

Target Full Cost
The total cost in developing, producing, and delivering a product or service.

Quick Check

1. In making short-term special decisions, you should:
   a. focus on total costs
   b. separate variable from fixed costs
   c. use a traditional absorption costing approach
   d. only focus on quantitative factors

2. Which of the following is relevant to Amazon.com's decision to accept a special order at a lower sale price from a large customer in China?
   a. the cost of Amazon.com's warehouses in the United States
   b. Amazon.com's investment in its Web site
   c. the cost of shipping the order to the customer
   d. founder Jeff Bezos's salary

3. In deciding whether to drop its electronics product line, Amazon.com would consider:
   a. the costs it could save by dropping the product line
   b. the revenues it would lose from dropping the product line
   c. how dropping the electronics product line would affect sales of its other products like CDs
   d. all of the above

4. In deciding which product lines to emphasize, Amazon.com should focus on the product line that has the highest:
   a. contribution margin per unit of the constraining factor
   b. contribution margin per unit of product
   c. contribution margin ratio
   d. profit per unit of product

5. When making outsourcing decisions:
   a. the manufacturing unit cost of making the product in-house is relevant
   b. the variable cost of producing the product in-house is relevant
   c. avoidable fixed costs are irrelevant
   d. expected use of the freed capacity is irrelevant

6. When companies are price-setters, their products and services:
   a. are priced by managers using a target-pricing emphasis
   b. tend to be unique
   c. tend to have a lot of competitors
   d. tend to be commodities

7. When pricing a product or service, managers must consider which of the following?
   a. only variable costs
   b. only period costs
   c. only manufacturing costs
   d. all costs

Short-Term Business Decisions

8. Which of the following costs are irrelevant to business decisions?
   a. sunk costs
   b. costs that differ between alternatives
   c. variable costs
   d. avoidable costs

9. When deciding whether to sell as is or process a product further, managers should ignore which of the following?
   a. the revenue if the product is processed further
   b. the cost of processing further
   c. the costs of processing the product thus far
   d. the revenue if the product is sold as is

10. When making decisions, managers should:
    a. consider sunk costs in their decisions
    b. consider costs that do not differ between alternatives
    c. consider only variable costs
    d. consider revenues that differ between alternatives

Answers are given after Apply Your Knowledge (p. 1109).

Assess Your Progress

Short Exercises

1 Describe and identify information relevant to business decisions

S21-1 You are trying to decide whether to trade in your inkjet printer for a more recent model. Your usage pattern will remain unchanged, but the old and new printers use different ink cartridges. Are the following items relevant or irrelevant to your decision?

a. The price of the new printer
b. The price you paid for the old printer
c. The trade-in value of the old printer
d. Paper costs
e. The difference between ink cartridges' costs

2 Make special order and pricing decisions

S21-2 Consider the ACDelco special sales order example on pages 1062–1064. Suppose that:

a. ACDelco's variable manufacturing cost is $1.35 per oil filter (instead of $1.20).
b. ACDelco would have to buy a special stamping machine that costs $9,000 to mark the customer's logo on the special-order oil filters. The machine would be scrapped when the special order is complete.

Would you recommend that ACDelco accept the special order under these conditions?

2 Make special order and pricing decisions

S21-3 SnowDreams operates a Rocky Mountain ski resort. The company is planning their lift ticket pricing for the coming ski season. Investors would like to earn a 15% return on the company's $100 million of assets. The company primarily incurs fixed costs to groom the runs and operate the lifts. SnowDreams projects fixed costs to be $33,750,000 for the ski season. The resort serves about 750,000 skiers and snowboarders each season. Variable costs are about $10 per guest. Currently, the resort has such a favorable reputation among skiers and snowboarders that they have some control over the lift ticket prices.

1. Would SnowDreams emphasize target pricing or cost-plus pricing. Why?
2. If other resorts in the area charge $70 per day, what price should SnowDreams charge?

2 Make special order and pricing decisions

S21-4 Consider SnowDreams from Short Exercise 21-3. Assume that SnowDreams' reputation has diminished and other resorts in the vicinity are only charging $65 per lift ticket. SnowDreams has become a price-taker and won't be able to charge more than its competitors. At the market price, SnowDreams managers believe they will still serve 750,000 skiers and snowboarders each season.

1. If SnowDreams can't reduce its costs, what profit will it earn? State your answer in dollars and as a percent of assets. Will investors be happy with the profit level?
2. Assume SnowDreams has found ways to cut its fixed costs to $30 million. What is its new target variable cost per skier/snowboarder?

[3] Make dropping a product and product-mix decisions

S21-5 Knight Fashion in New York operates three departments: Men's, Women's, and Accessories. Knight Fashion allocates fixed expenses (building depreciation and utilities) based on the square feet occupied by each department. Departmental operating income data for the third quarter of 2007 are as follows:

	Department			
	Men's	Women's	Accessories	Total
Sales revenue	$105,000	$54,000	$100,000	$259,000
Variable expenses	60,000	30,000	80,000	170,000
Fixed expenses	25,000	20,000	25,000	70,000
Total expenses	85,000	50,000	105,000	240,000
Operating income (loss)	$20,000	$4,000	$(5,000)	$19,000

The store will remain in the same building regardless of whether any of the departments are dropped. Should Knight Fashion drop any of the departments? Give your reason.

[3] Make dropping a product and product-mix decisions

S21-6 Consider Knight Fashion from Short Exercise 21-5. Assume that the fixed expenses assigned to each department include only direct fixed costs of the department:

- Salary of the department's manager
- Cost of advertising directly related to that department

If Knight Fashion drops a department, it will not incur these fixed expenses. Under these circumstances, should Knight Fashion drop any of the departments? Give your reason.

[3] Make dropping a product and product-mix decisions

S21-7 Consider Knight Fashion from Short Exercises 21-5 and 21-6. Assume once again, that Knight Fashion allocates all fixed costs based on square footage. If Knight Fashion drops one of the current departments, it plans to replace the dropped department with a shoe department. The company expects the shoe department to produce $80,000 in sales and have $50,000 of variable costs. Because the shoe business would be new to Knight Fashion, the company would have to incur an additional $7,000 of fixed costs (advertising, depreciation on new shoe display racks, and so forth) per period related to the department. What should Knight Fashion do now?

[3] Make dropping a product and product-mix decisions

S21-8 StoreAll produces plastic storage bins for household storage needs. The company makes two sizes of bins: large (50 gallon) and regular (35 gallon). Demand for the product is so high that StoreAll can sell as many of each size as it can produce. The company uses the same machinery to produce both sizes. The machinery can only be run for 3,000 hours per period. StoreAll can produce 10 large bins every hour, whereas it can

continued . . .

produce 15 regular bins in the same amount of time. Fixed costs amount to $100,000 per period. Sales prices and variable costs are as follows:

	Regular	Large
Sales price per unit	$8.00	$10.00
Variable cost per unit	$3.00	$ 4.00

1. Which product should StoreAll emphasize? Why?
2. To maximize profits, how many of each size bin should StoreAll produce?
3. Given this product mix, what will the company's operating income be?

Make dropping a product and product-mix decisions

S21-9 Consider StoreAll in Short Exercise 21-8. Assume demand for regular bins is limited to 30,000 units and demand for large bins is limited to 25,000 units.

1. How many of each size bin should StoreAll make now?
2. Given this product mix, what will the company's operating income be?
3. Explain why the operating income is less than it was when StoreAll was producing its optimal product mix in S21-8.

Make outsourcing and sell as is or process further decisions

S21-10 Suppose an Olive Garden restaurant is considering whether to (1) bake bread for its restaurant in-house or (2) buy the bread from a local bakery. The chef estimates that variable costs of making each loaf include $0.50 of ingredients, $0.25 of variable overhead (electricity to run the oven), and $0.75 of direct labor for kneading and forming the loaves. Allocating fixed overhead (depreciation on the kitchen equipment and building) based on direct labor assigns $1.00 of fixed overhead per loaf. None of the fixed costs are avoidable. The local bakery would charge $1.75 per loaf.

1. What is the unit cost of making the bread in-house (use absorption costing)?
2. Should Olive Garden bake the bread in-house or buy from the local bakery? Why?
3. In addition to the financial analysis, what else should Olive Garden consider when making this decision?

Make outsourcing and sell as is or process further decisions

S21-11 U.S. Food in Lexington, Kentucky, manufactures and markets snack foods. Betsy Gonzalez manages the company's fleet of 200 delivery trucks. Gonzalez has been charged with "reengineering" the fleet-management function. She has an important decision to make.

- Should she continue to manage the fleet in-house with the five employees reporting to her? To do so, she will have to acquire new fleet-management software to streamline U.S. Food's fleet-management process.
- Should she outsource the fleet-management function to Fleet Management Services, a company that specializes in managing fleets of trucks for other companies? Fleet Management Services would

continued ...

take over the maintenance, repair, and scheduling of U.S. Food's fleet (but U.S. Food would retain ownership). This alternative would require Gonzalez to lay off her five employees. However, her own job would be secure as she would be U.S. Food's liaison with Fleet Management Services.

Assume that Gonzalez's records show the following data concerning U.S. Food's fleet:

Book value of U.S. Food's trucks, with an estimated five-year life	$3,500,000
Annual leasing fee for new fleet-management software	8,000
Annual maintenance of trucks	145,500
Fleet Supervisor Gonzalez's annual salary	60,000
Total annual salaries of U.S. Food's five other fleet-management employees	150,000

Suppose that Fleet Management Services offers to manage U.S. Food's fleet for an annual fee of $290,000.

Which alternative will maximize U.S. Food's short-term operating income?

S21-12 Refer to U.S. Food in Short Exercise 21-11. What qualitative factors should Gonzalez consider before making a final decision?

S21-13 Auto Components has an inventory of 500 obsolete remote entry keys that are carried in inventory at a manufacturing cost of $80,000. Production Supervisor Terri Smith must decide whether to:
- process the inventory further at a cost of $20,000, with the expectation of selling it for $28,000, or
- scrap the inventory for a sale price of $6,000.

What should Smith do? Present figures to support your decision.

S21-14 Chocolite processes cocoa beans into cocoa powder at a processing cost of $10,000 per batch. Chocolite can sell the cocoa powder as is or it can process the cocoa powder further into either chocolate syrup or boxed assorted chocolates. Once processed, each batch of cocoa beans would result in the following sales revenue:

Cocoa powder	$15,000
Chocolate syrup	$100,000
Boxed assorted chocolates	$200,000

The cost of transforming the cocoa powder into chocolate syrup would be $70,000. Likewise, the company would incur $180,000 to transform the cocoa powder into boxed assorted chocolates. The company president has decided to make boxed assorted chocolates owing to its high sales value and to the fact that the cocoa bean processing cost of $10,000 eats up most of the cocoa powder profits. Has the president made the right or wrong decision? Explain your answer. Be sure to include the correct financial analysis in your response.

Exercises

Describe and identify information relevant to business decisions

E21-15 Joe Roberts, production manager for Fabricut, invested in computer-controlled production machinery last year. He purchased the machinery from Advanced Design at a cost of $2 million. A representative from Advanced Design has recently contacted Joe because the company has designed an even more efficient piece of machinery. The new design would double the production output of the year-old machinery but cost Fabricut another $3 million. Roberts is afraid to bring this new equipment to the company president's attention because he convinced the president to invest $2 million in the machinery last year.

Requirement

Explain what is relevant and irrelevant to Roberts's dilemma. What should he do?

Make special order and pricing decisions

E21-16 Suppose the Baseball Hall of Fame in Cooperstown, New York, has approached Sports-Cardz with a special order. The Hall of Fame wishes to purchase 50,000 baseball card packs for a special promotional campaign and offers $0.40 per pack, a total of $20,000. Sports-Cardz's total production cost is $0.60 per pack, as follows:

Variable costs:	
Direct materials	$0.14
Direct labor	0.08
Variable overhead	0.13
Fixed overhead	0.25
Total cost	$0.60

Sports-Cardz has enough excess capacity to handle the special order.

Requirements

1. Prepare an incremental analysis to determine whether Sports-Cardz should accept the special sales order.
2. Now assume that the Hall of Fame wants special hologram baseball cards. Sports-Cardz will spend $5,000 to develop this hologram, which will be useless after the special order is completed. Should Sports-Cardz accept the special order under these circumstances?

Make special order and pricing decisions

E21-17 Maui Jane Sunglasses sell for about $150 per pair. Suppose that the company incurs the following average costs per pair:

Direct materials	$40
Direct labor	12
Variable manufacturing overhead	8
Variable marketing expenses	4
Fixed manufacturing overhead	20*
Total costs	$84

$$*\frac{\$2,000,000 \text{ total fixed manufacturing overhead}}{100,000 \text{ pairs of sunglasses}}$$

continued ...

Maui Jane has enough idle capacity to accept a one-time-only special order from Lenscrafters for 20,000 pairs of sunglasses at $76 per pair. Maui Jane will not incur any variable marketing expenses for the order.

Requirements

1. How would accepting the order affect Maui Jane's operating income? In addition to the special order's effect on profits, what other (longer-term qualitative) factors should Maui Jane's managers consider in deciding whether to accept the order?
2. Maui Jane's marketing manager, Jim Revo, argues against accepting the special order because the offer price of $76 is less than Maui Jane's $84 cost to make the sunglasses. Revo asks you, as one of Maui Jane's staff accountants, to write a memo explaining whether his analysis is correct.

2 Make special order and pricing decisions

E21-18 Bennett Builders builds 1,500 square-foot starter tract homes in the fast-growing suburbs of Atlanta. Land and labor are cheap, and competition among developers is fierce. The homes are "cookie-cutter," with any upgrades added by the buyer after the sale. Bennett Builders' cost per developed sub-lot are as follows:

Land	$50,000
Construction	$125,000
Landscaping	$5,000
Variable marketing costs	$2,000

Bennett Builders would like to earn a profit of 15% of the variable cost of each home sale. Similar homes offered by competing builders sell for $200,000 each.

Requirements

1. Which approach to pricing should Bennett Builders emphasize? Why?
2. Will Bennett Builders be able to achieve his target profit levels?
3. Bathrooms and kitchens are typically the most important selling features of a home. Bennett Builders could differentiate the homes by upgrading bathrooms and kitchens. The upgrades would cost $20,000 per home, but would enable Bennett Builders to increase the selling prices by $35,000 per home (kitchen and bathroom upgrades typically add about 150% of their cost to the value of any home.) If Bennett Builders upgrades, what will the new cost-plus price per home be? Should the company differentiate its product in this manner?

3 Make dropping a product and product-mix decisions

E21-19 Top managers of Video Avenue are alarmed by their operating losses. They are considering dropping the VCR-tape product line. Company

continued . . .

accountants have prepared the following analysis to help make this decision:

	Total	DVD Discs	VCR Tapes
Sales revenue	$420,000	$300,000	$120,000
Variable expenses	230,000	150,000	80,000
Contribution margin	190,000	150,000	40,000
Fixed expenses:			
Manufacturing	125,000	70,000	55,000
Marketing and administrative	70,000	55,000	15,000
Total fixed expenses	195,000	125,000	70,000
Operating income (loss)	$ (5,000)	$ 25,000	$ (30,000)

Total fixed costs will not change if the company stops selling VCR tapes.
    Prepare an incremental analysis to show whether Video Avenue should drop the VCR-tape product line. Will dropping VCR tapes add $30,000 to operating income? Explain.

E21-20 Refer to Exercise 21-19. Assume that Video Avenue can avoid $30,000 of fixed expenses by dropping the VCR-tape product line (these costs are direct fixed costs of the VCR product line). Prepare an incremental analysis to show whether Video Avenue should stop selling VCR tapes.

E21-21 Lifemaster produces two types of exercise treadmills: Regular and Deluxe. The exercise craze is such that Lifemaster could use all its available machine hours producing either model. The two models are processed through the same production departments.
    What is the constraint? Which model should Lifemaster produce? (*Hint:* Use the allocation of fixed manufacturing overhead to determine the proportion of machine hours used by each product.) If Lifemaster should produce both models, compute the mix that will maximize operating income.

	Per Unit	
	Deluxe	Regular
Sale price	$1,000	$ 550
Costs:		
Direct materials	$ 290	$ 100
Direct labor	80	180
Variable manufacturing overhead	240	80
Fixed manufacturing overhead*	120	40
Variable operating expenses	115	65
Total cost	845	465
Operating income	$ 155	$ 85

*Allocated on the basis of machine hours.

[3] Make dropping a product and product-mix decisions

3 Make dropping a product and product-mix decisions

E21-22 Vivace sells both designer and moderately priced fashion accessories. Top management is deciding which product line to emphasize. Accountants have provided the following data:

	Per Item	
	Designer	Moderately Priced
Average sale price................................	$200	$84
Average variable expenses....................	85	24
Average contribution margin................	115	60
Average fixed expenses (allocated)........	20	10
Average operating income....................	$95	$50

The Vivace store in Reno, Nevada, has 10,000 square feet of floor space. If Vivace emphasizes moderately priced goods, it can display 650 items in the store. If Vivace emphasizes designer wear, it can only display 300 designer items. These numbers are also the average monthly sales in units.

Prepare an analysis to show which product to emphasize.

3 Make dropping a product and product-mix decisions

E21-23 Each morning, Max Imery stocks the drink case at Max's Beach Hut in Myrtle Beach, South Carolina. Max's Beach Hut has 100 linear feet of refrigerated display space for cold drinks. Each linear foot can hold either six 12-ounce cans or four 20-ounce plastic or glass bottles. Max's Beach Hut sells three types of cold drinks:

1. Coca-Cola in 12-oz. cans, for $1.50 per can
2. Coca-Cola in 20-oz. plastic bottles, for $1.75 per bottle
3. SoBe in 20-oz. glass bottles, for $2.20 per bottle

Max's Beach Hut pays its suppliers:

1. $0.25 per 12-oz. can of Coca-Cola
2. $0.40 per 20-oz. bottle of Coca-Cola
3. $0.75 per 20-oz. bottle of SoBe

Max's Beach Hut's monthly fixed expenses include:

Hut rental..	$ 375
Refrigerator rental...	75
Max's salary..	1,550
Total fixed expenses..	$2,000

Max's Beach Hut can sell all the drinks stocked in the display case each morning.

1. What is Max's Beach Hut's constraining factor? What should Max stock to maximize profits?
2. Suppose Max's Beach Hut refuses to devote more than 60 linear feet to any individual product. Under this condition, how many linear feet of each drink should Imery stock? How many units of each product will be available for sale each day?

Make outsourcing and sell as is or process further decisions

E21-24 Fiber Systems manufactures an optical switch that it uses in its final product. The switch has the following manufacturing costs per unit:

Direct materials	$ 9.00
Direct labor	1.50
Variable overhead	2.00
Fixed overhead	6.50
Manufacturing product cost	$19.00

Another company has offered to sell Fiber Systems the switch for $14 per unit. If Fiber Systems buys the switch from the outside supplier, the manufacturing facilities that will be idled cannot be used for any other purpose, yet none of the fixed costs are avoidable. Should Fiber Systems make or buy the switch?

Make outsourcing and sell as is or process further decisions

E21-25 Refer to Exercise 21-24. Fiber Systems needs 80,000 optical switches. By outsourcing them, Fiber Systems can use its idle facilities to manufacture another product that will contribute $220,000 to operating income. Identify the *incremental* costs that Fiber Systems will incur to acquire 80,000 switches under three alternative plans. Which plan makes the best use of Fiber System's facilities? Support your answer.

Make outsourcing and sell as is or process further decisions

E21-26 Refer to DefTone's outsourcing decision on pages 1079–1082. DefTone's sales have increased, and as a result, the company needs 400,000 liners, rather than 250,000. DefTone has enough existing capacity to make all of the liners it needs. In addition, due to volume discounts, its variable costs of making each liner will decline to $0.28 per liner. Assume that by outsourcing, DefTone can reduce its fixed costs by $10,000. There is no alternative use for the factory space freed through outsourcing so it will just remain idle. What is the maximum DefTone will pay to outsource production of its CD liners?

Make outsourcing and sell as is or process further decisions

E21-27 Dairymaid processes organic milk into plain yogurt. Dairymaid sells plain yogurt to hospitals, nursing homes, and restaurants in bulk, one-gallon containers. Each batch, processed at a cost of $800, yields 500 gallons of plain yogurt. Dairymaid sells the one-gallon tubs for $6 each, and spends $0.10 for each plastic tub. Dairymaid has recently begun to reconsider its strategy. Dairymaid wonders if it would be more profitable to sell individual-size portions of fruited organic yogurt at local food stores. Dairymaid could further process each batch of plain yogurt into 10,667 individual portions (3/4 cup each) of fruited yogurt. A recent market analysis indicates that demand for the product exists. Dairymaid would sell each individual portion for $0.50. Packaging would cost $0.08 per portion, and fruit would cost $0.10 per portion. Fixed costs would not change. Should Dairymaid continue to sell only the gallon-size plain yogurt (sell as is), or convert the plain yogurt into individual-size portions of fruited yogurt (process further)? Why?

Problems (Problem Set A)

Make special order and pricing decisions

P21-28A Buoy manufactures flotation vests in Tampa, Florida. Buoy's contribution-margin income statement for the most recent month contains the following data:

Sales in units	31,000
Sales revenue	$434,000
Variable expenses:	
Manufacturing	$ 93,000
Marketing and administrative	107,000
Total variable expenses	200,000
Contribution margin	234,000
Fixed expenses:	
Manufacturing	126,000
Marketing and administrative	90,000
Total fixed expenses	216,000
Operating income	$ 18,000

Suppose Overton's wishes to buy 5,000 vests from Buoy. Acceptance of the order will not increase Buoy's variable marketing and administrative expenses. The Buoy plant has enough unused capacity to manufacture the additional vests. Overton's has offered $10.00 per vest, which is below the normal sale price of $14.

Requirements
1. Prepare an incremental analysis to determine whether Buoy should accept this special sales order.
2. Identify long-term factors Buoy should consider in deciding whether to accept the special sales order.

Make special order and pricing decisions

P21-29A GreenThumb operates a commercial plant nursery, where it propagates plants for garden centers throughout the region. GreenThumb has $5,000,000 in assets. Its yearly fixed costs are $600,000 and the variable costs for the potting soil, container, label, seedling, and labor for each gallon-size plant total $1.25. GreenThumb's volume is currently 500,000 units. Competitors offer the same plants, at the same quality, to garden centers for $3.50 each. Garden centers then mark them up to sell to the public for $8 to $10, depending on the type of plant.

Requirements
1. GreenThumb's owners want to earn a 12% return on the company's assets. What is GreenThumb's target full cost?
2. Given GreenThumb's current costs, will its owners be able to achieve their target profit?

continued ...

3. Assume GreenThumb has identified ways to cut its variable costs to $1.10 per unit. What is its new target fixed cost? Will this decrease in variable costs allow the company to achieve its target profit?

4. GreenThumb started an aggressive advertising campaign strategy to differentiate its plants from those grown by other nurseries. Monrovia Plants made this strategy work so GreenThumb has decided to try it, too. GreenThumb doesn't expect volume to be affected, but it hopes to gain more control over pricing. If GreenThumb has to spend $100,000 this year to advertise, and its variable costs continue to be $1.10 per unit, what will its cost-plus price be? Do you think GreenThumb will be able to sell its plants to garden centers at the cost-plus price? Why?

P21-30A Members of the board of directors of Security Systems have received the following operating income data for the year just ended.

	Product Line		
	Industrial Systems	Household Systems	Total
Sales revenue............................	$300,000	$310,000	$610,000
Cost of goods sold:			
Variable..............................	$38,000	$ 42,000	$ 80,000
Fixed...................................	210,000	69,000	279,000
Total cost of goods sold.......	248,000	111,000	359,000
Gross profit	52,000	199,000	251,000
Marketing and administrative expenses:			
Variable............................	66,000	71,000	137,000
Fixed	40,000	22,000	62,000
Total marketing and administrative expenses...	106,000	93,000	199,000
Operating income (loss)	$(54,000)	$106,000	$ 52,000

Members of the board are surprised that the industrial-systems product line is losing money. They commission a study to determine whether the company should drop the line. Company accountants estimate that dropping industrial systems will decrease fixed cost of goods sold by $80,000 and decrease fixed marketing and administrative expenses by $12,000.

Requirements
1. Prepare an incremental analysis to show whether Security Systems should drop the industrial-systems product line.
2. Prepare contribution margin income statements to show Security Systems' total operating income under the two alternatives: (a) with the industrial systems line and (b) without the line. Compare the *difference* between the two alternatives' income numbers to your answer to Requirement 1. What have you learned from this comparison?

3 Make dropping a product and product-mix decisions

3 Make dropping a product and product-mix decisions

P21-31A Brun located in St. Cloud, Minnesota, produces two lines of electric toothbrushes: deluxe and standard. Because Brun can sell all the toothbrushes it can produce, the owners are expanding the plant. They are deciding which product line to emphasize. To make this decision, they assemble the following data.

	Per Unit	
	Deluxe Toothbrush	Standard Toothbrush
Sale price	$80	$48
Variable expenses	20	18
Contribution margin	$60	$30
Contribution margin ratio	75%	62.5%

After expansion, the factory will have a production capacity of 4,500 machine hours per month. The plant can manufacture either 60 standard electric toothbrushes or 24 deluxe electric toothbrushes per machine hour.

Requirements
1. Identify the constraining factor for Brun.
2. Prepare an analysis to show which product line to emphasize.

4 Make outsourcing and sell as is or process further decisions

P21-32A X-Perience manufactures snowboards. Its cost of making 1,800 bindings is:

Direct materials	$17,520
Direct labor	3,100
Variable overhead	2,080
Fixed overhead	6,800
Total manufacturing costs for 1,800 bindings	$29,500

Suppose O'Brien will sell bindings to X-Perience for $14 each. X-Perience would pay $1 per unit to transport the bindings to its manufacturing plant, where it would add its own logo at a cost of $0.20 per binding.

Requirements
1. X-Perience's accountants predict that purchasing the bindings from O'Brien will enable the company to avoid $2,200 of fixed overhead. Prepare an analysis to show whether X-Perience should make or buy the bindings.
2. The facilities freed by purchasing bindings from O'Brien can be used to manufacture another product that will contribute $3,100 to profit. Total fixed costs will be the same as if X-Perience had produced the bindings. Show which alternative makes the best use of X-Perience's facilities: (a) make bindings, (b) buy bindings and leave facilities idle, or (c) buy bindings and make another product.

4 Make outsourcing and sell as is or process further decisions

P21-33A Vision Chemical has spent $240,000 to refine 72,000 gallons of acetone, which can be sold for $2.16 a gallon. Alternatively, Vision Chemical can process the acetone further. This processing will yield a total of 60,000 gallons of lacquer thinner that can be sold for $3.20 a gallon. The additional processing will cost $0.62 per gallon of lacquer thinner. To sell the lacquer thinner, Vision Chemical must pay shipping of $0.22 a gallon and administrative expenses of $0.10 a gallon on the thinner.

Requirements
1. Diagram Vision's decision, using Exhibit 21-23 as a guide.
2. Identify the sunk cost. Is the sunk cost relevant to Vision's decision?
3. Should Vision sell the acetone or process it into lacquer thinner? Show the expected net revenue difference between the two alternatives.

Problems (Problem Set B)

2 Make special order and pricing decisions

P21-34B United Packaging's contribution margin income statement follows:

Sales in units	360,000
Sales revenue	$432,000
Variable expenses:	
Manufacturing	$108,000
Marketing and administrative	53,000
Total variable expenses	161,000
Contribution margin	271,000
Fixed expenses:	
Manufacturing	156,000
Marketing and administrative	40,000
Total fixed expenses	196,000
Operating income	$ 75,000

Wallace Farms wants to buy 5,000 produce boxes from United Packaging. Acceptance of the order will not increase any of United Packaging's variable marketing and administrative expenses. United Packaging's plant has enough unused capacity to manufacture the additional boxes. Wallace Farms has offered $0.80 per box, which is considerably below the normal sale price of $1.20.

Requirements
1. Prepare an incremental analysis to determine whether United Packaging should accept this special sales order.
2. Identify long-term factors that United Packaging should consider in deciding whether to accept the special sales order.

2 Make special order and pricing decisions

P21-35B Softies produces facial tissues. Softies has $50 million in assets. Its yearly fixed costs are $12 million and the variable cost of producing and selling each box of tissues is $0.25. Softies currently sells 30 million boxes of tissues. Generic facial tissues, such as Softies' product, generally sell to retailers for $0.75 per box, while name brands, such as Kleenex and Puffs, sell to retailers for $1.00 per box.

Requirements
1. Softies' stockholders expect a 10% return on the company's assets. What is Softies' target full cost?
2. Given Softies' current costs, will its owners achieve their target profit?
3. Softies has identified ways to cut their fixed costs by $500,000. What is their new target variable cost per unit? Will Softies be able to reach their target profit?
4. Softies started an aggressive advertising campaign to transform its product into a name brand able to compete with Kleenex and Puffs. Softies doesn't feel volume will be affected, but it hopes it will gain more control over pricing. If Softies spends $3,000,000 a year to advertise, what will their cost-plus price be? (Continue to assume that fixed costs have declined by $500,000, but Softies was unable to reduce its variable cost per unit below $0.25.) Do you think Softies will be able to sell their facial tissues to retailers at the cost-plus price?

3 Make dropping a product and product-mix decisions

P21-36B The following operating income data of Abalone Seafood highlight the losses of the fresh seafood product line:

	Total	Product Line Fresh Seafood	Product Line Frozen Seafood
Sales revenue...............	$730,500	$190,500	$540,000
Cost of goods sold:			
Variable...............	$138,000	$ 44,000	$ 94,000
Fixed...................	61,000	20,000	41,000
Total cost of goods sold.......	199,000	64,000	135,000
Gross profit	531,500	126,500	405,000
Marketing and administrative expenses:			
Variable...............	223,000	98,000	125,000
Fixed...................	93,000	38,000	55,000
Total marketing and administrative expenses.....	316,000	136,000	180,000
Operating income (loss)..........	$215,500	$ (9,500)	$225,000

    Abalone Seafood is considering discontinuing the fresh seafood product line. The company's accountants estimate that dropping the

continued ...

fresh seafood line will decrease fixed cost of goods sold by $16,000 and decrease fixed marketing and administrative expenses by $10,000.

Requirements

1. Prepare an incremental analysis to show whether Abalone Seafood should drop the fresh seafood product line.
2. Prepare contribution margin income statements to compare Abalone Seafood's total operating income (a) with the fresh seafood product line and (b) without it. Compare the *difference* between the two alternatives' income numbers to your answer to Requirement 1. What have you learned from this comparison?

3 Make dropping a product and product-mix decisions

P21-37B Easy Living of Charlotte, North Carolina, specializes in outdoor furniture and spas. Owner Linda Spring is expanding the store. She is deciding which product line to emphasize. To make this decision, she assembles the following data:

	Per Unit	
	Spas	Patio Sets
Sale price	$1,000	$800
Variable expenses	480	440
Contribution margin	$ 520	$360
Contribution margin ratio	52%	45%

After renovation, the store will have 8,000 square feet of floor space. By devoting the new floor space to patio sets, Easy Living can display 60 patio sets. Alternatively, Easy Living could display 30 spas. Spring expects monthly sales to equal the maximum number of units displayed.

Requirements

1. Identify the constraining factor for Easy Living.
2. Prepare an analysis to show which product line to emphasize.

4 Make outsourcing and sell as is or process further decisions

P21-38B Morning Grain makes organic cereal. Costs of producing 140,000 boxes of cereal each year follow:

Direct materials	$220,000
Direct labor	140,000
Variable overhead	60,000
Fixed overhead	440,000
Total manufacturing costs	$860,000

Suppose Kellogg will sell Morning Grain the cereal for $4.00 a box. Morning Grain would also pay $0.19 a box to transport the cereal to its warehouse.

continued . . .

Requirements

1. Morning Grain's accountants predict that purchasing the cereal from Kellogg will enable the company to avoid $140,000 of fixed overhead. Prepare an analysis to show whether Morning Grain should make or buy the cereal.

2. Assume that the Morning Grain facilities freed up by purchasing the cereal from Kellogg can be used to manufacture snack bars that will contribute $180,000 to profit. Total fixed costs will be the same as if Morning Grain used the plant to make cereal. Prepare an analysis to show which alternative makes the best use of Morning Grain's facilities: (a) make cereal, (b) buy cereal and leave facilities idle, or (c) buy cereal and make snack bars.

P21-39B Acme Petroleum has spent $200,000 to refine 60,000 gallons of petroleum distillate. Suppose Acme Petroleum can sell the distillate for $6.00 a gallon. Alternatively, it can process the distillate further and produce cleaner fluid. The additional processing will cost another $1.75 a gallon, and the cleaner can be sold for $8.50 a gallon. To sell cleaner fluid, Acme Petroleum must pay a sales commission of $0.10 a gallon and a transportation charge of $0.15 a gallon.

Requirements

1. Diagram Acme Petroleum's alternatives, using Exhibit 21-23 (sell as is or process further) as a guide.
2. Identify the sunk cost. Is the sunk cost relevant to Acme Petroleum's decision?
3. Prepare an analysis to indicate whether Acme Petroleum should sell the distillate or process it into cleaner fluid. Show the expected net revenue difference between the two alternatives.

Apply Your Knowledge

Decision Case

Case 21-40. BKFin.com provides banks access to sophisticated financial information and analysis systems over the Web. The company combines these tools with benchmarking data access, including e-mail and wireless communications, so that banks can instantly evaluate individual loan applications and entire loan portfolios.

BKFin.com's CEO Jon Wise is happy with the company's growth. To better focus on client service, Wise is considering outsourcing some functions. CFO Jenny Lee suggests that the company's e-mail may be the place to start. She recently attended a conference and learned that companies like Continental Airlines, DellNet, GTE, and NBC were outsourcing their e-mail function. Wise asks Lee to identify costs related to BKFin.com's in-house Microsoft Exchange mail application, which has 2,300 mailboxes. This information follows:

Variable costs:	
E-mail license	$7 per mailbox per month
Virus protection license	$1 per mailbox per month
Other variable costs	$8 per mailbox per month
Fixed costs:	
Computer hardware costs	$94,300 per month
$8,050 monthly salary for two information technology staff members who work only on e-mail	$16,100 per month

Requirements

1. Compute the *total cost* per mailbox per month of BKFin.com's current e-mail function.

2. Suppose Mail.com, a leading provider of Internet messaging outsourcing services, offers to host BKFin.com's e-mail function for $9 per mailbox per month. If BKFin.com outsources its e-mail to Mail.com, BKFin.com will still need the virus protection software, its computer hardware, and one information technology staff member, who would be responsible for maintaining virus protection, quarantining suspicious e-mail, and managing content (e.g., screening e-mail for objectionable content). Should CEO Wise accept Mail.com's offer?

3. Suppose for an additional $5 per mailbox per month, Mail.com will also provide virus protection, quarantine, and content-management services. Outsourcing these additional functions would mean that BKFin.com would not need either an e-mail information technology staff member or the separate virus protection license. Should CEO Wise outsource these extra services to Mail.com?

Ethical Issue

Case 21-41. Mary Tan is the controller for Duck Associates, a property management company in Portland, Oregon. Each year Tan and payroll clerk Toby Stock meet with the external auditors about payroll accounting. This year, the auditors suggest that Tan consider outsourcing Duck Associates' payroll accounting to a company specializing in payroll processing services. This would allow Tan and her staff to focus on their primary responsibility: accounting for the properties under management. At present, payroll requires 1.5 employee positions—payroll clerk Toby Stock and a bookkeeper who spends half her time entering payroll data in the system.

Tan considers this suggestion, and she lists the following items relating to outsourcing payroll accounting:

a. The current payroll software that was purchased for $4,000 three years ago would not be needed if payroll processing were outsourced.

b. Duck Associates' bookkeeper would spend half her time preparing the weekly payroll input form that is given to the payroll processing service. She is paid $450 a week.

c. Duck Associates would no longer need payroll clerk Toby Stock, whose annual salary is $42,000.

d. The payroll processing service would charge $2,000 a month.

Requirements

1. Would outsourcing the payroll function increase or decrease Duck Associates' operating income?

2. Tan believes that outsourcing payroll would simplify her job, but she does not like the prospect of having to lay off Stock, who has become a close personal friend. She does not believe there is another position available for Stock at his current salary. Can you think of other factors that might support keeping Stock, rather than outsourcing payroll processing? How should each of the factors affect Tan's decision if she wants to do what is best for Duck Associates and act ethically?

Team Project

Case 21-42. John Menard is the founder and sole owner of Menards. Analysts have estimated that his chain of home improvement stores scattered around nine midwestern states generate about $3 billion in annual sales. But how can Menards compete with giant Home Depot?

Suppose Menard is trying to decide whether to invest $45 million in a state-of-the-art manufacturing plant in Eau Claire, Wisconsin. Menard expects the plant would operate for 15 years, after which it would have no residual value. The plant would produce Menards' own line of Formica countertops, cabinets, and picnic tables.

Suppose Menards would incur the following unit costs in producing its own product lines:

	Per Unit		
	Countertops	Cabinets	Picnic Tables
Direct materials	$15	$10	$25
Direct labor	10	5	15
Variable manufacturing overhead	5	2	6

Rather than making these products, assume Menards could buy them from outside suppliers. Suppliers would charge Menards $40 per countertop, $25 per cabinet, and $65 per picnic table.

Whether Menard makes or buys these products, assume that he expects the following annual sales:

- Countertops—487,200 at $130 each
- Picnic tables—100,000 at $225 each
- Cabinets—150,000 at $75 each

If "making" is sufficiently more profitable than outsourcing, Menard will build the new plant. John Menard has asked your consulting group for a recommendation. Menard uses the straight-line depreciation method.

Requirements

1. Are the following items relevant or irrelevant in Menard's decision to build a new plant that will manufacture his own products?
   a. The unit sale prices of the countertops, cabinets, and picnic tables (the sale prices that Menards charges its customers)
   b. The prices outside suppliers would charge Menards for the three products, if Menards decides to outsource the products rather than make them
   c. The $45 million to build the new plant
   d. The direct materials, direct labor, and variable overhead Menards would incur to manufacture the three product lines
   e. Menard's salary

2. Determine whether Menards should make or outsource the countertops, cabinets, and picnic tables, *assuming that the company has already built the plant and, therefore, has the manufacturing capacity to produce these products.* In other words, what is the annual difference in cash flows if Menards decides to make rather than outsource each of these three products?

3. Write a memo giving your recommendation to Menard. The memo should clearly state your recommendation, along with a brief summary of the reasons for your recommendation.

Quick Check Answers

1. *b*   2. *c*   3. *d*   4. *a*   5. *b*   6. *b*   7. *d*   8. *a*   9. *c*   10. *d*

For Internet Exercises, Excel in Practice, and additional online activities, go to this book's Web site at www.prenhall.com/bamber.

22 Capital Investment Decisions and the Time Value of Money

Learning Objectives

1. Describe the importance of capital investments and the capital budgeting process

2. Use the payback and accounting rate of return methods to make capital investment decisions

3. Use the time value of money to compute the present and future values of single lump sums and annuities

4. Use discounted cash flow models to make capital investment decisions

5. Compare and contrast the four capital budgeting methods

On the slopes of Deer Valley Ski Resort in Park Valley, Utah—site of the 2002 Winter Olympics slalom competition—management accounting seems a world away. But the counter where you rent your skis, the chairlift that whisks you up the mountain, and the restaurant that serves you dinner are all part of the resort's recent expansion. How did Deer Valley's developers decide to spend $13 million to expand Snow Park Lodge?

Director of Finance Jim Madsen explains that when the resort reaches a target number of skiers per day and a target level of profit, the owners expand. But each expansion must meet two requirements. First, the project must be profitable. Second, Deer Valley must expect to get its money back on the investment in a relatively short time. To figure out which projects meet these

requirements, Deer Valley's managers compare the amount of the investment needed to expand the resort with the additional revenues expected from expansion. The resort managers make this comparison using two capital budgeting techniques:

1. *Net present value*—to predict whether the investment will be profitable
2. *Payback period*—to predict how long it will take to "get the money back"

In this chapter, we'll see how companies like Deer Valley use net present value, payback period, and other capital investment analysis techniques to decide which long-term capital investments to make.

Capital Budgeting

> **1** Describe the importance of capital investments and the capital budgeting process

The process of making capital investment decisions is often referred to as **capital budgeting**. Companies make capital investments when they acquire *capital assets*—assets used for a long period of time. Capital investments include buying new equipment, building new plants, automating production, and developing major commercial Web sites. In addition to affecting operations for many years, capital investments usually require large sums of money. Deer Valley's decision to spend $13 million to expand Snow Park Lodge will tie up resources for years to come. So will Chrysler's recent decision to spend $419 million revamping its Belvidere manufacturing plant.

Capital investment decisions affect all businesses as they try to become more efficient by automating production and implementing new technologies. Grocers and retailers, such as Wal-Mart, have invested in expensive self-scan check-out machines while airlines, such as Delta and Continental, have invested in self check-in kiosks. These new technologies cost money. How do managers decide whether these expansions in plant and equipment will be good investments? They use capital budgeting analysis. Some companies, such as Georgia Pacific, employ staff solely dedicated to capital budgeting analysis. They spend thousands of hours a year determining which capital investments to pursue.

Four Popular Methods of Capital Budgeting Analysis

In this chapter, we discuss four popular methods of analyzing potential capital investments:

1. Payback period
2. Accounting rate of return (ARR)
3. Net present value (NPV)
4. Internal rate of return (IRR)

The first two methods, payback period and accounting rate of return, are fairly quick and easy and work well for capital investments that have a relatively short life span, such as computer equipment and software that may have a useful life of only three to five years. Management often uses the payback period and accounting rate of return to screen potential investments from those that are less desirable. The payback period provides management with valuable information on how fast the cash invested will be recouped. The accounting rate of return shows the effect of the investment on the company's accrual-based income. However, these two methods are inadequate if the capital investments have a longer life span. Why? Because these methods do not consider the time value of money. The last two methods, net present value and internal rate of return, factor in the time value of money so they are more appropriate for longer-term capital investments, such as Deer Valley's expansion of its lodge, ski runs, and chairlifts. Management often uses a combination of methods to make final capital investment decisions.

Capital budgeting is not an exact science. Although the calculations these methods require may appear precise, remember that they are based on predictions about an uncertain future. These predictions must consider many unknown factors, such as changing consumer preferences, competition, and government regulations. The further into the future the decision extends, the more likely that actual results will differ from predictions. Long-term decisions are riskier than short-term decisions.

Focus on Cash Flows

Generally accepted accounting principles (GAAP) are based on accrual accounting, but capital budgeting focuses on cash flows. The desirability of a capital asset depends on its ability to generate *net cash inflows*—that is, inflows in excess of outflows—over the asset's useful life. Recall that operating income based on accrual accounting contains noncash expenses, such as depreciation expense and bad-debt expense. The capital investment's *net cash inflows*, therefore, will differ from its operating income. Of the four capital budgeting methods covered in this chapter, only the accounting rate of return method uses accrual-based accounting income. The other three methods use the investment's projected *net cash inflows*.

What do the projected *net cash inflows* include? Cash *inflows* include future cash revenue generated from the investment, any future savings in ongoing cash operating costs resulting from the investment, and any future residual value of the asset. To determine the investment's *net* cash inflows, the inflows are *netted* against the investment's *future cash outflows*, such as the investment's ongoing cash operating costs and refurbishment, repairs, and maintenance costs. The initial investment itself is also a significant cash outflow. However, in our calculations, *we will always refer the amount of the investment separately from all other cash flows related to the investment*. The projected net cash inflows are "given" in our examples and in the assignment material. In reality, much of capital investment analysis revolves around projecting these figures as accurately as possible using input from employees throughout the organization (production, marketing, and so forth, depending on the type of capital investment).

Capital Budgeting Process

The first step in the capital budgeting process is to identify potential investments—for example, new technology and equipment that may make the company more efficient, competitive, and profitable. Employees, consultants, and outside sales vendors often offer capital investment proposals to management. After identifying potential capital investments, managers project the investments' net cash inflows and then analyze the investments using one or more of the four methods listed above. Sometimes the analysis involves a two-stage process: In the first stage, managers screen the investments using one or both of the methods that do *not* incorporate the time value of money: payback period or accounting rate of return. These simple methods quickly weed out undesirable investments. Potential investments that "pass the initial test" go on to a second stage of analysis. In the second stage, managers further analyze the potential investments using the net present value or internal rate of return methods. Because these methods consider the time value of money, they provide more accurate information about the potential investment's profitability.

Some companies can pursue all of the potential investments that meet or exceed their decision criteria. However, because of limited resources, other companies must engage in **capital rationing**, and choose among alternative capital investments. Based on the availability of funds, managers determine if and when to make specific capital investments. For example, management may decide to wait three years to buy a certain piece of equipment because they consider other investments more important. In the intervening three years, the company will reassess whether it should still invest in the equipment. Perhaps technology has changed, and even better equipment is available. Perhaps consumer tastes have changed so the company no longer needs the equipment. Because of changing factors, long-term capital budgets are rarely set in stone.

Most companies perform **post-audits** of their capital investments. After investing in the assets, they compare the actual net cash inflows generated from the investment to the projected net cash inflows. Post-audits help companies determine whether the investments are going as planned and deserve continued support, or whether they should abandon the project and sell the assets. Managers also use feedback from post-audits to better estimate net cash inflow projections for future projects. If managers expect routine post-audits, they will more likely submit realistic net cash inflow estimates with their capital investment proposals.

Using Payback and Accounting Rate of Return to Make Capital Investment Decisions

 Use the payback and accounting rate of return methods to make capital investment decisions

Payback Period

Payback is the length of time it takes to recover, in net cash inflows, the cost of the capital outlay. The payback model measures how quickly managers expect to recover their investment dollars. The shorter the payback period, the more attractive the asset, *all else being equal*. Computing the payback period depends on whether net cash inflows are equal each year, or whether they differ over time. We consider each in turn.

Payback with Equal Annual Net Cash Inflows

Tierra Firma makes camping gear. The company is considering investing $240,000 in hardware and software to develop a business-to-business (B2B) portal. Employees throughout the company will use the B2B portal to access company-approved suppliers. Tierra Firma expects the portal to save $60,000 a year for the six years of its useful life. The savings will arise from reducing the number of purchasing personnel the company employs and from lower prices on the goods and services purchased. Net cash inflows arise from an increase in revenues, a decrease in expenses, or both. In Tierra Firma's case, the net cash inflows result from lower expenses.

When net cash inflows are equal each year, managers compute the payback period as follows:

$$\text{Payback period} = \frac{\text{Amount invested}}{\text{Expected annual net cash inflow}}$$

Tierra Firma computes the investment's payback as follows:

$$\text{Payback period for B2B portal} = \frac{\$240,000}{\$60,000} = 4 \text{ years}$$

Exhibit 22-1 verifies that Tierra Firma expects to recoup the $240,000 investment in the B2B portal by the end of Year 4, when the accumulated net cash inflows total $240,000.

EXHIBIT 22-1 Payback—Equal Annual Net Cash Inflows

| | | Net Cash Inflows | | | |
| | | B2B Portal | | Web Site Development | |
Year	Amount Invested	Annual	Accumulated	Annual	Accumulated
0	240,000	—	—	—	—
1	—	$60,000	$60,000	$80,000	$80,000
2	—	60,000	120,000	80,000	160,000
3	—	60,000	180,000	80,000	240,000
4	—	60,000	240,000		
5	—	60,000	300,000		
6	—	60,000	360,000		

Tierra Firma is also considering investing $240,000 to develop a Web site. The company expects the Web site to generate $80,000 in net cash inflows each year of its three-year life. The payback period is computed as follows:

$$\text{Payback period for Web site development} = \frac{\$240,000}{\$80,000} = 3 \text{ years}$$

Exhibit 22-1 verifies that Tierra Firma will recoup the $240,000 investment for Web site development by the end of Year 3, when the accumulated net cash inflows total $240,000.

Payback with Unequal Net Cash Inflows

The payback equation only works when net cash inflows are the same each period. When periodic cash flows are unequal, you must accumulate net cash inflows until the amount invested is recovered. Assume that Tierra Firma is considering an alternate investment, the Z80 portal. The Z80 portal differs from the B2B portal and Web site in two respects: (1) it has *unequal* net cash inflows during its life and (2) it has a $30,000 residual value at the end of its life. The Z80 portal will generate net cash inflows of $100,000 in Year 1, $80,000 in Year 2, $50,000 each year in Years 3 through 5, $30,000 in Year 6, and $30,000 when it is sold at the end of its life. Exhibit 22-2 shows the payback schedule for these unequal annual net cash inflows.

EXHIBIT 22-2   Payback: Unequal Annual Net Cash Inflows

		Net Cash Inflows Z80 Portal	
Year	Amount Invested	Annual	Accumulated
0	$240,000	—	—
1	—	100,000	$100,000
2	—	80,000	180,000
3	—	50,000	230,000
4	—	50,000	280,000
5	—	50,000	330,000
6	—	30,000	360,000
Residual Value		30,000	390,000

By the end of Year 3, the company has recovered $230,000 of the $240,000 initially invested. At the end of Year 3, they are only $10,000 short of payback. Because the expected net cash inflow in Year 4 is $50,000, by the end of Year 4 the company will have recovered *more* than the initial investment. Therefore, the payback period is somewhere between three and four years. Assuming that the cash flow occurs evenly throughout the fourth year, the payback period is calculated as follows:

$$\text{Payback} = 3 \text{ years} + \frac{\$10,000 \text{ (amount needed to complete recovery in Year 4)}}{\$50,000 \text{ (net cash inflow in Year 4)}}$$
$$= 3.2 \text{ years}$$

Criticism of the Payback Period Method

A major criticism of the payback method is that it focuses only on time, not on profitability. The payback period considers only those cash flows that occur *during* the payback period. This method ignores any cash flows that occur *after* that period, including any residual value. For example, Exhibit 22-1 shows that the B2B portal will continue to generate net cash inflows for two years after its payback period. These additional net cash inflows amount to $120,000 ($60,000 × 2 years), yet the payback method ignores this extra cash. A similar situation occurs with the Z80 portal. As shown in Exhibit 22-2, the Z80 portal will provide an additional $150,000 of net cash inflows, including residual value, after its payback period of 3.2 years ($120,000 during its remaining life plus $30,000 residual value). However, the Web site's useful life, as shown in Exhibit 22-1, is the *same* as its payback period (three years). No cash flows are ignored, yet the Web site will merely cover its cost and provide no profit. Because this is the case, the company has little or no reason to invest in the Web site.

Exhibit 22-3 compares the payback period of the three investments. As the exhibit illustrates, the payback method does not consider the asset's profitability. The method only tells management how quickly they will recover their cash. Even though the Web site has a shortest payback period, both the B2B portal and the Z80 portal are better investments because they provide profit. The key point is that the investment with the shortest payback period is best *only if all other factors are the same*. Therefore, managers usually use the payback method as a screening device to "weed out" investments that will take too long to recoup. They rarely use payback

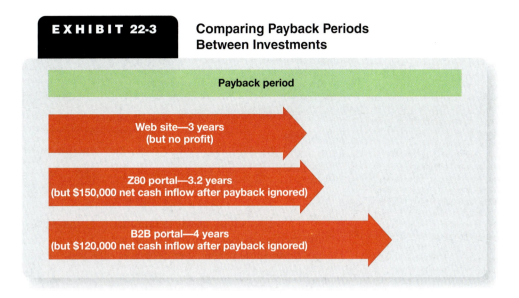

EXHIBIT 22-3 Comparing Payback Periods Between Investments

period as the sole method for deciding whether to invest in the asset. When using the payback period method, managers are guided by following decision rule:

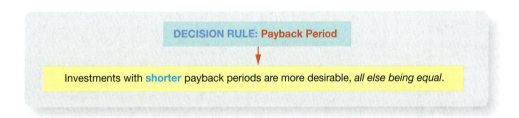

Accounting Rate of Return (ARR)

Companies are in business to earn profits. One measure of profitability is the **accounting rate of return (ARR)** on an asset:

$$\frac{\text{Accounting}}{\text{rate of return}} = \frac{\text{Average annual operating income from asset}}{\text{Average amount invested in asset}}$$

The ARR focuses on the *operating income, not the net cash inflow,* an asset generates. The ARR measures the *average* rate of return over the asset's entire life. Let's first consider investments with no residual value.

Investments with No Residual Value

Recall the B2B portal, which costs $240,000, has equal annual net cash inflows of $60,000, a six-year useful life, and no residual value.

Let's first consider the average annual operating income in the numerator. The average annual operating income of an asset is simply the asset's total operating income over the course of its operating life divided by its lifespan (number of years). Operating income is based on *accrual accounting*. Therefore, any noncash expenses, such as depreciation expense, must be subtracted from the asset's net cash inflows to arrive at its operating income. The B2B portal's average annual operating income is calculated as follows[1].

Total net cash inflows during operating life of asset ($60,000 × 6 years)	$360,000
Less: Total depreciation during operating life of asset (cost − any salvage value)	(240,000)
Total operating income during operating life	$120,000
Divide by: Asset's operating life (in years)	÷ 6 years
Average annual operating income from asset	$ 20,000

Now let's look at the denominator of the ARR equation. The *average* amount invested in an asset is its *net book value halfway* through the asset's useful life. The net book value of the asset decreases each year because of depreciation, as shown in Exhibit 22-4.

EXHIBIT 22-4 Net Book Value of B2B and Z80 Portals

	Net Book Value of B2B Portal (no residual value)	Net Book Value of Z80 Portal (residual value of $30,000)
Initial investment	$240,000	$240,000
(Annual depreciation expense)	($40,000* annual depreciation)	($35,000** annual depreciation)
End of Year 1	$200,000	$205,000
End of Year 2	160,000	170,000
End of Year 3 (halfway point)	120,000	135,000
End of Year 4	80,000	100,000
End of Year 5	40,000	65,000
End of Year 6	0	30,000

*$240,000 ÷ 6 years = $40,000 annual depreciation
**($240,000 − $30,000 residual value) ÷ 6 years = $35,000 annual depreciation

If the asset has no residual value, the average investment is half the asset's cost. Because the B2B portal does not have a residual value, the *average* amount invested is $120,000 ($240,000 invested ÷ 2). Exhibit 22-4 confirms this result. Notice that at the end of Year 3, the B2B's net book value is $120,000.

We calculate the B2B's ARR as:

$$\text{Accounting rate of return} = \frac{\$20,000}{\$240,000/2} = \frac{\$20,000}{\$120,000} = 0.167 = 16.7\%$$

Investments with a Residual Value

Now consider the Z80 portal (data from Exhibit 22-2). Recall the Z80 portal differed from the B2B portal only in that it had unequal net cash inflows during its life and a $30,000 residual value at the end of its life. Its average annual operating income is calculated as follows:

---

[1] If an asset has *equal* annual net cash inflows, like the B2B portal, another way to compute the average annual operating income ($20,000) is to subtract annual depreciation ($40,000) from annual net cash inflows ($60,000).

Total net cash inflows *during* operating life of asset (does not include the residual value at end of life)[2] (Year 1 + Year 2, etc.)	$360,000
Less: Total depreciation during operating life of asset (cost − any salvage value) ($240,000 cost − $30,000 salvage value)	(210,000)
Total operating income during operating life of asset	$150,000
Divide by: Asset's operating life (in years)	÷ 6 years
Average annual operating income from asset	$ 25,000

Notice that the Z80 portal's average annual operating ($25,000) income is higher than the B2B portal's operating income ($20,000). Since the Z80 asset has a residual value at the end of its life, less depreciation is expensed each year, leading to a higher average annual operating income.

Now let's look at the denominator of the ARR equation, the average amount invested in the asset. Recall from our previous discussion that the *average* amount invested in an asset is its *net book value halfway* through the asset's useful life. If the asset does have a residual value, the net book value of the asset halfway through its life is *greater* than half the asset's cost. Recall the Z80 portal has a $30,000 residual value. To calculate the average investment, the residual value is simply *added* to the amount invested:

$$\text{Average amount invested} = (\text{Amount invested in asset} + \text{Residual value})/2$$
$$\$135,000 = (\$240,000 + \$30,000)/2$$

Again, Exhibit 22-4 confirms this result. The Z80's net book value at the end of Year 3 is $135,000.

We calculate the Z80's ARR as:

$$\frac{\text{Accounting}}{\text{rate of return}} = \frac{\$25,000}{(\$240,000+\$30,000)/2} = \frac{\$25,000}{\$135,000} = 0.185 = 18.5\%$$

Companies that use the ARR model set a minimum required accounting rate of return. If Tierra Firma requires an ARR of at least 20%, then its managers would not approve an investment in the B2B portal or the Z80 portal because the ARR for both investments is less than 20%.

The decision rule is:

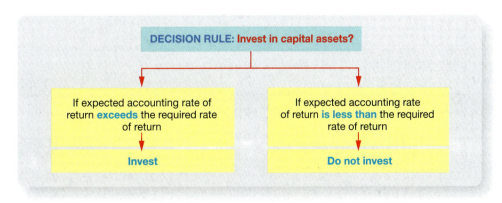

---

[2]The residual value is not included in the net cash inflows *during* the asset's operating life because we are trying to find the asset's average *annual operating* income. We assume that the asset will be sold for its expected residual value ($30,000) at the *end* of its life, resulting in no additional accounting gain or loss.

In summary, the payback period focuses on the time it takes for the company to recoup its cash investment but ignores all cash flows occurring after the payback period. Because it ignores any additional cash flows (including any residual value), the method does not consider the profitability of the project.

The ARR, however, measures the profitability of the asset over its entire life using accrual accounting figures. It is the only method that uses accrual accounting rather than net cash inflows in its computations. The payback period and ARR methods are simple and quick to compute so managers often use them to screen out undesirable investments. However, both methods ignore the time value of money.

Decision Guidelines

Capital Budgeting

Amazon.com started as a virtual retailer. It held no inventory. Instead, it bought books and CDs only as needed to fill customer orders. As the company grew, its managers decided to invest in their own warehouse facilities. Why? Owning warehouse facilities allows Amazon.com to save money by buying in bulk. Also, shipping all items in the customer's order in one package, from one location, saves shipping costs. Here are some of the guidelines Amazon.com's managers used as they made the major capital budgeting decision to invest in building warehouses.

Decision	Guideline
Why is this decision important?	Capital budgeting decisions typically require large investments and affect operations for years to come.
What method shows us how soon we will recoup our cash investment?	The payback method shows managers how quickly they will recoup their investment. The method highlights investments that are too risky due to long payback periods. However, it doesn't reveal any information about the investment's profitability.
Does any method consider the impact of the investment on accrual accounting income?	The accounting rate of return is the only capital budgeting method that shows how the investment will affect accrual accounting income, which is important to financial statement users. All other methods of capital investment analysis focus on the investment's net cash inflows.
How do we compute the payback period if cash flows are *equal*?	$$\text{Payback period} = \frac{\text{Amount invested}}{\text{Expected annual net cash inflow}}$$
How do we compute the payback period if cash flows are *unequal*?	Accumulate net cash inflows until the amount invested is recovered.
How do we compute the ARR?	$$\text{Accounting rate of return} = \frac{\text{Average annual operating income from asset}}{\text{Average amount invested in asset}}$$

Summary Problem 1

Zetamax is considering buying a new bar-coding machine for its Austin, Texas, plant. The company screens its potential capital investments using the payback period and accounting rate of return methods. If a potential investment has a payback period of less than four years and a minimum 12% accounting rate of return, it will be considered further. The data for the machine follow:

Cost of machine	$48,000
Estimated residual value	$ 0
Estimated annual net cash inflow (each year for 5 years)	$13,000
Estimated useful life	5 years

Requirements

1. Compute the bar-coding machine's payback period.

2. Compute the bar-coding machine's ARR.

3. Should Zetamax turn down this investment proposal or consider it further?

Solution

Requirement 1

$$\text{Payback period} = \frac{\text{Amount invested}}{\text{Expected annual net cash inflow}} = \frac{\$48,000}{\$13,000} = 3.7 \text{ years (rounded)}$$

Requirement 2

$$\text{Accounting rate of return} = \frac{\text{Average annual operating income from asset}}{\text{Average amount invested in asset}}$$

$$= \frac{\$3,400*}{(\$48,000 + \$0)/2}$$

$$= \frac{\$3,400}{\$24,000}$$

$$= 0.142 \text{ (rounded)}$$

$$= 14.2\%$$

*Total net cash inflows during life ($13,000 × 5 years)	$65,000
Less: total depreciation during life	(48,000)
Total operating income during life	$17,000
Divided by: life of asset	÷ 5 years
Average annual operating income	$ 3,400

Requirement 3

The bar-coding machine proposal passes both initial screening tests. The payback period is slightly less than four years, and the accounting rate of return is higher than 12%. Zetamax should further analyze the proposal using a method that incorporates the time value of money.

A Review of the Time Value of Money

A dollar received today is worth more than a dollar to be received in the future. Why? Because you can invest today's dollar and earn extra income. The fact that invested money earns income over time is called the **time value of money**, and this explains why we would prefer to receive cash sooner rather than later. The time value of money means that the timing of capital investments' net cash inflows is important. Two methods of capital investment analysis incorporate the time value of money: the NPV and IRR. This section reviews time value of money to make sure you have a firm foundation for discussing these two methods.

Factors Affecting the Time Value of Money

The time value of money depends on several key factors:

1. the principal amount (p)
2. the number of periods (n)
3. the interest rate (i)

The principal (p) refers to the amount of the investment or borrowing. Because this chapter deals with capital investments, we'll primarily discuss the principal in terms of investments. However, the same concepts apply to borrowings (which you probably discussed in your financial accounting course when you studied bonds payable). We state the principal as either a single lump sum or an annuity. For example, if you want to save money for a new car after college, you may decide to invest a single lump sum of $10,000 in a certificate of deposit (CD). However, you may not currently have $10,000 to invest. Instead, you may invest funds as an annuity, depositing $2,000 at the end of each year in a bank savings account. An **annuity** is a stream of *equal installments* made at *equal time intervals*.[3]

The number of periods (n) is the length of time from the beginning of the investment until termination. All else being equal, the shorter the investment period, the lower the total amount of interest earned. If you withdraw your savings after four years, rather than five years, you will earn less interest. If you begin to save for retirement at age 22 rather than age 45, you will earn more interest before you retire (you let time do the work). In this chapter, the number of periods is stated in years.[4]

The interest rate (i) is the annual percentage earned on the investment. **Simple interest** means that interest is calculated *only* on the principal amount. **Compound interest** means that interest is calculated on the principal *and* on all interest earned to date. *Compound interest assumes that all interest earned will remain invested at the same interest rate, not withdrawn and spent*. Exhibit 22-5 compares simple interest (6%) on a 5-year, $10,000 CD with interest compounded yearly (rounded to the nearest dollar). As you can see, the amount of compound interest earned yearly grows as the base on which it is calculated (principal plus cumulative interest to date) grows. Over the life of this investment, the total amount of compound interest is about 10% more than the total amount of simple interest. Most investments yield compound interest so we assume compound interest, rather than simple interest, for the rest of this chapter.

---

[3] An *ordinary annuity* is an annuity in which the installments occur at the *end* of each period. An *annuity due* is an annuity in which the installments occur at the *beginning* of each period. Throughout this chapter we use ordinary annuities since they are better suited to capital budgeting cash flow assumptions.
[4] The number of periods can also be stated in days, months, or quarters. If so, the interest rate needs to be adjusted to reflect the number of time periods in the year.

Capital Investment Decisions and the Time Value of Money

EXHIBIT 22-5 — Simple Versus Compound Interest for a Principal Amount of $10,000, at 6%, over 5 Years

Year	Simple Interest Calculation	Simple Interest	Compound Interest Calculation	Compound Interest
1	$10,000 × 6% =	$ 600	$10,000 × 6% =	$ 600
2	$10,000 × 6% =	600	($10,000 + 600) × 6% =	636
3	$10,000 × 6% =	600	($10,000 + 600 + 636) × 6% =	674
4	$10,000 × 6% =	600	($10,000 + 600 + 636 + 674) × 6% =	715
5	$10,000 × 6% =	600	($10,000 + 600 + 636 + 674 + 715) × 6% =	758
	Total interest	$3,000	Total interest	$3,383

Fortunately, time value calculations involving compound interest do not have to be as tedious as shown in Exhibit 22-5. Formulas and tables (or proper use of business calculators programmed with these formulas, or spreadsheet software such as Microsoft Excel) simplify the calculations. In the next sections, we will discuss how to use these tools to perform time value calculations.

Future Values and Present Values: Points Along the Time Continuum

Consider the time line in Exhibit 22-6. The future value or present value of an investment simply refers to the value of an investment at different points in time.

EXHIBIT 22-6 — Present Value and Future Value Along the Time Continuum

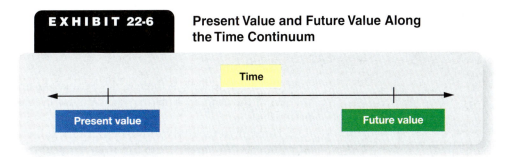

We can calculate the future value or the present value of any investment by knowing (or assuming) information about the three factors we listed earlier: (1) the principal amount, (2) the period of time, and (3) the interest rate. For example, in Exhibit 22-5, we calculated the interest that would be earned on (1) a $10,000 principal, (2) invested for 5 years, (3) at 6% interest. The future value of the investment is simply its worth at the end of the five-year time frame—the original principal *plus* the interest earned. In our example, the future value of the investment is:

$$\text{Future value} = \text{Principal} + \text{Interest Earned}$$
$$= \$10,000 + \$3,383$$
$$= \$13,383$$

If we invest $10,000 *today*, its *present value* is simply $10,000. So another way of stating the future value is:

$$\text{Future value} = \text{Present value} + \text{Interest Earned}$$

We can rearrange the equation as follows:

Present value = Future value − Interest Earned
$10,000 = $13,383 − $3,383

The only difference between present value and future value is the amount of interest that is earned in the intervening time span.

Future Value and Present Value Factors

Calculating each period's compound interest, as we did in Exhibit 22-5, and then adding it to the present value to figure the future value (or subtracting it from the future value to figure the present value) is tedious. Fortunately, mathematical formulas simplify future value and present value calculations. Mathematical formulas have been developed which specify future values and present values for unlimited combinations of interest rates (i) and time periods (n). Separate formulas exist for single lump-sum investments and annuities

These formulas are programmed into most business calculators so that the user only needs to correctly enter the principal amount, interest rate, and number of time periods to find present or future values. These formulas are also programmed into spreadsheets functions in Microsoft Excel. Because the specific steps to operate business calculators differ between brands, we will use tables instead. These tables contain the results of the formulas for various interest rate and time period combinations.

The formulas and resulting tables are shown in Appendix 22A:

1. Present Value of $1 (Appendix 22A, Table A, p. 1164)—*used for lump-sum amounts*
2. Present Value of Annuity of $1 (Appendix 22A, Table B, p. 1165)—*used for annuities*
3. Future Value of $1 (Appendix 22A, Table C, p. 1166)—*used for lump-sum amounts*
4. Future Value of Annuity of $1 (Appendix 22A, Table D, p. 1167)—*used for annuities*

Take a moment to look at these tables because we are going to use them throughout the rest of the chapter. Note that the columns are interest rates (i) and the rows are periods (n).

The data in each table, known as future value factors (FV factors) and present value factors (PV factors), are for an investment (or loan) of $1. To find the future value of an amount other than $1, you simply multiply the FV factor by the principal amount. To find the present value of an amount other than $1, you multiply the PV factor by the principal amount.

The annuity tables are derived from the lump-sum tables. For example, the Annuity PV factors (in the Present Value of Annuity of $1 table) are the *sums* of the PV factors found in the Present Value of $1 tables for a given number of time periods. The annuity tables allow us to perform "one-step" calculations rather than separately computing the present value of each annual cash installment and then summing the individual present values. (See the next Stop & Think).

Calculating Future Values of Single Sums and Annuities Using FV Factors

Let's go back to our $10,000 lump-sum investment. If we want to know the future value of the investment five years from now at an interest rate of 6%, we determine the FV factor from the table labeled Future Value of $1 (Appendix 22A, Table C). We use this table for lump-sum amounts. We look down the 6% column, and across

Stop & Think

Show that the *annuity* PV factors in Appendix 22A, Table B are simply the *sums* of the PV factors in Appendix 22A, Table A. Use an annuity of $1 made at the end of each of 3 years at an interest rate of 6%.

Answer: The *annuity* PV factor for $1 ($n = 3$, $i = 6\%$) (Appendix 22A, Table B) is **2.673**. This is the same as the *sum* of the individual PV factors for $1 at ($i = 6\%$) found in Appendix 22A, Table A:

Period (n)	PV factor for $1 at $i = 6\%$ (from Appendix 22A, Table A)
1	.943
2	.890
3	.840
Total	2.673

---

the 5 periods row, and find the future value factor is 1.338. We finish our calculations as follows:

$$\text{Future value} = \text{Principal amount} \times (\text{FV factor for } i = 6\%, n = 5)$$
$$= \$10{,}000 \times (1.338)$$
$$= \$13{,}380$$

This figure agrees with our earlier calculation of the investment's future value ($13,383) in Exhibit 22-5. (The difference of $3 is due to two facts: (1) the tables round the FV and PV factors to three decimal places and (2) we rounded our earlier yearly interest calculations in Exhibit 22-5 to the nearest dollar.)

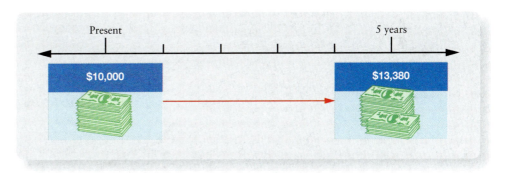

Let's also consider our alternative investment strategy, investing $2,000 at the end of each year for five years. The procedure for calculating the future value of an *annuity* is quite similar to calculating the future value of a lump-sum amount. This time, we use the Future Value of Annuity of $1 table (Appendix 22A, Table D). Assuming 6% interest, we once again look down the 6% column. Because we will be making five annual installments, we look across the row marked 5 periods. The Annuity FV factor is 5.637. We finish the calculation as follows:

$$\text{Future value} = \text{Amount of each cash installment} \times (\text{Annuity FV factor for } i = 6\%, n = 5)$$
$$= \$2{,}000 \times (5.637)$$
$$= \$11{,}274$$

This is considerably less than the future value ($13,380) of the lump sum of $10,000, even though we have invested $10,000 out-of-pocket either way.

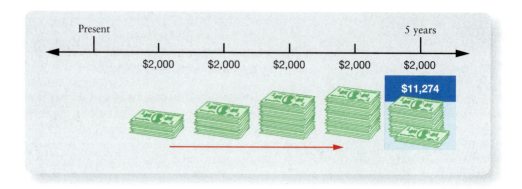

Stop & Think

Explain why the future value of the annuity ($11,274) is less than the future value of the lump sum ($13,380). Prove the $11,274 future value is correct by calculating interest using the "long-hand" method shown earlier.

Answer: Even though you invested $10,000 out-of-pocket, the timing of the investment significantly affects the amount of interest earned. The $10,000 lump sum invested immediately earns interest for the full five years. However, the annuity doesn't begin earning interest until Year 2 (because the first installment isn't made until the *end* of Year 1). Additionally, the amount invested begins at $2,000 and doesn't reach a full $10,000 until the end of Year 5. Therefore, the base on which the interest is earned is smaller than the lump-sum investment for the entire five-year period. As shown here, the $11,274 future value of a $2,000 annuity for five years is correct.

Year	Interest Earned During Year (6%) (rounded)	Investment Installment (end of year)	Cumulative Balance at End of Year (investments plus interest earned to date)*
1	$ 0	$2,000	$2,000
2	120	2,000	4,120
3	247	2,000	6,367
4	382	2,000	8,749
5	525	2,000	11,274

*This is the base on which the interest is earned the next year.

Calculating Present Values of Single Sums and Annuities Using PV Factors

The process for calculating present values—often called **discounting cash flows**—is similar to the process for calculating future values. The difference is the point in time at which you are assessing the investment's worth. Rather than determining its value at a future date, you are determining its value at an earlier point in time (today). For our example, let's assume you've just won the lottery after purchasing one $5 lottery ticket. The state offers you three payout options for your after-tax prize money:

Option #1: $1,000,000 now

Option #2: $150,000 at the end of each year for the next 10 years

Option #3: $2,000,000 10 years from now

Which alternative should you take? You might be tempted to wait 10 years to "double" your winnings. You may be tempted to take the money now and spend it. However, let's assume you plan to prudently invest all money received—no matter when you receive it—so that you have financial flexibility in the future (for example, for buying a house, retiring early, taking exotic vacations, and so forth). How can you choose among the three payment alternatives, when the total amount of each option varies ($1,000,000 versus $1,500,000 versus $2,000,000) and the timing of the cash flows varies (now versus some each year versus later)? Comparing these three options is like comparing apples to oranges—we just can't do it—unless we find some common basis for comparison. Our common basis for comparison will be the prize-money's worth at a certain point in time—namely, today. In other words, if we convert each payment option to its *present value*, we can compare apples to apples.

We already know the principal amount and timing of each payment option so the only assumption we'll have to make is the interest rate. The interest rate will vary, depending on the amount of risk you are willing to take with your investment. Riskier investments (such as stock investments) command higher interest rates; safer investments (such as FDIC-insured bank deposits) yield lower interest rates. Let's say that after investigating possible investment alternatives, you choose an investment contract with an 8% annual return. We already know that the present value of Option #1 is $1,000,000. Let's convert the other two payment options to their present values so that we can compare them. We'll need to use the Present Value of Annuity of $1 table (Appendix 22A, Table B) to convert payment Option #2 (since it's an annuity) and the Present Value of $1 table (Appendix 22A, Table A) to convert payment Option #3 (since it's a single-lump-sum). To obtain the PV factors, we'll look down the 8% column and across the 10 period row. Then, we finish the calculations as follows:

Option #2

Present value = Amount of each cash installment × (Annuity PV factor for $i = 8\%, n = 10$)

Present value = $150,000 × (6.710)

Present value = $1,006,500

Option #3

Present value = Principal amount × (PV factor for $i = 8\%, n = 10$)

Present value = $2,000,000 × (0.463)

Present value = $926,000

Exhibit 22-7 shows that we have converted each payout option to a common basis—its worth *today*—so we can make a valid comparison among the options.

EXHIBIT 22-7   **Present Value of Lottery Payout Options**

Payment Options	Present Value of Lottery Payout ($i = 8\%$, $n = 10$)
Option #1	$ 1,000,000
Option #2	$ 1,006,500
Option #3	$ 926,000

Based on this comparison, we should choose Option #2 because its worth, in today's dollars, is the highest of the three options.

Stop & Think

Suppose you decide to invest your lottery winnings very conservatively. You decide to invest in a risk-free investment that only earns 3%. Would you still choose payout Option #2? Explain your decision.

Answer: Using a 3% interest rate, the present values of the payout options are:

Payment Options	Present Value of Lottery Payout (Present value calculation, $i = 3\%$, $n = 10$)
Option #1	$1,000,000 (same because the payout is today)
Option #2	$1,279,500 (= $150,000 × 8.530)
Option #3	$1,488,000 (= $2,000,000 × .744)

When the lottery payout is invested at 3%, rather than 8%, the present values change. Option #3 is now the best alternative because its present value is the highest. Present values and future values are extremely sensitive to changes in interest rate assumptions, especially when the investment period is relatively long.

Now that you have studied time value of money concepts, we will discuss the two capital budgeting methods that incorporate the time value of money: net present value (NPV) and internal rate of return (IRR).

Using Discounted Cash-Flow Models to Make Capital Budgeting Decisions

 Use discounted cash-flow models to make capital investment decisions

Neither the payback period nor the ARR recognizes the time value of money. That is, these models fail to consider the *timing* of the net cash inflows an asset generates. *Discounted cash-flow models*—the NPV and the IRR—overcome this weakness. These models incorporate compound interest by assuming that companies will reinvest future cash flows when they are received. Over 85% of large industrial firms in the United States use discounted cash-flow methods to make capital investment decisions. Companies that provide services, like Deer Valley, also use these models.

The NPV and IRR methods rely on present value calculations to *compare* the amount of the investment (the investment's initial cost) with its expected net cash inflows. Recall from page 1113 that an investment's *net cash inflows* includes all *future* cash flows related to the investment, such as future increased sales or cost savings netted against the investment's cash operating costs. Because the cash outflow for the investment occurs *now*, but the net cash inflows from the investment occur in the *future*, companies can only make valid "apple-to-apple" comparisons if they convert the cash flows to the *same point in time*—namely the present value. Companies use the present value to make the comparison (rather than the future value) because the investment's initial cost is already stated at its present value.[4]

As shown in Exhibit 22-8, in a favorable investment, the present value of the investment's net cash inflows exceeds the initial cost of the investment. In terms of our earlier

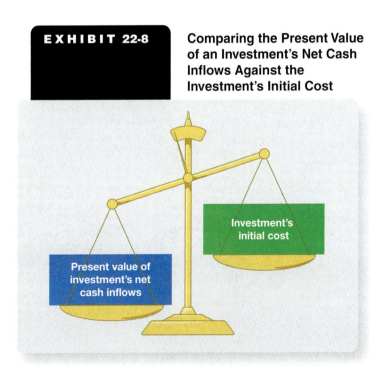

EXHIBIT 22-8 Comparing the Present Value of an Investment's Net Cash Inflows Against the Investment's Initial Cost

---

[4]If the investment is to be purchased through lease payments, rather than a current cash outlay, we would still use the current cash price of the investment as its initial cost. If no current cash price is available, we would discount the future lease payments back to their present value to estimate the investment's current cash price.

lottery example, the lottery ticket turned out to be a "good investment" because the present value of its net cash inflows (the present value of the lottery payout under *any* of the three payout options) exceeded the cost of the investment (the lottery ticket cost $5 to purchase). Let's begin our discussion by taking a closer look at the NPV method.

Net Present Value (NPV)

Allegra is considering producing CD players and digital video recorders (DVRs). The products require different specialized machines that each cost $1 million. Each machine has a five-year life and zero residual value. The two products have different patterns of predicted net cash inflows:

	Annual Net Cash Inflows	
Year	CD Players	DVRs
1	$ 305,450	$ 500,000
2	305,450	350,000
3	305,450	300,000
4	305,450	250,000
5	305,450	40,000
Total	$1,527,250	$1,440,000

The CD-player project generates more net cash inflows, but the DVR project brings in cash sooner. To decide how attractive each investment is, we find its **net present value (NPV)**. The NPV is the *difference* between the present value of the investment's net cash inflows and the investment's cost. We *discount* the net cash inflows—just as we did in the lottery example—using Allegra's minimum desired rate of return. This rate is called the **discount rate** because it is the interest rate used for the present value calculations. It's also called the **required rate of return** or **hurdle rate** because the investment must meet or exceed this rate to be acceptable. The discount rate depends on the riskiness of investments. The higher the risk, the higher the discount rate. Allegra's discount rate for these investments is 14%.

We then compare the present value of the net cash inflows to the investment's initial cost to decide which projects meet or exceed management's minimum desired rate of return. In other words, management is deciding whether the $1 million is worth more (because they would give it up now to invest in the project) or whether the project's future net cash inflows are worth more. They can only make a valid comparison between the two sums of money by comparing them at the *same* point in time—namely, at their present value.

NPV with Equal Periodic Net Cash Inflows (Annuity)

Allegra expects the CD-player project to generate $305,450 of net cash inflows each year for five years. Because these cash flows are equal in amount, and occur every year, they are an annuity. Therefore, we use the Present Value of Annuity of $1 table (Appendix 22A, Table B) to find the appropriate Annuity PV factor for $i = 14\%$, $n = 5$:

The present value of the net cash inflows from Allegra's CD-player project is:

> Present value = Amount of each net cash inflow × (Annuity PV factor for $i = 14\%$, $n = 5$)
> = $305,450 × (3.433)
> = $1,048,610

Next, we simply subtract the investment's initial cost ($1 million) from the present value of the net cash inflows ($1,048,610). The difference of $48,610 is the *net present value* (NPV), as shown in Exhibit 22-9.

EXHIBIT 22-9 — NPV of Equal Net Cash Inflows—CD-Player Project

	Annuity PV Factor (i = 14%, n = 5)	Net Cash Inflow	Present Value
Present value of annuity of equal annual net cash inflows for 5 years at 14%	3.433* ×	$305,450 =	$1,048,610
Investment			(1,000,000)
Net present value of the CD-player project			$ 48,610

*Annuity PV Factor is found in Appendix 22A, Table B.

A *positive* NPV means that the project earns *more* than the required rate of return. A negative NPV means that the project fails to earn the required rate of return. This leads to the following decision rule:

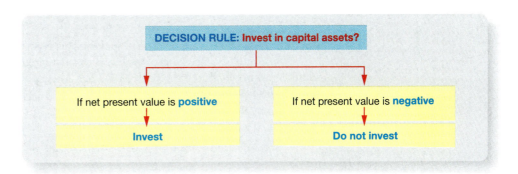

In Allegra's case, the CD-player project is an attractive investment. The $48,610 positive NPV means that the CD-player project earns *more than* Allegra's 14% target rate of return.

Another way managers can use present value analysis is to start the capital budgeting process by computing the total present value of the net cash inflows from the project to determine the *maximum* the company can invest in the project and still earn the target rate of return. For Allegra, the present value of the net cash inflows is $1,048,610. This means that Allegra can invest a maximum of $1,048,610 and still earn the 14% target rate of return. Because Allegra's managers believe they can undertake the project for $1 million, the project is an attractive investment.

NPV with Unequal Periodic Net Cash Inflows

In contrast to the CD-player project, the net cash inflows of the DVR project are unequal—$500,000 in Year 1, $350,000 in Year 2, and so on. Because these amounts vary by year, Allegra's managers *cannot* use the annuity table to compute the present value of the DVR project. They must compute the present value of each individual year's net cash inflows *separately (as separate lump sums received in different years)*, using the Present Value of $1 table (Appendix 22A, Table A). Exhibit 22-10 shows that the $500,000 net cash inflow received in Year 1 is discounted using a PV factor of $i = 14\%$, $n = 1$, while the $350,000 net cash inflow received in Year 2 is discounted using a PV factor of $i = 14\%$, $n = 2$, and so forth. After separately discounting each of the five year's net cash inflows, we find the *total* present value of the DVR project's net cash inflows is $1,078,910. Finally, we subtract the investment's cost ($1 million) to arrive at the DVR project's NPV: $78,910.

EXHIBIT 22-10   NPV with Unequal Net Cash Inflows—DVR Project

	PV Factor (i = 14%)		Net Cash Inflow		Present Value
Present value of each year's net cash inflows discounted at 14%:					
Year 1 (n = 1)	0.877 †	×	$500,000	=	$438,500
Year 2 (n = 2)	0.769	×	350,000	=	269,150
Year 3 (n = 3)	0.675	×	300,000	=	202,500
Year 4 (n = 4)	0.592	×	250,000	=	148,000
Year 5 (n = 5)	0.519	×	40,000	=	20,760
Total present value of net cash inflows					1,078,910
Investment					(1,000,000)
Net present value of the DVR project					$ 78,910

†PV Factors are found in Appendix 22A, Table A.

Because the NPV is positive, Allegra expects the DVR project to earn more than the 14% target rate of return, making this is an attractive investment.

You could also use Microsoft Excel to calculate the NPV. To do so, first open a blank workbook. Enter the cash flows for Allegra's CD-player project into a column, like shown below:

Year	Cash Flow
0	$(1,000,000)
1	$305,450
2	$305,450
3	$305,450
4	$305,450
5	$305,450

Then, select Insert from the Menu Line, and Function from the pull down menu.

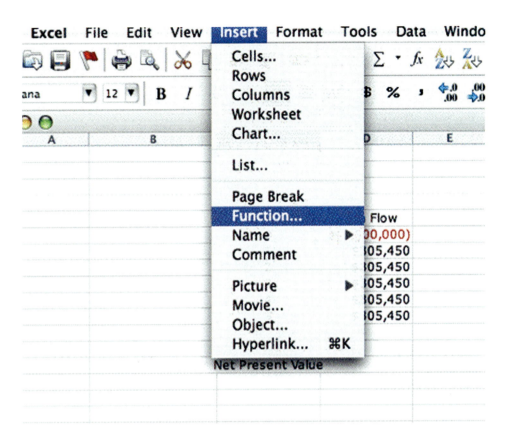

From the Paste Function dialog box, select Financial for Function category, and NPV for the actual function.

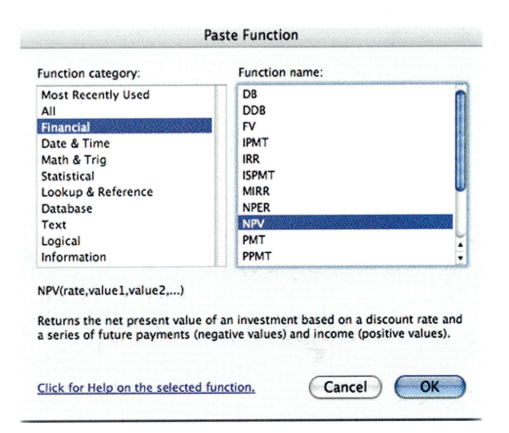

In the NPV dialog box, enter the 14% discount rate, and then select the cells in which you entered the cash inflows:

NPV

Rate	14%		= 0.14
Value1	D7:D11		= {305450;305450;:
Value2			= number

= 1048634.582

Returns the net present value of an investment based on a discount rate and a series of future payments (negative values) and income (positive values).

Value1: value1,value2,... are 1 to 29 payments and income, equally spaced in time and occurring at the end of each period.

Formula result = 1048634.582   Cancel   OK

Click OK, and Microsoft Excel calculates the present value of the cash inflows for you.

	A	B	C	D	E
1					
2					
3					
4					
5			Year	Cash Flow	
6			0	($1,000,000)	
7			1	$305,450	
8			2	$305,450	
9			3	$305,450	
10			4	$305,450	
11			5	$305,450	
12					
13					
14			Net Present Value	$1,048,634.58	
15					
16					

Next, use Excel to subtract the present value of the cost to derive the Net Present Value of the Investment.

Year	Cash Flow
0	($1,000,000)
1	$305,450
2	$305,450
3	$305,450
4	$305,450
5	$305,450

Present Value of Inflows	$1,048,635
Cost	($1,000,000)
Net Present Value	$48,635

The difference between the NPV derived using Excel verses the amount derived using the tables in Appendix 22A is simply due to mathematical rounding.

You can follow the same procedure to calculate the NPV with uneven cash flows, such as used in the DVR project.

First of all, Insert the NPV Function:

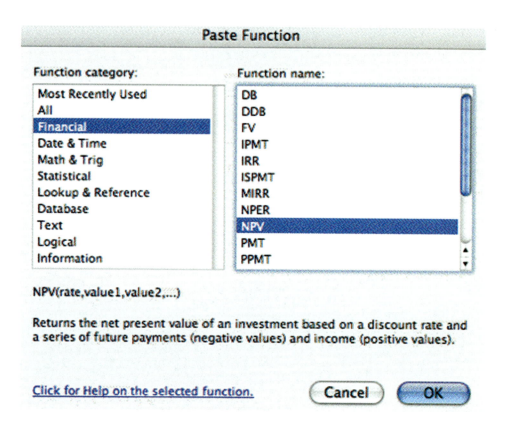

Then, select the discount rate and the cells with the cash inflows:

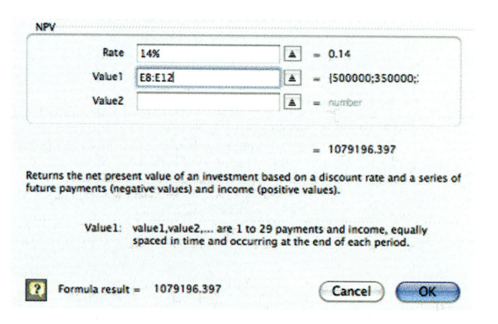

Click OK, and Excel displays the Present Value of the Cash Inflows in the cell:

Year	Cash Flow
0	($1,000,000)
1	$500,000
2	$350,000
3	$300,000
4	$250,000
5	$40,000
Present Value of Cash Inflows	$1,079,196.40

Next, use Excel to subtract the present value of the cash payment to derive the NPV of the investment.

Year	Cash Flow
0	($1,000,000)
1	$500,000
2	$350,000
3	$300,000
4	$250,000
5	$40,000
Present Value of Cash Inflows	$1,079,196
Present Value of Cost	($1,000,000)
Net Present Value	$79,196

Again, the difference between the NPV derived using Excel versus the amount derived using the tables in Appendix 22A is simply due to mathematical rounding.

Capital Rationing and the Profitability Index

Exhibits 22-9 and 22-10 show that both the CD-player and DVR projects have positive NPVs. Therefore, both are attractive investments. Because resources are limited, companies are not always able to invest in all capital assets that meet their investment criteria. For example, Allegra may not have the funds to invest in both the DVR and CD-player projects at this time. In this case, Allegra should choose the DVR project because it yields a higher NPV. The DVR project should earn an additional $78,910 beyond the 14% required rate of return, while the CD-player project returns an additional $48,610.

This example illustrates an important point. The CD-player project promises more *total* net cash inflows. But the *timing* of the DVR cash flows—loaded near the beginning of the project—gives the DVR investment a higher NPV. The DVR project is more attractive because of the time value of money. Its dollars, which are received sooner, are worth more now than the more-distant dollars of the CD-player project.

If Allegra had to choose between the CD and DVR project, they would choose the DVR project because it yields a higher NPV ($78,910). However, comparing the NPV of the two projects is *only* valid because both projects require the same initial cost—$1 million. In contrast, Exhibit 22-11 summarizes three capital investment options faced by Raycor, a sporting goods manufacturer. Each capital project requires a different initial investment. All three projects are attractive because each yields a positive NPV. Assuming Raycor can only invest in one project at this time, which one should it choose? Project B yields the highest NPV, but it also requires a larger initial investment than the alternatives.

EXHIBIT 22-11   Raycor's Capital Investment Options

	Project A	Project B	Project C
Present value of net cash inflows	$150,000	$238,000	$182,000
Investment	(125,000)	(200,000)	(150,000)
Net present value (NPV)	$ 25,000	$ 38,000	$ 32,000

To choose among the projects, Raycor computes the **profitability index** (also known as the **present value index**). The profitability index is computed as:

Profitability index = Present value of net cash inflows ÷ Investment

The profitability index computes the number of dollars returned for every dollar invested, *with all calculations performed in present value dollars*. It allows us to compare alternative investments in present value terms (like the NPV method) but also considers differences in the investments' initial cost. Let's compute the profitability index for all three alternatives.

Present value of net cash inflows		÷ Investment		= Profitability Index
Project A:	$150,000	÷ $125,000	=	1.20
Project B:	$238,000	÷ $200,000	=	1.19
Project C:	$182,000	÷ $150,000	=	1.21

The profitability index shows that Project C is the best of the three alternatives because it returns $1.21 (in present value dollars) for every $1.00 invested. Projects A and B return slightly less.

Let's also compute the profitability index for Allegra's CD-player and DVR projects:

CD-player:	$1,048,610	÷ $1,000,000 =	1.048
DVR:	$1,078,910	÷ $1,000,000 =	1.078

The profitability index confirms our prior conclusion that the DVR project is more profitable than the CD-player project. The DVR project returns $1.078 (in present value dollars) for every $1.00 invested (beyond the 14% return already used to discount the cash flows). We did not need the profitability index to determine that the DVR project was preferable because both projects required the same investment ($1 million).

NPV of a Project with Residual Value

Many assets yield cash inflows at the end of their useful lives because they have residual value. Companies discount an investment's residual value to its present value when determining the *total* present value of the project's net cash inflows. The residual value is discounted as a single lump sum—not an annuity—because it will be received only once, when the asset is sold.

Suppose Allegra expects the CD project equipment will be worth $100,000 at the end of its five-year life. To determine the CD-player project's NPV, we discount the residual value ($100,000) using the Present Value of $1 table ($i = 14\%$, $n = 5$). (See Appendix 22A, Table A, page 1164) We then *add* its present value ($51,900) to the present value of the CD project's other net cash inflows ($1,048,610) as shown in Exhibit 22-12:

EXHIBIT 22-12   NPV of a Project with Residual Value

	PV Factor ($i = 14\%$, $n = 5$)		Net Cash Inflow	Present Value
Present value of annuity	3.433	×	$305,450 =	$ 1,048,610
Present value of residual value (single lump sum)	0.519	×	100,000 =	51,900
Total present value of net cash inflows				$ 1,100,510
Investment				$(1,000,000)
Net present value (NPV)				$ 100,510

Because of the expected residual value, the CD-player project is now more attractive than the DVR project. If Allegra could pursue only the CD or DVR project, it would now choose the CD project because its NPV ($100,510) is higher than the DVR project ($78,910) and both projects require the same investment ($1 million).

Sensitivity Analysis

Capital budgeting decisions affect cash flows far into the future. Allegra's managers might want to know whether their decision would be affected by any of their major assumptions. For example:

- Changing the discount rate from 14% to 12% or to 16%
- Changing the net cash flows by 10%

After entering the basic information for NPV analysis into spreadsheet software, managers perform sensitivity analyses with just a few keystrokes. The software quickly recalculates and displays the results.

Internal Rate of Return (IRR)

Another discounted cash-flow model for capital budgeting is the internal rate of return. The **internal rate of return (IRR)** is the rate of return (based on discounted cash flows) a company can expect to earn by investing in the project. *It is the interest rate that makes the NPV of the investment equal to zero:*

$$\text{NPV} = 0$$

Let's look at this concept in another light by substituting in the definition of NPV:

$$\text{Present value of the investment's net cash inflows} - \text{Investment's cost} = 0$$

Finally, we rearrange the equation:

$$\text{Investment's cost} = \text{Present value of investment's net cash inflows}$$

In other words, the IRR is the *interest rate* that makes the cost of the investment equal to the present value of the investment's net cash inflows. The higher the IRR, the more desirable the project.

IRR with Equal Periodic Net Cash Inflows (Annuity)

Let's first consider Allegra's CD-player project, which would cost $1 million and result in five equal yearly cash inflows of $305,450. We compute the IRR of an investment with equal periodic cash flows (annuity) by taking the following steps:

1. The IRR is the interest rate that makes the cost of the investment *equal to* the present value of the investment's net cash inflows, so we set up the following equation:

   Investment's cost = Present value of investment's net cash inflows
   Investment's cost = Amount of each equal net cash inflow × Annuity PV factor ($i = ?, n =$ given)

2. Next, we plug in the information we do know—the investment cost ($1,000,000), the equal annual net cash inflows ($305,450), and the number of periods (five years):

   $$\$1,000,000 = \$305,450 \times \text{Annuity PV factor } (i = ?, n = 5)$$

3. We then rearrange the equation and solve for the Annuity PV factor ($i = ?, n = 5$):

   $$\$1,000,000 \div \$305,450 = \text{Annuity PV factor } (i = ?, n = 5)$$
   $$3.274 = \text{Annuity PV factor } (i = ?, n = 5)$$

4. Finally, we find the interest rate that corresponds to this Annuity PV factor. Turn to the Present Value of Annuity of $1 table (Appendix 22A, Table B). Scan the row corresponding to the project's expected life—five years, in our example. Choose the column(s) with the number closest to the Annuity PV factor you calculated in Step 3. The 3.274 annuity factor is in the 16% column. Therefore, the IRR of the CD-player project is 16%. Allegra expects the project to earn an internal rate of return of 16% over its life. Exhibit 22-13 confirms this result: Using a 16% discount rate, the project's NPV is zero. In other words, 16% is the discount rate that makes the investment cost equal to the present value of the investment's net cash inflows.

EXHIBIT 22-13   IRR—CD-Player Project

	Annuity PV Factor ($i = 16\%, n = 5$)	Net Cash Inflow	Total Present Value
Present value of annuity of equal annual net cash inflows for 5 years at 16%	3.274 ×	$305,450 =	$1,000,000†
Investment			(1,000,000)
Net present value of the CD-player project			$ 0‡

†Slight rounding error.
‡The zero difference proves that the IRR is 16%.

To decide whether the project is acceptable, compare the IRR with the minimum desired rate of return. The decision rule is:

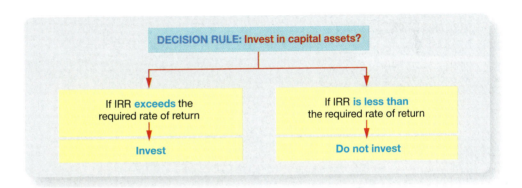

Recall that Allegra's hurdle rate is 14%. Because the CD project's IRR (16%) is higher than the hurdle rate (14%), Allegra would invest in the project.

In the CD-player project, the exact Annuity PV factor (3.274) appears in the Present Value of an Annuity of $1 table (Appendix 22A, Table B). Many times, the exact factor will not appear in the table. For example, let's find the IRR of Tierra Firma's B2B Portal. Recall the B2B portal had a six-year life with annual net cash inflows of $60,000. The investment cost $240,000. We find its Annuity PV factor using the same steps shown on page 1134:

Investment's cost	= Present value of investment's net cash inflows
Investment's cost	= Amount of each equal net cash inflow × Annuity PV factor ($i = ?, n =$ given)
$240,000	= $60,000 × Annuity PV factor ($i = ?, n = 6$)
$240,000 ÷ $60,000	= Annuity PV factor ($i = ?, n = 6$)
4.00	= Annuity PV factor ($i = ?, n = 6$)

Now look in the Present Value of Annuity of $1 table in the row marked 6 periods (Appendix 22A, Table B). You will not see 4.00 under any column. The closest two factors are 3.889 (at 14%) and 4.111 (at 12%). Thus, the B2B portal's IRR must be somewhere between 12% and 14%. If we need a more precise figure, we could use a business calculator or Microsoft Excel to find the portal's exact IRR of 12.978%. If Tierra Firma had a 14% hurdle rate, it would *not* invest in the B2B portal because the portal's IRR is less than 14%.

IRR with Unequal Periodic Cash Flows

Because the DVR project has unequal cash inflows, Allegra cannot use the Present Value of Annuity of $1 table to find the asset's IRR. Rather, Allegra must use a trial-and-error procedure to determine the discount rate making the project's NPV equal to zero. For example, because the company's minimum required rate of return is 14%, Allegra might start by calculating whether the DVR project earns at least 14%. Recall from Exhibit 22-10 that the DVR's NPV using a 14% discount rate is $78,910. Since the NPV is *positive*, the IRR must be *higher* than 14%. Allegra continues the trial-and-error process using *higher* discount rates until they find the rate that brings the net present value of the DVR project to *zero*. Exhibit 22-14 shows that at 16%, the DVR has an NPV of $40,390, therefore, the IRR must be higher than 16%. At 18%, the NPV is $3,980, which is very close to zero. Thus, the IRR must be slightly higher than 18%. If we use a business calculator, rather than the trial-and-error procedure, we would find the IRR is 18.23%.

The DVR's internal rate of return is higher than Allegra's 14% hurdle rate so the DVR project is attractive.

EXHIBIT 22-14 Finding the DVR's IRR Through Trial-and-Error

	Net Cash Inflow		PV Factor (for i = 16%)		Present Value at 16%	Net Cash Inflow		PV Factor (for i = 18%)		Present Value at 18%
Year 1 (n = 1)	$500,000	×	0.862*	=	$ 431,000	$500,000	×	0.847*	=	$ 423,500
Year 2 (n = 2)	350,000	×	0.743	=	260,050	350,000	×	0.718	=	251,300
Year 3 (n = 3)	300,000	×	0.641	=	192,300	300,000	×	0.609	=	182,700
Year 4 (n = 4)	250,000	×	0.552	=	138,000	250,000	×	0.516	=	129,000
Year 5 (n = 5)	40,000	×	0.476	=	19,040	40,000	×	0.437	=	17,480
Total present value of net cash inflows					$1,040,390					$1,003,980
Investment					(1,000,000)					(1,000,000)
Net present value (NPV)					$ 40,390					$ 3,980

*PV Factors are found in Appendix 22A, Table A.

You could also use Microsoft Excel to calculate the Internal Rate of Return. To do so, first open a blank workbook. Enter the cash flows for Allegra's CD-player project into a column, like shown below:

Year	Cash Flow
0	$(1,000,000)
1	$305,450
2	$305,450
3	$305,450
4	$305,450
5	$305,450

Then, select Insert from the Menu Line, and Function from the pull down menu.

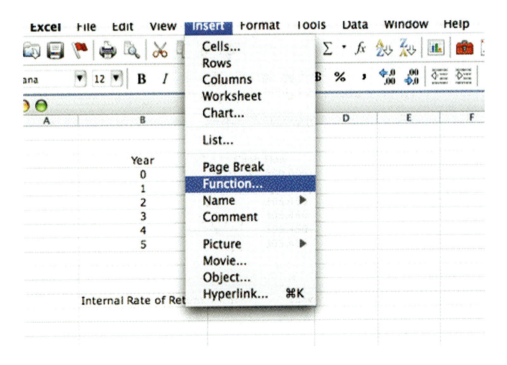

From the Paste Function dialog box, select Financial for function type, and IRR for the actual function.

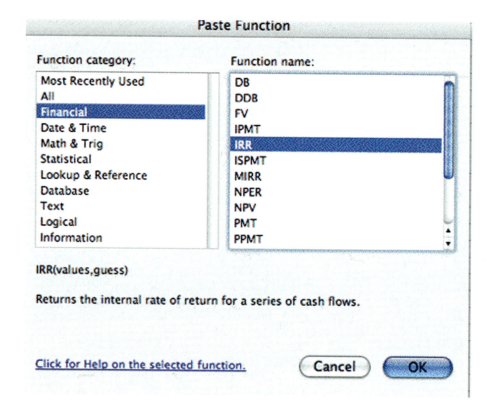

In the IRR dialog box, select the cells in which you entered the cash flows:

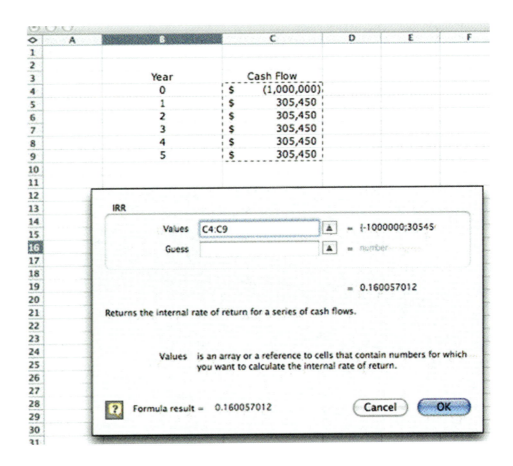

Click OK, and Microsoft Excel calculates the IRR for you.

	A	B	C	D
1				
2				
3		Year	Cash Flow	
4		0	$ (1,000,000)	
5		1	$ 305,450	
6		2	$ 305,450	
7		3	$ 305,450	
8		4	$ 305,450	
9		5	$ 305,450	
10				
11				
12				
13		Internal Rate of Return		16%
14				

You can follow the same procedure to calculate the Internal Rate of Return with uneven cash flows, such as used in the DVR project.

First, here's how Excel would display the cash flows and the IRR function:

	A	B	C	D
1				
2				
3		Year	Cash Flow	
4		0	$ (1,000,000)	
5		1	$ 500,000	
6		2	$ 350,000	
7		3	$ 300,000	
8		4	$ 250,000	
9		5	$ 40,000	
10				
11				
12				
13		Internal Rate of Return	=IRR(C4:C9)	
14				
15				

When Excel calculates the IRR, we see that the IRR is precisely 18.23%.

	A	B	C	D
1				
2				
3		Year	Cash Flow	
4		0	$ (1,000,000)	
5		1	$ 500,000	
6		2	$ 350,000	
7		3	$ 300,000	
8		4	$ 250,000	
9		5	$ 40,000	
10				
11				
12				
13		Internal Rate of Return	18.23%	
14				
15				

Comparing Capital Budgeting Methods

5 Compare and contrast the four capital budgeting methods

We have discussed four capital budgeting methods commonly used by companies to make capital investment decisions. Two of these methods do not incorporate the time value of money: payback period and ARR. Exhibit 22-15 summarizes the similarities and differences between these two methods.

The discounted cash-flow methods are superior because they consider both the time value of money and profitability. These methods compare an investment's initial cost

EXHIBIT 22-15 Capital Budgeting Methods That *Ignore* the Time Value of Money

Payback period	Accounting rate of return
• Simple to compute • Focuses on the time it takes to recover the company's cash investment • Ignores any cash flows occurring after the payback period, including any residual value • Highlights risks of investments with longer cash recovery periods • Ignores the time value of money	• The only method that uses accrual accounting figures • Shows how the investment will affect operating income, which is important to financial statement users • Measures the profitability of the asset over its entire life • Ignores the time value of money

(cash outflow) with its future net cash inflows—all converted to the *same point in time*—the present value. Profitability is built into the discounted cash-flow methods because they consider *all* cash inflows and outflows over the project's life. Exhibit 22-16 considers the similarities and differences between the two discounted cash-flow methods.

EXHIBIT 22-16 Capital Budgeting Methods That *Incorporate* the Time Value of Money

Net present value	Internal rate of return
• Incorporates the time value of money and the asset's net cash flows over its entire life • Indicates whether or not the asset will earn the company's minimum required rate of return • Shows the excess or deficiency of the asset's present value of net cash inflows over its initial investment cost • The profitability index should be computed for capital rationing decisions when the assets require different initial investments	• Incorporates the time value of money and the asset's net cash flows over its entire life • Computes the project's unique rate of return • No additional steps needed for capital rationing decisions

Managers often use more than one method to gain different perspectives on risks and returns. For example, Deer Valley's owners could decide to pursue capital projects with positive NPVs, provided that those projects have a payback of four years or less.

Stop & Think

A pharmaceutical company is considering two research projects that require the same initial investment. Project A has an NPV of $232,000 and a 3-year payback period. Project B has an NPV of $237,000 and a payback period of 4.5 years. Which project would you choose?

Answer: Many managers would choose project A. NPV is a better guide to decision making than payback period. But managers would consider the 2.2% [($237,000 − $232,000)/$232,000] difference between the NPVs to be insignificant. In contrast, the 50% [(4.5 years − 3.0 years)/3.0 years] difference between payback periods *is* significant. The uncertainty of receiving operating cash flows increases with each passing year. Managers often forgo small differences in expected cash inflows to decrease the risk of investments.

Decision Guidelines

CAPITAL BUDGETING

Here are more of the guidelines Amazon.com's managers used as they made the major capital budgeting decision to invest in building warehouses.

Decision	Guideline
Which capital budgeting methods are best?	Discounted cash-flow methods (NPV and IRR) are best because they incorporate both profitability and the time value of money.
Why do the NPV and IRR models use the present value?	Because an investment's cash inflows and cash outflows occur at different points in time, they must be converted to a common point in time to make a valid comparison (that is, to determine whether inflows exceed cash outflows). These methods use the *present* value as the common point in time.
How do we know if investing in warehouse facilities will be worthwhile?	Investment in warehouse facilities may be worthwhile if the NPV is positive or the IRR exceeds the required rate of return.
How do we compute the net present value with: • Equal annual cash flows?	Compute the present value of the investment's net cash inflows using the Present Value of an Annuity of $1 table and then subtract the investment's cost.
• Unequal annual cash flows?	Compute the present value of each year's net cash inflows using the Present Value of $1 (lump sum) table, sum the present value of the inflows, and then subtract the investment's cost.
How do we compute the internal rate of return with • Equal annual cash flows?	Find the interest rate that yields the following PV factor: $$\text{Annuity PV factor} = \frac{\text{Investment cost}}{\text{Expected annual net cash inflow}}$$
• Unequal annual cash flows?	Trial and error, spreadsheet software, or business calculator

Summary Problem 2

Recall from Summary Problem 1 that Zetamax is considering buying a new bar-coding machine. The investment proposal passed the initial screening tests (payback period and accounting rate of return) so the company now wants to analyze the proposal using the discounted cash flow methods. Recall that the bar-coding machine costs $48,000, has a five-year life, and no residual value. The estimated net cash inflows are $13,000 per year over its life. The company's hurdle rate is 16%.

Requirements

1. Compute the bar-coding machine's NPV.
2. Find the bar-coding machine's IRR (exact percentage not required).
3. Should Zetamax buy the bar-coding machine? Why?

Solution

Requirement 1

Present value of annuity of equal annual net cash inflows at 16% ($13,000 × 3.274*)	$42,562
Investment	(48,000)
Net present value	$(5,438)

*Annuity PV factor ($i = 16\%, n = 5$)

Requirement 2

$$\text{Investment cost} = \text{Amount of each equal cash inflow} \times \text{Annuity PV factor } (i = ?, n = 5)$$
$$\$48{,}000 = \$13{,}000 \times \text{Annuity PV factor } (i = ?, n = 5)$$
$$\$48{,}000 \div \$13{,}000 = \text{Annuity PV factor } (i = ?, n = 5)$$
$$3.692 = \text{Annuity PV factor } (i = ?, n = 5)$$

Because the cash flows occur for five years, we look for the PV factor 3.692 in the row marked $n = 5$ on the Present Value of Annuity of $1 table (Appendix 22A, Table B). The PV factor is 3.605 at 12% and 3.791 at 10%. Therefore, the bar-coding machine has an IRR that falls between 10% and 12%. (*Optional:* Using a business calculator, we find an 11.038% internal rate of return.)

Requirement 3

Decision: Do not buy the bar-coding machine. It has a negative NPV and its IRR falls below the company's required rate of return. Both methods consider profitability and the time value of money.

Review Capital Investment Decisions and the Time Value of Money

Accounting Vocabulary

Accounting Rate of Return
A measure of profitability computed by dividing the average annual operating income from an asset by the average amount invested in the asset.

Annuity
A stream of equal installments made at equal time intervals.

Capital Budgeting
The process of making capital investment decisions. Companies make capital investments when they acquire *capital assets*—assets used for a long period of time.

Capital Rationing
Choosing among alternative capital investments due to limited funds.

Compound Interest
Interest computed on the principal *and* all interest earned to date.

Discount Rate
Management's minimum desired rate of return on an investment. Also called the hurdle rate and required rate of return.

Internal Rate of Return (IRR)
The rate of return (based on discounted cash flows) that a company can expect to earn by investing in a capital asset. The interest rate that makes the NPV of the investment equal to zero.

Net Present Value (NPV)
The *difference* between the present value of the investment's net cash inflows and the investment's cost.

Payback
The length of time it takes to recover, in net cash inflows, the cost of a capital outlay.

Post-Audits
Comparing a capital investment's actual net cash inflows to its projected net cash inflows.

Profitability Index
An index that computes the number of dollars returned for every dollar invested, *with all calculations performed in present value dollars*. Computed as present value of net cash inflows divided by investment.

Simple Interest
Interest computed *only* on the principal amount.

Time Value of Money
The fact that money can be invested to earn income over time.

Quick Check

1. Which of the following methods uses accrual accounting, rather than net cash flows, as a basis for calculations?
   a. payback
   b. ARR
   c. NPV
   d. IRR

2. Which of the following methods does not consider the investment's profitability?
   a. payback
   b. ARR
   c. NPV
   d. IRR

3. Which of the following is true regarding capital rationing decisions?
   a. Companies should always choose the investment with the shortest payback period.
   b. Companies should always choose the investment with the highest NPV.
   c. Companies should always choose the investment with the highest ARR.
   d. None of the above.

4. Your rich aunt has promised to give you $3,000 a year at the end of each of the next four years to help you pay for college. Using a discount rate of 10%, the present value of the gift can be stated as:
   a. PV = $3,000 (PV factor, $i = 4\%, n = 10$)
   b. PV = $3,000 × 10% × 5
   c. PV = $3,000 (Annuity PV factor, $i = 10\%, n = 4$)
   d. PV = $3,000 (Annuity FV factor, $i = 10\%, n = 4$)

5. Which of the following affects the present value of an investment?
   a. the interest rate
   b. the number of time periods (length of the investment)
   c. the type of investment (annuity versus single lump sum)
   d. all of the above

6. In computing the IRR on the Snow Park Lodge expansion, Deer Valley would consider all of the following *except?*
   a. predicted cash inflows over the life of the expansion
   b. the cost of the expansion
   c. present value factors
   d. depreciation on the assets built in the expansion

7. The IRR is
   a. the same as the ARR
   b. the firm's hurdle rate
   c. the interest rate at which the NPV of the investment is zero
   d. none of the above

8. Suppose Amazon.com is considering investing in warehouse-management software that costs $500,000, has $50,000 residual value, and should lead to cost savings of $120,000 per year for its five-year life. In calculating the ARR, which of the following figures should be used as the equation's denominator (average amount invested in the asset)?

    a. $225,000

    b. $500,000

    c. $250,000

    d. $275,000

9. Using the information from Question 8, which of the following figures should be used in the equation's numerator (average annual operating income)?

    a. $120,000

    b. $20,000

    c. $30,000

    d. $10,000

10. Which of the following is the most reliable method for making capital budgeting decisions?

    a. NPV method

    b. ARR method

    c. payback method

    d. post-audit method

Answers are given after Apply Your Knowledge (p. 1153)

Assess Your Progress

Short Exercises

1 Describe the importance of capital investments and the capital budgeting process

S22-1 Place the following activities in sequence to illustrate the capital budgeting process:
a. Budget capital investments
b. Project investments' cash flows
c. Perform post-audits
d. Make investments
e. Use feedback to reassess investments already made
f. Identify potential capital investments
g. Screen/analyze investments using one or more of the methods discussed

2 Use the payback and accounting rate of return methods to make capital investment decisions

S22-2 Consider how Deer Valley (from the chapter-opening story) could use capital budgeting to decide whether the $13 million Snow Park Lodge expansion would be a good investment.

Assume Deer Valley's managers developed the following estimates concerning the expansion (all numbers assumed):

Number of additional skiers per day	120
Average number of days per year that weather conditions allow skiing at Deer Valley	150
Useful life of expansion (in years)	10
Average cash spent by each skier per day	$245
Average variable cost of serving each skier per day	$ 85
Cost of expansion	$13,000,000
Discount rate	12%

Assume that Deer Valley uses the straight-line depreciation method and expects the lodge expansion to have a residual value of $1 million at the end of its 10-year life.

Requirements
1. Compute the average annual net cash inflow from the expansion.
2. Compute the average annual operating income from the expansion.

2 Use the payback and accounting rate of return methods to make capital investment decisions

S22-3 Refer to the Deer Valley Snow Park Lodge expansion project in S22-2. Compute the payback period for the expansion project.

2 Use the payback and accounting rate of return methods to make capital investment decisions

S22-4 Refer to the Deer Valley Snow Park Lodge expansion project in S22-2. What is the ARR?

S22-5 Refer to the Deer Valley Snow Park Lodge expansion project in S22-2. *Assume the expansion has zero residual value.*

Requirements
1. Will the payback period change? Explain and recalculate if necessary.
2. Will the project's ARR change? Explain and recalculate if necessary.
3. Assume Deer Valley screens its potential capital investments using the following decision criteria:

Maximum payback period	5 years
Minimum accounting rate of return	18%

Will Deer Valley consider this project further, or reject it?

S22-6 Suppose Deer Valley is deciding whether to purchase new accounting software. The payback period for the $30,000 software package is four years, and the software's expected life is six years. Assuming equal yearly cash flows, what are the expected annual cash savings from the new software?

S22-7 Your grandfather would like to share some of his fortune with you. He offers you to give you money under one of the following scenarios (you get to choose):
1. $8,000 a year at the end of each of the next eight years
2. $50,000 (lump sum) now
3. $100,000 (lump sum) eight years from now

Calculate the present value of each scenario using a 6% discount rate. Which scenario yields the highest present value? Would your preference change if you used a 12% discount rate?

S22-8 Assume you make the following investments:
a. You invest $5,000 for four years at 12% interest. What is the investment's value at the end of four years?
b. In a different account earning 12% interest, you invest $1,250 at the end of each year for four years. What is the investment's value at the end of four years?
c. What general "rule-of-thumb" explains the difference in the investments' future values?

S22-9 Refer to the lottery payout options on page 1128. Rather than comparing the payout options at their present values (as done in the chapter), compare the payout options at their future value, 10 years from now.
a. Using an 8% interest rate, what is the future value of each payout option?
b. Rank your preference among payout options.
c. Does computing the future value, rather than the present value of the options, change your preference between payout options? Explain.

3 Use the time value of money to compute the present and future values of single lump sums and annuities

S22-10 Use the Present Value of $1 table (Appendix 22A, Table A) to determine the present value of $1 received one year from now. Assume a 14% interest rate. Use the same table to find the present value of $1 received two years from now. Continue this process for a total of five years.

a. What is the *total* present value of the cash flows received over the five-year period?

b. Could you characterize this stream of cash flows as an annuity? Why, or why not?

c. Use the Present Value of Annuity of $1 table (Appendix 22A, Table B) to determine the present value of the same stream of cash flows. Compare your results to your answer to Part a.

d. Explain your findings.

4 Use discounted cash flow models to make capital investment decisions

S22-11 Refer to the Deer Valley Snow Park Lodge expansion project in S22-2. What is the project's NPV? Is the investment attractive? Why?

4 Use discounted cash flow models to make capital investment decisions

S22-12 Refer to S22-11. *Assume the expansion has no residual value.* What is the project's NPV? Is the investment still attractive? Why?

S22-13 Refer to S22-12. *Continue to assume the expansion has no residual value.* What is the project's IRR? Is the investment attractive? Why?

5 Compare and contrast the four capital budgeting methods

S22-14 Use your results from S22-5, 22-12, and 22-13 to write a memo to Deer Valley's Director of Finance Jim Madsen, recommending whether Deer Valley should undertake the expansion, *assuming no residual value.* Cover the strengths and weaknesses of each capital budgeting method cited in your memo. Use the following format:

Date: _____

To: Mr. Jim Madsen, Director of Finance

From: _____

Subject: _____

Exercises

1 Describe the importance of capital investments and the capital budgeting process

5 Compare and contrast the four capital budgeting methods

E22-15 You have just started a business and want your new employees to be well informed about capital budgeting. Write a memo to your employees (1) explaining why capital budgeting is important, (2) briefly describing the four different methods of analyzing capital investments along with some of their strengths and weaknesses, and (3) explaining why your company will post-audit all capital investments.

2 Use the payback and accounting rate of return methods to make capital investment decisions

E22-16 Quiksilver is considering acquiring a manufacturing plant. The purchase price is $1,236,100. The owners believe the plant will generate net cash inflows of $309,025 annually. It will have to be replaced in eight years. Use the payback method to determine whether Quiksilver should purchase this plant.

2 Use the payback and accounting rate of return methods to make capital investment decisions

E22-17 Sikes Hardware is adding a new product line that will require an investment of $1,454,000. Managers estimate that this investment will have a 10-year life and generate net cash inflows of $310,000 the first year, $280,000 the second year, and $240,000 each year thereafter for eight years. Compute the payback period.

2 Use the payback and accounting rate of return methods to make capital investment decisions

E22-18 Engineered Products is shopping for new equipment. Managers are considering two investments. Equipment manufactured by Atlas costs $1,000,000 and will last for five years, with no residual value. The Atlas equipment will generate annual operating income of $160,000. Equipment manufactured by Veras costs $1,200,000 and will remain useful for six years. It promises annual operating income of $240,500, and its expected residual value is $100,000.

Which equipment offers the higher ARR?

2 Use the payback and accounting rate of return methods to make capital investment decisions

E22-19 Refer to the Sikes Hardware information in E22-17. Compute the ARR for the investment.

3 Use the time value of money to compute the present and future values of single lump sums and annuities

E22-20 Assume you want to retire early at age 52. You plan to save using one of the following two strategies: (1) save $3,000 a year in an IRA beginning when you are 22 and ending when you are 52 (30 years) or (2) wait until you are 40 to start saving and then save $7,500 per year for the next 12 years. Assume you will earn the historic stock market average of 10% per year.

Requirements

1. How much "out-of-pocket" cash will you invest under the two options?
2. How much savings will you have accumulated at age 52 under the two options?

continued ...

3. Explain the results.
4. If you were to let the savings continue to grow for 10 more years (with no further out-of-pocket investments), what would the investments be worth when you are age 62?

E22-21 Your best friend just received a gift of $5,000 from his favorite aunt. He wants to save the money to use as "starter" money after college. He can invest it (1) risk-free at 3%, (2) taking on moderate risk at 8%, or (3) taking on high risk at 16%. Help your friend project the investment's worth at the end of four years under each investment strategy and explain the results to him.

E22-22 Janet wants to take the next five years off work to travel around the world. She estimates her annual cash needs at $30,000 (if she needs more, she'll work odd jobs). Janet believes she can invest her savings at 8% until she depletes her funds.

Requirements
1. How much money does Janet need now to fund her travels?
2. After speaking with a number of banks, Janet learns she'll only be able to invest her funds at 6%. How much does she need now to fund her travels?

E22-23 Congratulations! You've won a state lotto. The state lottery offers you the following (after-tax) payout options:

Option #1: $12,000,000 after five years

Option #2: $2,250,000 per year for the next five years

Option #3: $10,000,000 after three years

Assuming you can earn 8% on your funds, which option would you prefer?

E22-24 Use the NPV method to determine whether Salon Products should invest in the following projects:
- *Project A*: Costs $272,000 and offers eight annual net cash inflows of $60,000. Salon Products requires an annual return of 14% on projects like A.
- *Project B*: Costs $380,000 and offers nine annual net cash inflows of $70,000. Salon Products demands an annual return of 12% on investments of this nature.

What is the NPV of each project? What is the maximum acceptable price to pay for each project?

Use discounted cash flow models to make capital investment decisions

E22-25 Bevil Industries is deciding whether to automate one phase of its production process. The manufacturing equipment has a six-year life and will cost $900,000. Projected net cash inflows are as follows:

Year 1	$260,000
Year 2	$250,000
Year 3	$225,000
Year 4	$210,000
Year 5	$200,000
Year 6	$175,000

Requirements

1. Compute this project's NPV using Bevil Industries's 14% hurdle rate. Should Bevil Industries invest in the equipment?

2. Bevil Industries could refurbish the equipment at the end of six years for $100,000. The refurbished equipment could be used one more year, providing $75,000 of net cash inflows in Year 7. Additionally, the refurbished equipment would have a $50,000 residual value at the end of Year 7. Should Bevil Industries invest in the equipment and refurbishing it after six years? Hint: In addition to your answer to Requirement 1, discount the additional cash outflow and inflows back to the present value.

Use discounted cash flow models to make capital investment decisions

E22-26 Refer to Salon Products in E22-24. Compute the IRR of each project, and use this information to identify the better investment.

Use discounted cash flow models to make capital investment decisions

E22-27 Ritter Razors is considering an equipment investment that will cost $950,000. Projected net cash inflows over the equipment's three-year life are as follows: Year 1: $500,000, Year 2: $400,000, and Year 3: $300,000. Ritter wants to know the equipment's IRR.

Requirements

Use trial and error to find the IRR within a 2% range. (*Hint*: Use Ritter's hurdle rate of 10% to begin the trial-and-error process.)

Optional: Use a business calculator to compute the exact IRR.

Use discounted cash flow models to make capital investment decisions

E22-28 Sheffield Manufacturing is considering three capital investment proposals. At this time, Sheffield Manufacturing only has funds available to pursue one of the three investments. Which investment should Sheffield Manufacturing pursue at this time? Why?

	Equipment A	Equipment B	Equipment C
Present value of net cash inflows	$1,695,000	$1,960,000	$2,200,000
Investment	($1,500,000)	($1,750,000)	($2,000,000)
NPV	$ 195,000	$ 210,000	$ 200,000

5 Compare and contrast the four capital budgeting methods

E22-29 Fill in each statement with the appropriate capital budgeting method: Payback period, ARR, NPV, or IRR.

a. _____ and _____ incorporate the time value of money.
b. _____ focuses on time, not profitability.
c. _____ uses accrual accounting income.
d. _____ finds the discount rate which brings the investment's NPV to zero.
e. In capital rationing decisions, the profitability index must be computed to compare investments requiring different initial investments when the _____ method is used.
f. _____ ignores salvage value.
g. _____ uses discounted cash flows to determine the asset's unique rate of return.
h. _____ highlights risky investments.
i. _____ measures profitability, but ignores the time value of money.

Problems (Problem Set A)

1 Describe the importance of capital investments and the capital budgeting process

P22-30A Look through the business section of the newspaper. Find a company that has recently made a capital investment. Summarize the company's decision and then answer the following questions. Why do you think this is a capital investment decision? What effect will the decision have on the company? What methods might the company have used to make their decision? What information would the company have used in making their decision?

3 Use the time value of money to compute the present and future values of single lump sums and annuities

P22-31A You are planning for a very early retirement. You would like to retire at age 40 and have enough money saved to be able to draw $225,000 per year for the next 40 years (based on family history, you think you'll live to age 80). You plan to save by making 15 equal annual installments (from age 25 to age 40) into a fairly risky investment fund that you expect will earn 12% per year. You will leave the money in this fund until it is completely depleted when you are 80 years old. To make your plan work:

1. How much money must you accumulate by retirement? (*Hint:* Find the present value of the $225,000 withdrawals.)
2. How does this amount compare to the total amount you will draw out of the investment during retirement? How can these numbers be so different?

continued . . .

3. How much must you pay into the investment each year for the first 15 years? (*Hint:* Your answer from Requirement 1 becomes the future value of this annuity.)
4. How does the total "out-of-pocket" savings compare to the investment's value at the end of the 15-year savings period and the withdrawals you will make during retirement?

P22-32A Water World is considering purchasing a water park in San Antonio, Texas, for $1,850,000. The new facility will generate annual net cash inflows of $520,000 for eight years. Engineers estimate that the facility will remain useful for eight years and have no residual value. The company uses straight-line depreciation, and its stockholders demand an annual return of 12% on investments of this nature.

Requirements
1. Compute the payback period, the ARR, the NPV of this investment, and its IRR.
2. Recommend whether the company should invest in this project.

P22-33A Locos operates a chain of sandwich shops. The company is considering two possible expansion plans. Plan A would open eight smaller shops at a cost of $8,440,000. Expected annual net cash inflows are $1,600,000, with zero residual value at the end of 10 years. Under Plan B, Locos would open three larger shops at a cost of $8,340,000. This plan is expected to generate net cash inflows of $1,100,000 per year for 10 years, the estimated life of the properties. Estimated residual value is $1,000,000. Locos uses straight-line depreciation and requires an annual return of 8%

Requirements
1. Compute the payback period, the ARR, and the NPV of these two plans. What are the strengths and weaknesses of these capital budgeting models?
2. Which expansion plan should Locos choose? Why?
3. Estimate Plan A's IRR. How does the IRR compare with the company's required rate of return?

Problems (Problem Set B)

P22-34B Look through a recent copy of a business magazine, such as *Forbes* or *Fortune*. Find a company that has recently made a capital investment. Summarize the company's decision and then answer the following questions. Why do you think this is a capital investment decision? What

continued . . .

effect will the decision have on the company? What methods might the company have used to make their decision? What information would the company have used in making their decision?

P22-35B You are planning for an early retirement. You would like to retire at age 50 and have enough money saved to be able to draw $225,000 per year for the next 30 years (based on family history, you think you'll live to age 80). You plan to save by making 25 equal annual installments (from age 25 to age 50) into a fairly risky investment fund that you expect will earn 12% per year. You will leave the money in this fund until it is completely depleted when you are 80 years old. To make your plan work:

1. How much money must you accumulate by retirement? (*Hint*: Find the present value of the $225,000 withdrawals. You may want to draw a timeline showing the savings period and the retirement period.)
2. How does this amount compare the total amount you will draw out of the investment during retirement? How can these numbers be so different?
3. How much must you pay into the investment each year for the first 25 years? (*Hint*: Your answer from Question 1 becomes the future value of this annuity.)
4. How does the total "out-of-pocket" savings compare to the investment's value at the end of the 25-year savings period and the withdrawals you will make during retirement?

P22-36B Zippi manufactures motorized scooters in Oakland, California. The company is considering an expansion. The plan calls for a construction cost of $5,200,000. The expansion will generate annual net cash inflows of $675,000 for 10 years. Engineers estimate that the new facilities will remain useful for 10 years and have no residual value. The company uses straight-line depreciation, and its stockholders demand an annual return of 10% on investments of this nature.

Requirements
1. Compute the payback period, the ARR, the NPV of this investment, and its IRR.
2. Recommend whether the company should invest in this project.

P22-37B Java Café is considering two possible expansion plans. Plan A is to open 8 cafés at a cost of $4,180,000. Expected annual net cash inflows are $780,000, with residual value of $820,000 at the end of seven years. Under plan B, Java Café would open 12 cafés at a cost of $4,200,000.

continued . . .

This investment is expected to generate net cash inflows of $994,000 each year for seven years, which is the estimated useful life of the properties. Estimated residual value of the Plan B cafés is zero. Java Café uses straight-line depreciation and requires an annual return of 14%.

Requirements
1. Compute the payback period, the ARR, and the NPV of each plan. What are the strengths and weaknesses of these capital budgeting models?
2. Which expansion plan should Java Café adopt? Why?
3. Estimate the IRR for Plan B. How does Plan B's IRR compare with Java Café's required rate of return?

Apply Your Knowledge

Decision Case

Case 22-38. Ted Christensen, a second-year business student at the University of Utah, will graduate in two years with an accounting major and a Spanish minor. Christensen is trying to decide where to work this summer. He has two choices: work full-time for a bottling plant or work part-time in the accounting department of a meat-packing plant. He probably will work at the same place next summer as well. He is able to work 12 weeks during the summer.

The bottling plant will pay Christensen $380 per week this year and 7% more next summer. At the meat-packing plant, he could work 20 hours per week at $8.75 per hour. By working only part-time, he could take two accounting courses this summer. Tuition is $225 per hour for each of the four-hour courses. Christensen believes that the experience he gains this summer will qualify him for a full-time accounting position with the meat-packing plant next summer. That position will pay $550 per week.

Christensen sees two additional benefits of working part-time this summer. First, he could reduce his studying workload during the fall and spring semesters by one course each term. Second, he would have the time to work as a grader in the university's accounting department during the 15-week fall term. Grading pays $50 per week.

Requirements

1. Suppose that Christensen ignores the time value of money in decisions that cover this short a time period. Suppose also that his sole goal is to make as much money as possible between now and the end of next summer. What should he do? What nonquantitative factors might Ted consider? What would *you* do if you were faced with these alternatives?

2. Now suppose that Christensen considers the time value of money for all cash flows that he expects to receive one year or more in the future. Which alternative does this consideration favor? Why?

Quick Check Answers

1. *b* 2. *a* 3. *d* 4. *c* 5. *d* 6. *d* 7. *c* 8. *d* 9. *c* 10. *a*

For Internet Exercises, Excel in Practice, and additional online activities, go to this book's Web site at www.prenhall.com/bamber.

Appendix 22A

Present Value Tables and Future Value Tables

Table A Present Value of $1

						Present Value							
Periods	1%	2%	3%	4%	5%	6%	8%	10%	12%	14%	16%	18%	20%
1	0.990	0.980	0.971	0.962	0.952	0.943	0.926	0.909	0.893	0.877	0.862	0.847	0.833
2	0.980	0.961	0.943	0.925	0.907	0.890	0.857	0.826	0.797	0.769	0.743	0.718	0.694
3	0.971	0.942	0.915	0.889	0.864	0.840	0.794	0.751	0.712	0.675	0.641	0.609	0.579
4	0.961	0.924	0.888	0.855	0.823	0.792	0.735	0.683	0.636	0.592	0.552	0.516	0.482
5	0.951	0.906	0.863	0.822	0.784	0.747	0.681	0.621	0.567	0.519	0.476	0.437	0.402
6	0.942	0.888	0.837	0.790	0.746	0.705	0.630	0.564	0.507	0.456	0.410	0.370	0.335
7	0.933	0.871	0.813	0.760	0.711	0.665	0.583	0.513	0.452	0.400	0.354	0.314	0.279
8	0.923	0.853	0.789	0.731	0.677	0.627	0.540	0.467	0.404	0.351	0.305	0.266	0.233
9	0.914	0.837	0.766	0.703	0.645	0.592	0.500	0.424	0.361	0.308	0.263	0.225	0.194
10	0.905	0.820	0.744	0.676	0.614	0.558	0.463	0.386	0.322	0.270	0.227	0.191	0.162
11	0.896	0.804	0.722	0.650	0.585	0.527	0.429	0.350	0.287	0.237	0.195	0.162	0.135
12	0.887	0.788	0.701	0.625	0.557	0.497	0.397	0.319	0.257	0.208	0.168	0.137	0.112
13	0.879	0.773	0.681	0.601	0.530	0.469	0.368	0.290	0.229	0.182	0.145	0.116	0.093
14	0.870	0.758	0.661	0.577	0.505	0.442	0.340	0.263	0.205	0.160	0.125	0.099	0.078
15	0.861	0.743	0.642	0.555	0.481	0.417	0.315	0.239	0.183	0.140	0.108	0.084	0.065
20	0.820	0.673	0.554	0.456	0.377	0.312	0.215	0.149	0.104	0.073	0.051	0.037	0.026
25	0.780	0.610	0.478	0.375	0.295	0.233	0.146	0.092	0.059	0.038	0.024	0.016	0.010
30	0.742	0.552	0.412	0.308	0.231	0.174	0.099	0.057	0.033	0.020	0.012	0.007	0.004
40	0.672	0.453	0.307	0.208	0.142	0.097	0.046	0.022	0.011	0.005	0.003	0.001	0.001

The factors in the table were generated using the following formula:

$$\text{Present Value of \$1} = \frac{1}{(1+i)^n}$$

where:

i = annual interest rate

n = number of periods

Table B Present Value of Annuity of $1

Present Value

Periods	1%	2%	3%	4%	5%	6%	8%	10%	12%	14%	16%	18%	20%
1	0.990	0.980	0.971	0.962	0.952	0.943	0.926	0.909	0.893	0.877	0.862	0.847	0.833
2	1.970	1.942	1.913	1.886	1.859	1.833	1.783	1.736	1.690	1.647	1.605	1.566	1.528
3	2.941	2.884	2.829	2.775	2.723	2.673	2.577	2.487	2.402	2.322	2.246	2.174	2.106
4	3.902	3.808	3.717	3.630	3.546	3.465	3.312	3.170	3.037	2.914	2.798	2.690	2.589
5	4.853	4.713	4.580	4.452	4.329	4.212	3.993	3.791	3.605	3.433	3.274	3.127	2.991
6	5.795	5.601	5.417	5.242	5.076	4.917	4.623	4.355	4.111	3.889	3.685	3.498	3.326
7	6.728	6.472	6.230	6.002	5.786	5.582	5.206	4.868	4.564	4.288	4.039	3.812	3.605
8	7.652	7.325	7.020	6.733	6.463	6.210	5.747	5.335	4.968	4.639	4.344	4.078	3.837
9	8.566	8.162	7.786	7.435	7.108	6.802	6.247	5.759	5.328	4.946	4.607	4.303	4.031
10	9.471	8.983	8.530	8.111	7.722	7.360	6.710	6.145	5.650	5.216	4.833	4.494	4.192
11	10.368	9.787	9.253	8.760	8.306	7.887	7.139	6.495	5.938	5.553	5.029	4.656	4.327
12	11.255	10.575	9.954	9.385	8.863	8.384	7.536	6.814	6.194	5.660	5.197	4.793	4.439
13	12.134	11.348	10.635	9.986	9.394	8.853	7.904	7.103	6.424	5.842	5.342	4.910	4.533
14	13.004	12.106	11.296	10.563	9.899	9.295	8.244	7.367	6.628	6.002	5.468	5.008	4.611
15	13.865	12.849	11.938	11.118	10.380	9.712	8.559	7.606	6.811	6.142	5.575	5.092	4.675
20	18.046	16.351	14.878	13.590	12.462	11.470	9.818	8.514	7.469	6.623	5.929	5.353	4.870
25	22.023	19.523	17.413	15.622	14.094	12.783	10.675	9.077	7.843	6.873	6.097	5.467	4.948
30	25.808	22.396	19.600	17.292	15.373	13.765	11.258	9.427	8.055	7.003	6.177	5.517	4.979
40	32.835	27.355	23.115	19.793	17.159	15.046	11.925	9.779	8.244	7.105	6.234	5.548	4.997

The factors in the table were generated using the following formula:

$$\text{Present Value of Annuity of \$1} = \frac{1}{i}\left[1 - \frac{1}{(1+i^n)}\right]$$

where:

i = annual interest rate

n = number of periods

Table C Future Value of $1

Future Value

Periods	1%	2%	3%	4%	5%	6%	8%	10%	12%	14%	16%	18%	20%
1	1.010	1.020	1.030	1.040	1.050	1.060	1.080	1.100	1.120	1.140	1.160	1.180	1.200
2	1.020	1.040	1.061	1.082	1.103	1.124	1.166	1.210	1.254	1.300	1.346	1.392	1.440
3	1.030	1.061	1.093	1.125	1.158	1.191	1.260	1.331	1.405	1.482	1.531	1.643	1.728
4	1.041	1.082	1.126	1.170	1.216	1.262	1.360	1.464	1.574	1.689	1.811	1.939	2.074
5	1.051	1.104	1.159	1.217	1.276	1.338	1.469	1.611	1.762	1.925	2.100	2.288	2.488
6	1.062	1.126	1.194	1.265	1.340	1.419	1.587	1.772	1.974	2.195	2.436	2.700	2.986
7	1.072	1.149	1.230	1.316	1.407	1.504	1.714	1.949	2.211	2.502	2.826	3.185	3.583
8	1.083	1.172	1.267	1.369	1.477	1.594	1.851	2.144	2.476	2.853	3.278	3.759	4.300
9	1.094	1.195	1.305	1.423	1.551	1.689	1.999	2.358	2.773	3.252	3.803	4.435	5.160
10	1.105	1.219	1.344	1.480	1.629	1.791	2.159	2.594	3.106	3.707	4.411	5.234	6.192
11	1.116	1.243	1.384	1.539	1.710	1.898	2.332	2.853	3.479	4.226	5.117	6.176	7.430
12	1.127	1.268	1.426	1.601	1.796	2.012	2.518	3.138	3.896	4.818	5.936	7.288	8.916
13	1.138	1.294	1.469	1.665	1.886	2.133	2.720	3.452	4.363	5.492	6.886	8.599	10.699
14	1.149	1.319	1.513	1.732	1.980	2.261	2.937	3.798	4.887	6.261	7.988	10.147	12.839
15	1.161	1.346	1.558	1.801	2.079	2.397	3.172	4.177	5.474	7.138	9.266	11.974	15.407
20	1.220	1.486	1.806	2.191	2.653	3.207	4.661	6.728	9.646	13.743	19.461	27.393	38.338
25	1.282	1.641	2.094	2.666	3.386	4.292	6.848	10.835	17.000	26.462	40.874	62.669	95.396
30	1.348	1.811	2.427	3.243	4.322	5.743	10.063	17.449	29.960	50.950	85.850	143.371	237.376
40	1.489	2.208	3.262	4.801	7.040	10.286	21.725	45.259	93.051	188.884	378.721	750.378	1,469.772

The factors in the table were generated using the following formula:

Future Value of $1 = $(1+i)^n$

where:

i = annual interest rate

n = number of periods

Table D Future Value of Annuity of $1

Future Value

Periods	1%	2%	3%	4%	5%	6%	8%	10%	12%	14%	16%	18%	20%
1	1.000	1.000	1.000	1.000	1.000	1.000	1.000	1.000	1.000	1.000	1.000	1.000	1.000
2	2.010	2.020	2.030	2.040	2.050	2.060	2.080	2.100	2.120	2.140	2.160	2.180	2.200
3	3.030	3.060	3.091	3.122	3.153	3.184	3.246	3.310	3.374	3.440	3.506	3.572	3.640
4	4.060	4.122	4.184	4.246	4.310	4.375	4.506	4.641	4.779	4.921	5.066	5.215	5.368
5	5.101	5.204	5.309	5.416	5.526	5.637	5.867	6.105	6.353	6.610	6.877	7.154	7.442
6	6.152	6.308	6.468	6.633	6.802	6.975	7.336	7.716	8.115	8.536	8.977	9.442	9.930
7	7.214	7.434	7.662	7.898	8.142	8.394	8.923	9.487	10.089	10.730	11.414	12.142	12.916
8	8.286	8.583	8.892	9.214	9.549	9.897	10.637	11.436	12.300	13.233	14.240	15.327	16.499
9	9.369	9.755	10.159	10.583	11.027	11.491	12.488	13.579	14.776	16.085	17.519	19.086	20.799
10	10.462	10.950	11.464	12.006	12.578	13.181	14.487	15.937	17.549	19.337	21.321	23.521	25.959
11	11.567	12.169	12.808	13.486	14.207	14.972	16.645	18.531	20.655	23.045	25.733	28.755	32.150
12	12.683	13.412	14.192	15.026	15.917	16.870	18.977	21.384	24.133	27.271	30.850	34.931	39.581
13	13.809	14.680	15.618	16.627	17.713	18.882	21.495	24.523	28.029	32.089	36.786	42.219	48.497
14	14.947	15.974	17.086	18.292	19.599	21.015	24.215	27.975	32.393	37.581	43.672	50.818	59.196
15	16.097	17.293	18.599	20.024	21.579	23.276	27.152	31.772	37.280	43.842	51.660	60.965	72.035
20	22.019	24.297	26.870	29.778	33.066	36.786	45.762	57.275	72.052	91.025	115.380	146.630	186.690
25	28.243	32.030	36.459	41.646	47.727	54.865	73.106	98.347	133.330	181.870	249.210	342.600	471.980
30	34.785	40.568	47.575	56.085	66.439	79.058	113.280	164.490	241.330	356.790	530.310	790.950	1,181.900
40	48.886	60.402	75.401	95.026	120.800	154.760	259.060	442.590	767.090	1,342.000	2,360.800	4,163.200	7,343.900

The factors in the table were generated using the following formula:

$$\text{Future Value of Annuity of \$1} = \frac{(1+i)^n - 1}{i}$$

where:

i = annual interest rate

n = number of periods

23 The Master Budget and Responsibility Accounting

Learning Objectives

1. Learn why managers use budgets
2. Prepare an operating budget
3. Prepare a financial budget
4. Use sensitivity analysis in budgeting
5. Prepare performance reports for responsibility centers

Over 20% of sales of books, music, and electronics occur online. If you're one of the millions of customers worldwide who point and click to buy your books and CDs on Amazon.com, then you're part of Amazon.com's strategy to "get big fast." This strategy increased Amazon.com's sales, but at a cost. Spending was out of control. There was no budget, and managers spared no expense to help the company grow. As a result, Amazon.com lost more than $860 *million* dollars in 2000.

Founder and CEO Jeff Bezos had to turn this sea of red ink into income. Bezos set up a *budget* for Amazon.com's plan of action. Now, each division budgets both sales and expenses. In weekly meetings, managers compare actual results to the budget, which helps them correct problems quickly.

The result? Between 2000 and 2002, Amazon.com's sales increased 42%. With such an increase in sales, you'd expect expenses to also increase. But Amazon.com's new budget helped managers *cut* operating expenses. How did they decrease expenses when sales were increasing so dramatically? The budget helped Amazon.com reduce order-filling and distribution costs by 5%. Switching to lower-cost computer systems reduced "technical and content" operating costs by 20%. The result? Amazon.com reported its first-ever income from operations in 2002. By 2004, income from operations had risen to over $588 million. ■

Sources: Katrina Brooker, "Beautiful Dreamer," *Fortune*, December 18, 2000, pp. 234–239; Fred Vogelstein, "Bezos," *Fortune*, September 2, 2002, pp. 186–187; Fred Vogelstein, "What Went Right 2002," *Fortune*, December 30, 2002, p. 166; Nick Wingfield, "Survival Strategy: Amazon Takes Page from Wal-Mart to Prosper on Web," *Wall Street Journal*, November 22, 2002, A1; Fred Vogelstein, "Mighty Amazon," *Fortune*, May 26, 2003, pp. 60–74.

Perhaps, like Amazon.com, you've prepared a budget to ensure that you have enough cash to pay your expenses. The budget forces you to plan. If your budgeted cash inflow falls short of expenses, you can:

- increase your cash inflow (by taking on a job or a student loan), or
- cut your expenses.

In addition to planning, your personal budget can help you control expenses. To stay within your grocery budget, you may buy macaroni and cheese instead of shrimp. At the end of the month, if your bank balance is less than expected, you can compare your actual cash inflows and expenses to your budget to see why. You need to know whether cash inflows are lower than expected or expenses are higher than expected to know what corrective action to take.

As Amazon.com learned, it's easy for spending to get out of control if you don't have a budget. That's why everyone, from individuals like you to complex international organizations like Amazon.com, uses budgets. Careful budgeting helps both individuals and businesses stay out of trouble by reducing the risk that they will spend more than they earn.

As you'll see throughout this chapter, knowing how costs behave continues to be important when forming budgets. Total fixed costs will not change as volume changes within the relevant range. However, total variable costs must be adjusted when sales volume is expected to fluctuate.

Why Managers Use Budgets

Let's continue our study of budgets by moving from your personal budget to see how a small service business develops a simple budget. Assume you begin an online service that provides travel itineraries for leisure travelers. You want to earn $550 a

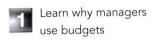

1 Learn why managers use budgets

month to help with your college expenses. You expect to sell 20 itineraries per month at a price of $30 each. Over the past six months, you paid your Internet service provider an average of $18 a month, and you spent an additional $20 per month on reference materials. You expect these monthly costs to remain about the same. These are your monthly fixed costs. Finally, you spend 5% of your sales revenues for banner ads on other travel Web sites. Because advertising costs fluctuate with sales revenue, these costs are variable.

Exhibit 23-1 shows how to compute budgeted revenues and then subtract budgeted expenses to arrive at budgeted operating income.

EXHIBIT 23-1 Service Company Budget

CUSTOM TRAVEL ITINERARIES
Budget for May 2009

Budgeted sales revenue (20 × $30)		$600
Less budgeted expenses:		
Internet-access expense	$18	
Reference-materials expense	20	
Advertising expense (5% × $600)	30	68
Budgeted operating income		$532

If business goes according to plan, you will not meet your $550 per month operating income goal. You will have to increase revenue (perhaps through word-of-mouth advertising) or cut expenses (perhaps by finding a less-expensive Internet-access provider).

Using Budgets to Plan and Control

Large international for-profit companies, such as Amazon.com, and nonprofit organizations, such as Habitat for Humanity, use budgets for the same reasons as you do in your personal life or in your small business—to plan and control actions and the related revenues and expenses. Exhibit 23-2 shows how managers use budgets in fulfilling their major responsibilities. First, they develop strategies—overall business goals like Amazon.com's goal to expand its international operations, or Gateway's goal to be a value leader in the personal computer market, while diversifying into other markets. Then, companies plan and budget for specific actions to achieve those goals. The next step is to act. For example, Amazon.com recently planned for and then added the Marketplace auction feature to its Web sites for the United Kingdom, Germany, and Japan. And Gateway is leaning on its suppliers to cut costs, while at the same time it is pumping out new products like plasma TVs and audio and video gear.

After acting, managers compare actual results with the budget. This feedback allows them to determine what, if any, corrective action to take. If Amazon.com spent more than expected to add the Marketplace to its international Web sites, managers must cut other costs or increase revenues. These decisions affect the company's future strategies and plans.

Amazon.com has a number of budgets. Its managers develop budgets for their own divisions. Software then "rolls up" the division budgets to create an organization-wide budget for the company as a whole. Managers also prepare both long-term and short-term budgets. Boeing's long-term budget forecasts demand for planes for the next 20 years.

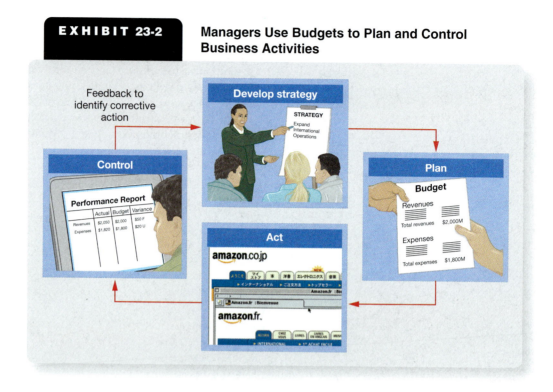

EXHIBIT 23-2 Managers Use Budgets to Plan and Control Business Activities

However, most companies (including Boeing) budget their cash flows monthly, weekly, and even daily to ensure that they have enough cash. They also budget revenues and expenses—and operating income—for months, quarters, and years. This chapter focuses on short-term budgets of one year or less. Chapter 22 explained how companies budget for major capital expenditures on property, plant, and equipment.

Benefits of Budgeting

Exhibit 23-3 summarizes three key benefits of budgeting. Budgeting forces managers to plan, promotes coordination and communication, and provides a benchmark for evaluating actual performance.

EXHIBIT 23-3 Benefits of Budgeting

Budgets force managers to plan.

Budgets promote coordination and communication.

Budgets provide a benchmark that motivates employees and helps managers evaluate performance.

Planning

Exhibit 23-1 shows that your expected income from the online travel itinerary business falls short of the target. The sooner you learn of the expected shortfall, the more time you have to plan how to increase revenues or cut expenses. The better your plan, and the more time you have to act on the plan, the more likely you will find a way to meet your target. Amazon.com's budget required that managers plan the expansion of the Web sites tailored for customers in Germany, France, and Japan.

Coordination and Communication

The master budget coordinates a company's activities. It forces managers to consider relations among operations across the entire value chain. For example, Amazon.com stimulates sales by offering free shipping on orders over a specified dollar amount. The budget encourages managers to ensure that the extra profits from increased sales outweigh the revenue lost from not charging for shipping.

Budgets also communicate a consistent set of plans throughout the company. For example, the initial Amazon.com budget communicated the message that all employees should help control costs.

Benchmarking

Budgets provide a benchmark that motivates employees and helps managers evaluate performance. In most companies, part of the manager's performance evaluation depends on how actual results compare to the budget. So, for example, the budgeted expenses for international expansion encourage Amazon.com's employees to increase the efficiency of international warehousing operations and to find less-expensive technology to support the Web sites.

Let's return to your online travel business. Suppose that comparing actual results to the budget in Exhibit 23-1 leads to the performance report in Exhibit 23-4.

EXHIBIT 23-4 Summary Performance Report

	Actual	Budget	Variance (Actual–Budget)
Sales revenue	$550	$600	$(50)
Less: Total expenses	90	68	(22)
Net income	$460	$532	$(72)

This report should prompt you to investigate why actual sales are $50 less than budgeted ($550 − $600). There are three possibilities:

1. The budget was unrealistic.
2. You did a poor selling job.
3. Uncontrollable factors (such as a sluggish economy) reduced sales.

All three may have contributed to the poor results.

You will also want to know why expenses are $22 higher than expected ($90 − $68). Did your Internet service provider increase rates? Did you have to buy more reference materials than planned? Did you spend more than 5% of your revenue on Web banner ads? You need to know the answers to these kinds of questions to decide how to get your business back on track.

Preparing the Master Budget

Now that you know *why* managers go to the trouble of developing budgets, let's consider the steps they take to prepare a budget.

Components of the Master Budget

The **master budget** is the set of budgeted financial statements and supporting schedules for the entire organization. Exhibit 23-5 shows the order in which managers prepare the components of the master budget for a merchandiser such as Amazon.com.

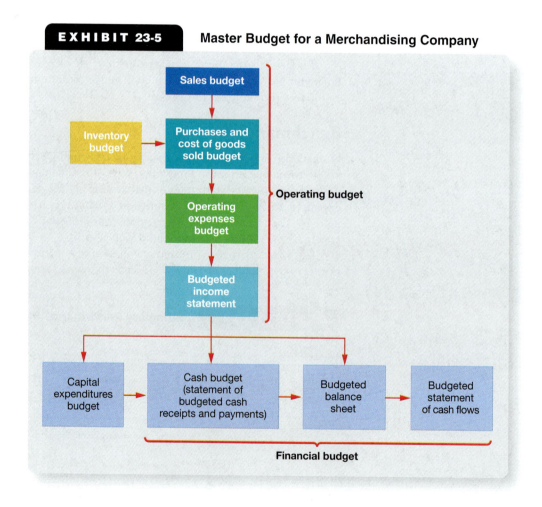

EXHIBIT 23-5 Master Budget for a Merchandising Company

The exhibit shows that the master budget includes three types of budgets:

1. The operating budget
2. The capital expenditures budget
3. The financial budget

Let's consider each, in turn.

The first component of the **operating budget** is the sales budget, the cornerstone of the master budget. Why? Because sales affect most other components of the master budget. After projecting sales revenue, cost of goods sold, and operating expenses, management prepares the end result of the operating budget: the budgeted income statement that projects operating income for the period.

The second type of budget is the **capital expenditures budget**. This budget presents the company's plan for purchasing property, plant, equipment, and other long-term assets.

The third type is the **financial budget**. Prior components of the master budget, including the budgeted income statement and the capital expenditures budget, along with plans for raising cash and paying debts, provide information for the first element of the financial budget: the cash budget. The cash budget, which projects cash inflows and outflows, feeds into the budgeted period-end balance sheet, which, in turn, feeds into the budgeted statement of cash flows. These budgeted financial statements look exactly like ordinary statements. The only difference is that they list budgeted (projected) rather than actual amounts.

Data for Whitewater Sporting Goods' Master Budget

We'll use Whitewater Sporting Goods Store No. 18 to see how managers prepare operating and financial budgets. Chapter 22 explained the capital budgeting process. Here is the information you have. We'll refer back to this information as we create the operating and financial budgets.

1. **You manage Whitewater Sporting Goods Store No. 18, which carries a complete line of outdoor recreation gear.** You are to prepare the store's master budget for April, May, June, and July, the main selling season. The division manager and the head of the accounting department will arrive from headquarters next week to review the budget with you.

2. Cash collections follow sales because the company sells on account.

3. Your store's balance sheet at March 31, 2009, the beginning of the budget period, appears in Exhibit 23-6.

EXHIBIT 23-6 Balance Sheet

WHITEWATER SPORTING GOODS STORE NO. 18
Balance Sheet
March 31, 2009

Assets		Liabilities	
Current assets:		Current liabilities:	
Cash.................................	$ 15,000	Accounts payable............	$ 16,800
Accounts receivable............	16,000	Salary and commissions	
Inventory.........................	48,000	payable..................	4,250
Prepaid insurance..............	1,800	Total liabilities................	21,050
Total current assets............	80,800		
Plant assets:		**Stockholders' Equity**	
Equipment and fixtures.......	32,000	Stockholders' equity..............	78,950
Accumulated depreciation.....	(12,800)		
Total plant assets................	19,200	Total liabilities and stockholders'	
Total assets......................	$100,000	equity..........................	$100,000

4. **Sales in March were $40,000.** The sales force predicts these future monthly sales:

April	$50,000
May	80,000
June	60,000
July	50,000

   Sales are 60% cash and 40% on credit. Whitewater collects all credit sales the month after the sale. The $16,000 of accounts receivable at March 31 arose from credit sales in March (40% of $40,000). Uncollectible accounts are immaterial.

5. **Whitewater maintains inventory equal to $20,000 plus 80% of the budgeted cost of goods sold for the following month.** Target ending inventory on July 31 is $42,400. Cost of goods sold averages 70% of sales. This is a variable cost. Inventory on March 31 is $48,000:

   $$\text{March 31 inventory} = \$20,000 + 0.80 \times (0.70 \times \text{April sales of } \$50,000)$$
   $$= \$20,000 + (0.80 \times \$35,000)$$
   $$= \$20,000 + \$28,000$$
   $$= \$48,000$$

   Whitewater pays for inventory as follows: 50% during the month of purchase and 50% during the next month. Accounts payable consists of inventory purchases only. March purchases were $33,600 so accounts payable at the end of March totals $16,800 ($33,600 × 0.50).

6. **Monthly payroll has two parts: a salary of $2,500 plus sales commissions equal to 15% of sales.** This is a mixed cost, with both a fixed and variable component. The company pays half this amount during the month and half early in the following month. Therefore, at the end of each month, Whitewater reports salary and commissions payable equal to half the month's payroll. The $4,250 liability on the March 31 balance sheet is half the March payroll of $8,500:

   $$\text{March payroll} = \text{Salary of } \$2,500$$
   $$+ \text{Sales commissions of } \$6,000 \ (0.15 \times \$40,000)$$
   $$= \$8,500$$

   $$\text{March 31 salary and commissions payable} = 0.50 \times \$8,500 = \$4,250$$

7. Other monthly expenses are as follows:

Rent expense (fixed cost)	$2,000, paid as incurred
Depreciation expense, including truck (fixed cost)	500
Insurance expense (fixed cost)	200 expiration of prepaid amount
Miscellaneous expenses (variable cost)	5% of sales, paid as incurred

8. **Whitewater plans to purchase a used delivery truck in April for $3,000 cash.**

9. **Whitewater requires each store to maintain a minimum cash balance of $10,000 at the end of each month.** The store can borrow money on six-month notes payable of $1,000 each at an annual interest rate of 12%. Management borrows no more than the amount needed to maintain the $10,000 minimum. Total interest expense will vary as the amount of borrowing varies from month

to month. Notes payable require six equal monthly payments of principal, plus monthly interest on the entire unpaid principal. Borrowing and all principal and interest payments occur at the end of the month.

10. Income taxes are the responsibility of corporate headquarters, so you can ignore tax.

As you prepare the master budget, remember that you are developing the store's operating and financial plan for the next four months. The steps in this process may seem mechanical, but you must think carefully about pricing, product lines, job assignments, needs for additional equipment, and negotiations with banks. Successful managers use this opportunity to make decisions that affect the future course of business.

Preparing the Operating Budget

2 Prepare an operating budget

The first three components of the operating budget as shown in Exhibit 23-5, are:

1. Sales budget (Exhibit 23-7)
2. Inventory, purchases, and cost of goods sold budget (Exhibit 23-8)
3. Operating expenses budget (Exhibit 23-9)

The results of these three budgets feed into the fourth element of the operating budget: the budgeted income statement (Exhibit 23-10). We consider each, in turn.

The Sales Budget

The forecast of sales revenue is the cornerstone of the master budget because the level of sales affects expenses and almost all other elements of the master budget. Budgeted total sales for each product is the sales price multiplied by the expected number of units sold. The overall sales budget in Exhibit 23-7 is the sum of the budgets for the individual products. Trace the April through July total sales ($240,000) to the budgeted income statement in Exhibit 23-10.

EXHIBIT 23-7 Sales Budget

WHITEWATER SPORTING GOODS STORE NO. 18
Sales Budget

	April	May	June	July	April–July Total
Cash sales, 60%	$30,000	$48,000	$36,000	$30,000	
Credit sales, 40%	20,000	32,000	24,000	20,000	
Total sales, 100%	$50,000	$80,000	$60,000	$50,000	$240,000

The Inventory, Purchases, and Cost of Goods Sold Budget

This budget determines cost of goods sold for the budgeted income statement, ending inventory for the budgeted balance sheet, and purchases for the cash budget. The familiar cost-of-goods-sold computation specifies the relations among these items:

$$\text{Beginning inventory} + \text{Purchase} - \text{Ending inventory} = \text{Cost of goods sold}$$

Beginning inventory is known from last month's balance sheet; budgeted cost of goods sold is 70% of sales; and budgeted ending inventory is a computed amount. You must solve for the budgeted purchases figure. To do this, rearrange the previous equation to isolate purchases on the left side:

$$\text{Purchases} = \text{Cost of goods sold} + \text{Ending inventory} - \text{Beginning inventory}$$

This equation makes sense. How much does Whitewater Sporting Goods have to purchase? Enough to cover sales and desired ending inventory, less the amount of beginning inventory already on hand at the start of the period. Exhibit 23-8 shows Whitewater Sporting Goods' inventory, purchases, and cost of goods sold budget.

EXHIBIT 23-8 Inventory, Purchases, and Cost of Goods Sold Budget

WHITEWATER SPORTING GOODS STORE NO. 18
Inventory, Purchases, and Cost of Goods Sold Budget

	April	May	June	July	April–July Total
Cost of goods sold					
(0.70 × sales, from sales budget in Exhibit 23-7)	$35,000	$56,000	$42,000	$35,000	$168,000
+ Desired ending inventory					
($20,000 + 0.80 × Cost of goods sold for the next month)	64,800*	53,600	48,000	42,400‡	
= Total inventory required	99,800	109,600	90,000	77,400	
− Beginning inventory	(48,000)†	(64,800)	(53,600)	(48,000)	
= Purchases	$51,800	$44,800	$36,400	$29,400	

*$20,000 + (0.80 × $56,000) = $64,800.
†Balance at March 31 (Exhibit 23-6).
‡Given in item 5 on page 1176.

Trace the total budgeted cost of goods sold from Exhibit 23-8 ($168,000) to the budgeted income statement in Exhibit 23-10. We will use the budgeted inventory and purchases amounts later.

The Operating Expenses Budget

Exhibit 23-9 shows the operating expense budget. Study each expense to make sure you know how it is computed. For example, sales commissions fluctuate with sales. Other expenses, such as rent and insurance, are the same each month (fixed).

Trace the April through July totals from the operating expenses budget in Exhibit 23-9 (salary and commissions of $46,000, rent expense of $8,000, and so on) to the budgeted income statement in Exhibit 23-10.

EXHIBIT 23-9   Operating Expenses Budget

WHITEWATER SPORTING GOODS STORE NO. 18
Operating Expenses Budget

	April	May	June	July	April–July Total
Salary, fixed amount (item 6, page 1176)	$ 2,500	$ 2,500	$ 2,500	$ 2,500	
Commission, 15% of sales from sales budget (item 6, page 1176 and Exhibit 23-7)	7,500	12,000	9,000	7,500	
Total salary and commissions	10,000	14,500	11,500	10,000	$ 46,000
Rent expense, fixed amount (item 7, page 1176)	2,000	2,000	2,000	2,000	8,000
Depreciation expense, fixed amount (item 7, page 1176)	500	500	500	500	2,000
Insurance expense, fixed amount (item 7, page 1176)	200	200	200	200	800
Miscellaneous expenses, 5% of sales from sales budget (item 7, page 1176 and Exhibit 23-7)	2,500	4,000	3,000	2,500	12,000
Total operating expenses	$15,200	$21,200	$17,200	$15,200	$ 68,800

The Budgeted Income Statement

Use the sales budget (Exhibit 23-7), the inventory, purchases, and cost of goods sold budget (Exhibit 23-8), and the operating expenses budget (Exhibit 23-9) to prepare the budgeted income statement in Exhibit 23-10. (We explain the computation of interest expense as part of the cash budget in the next section.)

Take this opportunity to solidify your understanding of operating budgets by carefully working out Summary Problem 1.

EXHIBIT 23-10   Budgeted Income Statement

WHITEWATER SPORTING GOODS STORE NO.18
Budgeted Income Statement
Four Months Ending July 31, 2009

		Amount	Source
Sales revenue		$240,000	Sales budget (Exhibit 23-7)
Cost of goods sold		168,000	Inventory, Purchases, and Cost of Goods
Gross profit		72,000	Sold budget (Exhibit 23-8)
Operating expenses:			
Salary and commissions	$ 46,000		Operating expenses budget (Exhibit 23-9)
Rent expense	8,000		Operating expenses budget (Exhibit 23-9)
Depreciation expense	2,000		Operating expenses budget (Exhibit 23-9)
Insurance expense	800		Operating expenses budget (Exhibit 23-9)
Miscellaneous expenses	12,000	68,800	Operating expenses budget (Exhibit 23-9)
Operating income		3,200	
Interest expense		225*	Cash budget (Exhibit 23-14)
Net income		$ 2,975	

*$90 + $75 + $60

Summary Problem 1

Review the Whitewater Sporting Goods example. You now think July sales might be $40,000 instead of the projected $50,000 in Exhibit 23-7. You want to see how this change in sales affects the budget.

Requirement

Revise the sales budget (Exhibit 23-7), the inventory, purchases, and cost of goods sold budget (Exhibit 23-8), and the operating expenses budget (Exhibit 23-9). Prepare a revised budgeted income statement for the four months ended July 31, 2009.

Note: You need not repeat the parts of the revised schedules that do not change. Assume that interest does not change.

Solution

Although not required, this solution repeats the budgeted amounts for April, May, and June. Revised figures appear in color for emphasis.

WHITEWATER SPORTING GOODS STORE NO. 18
Revised—Sales Budget

	April	May	June	July	Total
Cash sales, 60%	$30,000	$48,000	$36,000	$24,000	
Credit sales, 40%	20,000	32,000	24,000	16,000	
Total sales, 100%	$50,000	$80,000	$60,000	$40,000	$230,000

WHITEWATER SPORTING GOODS STORE NO. 18
Revised—Inventory, Purchases, and Cost of Goods Sold Budget

	April	May	June	July	Total
Cost of goods sold (0.70 × sales, from revised sales budget)	$35,000	$56,000	$42,000	$28,000	$161,000
+ Desired ending inventory ($20,000 + 0.80 × cost of goods sold for next month)	64,800	53,600	42,400	42,400[†]	
= Total inventory required	99,800	109,600	84,400	70,400	
− Beginning inventory	(48,000)*	(64,800)	(53,600)	(42,400)	
= Purchases	$51,800	$44,800	$30,800	$28,000	

*Balance at March 31, (Exhibit 23-6).
[†]Given in item 5 on page 1176

WHITEWATER SPORTING GOODS STORE NO. 18
Revised—Operating Expenses Budget

	April	May	June	July	Total
Salary, fixed amount	$ 2,500	$ 2,500	$ 2,500	$ 2,500	
Commission, 15% of sales from revised sales budget	7,500	12,000	9,000	6,000	
Total salary and commissions	10,000	14,500	11,500	8,500	$44,500
Rent expense, fixed amount	2,000	2,000	2,000	2,000	8,000
Depreciation expense, fixed amount	500	500	500	500	2,000
Insurance expense, fixed amount	200	200	200	200	800
Miscellaneous expenses, 5% of sales from revised sales budget	2,500	4,000	3,000	2,000	11,500
Total operating expenses	$15,200	$21,200	$17,200	$13,200	$66,800

WHITEWATER SPORTING GOODS STORE NO. 18
Revised Budgeted Income Statement
Four Months Ending July 31, 2009

		Amount	Source
Sales revenue		$230,000	Revised sales budget
Cost of goods sold		161,000	Revised inventory, purchases, and cost of goods sold budget
Gross profit		69,000	
Operating expenses:			
Salary and commissions	$44,500		Revised operating expenses budget
Rent expense	8,000		Revised operating expenses budget
Depreciation expense	2,000		Revised operating expenses budget
Insurance expense	800		Revised operating expenses budget
Miscellaneous expenses	11,500	66,800	Revised operating expenses budget
Operating income		2,200	
Interest expense		225	Given, Exhibit 23-10
Net income		$ 1,975	

Preparing the Financial Budget

3 Prepare a financial budget

Armed with a clear understanding of Whitewater Sporting Goods' operating budget, you're now ready to prepare the financial budget. Exhibit 23-5 shows that the financial budget includes the cash budget, the budgeted balance sheet, and the budgeted statement of cash flows. We start with the cash budget.

Preparing the Cash Budget

The **cash budget**, or **statement of budgeted cash receipts and payments**, details how the business expects to go from the beginning cash balance to the desired ending balance. The cash budget has four major parts:

- Cash collections from customers (Exhibit 23-11)
- Cash payments for purchases (Exhibit 23-12)
- Cash payments for operating expenses (Exhibit 23-13)
- Cash payments for capital expenditures (for example, the $3,000 capital expenditure to acquire the delivery truck)

Cash collections and payments depend on revenues and expenses, which appear in the operating budget. This is why you cannot prepare the cash budget until you have finished the operating budget.

Budgeted Cash Collections from Customers

Exhibit 23-11 shows that April's budgeted cash collections consist of two parts: (1) April's cash sales from the sales budget in Exhibit 23-7 ($30,000) plus (2) collections of March's credit sales ($16,000 from the March 31 balance sheet, Exhibit 23-6). Trace April's $46,000 ($30,000 + $16,000) total cash collections to the cash budget in Exhibit 23-14.

EXHIBIT 23-11 Budgeted Cash Collections

WHITEWATER SPORTING GOODS STORE NO. 18
Budgeted Cash Collections from Customers

	April	May	June	July	April–July Total
Cash sales from sales budget (Exhibit 23-7)	$30,000	$48,000	$36,000	$30,000	
Collections of last month's credit sales, from sales budget (Exhibit 23-7)	16,000*	20,000	32,000	24,000	
Total collections	$46,000	$68,000	$68,000	$54,000	$236,000

*March 31 accounts receivable (Exhibit 23-6).

Budgeted Cash Payments for Purchases

Exhibit 23-12 uses the inventory, purchases, and cost of goods sold budget from Exhibit 23-8 and payment information from item 5 to compute budgeted cash payments for purchases of inventory. April's cash payments for purchases consist of two parts: (1) payment of 50% of March's purchases ($16,800 accounts payable balance from the March 31 balance sheet, Exhibit 23-6) plus (2) payment for 50% of April's

EXHIBIT 23-12 Budgeted Cash Payments for Purchases

WHITEWATER SPORTING GOODS STORE NO. 18
Budgeted Cash Payments for Purchases

	April	May	June	July	April–July Total
50% of last month's purchases from inventory, purchases, and cost of goods sold budget (Exhibit 23-8)	$16,800*	$25,900	$22,400	$18,200	
50% of this month's purchases from inventory, purchases, and cost of goods sold budget (Exhibit 23-8)	25,900	22,400	18,200	14,700	
Total payments for purchases	$42,700	$48,300	$40,600	$32,900	$164,500

*March 31 accounts payable (Exhibit 23-6).

purchases ($25,900 = 50% × $51,800 from Exhibit 23-8). Trace April's $42,700 ($16,800 + $25,900) cash outlay for purchases to the cash budget in Exhibit 23-14.

Budgeted Cash Payments for Operating Expenses

Exhibit 23-13 uses items 6 and 7 and the operating expenses budget (Exhibit 23-9) to compute cash payments for operating expenses. April's cash payments for operating expenses consist of four items:

Payment of 50% of March's salary and commissions (from March 31 balance sheet, Exhibit 23-6)	$ 4,250
Payment of 50% of April's salary and commissions (50% × $10,000, Exhibit 23-9)	5,000
Payment of rent expense (Exhibit 23-9)	2,000
Payment of miscellaneous expenses (Exhibit 23-9)	2,500
Total April cash payments for operating expenses	$13,750

Follow April's $13,750 cash payments for operating expenses from Exhibit 23-13 to the cash budget in Exhibit 23-14.

EXHIBIT 23-13 Budgeted Cash Payments for Operating Expenses

WHITEWATER SPORTING GOODS STORE NO. 18
Budgeted Cash Payments for Operating Expenses

	April	May	June	July	April–July Total
Salary and commissions:					
50% of last month's expenses, from operating expenses budget (Exhibit 23-9)	$ 4,250*	$ 5,000	$ 7,250	$ 5,750	
50% of this month's expenses, from operating expenses budget (Exhibit 23-9)	5,000	7,250	5,750	5,000	
Total salary and commissions	9,250	12,250	13,000	10,750	
Rent expense, from operating expenses budget (Exhibit 23-9)	2,000	2,000	2,000	2,000	
Miscellaneous expenses, from operating expenses budget (Exhibit 23-9)	2,500	4,000	3,000	2,500	
Total payments for operating expenses	$13,750	$18,250	$18,000	$15,250	$65,250

*March 31 salary and commissions payable (Exhibit 23-6).

Stop & Think

Why are depreciation expense and insurance expense from the operating expenses budget (Exhibit 23-9) *excluded* from the budgeted cash payments for operating expenses in Exhibit 23-13?

Answer: These expenses do not require cash outlays in the current period. Depreciation is the periodic write-off of the cost of the equipment and fixtures that Whitewater Sporting Goods acquired previously. Insurance expense is the expiration of prepaid insurance.

The Cash Budget

To prepare the cash budget in Exhibit 23-14, start with the beginning cash balance and add the budgeted cash collections from Exhibit 23-11 to determine the cash available. Then, subtract cash payments for purchases (Exhibit 23-12), operating expenses (Exhibit 23-13), and any capital expenditures. This yields the ending cash balance before financing.

Item 9 (on pages 1176–1177) states that Whitewater Sporting Goods requires a minimum cash balance of $10,000. April's $1,550 budgeted cash balance before financing falls $8,450 short of the minimum required ($10,000 − $1,550). Because Whitewater Sporting Goods borrows in $1,000 notes, the company will have to borrow $9,000 to cover April's expected shortfall. The budgeted ending cash balance equals the "ending cash balance before financing," adjusted for the total effects

EXHIBIT 23-14 Cash Budget

WHITEWATER SPORTING GOODS STORE NO. 18
Cash Budget
Four Months Ending July 31, 2009

	April	May	June	July
Beginning cash balance	$15,000*	$10,550	$10,410	$18,235
Cash collections (Exhibit 23-11)	46,000	68,000	68,000	54,000
Cash available	$61,000	$78,550	$78,410	$72,235
Cash payments:				
Purchases of inventory (Exhibit 23-12)	$42,700	$48,300	$40,600	$32,900
Operating expenses (Exhibit 23-13)	13,750	18,250	18,000	15,250
Purchase of delivery truck (item 8, page 1176)	3,000	—	—	—
Total cash payments	59,450	66,550	58,600	48,150
(1) Ending cash balance before financing	1,550	12,000	19,810	24,085
Less: Minimum cash balance desired	(10,000)	(10,000)	(10,000)	(10,000)
Cash excess (deficiency)	$ (8,450)	$ 2,000	$ 9,810	$14,085
Financing of cash deficiency (see notes *a–c*):				
Borrowing (at end of month)	$ 9,000			
Principal payments (at end of month)		$ (1,500)	$ (1,500)	$ (1,500)
Interest expense (at 12% annually)		(90)	(75)	(60)
(2) Total effects of financing	9,000	(1,590)	(1,575)	(1,560)
Ending cash balance (1) + (2)	$10,550	$10,410	$18,235	$22,525

*March 31 cash balance (Exhibit 23-6).
Notes
^{a}Borrowing occurs in multiples of $1,000 and only for the amount needed to maintain a minimum cash balance of $10,000.
^{b}Monthly principal payments: $9,000 ÷ 6 = $1,500.
^{c}Interest expense:
  May: $9,000 × (0.12 × 1/12) = $90
  June: ($9,000 − $1,500) × (0.12 × 1/12) = $75
  July: ($9,000 − $1,500 − $1,500) × (0.12 × 1/12) = $60

of the financing (a $9,000 inflow in April). Exhibit 23-14 shows that Whitewater expects to end April with $10,550 of cash ($1,550 + $9,000). The exhibit also shows the cash balance at the end of May, June, and July.

Item 9 states that Whitewater must repay the notes in six equal installments. Thus, May through July show principal repayments of $1,500 ($9,000 ÷ 6) per month. Whitewater also pays interest expense on the outstanding notes payable, at 12% per year. The June interest expense is $75 [($9,000 principal − $1,500 repayment at the end of May) × 12% × 1/12]. Interest expense for the four months totals $225 ($90 + $75 + $60). This interest expense appears on the budgeted income statement in Exhibit 23-10.

The cash balance at the end of July ($22,525) is the cash balance in the July 31 budgeted balance sheet in Exhibit 23-15.

The Budgeted Balance Sheet

To prepare the budgeted balance sheet, project each asset, liability, and stockholders' equity account based on the plans outlined in the previous exhibits.

Study the budgeted balance sheet in Exhibit 23-15 to make certain you understand the computation of each figure. For example, on the budgeted balance sheet as of July 31, 2009, budgeted cash equals the ending cash balance from the cash budget in Exhibit 23-14 ($22,525). Accounts receivable as of July 31 equal July's credit sales of $20,000, shown in the sales budget (Exhibit 23-7). July 31 inventory of $42,400 is July's desired ending inventory in the inventory, purchases, and cost of goods sold budget in Exhibit 23-8. Detailed computations for each of the other accounts appear in Exhibit 23-15.

The Budgeted Statement of Cash Flows

The final step is preparing the budgeted statement of cash flows. Use the information from the schedules of cash collections and payments, the cash budget, and the beginning balance of cash to project cash flows from operating, investing, and financing activities. Take time to study Exhibit 23-16 on page 1187, and make sure you understand the origin of each figure.

Getting Employees to Accept the Budget

What is the most important part of Whitewater Sporting Goods' budgeting system? Despite all the numbers we have crunched, it is not the mechanics. It is getting managers and employees to accept the budget so Whitewater Sporting Goods can reap the planning, coordination, and control benefits illustrated in Exhibit 23-3.

Few people enjoy having their work monitored and evaluated. So if managers use the budget as a benchmark to evaluate employees' performance, managers must first motivate employees to accept the budget's goals. Here's how they can do it:

- Managers must support the budget themselves, or no one else will.
- Show employees how budgets can help them achieve better results.
- Have employees participate in developing the budget.

But these principles alone are not enough. As the manager of Store No. 18, your performance is evaluated by comparing actual results to the budget. When you develop your store's budget, you may be tempted to build in *slack*. For example, you might want to budget fewer sales and higher purchases than you expect. This increases the chance that actual performance will be better than the budget and that you will receive a good evaluation. But adding slack into the budget makes it less accurate—and less useful for planning and control. When the division manager and the head of the accounting department arrive from headquarters next week, they will scour your budget to find any slack you may have inserted.

EXHIBIT 23-15 | Budgeted Balance Sheet

WHITEWATER SPORTING GOODS STORE NO. 18
Budgeted Balance Sheet
July 31, 2009

Assets		
Current assets:		
Cash (Exhibit 23-14)	$22,525	
Accounts receivable (sales budget, Exhibit 23-7)	20,000	
Inventory (inventory, purchases, and cost of goods sold budget, Exhibit 23-8)	42,400	
Prepaid insurance (beginning balance of $1,800 − $800* for four months' expiration; operating expenses budget, Exhibit 23-9)	1,000	
Total current assets		$ 85,925
Plant assets:		
Equipment and fixtures (beginning balance of $32,000* + $3,000 truck acquisition; item 8, page 1176)	$35,000	
Accumulated depreciation (beginning balance of $12,800* + $2,000 for four months' depreciation; operating expenses budget, Exhibit 23-9)	(14,800)	
Total plant assets		20,200
Total assets		$106,125
Liabilities		
Current liabilities:		
Account payable (0.50 × July purchases of $29,400; inventory, purchases, and cost of goods sold budget, Exhibit 23-8)	$14,700	
Short-term note payable ($9,000 − $4,500 paid back; Exhibit 23-14)	4,500	
Salary and commissions payable (0.50 × July expenses of $10,000; operating expenses budget, Exhibit 23-9)	5,000	
Total liabilities		$ 24,200
Stockholders' Equity		
Stockholders' equity (beginning balance of $78,950* + $2,975 net income; Exhibit 23-10)		81,925
Total liabilities and stockholders' equity		$106,125

*March 31, 2009, Balance Sheet (Exhibit 23-6).

Using Information Technology for Sensitivity Analysis and Rolling Up Unit Budgets

Exhibits 23-7 through 23-16 show that the manager must prepare many calculations to develop the master budget for just one of the retail stores in the Whitewater Sporting Goods merchandising chain. No wonder managers embrace information

EXHIBIT 23-16 | Budgeted Statement of Cash Flows

WHITEWATER SPORTING GOODS STORE NO.18
Budgeted Statement of Cash Flows
Four Months Ending July 31, 2009

Cash flows from operating activities:		
Receipts:		
Collections from customers (Exhibit 23-11)	$ 236,000	
Total cash receipts		$236,000
Payments:		
Purchases of inventory (Exhibit 23-12)	$(164,500)	
Operating expenses (Exhibit 23-13)	(65,250)	
Payment of interest expense (Exhibits 23-14 and 23-10)	(225)	
Total cash payments		(229,975)
Net cash inflow from operating activities		6,025
Cash flows from investing activities:		
Acquisition of delivery truck (item 8, page 1176)	$ (3,000)	
Net cash outflow from investing activities		(3,000)
Cash flows from financing activities:		
Proceeds from issuance of notes payable (Exhibit 23-14)	$ 9,000	
Payment of notes payable (Exhibit 23-14)	(4,500)	
Net cash inflow from financing activities		4,500
Net increase in cash		$ 7,525
Cash balance, April 1, 2009 (Exhibit 23-6 and 23-14)		15,000
Cash balance, July 31, 2009 (Exhibits 23-14 and 23-15)		$ 22,525

technology to help prepare budgets! Let's see how advances in information technology make it more cost-effective for managers to:

- Conduct sensitivity analysis on their own unit's budget
- Roll up individual unit budgets to create the companywide budget

Sensitivity Analysis

The master budget models the company's *planned* activities. Top management pays special attention to ensure that the results of the budgeted income statement (Exhibit 23-10), the cash budget (Exhibit 23-14), and the budgeted balance sheet (Exhibit 23-15) support key strategies.

But actual results often differ from plans so management wants to know how budgeted income and cash flows would change if key assumptions turned out to be incorrect. Chapter 20 defined *sensitivity analysis* as a *what-if* technique that asks *what* a result will be *if* a predicted amount is not achieved or *if* an underlying assumption changes. *What if* the stock market crashes? How will this affect Amazon.com's sales? Will it have to postpone the planned expansion in Asia and Europe? *What* will be Whitewater Sporting Goods Store No. 18's cash balance on July 31 *if* the period's sales are 45% cash, not 60% cash? Will Whitewater Sporting Goods have to borrow more cash?

Most companies use computer spreadsheet programs (or special budget software) to prepare master budget schedules and statements. One of the earliest spreadsheet programs was developed by graduate business students who realized that computers could take the drudgery out of hand-computed master budget sensitivity analyses. Today, managers answer what-if questions simply by changing a

4 Use sensitivity analysis in budgeting

number. At the press of a key, the computer screen flashes a revised budget that includes all the effects of the change.

Technology makes it cost-effective to perform more comprehensive sensitivity analyses. Armed with a better understanding of how changes in sales and costs are likely to affect the company's bottom line, today's managers can react quickly if key assumptions underlying the master budget (such as sales price or quantity) turn out to be wrong.

Rolling Up Individual Unit Budgets into the Companywide Budget

Whitewater Sporting Goods Store No. 18 is just one of the company's many retail stores. As Exhibit 23-17 shows, Whitewater Sporting Goods' headquarters must roll up the budget data from Store No. 18, along with budgets for each of the other stores, to prepare the companywide master budget. This roll-up can be difficult for companies whose units use different spreadsheets to prepare the budgets.

Companies like Sunoco turn to budget-management software to solve this problem. Often designed as a component of the company's Enterprise Resource Planning (ERP) system (or data warehouse), this software helps managers develop and analyze budgets.

Across the globe, managers sit at their desks, log into the company's budget system, and enter their numbers. The software allows them to conduct sensitivity analyses on their own unit's data. When the manager is satisfied with her budget, she can enter it in the companywide budget with the click of a mouse. Her unit's budget automatically rolls up with budgets from all other units around the world.

Whether at headquarters or on the road, top executives can log into the budget system and conduct their own sensitivity analyses on individual units' budgets or on

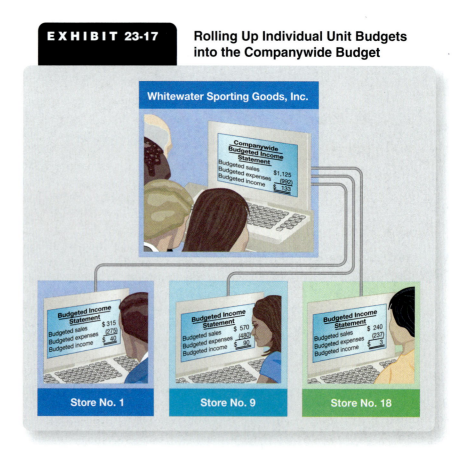

EXHIBIT 23-17 Rolling Up Individual Unit Budgets into the Companywide Budget

the companywide budget. Managers can spend less time compiling and summarizing data and more time analyzing it to ensure that the budget leads the company to achieve its key strategic goals.

Stop & Think

Consider two budget situations: (1) Whitewater Sporting Goods' marketing analysts produce a near-certain forecast for four-month sales of $4,500,000 for the company's 20 stores. (2) Much uncertainty exists about the period's sales. The most likely amount is $4,500,000, but marketing considers any amount between $3,900,000 and $5,100,000 to be possible. How will the budgeting process differ in these two circumstances?

Answer: Whitewater Sporting Goods will prepare a master budget for the expected sales level of $4,500,000 in either case. Because of the uncertainty in the second situation, executives will want a set of budgets covering the entire range of volume rather than a single level. Whitewater's managers may prepare budgets based on sales of, for example, $3,900,000, $4,200,000, $4,500,000, $4,800,000, and $5,100,000. These budgets will help managers plan for sales levels throughout the forecasted range.

Responsibility Accounting

You've now seen how managers set strategic goals and then develop plans and budget resources for activities that will help reach those goals. Let's look more closely at how managers *use* budgets to control operations.

Each manager is responsible for planning and controlling some part of the firm's activities. A **responsibility center** is a part or subunit of an organization whose manager is accountable for specific activities. Lower-level managers are often responsible for budgeting and controlling costs of a single value-chain function. For example, one manager is responsible for planning and controlling the *production* of Pace picante sauce at the plant, while another is responsible for planning and controlling the *distribution* of the product to customers. Lower-level managers report to higher-level managers, who have broader responsibilities. Managers in charge of production and distribution report to senior managers responsible for profits (revenues minus costs) earned by an entire product line.

Four Types of Responsibility Centers

Responsibility accounting is a system for evaluating the performance of each responsibility center and its manager. Responsibility accounting performance reports compare plans (budgets) with actions (actual results) for each center. Superiors then evaluate how well each manager: (1) used the budgeted resources to achieve the responsibility center's goals and thereby (2) controlled the operations for which he or she was responsible.

Exhibit 23-18 illustrates four types of responsibility centers.

1. **In a cost center, managers are accountable for costs (expenses) only.** Manufacturing operations, such as the Pace picante sauce production lines, are cost centers. The line foreman controls costs by ensuring that employees work efficiently. The foreman is *not* responsible for generating revenues because he is not involved in selling the product. The plant manager evaluates the foreman on his ability to control *costs* by comparing actual costs to budgeted costs. All else

EXHIBIT 23-18 Four Types of Responsibility Centers

In a **cost center**, such as a production line for Pace picante sauce, managers are responsible for costs.

In a **revenue center**, such as the Midwest sales region, managers are responsible for generating sales revenue.

In a **profit center**, such as a line of products, managers are responsible for generating income.

In an **investment center**, such as Campbell Soups and Sauces division, managers are responsible for income and invested capital.

being equal (for example, holding quality constant), the foreman is likely to receive a more favorable evaluation if actual costs are less than budgeted costs.

2. **In a revenue center, managers are primarily accountable for revenues.** Examples include the Midwest and Southeast sales regions of businesses, such as Pace Foods and Reebok. These managers of revenue centers may also be responsible for the costs of their own sales operations. Revenue center performance reports compare actual with budgeted revenues and may include the costs incurred by the revenue center itself. All else being equal, the manager is likely to receive a more favorable evaluation if actual revenues exceed the budget.

3. **In a profit center, managers are accountable for both revenues and costs (expenses) and, therefore, profits.** The (higher-level) manager responsible for the entire Pace product line would be accountable for increasing sales revenue *and* controlling costs to achieve the profit goals. Profit center reports include both revenues and expenses to show the profit center's income. Superiors evaluate the manager's performance by comparing actual revenues, expenses, and profits to the budget. All else being equal, the manager is likely to receive a more favorable evaluation if actual profits exceed the budget.

4. **In an investment center, managers are accountable for investments, revenues, and costs (expenses).** Examples include the Saturn division of General Motors and the North American Sauces and Beverages Division (which includes Pace Foods) of Campbell Soup. Managers of investment centers are responsible for (1) generating sales, (2) controlling expenses, and (3) managing the amount of investment required to earn the income (revenues minus expenses). For example, Bell South considers its information technology (IT) department an investment center. Managers are responsible for keeping IT costs within the budget while using the department's assets to generate revenue from projects, such as Bell South's FastAccess DSL service or its e-business operations.

Top management often evaluates investment center managers based on return on investment (ROI), residual income, or economic value added (EVA). Chapter 25 explains how these measures are calculated and used. All else being equal, the manager will receive a more favorable evaluation if the division's actual ROI, residual income, or EVA exceeds the amount budgeted.

Responsibility Accounting Performance Reports

Exhibit 23-19 shows how an organization like Campbell Soup Company may assign responsibility.

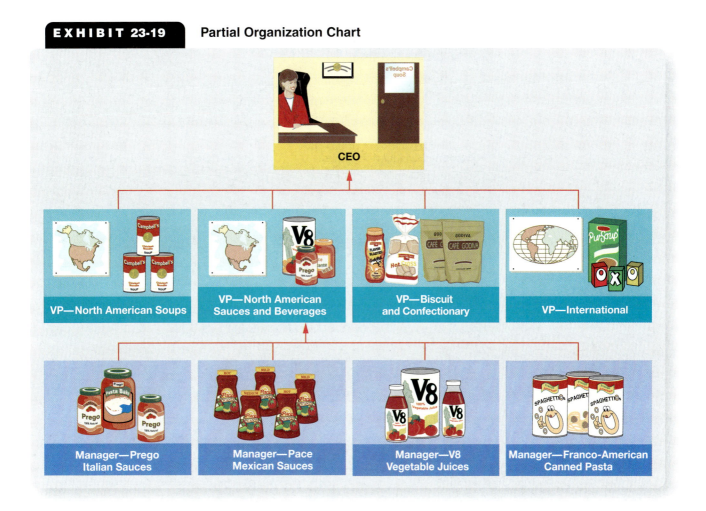

EXHIBIT 23-19 Partial Organization Chart

At the top level, the CEO oversees each of the four divisions. Division managers generally have broad responsibility, including deciding how to use assets to maximize ROI. Most companies consider divisions as *investment centers*.

Each division manager supervises all the product lines in that division. Exhibit 23-19 shows that the VP of North American Sauces and Beverages oversees the Prego Italian sauces, Pace Mexican sauces, V8 juice, and Franco-American canned pasta product lines. Product lines are generally considered *profit centers*. Thus, the manager of the Pace Foods product line is responsible for evaluating lower-level managers of both:

- *Cost centers* (such as plants that make Pace Foods products) and
- *Revenue centers* (such as managers responsible for selling Pace Foods products)

5 Prepare performance reports for responsibility centers

Exhibit 23-20 illustrates responsibility accounting performance reports for each level of management shown in Exhibit 23-19. Exhibit 23-20 uses assumed numbers to illustrate reports like those:

- The CEO may use to evaluate divisions
- The divisional VPs may use to evaluate individual product lines
- The product-line managers may use to evaluate the development, production, marketing, and distribution of their products

At each level, the reports compare actual results with the budget.

EXHIBIT 23-20 Responsibility Accounting Performance Reports at Various Levels

CEO'S QUARTERLY RESPONSIBILITY REPORT
(in millions of dollars)

Operating Income of Divisions and Corporate Headquarters Expense	Budget	Actual	Variance Favorable/ (Unfavorable)
North American Soups	$ 218	$ 209	$ (9)
North American Sauces and Beverages	70	84	14
Biscuits and Confectionary	79	87	8
International Soups and Sauces	35	34	(1)
Corporate Headquarters Expense	(33)	(29)	4
Operating Income	$ 369	$ 385	$16

VP—NORTH AMERICAN SAUCES AND BEVERAGES QUARTERLY RESPONSIBILITY REPORT
(in millions of dollars)

Operating Income of Product Lines	Budget	Actual	Variance Favorable/ (Unfavorable)
Italian Sauces	$ 20	$ 18	$ (2)
Mexican Sauces	25	38	13
Vegetable Juices	10	15	5
Canned Pastas	15	13	(2)
Operating Income	$ 70	$ 84	$14

MANAGER—MEXICAN SAUCES QUARTERLY RESPONSIBILITY REPORT
(in millions of dollars)

Revenue and Expenses	Budget	Actual	Variance Favorable/ (Unfavorable)
Sales revenue	$ 80	$ 84	$ 4
Cost of goods sold	(36)	(30)	6
Gross profit	44	54	10
Marketing expenses	(12)	(9)	3
Research and development expenses	(2)	(3)	(1)
Other expenses	(5)	(4)	1
Operating income	$ 25	$ 38	$13

Start with the lowest level and move to the top. Follow the $25 million budgeted operating income from the Mexican sauces product-line report to the report of the VP–North American Sauces and Beverages. The VP's report summarizes the budgeted and actual operating incomes for each of the four product lines he supervises.

Now, trace the $70 million budgeted operating income from the VP's report to the CEO's report. The CEO's report includes a summary of each division's budgeted and actual profits, as well as the costs incurred by corporate headquarters, which are not assigned to any of the divisions.

Management by Exception

The variances reported in Exhibit 23-20 aid **management by exception**, which directs executives' attention to important differences between actual and budgeted amounts. Look at the CEO's report. The International Soups and Sauces Division's actual operating income of $34 million is very close to the budgeted $35 million. Unless there are other signs of trouble, the CEO will not waste time investigating such a small variance.

In contrast, the North American Sauces and Beverages Division earned much more profit than budgeted. The CEO will want to know why. Suppose the VP of the division believes a national sales promotion was especially effective. That promotion may be repeated or adapted by other divisions. To identify the reason for exceptional results, so that other parts of the organization may benefit, is one reason why managers investigate large favorable variances (not just large unfavorable ones). Another is to ensure that employees are not skimping on ingredients, marketing, or R&D, which could hurt the company's long-term success.

A CEO who received the report at the top of Exhibit 23-20 would likely concentrate on improving the North American Soups Division because its actual income fell $9 million below budget. The CEO will want to see which product lines caused the shortfall so that he or she and the VP of the division can work together to correct any problems.

Exhibit 23-20 also shows how summarized data may hide problems. Although the North American Sauces and Beverages Division as a whole performed well, the Italian sauces and canned pasta lines did not. If the CEO received only the condensed report at the top of the exhibit, he or she would rely on division managers to spot and correct problems in individual product lines.

Not a Question of Blame

Responsibility accounting assigns managers responsibility for their unit's actions and provides a way to evaluate both their and their unit's performance. But superiors should not misuse responsibility accounting to find fault or place blame. The question is not "Who is to blame for an unfavorable variance?" Instead, the question is "Who can best explain why a specific variance occurred?" Consider the North American Soups Division in Exhibit 23-20. Suppose a tornado devastated the primary production plant. It may be that the remaining plants operated very efficiently, and this efficiency kept the income variance down to $9 million. If so, the North American Soups Division and its VP may actually have done a good job.

Other Performance Measures

Top management uses responsibility accounting performance reports to assess each responsibility center's *financial* performance. Top management also often assesses each responsibility center's nonfictional *operating* performance. Typical nonfinancial performance measures include customer satisfaction ratings, delivery time, product quality, employee expertise, and so forth. Chapter 25 discusses the broader view of performance evaluation, known as the "balanced scorecard." In that chapter, we will look at how managers use both financial and nonfinancial performance measures to form a "balanced view" of each responsibility center's performance.

The "Decision Guidelines" review budgets and how managers use them in responsibility accounting. Study these guidelines before working on Summary Problem 2.

Decision Guidelines

THE MASTER BUDGET AND RESPONSIBILITY ACCOUNTING

Amazon.com's initial strategy was to "get big fast." But without a budget, spending got out of control. So founder and CEO Jeff Bezos added a second strategic goal—to become the world's most cost-efficient, high-quality e-tailer. Today, Amazon.com's managers use budgets to help reach both the growth and cost-efficiency goals. Let's consider some of the decisions Amazon.com made as it set up its budgeting process.

Decision	Guidelines
What benefits should Amazon.com expect to obtain from developing a budget?	Requires managers to *plan* how to increase sales and how to cut costs. Promotes *coordination and communication*, such as communicating the importance of the cost-efficiency goal. Provides a *benchmark* that motivates employees and helps managers evaluate how well employees contributed to the sales growth and cost-efficiency goals.
In what order should Amazon.com's managers prepare the components of the master budget?	Begin with the *operating budget*. • Start with the *sales budget*, which feeds into all other budgets. • The sales and *ending inventory budgets* determine the *purchases and cost of goods sold budget*. • The sales, cost of goods sold, and *operating expense budgets* determine the *budgeted income statement*. Next, prepare the *capital expenditures budget*. Finally, prepare the *financial budget*. • Start with the *cash budget*. • The cash budget provides the ending cash balance for the *budgeted balance sheet* and the details for the *budgeted statement of cash flows*.
What extra steps should Amazon.com take given the uncertainty of Internet-based sales forecasts?	Prepare a *sensitivity analysis* and project budgeted results at different sales levels.
How does Amazon.com compute budgeted purchases?	$$\text{Beginning inventory} + \text{Purchases} - \text{Ending inventory} = \text{Cost of goods sold}$$ so $$\text{Purchases} = \text{Cost of goods sold} + \text{Ending inventory} - \text{Beginning inventory}$$
What kind of a responsibility center does each manager supervise?	Cost center: Manager is responsible for costs. Revenue center: Manager is responsible for revenues. Profit center: Manager is responsible for both revenues and costs, and, therefore, profits. Investment center: Manager is responsible for revenues, costs, and the amount of the investment required to earn the income.
How should Amazon.com evaluate managers?	Compare actual performance with the budget for the manager's responsibility center. *Management by exception* focuses on large differences between budgeted and actual results.

Summary Problem 2

Continue the revised Whitewater Sporting Goods illustration from Summary Problem 1. Now that you think July sales will be $40,000 instead of $50,000, as projected in Exhibit 23-7, how will this affect the financial budget?

Requirements

Revise the schedule of budgeted cash collections (Exhibit 23-11), the schedule of budgeted cash payments for purchases (Exhibit 23-12), and the schedule of budgeted cash payments for operating expenses (Exhibit 23-13). Prepare a revised cash budget, a revised budgeted balance sheet at July 31, 2009, and a revised budgeted statement of cash flows for the four months ended July 31, 2009. *Note:* You need not repeat the parts of the revised schedule that do not change.

Solution

Although not required, this solution repeats the budgeted amounts for April, May, and June. Revised figures appear in color for emphasis.

WHITEWATER SPORTING GOODS STORE NO. 18
Revised—Budgeted Cash Collections from Customers

	April	May	June	July	Total
Cash sales, from revised sales budget	$30,000	$48,000	$36,000	$24,000	
Collections of last month's credit sales, from revised sales budget	16,000*	20,000	32,000	24,000	
Total collections	$46,000	$68,000	$68,000	$48,000	$230,000

*March 31 accounts receivable (Exhibit 23-6)

WHITEWATER SPORTING GOODS STORE NO. 18
Revised—Budgeted Cash Payments for Purchases

	April	May	June	July	Total
50% of last month's purchases, from revised inventory, purchases, and cost of goods sold budget	$16,800*	$25,900	$22,400	$15,400	
50% of this month's purchases, from revised inventory, purchases, and cost of goods sold budget	25,900	22,400	15,400	14,000	
Total payments for purchases	$42,700	$48,300	$37,800	$29,400	$158,200

*March 31 accounts payable (Exhibit 23-6)

WHITEWATER SPORTING GOODS STORE NO. 18
Revised—Budgeted Cash Payments for Operating Expenses

	April	May	June	July	Total
Salary and commissions:					
50% of last month's expenses, from revised operating expenses budget	$ 4,250*	$ 5,000	$ 7,250	$ 5,750	
50% of this month's expenses, from revised operating expenses budget	5,000	7,250	5,750	4,250	
Total salary and commissions	9,250	12,250	13,000	10,000	
Rent expense, from revised operating expenses budget	2,000	2,000	2,000	2,000	
Miscellaneous expenses, from revised operating expenses budget	2,500	4,000	3,000	2,000	
Total payments for operating expenses	$13,750	$18,250	$18,000	$14,000	$64,000

*March 31 salary and commissions payable (Exhibit 23-6).

WHITEWATER SPORTING GOODS STORE NO. 18
Revised Cash Budget
Four Months Ending July 31, 2009

	April	May	June	July
Beginning cash balance	$15,000*	$10,550	$10,410	$21,035
Cash collections (revised budgeted cash collections)	46,000	68,000	68,000	48,000
Cash available	$61,000	78,550	78,410	69,035
Cash payments:				
Purchases of inventory (revised budgeted cash payments for purchases)	$42,700	$48,300	$37,800	$29,400
Operating expenses (revised budgeted cash payments for operating expenses)	13,750	18,250	18,000	14,000
Purchase of delivery truck (item 8, page 1176)	3,000	—	—	—
Total cash payments	59,450	66,550	55,800	43,400
(1) Ending cash balance before financing	1,550	12,000	22,610	25,635
Less: Minimum cash balance desired	(10,000)	(10,000)	(10,000)	(10,000)
Cash excess (deficiency)	$ (8,450)	$ 2,000	$12,610	$15,635
Financing of cash deficiency (see notes a–c):				
Borrowing (at end of month)	$ 9,000			
Principal payments (at end of month)		$ (1,500)	$ (1,500)	$ (1,500)
Interest expense (at 12% annually)		(90)	(75)	(60)
(2) Total effects of financing	9,000	(1,590)	(1,575)	(1,560)
Ending cash balance (1) + (2)	$10,550	$10,410	$21,035	$24,075

*March 31 cash balance (Exhibit 23-6).

Notes
[a] Borrowing occurs in multiples of $1,000 and only for the amount needed to maintain a minimum cash balance of $10,000.
[b] Monthly principal payments: $9,000 ÷ 6 = $1,500.
[c] Interest expense: May: $9,000 × (0.12 × 1/12) = $90; June: ($9,000 − $1,500) × (0.12 × 1/12) = $75; July: ($9,000 − $1,500 − $1,500) × (0.12 × 1/12) = $60

WHITEWATER SPORTING GOODS STORE NO. 18
Revised Budgeted Balance Sheet
July 31, 2009

Assets		
Current assets:		
Cash (revised cash budget)	$24,075	
Accounts receivable (revised sales budget)	16,000	
Inventory	42,400	
Prepaid insurance	1,000	
Total current assets		$ 83,475
Plant assets:		
Equipment and fixtures	$35,000	
Accumulated depreciation	(14,800)	
Total plant assets		20,200
Total assets		$103,675
Liabilities		
Current liabilities:		
Accounts payable (0.50 × July purchases of $28,000; revised inventory, purchases, and cost of goods sold budget)	$14,000	
Short-term note payable	4,500	
Salary and commissions payable (0.50 × July expenses of $8,500; revised operating expenses budget)	4,250	
Total liabilities		$ 22,750
Stockholders' Equity		
Stockholders' equity (beginning balance of $78,950* + $1,975 net income, revised budgeted income statement)		80,925
Total liabilities and stockholders' equity		$103,675

*March 31, 2009, balance sheet (Exhibit 23-6).

WHITEWATER SPORTING GOODS STORE NO.18
Revised Budgeted Statement of Cash Flows
Four Months Ending July 31, 2009

Cash flows from operating activities:		
Receipts:		
Collections (revised budgeted cash collections)	$230,000	
Total cash receipts		$230,000
Payments:		
Purchases of inventory (revised budgeted cash payments for purchases)	(158,200)	
Operating expenses (revised budgeted cash payments for operating expenses)	(64,000)	
Payment of interest expense	(225)	
Total cash payments		(222,425)
Net cash inflow from operating activities		7,575
Cash flows from investing activities:		
Acquisition of delivery truck	$ (3,000)	
Net cash outflow from investing activities		(3,000)
Cash flows from financing activities:		
Proceeds from issuance of notes payable	$ 9,000	
Payment of notes payable	(4,500)	
Net cash inflow from financing activities		4,500
Net increase in cash		$ 9,075
Cash balance, April 1, 2009 (Exhibit 23-6)		15,000
Cash balance, July 31, 2009 (revised cash budget)		$ 24,075

Review: The Master Budget and Responsibility Accounting

Accounting Vocabulary

Capital Expenditures Budget
A company's plan for purchases of property, plant, equipment, and other long-term assets.

Cash Budget
Details how the business expects to go from the beginning cash balance to the desired ending balance. Also called the statement of budgeted cash receipts and payments.

Financial Budget
The cash budget (cash inflows and outflows), the budgeted period-end balance sheet, and the budgeted statement of cash flows.

Management by Exception
Directs management's attention to important differences between actual and budgeted amounts.

Master Budget
The set of budgeted financial statements and supporting schedules for the entire organization. Includes the operating budget, the capital expenditures budget, and the financial budget.

Operating Budget
Projects sales revenue, cost of goods sold, and operating expenses, leading to the budgeted income statement that projects operating income for the period.

Responsibility Accounting
A system for evaluating the performance of each responsibility center and its manager.

Responsibility Center
A part or subunit of an organization whose manager is accountable for specific activities.

Quick Check

1. Amazon.com expected to receive which of the following benefits when it started its budgeting process?
   a. The planning required to develop the budget helps managers foresee and avoid potential problems before they occur.
   b. The budget helps motivate employees to achieve Amazon.com's sales growth and cost-reduction goals.
   c. The budget provides Amazon.com's managers with a benchmark against which to compare actual results for performance evaluation.
   d. All of the above.

2. Which of the following is the cornerstone (or most critical element) of the master budget?
   a. the sales budget
   b. the inventory budget
   c. the purchases and cost of goods sold budget
   d. the operating expenses budget

3. The income statement is part of which element of Amazon.com's master budget?
   a. the operating budget
   b. the capital expenditures budget
   c. the financial budget
   d. none of the above

Use the following information to answer Questions 4 through 6. Suppose Amazon.com sells 1 million hardcover books a day at an average price of $30 and 1.5 million paperback books a day at an average price of $15. Assume that Amazon.com's purchase price for the books is 60% of the selling price it charges retail customers. Amazon.com has no beginning inventory, but it wants to have a three-day supply of ending inventory. Assume that operating expenses are $0.5 million per day.

4. Compute Amazon.com's budgeted sales for the next (seven-day) week.
   a. $52.5 million
   b. $210 million
   c. $220.5 million
   d. $367.5 million

5. Determine Amazon.com's budgeted purchases for the next (seven-day) week.
   a. $220.5 million
   b. $315 million
   c. $367.5 million
   d. $525 million

6. What is Amazon.com's budgeted operating income for a (seven-day) week?
   a. $52.5 million
   b. $56 million
   c. $143.5 million
   d. $147 million

7. Which of the following expenses would *not* appear in Amazon.com's cash budget?
    a. depreciation expense
    b. wages expense
    c. interest expense
    d. marketing expense

8. IT has made it easier for Amazon.com's managers to perform all of the following tasks *except*:
    a. sensitivity analyses
    b. rolling up individual units' budgets into the companywide budget
    c. removing slack from the budget
    d. preparing responsibility center performance reports that identify variances between actual and budgeted revenues and costs

9. Which of the following managers is at the highest level of the organization?
    a. cost center manager
    b. revenue center manager
    c. profit center manager
    d. investment center manager

10. Suppose Amazon.com budgets $5 million for customer service costs but actually spends $4 million. Which of the following is true?
    a. Because this $1 million variance is favorable, management does not need to investigate further.
    b. Management will investigate this $1 million favorable variance to ensure that the cost savings do not reflect skimping on customer service.
    c. Management will investigate this $1 million unfavorable variance to try to identify and then correct the problem that led to the unfavorable variance.
    d. Management should investigate every variance, especially unfavorable ones.

Answers are given after Apply Your Knowledge (p. 1219).

Assess Your Progress

Short Exercises

[1] Learn why managers use budgets

S23-1 Consider the budget for your travel itinerary business (page 1171). Explain how you benefit from preparing the budget.

[2] Prepare an operating budget

[3] Prepare a financial budget

S23-2 In what order should you prepare the following components of the master budget?

Budgeted income statement	Operating expense budget	Cash budget
Budgeted statement of cash flows	Purchases and cost of goods sold budget	Capital expenditures budget
Budgeted balance sheet	Sales budget	Inventory budget

Which are components of the operating budget? Which are components of the financial budget?

[2] Prepare an operating budget

S23-3 In a series of Short Exercises, you will prepare parts of the master budget for Grippers, which sells its rock-climbing shoes worldwide. We will concentrate on Grippers' budget for January and February.

Grippers expects to sell 4,000 pairs of shoes for $185 each in January, and 3,500 pairs of shoes for $220 each in February. All sales are cash only. Prepare the sales budget for January and February.

[2] Prepare an operating budget

S23-4 In S23-3, Grippers expects cost of goods sold to average 65% of sales revenue, and the company expects to sell 4,300 pairs of shoes in March for $240 each. Grippers' target ending inventory is $10,000 plus 50% of the next month's cost of goods sold. Use this information and the sales budget from S23-3 to prepare Grippers' inventory, purchases, and cost of goods sold budget for January and February.

[2] Prepare an operating budget
[4] Use sensitivity analysis in budgeting

S23-5 Turn to the Whitewater Sporting Goods example on pages 1175–1180. Suppose June sales are expected to be $40,000 rather than $60,000. Revise Whitewater Sporting Goods' sales budget. What other components of Whitewater Sporting Goods' master budget would be affected by this change in the sales budget?

[2] Prepare an operating budget
[4] Use sensitivity analysis in budgeting

S23-6 Refer to the original Whitewater Sporting Goods example on pages 1175–1180. Suppose cost of goods sold averages 75% of sales rather than 70%. Revise Whitewater Sporting Goods' inventory, purchases, and cost of goods sold budget for April and May. What other components of Whitewater Sporting Goods' master budget would be affected by the change in the budgeted cost of goods sold?

[2] Prepare an operating budget
[3] Prepare a financial budget
[4] Use sensitivity analysis in budgeting

S23-7 Turn to the original Whitewater Sporting Goods example on pages 1175–1180. Suppose 70% of sales are cash and 30% are credit. Revise Whitewater's sales budget and budgeted cash collections from customers for April and May.

continued . . .

3 Prepare a financial budget

4 Use sensitivity analysis in budgeting

S23-8 Refer to the original Whitewater Sporting Goods example on pages 1175–1180. Suppose Whitewater Sporting Goods pays for 60% of inventory purchases in the month of the purchase and 40% during the next month. Revise Whitewater Sporting Goods' budgeted cash payments for purchases of inventory for April and May. (*Hint:* Assume these new percentages also apply to March purchases of $33,600 given in item 5 on page 1176.)

3 Prepare a financial budget

S23-9 You prepared Grippers' sales budget in S23-3. Now assume that Grippers' sales are 25% cash and 75% on credit. Grippers' collection history indicates that credit sales are collected as follows:

30% in the month of the sale
60% in the month after the sale
6% two months after the sale
4% are never collected

November sales totaled $391,500 and December sales were $398,250. Prepare a schedule for the budgeted cash collections for January and February.

3 Prepare a financial budget

S23-10 Refer to S23-9. Grippers has $8,300 cash on hand on January 1. The company requires a minimum cash balance of $7,500. January cash collections are $548,330 (as you calculated in S23-9). Total cash payments for January are $583,200. Prepare a cash budget for January. Will Grippers need to borrow cash by the end of January?

5 Prepare performance reports for responsibility centers

S23-11 Fill in the blanks with the phrase that best completes the sentence.

A cost center	A responsibility center	Lower
An investment center	A revenue center	Higher
A profit center		

a. The maintenance department at the San Diego Zoo is _____.
b. The concession stand at the San Diego Zoo is _____.
c. The menswear department at Bloomingdale's, which is responsible for buying and selling merchandise, is _____.
d. A production line at a Palm Pilot plant is _____.
e. _____ is any segment of the business whose manager is accountable for specific activities.
f. Gatorade, a division of Quaker Oats, is _____.
g. The sales manager in charge of Nike's northwest sales territory oversees _____.
h. Managers of cost and revenue centers are at _____ levels of the organization than are managers of profit and investment centers.

5 Prepare performance reports for responsibility centers

S23-12 In Exhibit 23-20, the next to last line of the CEO's report consists entirely of expenses. Describe the kinds of expenses that would be included in this category.

5 Prepare performance reports for responsibility centers

S23-13 Look at the performance report in Exhibit 23-20. On which variances should the manager of the Mexican sauces product line focus his efforts, according to the management by exception principle? For these variances, compute the variance as a percent of the budgeted amount, and suggest some questions the manager may want to investigate.

5 Prepare performance reports for responsibility centers

S23-14 Exhibit 23-20 shows that the Mexican sauces product line had a favorable marketing expense variance. Does this favorable variance necessarily mean that the manager of the Mexican sauces line is doing a good job? Explain.

Exercises

1 Learn why managers use budgets

E23-15 Hanna White owns a chain of travel goods stores. Last year, her sales staff sold 10,000 suitcases at an average sale price of $150. Variable expenses were 80% of sales revenue, and the total fixed expense was $100,000. This year, the chain sold more expensive product lines. Sales were 8,000 suitcases at an average price of $200. The variable expense percentage and the total fixed expense were the same both years. White evaluates the chain manager by comparing this year's income with last year's income.

Prepare a performance report for this year, similar to Exhibit 23-4. How would you improve White's performance evaluation system to better analyze this year's results?

2 Prepare an operating budget

E23-16 Leno sells tire rims. Its sales budget for the nine months ended September 30 follows:

	Quarter Ended			Nine-Month Total
	March 31	June 30	Sep. 30	
Cash sales, 30%......	$ 30,000	$ 45,000	$ 37,500	$112,500
Credit sales, 70%	70,000	105,000	87,500	262,500
Total sales, 100% ...	$100,000	$150,000	$125,000	$375,000

In the past, cost of goods sold has been 60% of total sales. The director of marketing and the financial vice president agree that each quarter's ending inventory should not be below $20,000 plus 10% of cost of goods sold for the following quarter. The marketing director expects sales of $220,000 during the fourth quarter. The January 1 inventory was $19,000.

Prepare an inventory, purchases, and cost of goods sold budget for each of the first three quarters of the year. Compute cost of goods sold for the entire nine-month period. (Use Exhibit 23-8 as a model.)

2 Prepare an operating budget

E23-17 Wheels is an exotic car dealership. Suppose that its Miami office projects that 2009 quarterly sales will increase by 3% in Quarter 1, by 4% in Quarter 2, by 6% in Quarter 3, and by 5% in Quarter 4. Management expects operating expenses to be 80% of revenues during each of the first two quarters, 79% of revenues during the third quarter, and 81% during the fourth. The office manager expects to borrow $100,000 on July 1, with quarterly principal payments of $10,000 beginning on September 30 and interest paid at an annual rate of 13%. Assume that fourth-quarter 2008 sales were $4,000,000.

Prepare a budgeted income statement for each of the four quarters of 2009 and for the entire year. Present the 2009 budget as follows:

Quarter 1	Quarter 2	Quarter 3	Quarter 4	Full Year

E23-18 Aqua Pure is a distributor of bottled water. For each of the Items a through c, compute the amount of cash receipts or payments Aqua Pure will budget for September. The solution to one item may depend on the answer to an earlier item.

  a. Management expects to sell equipment that costs $14,000 at a gain of $2,000. Accumulated depreciation on this equipment is $7,000.
  b. Management expects to sell 7,500 cases of water in August and 9,200 in September. Each case sells for $12. Cash sales average 30% of total sales, and credit sales make up the rest. On average, three-fourths of credit sales are collected in the month of sale, with the balance collected the following month.
  c. The company pays rent and property taxes of $4,200 each month. Commissions and other selling expenses average 25% of sales. Aqua Pure pays two-thirds of commissions and other selling expenses in the month incurred, with the balance paid in the following month.

E23-19 Battery Power, a family-owned battery store, began October with $10,500 cash. Management forecasts that collections from credit customers will be $11,000 in October and $15,000 in November. The store is scheduled to receive $6,000 cash on a business note receivable in October. Projected cash payments include inventory purchases ($13,000 in October and $13,900 in November) and operating expenses ($3,000 each month).

Battery Power's bank requires a $10,000 minimum balance in the store's checking account. At the end of any month when the account balance dips below $10,000, the bank automatically extends credit to the store in multiples of $1,000. Battery Power borrows as little as possible and pays back loans in quarterly installments of $2,000, plus 4% interest on the entire unpaid principal. The first payment occurs three months after the loan.

Requirements
1. Prepare Battery Power's cash budget for October and November.
2. How much cash will Battery Power borrow in November if collections from customers that month total $12,000 instead of $15,000?

E23-20 You recently began a job as an accounting intern at Outdoor Adventures. Your first task was to help prepare the cash budget for February and March. Unfortunately, the computer with the budget file crashed, and you did not have a backup or even a hard copy. You ran a program to salvage bits of data from the budget file. After entering the following data in the budget, you may have just enough information to reconstruct the budget.

Outdoor Adventures eliminates any cash deficiency by borrowing the exact amount needed from State Street Bank, where the current interest rate is 8%. Outdoor Adventures pays interest on its outstanding debt at the end of each month. The company also repays all borrowed amounts at the end of the month, as cash becomes available.

continued . . .

Complete the following cash budget:

OUTDOOR ADVENTURES LTD.
Cash Budget
February and March

	February	March
Beginning cash balance	$ 16,900	$?
Cash collections	?	79,600
Cash from sale of plant assets	0	1,800
Cash available	106,900	?
Cash payments:		
Purchase of inventory	$?	$41,000
Operating expenses	47,200	?
Total payments	98,000	?
(1) Ending cash balance before financing	?	25,100
Minimum cash balance desired	20,000	20,000
Cash excess (deficiency)	$?	$?
Financing of cash deficiency:		
Borrowing (at end of month)	$?	$?
Principal repayments (at end of month)	?	?
Interest expense	?	?
(2) Total effects of financing	?	?
Ending cash balance (1) + (2)	$?	$?

3 Prepare a financial budget

E23-21 Use the following to prepare a budgeted balance sheet for Marine.com at March 31, 2009. Show computations for the cash and owners' equity amounts.

    a. March 31 inventory balance, $15,000.
    b. March payments for inventory, $4,600.
    c. March payments of accounts payable and accrued liabilities, $8,200.
    d. March 31 accounts payable balance, $4,300.
    e. February 28 furniture and fixtures balance, $34,800; accumulated depreciation balance, $29,870.
    f. February 28 owners' equity, $26,700.
    g. March depreciation expense, $600.
    h. Cost of goods sold, 60% of sales.
    i. Other March expenses, including income tax, total $5,000; paid in cash.
    j. February 28 cash balance, $11,400.
    k. March budgeted sales, $12,200.
    l. March 31 accounts receivable balance, one-fourth of March sales.
    m. March cash receipts, $14,300.

5 Prepare performance reports for responsibility centers

E23-22 Identify each responsibility center as a cost center, a revenue center, a profit center, or an investment center.
  a. The bakery department of a Publix supermarket reports income for the current year.
  b. Pace Foods is a subsidiary of Campbell Soup Company.
  c. The personnel department of State Farm Insurance Companies prepares its budget and subsequent performance report on the basis of its expected expenses for the year.
  d. The shopping section of Burpee.com reports both revenues and expenses.
  e. Burpee.com's investor relations Web site provides operating and financial information to investors and other interested parties.
  f. The manager of a BP service station is evaluated based on the station's revenues and expenses.
  g. A charter airline records revenues and expenses for each airplane each month. Each airplane's performance report shows its ratio of operating income to average book value.
  h. The manager of the southwest sales territory is evaluated based on a comparison of current period sales against budgeted sales.

5 Prepare performance reports for responsibility centers

E23-23 InTouch is a Seattle company that sells cell phones and PDAs on the Web. InTouch has assistant managers for its digital and video cell phone operations. These assistant managers report to the manager of the total cell phone product line, who, with the manager of PDAs, reports to the manager for all sales of handheld devices, Beth Beverly. Beverly received the following data for November operations:

	Cell Phones		PDAs
	Digital	Video	
Revenues, budget............	$204,000	$800,000	$300,000
Expenses, budget............	140,000	390,000	225,000
Revenues, actual.............	214,000	840,000	290,000
Expenses, actual.............	135,000	400,000	230,000

Arrange the data in a performance report similar to Exhibit 23-20. Show November results, in thousands of dollars, for digital cell phones, for the total cell phone product line, and for all devices. Should Beverly investigate the performance of digital cell phone operations?

Problems (Problem Set A)

2 Prepare an operating budget

P23-24A The budget committee of Vinning Office Supply has assembled the following data. As the business manager, you must prepare the budgeted income statements for May and June 2009.
  a. Sales in April were $42,100. You forecast that monthly sales will increase 2.0% in May and 2.4% in June.
  b. Vinning Office Supply maintains inventory of $9,000 plus 25% of sales budgeted for the following month. Monthly purchases average

continued...

50% of sales revenues in that same month. Actual inventory on April 30 is $14,000. Sales budgeted for July are $42,400.

c. Monthly salaries amount to $4,000. Sales commissions equal 4% of sales for that month. Combine salaries and commissions into a single figure.

d. Other monthly expenses are:

Rent expense.............................	$3,000, paid as incurred
Depreciation expense	$ 600
Insurance expense.......................	$ 200, expiration of prepaid amount
Income tax................................	20% of operating income

Prepare Vinning Office Supply's budgeted income statements for May and June. Show cost of goods sold computations. Round *all* amounts to the nearest $100. (Round amounts ending in $50 or more upward, and amounts ending in less than $50 downward.) For example, budgeted May sales are $42,900 ($42,100 × 1.02), and June sales are $43,900 ($42,900 × 1.024).

P23-25A Refer to Problem 23-24A. Vinning Office Supply's sales are 70% cash and 30% credit. (Use the rounded sales on the last line of P23-24A.) Credit sales are collected in the month after sale. Inventory purchases are paid 50% in the month of purchase and 50% the following month. Salaries and sales commissions are also paid half in the month earned and half the next month. Income tax is paid at the end of the year.

The April 30, 2009, balance sheet showed the following balances:

Cash..	$11,000
Accounts payable	7,400
Salary and commissions payable	2,850

Requirements

1. Prepare schedules of (a) budgeted cash collections, (b) budgeted cash payments for purchases, and (c) budgeted cash payments for operating expenses. Show amounts for each month and totals for May and June. *Round* your computations to the nearest dollar.
2. Prepare a cash budget similar to Exhibit 23-14. If no financing activity took place, what is the budgeted cash balance on June 30, 2009?

P23-26A Alliance Printing of Baltimore has applied for a loan. Bank of America has requested a budgeted balance sheet at April 30, 2009, and a budgeted statement of cash flows for April. As Alliance Printing's controller, you have assembled the following information:

a. March 31 equipment balance, $52,400; accumulated depreciation, $41,300.

b. April capital expenditures of $42,800 budgeted for cash purchase of equipment.

c. April depreciation expense, $900.

d. Cost of goods sold, 60% of sales.

continued . . .

e. Other April operating expenses, including income tax, total $13,200, 25% of which will be paid in cash and the remainder accrued at April 30.
f. March 31 stockholders' equity, $93,700.
g. March 31 cash balance, $40,600.
h. April budgeted sales, $90,000, 70% of which is for cash. Of the remaining 30%, half will be collected in April and half in May.
i. April cash collections on March sales, $29,700.
j. April cash payments of March 31 liabilities incurred for March purchases of inventory, $17,300.
k. March 31 inventory balance, $29,600.
l. April purchases of inventory, $10,000 for cash and $36,800 on credit. Half of the credit purchases will be paid in April and half in May.

Requirements

1. Prepare the budgeted balance sheet for Alliance Printing at April 30, 2009. Show separate computations for cash, inventory, and stockholders' equity balances.
2. Prepare the budgeted statement of cash flows for April.
3. Suppose that Alliance Printing has become aware of more efficient (and more expensive) equipment than it budgeted for purchase in April. What is the total amount of cash available for equipment purchases in April, before financing, if the minimum desired ending cash balance is $21,000? (For this requirement, disregard the $42,800 initially budgeted for equipment purchases.)

3 Prepare a financial budget

4 Use sensitivity analysis in budgeting

P23-27A Refer to Problem 23-26A. Before granting a loan to Alliance Printing, Bank of America asks for a sensitivity analysis assuming April sales are only $60,000 rather than the $90,000 originally budgeted. (While the cost of goods sold will change, assume that purchases, depreciation, and the other operating expenses will remain the same as in Problem 23-26A.)

Requirements

1. Prepare a revised budgeted balance sheet for Alliance Printing, showing separate computations for cash, inventory, and owners' equity balances.
2. Suppose Alliance Printing has a minimum desired cash balance of $23,000. Will the company need to borrow cash in April?
3. In this sensitivity analysis, sales declined by 33 1/3% ($30,000 ÷ $90,000). Is the decline in expenses and income more or less than 33 1/3%? Explain why.

5 Prepare performance reports for responsibility centers

P23-28A Is each of the following most likely a cost center, a revenue center, a profit center, or an investment center?
a. Shipping department of Amazon.com.
b. Eastern district of a salesperson's territory.
c. Child care department of a church or synagogue.
d. Catering operation of Sonny's BBQ restaurant.
e. Executive headquarters of the United Way.

continued . . .

f. Accounts payable section of the accounting department at Home Depot.
g. Proposed new office of Coldwell Banker, a real-estate firm.
h. Disneyland.
i. The Empire State Building in New York City.
j. Branch warehouse of Dalton Carpets.
k. Information systems department for Habitat for Humanity.
l. Service department of Audio Forest stereo shop.
m. Investments department of Citibank.
n. Assembly-line supervisors at Dell Computer.
o. American subsidiary of a Japanese manufacturer.
p. Surgery unit of a privately owned hospital.
q. Research and development department of Cisco Systems.
r. Childrenswear department at a Target store.
s. Typesetting department of Northend Press, a printing company.
t. Prescription-filling department of Drugstore.com.
u. Order-taking department at L.L.Bean.
v. Personnel department of Goodyear Tire and Rubber Company.
w. Grounds maintenance department at Augusta National golf course.

P23-29A Winnie's World operates a chain of pet stores in the Midwest. The manager of each store reports to the region manager, who, in turn, reports to the headquarters in Milwaukee, Wisconsin. The *actual* income statements for the Dayton store, the Ohio region (including the Dayton store), and the company as a whole (including the Ohio region) for July 2009 are:

	Dayton	Ohio	Companywide
Revenue	$148,900	$1,647,000	$4,200,000
Expenses:			
Region manager/headquarters office	$ —	$ 60,000	$ 116,000
Cost of materials	81,100	871,900	1,807,000
Salary expense	38,300	415,100	1,119,000
Depreciation expense	7,200	91,000	435,000
Utilities expense	4,000	46,200	260,000
Rent expense	2,400	34,700	178,000
Total expenses	133,000	1,518,900	3,915,000
Operating income	$ 15,900	$ 128,100	$ 285,000

Budgeted amounts for July were as follows:

	Dayton	Ohio	Companywide
Revenue	$162,400	$1,769,700	$4,450,000
Expenses:			
Region manager/headquarters office	$ —	$ 65,600	$ 118,000
Cost of materials	86,400	963,400	1,972,000

continued . . .

	Dayton	Ohio	Companywide
Salary expense	38,800	442,000	1,095,000
Depreciation expense	7,200	87,800	449,000
Utilities expense	4,400	54,400	271,000
Rent expense	3,600	32,300	174,000
Total expenses	140,400	1,645,500	4,079,000
Operating income	$ 22,000	$ 124,200	$ 371,000

Requirements

1. Prepare a report for July 2009 that shows the performance of the Dayton store, the Ohio region, and the company as a whole. Follow the format of Exhibit 23-20.

2. As the Ohio region manager, would you investigate the Dayton store on the basis of this report? Why or why not?

3. Briefly discuss the benefits of budgeting. Base your discussion on Winnie's World's performance report.

Problems (Problem Set B)

Prepare an operating budget

P23-30B Representatives of the various departments of Go Sports have assembled the following data. As the business manager, you must prepare the budgeted income statements for August and September 2009.

a. Sales in July were $196,000. You forecast that monthly sales will increase 3% in August and 2% in September.

b. Go Sports tries to maintain inventory of $50,000 plus 20% of sales budgeted for the following month. Monthly purchases average 60% of sales revenue in that same month. Actual inventory on July 31 is $90,000. Sales budgeted for October are $220,000.

c. Monthly salaries amount to $15,000. Sales commissions equal 6% of sales for that month. Combine salaries and commissions into a single figure.

d. Other monthly expenses are:

Rent expense	$13,000, paid as incurred
Depreciation expense	$ 4,000
Insurance expense	$ 1,000, expiration of prepaid amount
Income tax	30% of operating income

Prepare Go Sports' budgeted income statements for August and September. Show cost of goods sold computations. Round *all* amounts to the nearest $1,000. For example, budgeted August sales are $202,000 ($196,000 × 1.03) and September sales are $206,000 ($202,000 × 1.02).

Prepare a financial budget

P23-31B Refer to P23-30B. Go Sports' sales are 50% cash and 50% credit. (Use sales on the last two lines of P23-30B.) Credit sales are collected in the

continued ...

month after the sale. Inventory purchases are paid 60% in the month of purchase and 40% the following month. Salaries and sales commissions are paid three-fourths in the month earned and one-fourth the next month. Income tax is paid at the end of the year.

The July 31, 2009 balance sheet showed the following balances:

Cash	$22,000
Accounts payable	52,000
Salaries and commissions payable	6,750

Requirements

1. Prepare schedules of (a) budgeted cash collections from customers, (b) budgeted cash payments for purchases, and (c) budgeted cash payments for operating expenses. Show amounts for each month and totals for August and September. Round your computations to the *nearest dollar*.
2. Prepare a cash budget similar to Exhibit 23-14. If no financing activity took place, what is the budgeted cash balance on September 30, 2009?

3 Prepare a financial budget

P23-32B The Music Box has applied for a loan. First Central Bank has requested a budgeted balance sheet at June 30, 2009, and a budgeted statement of cash flows for June. As the controller (chief accounting officer) of The Music Box, you have assembled the following information:

a. May 31 equipment balance, $80,800; accumulated depreciation, $12,400.
b. June capital expenditures of $16,400 budgeted for cash purchase of equipment.
c. June depreciation expense, $400.
d. Cost of goods sold, 50% of sales.
e. Other June operating expenses, including income tax, total $34,000, 75% of which will be paid in cash and the remainder accrued at June 30.
f. May 31 stockholders' equity, $137,500.
g. May 31 cash balance, $50,200.
h. June budgeted sales, $85,000, 40% of which is for cash; of the remaining 60%, half will be collected in June and half in July.
i. June cash collections on May sales, $15,300.
j. June cash payments of liabilities for May inventory purchases on credit, $8,300.
k. May 31 inventory balance, $11,900.
l. June purchases of inventory, $11,000 for cash and $37,200 on credit. Half the credit purchases will be paid in June and half in July.

Requirements

1. Prepare the budgeted balance sheet for The Music Box at June 30, 2009. Show separate computations for cash, inventory, and stockholders' equity balances.

continued . . .

2. Prepare the budgeted statement of cash flows for June.
3. On the basis of this data, if you were a First Central Bank loan officer, would you grant The Music Box a loan? Give your reason.

3 Prepare a financial budget

4 Use sensitivity analysis in budgeting

P23-33B Refer to P23-32B. Before granting a loan to The Music Box, First Central Bank asks for a sensitivity analysis, assuming that June sales are only $65,000 rather than the $85,000 originally budgeted. (While cost of goods sold will change, assume that purchases, depreciation, and the other operating expenses will remain the same as in P23-32B.)

Requirements
1. Prepare a revised budgeted balance sheet for The Music Box, showing separate computations for cash, inventory, and owners' equity balances.
2. Suppose The Music Box has a minimum desired cash balance of $35,000. Will the company borrow cash in June?
3. How would this sensitivity analysis affect First Central's loan decision?

5 Prepare performance reports for responsibility centers

P23-34B Is each of the following most likely a cost center, a revenue center, a profit center, or an investment center?
   a. Purchasing department of Milliken, a textile manufacturer.
   b. Quality control department of Mayfield Dairies.
   c. European subsidiary of Coca-Cola.
   d. Payroll department of the University of Wisconsin.
   e. Lighting department in a Sears store.
   f. Children's nursery in a church or synagogue.
   g. Personnel department of E*Trade, the online broker.
   h. igourmet.com, an e-tailer of gourmet cheeses.
   i. Service department of an automobile dealership.
   j. Customer service department of Procter & Gamble.
   k. Proposed new office of Deutsche Bank.
   l. Southwest region of Pizza Inns.
   m. Delta Air Lines.
   n. Order-taking department at Lands' End.
   o. Editorial department of the *Wall Street Journal*.
   p. A Ford Motor Company production plant.
   q. Police department of Boston.
   r. Century 21 Real Estate.
   s. A small pet-grooming business.
   t. Northeast sales territory for Boise-Cascade.
   u. Different product lines of Broyhill, a furniture manufacturer.
   v. McDonald's restaurants under the supervision of a regional manager.
   w. Job superintendents of a home builder.

1 Learn why managers use budgets

5 Prepare performance reports for responsibility centers

P23-35B Etown is a chain of home electronics stores. Each store has a manager who answers to a city manager, who, in turn, reports to a statewide manager. The actual income statements of Store No. 23, all stores in the Dallas area (including Store No. 23), and all stores in the state of Texas (including all Dallas stores) are summarized as follows for April:

	Store No. 23	Dallas	State of Texas
Sales revenue	$43,300	$486,000	$3,228,500
Expenses:			
City/state manager's office expenses	$ —	$ 18,000	$ 44,000
Cost of goods sold	15,000	171,300	1,256,800
Salary expense	4,000	37,500	409,700
Depreciation expense	3,700	13,100	320,000
Utilities expense	1,900	19,300	245,600
Rent expense	700	16,600	186,000
Total expenses	25,300	275,800	2,462,100
Operating income	$18,000	$210,200	$ 766,400

Budgeted amounts for April were as follows:

	Store No. 23	Dallas	State of Texas
Sales revenue	$39,000	$470,000	$3,129,000
Expenses:			
City/state manager's office expenses	$ —	$ 19,000	$ 45,000
Cost of goods sold	12,100	160,800	1,209,000
Salary expense	6,000	37,900	412,000
Depreciation expense	3,200	23,400	320,000
Utilities expense	1,000	15,000	240,000
Rent expense	700	15,700	181,000
Total expenses	23,000	271,800	2,407,000
Operating income	$16,000	$198,200	$ 722,000

Requirements

1. Prepare a report for April that shows the performance of Store No. 23, all the stores in the Dallas area, and all the stores in Texas. Follow the format of Exhibit 23-20.
2. As the city manager of Dallas, would you investigate Store No. 23 on the basis of this report? Why or why not?
3. Briefly discuss the benefits of budgeting. Base your discussion on Etown's performance report.

Apply Your Knowledge

Decision Cases

1 Learn why managers use budgets

Case 23-36. Donna Tse has recently accepted the position of assistant manager at Cycle World, a bicycle store in St. Louis. She has just finished her accounting courses. Cycle World's manager and owner, Jeff Towry, asks Tse to prepare a budgeted income statement for 2009 based on the information he has collected. Tse's budget follows:

CYCLE WORLD
Budgeted Income Statement
For the Year Ending July 31, 2009

Sales revenue		$244,000
Cost of goods sold		177,000
Gross profit		67,000
Operating expenses:		
Salary and commission expense	$46,000	
Rent expense	8,000	
Depreciation expense	2,000	
Insurance expense	800	
Miscellaneous expenses	12,000	68,800
Operating loss		(1,800)
Interest expense		225
Net loss		$ (2,025)

Requirements

Tse does not want to give Towry this budget without making constructive suggestions for steps Towry could take to improve expected performance. Write a memo to Towry outlining your suggestions. Your memo should take the following form:

> Date: _____
>
> **To:** Mr. Jeff Towry, Manager
>   Cycle World
>
> **From:** Donna Tse
>
> **Subject:** Cycle World's 2009 budgeted income statement

2 Prepare an operating budget

3 Prepare a financial budget

Case 23-37. Each autumn, as a hobby, Suzanne De Angelo weaves cotton place mats to sell through a local craft shop. The mats sell for $20 per set of four. The shop charges a 10% commission and remits the net proceeds to De Angelo at the end of December. De Angelo has woven and sold 25 sets each of the last two years. She has enough cotton in inventory to make another 25 sets. She paid $7 per set for the cotton. De Angelo uses a four-harness loom that she purchased for cash exactly two years

The Master Budget and Responsibility Accounting

ago. It is depreciated at the rate of $10 per month. The accounts payable relate to the cotton inventory and are payable by September 30.

De Angelo is considering buying an eight-harness loom so that she can weave more intricate patterns in linen. The new loom costs $1,000; it would be depreciated at $20 per month. Her bank has agreed to lend her $1,000 at 18% interest, with $200 principal plus accrued interest payable each December 31. De Angelo believes she can weave 15 linen place mat sets in time for the Christmas rush if she does not weave any cotton mats. She predicts that each linen set will sell for $50. Linen costs $18 per set. De Angelo's supplier will sell her linen on credit, payable December 31.

De Angelo plans to keep her old loom whether or not she buys the new loom. The balance sheet for her weaving business at August 31, 2009, is as follows:

SUZANNE DE ANGELO, WEAVER
Balance Sheet
August 31, 2009

Current assets:			Current liabilities:	
Cash		$ 25	Accounts payable	$ 74
Inventory of cotton		175		
		200		
Fixed assets:				
Loom		500	Stockholders' equity	386
Accumulated depreciation		(240)		
		260		
Total assets		$460	Total liabilities and owner's equity	$460

Requirements

1. Prepare a cash budget for the four months ending December 31, 2009, for two alternatives: weaving the place mats in cotton using the existing loom and weaving the place mats in linen using the new loom. For each alternative, prepare a budgeted income statement for the four months ending December 31, 2009, and a budgeted balance sheet at December 31, 2009.
2. On the basis of financial considerations only, what should De Angelo do? Give your reason.
3. What nonfinancial factors might De Angelo consider in her decision?

Ethical Issue

2 Prepare an operating budget

5 Prepare performance reports for responsibility centers

Case 23-38. Residence Suites operates a regional hotel chain. Each hotel is operated by a manager and an assistant manager/controller. Many of the staff who run the front desk, clean the rooms, and prepare the breakfast buffet work part-time or have a second job so turnover is high.

Assistant manager/controller Terry Dunn asked the new bookkeeper to help prepare the hotel's master budget. The master budget is prepared once a year and submitted to company headquarters for approval. Once approved, the master budget is used to evaluate the hotel's performance. These performance evaluations affect hotel managers' bonuses and they also affect company decisions on which hotels deserve extra funds for capital improvements.

When the budget was almost complete, Dunn asked the bookkeeper to increase amounts budgeted for labor and supplies by 15%. When asked why, Dunn responded that hotel manager Clay Murry told her to do this when she began working at the hotel. Murry explained that this budgetary cushion gave him flexibility in running the hotel. For example, because company headquarters tightly controls capital improvement funds, Murry can use the extra money budgeted for labor and supplies to replace broken televisions or pay "bonuses" to keep valued employees. Dunn initially accepted this explanation because she had observed similar behavior at the hotel where she worked previously.

Put yourself in Dunn's position. In deciding how to deal with the situation, answer the following questions:

1. What is the ethical issue?
2. What are my options?
3. What are the possible consequences?
4. What should I do?

Team Project

1. Learn why managers use budgets
2. Prepare an operating budget
5. Prepare performance reports for responsibility centers

Case 23-39. Xellnet provides e-commerce software for the pharmaceuticals industry. Xellnet is organized into several divisions. A companywide planning committee sets general strategy and goals for the company and its divisions, but each division develops its own budget.

Rick Watson is the new division manager of wireless communications software. His division has two departments: development and sales. Carrie Pronai manages the 20 or so programmers and systems specialists typically employed in the development department to create and update the division's software applications. Liz Smith manages the sales department.

Xellnet considers the divisions to be investment centers. To earn his bonus next year, Watson must achieve a 30% return on the $3 million invested in his division. Within the wireless division, development is a cost center, while sales is a revenue center.

Budgeting is in progress. Pronai met with her staff and is now struggling with two sets of numbers. Alternative A is her best estimate of next year's costs. However, unexpected problems can arise when writing software, and finding competent programmers is an ongoing challenge. She knows that Watson was a programmer before he earned an MBA so he should be sensitive to this uncertainty. Consequently, she is thinking of increasing her budgeted costs (Alternative B). Her department's bonuses largely depend on whether the department meets its budgeted costs.

XELLNET
Wireless Division
Development Budget 2009

	Alternative A	Alternative B
Salaries expense (including overtime and part time)	$ 2,400,000	$2,640,000
Software expense	120,000	132,000
Travel expense	65,000	71,500
Depreciation expense	255,000	255,000
Miscellaneous expense	100,000	110,000
Total expense	$ 2,940,000	$3,208,500

Liz Smith is also struggling with her sales budget. Companies have made their initial investments in communications software so it is harder to win new customers. If things go well, she believes her sales team can maintain the level of growth achieved over the last few years. This is Alternative A in the sales budget. However, if Smith is too optimistic, sales may fall short of the budget. If this happens, her team will not receive bonuses. Therefore, Smith is considering reducing the sales numbers and submitting Alternative B.

XELLNET
Wireless Division
Sales Budget 2009

	Alternative A	Alternative B
Sales revenue	$ 5,000,000	$4,500,000
Salaries expense	360,000	360,000
Travel expense	240,000	210,500

Split your team into three groups. Each group should meet separately before the entire team meets.

Requirements
1. The first group plays the role of Development Manager Carrie Pronai. Before meeting with the entire team, determine which set of budget numbers you are going to present to Rick Watson. Write a memo supporting your decision. Use the format shown in Case 23-36. Give this memo to the third group before the team meeting.

2. The second group plays the role of Sales Manager Liz Smith. Before meeting with the entire team, determine which set of budget numbers you are going to

present to Rick Watson. Write a memo supporting your decision. Use the format shown in Case 23-36. Give this memo to the third group before the team meeting.

3. The third group plays the role of Division Manager Rick Watson. Before meeting with the entire team, use the memos that Pronai and Smith provided you to prepare a division budget based on the sales and development budgets. Your divisional overhead costs (additional costs beyond those incurred by the development and sales departments) are approximately $390,000. Determine whether the wireless division can meet its targeted 30% return on assets given the budgeted alternatives submitted by your department managers.

During the meeting of the entire team, the group playing Watson presents the division budget and considers its implications. Each group should take turns discussing its concerns with the proposed budget. The team as a whole should consider whether the division budget must be revised. The team should prepare a report that includes the division budget and a summary of the issues covered in the team meeting.

Quick Check Answers

1. *d* 2. *a* 3. *a* 4. *d* 5. *b* 6. *c* 7. *a* 8. *c* 9. *d* 10. *b*

For Internet Exercises, Excel in Practice, and additional online activities, go to this book's Web site at www.prenhall.com/bamber.

24 Flexible Budgets and Standard Costs

Learning Objectives

1. Prepare a flexible budget for the income statement

2. Prepare an income statement performance report

3. Identify the benefits of standard costs and learn how to set standards

4. Compute standard cost variances for direct materials and direct labor

5. Analyze manufacturing overhead in a standard cost system

6. Record transactions at standard cost and prepare a standard cost income statement

Suppose you bought soft drinks for a party. Your budget was $30, but you actually spent $35. You need to stay within your budget in the future. It would be helpful to know *why* you spent more than the $30 budget. Here are some possibilities.

1. If each case of drinks costs more than the budget, then you might:

   - Find a cheaper price at a place like Costco, or wait for the drinks to go on sale.
   - Buy less-expensive store-brand drinks.

2. If you bought a larger quantity of soft drinks than you budgeted, why did you need this larger quantity?

   - If too many folks came to the party, next time you can restrict the invitation list.
   - If each guest drank more than you budgeted, perhaps you can cut per-guest consumption. Start the party later or end it earlier, or reduce the salty snacks.

3. If the budget for soft drinks was too low, you may need to increase the budget.

This chapter builds on your knowledge of budgeting. A budget variance is the difference between an actual amount and a budgeted figure. This chapter shows how managers use variances to operate a business. It's important to know *why* actual costs differ from the budget. That will enable you to identify problems and decide what action to take.

In this chapter, you'll learn how to figure out *why* actual results differ from your budget. This is the first step in correcting problems. You'll also learn to use another management tool—standard costing.

How Managers Use Flexible Budgets

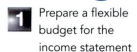

Prepare a flexible budget for the income statement

Pluto Pools installs swimming pools. At the beginning of the year, Pluto managers prepared a master budget. The master budget is a **static budget**, which means that it's prepared for only *one* level of sales volume. The static budget doesn't change after it's developed.

Exhibit 24-1 shows that Pluto's actual operating income is $16,000. This is $4,000 higher than expected from the static budget. This is a $4,000 favorable variance for June operating income. A **variance** is the difference between an actual amount and the budget. The variances in the third column of Exhibit 24-1 are:

- Favorable (F) if an actual amount increases operating income
- Unfavorable (U) if an actual amount decreases operating income

EXHIBIT 24-1   Actual Results Versus Static Budget

PLUTO POOLS
Comparison of Actual Results with Static Budget
Month Ended June 30, 2009

	Actual Results	Static Budget	Variance
Output units (pools installed)	10	8	2 F
Sales revenue	$121,000	$96,000	$25,000 F
Cost	(105,000)	(84,000)	(21,000) U
Operating income	$ 16,000	$12,000	$ 4,000 F

Pluto Pools' variance for operating income is favorable because Pluto installed 10 rather than 8 pools during June. But there's more to this story. Pluto Pools needs a flexible budget to show *why* operating income was favorable during June. Let's see how to prepare and use a flexible budget.

What Is a Flexible Budget?

The report in Exhibit 24-1 is hard to analyze because the static budget is based on 8 pools, but actual results are for 10 pools. This report raises more questions than it answers—for example:

- Why did the $21,000 unfavorable cost variance occur?
- Did workers waste materials?
- Did the cost of materials suddenly increase?
- How much of the additional cost arose because Pluto installed 10 rather than 8 pools?

We need a flexible budget to help answer these questions.

A **flexible budget** summarizes costs and revenues for several different volume levels within a relevant range. Flexible budgets separate variable costs from fixed costs; it is the variable costs that put the "flex" in the flexible budget. To create a flexible budget, you need to know your:

- Budgeted selling price per unit
- Variable cost per unit
- Total fixed costs
- Different volume levels within the relevant range

Exhibit 24-2 is a flexible budget for Pluto's revenues and costs to show what will happen if sales reach 5, 8, or 10 pools during June. The budgeted sale price per pool is $12,000. Budgeted variable costs (such as direct materials and direct labor) are $8,000 per pool, and budgeted fixed costs total $20,000. The formula for total cost is:

$$\text{Total cost} = \left(\begin{array}{c} \text{Number of} \\ \text{output units} \end{array} \times \begin{array}{c} \text{Variable cost} \\ \text{per output unit} \end{array} \right) + \text{Total fixed cost}$$

EXHIBIT 24-2 Flexible Budget

PLUTO POOLS
Flexible Budget
Month Ended June 30, 2009

	Flexible Budget per Output Unit	Outputs Units (Pools Installed)		
		5	8	10
Sales revenue	$12,000	$60,000	$96,000	$120,000
Variable costs	8,000	40,000	64,000	80,000
Fixed costs*		20,000	20,000	20,000
Total costs		60,000	84,000	100,000
Operating income		$ 0	$12,000	$ 20,000

*Fixed costs are usually given as a total amount rather than as a cost per unit.

Notice in Exhibit 24-2 that sales revenue and variable costs increase as more pools are installed. But fixed costs remain constant regardless of the number of pools installed within the relevant range of 5 to 10 pools. Remember: *The cost formula applies only to a specific relevant range.* Why? Because fixed costs and the variable cost per pool may change outside this range. In our example, Pluto's relevant range is 5 to 10 pools. If the company installs 12 pools, it will have to rent additional equipment, so fixed costs will exceed $20,000. Pluto will also have to pay workers for overtime pay, so the variable cost per pool will be more than $8,000.

Using the Flexible Budget: Why Do Actual Results Differ from the Static Budget?

2 Prepare an income statement performance report

It's not enough to know that a variance occurred. That's like knowing you have a fever. The doctor needs to know *why* your temperature is above normal.

Managers must know *why* a variance occurred—to pinpoint problems and take corrective action. As you can see in Exhibit 24-1, the static budget underestimated both sales and total costs. The variance in Exhibit 24-1 is called a static budget variance because actual activity differed from what was expected in the static budget. To develop more useful information, managers divide the static budget variance into two broad categories:

- **Sales volume variance**—arises because the number of units actually sold differed from the number of units on which the static budget was based.
- **Flexible budget variance**—arises because the company had more or less revenue, or more or less cost, than expected for the *actual* level of output.

Exhibit 24-3 diagrams these variances.

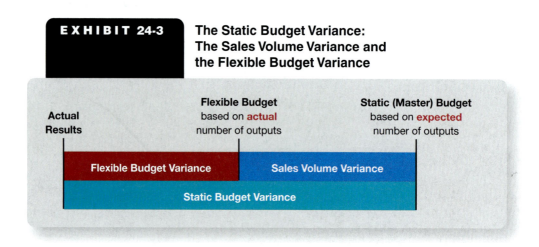

EXHIBIT 24-3 The Static Budget Variance: The Sales Volume Variance and the Flexible Budget Variance

Here's how to compute the two variances:

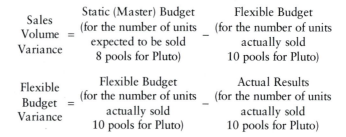

We've seen that Pluto Pools budgeted for 8 pools during June. Actual production was 10 pools. We will need to compute a sales volume variance for Pluto, and there may also be a flexible budget variance. Exhibit 24-4 is Pluto's income statement performance report for June.

EXHIBIT 24-4 Income Statement Performance Report

PLUTO POOLS
Income Statement Performance Report
Month Ended June 30, 2009

	1 Actual Results at Actual Prices	2 (1) − (3) Flexible Budget Variance	3 Flexible Budget for Actual Number of Output Units*	4 (3) − (5) Sales Volume Variance	5 Static (Master) Budget*
Output Units (pools installed)	10	0	10	2 F	8
Sales revenue	$121,000	$1,000 F	$120,000	$24,000 F	$96,000
Variable costs	83,000	3,000 U	80,000	16,000 U	64,000
Fixed costs	22,000	2,000 U	20,000	0	20,000
Total costs	105,000	5,000 U	100,000	16,000 U	84,000
Operating income	$ 16,000	$4,000 U	$ 20,000	$ 8,000 F	$12,000
		Flexible budget variance, $4,000 U		Sales volume variance, $8,000 F	
		Static budget variance, $4,000 F			

*Budgeted sale price is $12,000 per pool, budgeted variable cost is $8,000 per pool, and budgeted total monthly fixed costs are $20,000.

Column 1 of the performance report shows actual results—based on the 10 pools installed. Operating income was $16,000 for June.

Column 3 is Pluto's flexible budget for the 10 pools actually installed. Operating income should have been $20,000.

Column 5 gives the static budget for the 8 pools expected for June. Pluto hoped to earn $12,000.

The budget variances appear in columns 2 and 4 of the exhibit. Let's begin with the static budget in column 5. These data come from Exhibit 24-2.

The flexible budget for 10 units is in column 3. The differences between the static budget and the flexible budget—column 4—arise only because Pluto installed 10 pools rather than 8 during June. Column 4 shows the sales volume variances. Operating income is favorable by $8,000 because Pluto installed 10 pools rather than 8.

Column 1 of Exhibit 24-4 gives the actual results for June—10 pools and operating income of $16,000. OOPS! Operating income is $4,000 less than Pluto would have expected for 10 pools. Why did operating income not measure up to the flexible budget?

- It wasn't because the selling price of swimming pools took a dive. Sales revenue was $1,000 more than expected for 10 pools.
- Variable costs were $3,000 too high for 10 pools.
- Fixed costs were $2,000 too high for 10 pools.

Overall, expenses rose by $5,000 above the flexible budget, while sales revenue was only $1,000 more than the budget. That's why operating income didn't measure up.

The static budget is developed *before* the period. The performance report in Exhibit 24-4 is not developed until the *end* of the period. Why? Because *flexible budgets used in performance reports are based on the actual number of outputs, and the actual outputs aren't known until the end of the period.*

Decision Guidelines

FLEXIBLE BUDGETS

You and your roommate have started a business that prints T-shirts (for example, for school and student organizations). How can you use flexible budgets to plan and control your costs?

Decision	Guidelines
How to estimate sales revenue, costs, and profits over your relevant range? How to prepare a flexible budget for total costs?	Prepare a set of flexible budgets for different sales levels. $$\text{Total cost} = \left(\begin{array}{c} \text{Number} \\ \text{of T-shirts} \end{array} \times \begin{array}{c} \text{Variable cost} \\ \text{per T-shirt} \end{array} \right) + \begin{array}{c} \text{Fixed} \\ \text{cost} \end{array}$$
How to use budgets to help control costs?	Prepare an income statement performance report, as in Exhibit 24-4.
On which output level is the budget based?	Static (master) budget—*expected* number of T-shirts, estimated before the period Flexible budget—*actual* number of T-shirts, not known until the end of the period
Why does your actual income differ from budgeted income?	Prepare an income statement performance report comparing actual results, flexible budget for actual number of T-shirts sold, and static (master) budget, as in Exhibit 24-4.
• How much of the difference arises because the actual number of T-shirts sold doesn't equal budgeted sales?	Compute the sales volume variance (SVV) by comparing the flexible budget with the static budget. • Favorable SVV—Actual number of T-shirts sold > Expected number of T-shirts sold • Unfavorable SVV—Actual number of T-shirts sold < Expected number of T-shirts sold

• How much of the difference occurs because revenues and costs are not what they should have been for the actual number of T-shirts sold?	Compute the flexible budget variance (FBV) by comparing actual results with the flexible budget.
	• Favorable FBV—Actual sales revenue > Flexible budget sales revenue
	    Actual costs < Flexible budget costs
	• Unfavorable FBV—Actual sales revenue < Flexible budget sales revenue
	    Actual costs > Flexible budget costs

What actions can you take to avoid an unfavorable sales volume variance?	• Design more attractive T-shirts to increase demand. • Provide marketing incentives to increase number of T-shirts sold.
What actions can you take to avoid an unfavorable flexible budget variance?	• Avoid an unfavorable flexible budget variance for *sales revenue* by maintaining (not discounting) your selling price. • Avoid an unfavorable flexible budget variance for *costs* by controlling variable costs, such as the cost of the T-shirts, dye, and labor, and by controlling fixed costs.

Summary Problem 1

Exhibit 24-4 shows that Pluto Pools installed 10 swimming pools during June. Now assume that Pluto installed 7 pools (instead of 10) and that the actual sale price averaged $12,500 per pool. Actual variable costs were $57,400, and actual fixed costs were $19,000.

Requirements
1. Prepare a revised income statement performance report using Exhibit 24-4 as a guide.
2. As the company owner, which employees would you praise or criticize after you analyze this performance report?

Solution
Requirement 1

PLUTO POOLS
Income Statement Performance Report—Revised
Month Ended June 30, 2009

	1 Actual Results at Actual Prices	2 (1) – (3) Flexible Budget Variance	3 Flexible Budget for Actual Number of Output Units	4 (3) – (5) Sales Volume Variance	5 Static (Master) Budget
Output Units (pools installed)	7	0	7	1 U	8
Sales revenue	$87,500	$3,500 F	$84,000	$12,000 U	$96,000
Variable costs	57,400	1,400 U	56,000	8,000 F	64,000
Fixed costs	19,000	1,000 F	20,000	—	20,000
Total costs	76,400	400 U	76,000	8,000 F	84,000
Operating income	$11,100	$3,100 F	$ 8,000	$ 4,000 U	$12,000

Flexible budget variance, $3,100 F
Sales volume variance, $4,000 U
Static budget variance, $900 U

Requirement 2
As the company owner, you should determine the *causes* of the variances before praising or criticizing employees. It is especially important to determine whether the variance is due to factors the manager can control. For example,

- The unfavorable sales volume variance could be due to an ineffective sales staff. Or it could be due to a long period of rain that brought work to a standstill.
- The $1,000 favorable flexible budget variance for fixed costs could be due to an employee finding less expensive equipment. Or the savings might have come from delaying a needed overhaul of equipment that could decrease the company's costs in the long run.

Smart managers use variances to raise questions and direct attention, not to fix blame.

Standard Costing

3 Identify the benefits of standard costs and learn how to set standards

Most companies use **standard costs** to develop their flexible budgets. Think of a standard cost as a budget for a single unit. For example, Pluto Pools' standard variable cost is $8,000 per pool (Exhibit 24-2). This $8,000 variable cost includes the standard cost of inputs like the direct materials, direct labor, and variable overhead needed for one pool.

In a standard cost system, each input has both a quantity standard and a price standard. Pluto Pools has a standard for the following:

- Amount of gunite—a concrete derivative—used per pool (this determines the quantity standard)
- Price it pays per cubic foot of gunite (this determines the price standard)

Let's see how managers set these price and quantity standards.

Price Standards

The price standard for direct materials starts with the base purchase cost of each unit of inventory. Accountants help managers set a price standard for materials after considering early-pay discounts, freight in, and receiving costs.

World-class businesses demand continuous reductions in costs. This can be achieved several ways. You can work with suppliers to cut their costs. You can use the Internet to solicit price quotes from suppliers around the world, and you can share information.

For direct labor, accountants work with human resource managers to determine standard labor rates. They must consider basic pay rates, payroll taxes, and fringe benefits. Job descriptions reveal the level of experience needed for each task.

Accountants work with production managers to estimate manufacturing overhead costs. Production managers identify an appropriate allocation base such as direct labor hours or direct labor cost, as you learned in Chapter 17. Accountants then compute the standard overhead rates. Exhibit 24-5 summarizes the setting of standard costs.

EXHIBIT 24-5 Summary of Standard Setting Issues

	Price Standard	Quality Standard
Direct Materials	Responsibility: Purchasing manager Factors: Purchase price, discounts, delivery requirements, credit policy	Responsibility: Production manager and engineers Factors: Product specifications, spoilage, production scheduling
Direct Labor	Responsibility: Human resource managers Factors: Wage rate based on experience requirements, payroll taxes, fringe benefits	Responsibility: Production manager and engineers Factors: Time requirements for the production level of experience needed
Manufacturing Overhead	Responsibility: Production managers Factors: Nature and amount of resources needed for support activities (e.g., moving materials, maintaining equipment, and inspecting output)	

Application

Let's see how Pluto Pools might determine its cost standards for materials, labor, and overhead.

The manager in charge of purchasing for Pluto Pools indicates that the purchase price, net of discounts, is $1.90 per cubic foot of gunite. Delivery, receiving, and inspection add an average of $0.10 per cubic foot. Pluto's hourly wage for workers is $8 and payroll taxes and fringe benefits total $2.50 per direct labor hour. Variable and fixed overhead will total $6,400 and $9,600, respectively, and overhead is allocated based on 3,200 estimated direct labor hours.

Requirement
Compute Pluto Pools' cost standards for direct materials, direct labor, and overhead.

Answer

Direct materials price standard for gunite:

Purchase price, net of discounts	$1.90 per cubic foot
Delivery, receiving, and inspection	0.10 per cubic foot
Total standard cost per cubic foot of gunite	$2.00 per cubic foot

Direct labor price (or rate) standard:

Hourly wage	$ 8.00 per direct labor hour
Payroll taxes and fringe benefits	2.50 per direct labor hour
Total standard cost per direct labor hour	$10.50 per direct labor hour

Variable overhead price (or rate) standard:

$$\frac{\text{Estimated variable overhead cost}}{\text{Estimated quantity of allocation base}} = \frac{\$6,400}{3,200 \text{ direct labor hours}}$$
$$= \underline{\$2.00} \text{ per direct labor hour}$$

Fixed overhead price (or rate) standard:

$$\frac{\text{Estimated fixed overhead cost}}{\text{Estimated quantity of allocation base}} = \frac{\$9,600}{3,200 \text{ direct labor hours}}$$
$$= \underline{\$3.00} \text{ per direct labor hour}$$

Quantity Standards

Production managers and engineers set direct material and direct labor *quantity standards*. To set its labor standards, Westinghouse Air Brake's Chicago plant analyzed every moment in the production of the brakes.

To eliminate unnecessary work, Westinghouse rearranged machines in tight U-shaped cells so that work could flow better. Workers no longer had to move parts all over the plant floor, as illustrated in this diagram.

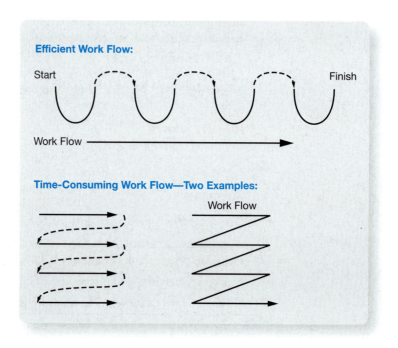

Westinghouse conducted time-and-motion studies to streamline various tasks. For example, the plant installed a conveyer at waist height to minimize bending and lifting. The result? Workers slashed one element of standard time by 90%.

Companies from Ritz-Carlton to Federal Express develop quantity standards based on "best practices." This is often called **benchmarking**. The *best practice* may be an internal benchmark from other plants or divisions within the company or it may be an external benchmark from other companies. Internal benchmarks are easy to obtain, but managers can also purchase external benchmark data. For example, Riverside Hospital in Columbus, Ohio, can compare its cost of performing an appendectomy with the "best practice" cost developed by a consulting firm that compares many different hospitals' costs for the same procedure.

Why Do Companies Use Standard Costs?

U.S. surveys show that more than 80% of responding companies use standard costing. Over half of responding companies in the United Kingdom, Ireland, Sweden, and Japan use standard costing. Why? Standard costing help managers:

- Prepare the budget
- Set target levels of performance
- Identify performance standards
- Set sales prices of products and services
- Decrease accounting costs

Standard cost systems might appear to be expensive. Indeed, the company must invest up front to develop the standards. But standards can save accounting costs. It is cheaper to value inventories at standard rather than actual costs. With standard costs, accountants avoid the LIFO, FIFO, or average-cost computations.

Variance Analysis

Once we establish standard costs, we can use the standards to assign costs to production. At least once a year, we will compare our actual production costs to the standards to locate variances. Exhibit 24-6 shows how to separate total variances for materials and labor into price and efficiency (quantity) variances. Study this exhibit carefully. It's used for the materials variances and the labor variances.

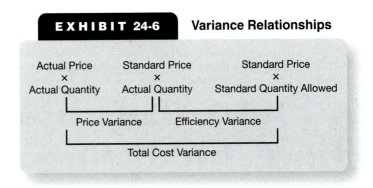

EXHIBIT 24-6 Variance Relationships

A **price variance** measures how well the business keeps unit prices of material and labor inputs within standards. As the name suggests, the price variance is the *difference in prices* (actual price per unit − standard price per unit) of an input, multiplied by the *actual quantity* of the input:

$$\text{Price Variance} = (\text{Actual Price} \times \text{Actual Quantity}) - (\text{Standard Price} \times \text{Actual Quantity})$$
$$\text{Or, Price Variance} = (\text{Actual Price} - \text{Standard Price}) \times \text{Actual Quantity}$$
$$= (AP - SP) \times AQ$$

An **efficiency** or **quantity variance** measures how well the business uses its materials or human resources. The efficiency variance is the difference in quantities (actual quantity of input used − standard quantity of input allowed for the actual number of outputs) multiplied by the standard price per unit of the input:

$$\text{Efficiency Variance} = (\text{Standard Price} \times \text{Actual Quantity}) - (\text{Standard Price} \times \text{Standard Quantity})$$
$$\text{Or, Efficiency Variance} = (\text{Actual Quantity} - \text{Standard Quantity}) \times \text{Standard Price}$$
$$= (AQ - SQ) \times SP$$

Exhibit 24-7 illustrates these variances and emphasizes two points.

- First, the price and efficiency variances sum to the flexible budget variance.
- Second, static budgets like column 5 of Exhibit 24-4 play no role in the price and efficiency variances.

The static budget is used only to compute the sales volume variance—never to compute the flexible budget variance or the price and efficiency cost variances for materials and labor.

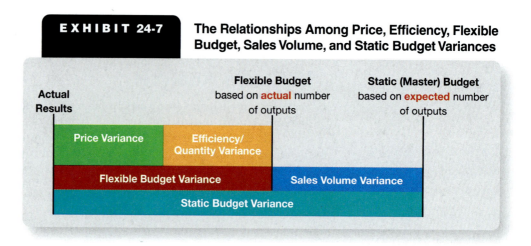

EXHIBIT 24-7 | The Relationships Among Price, Efficiency, Flexible Budget, Sales Volume, and Static Budget Variances

How Pluto Uses Standard Costing: Analyzing the Flexible Budget Variance

 Compute standard cost variances for direct materials and direct labor

Let's return to our Pluto Pools example. Exhibit 24-4 showed that the main cause for concern at Pluto is the $4,000 unfavorable flexible budget variance for total costs. The first step in identifying the causes of the cost variance is to identify the variable and fixed costs, as shown in Panel A of Exhibit 24-8.

Study Exhibit 24-8 carefully. Panel B shows how to compute the flexible budget amounts. Panel C shows how to compute actual materials and labor costs. Trace the following:

- Flexible budget amounts from Panel B to column (2) of Panel A
- Actual costs from Panel C to column (1) of Panel A

Column 3 of Panel A gives the flexible budget variances for direct materials and direct labor. For now, focus on materials and labor. We'll cover overhead later.

Direct Material Variances

Direct Materials Price Variance

Let's investigate the $2,800 unfavorable variance for direct materials. Recall that the direct materials standard price was $2.00 per cubic foot, and 10,000 cubic feet are needed for 10 pools (1,000 cubic feet per pool × 10 pools). The actual price of materials was $1.90 per cubic foot, and 12,000 cubic feet were actually used to make 10 pools. Using the formula, the **materials price variance** is $1,200 favorable. The calculation follows.

$$\begin{aligned}
\text{Materials Price Variance} &= (AP - SP) \times AQ \\
&= (\$1.90 \text{ per cubic foot} - \$2.00 \text{ per cubic foot}) \times 12,000 \text{ cubic feet} \\
&= -\$0.10 \text{ per cubic foot} \times 12,000 \text{ cubic feet} \\
&= \$1,200 \text{ F}
\end{aligned}$$

EXHIBIT 24-8 Data for Standard Costing Example

PANEL A—Comparison of Actual Results with Flexible Budget for 10 Swimming Pools

PLUTO POOLS
Data for Standard Costing Example
Month Ended June 30, 2009

	Actual Results at Actual Prices	Flexible Budget for 10 Pools	Flexible Budget Variance
Variable costs:			
Direct materials	$ 22,800*	$20,000†	$ 2,800 U
Direct labor	41,800*	42,000†	200 F
Variable overhead	9,000	8,000†	1,000 U
Marketing and administrative costs	9,400	10,000	600 F
Total variable costs	83,000	80,000	3,000 U
Fixed costs:			
Fixed overhead	12,300	9,600‡	2,700 U
Marketing and administrative expense	9,700	10,400	700 F
Total fixed costs	22,000	20,000	2,000 U
Total costs	$105,000	$100,000	$5,000 U

*See Panel C.
†See Panel B.
‡Fixed overhead was budgeted at $9,600 per month (Application Answer on page 1229).

PANEL B—Computation of Flexible Budget for Direct Materials, Direct Labor, and Variable Overhead for 7 Swimming Pools—Based on Standard Costs

	(1) Standard Quantity of Inputs Allowed for 10 Pools	(2) Standard Price per Unit of Input	(3) (1) × (2) Flexible Budget for 10 Pools
Direct materials	1,000 cubic feet per pool × 10 pools = 10,000 cubic feet	$ 2.00	$20,000
Direct labor	400 hours per pool × 10 pools = 4,000 hours	$10.50	42,000
Variable overhead	400 hours per pool × 10 pools = 4,000 hours	$ 2.00	8,000

PANEL C—Computation of Actual Costs for Direct Materials and Direct Labor for 10 Swimming Pools

	(1) Actual Quantity of Inputs Used for 10 Pools	(2) Actual Price per Unit of Input	(3) (1) × (2) Actual Cost for 10 Pools
Direct materials	12,000 cubic feet actually used	$1.90 actual cost/cubic foot	$22,800
Direct labor	3,800 hours actually used	$11.00 actual cost/hour	41,800

The $1,200 direct materials price variance is *favorable,* because the purchasing manager spent $0.10 *less* per cubic foot of gunite than budgeted ($1.90 actual price − $2.00 standard price). A negative amount means that the variance is favorable. A positive variance is unfavorable.

Direct Materials Efficiency Variance

Now let's see what portion of the unfavorable materials variance was due to the quantity used.

The standard quantity of inputs is the *quantity that should have been used* for the actual output. For Pluto, the *standard quantity of inputs (gunite) that workers should have used for the actual number of outputs* (10 pools) is:

1,000 cubic feet of gunite per pool × 10 pools installed = 10,000 cubic feet of gunite

Thus, the **direct materials efficiency variance** is:

$$\begin{aligned}
\text{Direct Materials Efficiency Variance} &= (AQ - SQ) \times SP \\
&= (12{,}000 \text{ cubic feet} - 10{,}000 \text{ cubic feet}) \times \$2.00 \text{ per cubic foot} \\
&= +2{,}000 \text{ cubic feet} \times \$2.00 \text{ per cubic foot} \\
&= \$4{,}000 \text{ U}
\end{aligned}$$

The $4,000 direct materials efficiency variance is *unfavorable,* because workers used 2,000 *more* cubic feet of gunite than they should have used on 10 pools. A positive amount means that the variance is unfavorable.

SUMMARY OF DIRECT MATERIAL VARIANCES Exhibit 24-9 summarizes how Pluto splits the $2,800 unfavorable direct materials flexible budget variance into price and efficiency effects.

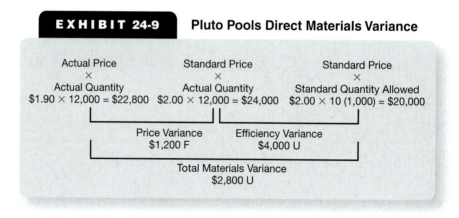

EXHIBIT 24-9 Pluto Pools Direct Materials Variance

In summary, Pluto spent $2,800 more than it should have for gunite because:

- A good price for the gunite increased profits by $1,200, but
- Inefficient use of the gunite reduced profits by $4,000.

Let's review who is responsible for each of these variances and consider why each variance may have occurred.

1. The purchasing manager is in the best position to explain the favorable price variance. Pluto's purchasing manager may have negotiated a good price for gunite.

2. The manager in charge of installing pools can explain why workers used so much gunite to install the 10 pools. Was the gunite of lower quality? Did workers waste materials? Did their equipment malfunction? Pluto's top management needs this information to decide what corrective action to take.

These variances raise questions that can help pinpoint problems. But be careful! A favorable variance doesn't always mean that a manager did a good job, nor does an unfavorable variance mean that a manager did a bad job. Perhaps Pluto's purchasing manager got a lower price by purchasing inferior-quality materials. This would lead to waste and spoilage. If so, the purchasing manager's decision hurt the company. This illustrates why good managers:

- Use variances as a guide for investigation rather than merely to assign blame
- Investigate favorable as well as unfavorable variances

Direct Labor Variances

Pluto uses a similar approach to analyze the direct labor flexible budget variance. Exhibit 24-10 shows how Pluto computes labor variances.

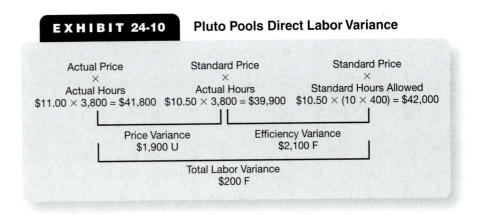

EXHIBIT 24-10 Pluto Pools Direct Labor Variance

Why did Pluto spend $200 less on labor than it should have used for 10 pools? To answer this question, Pluto computes the labor price and efficiency variances, in exactly the same way as it did for direct materials. Recall that the standard price for direct labor is $10.50 per hour, and 4,000 hours were budgeted for 10 pools (400 hours per pool × 10 pools). But actual direct labor cost was $11.00 per hour, and it took 3,800 hours to install 10 pools.

Direct Labor Price Variance

Using the formula, the **direct labor price variance** was $1,900 unfavorable. The calculation follows.

$$\text{Direct Labor Price Variance} = (AP - SP) \times AH$$
$$= (\$11.00 - \$10.50) \times 3{,}800 \text{ hours}$$
$$= \$1{,}900 \text{ U}$$

The $1,900 direct labor price variance is *unfavorable* because Pluto paid workers $0.50 *more* per hour than budgeted ($11.00 actual price − $10.50 standard price). The positive amount indicates an unfavorable variance.

DIRECT LABOR EFFICIENCY VARIANCE Now let's see how efficiently Pluto used its labor. The *standard quantity of direct labor hours that workers should have used to install 10 pools* is:

400 direct labor hours per pool × 10 pools installed = 4,000 direct labor hours

Thus, the **direct labor efficiency variance** is:

$$\text{Direct Labor Efficiency Variance} = (AH - SH) \times SP$$
$$= (3{,}800 \text{ hours} - 4{,}000 \text{ hours}) \times \$10.50 \text{ per hour}$$
$$= -200 \text{ hours} \times \$10.50$$
$$= -\$2{,}100 \text{ F}$$

The $2,100 direct labor efficiency variance is *favorable* because installers actually worked 200 *fewer* hours than the budget called for. If the calculation results in a negative amount, the variance is favorable.

SUMMARY OF DIRECT LABOR VARIANCES Exhibit 24-10 summarizes how Pluto computes the labor price and efficiency variances.

The $200 favorable direct labor variance suggests that labor costs were close to expectations. But to manage Pluto Pools' labor costs, we need to "peel the onion" to gain more insight:

- Pluto paid its employees an average of $11.00 per hour in June instead of the standard rate of $10.50—for an unfavorable price variance.
- Workers installed 10 pools in 3,800 hours instead of the budgeted 4,000 hours—for a favorable efficiency variance.

This situation reveals a trade-off. Pluto hired more experienced (and thus more expensive) workers and had an unfavorable price variance. But the installers turned out more work than expected, and the strategy was successful. The overall effect on profits was favorable. This possibility reminds us that managers should take care in using variances to evaluate performance. Go slow. Analyze the data. Then take action.

Manufacturing Overhead Variances

5 Analyze manufacturing overhead in a standard cost system

In this section of the chapter we use the terms *manufacturing overhead* and *overhead* interchangeably. The total overhead variance is the difference between:

Actual overhead cost and **Standard overhead allocated to production**

Exhibit 24-8 shows that Pluto actually incurred $21,300 of overhead: $9,000 variable and $12,300 fixed. The next step is to see how Pluto allocates overhead in a standard cost system.

Allocating Overhead in a Standard Cost System

In a standard costing system, the manufacturing overhead allocated to production is:

$$\text{Overhead allocated to production} = \text{Standard (predetermined) overhead rate} \times \text{Standard quantity of the allocation base allowed for }\textit{actual}\text{ output}$$

Let's begin by computing Pluto's standard overhead rate, as follows (data from page 1229):

$$\begin{aligned}
\text{Standard overhead rate} &= \frac{\text{Budgeted manufacturing overhead cost}}{\text{Budgeted direct labor hours}} \\
&= \frac{\text{Variable overhead} + \text{Fixed overhead}}{\text{Budgeted direct labor hours}} \\
&= \frac{\$6,400 + \$9,600}{3,200 \text{ direct labor hours}} \\
&= \frac{\$6,400}{3,200} + \frac{\$9,600}{3,200} \\
&= \$2.00 \text{ variable} + \$3.00 \text{ fixed} \\
&= \$5.00 \text{ per direct labor hour}
\end{aligned}$$

Now let's determine the standard quantity of direct labor hours that Pluto allowed for actual output (10 pools), as follows (data from Exhibit 24-8, Panel B):

$$\begin{aligned}
\text{Standard quantity of direct labor hours for actual output} &= 400 \text{ hours per pool} \times 10 \text{ pools} \\
&= 4,000 \text{ direct labor hours}
\end{aligned}$$

Thus, Pluto allocates the cost of overhead to production based on standard costs as follows:

$$\begin{aligned}
\text{Standard overhead allocated to production} &= \text{Standard overhead rate} \times \text{Standard quantity of the allocation base allowed for } actual \text{ output} \\
&= \$5.00 \text{ per hour} \times 4,000 \text{ hours} \\
&= \$20,000
\end{aligned}$$

Pluto computes its total overhead cost variance as follows:

$$\begin{aligned}
\text{Total overhead variance} &= \text{Actual overhead cost (Exhibit 24-8, Panel A)} - \text{Standard overhead allocated to production } (\$4,000 \text{ hours} \times \$5.00 \text{ per hour}) \\
&= \$21,300^* - \$20,000 \\
&= \$1,300 \text{ U}
\end{aligned}$$

*Variable ($9,000) + fixed ($12,300) = $21,300.

Pluto actually spent $1,300 more on overhead than it allocated to production. To see why this unfavorable variance occurred, Pluto "drills down" by splitting the total overhead variance into two components:

- The overhead flexible budget variance
- The production volume variance

Exhibit 24-11 shows the computation of the overhead variances, and the discussion that follows explains them.

Overhead Flexible Budget Variance

The **overhead flexible budget variance** tells how well managers controlled overhead costs. Pluto actually spent $21,300 on overhead ($9,000 variable + $12,300 fixed) to install the 10 pools. The flexible budget for 10 pools called for overhead of only

EXHIBIT 24-11 | Manufacturing Overhead Variances

PLUTO POOLS
Manufacturing Overhead Variances
Month Ended June 30, 2009

	(1) Actual Overhead Cost (Exhibit 24-8)	(2) (1) – (3) Flexible Budget Overhead for Actual Output (Exhibit 24-8)	(3) Standard Overhead Allocated to Production for Actual Output (Rates from page 1237)
Variable overhead	$ 9,000	$ 8,000	$2.00 × 4,000 direct labor hours = $ 8,000
Fixed overhead	12,300	9,600	$3.00 × 4,000 direct labor hours = $12,000
Total overhead	$21,300	$17,600	$5.00 × 4,000 direct labor hours = $20,000
	Flexible budget variance, $3,700 U		Production volume variance, $2,400 F
	Total manufacturing overhead variance, $1,300 U		

$17,600 ($8,000 variable + $9,600 fixed). So Pluto's **overhead flexible budget variance** is computed as follows:

$$\text{Overhead Flexible Budget Variance} = \text{Actual overhead cost} - \text{Flexible budget overhead for actual output}$$
$$= \$21,300 - \$17,600$$
$$= \$3,700\ U$$

Why did Pluto spend $3,700 more on overhead than it should have spent to install the 10 pools in June? You can see from Exhibit 24-11 that $1,000 ($9,000 − $8,000) of the variance is due to higher-than-expected spending on *variable* overhead. The remaining $2,700 ($12,300 − $9,600) is due to higher spending on *fixed* overhead. Pluto will investigate the reason for each of these variances.

Overhead Production Volume Variance

The second component of the total overhead variance is the **overhead production volume variance**. This variance arises when actual production differs from expected production. Pluto expected to install 8 pools during June, but actually installed 10. The **overhead production volume variance** is computed as follows:

$$\text{Overhead Production Volume Variance} = \text{Flexible budget overhead for actual output (10 pools)} - \text{Standard overhead allocated to (actual) production}$$
$$= \$17,600\ (\text{Exhibit 24-11, column 2}) - \$20,000\ (\text{Exhibit 24-11, column 3})$$
$$= \$2,400\ F$$

The production volume variance is favorable because Pluto's actual output (10 pools) exceeded expected output (8 pools). By installing 10 pools Pluto used its production capacity more fully than originally planned. If Pluto had installed 7 or fewer pools, the production volume variance would have been unfavorable because the company would have had unused production capacity.

Summary of Overhead Variances

Most companies compile cost information for the individual items of overhead, such as indirect materials, indirect labor, and utilities. Managers drill down by comparing actual to budgeted costs for each item. For example, Pluto's analysis might reveal that variable overhead costs were higher than expected because water rates increased or because workers used more water than expected. Perhaps spending on fixed overhead increased because Pluto purchased new equipment and its depreciation increased.

Standard Cost Accounting Systems

Journal Entries

6 Record transactions at standard cost and prepare a standard cost income statement

We use Pluto Pools' June transactions to demonstrate standard costing in a job costing context. Management needs to know about variances to address each problem. Therefore, Pluto records variances from standards as soon as possible. This means that Pluto records direct materials price variances when materials are purchased. It also means that Work in Process Inventory is debited (swimming pools are costed) at standard input quantities and standard prices. June's entries follow.

Purchase of direct materials

1.	Materials Inventory (12,000 cubic feet × $2.00)	24,000	
	Direct Materials Price Variance		1,200
	Accounts Payable (12,000 × $1.90)		22,800
	To record purchase of direct materials.		

The credit to Accounts Payable is for the *actual quantity* of gunite purchased (12,000 cubic feet) at the *actual price* ($1.90 per cubic foot). In contrast, the debit to Materials Inventory is recorded at the *standard price* ($2 per cubic foot). Maintaining Materials Inventory at the *standard price* ($2.00) allows Pluto to record the direct materials price variance at time of purchase. Recall that Pluto's direct materials price variance was $1,200 favorable (p. 1232). A favorable variance has a credit balance and is a contra expense. An unfavorable variance means extra expense and has a debit balance.

Use of direct materials

2.	Work in Process Inventory (10,000 cubic feet × $2.00)	20,000	
	Direct Materials Efficiency Variance	4,000	
	Materials Inventory (12,000 × $2.00)		24,000
	To record use of direct materials.		

Pluto debits Work in Process Inventory for the *standard cost* of the 10,000 cubic feet of direct materials that should have been used to install 10 pools. This maintains Work in Process Inventory at standard cost. Materials Inventory is credited for the *actual quantity* of materials put into production (12,000 cubic feet) costed at the *standard price*.

Pluto's direct materials efficiency variance was $4,000 unfavorable (page 1234). An unfavorable variance has a debit balance, which increases expense and decreases profits.

Direct labor cost incurred

3.	Manufacturing Wages (3,800 hours × $10.50)	39,900	
	Direct Labor Price Variance	1,900	
	Wages Payable (3,800 × $11.00)		41,800
	To record direct labor costs incurred.		

Manufacturing Wages is debited for the *standard price* ($10.50) of direct labor hours actually used (3,800). Wages Payable is credited for the *actual cost* (the *actual* hours worked at the *actual* wage rate) because this is the amount Pluto must pay the workers. The direct labor price variance is $1,900 unfavorable (page 1235), a debit amount.

Direct labor cost allocated to production

4.	Work in Process Inventory (4,000 hours × $10.50)	42,000	
	Direct Labor Efficiency Variance		2,100
	Manufacturing Wages (3,800 × $10.50)		39,900
	To allocate direct labor cost to production.		

Pluto debits Work in Process Inventory for the standard cost per direct labor hour ($10.50) that should have been used for 10 pools (4,000 hours), like direct materials entry 2. Manufacturing Wages is credited to close its prior debit balance. The direct labor efficiency variance is credited for the $2,100 favorable variance (page 1236). This maintains Work in Process Inventory at standard cost.

Actual overhead cost incurred

5.	Manufacturing Overhead (actual cost)	21,300	
	Accounts Payable, Accumulated Depreciation, etc.		21,300
	To record actual overhead costs incurred (Exhibit 24-11).		

This entry records Pluto's actual overhead cost for June.

Overhead allocated to production

6.	Work in Process Inventory (4,000 hours × $5.00)	20,000	
	Manufacturing Overhead		20,000
	To allocate overhead to production (See Exhibit 24-11).		

In standard costing, the overhead allocated to Work in Process Inventory is computed as the standard overhead rate ($5.00 per hour) × standard quantity of the allocation base allowed for actual output (4,000 hours for 10 pools).

Completion of production

7.	Finished Goods Inventory	82,000	
	Work in Process Inventory		82,000
	To record completion of 10 pools ($20,000 of materials + $42,000 of labor + $20,000 of manufacturing overhead), all at standard cost.		

This entry transfers the standard cost of the 10 pools completed during June from Work in Process to Finished Goods.

Cost of sales

	8.	Cost of Goods Sold	82,000	
		Finished Goods Inventory		82,000
		To record the cost of sales of 10 pools, at standard cost.		

Close the overhead account

	9.	Overhead Flexible Budget Variance	3,700	
		Overhead Production Volume Variance		2,400
		Manufacturing Overhead		1,300
		To record overhead variances and close the Manufacturing Overhead account. (Exhibit 24-11)		

Entry 9 closes the Manufacturing Overhead account and records the overhead variances. Exhibit 24-12 shows the relevant Pluto accounts after posting these entries.

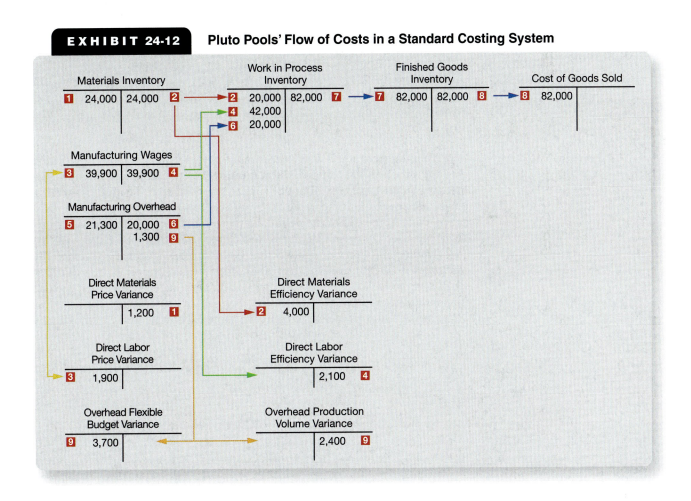

EXHIBIT 24-12 Pluto Pools' Flow of Costs in a Standard Costing System

Standard Cost Income Statement for Management

Pluto Pools' top management needs to know about the company's cost variances. Exhibit 24-13 shows a standard cost income statement that highlights the variances for management.

EXHIBIT 24-13 | Standard Cost Income Statement

PLUTO POOLS
Standard Cost Income Statement
Month Ended June 30, 2009

Sales revenue at standard (10 × $12,000)			$120,000
Sales revenue variance			1,000
Sales revenue at actual			121,000
Cost of goods sold at standard cost		$82,000	
Manufacturing cost variances (parentheses denote a credit balance):			
Direct materials price variance	$(1,200)		
Direct materials efficiency variance	4,000		
Direct labor rate variance	1,900		
Direct labor efficiency variance	(2,100)		
Overhead flexible budget variance	3,700		
Overhead production volume variance	(2,400)		
Total manufacturing variance		3,900	
Cost of goods sold at actual cost			85,900
Gross profit			35,100
Marketing and administrative expense*			(19,100)
Operating income			$ 16,000

*$9,400 + $9,700 from Exhibit 24-8, Panel A.

The statement starts with sales revenue at standard and adds the favorable sales revenue variance of $1,000 (Exhibit 24-4) to yield actual sales revenue. Next, the statement shows the cost of goods sold at standard cost. Then the statement separately lists each manufacturing cost variance, followed by cost of goods sold at actual cost. At the end of the period, all the variance accounts are closed to zero out their balances. Operating income is thus closed to Income Summary.

The income statement shows that the net effect of all the manufacturing cost variances is $3,900 unfavorable. Thus, June's operating income is $3,900 lower than it would have been if all the actual manufacturing costs had been equal to their standard costs.

The Decision Guidelines summarize standard costing and variance analysis.

Decision Guidelines

STANDARD COSTS AND VARIANCE ANALYSIS

Now you've seen how managers use standard costs and variances to identify potential problems. Variances help managers see *why* actual costs differ from the budget. This is the first step in determining how to correct problems. Let's review how Pluto Pools made some key decisions in setting up and using its standard cost system.

Decision	Guidelines
How to set standards?	Historical performance data
	Engineering analysis/time-and-motion studies
	Continuous improvement standards
	Benchmarking
How to compute a price variance for materials or labor?	$\text{Price variance} = \left(\begin{array}{c}\text{Actual price} \\ \text{per input unit}\end{array} - \begin{array}{c}\text{Standard price} \\ \text{per input unit}\end{array}\right) \times \begin{array}{c}\text{Actual quantity} \\ \text{of input}\end{array}$
How to compute an efficiency variance for materials or labor?	$\text{Efficiency variance} = \left(\begin{array}{c}\text{Actual quantity} \\ \text{of input}\end{array} - \begin{array}{c}\text{Standard quantity} \\ \text{of input for actual output}\end{array}\right) \times \begin{array}{c}\text{Standard price per input unit}\end{array}$
Who is best able to explain a	
Sales volume variance?	Marketing Department
Sales revenue variance?	Marketing Department
Direct material price variance?	Purchasing Department
Direct material efficiency variance?	Production Department
Direct labor price variance?	Human Resources Department
Direct labor efficiency variance?	Production Department
How to allocate manufacturing overhead in a standard costing system?	$\begin{array}{c}\text{Manufacturing overhead allocated}\end{array} = \left(\begin{array}{c}\text{Standard overhead rate}\end{array}\right) \times \left(\begin{array}{c}\text{Standard quantity of allocation base allowed for actual output}\end{array}\right)$
How to analyze over- or underallocated overhead?	Split over- or underallocated overhead into
	$\begin{array}{c}\text{Flexible budget variance}\end{array} = \begin{array}{c}\text{Actual overhead}\end{array} - \begin{array}{c}\text{Flexible budget overhead for actual output}\end{array}$
	$\begin{array}{c}\text{Production volume variance}\end{array} = \begin{array}{c}\text{Flexible budget overhead for actual output}\end{array} - \begin{array}{c}\text{Standard overhead allocated to actual output}\end{array}$
How to record standard costs in the accounts?	Materials Inventory: Actual quantity at standard price
	Work in Process Inventory (and Finished Goods Inventory and Cost of Goods Sold): Standard quantity of inputs allowed for actual outputs, at standard price of inputs
How to analyze cost variances?	Debit balance → more expense
	Credit balance → less expense

Summary Problem 2

Exhibit 24-8 indicates that Pluto Pools installed 10 swimming pools in June. Suppose Pluto had installed 7 pools instead of 10 and that *actual costs* were

Direct materials (gunite)............	7,400 cubic feet @ $2.00 per cubic foot
Direct labor...............................	2,740 hours @ $10.00 per hour
Variable overhead......................	$5,400
Fixed overhead.........................	$11,900

Requirements

1. Given these new data, prepare an exhibit similar to Exhibit 24-8. Ignore marketing and administrative expense.

2. Compute price and efficiency variances for direct materials and direct labor.

3. Compute the total variance, the flexible budget variance, and the production volume variance for manufacturing overhead. Standard total overhead allocated to production is $5.00 per direct labor hour.

Solution

Requirement 1

PANEL A—Comparison of Actual Results with Flexible Budget for 7 Swimming Pools

PLUTO POOLS
Revised Data for Standard Costing Example
Month Ended June 30, 2009

	Actual Results at Actual Prices	Flexible Budget for 7 Pools	Flexible Budget Variance
Variable costs:			
Direct materials	$14,800*	$14,000†	$ 800 U
Direct labor	27,400*	29,400†	2,000 F
Variable overhead	5,400	5,600†	200 F
Total variable costs	47,600	49,000	1,400 F
Fixed costs:			
Fixed overhead	11,900	9,600‡	2,300 U
Total costs	$59,500	$58,600	$ 900 U

*See Panel C.
†See Panel B.
‡Fixed overhead was budgeted at $9,600 per month.

PANEL B—Computation of Flexible Budget for Direct Materials, Direct Labor, and Variable Overhead for 7 Swimming Pools—Based on Standard Costs

	(1) Standard Quantity of Inputs Allowed for 7 Pools	(2) Standard Price per Unit of Input	(3) (1) × (2) Flexible Budget for 10 Pools
Direct materials	1,000 cubic feet per pool × 7 pools = 7,000 cubic feet	$ 2.00	$14,000
Direct labor	400 hours per pool × 7 pools = 2,800 hours	$10.50	29,400
Variable overhead	400 hours per pool × 7 pools = 2,800 hours	$ 2.00	5,600

PANEL C—Computation of Actual Costs for Direct Materials and Direct Labor for 7 Swimming Pools

	(1) Actual Quantity of Inputs Used for 7 Pools	(2) Actual Price per Unit of Input	(3) (1) × (2) Actual Cost for 7 Pools
Direct materials	7,400 cubic feet actually used	$2.00 actual cost/cubic foot	$14,800
Direct labor	2,740 hours actually used	$10.00 actual cost/hour	27,400

Requirement 2

$$\text{Price variance} = \left(\begin{array}{c}\text{Actual price} \\ \text{per input unit}\end{array} - \begin{array}{c}\text{Standard price} \\ \text{per input unit}\end{array}\right) \times \begin{array}{c}\text{Actual quantity} \\ \text{of input}\end{array}$$

Direct materials:

$$\text{Price variance} = (\$2.00 - \$2.00) \times 7{,}400 \text{ cubic feet} = \$0$$

Direct labor:

$$\text{Rate variance} = (\$10.00 - \$10.50) \times 2{,}740 \text{ hours} = \$1{,}370 \text{ F}$$

$$\text{Efficiency variance} = \left(\begin{array}{c}\text{Actual quantity} \\ \text{of input}\end{array} - \begin{array}{c}\text{Standard quantity} \\ \text{of input}\end{array}\right) \times \begin{array}{c}\text{Standard price per} \\ \text{input unit}\end{array}$$

Direct materials:

$$\text{Efficiency variance} = \left(\begin{array}{c}7{,}400 \\ \text{cubic feet}\end{array} - \begin{array}{c}7{,}000 \\ \text{cubic feet}\end{array}\right) \times \begin{array}{c}\$2.00 \text{ per} \\ \text{cubic foot}\end{array} = \$800 \text{ U}$$

Direct labor:

$$\text{Efficiency variance} = \left(\begin{array}{c}2{,}740 \\ \text{hours}\end{array} - \begin{array}{c}2{,}800 \\ \text{hours}\end{array}\right) \times \begin{array}{c}\$10.50 \text{ per} \\ \text{hours}\end{array} = \$630 \text{ F}$$

Requirement 3

Total overhead variance:	
Actual overhead cost ($5,400 variable + $11,900 fixed)..................	$17,300
Standard overhead allocated to actual output (2,800 standard direct labor hours × $5.00)	14,000
Total overhead variance..	$ 3,300 U
Overhead flexible budget variance:	
Actual overhead cost ($5,400 + $11,900)...	$17,300
Flexible budget overhead for actual output ($5,600 + $9,600)	15,200
Overhead flexible budget variance..	$ 2,100 U
Overhead production volume variance:	
Flexible budget overhead for actual output ($5,600 + $9,600)	$15,200
Standard overhead allocated to actual output (2,800 standard direct labor hours × $5.00)	14,000
Overhead production volume variance	$ 1,200 U

Review *Flexible Budgets and Standard Costs*

Accounting Vocabulary

Benchmarking
Using standards based on "best practice." Best practice may be an internal benchmark or an external benchmark from other companies.

Efficiency (quantity) Variance
Measure whether the quantity of materials or labor use to make the actual number of outputs is within the standard allowed for that number of outputs. This is computed as the difference in quantities (actual quantity of input used minus standard quantity of input allowed for the actual number of outputs) multiplied by the standard price per unit of the input.

Flexible Budget
A summarized budget that managers can easily compute for several different volume levels. Flexible budgets separate variable costs from fixed costs; it is the variable costs that put the "flex" in the flexible budget.

Flexible Budget Variance
The difference arising because the company actually earned more or less revenue, or incurred more or less cost, than expected for the actual level of output. This equals the difference between the actual amount and a flexible budget amount.

Master Budget
The budget prepared for only one level of sales volume. Also called the **static budget**.

Overhead Flexible Budget Variance
Shows how well management has controlled overhead costs. It is the difference between the actual overhead cost and the flexible budget overhead for the actual number of outputs.

Price (rate) Variance
Measures how well the business keeps unit prices of material and labor inputs within standards. This is computed as the difference in prices (actual price per unit minus standard price per unit) of an input multiplied by the actual quantity of the input.

Production Volume Variance
Arises when actual production differs from expected production. It is the difference between (1) the manufacturing overhead cost in the flexible budget or actual outputs and (2) the standard overhead allocated to production.

Sales Volume Variance
The difference arising only because the number of units actually sold differs from the static budget units. This equals the difference between a static budget amount and a flexible budget amount.

Standard Cost
A budget for a single unit.

Static Budget
The budget prepared for only one level of sales volume. Also called the **master budget**.

Variance
The difference between an actual amount and the budget. A variance is labeled as favorable if it increases operating income and unfavorable if it decreases operating income.

Quick Check

Questions 1 through 4 rely on the following data. ProNet Systems is a start-up company that makes connectors for high-speed Internet connections. The company has budgeted variable costs of $130 for each connector and fixed costs of $8,000 per month.

ProNet's static budget predicted production and sales of 100 connectors in August, but the company actually produced and sold only 75 connectors at a total cost of $23,000.

1. ProNet's total flexible budget cost for 75 connectors per month is
   a. $8,130
   b. $9,750
   c. $13,000
   d. $17,750

2. ProNet's sales volume variance for total costs is
   a. $5,250 F
   b. $3,250 F
   c. $3,250 U
   d. $5,250 U

3. ProNet's flexible budget variance for total costs is
   a. $5,250 U
   b. $5,250 F
   c. $3,250 U
   d. $3,250 F

4. ProNet Systems' managers could set direct labor standards based on:
   a. Past actual performance
   b. Continuous improvement
   c. Benchmarking
   d. Time-and-motion studies
   e. Any of the above

Questions 5 through 7 rely on the following data. ProNet Systems has budgeted 3 hours of direct labor per connector, at a standard cost of $15 per hour. During January, technicians actually worked 210 hours completing the 75 connectors. ProNet paid the technicians $15.50 per hour.

5. What is ProNet's direct labor price variance for August?
   a. $37.50 U
   b. $112.50 U
   c. $105.00 U
   d. $120.00 U

6. What is ProNet's direct labor efficiency variance for August?
   a. $75.00 F
   b. $232.50 F
   c. $225.00 F
   d. $1,350.00 F

7. The journal entry to record ProNet's *use* of direct labor in August is
   a. Manufacturing Wages
      Direct Labor Efficiency Variance
         Work in Process Inventory
   b. Manufacturing Wages
       Direct Labor Efficiency Variance
       Work in Process Inventory
   c. Work in Process Inventory
      Direct Labor Efficiency Variance
         Manufacturing Wages
   d. Work in Process Inventory
       Direct Labor Efficiency Variance
       Manufacturing Wages

8. ProNet Systems allocates manufacturing overhead based on machine hours. Each connector should require 10 machine hours. According to the static budget, ProNet expected to incur:

   1,000 machine hours per month (100 connectors × 10 machine hours per connector)

   $5,250 in variable manufacturing overhead costs

   $8,000 in fixed manufacturing overhead costs

   During August, ProNet actually used 825 machine hours to make the 75 connectors. ProNet's predetermined standard *total* manufacturing overhead rate is
   a. $5.25 per machine hour
   b. $13.25 per machine hour
   c. $8.00 per machine hour
   d. $16.06 per machine hour

9. The total manufacturing overhead variance is composed of:
   a. Flexible budget variance and production volume variance
   b. Price variance and production volume variance
   c. Efficiency variance and production volume variance
   d. Price variance and efficiency variance

10. When ProNet *uses* direct materials, the amount of the debit to Work in Process Inventory is based on:
    a. Standard quantity of the materials allowed for actual production × Standard price per unit of the materials
    b. Standard quantity of the materials allowed for actual production × Actual price per unit of the materials
    c. Actual quantity of the materials used × Actual price per unit of the materials
    d. Actual quantity of the materials used × Standard price per unit of the materials

    Answers are given after Apply Your Knowledge (p. 1265).

Assess Your Progress

Short Exercises

Matching terms
[1]

S24-1 Match each of the following terms to the definitions below.
  a. Flexible Budget
  b. Flexible Budget Variance
  c. Sales Volume Variance
  d. Static Budget
  e. Variance

  _____ 1. The budget prepared for only one level of sales volume. (p. 1222)
  _____ 2. The difference between an actual amount and the budget. (p. 1222)
  _____ 3. A summarized budget for several levels of volume that separates variable costs from fixed costs. (p. 1223)
  _____ 4. The difference arising only because the number of units actually sold differs from the static budget units. (p. 1224)
  _____ 5. The difference arising because the company actually earned more or less revenue, or incurred more or less cost, than expected for the actual level of output. (p. 1225)

Matching terms
[2]

S24-2 Match each of the following terms to the definitions below.
  a. Benchmarking
  b. Efficiency Variance
  c. Overhead Flexible Budget Variance
  d. Price Variance
  e. Production Volume Variance
  f. Standard Cost

  _____ 1. A budget for a single unit. (p. 1228)
  _____ 2. Using standards based on "best practice." (p. 1230)
  _____ 3. Measures how well the business keeps unit prices of material and labor inputs within standards. (p. 1231)
  _____ 4. Measures whether the quantity of materials or labor used to make the actual number of outputs is within the standard allowed for that number of outputs. (p. 1231)
  _____ 5. Shows how well management has controlled overhead costs. (p. 1237)
  _____ 6. Arises when actual production differs from expected production. (p. 1238)

Flexible budget preparation
[1]

S24-3 Boje, Inc. manufactures travel locks. The budgeted selling price is $15 per lock, the variable cost is $10 per lock, and budgeted fixed costs are $15,000. Prepare a flexible budget for output levels of 4,000 locks and 6,000 locks for the month ended April 30, 2007. (p. 1223)

Flexible budget variance
[2]

S24-4 Complete the flexible budget variance analysis for Boje, Inc. by filling in the blanks in the following partial Income Statement Performance Report for 5,000 travel locks. (p. 1225)

continued . . .

BOJE, INC.
Income Statement Performance Report
Month Ended April 30, 2007

	Actual Results at Actual Prices	Flexible Budget Variance	Flexible Budget for Actual Number of Output Units
Output units	5,000	——	5,000
Sales revenue	$80,000	——	$75,000
Variable costs	52,000	——	50,000
Fixed costs	16,000	——	15,000
Total costs	68,000	——	65,000
Operating income	$12,000	——	$10,000

Static budgets and flexible budgets

S24-5 Fill in the blanks with the phrase that best completes the sentence.

Actual number of outputs   Beginning of the period   Static budget variance

Expected number of outputs   End of the period

Sales volume variance   Flexible budget variance

a. The static budget is developed at the _____. (p. 1222)

b. The flexible budget used in an income statement performance report is based on the _____. (pp. 1223–1224)

c. The master budget is based on the _____. (p. 1222)

d. The flexible budget used in an income statement performance report is developed at the _____. (pp. 1224–1225)

e. The difference between actual costs and the costs that should have been incurred for the actual number of outputs is the _____. (p. 1224)

Calculate materials variances

S24-6 Longman, Inc. is a manufacturer of lead crystal glasses. The standard materials quantity is 1 pound per glass at a price of $0.40 per pound. The actual results for the production of 7,000 glasses was 1.1 pound per glass, at a price of $0.50 per pound. Calculate the materials price variance and the materials efficiency variance. (pp. 1232–1234)

Calculate labor variances

S24-7 Longman, Inc. manufactures lead crystal glasses. The standard direct labor time is 1/5 hour per glass, at a price of $14 per hour. The actual results for the production of 7,000 glasses was 1/4 hour, at a price of $13 per hour. Calculate the labor price variance and the labor efficiency variance. (pp. 1235–1236)

Interpreting material and labor variances

S24-8 Refer to S24-6 and S24-7. For each variance, who in Longman's organization is most likely responsible? Interpret the direct materials and direct labor variances for Longman's management. (pp. 1232–1236)

Flexible Budgets and Standard Costs   **1251**

Standard overhead rates

S24-9 Longman, Inc. manufactures lead crystal glasses. The following information relates to the company's overhead costs:

Static budget variable overhead	$7,000
Static budget fixed overhead	$3,000
Static budget direct labor hours	1,000 hours
Static budget number of glasses	5,000

Longman allocates manufacturing overhead to production based on standard direct labor hours. Last month, Longman reported the following actual results for the production of 7,000 glasses: actual variable overhead, $10,400; actual fixed overhead, $2,800. Compute the standard variable overhead rate and the standard fixed overhead rate. (p. 1238)

Compute overhead variances

S24-10 Refer to the Longman data in S24-9. Compute the overhead variances. (Use Exhibit 24-11 on p. 1238 as a guide.)

Materials journal entries

S24-11 The following materials variance analysis was performed for Longman. Record Longman's direct materials journal entries. (p. 1239)

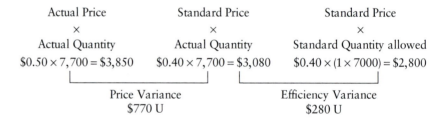

Labor journal entries

S24-12 The following labor variance analysis was performed for Longman. Record Longman's direct labor journal entries. (p. 1240)

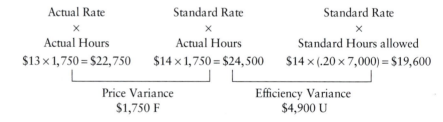

Journal entries for goods completed and sold

S24-13 Longman completed 70,000 glasses in 2008, at a standard cost of $364,000. The company sold all of them on account at a sale price of $8.00 each. There were no beginning or ending inventories of any kind. Record the journal entries for the completion and sale of the 70,000 glasses. (p. 1240)

Standard cost income statement

S24-14 Use the following information to prepare a standard cost income statement for Longman, using Exhibit 24-13 on page 1242 as a guide. Remember that unfavorable variances are added to cost of goods sold.

Cost of goods sold $364,000

Direct labor price variance $48,000 U

Direct materials efficiency variance $2,800 U

Overhead flexible budget variance $3,000 U

continued . . .

Direct labor efficiency variance $17,500 F

Sales Revenue $560,000

Marketing and administrative costs were $75,000

Direct materials price variance $7,700 U

Production volume variance $12,000 F

Exercises

Prepare a flexible budget

E24-15 ErgoNow sells its main product, ergonomic mouse pads, for $11 each. Its variable cost is $5.20 per pad. Fixed costs are $200,000 per month for volumes up to 60,000 pads. Above 60,000 pads, monthly fixed costs are $250,000. Prepare a monthly flexible budget for the product, showing sales revenue, variable costs, fixed costs, and operating income for volume levels of 40,000, 50,000, and 70,000 pads. (p. 1223)

Prepare an income statement performance report

E24-16 Ranger Pro Company managers received the following incomplete performance report: (p. 1225)

RANGER PRO COMPANY
Income Statement Performance Report
Year Ended July 31, 2009

	Actual Results at Actual Prices	Flexible Budget Variance	Flexible Budget for Actual Number of Output Units	Sales Volume Variance	Static (Master) Budget
Output units	36,000	—	36,000	4,000 F	—
Sales revenue	$216,000	—	$216,000	$24,000 F	—
Variable costs	84,000	—	80,000	9,000 U	—
Fixed costs	106,000	—	100,000	0	—
Total costs	190,000	—	180,000	9,000 U	—
Operating income	$ 26,000	—	$ 36,000	$15,000 F	—

Complete the performance report. Identify the employee group that may deserve praise and the group that may be subject to criticism. Give your reasons.

Prepare an income statement performance report

E24-17 Top managers of Kyler Industries predicted 2008 sales of 14,500 units of its product at a unit price of $8. Actual sales for the year were 14,000 units at $9.50 each. Variable costs were budgeted at $2.20 per unit, and actual variable costs were $2.30 per unit. Actual fixed costs of $42,000 exceeded budgeted fixed costs by $2,000. Prepare Kyler's income statement performance report in a format similar to that of Exercise E24-16. What variance contributed most to the year's favorable results? What caused this variance? (p. 1225)

Calculate materials and labor variances

E24-18 Urieta, Inc. produced 1,000 units of the company's product in 2009. The standard quantity of materials was 3 yards of cloth per unit at a standard price of $1 per yard. The accounting records showed that 2,800 yards of

continued ...

cloth were used and the company paid $1.10 per yard. Standard time was 2 direct labor hours per unit at a standard rate of $5 per direct labor hour. Employees worked 1,500 hours and were paid $4.75 per hour. Calculate the materials price variance and the materials efficiency variance, as well as the labor price and efficiency variances. (pp. 1232, 1234–1236)

Calculate materials variances

E24-19 The following direct materials variance computations are incomplete:

$$\text{Price variance} = (\$? - \$10) \times 9{,}600 \text{ pounds} = \$4{,}800 \text{ U}$$
$$\text{Efficiency variance} = (? - 10{,}400 \text{ pounds}) \times \$10 = ? \text{ F}$$
$$\text{Flexible budget variance} = \$?$$

Fill in the missing values, and identify the flexible budget variance as favorable or unfavorable. (pp. 1232, 1234)

Calculate materials and labor variances

E24-20 Great Fender, which uses a standard cost accounting system, manufactured 20,000 boat fenders during the year, using 145,000 feet of extruded vinyl purchased at $1.05 per foot. Production required 450 direct labor hours that cost $14.00 per hour. The materials standard was 7 feet of vinyl per fender, at a standard cost of $1.10 per foot. The labor standard was 0.025 direct labor hour per fender, at a standard price of $13.00 per hour. Compute the price and efficiency variances for direct materials and direct labor. Does the pattern of variances suggest Great Fender's managers have been making trade-offs? Explain. (pp. 1232, 1234, 1236)

Prepare journal entries

E24-21 Make the journal entries to record the purchase and use of direct materials and direct labor in E24-20. (pp. 1239–1240)

Prepare a standard cost income statement

E24-22 The managers of Ennis DVD Co., a contract manufacturer of DVD drives, are seeking explanations for the variances in the following report. Explain the meaning of each of Ennis's materials, labor, and overhead variances. (p. 1242)

ENNIS DVD CO.
Standard Cost Income Statement
Year Ended December 31, 2007

Sales revenue		$1,200,000
Cost of goods sold at standard cost		700,000
Manufacturing cost variances:		
Direct materials price variance	$10,000 F	
Direct materials efficiency variance	32,000 U	
Direct labor price variance	24,000 F	
Direct labor efficiency variance	10,000 U	
Overhead flexible budget variance	28,000 U	
Production volume variance	8,000 F	
Total manufacturing variances		28,000
Cost of goods sold at actual cost		728,000
Gross profit		472,000
Marketing and administrative costs		418,000
Operating income		$ 54,000

Compute overhead variances

E24-23 Tulsa Paint Company's budgeted production volume for the month was 30,000 gallons of paint. The standard overhead cost included $0.50 variable overhead per gallon and fixed overhead costs of $30,000.

Tulsa Paint actually produced 33,000 gallons of paint. Actual variable overhead was $16,200, and fixed overhead was $31,000. Compute the total overhead variance, the overhead flexible budget variance, and the production volume variance. (pp. 1237–1238)

Prepare a standard cost income statement

E24-24 The May 2008 revenue and cost information for Odessa Outfitters, Inc., follows:

Sales revenue	$560,000
Cost of goods sold (standard)	342,000
Direct materials price variance	1,000 F
Direct materials efficiency variance	6,000 F
Direct labor price variance	4,000 U
Direct labor efficiency variance	2,000 F
Overhead flexible budget variance	3,500 U
Production volume variance	8,000 F

Prepare a standard cost income statement for management through gross profit. (p. 1242) Report all standard cost variances for management's use. Has management done a good or poor job of controlling costs? Explain.

Problems (Group A)

Prepare an income statement performance report

P24-25A Cellular Technologies manufactures capacitors for cellular base stations and other communications applications. The company's March 2009 flexible budget income statements show output levels of 7,500, 9,000, and 11,000 units. The static budget was based on expected sales of 9,000 units.

CELLULAR TECHNOLOGIES
Flexible Budget Income Statement
Month Ended March 31, 2009

	Flexible Budget per Output Unit	Output Units (Capacitors)		
		7,500	9,000	11,000
Sales revenue	23	$172,500	$207,000	$253,000
Variable costs	12	90,000	108,000	132,000
Fixed costs		54,000	54,000	54,000
Total costs		144,000	162,000	186,000
Operating income		$ 28,500	$ 45,000	$ 67,000

continued . . .

The company sold 11,000 units during March, and its actual operating income was as follows:

CELLULAR TECHNOLOGIES
Income Statement
Month Ended March 31, 2009

Sales revenue	$257,000
Variable costs	134,250
Fixed costs	55,575
Total costs	189,825
Operating income	$ 67,175

Requirements

1. Prepare an income statement performance report for March. (p. 1225)
2. What was the effect on Cellular Technologies' operating income of selling 2,000 units more than the static budget level of sales? (p. 1223)
3. What is Cellular Technologies' static budget variance? (p. 1222) Explain why the income statement performance report provides more useful information to Cellular Technologies' managers than the simple static budget variance. (p. 1225) What insights can Cellular Technologies' managers draw from this performance report?

Preparing a flexible budget and computing standard cost variances

P24-26A Rocky Recliners manufactures leather recliners and uses flexible budgeting and a standard cost system. Rocky allocates overhead based on yards of direct materials. The company's performance report includes the following selected data:

	Static Budget (1,000 recliners)	Actual Results (980 recliners)
Sales (1,000 recliners × $500)	$500,000	
(980 recliners × $490)		$480,200
Variable manufacturing costs:		
Direct materials (6,000 yds. × $8.90)	53,400	
(6,150 yds. × $8.70)		53,505
Direct labor (10,000 hrs. × $9.00)	90,000	
(9,600 hrs. × $9.15)		87,840
Variable overhead (6,000 yds. × $5.00)	30,000	
(6,150 yds. × $6.40)		39,360
Fixed manufacturing costs:		
Fixed overhead	60,000	62,000
Total cost of goods sold	233,400	242,705
Gross profit	$266,600	$237,495

continued . . .

Requirements

1. Prepare a flexible budget based on the actual number of recliners sold. (p. 1223)
2. Compute the price variance and the efficiency variance for direct materials and for direct labor. (pp. 1232, 1240) For manufacturing overhead, compute the total variance, the flexible budget variance, and the production volume variance. (pp. 1237–1238)
3. Have Rocky's managers done a good job or a poor job controlling materials and labor costs? Why?
4. Describe how Rocky's managers can benefit from the standard costing system. (p. 1230)

Using incomplete cost and variance information to determine the number of direct labor hours worked

P24-27A Samantha's Shades manufactures lamp shades. Samantha Sanders, the manager, uses standard costs to judge performance. Recently, a clerk mistakenly threw away some of the records, and Sanders has only partial data for October. She knows that the direct labor flexible budget variance for the month was $1,050 U, the standard labor rate was $9 per hour, and the actual labor rate was $9.50 per hour. The standard direct labor hours for the actual October output were 4,475.

Requirements

1. Find the actual number of direct labor hours worked during October. First, calculate the standard labor cost. Next, calculate the actual labor cost by adding the unfavorable flexible budget variance of $1,050 to the standard labor cost. Finally, divide the actual labor cost by the actual labor rate per hour. (p. 1235)
2. Compute the direct labor price and efficiency variances. Do these variances suggest the manager may have made a trade-off? Explain. (pp. 1235–1236)

Computing and journalizing standard cost variances

P24-28A Bria manufactures coffee mugs that it sells to other companies for customizing with their own logos. Bria prepares flexible budgets and uses a standard cost system to control manufacturing costs. The standard unit cost of a coffee mug is based on static budget volume of 60,000 coffee mugs per month:

Direct materials (0.2 lbs. @ $0.25 per lb.)		$0.05
Direct labor (3 minutes @ $0.12 per minute)		0.36
Manufacturing overhead:		
Variable (3 minutes @ $0.06 per minute)	$0.18	
Fixed (3 minutes @ $0.14 per minute)	0.42	0.60
Total cost per coffee mug		$1.01

Actual cost and production information for July:

a. Actual production and sales were 62,700 coffee mugs.
b. Actual direct materials usage was 12,000 lbs., at an actual price of $0.18 per lb.

continued ...

c. Actual direct labor usage of 200,000 minutes at a total cost of $30,000.

d. Actual overhead cost was $40,800.

Requirements

1. Compute the price and efficiency variances for direct materials and direct labor. (pp. 1232, 1234)

2. Journalize the usage of direct materials and the assignment of direct labor, including the related variances. (pp. 1239–1241)

3. For manufacturing overhead, compute the total variance, the flexible budget variance, and the production volume variance. (*Hint:* Remember that the fixed overhead in the flexible budget equals the fixed overhead in the static budget.) (pp. 1237–1238)

4. Bria intentionally hired more-skilled workers during July. How did this decision affect the cost variances? Overall, was the decision wise? (p. 1234)

Computing standard cost variances and reporting to management

P24-29A HeadSmart manufactures headphone cases. During September 2008, the company produced and sold 106,000 cases and recorded the following cost data:

STANDARD COST INFORMATION:

	Quantity	Price
Direct materials	2 parts	$0.16 per part
Direct labor	0.02 hours	$8.00 per hour
Variable manufacturing overhead	0.02 hours	$10.00 per hour

Fixed manufacturing overhead ($32,000 for static budget volume of 100,000 units and 2,000 hours, or $16 per hour).

ACTUAL INFORMATION:

Direct materials (220,000 parts @ $0.21 per part = $46,200)

Direct labor (1,700 hrs. @ $8.10 per hr. = $13,770)

Manufacturing overhead $60,500

Requirements

1. Compute the price and efficiency variances for direct materials and direct labor. (pp. 1232, 1234)

2. For manufacturing overhead, compute the total variance, the flexible budget variance, and the production volume variance. (pp. 1237–1238)

3. Prepare a standard cost income statement through gross profit to report all variances to management. Sale price of the headset cases was $1.50 each. (p. 1242)

4. HeadSmart's management used more-experienced workers during September. Discuss the trade-off between the two direct labor variances. (pp. 1234–1235)

Problems (Group B)

Prepare an income statement performance report

2

P24-30B Nambe Clay, Inc., produces clay products for art in elementary school art programs. The company's flexible budget income statement for January 2009 shows output levels of 55,000, 60,000, and 65,000 clay kits. The static budget was based on 55,000 units.

NAMBE CLAY, INC.
Flexible Budget Income Statement
Month Ended January 31, 2009

	Flexible Budget per Output Unit	Output Units (kits)		
		55,000	60,000	65,000
Sales revenue	$3.00	$165,000	$180,000	$195,000
Variable costs	1.50	82,500	90,000	97,500
Fixed costs		70,000	70,000	70,000
Total costs		152,500	160,000	167,500
Operating income		$ 12,500	$ 20,000	$ 27,500

The company sold 60,000 clay kits during January 2009. Its actual operating income was as follows:

NAMBE CLAY, INC.
Income Statement
Month Ended January 31, 2009

Sales revenue	$185,000
Variable costs	$ 95,000
Fixed costs	69,000
Total costs	164,000
Operating income	$ 21,000

Requirements

1. Prepare an income statement performance report for January 2009. (p. 1225)
2. What accounts for most of the difference between actual operating income and static budget operating income? (p. 1223)
3. What is Nambe's static budget variance? (p. 1222) Explain why the income statement performance report provides Nambe's managers with more useful information than the simple static budget variance. (p. 1226) What insights can Nambe's managers draw from this performance report?

Preparing a flexible budget and computing standard cost variances

P24-31B Dawkins Co. assembles PCs and uses flexible budgeting and a standard cost system. Dawkins allocates overhead based on the number of direct materials parts. The company's performance report includes the following selected data:

	Static Budget (20,000 PCs)	Actual Results (22,000 PCs)
Sales (20,000 PCs × $400)	$8,000,000	
(22,000 PCs × $420)		$9,240,000
Variable manufacturing costs:		
Direct materials (200,000 parts @ $10.00)	2,000,000	
(214,200 parts @ $9.80)		2,099,160
Direct labor (40,000 hrs. @ $14.00)	560,000	
(41,000 hrs. @ $14.60)		598,600
Variable overhead (200,000 parts @ $4.00)	800,000	
(214,200 parts @ $4.10)		878,220
Fixed manufacturing costs:		
Fixed overhead	900,000	930,000
Total cost of goods sold	4,260,000	4,505,980
Gross profit	$3,740,000	$4,734,020

Requirements
1. Prepare a flexible budget based on the actual number of PCs sold. (p. 1223)
2. Compute the price variance and the efficiency variance for direct materials and for direct labor. (pp. 1232, 1234) For manufacturing overhead, compute the total variance, the flexible budget variance, and the production volume variance. (pp. 1237–1238)
3. Have Dawkins's managers done a good job or a poor job controlling materials and labor costs? Why?
4. Describe how Dawkins's managers can benefit from the standard costing system. (p. 1230)

Using incomplete cost and variance information to determine the number of direct labor hours worked

P24-32B Petra's Music manufactures harmonicas. Petra uses standard costs to judge performance. Recently, a clerk mistakenly threw away some of the records, and Petra has only partial data for October. She knows that the direct labor flexible budget variance for the month was $2,050 F and that the standard labor rate was $10 per hour. The actual labor rate was $9.50 per hour. The standard direct labor hours for actual October output were 6,000.

Requirements
1. Find the actual number of direct labor hours worked during October. First, calculate the standard labor cost. Next, calculate the actual labor cost by subtracting the favorable flexible budget variance of $2,050 from the standard labor cost. Finally, divide the actual labor cost by the actual labor rate per hour. (p. 1236)
2. Compute the direct labor price and efficiency variances. Do these variances suggest the manager may have made a trade-off? Explain. (pp. 1235–1236)

Computing and journalizing standard cost variances

P24-33B Mancini manufactures embroidered jackets. The company prepares flexible budgets and uses a standard cost system to control manufacturing costs. The standard unit cost of a jacket is based on static budget volume of 14,000 jackets per month:

Direct materials (3.0 sq. ft @ $4.00 per sq. ft)		$12.00
Direct labor (2 hours @ $9.40 per hour)		18.80
Manufacturing overhead:		
Variable (2 hours @ $0.65 per hour)	$1.30	
Fixed (2 hours @ $2.20 per hour)	4.40	5.70
Total cost per jacket		$36.50

Actual cost and production information:
a. Actual production was 13,600 jackets.
b. Actual direct materials usage was 2.8 square feet per jacket, at an actual price of $4.10 per square foot.
c. Actual direct labor usage of 25,000 hours at a total cost of $237,500.
d. Total actual overhead cost was $79,000.

Requirements
1. Compute the price and efficiency variances for direct materials and direct labor. (pp. 1232, 1234)
2. Journalize the usage of direct materials and the assignment of direct labor, including the related variances. (pp. 1239, 1241)
3. For manufacturing overhead, compute the total variance, the flexible budget variance, and the production volume variance. (*Hint:* Remember that the fixed overhead in the flexible budget equals the fixed overhead in the static budget.) (pp. 1237–1238)
4. Mancini's management intentionally purchased superior materials for November production. How did this decision affect the cost variances? Overall, was the decision wise? (p. 1235)

Computing standard cost variances and reporting to management

P24-34B Pecos Pecan Pads makes pressed pecan wood covers to prevent weed growth. During July 2009, the company produced and sold 44,000 rolls and recorded the following cost data:

STANDARD COST INFORMATION:

	Quantity	Price
Direct materials	3 lbs.	$1.10 per lb.
Direct labor	0.10 hours	$9.00 per hour
Variable manufacturing overhead	0.10 hours	$18.00 per hour
Fixed manufacturing overhead ($96,000 for static budget volume of 40,000 units and 4,000 hours, or $24 per hour)		

continued . . .

ACTUAL INFORMATION:

Direct materials (135,000 lbs. @ $1.00 per lb. = $135,000)

Direct labor (4,500 hrs. @ $8.75 per hr. = $39,375)

Manufacturing overhead $168,800

Requirements

1. Compute the price and efficiency variances for direct materials and direct labor. (pp. 1232, 1234)
2. For manufacturing overhead, compute the total variance, the flexible budget variance, and the production volume variance. (pp. 1237–1238)
3. Prepare a standard cost income statement through gross profit to report all variances to management. Sale price was $10.60 per roll. (p. 1242)
4. Pecos intentionally purchased cheaper materials during July. Was the decision wise? Discuss the trade-off between the two materials variances. (p. 1234)

Apply Your Knowledge

Decision Cases

Prepare an income statement performance report

Case 1. Movies Galore distributes DVDs to movie retailers, including dot.coms. Movies Galore's top management meets monthly to evaluate the company's performance. Controller Allen Walsh prepared the following performance report for the meeting.

MOVIES GALORE
Income Statement Performance Report
Month Ended July 31, 2008

	Actual Results	Static Budget	Variance
Sales revenue	$1,640,000	$1,960,000	$320,000 U
Variable costs:			
Cost of goods sold	775,000	980,000	205,000 F
Sales commisions	77,000	107,800	30,800 F
Shipping cost	43,000	53,900	10,900 F
Fixed costs:			
Salary cost	311,000	300,500	10,500 U
Depreciation cost	209,000	214,000	5,000 F
Rent cost	129,000	108,250	20,750 U
Advertising cost	81,000	68,500	12,500 U
Total costs	1,625,000	1,832,950	207,950 F
Operating income	$ 15,000	$ 127,050	$112,050 U

Walsh also revealed that the actual sale price of $20 per movie was equal to the budgeted sale price and that there were no changes in inventories for the month.

Management is disappointed by the operating income results. CEO Jilinda Robinson exclaims, "How can actual operating income be roughly 12% of the static budget amount when there are so many favorable variances?"

Requirements
1. Prepare a more informative performance report. Be sure to include a flexible budget for the actual number of DVDs bought and sold. (p. 1225)

2. As a member of Movies Galore's management team, which variances would you want investigated? Why?

3. Robinson believes that many consumers are postponing purchases of new movies until after the introduction of a new format for recordable DVD players. In light of this information, how would you rate the company's performance?

Compute standard cost variances for direct materials and direct labor

Case 2. Suppose you manage the local Scoopy's ice cream parlor. In addition to selling ice cream cones, you make large batches of a few flavors of milk shakes to sell throughout the day. Your parlor is chosen to test the company's "Made-for-You" system. This new system enables patrons to customize their milk shakes by choosing different flavors.

Customers like the new system and your staff appears to be adapting, but you wonder whether this new made-to-order system is as efficient as the old system in which you just made a few large batches. Efficiency is a special concern because your performance is evaluated in part on the restaurant's efficient use of materials and labor. Your superiors consider efficiency variances greater than 5% to be unacceptable.

You decide to look at your sales for a typical day. You find that the parlor used 390 lbs. of ice cream and 72 hours of direct labor to produce and sell 2,000 shakes. The standard quantity allowed for a shake is 0.2 pounds of ice cream and 0.03 hours (1.8 minutes) of direct labor. The standard prices are $1.50 per pound for ice cream and $8 an hour for labor.

Requirements

1. Compute the efficiency variances for direct labor and direct materials. (pp. 1232–1234, 1235–1236)

2. Provide likely explanations for the variances. Do you have reason to be concerned about your performance evaluation? Explain.

3. Write a memo to Scoopy's national office explaining your concern and suggesting a remedy. Your memo should take the following form:

Date: _____

To: Scoopy's National Office

From: _____

Subject: Made-for-You " System

Ethical Issues

Rita Lane is the accountant for Outdoor Living, a manufacturer of outdoor furniture that is sold through specialty stores and Internet companies. Lane is responsible for reviewing the standard costs. While reviewing the standards for the coming year, two ethical issues arise. Use the IMA's ethical guidelines, page 383, to identify the ethical dilemma in each situation. Identify the relevant factors in each situation and suggest what Lane should recommend to the controller.

Issue 1. Lane has been approached by Casey Henderson, a former colleague who worked with Lane when they were both employed by a public accounting firm. Henderson has recently started his own firm, Henderson Benchmarking Associates, which collects and sells data on industry benchmarks. He offers to provide Lane with benchmarks for the outdoor furniture industry free of charge if she will provide him with the last three years of Outdoor Living's standard and actual costs. Henderson explains that this is how he obtains most of his firm's benchmarking data. Lane always has a difficult time with the standard-setting process and believes that the benchmark data would be very useful.

Issue 2. Outdoor Living's management is starting a continuous improvement policy that requires a 10% reduction in standard costs each year for the next three years. Dan Jacobs, manufacturing foreman of the Teak furniture line, asks Lane to set loose standard costs this year before the continuous improvement policy is implemented. Jacobs argues that there is no other way to meet the tightening standards while maintaining the high quality of the Teak line.

Team Project

Lynx Corp. manufactures wood windows and doors. Lynx has been using a standard cost system that bases price and quantity standards on Lynx's historical long-run average performance. Suppose Lynx's controller has engaged your team of management consultants to advise her whether Lynx should use some basis other than historical performance for setting standards.

1. List the types of variances you recommend that Lynx compute (for example, direct materials price variance for glass). (pp. 1232, 1234, 1237–1238) For each variance, what specific standards would Lynx need to develop? (pp. 1228–1229) In addition to cost standards, do you recommend that Lynx develop any nonfinancial standards?

2. There are many approaches to setting standards other than simply using long-run average historical prices and quantities.

   a. List three alternative approaches that Lynx could use to set standards, and explain how Lynx could implement each alternative. (pp. 1229–1230)

   b. Evaluate each alternative method of setting standards, including the pros and cons of each method.

   c. Write a memo to Lynx's controller detailing your recommendations. First, should Lynx retain its historical data-based standard cost approach? If not, which of the alternative approaches should it adopt? Use the following format for your memo:

Date: _____

To: Controller, Lynx Corporation

From: _____, Management Consultants

Subject: Standard Costs

For Internet Exercises, Excel in Practice, and additional online activities, go to the Web site, www.prenhall.com/horngren.

Quick Check

1. d 2. b 3. a 4. e 5. c 6. c 7. d 8. b 9. a 10. a

25 Performance Evaluation and the Balanced Scorecard

Learning Objectives

1. Explain why and how companies decentralize

2. Explain why companies use performance evaluation systems

3. Describe the balanced scorecard and identify key performance indicators for each perspective

4. Use performance reports to evaluate cost, revenue, and profit centers

5. Use ROI, RI, and EVA to evaluate investment centers

To deliver over 3.6 billion packages a year in over 200 countries, United Parcel Service (UPS) employs over 370,000 people. But how does management successfully guide the actions of all of these employees? First, they divide—or decentralize—the company into three segments: domestic packaging, international packaging, and nonpackaging services (such as supply chain and logistics). They further break each packaging segment into geographic regions and each region into districts. Management gives each district manager authority to make decisions for her own district. Because top management wants *every* employee to know how his or her day-to-day job contributes to the company's goals, they implemented a system, called the balanced scorecard, for communicating strategy to all district managers and employees. Management can also use the balanced scorecard to measure whether each district is meeting its goals and to assess where they should make changes. According to one UPS executive, "The balanced scorecard provided a road map—the shared vision of our future goals—with action elements that let *everyone* contribute to our success."

In 2000, *Forbes* named UPS the "Company of the Year" and in 2004, *Fortune* rated UPS as the "World's Most Admired Company in its Industry" for the sixth consecutive year.

Sources: Robert Kaplan and David Norton, *The Strategy-Focused Organization: How Balanced Scorecard Companies Thrive in the New Business Environment,* Harvard Business School Press, Boston, 2001, pp. 21–22, 239–241; UPS Web site.

Many companies, such as UPS, decentralize their operations into subunits. Decentralization provides large companies with many advantages. Because top management is not directly involved in running the day-to-day operations of each subunit, they need a system—such as the balanced scorecard—for communicating the company's strategy to subunit managers and for measuring how well the subunits are achieving their goals. Let's first take a look at the advantages and disadvantages of decentralization.

Decentralized Operations

1 Explain why and how companies decentralize

In a small company, the owner or top manager often makes all planning and operating decisions. Small companies can use **centralized** decision making because of the smaller scope of their operations. However, when a company grows, it is impossible for a single person to manage the entire organization's daily operations. Therefore, most companies **decentralize** as they grow.

Companies that decentralize split their operations into different divisions or operating units. Top management delegates decision-making responsibility to the unit managers. Top management determines the type of decentralization that best suits the company's strategy. For example, decentralization may be based on geographic area, product line, customer base, business function, or some other business characteristic. Citizen's Bank segments its operations by state (different geographic areas). Sherwin-Williams segments by customer base (commercial and consumer paint divisions). PepsiCo segments by brands (Pepsi, Frito-Lay, Quaker, Gatorade, and Tropicana). And UPS segmented first by function (domestic packaging, international packaging, and nonpackaging services), then by geographic area.

Advantages of Decentralization

What advantages does decentralization offer large companies? Let's take a look.

Frees Top Management Time

By delegating responsibility for daily operations to unit managers, top management can concentrate on long-term strategic planning and higher-level decisions that affect the entire company.

Supports Use of Expert Knowledge

Decentralization allows top management to hire the expertise each business unit needs to excel in their own specific operations. For example, decentralizing by state allows

Citizens Bank to hire managers with specialized knowledge of the banking laws in each state. Such specialized knowledge can help unit managers make better decisions, than could the company's top managers, about product and business improvements within the business unit.

Improves Customer Relations

Unit managers focus on just one segment of the company. Therefore, they can maintain closer contact with important customers than can upper management. Thus, decentralization often leads to improved customer relations and quicker customer response time.

Provides Training

Decentralization also provides unit managers with training and experience necessary to become effective top managers. For example, in politics, presidential candidates often have experience as senators or state governors. Likewise, companies often choose CEOs based on their past performance as division managers.

Improves Motivation and Retention

Empowering unit managers to make decisions increases managers' motivation and retention, and improves job performance and satisfaction.

Disadvantages of Decentralization

Despite its advantages, decentralization can also cause potential problems, including those outlined in this section.

Duplication of Costs

Decentralization may cause the company to duplicate certain costs or assets. For example, each business unit may hire its own payroll department and purchase its own payroll software. Companies can often avoid such duplications by providing centralized services. For example, Doubletree Hotels segments its business by property, yet each property shares one centralized reservations office and one centralized Web site.

Problems Achieving Goal Congruence

Goal congruence occurs when unit managers' goals align with top management's goals. Decentralized companies often struggle to achieve goal congruence. Unit managers may not fully understand the "big picture" of the company. They may make decisions that are good for their division but could harm another division or the rest of the company. For example, the purchasing department may buy cheaper components to decrease product cost. However, cheaper components may hurt the product line's quality, and the company's brand, *as a whole*, may suffer. Later in this chapter, we'll see how managerial accountants can design performance evaluation systems that foster goal congruence.

As Exhibit 25-1 illustrates, the many advantages of decentralization usually outweigh the disadvantages.

Responsibility Centers

Decentralized companies delegate responsibility for specific decisions to each subunit, creating responsibility centers. Recall from Chapter 23 that a **responsibility center** is a part or subunit of an organization whose manager is accountable for specific activities. Exhibit 25-2 reviews the four most common types of responsibility centers.

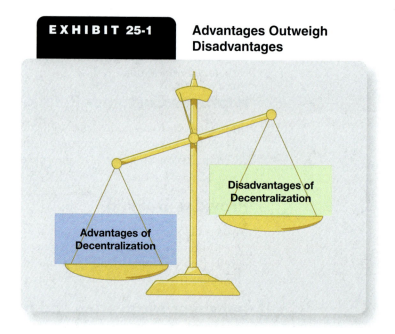

EXHIBIT 25-1 Advantages Outweigh Disadvantages

EXHIBIT 25-2 The Four Most Common Types of Responsibility Centers

Responsibility Center	Manager is responsible for...	Examples
Cost center	Controlling costs	Production line at Dell Computer; legal department and accounting departments at Nike
Revenue center	Generating sales revenue	Midwest sales region at Pace Foods; central reservation office at Delta
Profit center	Producing profit through generating sales and controlling costs	Product line at Anheuser-Busch; individual Home Depot stores
Investment center	Producing profit and managing the division's invested capital	Company divisions, such as Walt Disney World Resorts and Toon Disney

Performance Measurement

Once a company decentralizes operations, top management is no longer involved in running the subunits' day-to-day operations. Performance evaluation systems provide top management with a framework for maintaining control over the entire organization.

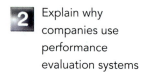
Explain why companies use performance evaluation systems

Goals of Performance Evaluation Systems

When companies decentralize, top management needs a system to communicate its goals to subunit managers. Additionally, top management needs to determine whether the decisions being made at the subunit level are effectively meeting company goals. We'll now consider the primary goals of performance evaluation systems.

Promoting Goal Congruence and Coordination

As previously mentioned, decentralization increases the difficulty of achieving goal congruence. Unit managers may not always make decisions consistent with the overall goals of the organization. A company will be able to achieve its goals only if each unit moves, in a synchronized fashion, toward the overall company goals. The performance measurement system should provide incentives for coordinating the subunits' activities and direct them toward achieving the overall company goals.

Communicating Expectations

To make decisions that are consistent with the company's goals, unit managers must know the goals and the specific part their unit plays in attaining those goals. The performance measurement system should spell out the unit's most critical objectives. Without a clear picture of what management expects, unit managers have little to guide their daily operating decisions.

Motivating Unit Managers

Unit managers are usually motivated to make decisions that will help to achieve top management's expectations. For additional motivation, upper management may offer bonuses to unit managers who meet or exceed performance targets. Top management must exercise extreme care in setting performance targets. For example, a manager measured solely by his ability to control costs may take whatever actions are necessary to achieve that goal, including sacrificing quality or customer service. But such actions would *not* be in the best interests of the firm as a whole. Therefore, upper management must consider the ramifications of the performance targets they set for unit managers.

Providing Feedback

In decentralized companies, top management is no longer involved in the day-to-day operations of each subunit. Performance evaluation systems provide upper management with the feedback they need to maintain control over the entire organization, even though they have delegated responsibility and decision-making authority to unit managers. If targets are not met at the unit level, upper management will take corrective actions, ranging from modifying unit goals (if the targets were unrealistic) to replacing the unit manager (if the targets are achievable, but the manager fails to reach them).

Benchmarking

Performance evaluation results are often used for **benchmarking**, which is the practice of comparing the company's achievements against the best practices in the industry. Comparing results against industry benchmarks is often more revealing than comparing results against budgets. To survive, a company must keep up with its competitors. Benchmarking helps the company determine whether or not it is performing at least as well as its competitors.

> **Stop & Think**
>
> Do companies, such as UPS, only benchmark subunit performance against competitors and industry standards?
>
> **Answer:** No. Companies also benchmark performance against the subunit's past performance. Historical trend data (measuring performance over time) helps managers assess whether their decisions are improving, having no effect, or adversely affecting subunit performance. Some companies also benchmark performance against other subunits with similar characteristics.

Limitations of Financial Performance Measurement

In the past, performance measurement revolved almost entirely around *financial* performance. Until 1995, 95% of UPS's performance measures were financial. On the one hand, this focus makes sense because the ultimate goal of a company is to generate profit. On the other hand, *current* financial performance tends to reveal the results of *past* actions rather than indicate *future* performance. For this reason, financial measures tend to be **lag indicators**, rather than **lead indicators**. Management needs to know the results of past decisions, but they also need to know how current decisions may affect the future. To adequately assess the company, managers need lead indicators in addition to lag indicators.

Another limitation of financial performance measures is that they tend to focus on the company's short-term achievements, rather than on long-term performance. Why is this the case? Because financial statements are prepared on a monthly, quarterly, or annual basis. To remain competitive, top management needs clear signals that assess and predict the company's performance over longer periods of time.

The Balanced Scorecard

3 Describe the balanced scorecard and identify key performance indicators for each perspective

In the early 1990s, Robert Kaplan and David Norton introduced the **balanced scorecard**.[1] The balanced scorecard recognizes that management must consider *both* financial performance measures (which tend to measure the results of actions already taken) and operational performance measures (which tend to drive future performance) when judging the performance of a company and its subunits. These measures should be linked with the company's goals and its strategy for achieving those goals. The balanced scorecard represents a major shift in corporate performance measurement: Rather than treating financial indicators as the sole measure of performance, they are now only one measure among a broader set. Keeping score of operating measures *and* traditional financial measures give management a "balanced" view of the organization.

Kaplan and Norton use the analogy of an airplane pilot to illustrate the necessity for a balanced scorecard approach to performance evaluation. The pilot of an airplane cannot rely on only one factor, such as wind speed, to fly a plane. Rather, the pilot must consider other critical factors, such as altitude, direction, and fuel level. Likewise, management cannot rely on only financial measures to guide the company. Management needs to consider other critical factors, such as customer satisfaction, operational efficiency, and employee excellence. Similar to the way a pilot uses cockpit instruments to measure critical factors, management uses *key performance indicators*—such as customer satisfaction ratings and revenue growth—to measure critical factors that affect

---

[1] Robert Kaplan and David Norton, "The Balanced Scorecard—Measures That Drive Performance," *Harvard Business Review on Measuring Corporate Performance*, Boston, 1991, pp. 123–145; Robert Kaplan and David Norton, *Translating Strategy into Action: The Balanced Scorecard*, Boston, Harvard Business School Press, 1996.

the success of the company. As shown in Exhibit 25-3, **key performance indicators (KPIs)** are summary performance measures that help managers assess whether the company is achieving its goals.

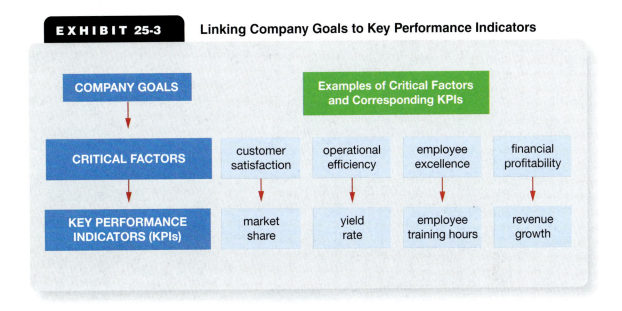

EXHIBIT 25-3 Linking Company Goals to Key Performance Indicators

The Four Perspectives of the Balanced Scorecard

The balanced scorecard views the company from four different perspectives, each of which evaluates a specific aspect of organizational performance:

1. Financial perspective
2. Customer perspective
3. Internal business perspective
4. Learning and growth perspective

Exhibit 25-4 illustrates how the company's strategy affects, and, in turn, is affected by all four perspectives. Additionally, it shows the cause-and-effect relationship linking the four perspectives.

Companies that adopt the balanced scorecard usually have specific objectives they wish to achieve within each of the four perspectives. Once management clearly identifies the objectives, they develop KPIs that will assess how well the objectives are being achieved. To focus attention on the most critical elements and prevent information overload, management should use only a few KPIs for each perspective. Let's now look at each of the perspectives and discuss the links between them.

Financial Perspective

This perspective helps managers answer the question, "How do we look to shareholders?" The ultimate goal of companies is to generate income for their owners. Therefore, company strategy revolves around increasing the company's profits through increasing revenue growth and increasing productivity. Companies grow revenue through introducing new products, gaining new customers, and increasing sales to existing customers. Companies increase productivity through reducing costs

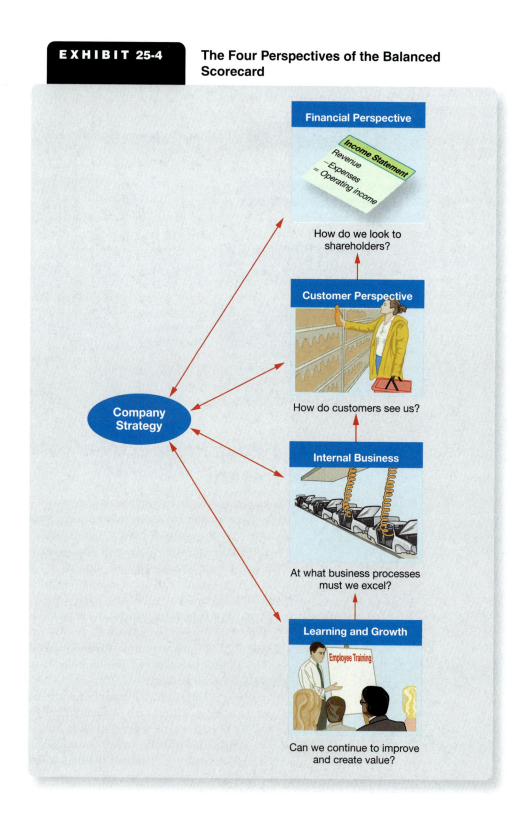

EXHIBIT 25-4 The Four Perspectives of the Balanced Scorecard

and using the company's assets more efficiently. Managers may implement seemingly sensible strategies and initiatives, but the test of their judgment is whether these decisions increase company profits. The financial perspective focuses management's attention on KPIs that assess financial objectives, such as revenue growth and cost cutting. Some commonly used KPIs include: *sales revenue growth, gross margin growth,* and *return on investment*. The latter portion of this chapter discusses in detail the most commonly used financial perspective KPIs.

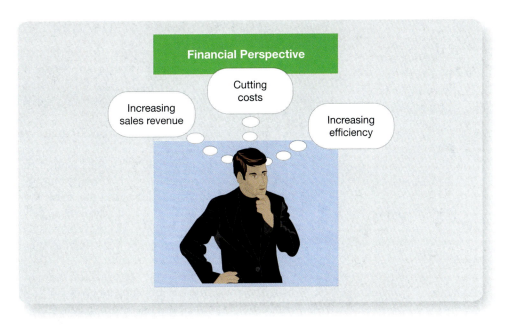

Customer Perspective

This perspective helps managers evaluate the question, "How do customers see us?" Customer satisfaction is a top priority for long-term company success. If customers aren't happy, they won't come back. Therefore, customer satisfaction is critical to achieving the company's financial goals outlined in the financial perspective of the balanced scorecard. Customers are typically concerned with four specific product or service attributes: (1) the product's price, (2) the product's quality, (3) the sales service quality, and (4) the product's delivery time (the shorter the better). Since each of these attributes is critical to making the customer happy, most companies have specific objectives for each of these attributes.

Businesses commonly use KPIs, such as *customer satisfaction ratings*, to assess how they are performing on these attributes. No doubt you have filled out a customer satisfaction survey. Because customer satisfaction is crucial, customer satisfaction ratings determine the extent to which bonuses are granted to Bahama Breeze restaurant managers. Other typical KPIs include *percentage of market share, increase in the number of customers, number of repeat customers*, and *rate of on-time deliveries*.

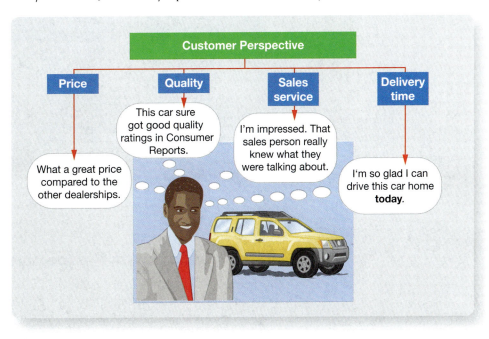

Internal Business Perspective

This perspective helps managers address the question, "At what business processes must we excel to satisfy customer and financial objectives?" The answer to this question incorporates three factors: innovation, operations, and post-sales service. All three factors critically affect customer satisfaction, which will affect the company's financial success.

Satisfying customers once does not guarantee future success, which is why the first important factor of the internal business perspective is innovation. Customers' needs and wants change as the world around them changes. Just a couple of years ago, digital cameras, flat-panel computer monitors, plasma screen televisions, and digital video recorders (DVRs) did not exist. Companies must continually improve existing products (such as adding cameras to cell phones) and develop new products (such as iPods and portable DVD players) to succeed in the future. Companies commonly assess innovation using KPIs, such as the *number of new products developed* or *new-product development time*.

The second important factor of the internal business perspective is operations. Efficient and effective internal operations allow the company to meet customers' needs and expectations. For example, the time it takes to manufacture a product (*manufacturing cycle time*) affects the company's ability to deliver quickly to meet a customer's demand. Production efficiency (*number of units produced per hour*) and product quality (*defect rate*) also affect the price charged to the customer. To remain competitive, companies must be at least as good as the industry leader at those internal operations that are essential to their business.

The third factor of the internal business perspective is post-sales service. How well does the company service customers after the sale? Claims of excellent post-sales service help to generate more sales. Management assesses post-sales service through the following typical KPIs: *number of warranty claims received, average repair time,* and *average wait time on the phone for a customer service representative*.

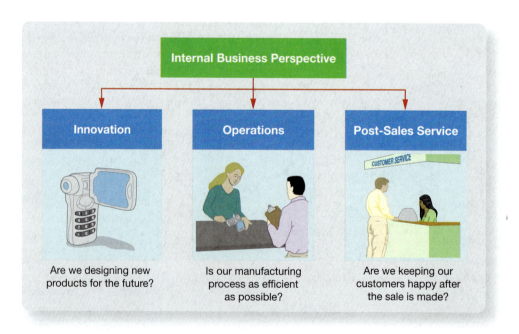

Learning and Growth Perspective

This perspective helps managers assess the question, "Can we continue to improve and create value?" The learning and growth perspective focuses on three factors: (1) employee capabilities, (2) information system capabilities, and (3) the company's "climate for action." The learning and growth perspective lays the foundation needed to improve internal business operations, sustain customer satisfaction, and generate financial success. Without skilled employees, updated technology, and a positive corporate culture, the company will not be able to meet the objectives of the other perspectives.

Let's consider each of these factors. First, because most routine work is automated, employees are freed up to be critical and creative thinkers who help achieve the company's goals. The learning and growth perspective measures employees' skills, knowledge, motivation, and empowerment. KPIs typically include *hours of employee training*, *employee satisfaction*, *employee turnover*, and *number of employee suggestions implemented*. Second, employees need timely and accurate information on customers, internal processes, and finances, therefore, other KPIs measure the maintenance and improvement of the company's information system. For example, KPIs might include the *percentage of employees having online access to information about customers*, and the *percentage of processes with real-time feedback on quality, cycle time, and cost*. Finally, management must create a corporate culture that supports

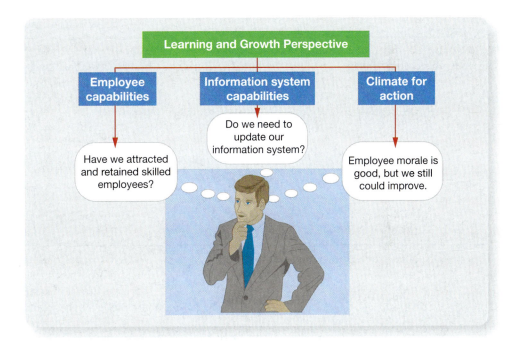

communication, change, and growth. For example, UPS used the balanced scorecard to communicate strategy to every employee and to show them how their daily work contributed to company success.

In summary, the balanced scorecard focuses performance measurement on progress toward the company's goals in each of the four perspectives. In designing the scorecard, managers start with the company's goals and its strategy for achieving those goals and then identify the *most* important measures of performance that will predict long-term success. Some of these measures are operational lead indicators, while others are financial lag indicators. Managers must consider the linkages between strategy and operations and how those operations will affect finances now and in the future.

So far, we have looked at why companies decentralize, why they need to measure subunit performance, and how the balanced scorecard can help. In the second half of the chapter, we'll focus on how companies measure the financial perspective of the balanced scorecard.

Decision Guidelines

UPS had to make the following types of decisions when it decentralized and developed its balanced scorecard for performance evaluation.

Decision	Guidelines
On what basis should the company be decentralized?	The manner of decentralization should fit the company's strategy. Many companies decentralize based on geographic region, product line, business function, or customer type.
Will decentralization have any negative impact on the company?	Decentralization usually provides many benefits; however, decentralization also has potential drawbacks: • Subunits may duplicate costs or assets. • Subunit managers may not make decisions that are favorable to the entire company.
How can responsibility accounting be incorporated at decentralized companies?	Subunit managers are given responsibility for specific activities and are only held accountable for the results of those activities. Subunits generally fall into one of the following four categories according to their responsibilities: 1. **Cost centers**—responsible for controlling costs 2. **Revenue centers**—responsible for generating revenue 3. **Profit centers**—responsible for controlling costs and generating revenue 4. **Investment centers**—responsible for controlling costs, generating revenue, and efficiently managing the division's invested capital (assets)
Is a performance evaluation system necessary?	While not mandatory, most companies will reap many benefits from implementing a well-designed performance evaluation system. Such systems will promote goal congruence, communicate expectations, motivate managers, provide feedback, and enable benchmarking.
Should the performance evaluation system include lag or lead measures?	Better performance evaluation systems include *both* lag and lead measures. Lag measures indicate the results of past actions, while lead measures project future performance.
What are the four balanced scorecard perspectives?	1) Financial perspective, 2) Customer perspective, 3) Internal Business perspective, and 4) Learning and Growth perspective.
Must all four perspectives be included in the company's balanced scorecard?	Every company's balanced scorecard will be unique to its business and strategy. Because each of the four perspectives is causally linked, most companies will benefit from developing performance measures for each of the four perspectives.

Summary Problem 1

Requirements

1. Each of the following describes a key performance indicator. Determine which of the following balanced scorecard perspectives is being addressed (financial, customer, internal business, learning and growth)
    a. Employee turnover
    b. Earnings per share
    c. Percentage of on-time deliveries
    d. Revenue growth rate
    e. Percentage of defects discovered during manufacturing
    f. Number of warranties claimed
    g. New product development time
    h. Number of repeat customers
    i. Number of employee suggestions implemented

2. Read the following company initiatives and determine which of the balanced scorecard perspectives is being addressed (financial, customer, internal business, learning and growth)
    a. Purchasing efficient production equipment
    b. Providing employee training
    c. Updating retail store lighting
    d. Paying quarterly dividends
    e. Updating the company's information system

Solution

Requirement 1
a. Learning and growth
b. Financial
c. Customer
d. Financial
e. Internal business
f. Internal business
g. Internal business
h. Customer
i. Learning and growth

Requirement 2
a. Internal business
b. Learning and growth
c. Customer
d. Financial
e. Learning and growth

Measuring the Financial Performance of Cost, Revenue, and Profit Centers

In this half of the chapter we'll take a more detailed look at how companies measure the financial perspective of the balanced scorecard for different subunits of the company. We'll focus now on the financial performance measurement of each type of responsibility center.

Responsibility accounting performance reports capture the financial performance of cost, revenue, and profit centers. Recall from Chapter 23 that responsibility accounting performance reports compare *actual* results with *budgeted* amounts and display a variance, or difference, between the two amounts. Because **cost centers** are only responsible for controlling costs, their performance reports only include information on actual versus budgeted *costs*. Likewise, performance reports for **revenue centers** only contain actual versus budgeted *revenue*. However, **profit centers** are responsible for both controlling costs and generating revenue. Therefore, their performance reports contain actual and budgeted information on both their *revenues and costs*.

Cost center performance reports typically focus on the *flexible budget variance*—the difference between actual results and the flexible budget (as described in Chapter 24). Exhibit 25-5 shows an example of a cost center performance report for a regional payroll processing department of House and Garden Depot, a home improvement warehouse chain. Because the payroll processing department only incurs expenses and does not generate revenue, it is classified as a cost center.

4 Use performance reports to evaluate cost, revenue, and profit centers

EXHIBIT 25-5 — Example of Cost Center Performance Report

HOUSE AND GARDEN DEPOT-NORTH FLORIDA REGION
Payroll Processing Department Performance Report
July 2008

	Actual	Flexible Budget	Flexible Budget Variance (U or F)	% Variance* (U of F)
Salary and wages	$18,500	$18,000	$ 500 U	2.8% U
Payroll benefits	6,100	5,000	1,100 U	22.0% U
Equipment depreciation	3,000	3,000	0	0%
Supplies	1,850	2,000	150 F	7.5% F
Other	1,900	2,000	100 F	5.0% F
Total Expenses	$31,350	$30,000	$1,350 U	4.5% U

*Flexible budget variance/flexible budget

Managers use **management by exception** to determine which variances in the performance report are worth investigating. For example, management may only investigate variances that exceed a certain dollar amount (for example, over $1,000) or a certain percentage of the budgeted figure (for example, over 10%). Smaller variances signal that operations are close to target and do not require management's immediate attention. For example, in the cost center performance report illustrated in Exhibit 25-5, management might only investigate "payroll benefits" because the variance exceeds both $1,000 and 10%. Companies that use standard costs can compute price and efficiency variances, as described in Chapter 24, to better understand why significant flexible budget variances occurred.

Revenue center performance reports often highlight both the flexible budget variance and the sales volume variance. The Paint Department at House and Garden Depot's Tallahassee store might look similar to Exhibit 25-6, with detailed sales volume and revenue shown for each brand and type of paint sold. (For simplicity, the exhibit shows volume and revenue for only one item.) The cash register bar-coding system provides management with the sales volume and sales revenue generated by individual products.

EXHIBIT 25-6   **Example of a Revenue Center Performance Report**

HOUSE AND GARDEN DEPOT—Tallahassee Store
Paint Department Performance Report
July 2008

Sales Revenue	Actual Sales	Flexible Budget Variance	Flexible Budget	Sales Volume Variance	Static (Master) Budget
Number of Gallons	2,480	–0–	2,480	155 (F)	2,325
Glidden – Flat	$40,920	$3,720 (U)	$44,640	$2,790 (F)	$41,850
Glidden – Semigloss					
Glidden – Glossy					

Recall from Chapter 24 that the sales volume variance is due strictly to volume differences—selling more or fewer units (gallons of paint) than originally planned. The flexible budget variance, however, is due strictly to differences in the sales price—selling units for a higher or lower price than originally planned. Both the sales volume variance and the flexible budget variance help revenue center managers understand why they have exceeded or fallen short of budgeted revenue.

Managers of profit centers are responsible for both generating revenue and controlling costs so their performance reports include both revenues and expenses. Exhibit 25-7 shows an example of a profit center performance report for the Tallahassee House and Garden Depot store.

EXHIBIT 25-7   **Example of a Profit Center Performance Report**

HOUSE AND GARDEN DEPOT
Tallahassee Store—Performance Report
July 2008

	Actual	Flexible Budget	Flexible Budget Variance	% Variance
Sales Revenue	$5,243,600	$5,000,000	$243,600 F	4.9% F
Operating expenses	4,183,500	4,000,000	183,500 F	4.6% F
Income from operations before service department charges	1,060,100	1,000,000	60,100 F	6.0% F
Service department charges (allocated)	84,300	75,000	9,300 U	12.4% U
Income from operations	$ 975,800	$ 925,000	$ 50,800 F	5.5% F

Notice how this profit center performance report contains a line called "Service department charges." Recall that one drawback of decentralization is that subunits may duplicate costs or assets. Many companies avoid this problem by providing centralized service departments where several subunits, such as profit centers, share assets or costs. For example, the payroll processing cost center shown in Exhibit 25-5 serves all of the House and Garden Depot stores in the north Florida region. In addition to centralized payroll departments, companies often provide centralized human resource departments, legal departments, and information systems.

When subunits share centralized services, should those services be "free" to the subunits? If they are free, the subunit's performance report will *not* include any charge for using those services. However, if they are not free, the performance report will show a charge, as you see in Exhibit 25-7. Most companies charge subunits for their use of centralized services because the subunit would incur a cost to buy those services on its own. For example, if House and Garden Depot didn't operate a centralized payroll department, the Tallahassee House and Garden Depot store would have to hire its own payroll department personnel and purchase any computers, payroll software, and supplies necessary to process the store's payroll. As an alternative, it could outsource payroll to a company, such as Paychex or ADP. In either event, the store would incur a cost for processing payroll. It only seems fair that the store is charged for using the centralized payroll processing department. Appendix 25A at the end of this chapter describes how companies allocate service department costs between subunits. Because the charges are the result of allocation, rather than a direct cost of the profit center, they are usually shown on a separate line rather than "buried" in the subunit's other operating expenses.

Regardless of the type of responsibility center, performance reports should focus on information, not blame. Analyzing budget variances helps managers understand the underlying reasons for the unit's performance. Once management understands these reasons, it may be able to take corrective actions. But some variances are uncontrollable. For example, the 2005 hurricanes in the Gulf Coast increased prices of gasoline (due to damaged oil refineries) and building materials (as people repaired hurricane-damaged homes). These price increases resulted in unfavorable cost variances for many companies. Managers should not be held accountable for conditions they cannot control. Responsibility accounting can help management identify the causes of variances, thus, allowing them to determine what was controllable, and what was not.

We have just looked at the detailed financial information presented in responsibility accounting performance reports. In addition to these *detailed* reports, upper management often uses *summary* measures—financial KPIs—to assess the financial performance of cost, revenue, and profit centers. Examples include the *cost per unit of output* (for cost centers), *revenue growth* (for revenue centers), and *gross margin growth* (for profit centers). KPIs, such as these, are used to address the financial perspective of the balanced scorecard for cost, revenue, and profit centers. In the next section we'll look at the most commonly used KPIs for investment centers.

Stop & Think

We have just seen that companies like House and Garden Depot use responsibility accounting performance reports to evaluate the financial performance of cost, revenue, and profit centers. Are these types of responsibility reports sufficient for evaluating the financial performance of investment centers? Why or why not?

Answer: Investment centers are responsible not only for generating revenue and controlling costs, but also for efficiently managing the subunit's invested capital. The performance reports we have just seen address how well the subunits control costs and generate revenue, but they do not address how well the subunits manage their assets. Therefore, these performance reports will be helpful but not sufficient for evaluating investment center performance.

Measuring the Financial Performance of Investment Centers

Investment centers are typically large divisions of a company, such as the Frito-Lay division of PepsiCo. The duties of an investment center manager are similar to those of a CEO. The CEO is responsible for maximizing income, in relation to the company's invested capital, by using company assets efficiently. Likewise, investment center managers are responsible not only for generating profit but also for making the best use of the investment center's assets.

How does an investment center manager influence the use of the division's assets? An investment center manager has the authority to open new stores or close old stores. The manager may also decide how much inventory to hold, what types of investments to make, how aggressively to collect accounts receivable, and whether to invest in new equipment. In other words, the manager has decision-making responsibility over all of the division's assets.

Companies cannot evaluate investment centers the way they evaluate profit centers, based only on operating income. Why? Because income does not indicate how *efficiently* the division is using its assets. The financial evaluation of investment centers must measure two factors: (1) how much income the division is generating and (2) how efficiently the division is using its assets.

Consider House and Garden Depot. In addition to its home improvement warehouse stores, House and Garden Depot operates a Landscaping Division and a Design Division. Operating income, total assets, and sales for the two divisions follow (in thousands of dollars):

House and Garden Depot	Landscaping Division	Design Division
Operating income	$ 450,000	$ 600,000
Total assets	2,500,000	4,000,000
Sales	7,500,000	10,000,000

Based on operating income alone, the Design Division (with operating income of $600,000) appears to be more profitable than the Landscaping Division (with operating income of $450,000). However, this comparison is misleading because it does not consider the assets invested in each division. The Design Division has more assets to use for generating income than does the Landscaping Division.

To adequately evaluate an investment center's financial performance, companies need summary performance measures—or KPIs—that include *both* the division's operating income *and* its assets. (See Exhibit 25-8.) In the next sections, we discuss three commonly used performance measures: return on investment (ROI), residual income (RI), and economic value added (EVA). All three measures incorporate both the division's assets and its operating income. For simplicity, we will leave the word *divisional* out of the equations. However, keep in mind that all of the equations use divisional data when evaluating a division's performance.

5 Use ROI, RI, and EVA to evaluate investment centers

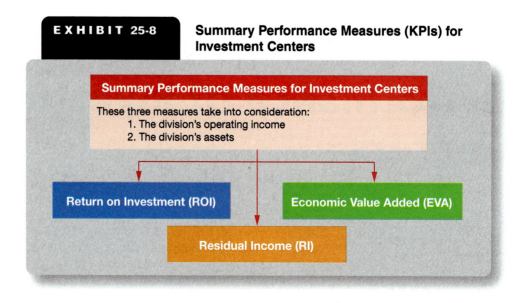

Return on Investment (ROI)

Return on Investment (ROI) is one of the most commonly used KPIs for evaluating an investment center's financial performance. Companies typically define ROI as follows:

$$ROI = \frac{\text{Operating income}}{\text{Total assets}}$$

ROI measures the amount of income an investment center earns relative to the amount of its assets. Let's calculate each division's ROI:

$$\text{Landscaping Division ROI} = \left(\frac{\$450,000}{\$2,500,000}\right) = 18\%$$

$$\text{Design Division ROI} = \left(\frac{\$600,000}{\$4,000,000}\right) = 15\%$$

Although the Design Division has a higher operating income than the Landscaping Division, the Design Division is actually *less* profitable than the Landscaping Division when we consider that the Design Division has more assets from which to generate its profit.

If you had $1,000 to invest, would you rather invest it in the Design Division or Landscaping Division? The Design Division earns a profit of $0.15 on every $1.00 of assets, but the Landscaping Division earns $0.18 on every $1.00 of assets. When top management decides how to invest excess funds, they often consider each division's ROI. A division with a higher ROI is more likely to receive extra funds because it has a "track record" of providing a higher return.

In addition to comparing ROI across divisions, management also compares a division's ROI across time to determine whether the division is becoming more or less profitable in relation to its assets. Additionally, management often benchmarks divisional ROI with other companies in the same industry to determine how each division is performing compared to its competitors.

To determine what is driving a division's ROI, management often restates the ROI equation in its expanded form. Notice that Sales is incorporated in the denominator of the first term, and in the numerator of the second term. When the two terms are multiplied together, Sales cancels out, leaving the original ROI formula.

$$\text{ROI} = \frac{\text{Operating income}}{\text{Sales}} \times \frac{\text{Sales}}{\text{Total assets}} = \frac{\text{Operating income}}{\text{Total assets}}$$

Why do managers rewrite the ROI formula this way? Because it helps them better understand how they can improve their ROI. The first term in the expanded equation is called the **profit margin**:

$$\text{Profit margin} = \frac{\text{Operating income}}{\text{Sales}}$$

The profit margin shows how much operating income the division earns on every $1.00 of sales so this term focuses on profitability. Let's calculate each division's sales margin:

$$\text{Landscaping Division's profit margin} = \left(\frac{\$450,000}{\$7,500,000}\right) = 6\%$$

$$\text{Design Division's profit margin} = \left(\frac{\$600,000}{\$10,000,000}\right) = 6\%$$

Both the Landscaping Division and the Design Division have a profit margin of 6%, meaning that both divisions earn a profit of $0.06 on every $1.00 of sales.

If both divisions have identical sales margins, then why do their ROIs differ (18% for Landscaping versus 15% for Design)? The answer is found in the second term of the expanded ROI equation, **capital turnover**:

$$\text{Capital turnover} = \frac{\text{Sales}}{\text{Total assets}}$$

Capital turnover shows how efficiently a division uses its assets to generate sales. Rather than focusing on profitability, capital turnover focuses on efficiency. Let's calculate each division's capital turnover:

$$\text{Landscaping Division's capital turnover} = \left(\frac{\$7,500,000}{\$2,500,000}\right) = 3$$

$$\text{Design Division's capital turnover} = \left(\frac{\$10,000,000}{\$4,000,000}\right) = 2.5$$

The Landscaping Division has a capital turnover of 3. This means that the Landscaping Division generates $3.00 of sales with every $1.00 of assets. The Design

Division's capital turnover is only 2.5. The Design Division generates only $2.50 of sales with every $1.00 of assets. The Landscaping Division uses its assets more efficiently in generating sales than the Design Division.

Let's put the two terms back together in the expanded ROI equation:

	Profit margin	×	Capital turnover	=	ROI
Landscaping Division:	6%	×	3	=	18%
Design Division:	6%	×	2.5	=	15%

As you can see, the expanded ROI equation gives management more insight into the division's ROI. Management can now see that both divisions are equally profitable on their sales (6%), but the Landscaping Division is doing a better job of generating sales with their assets than is the Design Division. Consequently, the Landscaping Division has a higher ROI.

If a manager is not satisfied with his division's capital turnover rate, how can he improve it? He might try to eliminate nonproductive assets—for example, by being more aggressive in collecting accounts receivables or decreasing inventory levels. He might decide to change retail-store layout to generate sales. For example, CVS successfully increased sales just by lowering shelves and changing the direction of the aisles.

What if management is not satisfied with the current profit margin? To increase the profit margin, management must increase the operating income earned on every dollar of sales. Management may cut product costs or selling and administrative costs, but it needs to be careful when trimming costs. Cutting costs in the short term can hurt long-term ROI. For example, sacrificing quality or cutting back on research and development could decrease costs in the short run, but may hurt long-term sales. The balanced scorecard helps management carefully consider the consequences of cost-cutting measures before acting on them.

ROI has one major drawback. Evaluating division managers based solely on ROI gives them an incentive to adopt *only* projects that will maintain or increase their current ROI. Let's say that top management has set a company-wide target ROI of 16%. Both divisions are considering investing in in-store video display equipment that shows customers how to use featured products. This equipment will increase sales because customers are more likely to buy the products when they see these infomercials. The equipment would cost each division $100,000 and is expected to provide each division with $17,000 of annual income. The *equipment's* ROI is:

$$\text{Equipment ROI} = \frac{\$17,000}{\$100,000} = 17\%$$

Upper management would want the divisions to invest in this equipment since the equipment will provide a 17% ROI, which is higher than the 16% target rate. But what will the managers of the divisions do? Because the Design Division currently has an ROI of 15%, the new equipment (with its 17% ROI) will *increase* the division's *overall* ROI. Therefore, the Design Division manager will buy the equipment. However, the Landscaping Division currently has an ROI of 18%. If the Landscaping Division invests in the equipment, its *overall* ROI will *decrease*. Therefore, the manager of the Landscaping Division will probably turn down the investment. In this case, goal congruence is *not* achieved—only one division will invest in equipment. Yet top management wants both divisions to invest in the equipment because the equipment return exceeds the 16% target ROI. Next, we discuss a performance measure that overcomes this problem with ROI.

Residual Income (RI)

Residual income (RI) is another commonly used KPI for evaluating an investment center's financial performance. Similar to ROI, RI considers both the division's operating income and its total assets. RI measures the division's profitability and the efficiency with which the division uses its assets. RI also incorporates another piece of information: top management's target rate of return (such as the 16% target return in the previous example). The target rate of return is the minimum acceptable rate of return that top management expects a division to earn with its assets.

RI compares the division's operating income with the minimum operating income expected by top management *given the size of the division's assets*. A positive RI means that the division's operating income exceeds top management's target rate of return. A negative RI means the division is not meeting the target rate of return. Let's look at the RI equation and then calculate the RI for both divisions using the 16% target rate of return from the previous example.

$$RI = \text{Operating income} - \text{Minimum acceptable income}$$

In this equation, the minimum acceptable income is defined as top management's target rate of return multiplied by the division's total assets. Thus,

$$RI = \text{Operating income} - (\text{Target rate of return} \times \text{Total assets})$$

$$\begin{aligned}\text{Landscaping Division RI} &= \$450{,}000 - (16\% \times \$2{,}500{,}000) \\ &= \$450{,}000 - \$400{,}000 \\ &= \$50{,}000\end{aligned}$$

The positive RI indicates that the Landscaping Division exceeded top management's 16% target return expectations. The RI calculation also confirms what we learned about the Landscaping Division's ROI. Recall that the Landscaping Division's ROI was 18%, which is higher than the targeted 16%.

Let's also calculate the RI for the Design Division:

$$\begin{aligned}\text{Design Division RI} &= \$600{,}000 - (16\% \times \$4{,}000{,}000) \\ &= \$600{,}000 - \$640{,}000 \\ &= (\$40{,}000)\end{aligned}$$

The Design Division's RI is negative. This means that the Design Division did not use its assets as effectively as top management expected. Recall that the Design Division's ROI of 15% fell short of the target rate of 16%.

Why would a company prefer to use RI over ROI for performance evaluation? The answer is that RI is more likely to lead to goal congruence than ROI. Let's once again consider the video display equipment that both divisions could buy. In both divisions, the equipment is expected to generate a 17% return. If the divisions are evaluated based on ROI, we learned that the Design Division will buy the equipment because it will increase the division's ROI. The Landscaping Division will probably not buy the equipment because it will lower the division's ROI.

However, if management evaluates divisions based on RI rather than ROI, what will the divisions do? The answer depends on whether the project yields a positive or negative RI. Recall that the equipment would cost each division $100,000 but will provide $17,000 of operating income each year. The RI provided by *just* the equipment would be:

$$\begin{aligned}\text{Equipment RI} &= \$17{,}000 - (\$100{,}000 \times 16\%) \\ &= \$17{,}000 - \$16{,}000 \\ &= \$1{,}000\end{aligned}$$

If purchased, this equipment will *improve* each division's current RI by $1,000. As a result, both divisions will be motivated to invest in the equipment. Goal congruence is achieved because both divisions will take the action that top management desires. That is, both divisions will invest in the equipment.

Another benefit of RI is that management may set different target returns for different divisions. For example, management might require a higher target rate of return from a division operating in a riskier business environment. If the design industry were riskier than the landscape industry, top management might decide to set a higher target return—perhaps 17%—for the Design Division.

Economic Value Added (EVA)

Economic Value Added (EVA), is a special type of RI calculation. Unlike the RI calculation we've just discussed, EVA looks at a division's RI through the eyes of the company's primary stakeholders: its investors and long-term creditors (such as bondholders). Since these stakeholders provide the company's capital, management often wishes to evaluate how efficiently a division is using its assets from these two stakeholders' viewpoints. EVA calculates RI for these stakeholders by specifically considering:

1. The income available to these stakeholders
2. The assets used to generate income for these stakeholders
3. The minimum rate of return required by these stakeholders (referred to as the **weighted average cost of capital**, or WACC)

Let's compare the EVA equation with the RI equation and then explain the differences in more detail:

$$RI = \text{Operating income} - (\text{Total assets} \times \text{Target rate of return})$$

$$EVA = \text{After-tax operating income} - [(\text{Total assets} - \text{Current liabilities}) \times \text{WACC\%}]$$

Both equations calculate whether any income was created by the division above and beyond expectations. They do this by comparing actual income with the minimum acceptable income. But note the differences in the EVA calculation:

1. The EVA calculation uses *after-tax operating income*, which is the income left over after subtracting income taxes. Why? Because the portion of income paid to the government is not available to investors and long-term creditors.

2. *Total assets is reduced by current liabilities.* Why? Because funds owed to short-term creditors, such as suppliers (accounts payable) and employees (wages payable), will be paid in the immediate future and will not be available for generating income in the long run. The division is not expected to earn a return for investors and long-term creditors on those funds that will soon be paid out to short-term creditors.

3. The *WACC* replaces management's target rate of return. Since EVA focuses on investors and creditors, it's *their* expected rate of return that should be used, not management's expected rate of return. The WACC, which represents the minimum rate of return expected by *investors and long-term creditors*, is based on company's cost of raising capital from both groups of stakeholders. The riskier the business, the higher the expected return. Detailed WACC computations are discussed in advanced accounting and finance courses.

In summary, EVA incorporates all the elements of RI from the perspective of investors and long-term creditors. Now that we've walked through the equation's components, let's calculate EVA for the Landscape and Design Divisions discussed earlier. We'll need the following additional information:

Effective income tax rate	30%
WACC	13%
Landscaping Division's current liabilities	$150,000
Design Division's current liabilities	$250,000

The 30% effective income tax rate means that the government takes 30% of the company's income, leaving only 70% to the company's stakeholders. Therefore, we calculate *after-tax operating income* by multiplying the division's operating income by 70%, or (100% − effective tax rate of 30%).

$$\text{EVA} = \text{After-tax operating income} - [(\text{Total assets} - \text{Current liabilities}) \times \text{WACC\%}]$$

Landscaping Division EVA	=	($450,000 × 70%)	−	[($2,500,000 − $150,000) × 13%]
	=	$315,000	−	($2,350,000 × 13%)
	=	$315,000	−	$305,500
	=	$9,500		

Design Division EVA	=	($600,000 × 70%)	−	[($4,000,000 − $250,000) × 13%]
	=	$420,000	−	($3,750,000 × 13%)
	=	$420,000	−	$487,500
	=	($67,500)		

These EVA calculations show that the Landscaping Division has generated income in excess of expectations for its investors and long-term debt-holders, whereas the Design Division has not.

Many firms, such as Coca-Cola, Quaker Oats, and J.C. Penney, measure the financial performance of their investment centers using EVA. EVA promotes goal congruence, just as RI does. Additionally, EVA looks at the income generated by the division in excess of expectations, solely from the perspective of investors and long-term creditors. Therefore, EVA specifically addresses the financial perspective of the balanced scorecard that asks, "How do we look to shareholders?"

Exhibit 25-9 summarizes the three performance measures and some of their advantages.

Limitations of Financial Performance Measures

We have just finished looking at three KPIs (ROI, RI, and EVA) commonly used to evaluate the financial performance of investment centers. As discussed in the following sections, all of these measures have drawbacks that management should keep in mind when evaluating the financial performance of investment centers.

Measurement Issues

The ROI, RI, and EVA calculations appear to be very straightforward; however, management must make some decisions before these calculations can be made. For

> **EXHIBIT 25-9** Three Investment Center Performance Measures: A Summary
>
> **ROI:**
>
> | Equation | $\text{ROI} = \dfrac{\text{Operating income}}{\text{Sales}} \times \dfrac{\text{Sales}}{\text{Total assets}} = \dfrac{\text{Operating income}}{\text{Total assets}}$ |
> |---|---|
> | Advantages | • The expanded equation provides management with additional information on profitability and efficiency
• Management can compare ROI across divisions and with other companies
• ROI is useful for resource allocation |
>
> **RI:**
>
> | Equation | RI = Operating income − (Total assets × Target rate of return) |
> |---|---|
> | Advantages | • Promotes goal congruence better than ROI
• Incorporates management's minimum required rate of return
• Management can use different target rates of return for divisions with different levels of risk |
>
> **EVA:**
>
> | Equation | EVA = (After-tax operating income) − [(Total assets − Current liabilities) × WACC%] |
> |---|---|
> | Advantages | • Considers income generated for investors and long-term creditors in excess of their expectations
• Promotes goal congruence |

example, all three equations use the term *total assets*. Recall that total assets is a balance sheet figure, which means that it is a snapshot at any given point in time. Because the total assets figure will be *different* at the beginning of the period and at the end of the period, most company's choose to use a simple average of the two figures in their ROI, RI, and EVA calculations.

Management must also decide if they really want to include *all* assets in the total asset figure. Many firms, such as Kohls and Aldi, are continually buying land on which to build future retail outlets. Until those stores are built and opened, the land (including any construction in progress) is a nonproductive asset, which is not adding to the company's operating income. Including nonproductive assets in the total asset figure will naturally drive down the ROI, RI, and EVA figures. Therefore, some firms will not include nonproductive assets in these calculations.

Another asset measurement issue is whether to use the gross book value of assets (the historical cost of the assets), or the net book value of assets (historical cost less accumulated depreciation). Many firms will use the net book value of assets because the figure is consistent with and easily pulled from the balance sheet. Because depreciation expense factors into the firm's operating income, the net book value concept is also consistent with the measurement of operating income. However, using the net book value of assets has a definite drawback. Over time, the net book value of assets decreases because accumulated depreciation continues to grow until the assets are fully depreciated. Therefore, ROI, RI, and EVA get *larger* over time *simply because of depreciation* rather than from actual improvements in operations. In addition, the rate of this depreciation effect will depend on the depreciation method used.

In general, calculating ROI based on the net book value of assets gives managers incentive to continue using old, outdated equipment because its low net book value results in a higher ROI. However, top management may want the division to invest in new technology to create operational efficiency (internal business perspective of the balanced scorecard) or to enhance its information systems (learning and growth perspective). The long-term effects of using outdated equipment may be devastating, as competitors use new technology to produce and sell at lower cost. Thus, to create goal congruence, some firms prefer calculating ROI based on the gross book value of assets. The same general rule holds true for RI and EVA calculations: All else being equal, using net book value will increase RI and EVA over time.

Short-Term Focus

One serious drawback of financial performance measures is their short-term focus. Companies usually prepare performance reports and calculate ROI, RI, and EVA figures over a one-year time frame or less. If upper management uses a short time frame, division managers have an incentive to take actions that will lead to an immediate increase in these measures, even if such actions may not be in the company's long-term interest (such as cutting back on R&D or advertising). On the other hand, some potentially positive actions considered by subunit managers may take longer than one year to generate income at the targeted level. Many **product life cycles** start slow, even incurring losses in the early stages, before generating profit. If managers are measured on short-term financial performance only, they may not introduce new products because they are not willing to wait several years for the positive effect to show up in their financial performance measures.

As a potential remedy, management can measure financial performance using a longer time horizon, such as three to five years. Extending the time frame gives subunit managers the incentive to think long term rather than short term and make decisions that will positively impact the company over the next several years.

The limitations of financial performance measures confirm the importance of the balanced scorecard. The deficiencies of financial measures can be overcome by taking a broader view of performance—including KPIs from all four balanced scorecard perspectives rather than concentrating on only the financial measures.

Decision Guidelines

When managers at UPS developed the financial perspective of their balanced scorecard, they had to make decisions such as these.

Decision	Guidelines
How should the financial section of the balanced scorecard be measured for cost, revenue, and profit centers?	Responsibility accounting performance reports measure the financial performance of cost, revenue, and profit centers. These reports typically highlight the variances between budgeted and actual performance.
How should the financial section of the balanced scorecard be measured for investment centers?	Investment centers require measures that take into account the division's operating income *and* the division's assets. Typical measures include: • Return on investment (ROI) • Residual income (RI) • Economic value added (EVA)
How is ROI computed and interpreted?	**ROI = Operating income ÷ Total assets** ROI measures the amount of income earned by a division relative to the size of its assets. The higher, the better.

Can managers learn more by writing the ROI formula in its expanded form?	In its expanded form, ROI is written as:
	ROI = Profit margin × Capital turnover
	where,
	    Profit margin = Operating income ÷ Sales
	    Capital turnover = Sales ÷ Total assets
	Profit margin focuses on profitability (the amount of income earned on every dollar of sales) while capital turnover focuses on efficiency (the amount of sales generated with every dollar of assets).

How is RI computed and interpreted?	**RI = Operating income − (Target rate of return × Total assets)** If RI is positive, the division is earning income at a rate that exceeds management's minimum expectations.
How does EVA differ from RI?	EVA is a special type of RI calculation that focuses on the income (in excess of expectations) created by the division for two specific stakeholders: investors and long-term creditors.
When calculating ROI, RI, or EVA, are there any measurement issues of concern?	If the net book value of assets is used to measure total assets, ROI, RI, and EVA will "artificially" rise over time due to the depreciation of the assets. Using gross book value to measure total assets eliminates this measurement issue. Many firms use the average balance of total assets, rather than the beginning or ending balance of assets, when they calculate ROI, RI, and EVA.

Summary Problem 2

Assume House and Garden Depot expects each division to earn a 16% target rate of return. House and Garden Depot's weighted average cost of capital (WACC) is 13%, and its effective tax rate is 30%. Assume the company's original Retail Division had the following results last year (in millions of dollars):

Operating income	$ 1,450
Total assets	16,100
Current liabilities	3,600
Sales	26,500

Requirements

1. Compute the Retail Division's profit margin, capital turnover, and ROI. Round your results to three decimal places. Interpret the results in relation to the Landscaping and Design Divisions discussed in the chapter.
2. Compute and interpret the Retail Division's RI.
3. Compute the Retail Division's EVA. What does this tell you?
4. What can you conclude based on all three financial performance KPIs?

Solution

Requirement 1

$$
\begin{aligned}
\text{ROI} &= \text{Profit margin} & \times & \quad \text{Capital turnover} \\
&= (\text{Operating income} \div \text{Sales}) & \times & \quad (\text{Sales} \div \text{Total assets}) \\
&= (\$1,450 \div \$26,500) & \times & \quad (\$26,500 \div \$16,100) \\
&= .055 & \times & \quad 1.646 \\
&= .091
\end{aligned}
$$

The original Retail Division is far from meeting top management's expectations. Its ROI is only 9.1%. The profit margin (5.5%) is slightly lower than the Landscaping and Design Divisions (6% each), but the capital turnover (1.646) is much lower than the other divisions (3.0 and 2.5). This means that the original Retail Division is not generating sales from its assets as efficiently as the Landscaping and Design Divisions. Division management needs to consider ways to increase the efficiency with which they use divisional assets.

Requirement 2

$$
\begin{aligned}
\text{RI} &= \text{Operating income} & - & \quad (\text{Target rate of return} \times \text{Total assets}) \\
&= \$1,450 & - & \quad (16\% \times \$16,100) \\
&= \$1,450 & - & \quad \$2,576 \\
&= (\$1,126)
\end{aligned}
$$

The negative RI confirms the ROI results: The division is not meeting management's target rate of return.

Requirement 3

$$\begin{aligned}
\text{EVA} &= \text{After-tax operating income} - [(\text{Total assets} - \text{Current liabilities}) \times \text{WACC\%}] \\
&= (\$1,450 \times 70\%) - [(\$16,100 - \$3,600) \times 13\%] \\
&= \$1,015 - (\$12,500 \times 13\%) \\
&= \$1,015 - \$1,625 \\
&= (\$610)
\end{aligned}$$

The negative EVA means that the division is not generating income for investors and long-term creditors at the rate desired by these stakeholders.

Requirement 4

All three investment center performance measures (ROI, RI, and EVA) point to the same conclusion: The original Retail Division is not meeting financial expectations. Either top management and stakeholders' expectations are unrealistic or the division is not *currently* performing up to par. Recall, however, that financial performance measures tend to be lag indicators—measuring the results of decisions made in the past. The division's managers may currently be implementing new initiatives to improve the division's future profitability. Lead indicators should be used to project whether such initiatives are pointing the company in the right direction.

Appendix 25A

Allocating Service Department Costs

How do companies charge subunits for their use of service departments? For example, suppose House and Garden Depot incurs $30,000 per month to operate the North Florida Region's centralized payroll department. To simplify the illustration, let's assume the region only has three stores: Tallahassee, Gainesville, and Jacksonville. How should the company split, or allocate, the $30,000 cost among the three stores? Splitting the cost equally—charging each store $10,000—may not be fair, especially if the three units don't use the services equally.

Ideally, the company should allocate the $30,000 based on each subunit's use of centralized payroll services. The company should use the primary activity that drives the cost of central payroll services as the allocation base. As you may recall from Chapter 19, companies identify cost drivers when they implement ABC. Thus, a company that has already implemented ABC should know what cost drivers would be suitable for allocating service department charges. For example, payroll processing cost may be driven by the number of employee payroll checks or direct deposits processed. The cost driver chosen for allocating the $30,000 might be the "number of employees" employed by each store, as shown in the following table.

Subunits Sharing Central Payroll Services	Number of Employees (allocation base)	Percentage of Total Employees	Service Department Charge ($30,000 × %)
Tallahassee	100	25%	$ 7,500
Gainesville	140	35%	10,500
Jacksonville	160	40%	12,000
Total	400	100%	$30,000

Most companies will use some type of usage related cost driver to allocate service department costs. The following table lists additional centralized services and common allocation bases.

Centralized Service Departments	Typical Allocation Base
Human resources	Number of employees
Legal	Number of hours spent on legal matters
Travel	Number of business trips booked

However, when usage data are not available or are too costly to collect, companies will resort to allocating service department costs based on each subunit's "ability to bear" the cost. In such cases, companies allocate the service department cost based on the relative amount of revenue or operating income each subunit generates. The following table illustrates this type of allocation.

Subunits Sharing Centralized Payroll Services	Unit Operating Income Before Service Department Charges	Percentage of Total Operating Income	Service Department Charge ($30,000 × %)
Tallahassee	$ 320,000	20%	$ 6,000
Gainesville	480,000	30%	9,000
Jacksonville	800,000	50%	15,000
Total	$1,600,000	100%	$30,000

This type of allocation is like a tax: the higher the subunit's income, the higher the charge.

Even usage-related allocation systems have limitations. What if the cost of running the service department is fixed rather than variable? Then, much of the cost cannot be attributed to a specific cost driver. In our payroll example, suppose $20,000 of the total $30,000 is straight-line depreciation on the equipment and software. Should the company still use the number of employees to allocate the entire $30,000 of cost? As another example, suppose the Tallahassee store downsizes and its relative percentage of employees drops from 25% to 10%, while the number of employees in each of the other two stores stays constant. If that happens, the Gainesville and Jacksonville stores will be charged higher costs even though they did nothing to cause an increase. These are just two examples of how the best allocation systems are still subject to inherent flaws. More complex service department allocation systems, such as the step-down and reciprocal methods, are discussed in more advanced accounting texts.

Review: Performance Evaluation and the Balanced Scorecard

Accounting Vocabulary

Balanced Scorecard
Measures that recognize management must consider both financial performance measures and operational performance measures when judging the performance of a company and its subunits.

Benchmarking
Comparing actual performance to similar companies in the same industry, to other divisions, or to world-class standards.

Capital Turnover
The amount of sales revenue generated for every dollar of invested assets; a component of the ROI calculation, computed as sales divided by total assets.

Centralized Companies
Companies in which all major planning and operating decisions are made by top management.

Cost Center
A subunit responsible only for controlling costs.

Decentralized Companies
Companies that are segmented into smaller operating units; unit managers make planning and operating decisions for their unit.

Economic Value Added (EVA)
A residual income measure calculating the amount of income generated by the company or its divisions in excess of stockholders and long-term creditors expectation s.

Goal Congruence
Aligning the goals of subunit managers with the goals of top management.

Investment Center
A subunit responsible for generating profits and efficiently managing the division's invested capital (assets).

Key Performance Indicator (KPI)
Summary performance measures that help managers assess whether the company is achieving its long-term and short-term goals.

Lag Indicators
Performance measures that indicate past performance.

Lead Indicators
Performance measures that forecast future performance.

Management by Exception
Directs management's attention to important differences between actual and budgeted amounts.

Product Life Cycle
The length of time between a product's initial development and its discontinuance in the market.

Profit Center
A subunit responsible for generating revenue and controlling costs.

Profit Margin
The amount of income earned on every dollar of sales; a component of the ROI calculation, computed as operating income divided by sales.

Residual Income (RI)
A measure of profitability and efficiency, computed as the excess of actual income over a specified minimum acceptable income.

Responsibility Center
A part or subunit of an organization whose manager is accountable for specific activities.

Return on Investment (ROI)
A measure of profitability and efficiency, computed as operating income divided by total assets.

Revenue Center
A subunit responsible only for generating revenue.

Weighted Average Cost of Capital (WACC)
The company's cost of capital; the target return used in EVA calculations to denote the return expected by stockholders and long-term creditors.

Quick Check

1. Which is *not* one of the potential advantages of decentralization?
    a. improves customer relations
    b. increases goal congruence
    c. improves motivation and retention
    d. supports use of expert knowledge

2. The Quaker Foods division of PepsiCo is most likely treated as a:
    a. cost center
    b. revenue center
    c. profit center
    d. investment center

3. Decentralization is often based on all the following except?
    a. geographic region
    b. product line
    c. revenue size
    d. business function

4. Manufacturing yield rate (number of units produced per unit of time) would be a typical measure for which of the following balanced scorecard perspectives:
    a. financial
    b. customer
    c. internal business
    d. learning and growth

5. Which of the following balanced scorecard perspectives essentially asks, "Can we continue to improve and create value?"
    a. financial
    b. customer
    c. internal business
    d. learning and growth

6. Assume the Residential Division of Kohler Faucets had the following results last year (in thousands of dollars):

Sales	$4,250,000
Operating income	850,000
Total assets	5,000,000
Current liabilities	250,000

Further assume that management's target rate of return is 12%, and the weighted average cost of capital is 10%. What is the division's profit margin?
    a. 20%
    b. 85%
    c. 17%
    d. 5%

7. Refer to the Kohler data in Question 6. What is the division's capital turnover?
   a. 20%
   b. 17%
   c. 85%
   d. 117%

8. Refer to the Kohler data in Question 6. What is the division's ROI?
   a. 17%
   b. 5.88%
   c. 17.89%
   d. 85%

9. Refer to the Kohler data in Question 6. What is the division's RI?
   a. $375,000
   b. $250,000
   c. $350,000
   d. $280,000

10. The performance evaluation of a cost center is typically based on its:
    a. sales volume variance
    b. ROI
    c. flexible budget variance
    d. static budget variance

Answers are given after Apply Your Knowledge (p. 1311).

Assess Your Progress

Short Exercises

1 Explain why and how companies decentralize

S25-1 Explain why companies decentralize. Describe some typical methods of decentralization.

1 Explain why and how companies decentralize

S25-2 Most decentralized subunits can be described as one of four different types of responsibility centers. List the four most common types of responsibility centers and describe their responsibilities.

1 Explain why and how companies decentralize

S25-3 Each of the following managers has been given certain decision-making authority. Classify each of the following managers according to the type of responsibility center they manage.
1. Manager of Holiday Inn's central reservation office
2. Managers of various corporate-owned Holiday Inn locations
3. Manager of the Holiday Inn corporate division
4. Manager of the housekeeping department at a Holiday Inn
5. Manager of the Holiday Inn Express corporate division
6. Manager of the complimentary breakfast buffet at a Holiday Inn Express

2 Explain why companies use performance evaluation systems

S25-4 Well-designed performance evaluation systems accomplish many goals. (See pp. 1270–1271). State which goal is being achieved by the following actions:
a. Comparing targets to actual results
b. Providing subunit managers with performance targets
c. Comparing actual results with industry standards
d. Providing bonuses to subunit managers who achieve performance targets
e. Aligning subunit performance targets with company strategy
f. Comparing actual results to the results of competitors
g. Taking corrective actions
h. Using the adage, "you get what you measure," when designing the performance evaluation system

3 Describe the balanced scorecard and identify key performance indicators for each perspective

S25-5 Classify each of the following key performance indicators according to the balanced scorecard perspective it addresses. Choose from financial perspective, customer perspective, internal business perspective, or learning and growth perspective.
a. Number of employee suggestions implemented
b. Revenue growth
c. Number of on-time deliveries
d. Percentage of sales force with access to real-time inventory levels

continued . . .

e. Customer satisfaction ratings
f. Number of defects found during manufacturing
g. Number of warranty claims
h. ROI
i. Variable cost per unit
j. Percentage of market share
k. Number of hours of employee training
l. Number of new products developed
m. Yield rate (number of units produced per hour)
n. Average repair time
o. Employee satisfaction
p. Number of repeat customers

S25-6 Describe management by exception and how it is used in the evaluation of cost, revenue, and profit centers.

S25-7 Which of the following corporate divisions is more profitable? Explain.

	Domestic	International
Operating income	$6 million	$10 million
Total assets	$20 million	$35 million

S25-8 Racer Sports Company makes snowboards, downhill skis, cross-country skis, skateboards, surfboards, and in-line skates. The company has found it beneficial to split operations into two divisions based on the climate required for the sport: snow sports and non-snow sports. The following divisional information is available for the past year:

	Sales	Operating Income	Total Assets	Current Liabilities
Snow sports	$5,000,000	$ 900,000	$4,000,000	$350,000
Non-snow sports	8,000,000	1,440,000	6,000,000	600,000

Racer's management has specified a target 15% rate of return. The company's weighted average cost of capital (WACC) is 12% and its effective tax rate is 35%.

Requirements
1. Calculate each division's ROI.
2. Top management has extra funds to invest. Which division will most likely receive those funds? Why?
3. Can you explain why one division's ROI is higher? How could management gain more insight?

5 Use ROI, RI, and EVA to evaluate investment centers

S25-9 Refer to the information about Racer Sports in S25-8. Compute each division's profit margin. Interpret your results.

5 Use ROI, RI, and EVA to evaluate investment centers

S25-10 Refer to the information about Racer Sports in S25-8.
1. Compute each division's capital turnover (round to two decimal places). Interpret your results.
2. Use your answers to Question 1, along with your answers to S25-9, to recalculate ROI using the expanded formula. Do your answers agree with your ROI calculations in S25-8?

5 Use ROI, RI, and EVA to evaluate investment centers

S25-11 Refer to the information about Racer Sports in S25-8. Compute each division's RI. Interpret your results. Are your results consistent with your answers to S25-8?

5 Use ROI, RI, and EVA to evaluate investment centers

S25-12 Refer to the information about Racer Sports in S25-8. Compute each division's EVA. Interpret your results.

Exercises

1 Explain why and how companies decentralize

E25-13 Grandma Jones Cookie Company sells homemade cookies made with organic ingredients. Her sales are strictly Web-based. The business is taking off more than Grandma Jones ever expected, with orders coming from across the country from both consumers and corporate event planners. Even by employing a full-time baker and a Web designer, Grandma Jones can no longer handle the business on her own. She wants your advice on whether she should decentralize and, if so, how she should do it. Explain some of the advantages and disadvantages of decentralization and offer her three ways she might decentralize her company.

2 Explain why companies use performance evaluation systems

E25-14 Explain the difference between lag and lead indicators. Are financial performance measures typically referred to as lag or lead indicators? Explain why, using L.L.Bean (a catalog clothing merchandiser) as an example. Are operational measures (such as customer satisfaction ratings, defect rate, number of on-time deliveries, and so forth) typically referred to as lag or lead indicators? Explain why, using L.L.Bean as an example.

2 Explain why companies use performance evaluation systems

E25-15 Well-designed performance evaluation systems accomplish many goals. Describe the potential benefits performance evaluation systems offer.

3 Describe the balanced scorecard and identify key performance indicators for each perspective

E25-16 Sketch a diagram depicting each of the four balanced scorecard perspectives and how they are linked together. Expand the diagram to include the primary factors underlying each of the perspectives.

E25-17 Imagine you are part of the top management team at Racer Sports Company (see Short Exercise 25-8). Using your answer to E25-16, develop two key performance indicators for each factor shown on your diagram.

3 Describe the balanced scorecard and identify key performance indicators for each perspective

E25-18 Classify each of the following key performance indicators according to the balanced scorecard perspective it addresses. Choose from financial perspective, customer perspective, internal business perspective, or learning and growth perspective.

a. Number of customer complaints
b. Number of information system upgrades completed
c. EVA
d. New product development time
e. Employee turnover rate
f. Percentage of products with online help manuals
g. Customer retention
h. Percentage of compensation based on performance
i. Percentage of orders filled each week
j. Gross margin growth
k. Number of new patents
l. Employee satisfaction ratings
m. Manufacturing cycle time (average length of production process)
n. Earnings growth
o. Average machine setup time
p. Number of new customers
q. Employee promotion rate
r. Cash flow from operations
s. Customer satisfaction ratings
t. Machine downtime
u. Finished products per day per employee
v. Percentage of employees with access to upgraded system
w. Wait time per order prior to start of production

4 Use performance reports to evaluate cost, revenue, and profit centers

E25-19 One subunit of Racer Sports Company had the following financial results last month:

Racer—Subunit X	Actual	Flexible Budget	Flexible Budget Variance (U or F)	% Variance* (U of F)
Direct materials	$28,100	$26,000		
Direct labor	13,500	14,000		
Indirect labor	26,000	23,000		
Utilities	12,000	11,000		
Depreciation	25,000	25,000		
Repairs and maintenance	4,300	5,000		
Total	$108,900	$104,000		

continued . . .

Requirements

1. Complete the performance evaluation report for this subunit (round to four decimals).
2. Based on the data presented, what type of responsibility center is this subunit?
3. Which items should be investigated if part of management's decision criteria is to investigate all variances exceeding $3,000 or 10%?
4. Should only unfavorable variances be investigated? Explain.

[4] Use performance reports to evaluate cost, revenue, and profit centers

E25-20 The accountant for a subunit of Racer Sports Company went on vacation before completing the subunit's monthly performance report. This is as far as she got:

Racer—Subunit X Revenue by Product	Actual	Flexible Budget Variance	Flexible Budget	Sales Volume Variance	Static (Master) Budget
Downhill Model RI	$ 326,000			$20,000 (F)	$ 300,000
Downhill Model RII	155,000		$165,000		150,000
Cross-country Model EXI	283,000	$2,000 (U)	285,000		300,000
Cross-country Model EXII	252,000		245,000	17,500 (U)	262,500
Snowboard Model LXI	425,000	5,000 (F)			400,000
Total	$1,441,000				$1,412,500

Requirements

1. Complete the performance evaluation report for this subunit.
2. Based on the data presented what type of responsibility center is this subunit?
3. Which items should be investigated if part of management's decision criteria is to investigate all variances exceeding $15,000? Interpret your results (What might be the cause of these variances? What impact might these variances have on company inventory levels and operations?).

[5] Use ROI, RI, and EVA to evaluate investment centers

E25-21 Zoro, a national manufacturer of lawn-mowing and snowblowing equipment, segments its business according to customer type: professional and residential. The following divisional information was available for the past year (in thousands of dollars):

	Sales	Operating Income	Total Assets	Current Liabilities
Residential	$ 555,000	$ 62,000	$188,000	$ 68,000
Professional	1,030,000	173,000	420,000	150,000

continued . . .

Management has a 25% target rate of return for each division. Zoro's weighted average cost of capital is 15% and its effective tax rate is 30%.

Requirements

1. Calculate each division's ROI. Round all of your answers to four decimal places.
2. Calculate each division's profit margin. Interpret your results.
3. Calculate each division's capital turnover. Interpret your results.
4. Use the expanded ROI formula to confirm your results from Requirement 1. What can you conclude?

E25-22 Refer to the data about Zoro in E25-21.

1. Calculate each division's RI. Interpret your results.
2. Calculate each division's EVA. Interpret your results.
3. Describe the conceptual and computational similarities and differences between RI and EVA.

Problems (Problem Set A)

P25-23A One subunit of Racer Sports Company had the following financial results last month:

Racer—Subunit X	Flexible Budget	Actual	Flexible Budget Variance (U or F)	Percentage Variance*
Sales	$450,000	$480,000		
Cost of goods sold	250,000	260,000		
Gross margin	$200,000	$220,000		
Operating expenses	50,000	53,000		
Operating income before service department charges	$150,000	$167,000		
Service department charges (allocated)	(25,000)	(35,000)		
Operating income	$125,000	$132,000		

*Flexible budget variance ÷ Flexible budget.

Requirements

1. Complete the performance evaluation report for this subunit (round to three decimal places).
2. Based on the data presented and your knowledge of the company (see S25-8), what type of responsibility center is this subunit?

continued . . .

3. Which items should be investigated if part of management's decision criteria is to investigate all variances equal to or exceeding $10,000 *and* exceeding 10% (both criteria must be met)?
4. Should only unfavorable variances be investigated? Explain.
5. Is it possible that the variances are due to a higher-than-expected sales volume? Explain.
6. Do you think management will place equal weight on each of the $10,000 variances? Explain.
7. Which balanced scorecard perspective is being addressed through this performance report? In your opinion, is this performance report a lead or lag indicator? Explain.
8. Give one key performance indicator for the three other balanced scorecard perspectives. Make sure to indicate which perspective is being addressed by the indicators you list. Are they lead or lag indicators? Explain.

P25-24A Sherwin-Wilkens is a national paint manufacturer and retailer. The company is segmented into five divisions: paint stores (branded retail locations), consumer (paint sold through stores like Sears, Home Depot, and Lowe's), automotive (sales to auto manufacturers), international, and administration. The following is selected divisional information for their two largest divisions: paint stores and consumer (in thousands of dollars).

	Sales	Operating Income	Total Assets	Current Liabilities
Paint stores	$3,980,000	$480,000	$1,400,000	$350,000
Consumer	1,295,000	190,000	1,595,000	600,000

Management has specified a 20% target rate of return. The company's weighted average cost of capital is 15%. The company's effective tax rate is 32%.

Requirements
1. Calculate each division's ROI. Round calculations to four decimal places.
2. Calculate each division's profit margin. Interpret your results.
3. Calculate each division's capital turnover. Interpret your results.
4. Use the expanded ROI formula to confirm your results from Requirement 1. Interpret your results.
5. Calculate each division's RI. Interpret your results and offer recommendation for any division with negative RI.
6. Calculate each division's EVA. Interpret your results.
7. Describe the conceptual and computational similarities and differences between RI and EVA.
8. Total asset data was provided in this problem. If you were to gather this information from an annual report, how would you measure

continued . . .

total assets? Describe your measurement choices and some of the pros and cons of those choices.

9. Describe some of the factors that management considers when setting their minimum target rate of return.
10. Explain why some firms prefer to use RI rather than ROI for performance measurement.
11. Explain why budget versus actual performance reports are insufficient for evaluating the performance of investment centers.

Use ROI, RI, and EVA to evaluate investment centers

P25-25A PepsiCo segments its company into four distinct divisions. The net revenues, operating profit, and total assets for these divisions are disclosed in the footnotes to PepsiCo's consolidated financial statements.

Requirements

1. Use the following steps to find the divisional data in PepsiCo's 2004 annual report:
   a. Go to the PepsiCo.com Web site.
   b. Go to the "investors" link.
   c. Go to the "annual reports" link.
   d. Click on the 2004 annual report.
   e. Look under "Notes to the Consolidated Financial Statements, Note 1—Basis of Presentation and Our Divisions."
2. What are Pepsi's four business divisions? Make a table listing each division, its net revenues, operating profit, and total assets.
3. Use the data you collected in Requirement 2 to calculate each division's profit margin. Interpret your results.
4. Use the data you collected in Requirement 2 to calculate each division's capital turnover. Interpret your results.
5. Use the data you collected in Requirement 2 to calculate each division's ROI. Interpret your results.
6. Can you calculate RI and/or EVA using the data presented? Why or why not?

Problems (Problem Set B)

1. Explain why and how companies decentralize
2. Explain why companies use performance evaluation systems
3. Describe the balanced scorecard and identify key performance indicators for each perspective
4. Use performance reports to evaluate cost, revenue, and profit centers

P25-26B Zoro is a national manufacturer of lawn-mowing and snowblowing equipment. One subunit of Zoro had the following financial results last month:

Zoro—Subunit X	Flexible Budget	Actual	Flexible Budget Variance (U or F)	Percentage Variance*
Sales	$520,000	$500,000		
Cost of goods sold	400,000	385,000		
Gross margin	$120,000	$115,000		
Operating expenses	30,000	22,000		
Operating income before service department charges	$90,000	$93,000		
Service department charges (allocated)	(15,000)	(30,000)		
Operating income	$75,000	$63,000		

*Flexible budget variance ÷ Flexible budget.

Requirements

1. Complete the performance evaluation report for the subunit (round to three decimal places).
2. Based on the data presented, what type of responsibility center is this subunit?
3. Which items should be investigated if part of management's decision criteria is to investigate all variances equal to or exceeding $5,000 *and* exceeding 10% (both criteria must be met)?
4. Should only unfavorable variances be investigated? Explain.
5. Is it possible that the variances are due to a higher-than-expected sales volume? Explain.
6. Will management place equal weight on each of the $15,000 variances? Explain.
7. Which balanced scorecard perspective is being addressed through this performance report? In your opinion, is this performance report a lead or lag indicator? Explain.
8. List one key performance indicator for the three other balanced scorecard perspectives. Make sure to indicate which perspective is being addressed by the indicators you list. Are they lead or lag indicators? Explain.

5 Use ROI, RI, and EVA to evaluate investment centers

P25-27B CVZ operates a national drugstore chain. The company is segmented into two divisions: retail pharmacy and PBM (pharmaceutical benefit management). The following is selected divisional information (in million of dollars).

	Sales	Operating Income	Total Assets	Current Liabilities
Retail	$29,730	$1,320	$13,120	$4,460
PBM	1,965	135	1,430	485

Management has specified a 10% target rate of return. The company's weighted average cost of capital is 9%. The company's effective tax rate is 32%.

Requirements
1. Calculate each division's ROI.
2. Calculate each division's profit margin. Interpret your results.
3. Calculated each division's capital turnover. Interpret your results.
4. Use the expanded ROI formula to confirm your results from Requirement 1.
5. Calculate each division's RI. Interpret your results.
6. Calculate each division's EVA. Interpret your results.
7. Describe the conceptual similarities and differences between RI and EVA.
8. Total asset data was provided for this problem. If you were to gather this information from an annual report, how would you measure total assets? Describe your measurement choices and some of the pros and cons of those choices.
9. Describe some of the factors that management considers when setting their minimum rate of return.
10. Explain why some firms prefer to use RI rather than ROI for performance measurement.
11. Explain why budget versus actual performance reports are insufficient for evaluating the performance of investment centers.

5 Use ROI, RI, and EVA to evaluate investment centers

P25-28B Coca-Cola segments its company into seven operating segments, or divisions. Six of the seven are strategic business units. The sixth segment is "corporate." The net operating revenues, operating income, and identifiable operating assets for these divisions are disclosed in the footnotes to Coca-Cola's consolidated financial statements.

Requirements

1. Use the following steps to find the divisional data in Coca-Cola's 2005 annual report:
   a. Go to the Coca-Cola Web site.
   b. Go to the "Coca-Cola Company" link.
   c. Go to the "investors" link.
   d. Go to the "financial information" link.
   e. Go to the "annual reports" link.
   f. Click on the 2005 annual report on Form 10K.
   g. Look under "Notes to the Consolidated Financial Statements, Note 20 (Operating Segments)."

2. What are Coca-Cola's five operating segments (other than corporate)? Make a table listing each operating segment, its net operating revenues, operating income, and identifiable operating assets.

3. Use the data you collected in Requirement 2 to calculate each division's profit margin. Interpret your results.

4. Use the data you collected in Requirement 2 to calculate each division's capital turnover. Interpret your results.

5. Use the data you collected in Requirement 2 to calculate each division's ROI. Interpret your results.

6. Can you calculate RI and/or EVA using the data presented? Why or why not?

Apply Your Knowledge

Decision Case

Case 25-29. Colgate-Palmolive operates two product segments. Using the company Web site, locate segment information for 2004 in the company's 2004 annual report. (*Hint:* Look under investor relations on the company Web site.)

Requirements

1. What are the two segments? Gather data about each segment's net sales, operating income, and identifiable assets.

2. Calculate ROI for each segment.

3. Which segment has the highest ROI? Explain why.

4. If you were on the top management team and could allocate extra funds to only one division, which division would you choose? Why?

Quick Check Answers

1. *b* 2. *d* 3. *c* 4. *c* 5. *d* 6. *a* 7. *c* 8. *a* 9. *b* 10. *c*

For Internet Exercises, Excel in Practice, and additional online activities, go to this book's Web site at www.prenhall.com/bamber.

Appendix A

2 0 0 5

ANNUAL REPORT

REPORT OF ERNST & YOUNG LLP
INDEPENDENT REGISTERED PUBLIC ACCOUNTING FIRM

The Board of Directors and Stockholders
Amazon.com, Inc.

We have audited the accompanying consolidated balance sheets of Amazon.com, Inc. as of December 31, 2005 and 2004, and the related consolidated statements of operations, stockholders' equity (deficit), and cash flows for each of the three years in the period ended December 31, 2005. Our audits also included the financial statement schedule listed in the Index at Item 15(a)(2). These financial statements and schedule are the responsibility of the Company's management. Our responsibility is to express an opinion on these financial statements and schedule based on our audits.

We conducted our audits in accordance with the standards of the Public Company Accounting Oversight Board (United States). Those standards require that we plan and perform the audit to obtain reasonable assurance about whether the financial statements are free of material misstatement. An audit includes examining, on a test basis, evidence supporting the amounts and disclosures in the financial statements. An audit also includes assessing the accounting principles used and significant estimates made by management, as well as evaluating the overall financial statement presentation. We believe that our audits provide a reasonable basis for our opinion.

In our opinion, the financial statements referred to above present fairly, in all material respects, the consolidated financial position of Amazon.com, Inc. at December 31, 2005 and 2004, and the consolidated results of its operations and its cash flows for each of the three years in the period ended December 31, 2005, in conformity with U.S. generally accepted accounting principles. Also, in our opinion, the related financial statement schedule, when considered in relation to the basic financial statements taken as a whole, presents fairly in all material respects the information set forth therein.

As discussed in Note 1 to the consolidated financial statements, the Company adopted Statement of Financial Accounting Standards No. 123 (revised 2004), Share-Based Payment, effective January 1, 2005.

We also have audited, in accordance with the standards of the Public Company Accounting Oversight Board (United States), the effectiveness of Amazon.com, Inc.'s internal control over financial reporting as of December 31, 2005, based on criteria established in Internal Control-Integrated Framework issued by the Committee of Sponsoring Organizations of the Treadway Commission and our report dated February 16, 2006 expressed an unqualified opinion thereon.

/s/ ERNST & YOUNG LLP

Seattle, Washington
February 16, 2006

AMAZON.COM, INC.
CONSOLIDATED STATEMENTS OF CASH FLOWS
(in millions)

	Year Ended December 31,		
	2005	2004	2003
CASH AND CASH EQUIVALENTS, BEGINNING OF PERIOD	$ 1,303	$ 1,102	$ 738
OPERATING ACTIVITIES:			
Net income	359	588	35
Adjustments to reconcile net income to net cash provided by operating activities:			
Depreciation of fixed assets, including internal-use software and website development, and other amortization	121	76	76
Stock-based compensation	87	58	88
Other operating expense (income)	7	(8)	3
Gains on sales of marketable securities, net	(1)	(1)	(10)
Remeasurements and other	(42)	1	130
Non-cash interest expense and other	5	5	13
Deferred income taxes	70	(257)	1
Cumulative effect of change in accounting principle	(26)	—	—
Changes in operating assets and liabilities:			
Inventories	(104)	(169)	(77)
Accounts receivable, net and other current assets	(84)	(2)	2
Accounts payable	274	286	168
Accrued expenses and other current liabilities	60	(14)	(26)
Additions to unearned revenue	156	110	102
Amortization of previously unearned revenue	(149)	(107)	(112)
Net cash provided by operating activities	733	566	393
INVESTING ACTIVITIES:			
Purchases of fixed assets, including internal-use software and website development	(204)	(89)	(46)
Acquisitions, net of cash acquired	(24)	(71)	—
Sales and maturities of marketable securities and other investments	836	1,427	813
Purchases of marketable securities	(1,386)	(1,584)	(536)
Proceeds from sale of subsidiary	—	—	5
Net cash (used in) provided by investing activities	(778)	(317)	236
FINANCING ACTIVITIES:			
Proceeds from exercises of stock options and other	66	60	163
Proceeds from long-term debt and other	11	—	—
Repayments of long-term debt and capital lease obligations	(270)	(157)	(495)
Net cash used in financing activities	(193)	(97)	(332)
Foreign-currency effect on cash and cash equivalents	(52)	49	67
Net (decrease) increase in cash and cash equivalents	(290)	201	364
CASH AND CASH EQUIVALENTS, END OF PERIOD	$ 1,013	$ 1,303	$ 1,102
SUPPLEMENTAL CASH FLOW INFORMATION:			
Cash paid for interest	$ 105	$ 108	$ 120
Cash paid for income taxes	12	4	2

See accompanying notes to consolidated financial statements.

AMAZON.COM, INC.
CONSOLIDATED STATEMENTS OF OPERATIONS
(in millions, except per share data)

	Year Ended December 31,		
	2005	2004	2003
Net sales	$8,490	$6,921	$5,264
Cost of sales	6,451	5,319	4,007
Gross profit	2,039	1,602	1,257
Operating expenses (1):			
Fulfillment	745	601	495
Marketing	198	162	128
Technology and content	451	283	257
General and administrative	166	124	104
Other operating expense (income)	47	(8)	3
Total operating expenses	1,607	1,162	987
Income from operations	432	440	270
Interest income	44	28	22
Interest expense	(92)	(107)	(130)
Other income (expense), net	2	(5)	7
Remeasurements and other	42	(1)	(130)
Total non-operating expense	(4)	(85)	(231)
Income before income taxes	428	355	39
Provision for income taxes	95	(233)	4
Income before change in accounting principle	333	588	35
Cumulative effect of change in accounting principle	26	—	—
Net income	$ 359	$ 588	$ 35
Basic earnings per share:			
Prior to cumulative effect of change in accounting principle	$ 0.81	$ 1.45	$ 0.09
Cumulative effect of change in accounting principle	0.06	—	—
	$ 0.87	$ 1.45	$ 0.09
Diluted earnings per share:			
Prior to cumulative effect of change in accounting principle	$ 0.78	$ 1.39	$ 0.08
Cumulative effect of change in accounting principle	0.06	—	—
	$ 0.84	$ 1.39	$ 0.08
Weighted average shares used in computation of earnings per share:			
Basic	412	406	395
Diluted	426	425	419

(1) Includes stock-based compensation as follows:

Fulfillment	$16	$10	$18
Marketing	6	4	5
Technology and content	45	32	50
General and administrative	20	12	15
Total stock-based compensation expense	$87	$58	$88

See accompanying notes to consolidated financial statements.

AMAZON.COM, INC.
CONSOLIDATED BALANCE SHEETS
(in millions, except per share data)

	December 31,	
	2005	2004
ASSETS		
Current assets:		
Cash and cash equivalents	$ 1,013	$ 1,303
Marketable securities	987	476
Cash, cash equivalents, and marketable securities	2,000	1,779
Inventories	566	480
Deferred tax assets, current portion	89	81
Accounts receivable, net and other current assets	274	199
Total current assets	2,929	2,539
Fixed assets, net	348	246
Deferred tax assets, long-term portion	223	282
Goodwill	159	139
Other assets	37	42
Total assets	$ 3,696	$ 3,248
LIABILITIES AND STOCKHOLDERS' EQUITY (DEFICIT)		
Current liabilities:		
Accounts payable	$ 1,366	$ 1,142
Accrued expenses and other current liabilities	563	478
Total current liabilities	1,929	1,620
Long-term debt and other	1,521	1,855
Commitments and contingencies		
Stockholders' equity (deficit):		
Preferred stock, $0.01 par value:		
Authorized shares—500		
Issued and outstanding shares—none	—	—
Common stock, $0.01 par value:		
Authorized shares—5,000		
Issued and outstanding shares—416 and 410 shares	4	4
Additional paid-in capital	2,263	2,123
Accumulated other comprehensive income	6	32
Accumulated deficit	(2,027)	(2,386)
Total stockholders' equity (deficit)	246	(227)
Total liabilities and stockholders' equity (deficit)	$ 3,696	$ 3,248

See accompanying notes to consolidated financial statements.

AMAZON.COM, INC.
CONSOLIDATED STATEMENTS OF STOCKHOLDERS' EQUITY (DEFICIT)
(in millions)

	Common Stock Shares	Common Stock Amount	Additional Paid-In Capital	Accumulated Other Comprehensive Income	Accumulated Deficit	Total Stockholders' Equity (Deficit)
Balance at December 31, 2002	388	$ 4	$1,643	$ 10	$(3,009)	$(1,352)
Net income	—	—	—	—	35	35
Foreign currency translation gains, net	—	—	—	15	—	15
Increase of net unrealized gains on available-for-sale securities	—	—	—	2	—	2
Net activity of terminated Euro Currency Swap	—	—	—	11	—	11
Comprehensive income						63
Exercise of common stock options, net and vesting of restricted stock	15	—	163	—	—	163
Income tax benefit on stock awards	—	—	2	—	—	2
Deferred stock-based compensation, net	—	—	4	—	—	4
Issuance of common stock – employee benefit plan	—	—	1	—	—	1
Stock compensation – restricted stock units	—	—	31	—	—	31
Stock compensation – variable accounting	—	—	52	—	—	52
Balance at December 31, 2003	403	4	1,896	38	(2,974)	(1,036)
Net income	—	—	—	—	588	588
Foreign currency translation losses, net	—	—	—	(1)	—	(1)
Decline of unrealized gains on available-for-sale securities, net of tax effect	—	—	—	(11)	—	(11)
Amortization of unrealized loss on terminated Euro Currency Swap, net of tax	—	—	—	6	—	6
Comprehensive income						582
Exercise of common stock options, net and vesting of restricted stock	6	—	60	—	—	60
Income tax benefit on stock awards	—	—	107	—	—	107
Deferred stock-based compensation, net	—	—	3	—	—	3
Issuance of common stock – employee benefit plan	1	—	3	—	—	3
Stock compensation – restricted stock units	—	—	49	—	—	49
Stock compensation – variable accounting	—	—	5	—	—	5
Balance at December 31, 2004	410	4	2,123	32	(2,386)	(227)
Net income	—	—	—	—	359	359
Foreign currency translation losses, net	—	—	—	(15)	—	(15)
Decline of unrealized gains on available-for-sale securities, net of tax effect	—	—	—	(14)	—	(14)
Amortization of unrealized loss on terminated Euro Currency Swap, net of tax	—	—	—	3	—	3
Comprehensive income						333
Exercise of common stock options, net and vesting of restricted stock	6	—	58	—	—	58
Change in accounting principle	—	—	(26)	—	—	(26)
Income tax benefit on stock awards	—	—	10	—	—	10
Issuance of common stock – employee benefit plan	—	—	4	—	—	4
Stock-based compensation	—	—	94	—	—	94
Balance at December 31, 2005	416	$ 4	$2,263	$ 6	$(2,027)	$ 246

See accompanying notes to consolidated financial statements.

AMAZON.COM, INC.
NOTES TO CONSOLIDATED FINANCIAL STATEMENTS (Excerpts)

Note 1—DESCRIPTION OF BUSINESS AND ACCOUNTING POLICIES

Description of Business

Amazon.com, Inc., a Fortune 500 company, opened its virtual doors on the World Wide Web in July 1995 and today offers Earth's Biggest Selection. We seek to be Earth's most customer-centric company, where customers can find and discover anything they might want to buy online, and endeavor to offer customers the lowest possible prices.

Amazon.com and its affiliates operate retail websites, including: *www.amazon.com, www.amazon.co.uk, www.amazon.de, www.amazon.co.jp, www.amazon.fr, www.amazon.ca,* and *www.joyo.com*. We have organized our operations into two principal segments: North America and International. The North America segment includes the operating results of *www.amazon.com* and *www.amazon.ca*. The International segment includes the operating results of *www.amazon.co.uk, www.amazon.de, www.amazon.fr, www.amazon.co.jp,* and *www.joyo.com*. In addition, we operate other websites, including *www.a9.com* and *www.alexa.com* that enable search and navigation; *www.imdb.com*, a comprehensive movie database; and Amazon Mechanical Turk at *www.mturk.com* which provides a web service for computers to integrate a network of humans directly into their processes.

Principles of Consolidation

The consolidated financial statements include the accounts of the Company, its wholly-owned subsidiaries, and those entities (relating to *www.joyo.com*) in which we have a variable interest. Intercompany balances and transactions have been eliminated.

Use of Estimates

The preparation of financial statements in conformity with GAAP requires estimates and assumptions that affect the reported amounts of assets and liabilities, revenues and expenses, and related disclosures of contingent liabilities in the consolidated financial statements and accompanying notes. Estimates are used for, but not limited to, valuation of investments, receivables valuation, sales returns, incentive discount offers, inventory valuation, depreciable lives of fixed assets, internally-developed software, valuation of acquired intangibles, deferred tax assets and liabilities, stock-based compensation, restructuring-related liabilities, and contingencies. Actual results could differ materially from those estimates.

Business Acquisitions

We acquired certain companies during 2005 for an aggregate cash purchase price of $29 million. Acquired intangibles totaled $10 million and have estimated useful lives of between one and three years. The excess of purchase price over the fair value of the net assets acquired was $19 million and is classified as "Goodwill" on our consolidated balance sheets. The results of operations of each of the acquired businesses have been included in our consolidated results from each transaction closing date forward. The effect of these acquisitions on consolidated net sales and operating income during 2005 was not significant.

In 2004, we acquired all of the outstanding shares of Joyo.com Limited, a British Virgin Islands company that operates an Internet retail website in the People's Republic of China ("PRC") in cooperation with a PRC subsidiary and PRC affiliates, at a purchase price of $75 million, including a cash payment of $71 million (net of cash acquired), the assumption of employee stock options, and transaction-related costs. Acquired intangibles were $6 million with estimated useful lives of between one and four years. The excess of purchase price over the fair value of the net assets acquired was $70 million and is classified as "Goodwill" on the consolidated balance sheets. The results of operations of Joyo.com have been included in our consolidated results from the acquisition date forward.

AMAZON.COM, INC.
NOTES TO CONSOLIDATED FINANCIAL STATEMENTS—(Continued)

The PRC regulates Joyo.com's business through regulations and license requirements restricting (i) the scope of foreign investment in the Internet, retail and delivery sectors, (ii) Internet content and (iii) the sale of certain media products. In order to meet the PRC local ownership and regulatory licensing requirements, Joyo.com's business is operated through a PRC subsidiary which acts in cooperation with PRC companies owned by nominee shareholders who are PRC nationals.

Joyo.com does not own any capital stock of the PRC affiliates, but is the primary beneficiary of future losses or profits through contractual rights. As a result, we consolidate the results of the PRC affiliates in accordance with FIN 46R, "Consolidation of Variable Interest Entities." The net assets and operating results for the PRC affiliates were not significant.

Accounting Change

As of January 1, 2005, we adopted SFAS No. 123(R) using the modified prospective method, which requires measurement of compensation cost for all stock-based awards at fair value on date of grant and recognition of compensation over the service period for awards expected to vest. The adoption of SFAS 123(R) resulted in a cumulative benefit from accounting change of $26 million, which reflects the net cumulative impact of estimating future forfeitures in the determination of period expense, rather than recording forfeitures when they occur as previously permitted. See "Note 1—Description of Business and Accounting Policies—Stock-based Compensation."

Cash and Cash Equivalents

We classify all highly liquid instruments, including money market funds that comply with Rule 2a-7 of the Investment Company Act of 1940, with a remaining maturity of three months or less at the time of purchase as cash equivalents.

Inventories

Inventories, consisting of products available for sale, are accounted for using the FIFO method, and are valued at the lower of cost or market value. This valuation requires us to make judgments, based on currently-available information, about the likely method of disposition, such as through sales to individual customers, returns to product vendors, or liquidations, and expected recoverable values of each disposition category. Based on this evaluation, we adjust the carrying amount of our inventories to lower of cost or market value.

We provide fulfillment-related services in connection with certain of our third parties and Amazon Enterprise Solutions programs. In those arrangements, as well as all other product sales by third parties, the third party maintains ownership of the related products.

Accounts Receivable, Net and Other Current Assets

Included in "Accounts receivable, net and other current assets" are prepaid expenses of $15 million and $12 million at December 31, 2005 and 2004, representing advance payments for insurance, licenses, and other miscellaneous expenses.

Allowance for Doubtful Accounts

We estimate losses on receivables based on known troubled accounts, if any, and historical experience of losses incurred. The allowance for doubtful accounts receivable was $43 million and $23 million at December 31, 2005 and 2004.

AMAZON.COM, INC.
NOTES TO CONSOLIDATED FINANCIAL STATEMENTS—(Continued)

Internal-use Software and Website Development

Costs incurred to develop software for internal use are required to be capitalized and amortized over the estimated useful life of the software in accordance with Statement of Position (SOP) 98-1, *Accounting for the Costs of Computer Software Developed or Obtained for Internal Use.* Costs related to design or maintenance of internal-use software are expensed as incurred. For the years ended 2005, 2004, and 2003, we capitalized $90 million (including $11 million of stock-based compensation), $44 million, and $30 million of costs associated with internal-use software and website development, which are partially offset by amortization of previously capitalized amounts of $50 million, $30 million, and $24 million.

Depreciation of Fixed Assets

Fixed assets include assets such as furniture and fixtures, heavy equipment, technology infrastructure, internal-use software and website development, and our DVD rental library. Depreciation is recorded on a straight-line basis over the estimated useful lives of the assets (generally two years or less for assets such as internal-use software and our DVD rental library, three years for our technology infrastructure, five years for furniture and fixtures, and ten years for heavy equipment). Depreciation expense is generally classified within the corresponding operating expense categories on the consolidated statements of operations, and certain assets, such as our DVD rental library, are amortized as "Cost of sales."

Leases and Asset Retirement Obligations

We account for our lease agreements pursuant to SFAS No 13, *Accounting for Leases*, which categorizes leases at their inception as either operating or capital leases depending on certain defined criteria. On certain of our lease agreements, we may receive rent holidays and other incentives. We recognize lease costs on a straight-line basis without regard to deferred payment terms, such as rent holidays that defer the commencement date of required payments. Additionally, incentives we receive are treated as a reduction of our costs over the term of the agreement. Leasehold improvements are capitalized at cost and amortized over the lesser of their expected useful life or the life of the lease, without assuming renewal features, if any, are exercised.

In accordance with Statement of Financial Accounting Standards (SFAS) No. 143, *Accounting for Asset Retirement Obligations,* we establish assets and liabilities for the present value of estimated future costs to return certain of our leased facilities to their original condition. Such assets are depreciated over the lease period into operating expense, and the recorded liabilities are accreted to the future value of the estimated restoration costs.

Goodwill

We evaluate goodwill for impairment, at a minimum, on an annual basis and whenever events and changes in circumstances suggest that the carrying amount may not be recoverable. Impairment of goodwill is tested at the reporting unit level by comparing the reporting unit's carrying amount, including goodwill, to the fair value of the reporting unit. The fair values of the reporting units are estimated using discounted projected cash flows. If the carrying amount of the reporting unit exceeds its fair value, goodwill is considered impaired and a second step is performed to measure the amount of impairment loss, if any. We conduct our annual impairment test as of October 1 of each year, and have determined there to be no impairment in 2005 or 2004. There were no events or circumstances from the date of our assessment through December 31, 2005 that would impact this assessment.

At December 31, 2005 and December 31, 2004, approximately 71% and 72% of our acquired goodwill was assigned to our International segment, the majority of which relates to our acquisition of Joyo.com in 2004.

AMAZON.COM, INC.
NOTES TO CONSOLIDATED FINANCIAL STATEMENTS—(Continued)

Unearned Revenue

Unearned revenue is recorded when payments are received in advance of performing our service obligations and is recognized ratably over the service period. Unearned revenue was $48 million and $41 million at December 31, 2005 and 2004. These amounts are included in "Accrued expenses and other current liabilities" on the consolidated balance sheets.

Note 3—FIXED ASSETS(partial)

Fixed assets, at cost, consist of the following (in millions):

	December 31, 2005	December 31, 2004
Gross Fixed Assets (1):		
Fulfillment and customer service (2)	$309	$263
Technology infrastructure	69	38
Internal-use software, content, and website development	138	79
Other corporate assets	55	43
Gross fixed assets	571	423
Accumulated Depreciation (1):		
Fulfillment and customer service	123	106
Technology infrastructure	27	15
Internal-use software, content, and website development	51	32
Other corporate assets	22	24
Total accumulated depreciation	223	177
Total fixed assets, net	$348	$246

Depreciation expense on fixed assets was $113 million [for 2005] and $75 million [for 2004]...

Note 4—LONG-TERM DEBT AND OTHER

Our long-term debt and other long-term liabilities are summarized as follows:

	December 31, 2005	December 31, 2004
	(in millions)	
4.75% Convertible Subordinated Notes due February 2009	$ 900	$ 900
6.875% PEACS due February 2010	580	935
Other long-term debt and capital lease obligations	44	22
	1,524	1,857
Less current portion of other long-term debt and capital lease obligations	(3)	(2)
Total long-term debt and other	$1,521	$1,855

Appendix B

Investments and International Operations

Investments in stock can be a few shares or the acquisition of an entire company. In Chapters 11 through 13 we discussed the stocks and bonds that companies issued to finance their operations. Here we examine stocks and bonds for the investor who bought them.

Stock Investments

Some Basics

The owner of the stock in a corporation is the *investor*. The corporation that issued the stock is the *investee*. If you own shares of McDonald's stock, you are the investor and McDonald's is the investee.

Classifying Investments

An investment is an asset to the investor. The investment may be short-term or long-term.

- **Short-term investments**—sometimes called **marketable securities**—are current assets. Short-term investments are liquid (readily convertible to cash), and the investor intends to convert them to cash within one year.
- **Long-term investments** are all investments that are not short-term. Long-term investments include stocks and bonds that the investor expects to hold longer than one year or that are not readily marketable—for instance, real estate held for sale.

Exhibit B-1 shows the positions of short-term and long-term investments on the balance sheet.

EXHIBIT B-1 Reporting Investments on the Balance Sheet

Assets		
Current Assets		
Cash	$X	
Short-term investments	X	
Accounts receivable	X	
Inventories	X	
Prepaid expenses	X	
Total current assets		$X
Long-term investments (or simply Investments)		X
Property, plant, and equipment		X
Intangible assets		X
Other assets		X

The balance sheet reports assets by order of liquidity, starting with cash. Short-term investments are the second-most-liquid asset. Long-term investments are less liquid than current assets but more liquid than property, plant, and equipment.

Trading and Available-for-Sale Investments

We begin stock investments with situations in which the investor owns less than 20% of the investee company. These investments in stock are classified as trading investments or as available-for-sale investments.

- **Trading investments** are to be sold in the very near future—days, weeks, or only a few months—with the intent of generating a profit on a quick sale. Trading investments are short-term.
- **Available-for-sale investments** are all less-than-20% investments other than trading investments. Available-for-sale investments are current assets if the business expects to sell them within the next year or within the operating cycle if longer than a year. All other available-for-sale investments are long-term.

The investor accounts for trading investments and available-for-sale investments separately. Let's begin with trading investments.

Trading Investments

The **market-value method** is used to account for trading investments because they will be sold in the near future at their current market value. Cost is the initial amount for a trading investment. Assume McDonald's Corporation has excess cash to invest. Suppose McDonald's buys 500 shares of Ford Motor Company stock for $50 per share on October 23, 2008. Assume further that McDonald's management plans to sell this stock within three months. This is a trading investment, which McDonald's records as follows:

2008			
Oct. 23	Short-Term Investment (500 × $50)	25,000	
	Cash		25,000
	Purchased investment.		

Short-Term Investment
25,000 |

Ford pays cash dividends, so McDonald's would receive a dividend on the investment. McDonald's entry to record receipt of a $2-per-share cash dividend is

2008			
Nov. 14	Cash (500 × $2.00)	1,000	
	Dividend Revenue		1,000
	Received cash dividend.		

Trading investments are reported on the balance sheet at current market value, not at cost. This requires a year-end adjustment of the trading investment to current market value. Assume that the Ford stock has decreased in value, and at December 31,

2008, McDonald's investment in Ford stock is worth $20,000 ($5,000 less than the purchase price). At year-end, McDonald's would make the following adjustment:

2008			
Dec. 31	Loss on Trading Investment ($25,000 − $20,000)	5,000	
	Short-Term Investment		5,000
	Adjusted trading investment to market value.		

```
         Short-Term Investment
         25,000  |  5,000
         20,000  |
```

Reporting Trading Investments

The T-account shows the $20,000 balance of Short-Term Investment. McDonald's would report its trading investment on the balance sheet at December 31, 2008, and the loss on trading investment on the 2008 income statement, as follows:

Balance Sheet (Partial):	Income Statement (Partial):
ASSETS	Other gains and losses:
Current assets:	Gain (loss) on trading
Short-term investments, at market value $20,000	investment .... $(5,000)

If the investment's market value had risen above $25,000, McDonald's would have debited Short-Term Investment and credited Gain on Trading Investment.

Selling a Trading Investment

When a company sells a trading investment, the gain or loss on the sale is the difference between the sale proceeds and the last carrying amount. If McDonald's sells the Ford stock for $18,000, McDonald's would record the sale as follows:

2009			
Jan. 19	Cash	18,000	
	Loss on Sale of Investment	2,000	
	Short-Term Investment		20,000
	Sold investment.		

```
         Short-Term Investment
         25,000  |  5,000
         20,000  | 20,000
```

For reporting on the income statement, McDonald's could combine all gains and losses ($5,000 loss + $2,000 loss) on short-term investments and report a single net amount under Other gains (losses). . . . $(7,000).

Long-Term Available-for-Sale Investments

The **market-value method** is used to account for available-for-sale investments because the company expects to resell the stock at its market value. Available-for-sale investments therefore are reported on the balance sheet at their *current market value,* just like trading investments.

Suppose Dell Corporation purchases 1,000 shares of Coca-Cola common stock at the market price of $33. Dell plans to hold this stock for longer than a year and classifies it as a long-term available-for-sale investment. Dell's entry to record the investment is

2008			
Feb. 23	Long-Term Available-for-Sale Investment (1,000 × $33)	33,000	
	Cash		33,000
	Purchased investment.		

Assume that Dell receives a $0.60 per share cash dividend on the Coca-Cola stock. Dell's entry for receipt of the dividend is

2008			
July 14	Cash (1,000 × $0.60)	600	
	Dividend Revenue		600
	Received dividend.		

Available-for-sale investments are accounted for at market value. This requires an adjustment to current market value. Assume that the market value of Dell's investment in Coca-Cola stock has risen to $36,000 on December 31, 2008. In this case, Dell makes the following adjustment:

2008			
Dec. 31	Allowance to Adjust Investment to Market ($36,000 − $33,000)	3,000	
	Unrealized Gain on Investment		3,000
	Adjusted investment to market value.		

Allowance to Adjust Investment to Market is a companion account to Long-Term Investment. The Allowance account brings the investment to current market value. Cost ($33,000) plus the Allowance ($3,000) equals the investment carrying amount ($36,000).

Long-Term Available-for-Sale Investment	Allowance to Adjust Investment to Market
33,000	3,000

Investment carrying amount = Market value of $36,000

Observe that the Long-Term Available-for-Sale account is carried at cost, not at market value. It takes the allowance account to adjust the investment carrying amount to market value.

Here the Allowance has a debit balance because the investment has increased in value. If the investment's value declines, the Allowance is credited. In that case, the investment carrying amount is cost *minus* the Allowance. The Allowance with a credit balance becomes a contra account.

Reporting Available-for-Sale Investments

The other side of the December 31 adjustment credits Unrealized Gain on Investment. If the investment declines, the company debits an Unrealized Loss. *Unrealized* means that the gain or loss resulted from a change in market value, not from a sale of the investment. A gain or loss on the sale of an investment is said to be *realized* when the company receives cash. For available-for-sale investments, the Unrealized Gain (or Loss) account is reported on the balance sheet as part of stockholders' equity, as shown here.

BALANCE SHEET (PARTIAL)

Assets		Stockholders' Equity	
Total current assets............................	$ XXX	Common stock	$ XXX
Long-term available-for-sale investments—at market value........	36,000	Retained earnings ...	XXX
Property, plant, and equipment, net	XXX	Unrealized gain on investments	3,000

Selling an Available-for-Sale Investment

The sale of an available-for-sale investment usually results in a *realized* gain or loss. Suppose Dell Corporation sells its investment in Coca-Cola stock for $32,000 during 2009. Dell would record the sale as follows:

2009			
May 19	Cash	32,000	
	Loss on Sale of Investment	1,000	
	Long-Term Available-for-Sale Investment (cost)		33,000
	Sold investment.		

Dell would report the Loss on Sale of Investment as an "Other gain or loss" on the income statement.

Equity-Method Investments

An investor with a stock holding between 20% and 50% of the investee's voting stock can *significantly influence* the investee's decisions. For this reason, investments in the range of 20% to 50% are common. For example, General Motors owns nearly 40% of Isuzu Motors. We use the **equity method** to account for 20% to 50% investments.

Recording the Initial Investment

Investments accounted for by the equity method are recorded initially at cost. Suppose Walgreen Co. pays $400,000 to purchase 20% of the common stock of

Drugstore.com. Walgreen then refers to Drugstore.com as an *affiliated company*. Walgreen's entry to record the purchase of this investment follows.

2008			
Jan. 6	Long-Term Equity-Method Investment	400,000	
	Cash		400,000
	Purchased equity-method investment.		

Adjusting the Investment Account for Investee Net Income

Under the equity method, the investor applies its percentage of ownership to record its share of the investee's net income. The investor debits the Investment account and credits Investment Revenue when the investee reports income. As the investee's equity increases, so does the Investment account on the investor's books.

Suppose Drugstore.com reported net income of $250,000 for the year. Walgreen would record 20% of this amount as an increase in the investment account, as follows:

2008			
Dec. 31	Long-Term Equity-Method Investment ($250,000 × 0.20)	50,000	
	Equity-Method Investment Revenue		50,000
	Recorded investment revenue.		

Receiving Dividends on an Equity-Method Investment

Walgreen records its proportionate part of cash dividends received from Drugstore.com. Suppose Drugstore.com declares and pays a cash dividend of $100,000. Walgreen receives 20% of this dividend and makes the following journal entry:

2009			
Jan. 17	Cash ($100,000 × 0.20)	20,000	
	Long-Term Equity-Method Investment		20,000
	Received dividend on equity-method investment.		

The Investment account is credited for the receipt of a dividend on an equity-method investment. Why? Because the dividend *decreases* the investee's equity. It also decreases the investor's investment.

Reporting Equity-Method Investments

After the preceding entries are posted, Walgreen's Investment account shows its equity in the net assets of Drugstore.com:

Long-Term Equity-Method Investment

2008			2009		
Jan. 6	Purchase	400,000	Jan. 17	Dividends received	20,000
Dec. 31	Net income	50,000			
2009					
Jan. 17	Balance	430,000			

Walgreen can report the long-term investment on the balance sheet and the revenue on the income statement as follows:

Balance Sheet (Partial):			Income Statement (Partial):	
ASSETS			Income from operations	$ XXX
Total current assets	$	XXX	Other revenue:	
Long-term equity-method investments		430,000	Equity-method investment revenue	50,000
Property, plant, and equipment, net		XXX	Net income	$ XXX

Selling an Equity-Method Investment

There is usually a gain or a loss on the sale of an equity-method investment. The gain or loss is the difference between the sale proceeds and the investment carrying amount. Suppose Walgreen sells one-tenth of the Drugstore.com common stock for $40,000. The sale is recorded as follows:

Feb. 13	Cash	40,000	
	Loss on Sale of Investment	3,000	
	Long-Term Equity-Method Investment		
	($430,000 × 1/10)		43,000
	Sold investment.		

The following T-account summarizes the accounting for equity-method investments:

Long-Term Equity-Method Investment	
Cost	Share of losses
Share of income	Share of dividend received

Joint Ventures

A *joint venture* is a separate entity owned by a group of companies. Joint ventures are common in international business. Companies such as ExxonMobil, British Telecom, and Toyota partner with companies in other countries. A participant in a joint venture accounts for its investment by the equity method.

Consolidated Subsidiaries

Most large corporations own controlling interests in other companies. A **controlling** (or **majority**) **interest** is more than 50% of the investee's voting stock. A greater-than-50% investment enables the investor to elect a majority of the board of directors and thereby control the investee. The corporation that controls the other company is called the **parent company**, and the company that is controlled by another corporation is called the **subsidiary**. A well-known example is Saturn Corporation, which is a subsidiary of General Motors, the parent company. Because GM owns Saturn Corporation, the stockholders of GM control Saturn. Exhibit B-2 shows some of the subsidiaries of three large automakers.

EXHIBIT B-2 — Selected Subsidiaries of Three Large Automobile Manufacturers

Parent Company	Selected Subsidiaries
General Motors Corporation	Saturn Corporation
	Hughes Aircraft Company
Ford Motor Company	Ford Aerospace Corporation
	Jaguar, Ltd.
DaimlerChrysler Corporation	Jeep/Eagle Corporation
	DaimlerChrysler Rail Systems

Consolidation Accounting

Consolidation accounting is the way to combine the financial statements of two or more companies that have the same owners. Most published financial reports include consolidated statements. **Consolidated statements** combine the balance sheets, income statements, and cash-flow statements of the parent company plus those of its majority-owned subsidiaries. The final outcome is a single set of statements as if the parent and its subsidiaries were the same entity.

In consolidation accounting, the assets, liabilities, revenues, and expenses of each subsidiary are added to the parent's accounts. For example, Saturn's cash balance is added to the cash balance of General Motors, and the overall sum is reported on GM's balance sheet. The consolidated financial statements bear only the name of the parent company, in this case General Motors Corporation.

Exhibit B-3 summarizes the accounting for investments in stock by showing which accounting method is used for each type of investment.

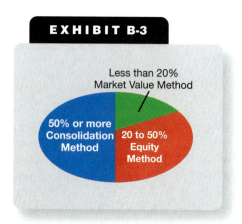

EXHIBIT B-3

Accounting Methods for Stock Investments by Percentage of Ownership

Goodwill and Minority Interest

Goodwill is an intangible asset that is recorded in the consolidation process. Goodwill is reported on the parent company's consolidated balance sheet. As we saw in Chapter 9, **goodwill** is the excess of the cost to acquire another company over the sum of the market value of its net assets.

A parent company may purchase less than 100% of a subsidiary company. For example, Nokia, the cellular telephone company, has a minority interest in (owns less than 100% of) several other companies. **Minority interest** is the portion (less than 50%) of a subsidiary's stock owned by outside stockholders. Nokia Corporation, the parent company, therefore reports on its consolidated balance sheet an account titled Minority Interest.

Bond Investments

The relationship between the issuing corporation (the debtor that borrowed money) and the bondholders (investors who own the bonds) may be diagrammed as follows:

Issuing Corporation Has	Bondholder Has
Bonds payable ⟷	Investment in bonds
Interest expense ⟷	Interest revenue

The dollar amount of a bond transaction is the same for both the issuing corporation and the bondholder because money passes from one to the other. However, the accounts debited and credited differ. For example, the corporation has bonds payable; the bondholder has an investment. The corporation has interest expense, and the bondholder has interest revenue. Chapter 13 covers bonds payable.

Virtually all investments in bonds are long-term. These are called **held-to-maturity investments**. Bond investments are recorded at cost. At maturity, the bondholders will receive the bonds' full face value. We must amortize any discount or premium, as we did for bonds payable in Chapter 13. Held-to-maturity investments are reported at their *amortized cost*.

Suppose an investor purchases $10,000 of 6% CBS bonds at a price of 94 (94% of maturity value) on July 1, 2008. The investor intends to hold the bonds as a long-term investment until their maturity. Interest dates are June 30 and December 31. These bonds mature on July 1, 2010, so they will be outstanding for 60 months. Let's amortize the discount by the straight-line method. The bondholder's entries for this investment follow.

2008			
July 1	Long-Term Investment in Bonds ($10,000 × 0.94)	9,400	
	Cash		9,400
	Purchased bond investment.		

At December 31, the year-end entries are

Dec. 31	Cash ($10,000 × 0.06 × 6/12)	300	
	Interest Revenue		300
	Received interest.		
Dec. 31	Long-Term Investment in Bonds [($10,000 − $9,400)/5 × 6/12]	60	
	Interest Revenue		60
	Amortized discount on bond investment.		

Reporting Bond Investments

The financial statements at December 31, 2008, report the following for this investment in bonds:

Balance sheet at December 31, 2008:	
Long-term investments in bonds ($9,400 + $60).....................	$9,460

Income statement for 2008:	
Other revenues:	
Interest revenue ($300 + $60).......	$ 360

Decision Guidelines

ACCOUNTING FOR LONG-TERM INVESTMENTS

Suppose you work for Bank of America. Your duties include accounting for the bank's investments. The following Decision Guidelines can serve as your checklist for using the appropriate method to account for each type of investment.

Decision	Guidelines
INVESTMENT TYPE	**ACCOUNTING METHOD**
Short-Term Investment Trading investment	Market value—report all gains (losses) on the income statement

Long-Term Investment
    Investor owns less than 20% of investee stock (available-for-sale investment)
	Market value—report *unrealized* gains (losses) on the balance sheet
	    —report *realized* gains (losses) from sale of the investment on the income statement

Investor owns between 20% and 50% of investee stock	Equity
Investor owns more than 50% of investee stock	Consolidation
Long-term investment in bonds (held-to-maturity investment)	Amortized cost

Summary Problem 1

Requirements

1. Identify the appropriate accounting method for each of the following situations:
    a. Investment in 25% of investee company's stock.
    b. Available-for-sale investment in stock.
    c. Investment in more than 50% of investee company's stock.

2. At what amount should the following available-for-sale investment portfolio be reported on the December 31 balance sheet? All the investments are less than 5% of the investee's stock.

Stock	Investment Cost	Current Market Value
Amazon.com	$ 5,000	$ 5,500
Intelysis	61,200	53,000
Procter & Gamble	3,680	6,230

Journalize any adjusting entry required by these data.

3. Investor paid $67,900 to acquire a 40% equity-method investment in the common stock of Investee. At the end of the first year, Investee's net income was $80,000, and Investee declared and paid cash dividends of $55,000. Journalize Investor's (a) purchase of the investment, (b) share of Investee's net income, (c) receipt of dividends from Investee, and (d) sale of Investee stock for $80,100.

Solutions

1. (a) Equity (b) Market value (c) Consolidation

2. Report the investments at market value, $64,730, as follows:

Stock	Investment Cost	Current Market Value
Amazon.com	$ 5,000	$ 5,500
Intelysis	61,200	53,000
Procter & Gamble	3,680	6,230
Totals	$69,880	$64,730

Adjusting entry:

Unrealized Loss on Investments ($69,880 − $64,730)	5,150	
Allowance to Adjust Investment to Market		5,150
To adjust investments to current market value.		

3. a.	Long-Term Equity-Method Investment		67,900	
	Cash			67,900
	Purchased equity-method investment.			
b.	Long-Term Equity-Method Investment ($80,000 × 0.40)		32,000	
	Equity-Method Investment Revenue			32,000
	Recorded investment revenue.			
c.	Cash ($55,000 × 0.40)		22,000	
	Long-Term Equity-Method Investment			22,000
	Received dividend on equity-method investment.			
d.	Cash		80,100	
	Long-Term Equity-Method Investment			
	($67,900 + $32,000 − $22,000)			77,900
	Gain on Sale of Investment			2,200
	Sold investment.			

Accounting for International Operations

Accounting across national boundaries is called *international accounting*. Did you know that Coca-Cola, IBM, and Bank of America earn most of their revenue outside the United States? It is common for U.S. companies to do a large part of their business abroad. McDonald's and AMR (American Airlines) are also very active in other countries. Exhibit B-4 shows the percentages of international sales for three leading companies.

EXHIBIT B-4 Extent of International Business

Company	Percentage of International Sales
McDonald's	65%
IBM	63%
AMR (American Airlines)	35%

Foreign Currencies and Foreign-Currency Exchange Rates

If Boeing, a U.S. company, sells a 747 jet to Air France, will Boeing receive U.S. dollars or euros? If the transaction is stated in dollars, Air France must buy dollars to pay Boeing in U.S. currency. If the transaction is in euros, Boeing will collect euros. To get dollars, Boeing must sell euros. In either case, a step has been added to the transaction: One company must convert domestic currency into foreign currency, or vice versa.

One nation's currency can be stated in terms of another's monetary unit. The price of a foreign currency is called the **foreign-currency exchange rate**. In Exhibit B-5, the U.S. dollar value of a European euro is $1.28. This means that one euro can be bought for $1.28. Other currencies are also listed in Exhibit B-5.

EXHIBIT B-5 Foreign-Currency Exchange Rates

Country	Monetary Unit	U.S Dollar Value	Country	Monetary Unit	U.S Dollar Value
Canada	Dollar	$0.90	Japan	Yen	$0.009
European Common Market	European currency unit	1.28	Mexico	Peso	0.090
Great Britain	Pound	1.90	Russia	Ruble	0.037

Source: *The Wall Street Journal,* Sept. 26, 2006, p. C11.

We use the exchange rate to *translate* the price of an item stated in one currency to its price in a second currency. Suppose an item costs 200 Canadian dollars. To compute its cost in U.S. dollars, we multiply the amount in Canadian dollars by the translation rate: 200 Canadian dollars × $0.90 = $180.

Currencies are described as "strong" or "weak." The exchange rate of a **strong currency** is rising relative to other nations' currencies. The exchange rate of a **weak currency** is falling relative to other currencies.

Foreign-Currency Transactions

Many companies conduct transactions in foreign currencies. D. E. Shipp Belting of Waco, Texas, provides an example. Shipp makes conveyor belts for several industries, including M&M Mars, which makes Snickers candy bars. Farmers along the Texas–Mexico border use Shipp conveyor belts to process vegetables. Shipp Belting conducts some of its business in pesos, the Mexican monetary unit.

Collecting Cash in a Foreign Currency

Consider Shipp Belting's sale of conveyor belts to Artes de Mexico, a vegetable grower in Matamoros. Suppose Artes orders conveyor belts valued at 1,000 pesos (approximately $90), and Artes will pay in pesos. Shipp will need to convert the pesos to dollars. Let's see how to account for this transaction.

Shipp Belting sells goods to Artes de Mexico for a price of 1,000 pesos on June 2. On that date, a peso was worth $0.090. One month later, on July 2, the peso has strengthened against the dollar and a peso is worth $0.100. Shipp still receives 1,000 pesos from Artes because that was the agreed price. Now the dollar value of Shipp's cash receipt is $10 more than the original amount, so Shipp ends up earning $10 more than expected. The following journal entries account for these transactions of Shipp Belting:

June 2	Accounts Receivable—Artes (1,000 pesos × $0.090)	90	
	Sales Revenue		90
	Sale on account.		

July 2	Cash (1,000 pesos × $0.100)	100	
	Accounts Receivable—Artes		90
	Foreign-Currency Gain		10
	Collection on account.		

Paying Cash in a Foreign Currency

Shipp Belting buys inventory from Gesellschaft Ltd., a Swiss company. The two companies decide on a price of 10,000 Swiss francs. On August 10, when Shipp receives the goods, the Swiss franc is priced at $0.72. When Shipp pays two weeks later, the Swiss franc has strengthened against the dollar and is now worth $0.78. This works to Shipp's disadvantage. Shipp would record the purchase and payment as follows:

Aug. 10	Inventory (10,000 Swiss francs × $0.72)	7,200	
	Accounts Payable—Gesellschaft Ltd.		7,200
	Purchase on account.		

Aug. 24	Accounts Payable—Gesellschaft Ltd.	7,200	
	Foreign-Currency Loss	600	
	Cash (10,000 Swiss francs × $0.78)		7,800
	Payment on account.		

In this case, the strengthening of the Swiss franc gave Shipp a foreign-currency loss.

Reporting Foreign-Currency Gains and Losses on the Income Statement

The Foreign-Currency Gain (Loss) account reports gains and losses on foreign-currency transactions. The company reports the *net amount* of these two accounts on the income statement as Other gains (losses). For example, Shipp Belting would combine the $600 foreign-currency loss and the $10 gain and report the net loss of $590 on the income statement, as follows:

Other gains (losses):	
Foreign-currency gain (loss), net ($600 − $10)	$(590)

These gains and losses fall into the "Other" category because they arise from outside activities. Buying and selling foreign currencies are not Shipp Belting's main business.

International Accounting Standards

In this text, we focus on generally accepted accounting principles in the United States. Most accounting methods are consistent throughout the world. Double-entry, the accrual system, and the basic financial statements (balance sheet, income statement, and so on) are used worldwide. But some differences exist among countries, as shown in Exhibit B-6.

EXHIBIT B-6 Some International Accounting Differences

Country	Inventories	Goodwill	Research and Development Costs
United States	Specific unit cost, FIFO, LIFO, weighted-average.	Written down when current value decreases.	Expensed as incurred.
Germany	LIFO is unacceptable for tax purposes and is not widely used.	Amortized over 5 years.	Expensed as incurred.
Japan	Similar to U.S.	Amortized over 5 years.	May be capitalized and amortized over 5 years.
United Kingdom (Great Britain)	LIFO is unacceptable for tax purposes and is not widely used.	Amortized over useful life or not amortized if life is indefinite.	Expense research costs. Some development costs may be capitalized.

The International Accounting Standards Committee (IASC), headquartered in London, operates much as the Financial Accounting Standards Board in the United States. It has the support of the accounting professions in many countries. However, the IASC has no authority to require compliance and must rely on cooperation by the various national accounting professions.

Decision Guidelines

FOREIGN-CURRENCY TRANSACTIONS

You've just opened a boutique to import clothing manufactured in China. Should you transact business in Chinese *renminbi* (the official currency unit), or in U.S. dollars? What foreign-currency gains or losses might occur? The Decision Guidelines will help you address these questions.

Decision	Guidelines
When to record a	
• Foreign-currency gain?	• When you receive foreign currency worth *more* U.S. dollars than the receivable on your books
	• When you pay foreign currency that costs *fewer* U.S. dollars than the payable on your books
• Foreign-currency loss?	• When you receive foreign currency worth *fewer* U.S. dollars than the receivable on your books
	• When you pay foreign currency that costs *more* U.S. dollars than the payable on your books

Summary Problem 2

Requirement

Journalize the following transactions of American Corp. Explanations are not required.

2008		
Nov. 16	Purchased equipment on account for 40,000 Swiss francs when the exchange rate was $0.73 per Swiss franc.	
27	Sold merchandise on account to a Belgian company for 7,000 euros. Each euro is worth $1.10.	
Dec. 22	Paid the Swiss company when the franc's exchange rate was $0.725.	
31	Adjusted for the change in the exchange rate of the euro. Its current exchange rate is $1.08.	
2009		
Jan. 4	Collected from the Belgian company. The euro exchange rate is $1.12.	

Solution

Entries for transactions stated in foreign currencies:

2008			
Nov. 16	Equipment (40,000 × $0.73)	29,200	
	Accounts Payable		29,200
27	Accounts Receivable (7,000 × $1.10)	7,700	
	Sales Revenue		7,700
Dec. 22	Accounts Payable	29,200	
	Cash (40,000 × $0.725)		29,000
	Foreign-Currency Gain		200
31	Foreign-Currency Loss [7,000 × ($1.10 – $1.08)]	140	
	Accounts Receivable		140
2009			
Jan. 4	Cash (7,000 × $1.12)	7,840	
	Accounts Receivable ($7,700 – $140)		7,560
	Foreign-Currency Gain		280

Exercises

Accounting for a trading investment

EB-1 Boston Today Publishers completed the following trading-investment transactions during 2007 and 2008:

2007		
Dec.	6	Purchased 1,000 shares of Subaru stock at a price of $52.25 per share, intending to sell the investment next month.
	23	Received a cash dividend of $1.10 per share on the Subaru stock.
	31	Adjusted the investment to its market value of $50 per share.
2008		
Jan.	27	Sold the Subaru stock for $48 per share.

Journalize Boston Today Publishers' investment transactions. Explanations are not required. (pp. B-2–B-3)

Accounting for an available-for-sale investment

EB-2 Raider Investments completed these long-term available-for-sale investment transactions during 2007:

2007		
Jan.	14	Purchased 300 shares of Fossil stock, paying $44 per share. Raider intends to hold the investment for the indefinite future.
Aug.	22	Received a cash dividend of $0.60 per share on the Fossil stock.
Dec.	31	Adjusted the Fossil investment to its current market value of $12,000.

1. Journalize Raider's investment transactions. Explanations are not required. (pp. B-4–B-5)
2. Show how to report the investment and any unrealized gain or loss on Raider's balance sheet at December 31, 2007. (p. B-5)

Accounting for the sale of an available-for-sale investment

EB-3 Use the data given in Exercise EB-2. On August 4, 2008, Raider Investments sold its investment in Fossil stock for $45 per share.
1. Journalize the sale. No explanation is required. (p. B-5)
2. How does the gain or loss that you recorded differ from the gain or loss that was recorded at December 31, 2007 (in Exercise EB-2)? (p. B-5)

Accounting for a 40% investment in another company

EB-4 Suppose on January 6, 2008, General Motors paid $500 million for its 40% investment in Isuzu. Assume Isuzu earned net income of $60 million and paid cash dividends of $50 million during 2008.
1. What method should General Motors use to account for the investment in Isuzu? Give your reason. (p. B-5)
2. Journalize these three transactions on the books of General Motors. Show all amounts in millions of dollars and include an explanation for each entry. (pp. B-5–B-6)
3. Post to the Long-Term Equity-Method Investment T-account. What is its balance after all the transactions are posted? (pp. B-5–B-6)

Working with a bond investment

EB-5 Smith Barney & Co. owns vast amounts of corporate bonds. Suppose Smith Barney buys $1,000,000 of Primo Corp. bonds at a price of 98. The Primo bonds pay stated interest at the annual rate of 8% and mature within five years.

1. How much did Smith Barney pay to purchase the bond investment? How much will Smith Barney collect when the bond investment matures? (pp. B-9–B-10)
2. How much cash interest will Smith Barney receive each year from Primo? (pp. B-9–B-10)
3. Compute Smith Barney's annual interest revenue on this bond investment. Use the straight-line method to amortize the discount on the investment. (pp. B-9–B-10)

Recording bond investment transactions

EB-6 Return to Exercise EB-5, the Smith Barney investment in Primo Corp. bonds. Journalize on Smith Barney's books, along with an explanation for each entry:

a. Purchase of the bond investment on January 2, 2007. Smith Barney expects to hold the investment to maturity. (pp. B-9–B-10)
b. Receipt of annual cash interest on December 31, 2007. (pp. B-9–B-10)
c. Amortization of discount on December 31, 2007. (pp. B-9–B-10)
d. Collection of the investment's face value at its maturity date on January 2, 2012. (Challenge) (Interest and amortization of discount for 2011 have already been recorded, so you may ignore these entries.)

Accounting for foreign-currency transactions

EB-7 Suppose Wilson & Co. sells athletic shoes to a Russian company on March 14. Wilson agrees to accept 2,000,000 Russian rubles. On the date of sale, the ruble is quoted at $0.030. Wilson collects half the receivable on April 19, when the ruble is worth $0.028. Then, on May 10, when the price of the ruble is $0.036, Wilson collects the final amount.

Journalize these three transactions for Wilson; include an explanation. Overall, how well did Wilson come out in terms of a net foreign-currency gain or loss? (pp. B-5–B-7)

Problems

Accounting for trading investments

PB-8 Jetway Corporation generated excess cash and invested in securities, as follows:

July 2	Purchased 3,500 shares of common stock as a trading investment, paying $12 per share.
Aug. 21	Received cash dividend of $0.40 per share on the trading investment.
Sep. 16	Sold the trading investment for $13.50 per share.
Oct. 8	Purchased trading investments for $136,000.
Dec. 31	Adjusted the trading securities to market value of $133,000.

continued...

Requirements
1. Record the transactions in the journal of Jetway Corporation. Explanations are not required. (pp. B-2–B-3)
2. Post to the Short-Term Investments account, and show how to report the short-term investments on Jetway's balance sheet at December 31, 2007. (p. B-3)

Accounting for available-for-sale and equity-method investments

PB-9 The beginning balance sheet of Media Source Co. included the following:

Long-Term Equity-Method Investments	$600,000

During the year Media Source completed these investment transactions:

Mar.	3	Purchased 5,000 shares of Flothru Software common stock as a long-term available-for-sale investment, paying $9 per share.
May	14	Received cash dividend of $0.80 per share on the Flothru investment.
Dec.	15	Received cash dividend of $80,000 from equity-method investments.
	31	Received annual reports from equity-method investee companies. Their total net income for the year was $600,000. Of this amount, Media Source's proportion is 25%.
	31	Adjusted the available-for-sale investment to market value of $44,000.

Requirements
1. Record the transactions in the journal of Media Source Co. (pp. B-4–B-7)
2. Post entries to T-accounts for Long-Term Available-for-Sale Investments and Allowance to Adjust Investment to Market. Then determine their balances at December 31.

   Post to a T-account for Long-Term Equity-Method Investment, and determine its December 31 balance. (pp. B-5–B-6)
3. Show how to report the Long-Term Available-for-Sale Investment and the Long-Term Equity-Method Investments on Media Source's balance sheet at December 31. (pp. B-5–B-7)

Accounting for a bond investment; amortizing discount by the straight-line method

PB-10 Financial institutions hold large quantities of bond investments. Suppose Solomon Brothers purchases $800,000 of 6% bonds of Buster Brown Corporation for 92 on January 1, 2004. These bonds pay interest on June 30 and December 31 each year. They mature on January 1, 2009.

Requirements
1. Journalize Solomon Brothers' purchase of the bonds as a long-term investment on January 1, 2004 (to be held to maturity). Then record the receipt of cash interest and amortization of discount on June 30 and December 31, 2004. The straight-line method is appropriate for amortizing discount. (pp. B-9–B-10)
2. Show how to report this long-term bond investment on Solomon Brothers' balance sheet at December 31, 2004. (pp. B-9–B-10)

Recording foreign-currency transactions and reporting the foreign-currency gain or loss

PB-11 Suppose Tommy Hilfiger completed the following transactions:

May	4	Sold clothing on account to a Mexican department store for $70,000. The customer agrees to pay in dollars.
	13	Purchased inventory on account from a Canadian company at a price of Canadian $60,000. The exchange rate of the Canadian dollar is $0.85, and payment will be in Canadian dollars.
	20	Sold goods on account to an English firm for 80,000 British pounds. Collection will be in pounds, and the exchange rate of the pound is $1.80.
	27	Collected from the Mexican company.
June	21	Paid the Canadian company. The exchange rate of the Canadian dollar is $0.82.
July	17	Collected from the English firm. The exchange rate of the British pound is $1.77.

Requirements

1. Record these transactions in Tommy Hilfiger's journal, and show how to report the net foreign-currency gain or loss on the income statement. Explanations are not required. (pp. B-5–B-7)
2. How will what you learned in this problem help you structure international transactions? (Challenge)

Appendix C

Present Value Tables

This appendix provides present value tables and future value tables (more complete than those in the Chapter 13).

EXHIBIT C-1 Present Value of $1

Present Value

Periods	1%	2%	3%	4%	5%	6%	7%	8%	9%	10%	12%
1	0.990	0.980	0.971	0.962	0.952	0.943	0.935	0.926	0.917	0.909	0.893
2	0.980	0.961	0.943	0.925	0.907	0.890	0.873	0.857	0.842	0.826	0.797
3	0.971	0.942	0.915	0.889	0.864	0.840	0.816	0.794	0.772	0.751	0.712
4	0.961	0.924	0.888	0.855	0.823	0.792	0.763	0.735	0.708	0.683	0.636
5	0.951	0.906	0.883	0.822	0.784	0.747	0.713	0.681	0.650	0.621	0.567
6	0.942	0.888	0.837	0.790	0.746	0.705	0.666	0.630	0.596	0.564	0.507
7	0.933	0.871	0.813	0.760	0.711	0.665	0.623	0.583	0.547	0.513	0.452
8	0.923	0.853	0.789	0.731	0.677	0.627	0.582	0.540	0.502	0.467	0.404
9	0.914	0.837	0.766	0.703	0.645	0.592	0.544	0.500	0.460	0.424	0.361
10	0.905	0.820	0.744	0.676	0.614	0.558	0.508	0.463	0.422	0.386	0.322
11	0.896	0.804	0.722	0.650	0.585	0.527	0.475	0.429	0.388	0.350	0.287
12	0.887	0.788	0.701	0.625	0.557	0.497	0.444	0.397	0.356	0.319	0.257
13	0.879	0.773	0.681	0.601	0.530	0.469	0.415	0.368	0.326	0.290	0.229
14	0.870	0.758	0.661	0.577	0.505	0.442	0.388	0.340	0.299	0.263	0.205
15	0.861	0.743	0.642	0.555	0.481	0.417	0.362	0.315	0.275	0.239	0.183
16	0.853	0.728	0.623	0.534	0.458	0.394	0.339	0.292	0.252	0.218	0.163
17	0.844	0.714	0.605	0.513	0.436	0.371	0.317	0.270	0.231	0.198	0.146
18	0.836	0.700	0.587	0.494	0.416	0.350	0.296	0.250	0.212	0.180	0.130
19	0.828	0.686	0.570	0.475	0.396	0.331	0.277	0.232	0.194	0.164	0.116
20	0.820	0.673	0.554	0.456	0.377	0.312	0.258	0.215	0.178	0.149	0.104
21	0.811	0.660	0.538	0.439	0.359	0.294	0.242	0.199	0.164	0.135	0.093
22	0.803	0.647	0.522	0.422	0.342	0.278	0.226	0.184	0.150	0.123	0.083
23	0.795	0.634	0.507	0.406	0.326	0.262	0.211	0.170	0.138	0.112	0.074
24	0.788	0.622	0.492	0.390	0.310	0.247	0.197	0.158	0.126	0.102	0.066
25	0.780	0.610	0.478	0.375	0.295	0.233	0.184	0.146	0.116	0.092	0.059
26	0.772	0.598	0.464	0.361	0.281	0.220	0.172	0.135	0.106	0.084	0.053
27	0.764	0.586	0.450	0.347	0.268	0.207	0.161	0.125	0.098	0.076	0.047
28	0.757	0.574	0.437	0.333	0.255	0.196	0.150	0.116	0.090	0.069	0.042
29	0.749	0.563	0.424	0.321	0.243	0.185	0.141	0.107	0.082	0.063	0.037
30	0.742	0.552	0.412	0.308	0.231	0.174	0.131	0.099	0.075	0.057	0.033
40	0.672	0.453	0.307	0.208	0.142	0.097	0.067	0.046	0.032	0.022	0.011
50	0.608	0.372	0.228	0.141	0.087	0.054	0.034	0.021	0.013	0.009	0.003

EXHIBIT C-1 Present Value of $1 (con't)

Present Value

14%	15%	16%	18%	20%	25%	30%	35%	40%	45%	50%	Periods
0.877	0.870	0.862	0.847	0.833	0.800	0.769	0.741	0.714	0.690	0.667	1
0.769	0.756	0.743	0.718	0.694	0.640	0.592	0.549	0.510	0.476	0.444	2
0.675	0.658	0.641	0.609	0.579	0.512	0.455	0.406	0.364	0.328	0.296	3
0.592	0.572	0.552	0.516	0.482	0.410	0.350	0.301	0.260	0.226	0.198	4
0.519	0.497	0.476	0.437	0.402	0.328	0.269	0.223	0.186	0.156	0.132	5
0.456	0.432	0.410	0.370	0.335	0.262	0.207	0.165	0.133	0.108	0.088	6
0.400	0.376	0.354	0.314	0.279	0.210	0.159	0.122	0.095	0.074	0.059	7
0.351	0.327	0.305	0.266	0.233	0.168	0.123	0.091	0.068	0.051	0.039	8
0.308	0.284	0.263	0.225	0.194	0.134	0.094	0.067	0.048	0.035	0.026	9
0.270	0.247	0.227	0.191	0.162	0.107	0.073	0.050	0.035	0.024	0.017	10
0.237	0.215	0.195	0.162	0.135	0.086	0.056	0.037	0.025	0.017	0.012	11
0.208	0.187	0.168	0.137	0.112	0.069	0.043	0.027	0.018	0.012	0.008	12
0.182	0.163	0.145	0.116	0.093	0.055	0.033	0.020	0.013	0.008	0.005	13
0.160	0.141	0.125	0.099	0.078	0.044	0.025	0.015	0.009	0.006	0.003	14
0.140	0.123	0.108	0.084	0.065	0.035	0.020	0.011	0.006	0.004	0.002	15
0.123	0.107	0.093	0.071	0.054	0.028	0.015	0.008	0.005	0.003	0.002	16
0.108	0.093	0.080	0.060	0.045	0.023	0.012	0.006	0.003	0.002	0.001	17
0.095	0.081	0.069	0.051	0.038	0.018	0.009	0.005	0.002	0.001	0.001	18
0.083	0.070	0.060	0.043	0.031	0.014	0.007	0.003	0.002	0.001		19
0.073	0.061	0.051	0.037	0.026	0.012	0.005	0.002	0.001	0.001		20
0.064	0.053	0.044	0.031	0.022	0.009	0.004	0.002	0.001			21
0.056	0.046	0.038	0.026	0.018	0.007	0.003	0.001	0.001			22
0.049	0.040	0.033	0.022	0.015	0.006	0.002	0.001				23
0.043	0.035	0.028	0.019	0.013	0.005	0.002	0.001				24
0.038	0.030	0.024	0.016	0.010	0.004	0.001	0.001				25
0.033	0.026	0.021	0.014	0.009	0.003	0.001					26
0.029	0.023	0.018	0.011	0.007	0.002	0.001					27
0.026	0.020	0.016	0.010	0.006	0.002	0.001					28
0.022	0.017	0.014	0.008	0.005	0.002						29
0.020	0.015	0.012	0.007	0.004	0.001						30
0.005	0.004	0.003	0.001	0.001							40
0.001	0.001	0.001									50

EXHIBIT C-2   Present Value of Annuity of $1

Present Value

Periods	1%	2%	3%	4%	5%	6%	7%	8%	9%	10%	12%
1	0.990	0.980	0.971	0.962	0.952	0.943	0.935	0.926	0.917	0.909	0.893
2	1.970	1.942	1.913	1.886	1.859	1.833	1.808	1.783	1.759	1.736	1.690
3	2.941	2.884	2.829	2.775	2.723	2.673	2.624	2.577	2.531	2.487	2.402
4	3.902	3.808	3.717	3.630	3.546	3.465	3.387	3.312	3.240	3.170	3.037
5	4.853	4.713	4.580	4.452	4.329	4.212	4.100	3.993	3.890	3.791	3.605
6	5.795	5.601	5.417	5.242	5.076	4.917	4.767	4.623	4.486	4.355	4.111
7	6.728	6.472	6.230	6.002	5.786	5.582	5.389	5.206	5.033	4.868	4.564
8	7.652	7.325	7.020	6.733	6.463	6.210	5.971	5.747	5.535	5.335	4.968
9	8.566	8.162	7.786	7.435	7.108	6.802	6.515	6.247	5.995	5.759	5.328
10	9.471	8.983	8.530	8.111	7.722	7.360	7.024	6.710	6.418	6.145	5.650
11	10.368	9.787	9.253	8.760	8.306	7.887	7.499	7.139	6.805	6.495	5.938
12	11.255	10.575	9.954	9.385	8.863	8.384	7.943	7.536	7.161	6.814	6.194
13	12.134	11.348	10.635	9.986	9.394	8.853	8.358	7.904	7.487	7.103	6.424
14	13.004	12.106	11.296	10.563	9.899	9.295	8.745	8.244	7.786	7.367	6.628
15	13.865	12.849	11.938	11.118	10.380	9.712	9.108	8.559	8.061	7.606	6.811
16	14.718	13.578	12.561	11.652	10.838	10.106	9.447	8.851	8.313	7.824	6.974
17	15.562	14.292	13.166	12.166	11.274	10.477	9.763	9.122	8.544	8.022	7.120
18	16.398	14.992	13.754	12.659	11.690	10.828	10.059	9.372	8.756	8.201	7.250
19	17.226	15.678	14.324	13.134	12.085	11.158	10.336	9.604	8.950	8.365	7.366
20	18.046	16.351	14.878	13.590	12.462	11.470	10.594	9.818	9.129	8.514	7.469
21	18.857	17.011	15.415	14.029	12.821	11.764	10.836	10.017	9.292	8.649	7.562
22	19.660	17.658	15.937	14.451	13.163	12.042	11.061	10.201	9.442	8.772	7.645
23	20.456	18.292	16.444	14.857	13.489	12.303	11.272	10.371	9.580	8.883	7.718
24	21.243	18.914	16.936	15.247	13.799	12.550	11.469	10.529	9.707	8.985	7.784
25	22.023	19.523	17.413	15.622	14.094	12.783	11.654	10.675	9.823	9.077	7.843
26	22.795	20.121	17.877	15.983	14.375	13.003	11.826	10.810	9.929	9.161	7.896
27	23.560	20.707	18.327	16.330	14.643	13.211	11.987	10.935	10.027	9.237	7.943
28	24.316	21.281	18.764	16.663	14.898	13.406	12.137	11.051	10.116	9.307	7.984
29	25.066	21.844	19.189	16.984	15.141	13.591	12.278	11.158	10.198	9.370	8.022
30	25.808	22.396	19.600	17.292	15.373	13.765	12.409	11.258	10.274	9.427	8.055
40	32.835	27.355	23.115	19.793	17.159	15.046	13.332	11.925	10.757	9.779	8.244
50	39.196	31.424	25.730	21.482	18.256	15.762	13.801	12.234	10.962	9.915	8.305

EXHIBIT C-2 Present Value of Annuity of $1 (con't)

Present Value

14%	15%	16%	18%	20%	25%	30%	35%	40%	45%	50%	Periods
0.877	0.870	0.862	0.847	0.833	0.800	0.769	0.741	0.714	0.690	0.667	1
1.647	1.626	1.605	1.566	1.528	1.440	1.361	1.289	1.224	1.165	1.111	2
2.322	2.283	2.246	2.174	2.106	1.952	1.816	1.696	1.589	1.493	1.407	3
2.914	2.855	2.798	2.690	2.589	2.362	2.166	1.997	1.849	1.720	1.605	4
3.433	3.352	3.274	3.127	2.991	2.689	2.436	2.220	2.035	1.876	1.737	5
3.889	3.784	3.685	3.498	3.326	2.951	2.643	2.385	2.168	1.983	1.824	6
4.288	4.160	4.039	3.812	3.605	3.161	2.802	2.508	2.263	2.057	1.883	7
4.639	4.487	4.344	4.078	3.837	3.329	2.925	2.598	2.331	2.109	1.922	8
4.946	4.772	4.607	4.303	4.031	3.463	3.019	2.665	2.379	2.144	1.948	9
5.216	5.019	4.833	4.494	4.192	3.571	3.092	2.715	2.414	2.168	1.965	10
5.553	5.234	5.029	4.656	4.327	3.656	3.147	2.752	2.438	2.185	1.977	11
5.660	5.421	5.197	4.793	4.439	3.725	3.190	2.779	2.456	2.197	1.985	12
5.842	5.583	5.342	4.910	4.533	3.780	3.223	2.799	2.469	2.204	1.990	13
6.002	5.724	5.468	5.008	4.611	3.824	3.249	2.814	2.478	2.210	1.993	14
6.142	5.847	5.575	5.092	4.675	3.859	3.268	2.825	2.484	2.214	1.995	15
6.265	5.954	5.669	5.162	4.730	3.887	3.283	2.834	2.489	2.216	1.997	16
6.373	6.047	5.749	5.222	4.775	3.910	3.295	2.840	2.492	2.218	1.998	17
6.467	6.128	5.818	5.273	4.812	3.928	3.304	2.844	2.494	2.219	1.999	18
6.550	6.198	5.877	5.316	4.844	3.942	3.311	2.848	2.496	2.220	1.999	19
6.623	6.259	5.929	5.353	4.870	3.954	3.316	2.850	2.497	2.221	1.999	20
6.687	6.312	5.973	5.384	4.891	3.963	3.320	2.852	2.498	2.221	2.000	21
6.743	6.359	6.011	5.410	4.909	3.970	3.323	2.853	2.498	2.222	2.000	22
6.792	6.399	6.044	5.432	4.925	3.976	3.325	2.854	2.499	2.222	2.000	23
6.835	6.434	6.073	5.451	4.937	3.981	3.327	2.855	2.499	2.222	2.000	24
6.873	6.464	6.097	5.467	4.948	3.985	3.329	2.856	2.499	2.222	2.000	25
6.906	6.491	6.118	5.480	4.956	3.988	3.330	2.856	2.500	2.222	2.000	26
6.935	6.514	6.136	5.492	4.964	3.990	3.331	2.856	2.500	2.222	2.000	27
6.961	6.534	6.152	5.502	4.970	3.992	3.331	2.857	2.500	2.222	2.000	28
6.983	6.551	6.166	5.510	4.975	3.994	3.332	2.857	2.500	2.222	2.000	29
7.003	6.566	6.177	5.517	4.979	3.995	3.332	2.857	2.500	2.222	2.000	30
7.105	6.642	6.234	5.548	4.997	3.999	3.333	2.857	2.500	2.222	2.000	40
7.133	6.661	6.246	5.554	4.999	4.000	3.333	2.857	2.500	2.222	2.000	50

EXHIBIT C-3 Future Value of $1

Future Value

Periods	1%	2%	3%	4%	5%	6%	7%	8%	9%	10%	12%	14%	15%
1	1.010	1.020	1.030	1.040	1.050	1.060	1.070	1.080	1.090	1.100	1.120	1.140	1.150
2	1.020	1.040	1.061	1.082	1.103	1.124	1.145	1.166	1.188	1.210	1.254	1.300	1.323
3	1.030	1.061	1.093	1.125	1.158	1.191	1.225	1.260	1.295	1.331	1.405	1.482	1.521
4	1.041	1.082	1.126	1.170	1.216	1.262	1.311	1.360	1.412	1.464	1.574	1.689	1.749
5	1.051	1.104	1.159	1.217	1.276	1.338	1.403	1.469	1.539	1.611	1.762	1.925	2.011
6	1.062	1.126	1.194	1.265	1.340	1.419	1.501	1.587	1.677	1.772	1.974	2.195	2.313
7	1.072	1.149	1.230	1.316	1.407	1.504	1.606	1.714	1.828	1.949	2.211	2.502	2.660
8	1.083	1.172	1.267	1.369	1.477	1.594	1.718	1.851	1.993	2.144	2.476	2.853	3.059
9	1.094	1.195	1.305	1.423	1.551	1.689	1.838	1.999	2.172	2.358	2.773	3.252	3.518
10	1.105	1.219	1.344	1.480	1.629	1.791	1.967	2.159	2.367	2.594	3.106	3.707	4.046
11	1.116	1.243	1.384	1.539	1.710	1.898	2.105	2.332	2.580	2.853	3.479	4.226	4.652
12	1.127	1.268	1.426	1.601	1.796	2.012	2.252	2.518	2.813	3.138	3.896	4.818	5.350
13	1.138	1.294	1.469	1.665	1.886	2.133	2.410	2.720	3.066	3.452	4.363	5.492	6.153
14	1.149	1.319	1.513	1.732	1.980	2.261	2.579	2.937	3.342	3.798	4.887	6.261	7.076
15	1.161	1.346	1.558	1.801	2.079	2.397	2.759	3.172	3.642	4.177	5.474	7.138	8.137
16	1.173	1.373	1.605	1.873	2.183	2.540	2.952	3.426	3.970	4.595	6.130	8.137	9.358
17	1.184	1.400	1.653	1.948	2.292	2.693	3.159	3.700	4.328	5.054	6.866	9.276	10.76
18	1.196	1.428	1.702	2.026	2.407	2.854	3.380	3.996	4.717	5.560	7.690	10.58	12.38
19	1.208	1.457	1.754	2.107	2.527	3.026	3.617	4.316	5.142	6.116	8.613	12.06	14.23
20	1.220	1.486	1.806	2.191	2.653	3.207	3.870	4.661	5.604	6.728	9.646	13.74	16.37
21	1.232	1.516	1.860	2.279	2.786	3.400	4.141	5.034	6.109	7.400	10.80	15.67	18.82
22	1.245	1.546	1.916	2.370	2.925	3.604	4.430	5.437	6.659	8.140	12.10	17.86	21.64
23	1.257	1.577	1.974	2.465	3.072	3.820	4.741	5.871	7.258	8.954	13.55	20.36	24.89
24	1.270	1.608	2.033	2.563	3.225	4.049	5.072	6.341	7.911	9.850	15.18	23.21	28.63
25	1.282	1.641	2.094	2.666	3.386	4.292	5.427	6.848	8.623	10.83	17.00	26.46	32.92
26	1.295	1.673	2.157	2.772	3.556	4.549	5.807	7.396	9.399	11.92	19.04	30.17	37.86
27	1.308	1.707	2.221	2.883	3.733	4.822	6.214	7.988	10.25	13.11	21.32	34.39	43.54
28	1.321	1.741	2.288	2.999	3.920	5.112	6.649	8.627	11.17	14.42	23.88	39.20	50.07
29	1.335	1.776	2.357	3.119	4.116	5.418	7.114	9.317	12.17	15.86	26.75	44.69	57.58
30	1.348	1.811	2.427	3.243	4.322	5.743	7.612	10.06	13.27	17.45	29.96	50.95	66.21
40	1.489	2.208	3.262	4.801	7.040	10.29	14.97	21.72	31.41	45.26	93.05	188.9	267.9
50	1.645	2.692	4.384	7.107	11.47	18.42	29.46	46.90	74.36	117.4	289.0	700.2	1,084

EXHIBIT C-4   Future Value of Annuity $1

Future Value

Periods	1%	2%	3%	4%	5%	6%	7%	8%	9%	10%	12%	14%	15%
1	1.000	1.000	1.000	1.000	1.000	1.000	1.000	1.000	1.000	1.000	1.000	1.000	1.000
2	2.010	2.020	2.030	2.040	2.050	2.060	2.070	2.080	2.090	2.100	2.120	2.140	2.150
3	3.030	3.060	3.091	3.122	3.153	3.184	3.215	3.246	3.278	3.310	3.374	3.440	3.473
4	4.060	4.122	4.184	4.246	4.310	4.375	4.440	4.506	4.573	4.641	4.779	4.921	4.993
5	5.101	5.204	5.309	5.416	5.526	5.637	5.751	5.867	5.985	6.105	6.353	6.610	6.742
6	6.152	6.308	6.468	6.633	6.802	6.975	7.153	7.336	7.523	7.716	8.115	8.536	8.754
7	7.214	7.434	7.662	7.898	8.142	8.394	8.654	8.923	9.200	9.487	10.09	10.73	11.07
8	8.286	8.583	8.892	9.214	9.549	9.897	10.26	10.64	11.03	11.44	12.30	13.23	13.73
9	9.369	9.755	10.16	10.58	11.03	11.49	11.98	12.49	13.02	13.58	14.78	16.09	16.79
10	10.46	10.95	11.46	12.01	12.58	13.18	13.82	14.49	15.19	15.94	17.55	19.34	20.30
11	11.57	12.17	12.81	13.49	14.21	14.97	15.78	16.65	17.56	18.53	20.65	23.04	24.35
12	12.68	13.41	14.19	15.03	15.92	16.87	17.89	18.98	20.14	21.38	24.13	27.27	29.00
13	13.81	14.68	15.62	16.63	17.71	18.88	20.14	21.50	22.95	24.52	28.03	32.09	34.35
14	14.95	15.97	17.09	18.29	19.60	21.02	22.55	24.21	26.02	27.98	32.39	37.58	40.50
15	16.10	17.29	18.60	20.02	21.58	23.28	25.13	27.15	29.36	31.77	37.28	43.84	47.58
16	17.26	18.64	20.16	21.82	23.66	25.67	27.89	30.32	33.00	35.95	42.75	50.98	55.72
17	18.43	20.01	21.76	23.70	25.84	28.21	30.84	33.75	36.97	40.54	48.88	59.12	65.08
18	19.61	21.41	23.41	25.65	28.13	30.91	34.00	37.45	41.30	45.60	55.75	68.39	75.84
19	20.81	22.84	25.12	27.67	30.54	33.76	37.38	41.45	46.02	51.16	63.44	78.97	88.21
20	22.02	24.30	26.87	29.78	33.07	36.79	41.00	45.76	51.16	57.28	72.05	91.02	102.4
21	23.24	25.78	28.68	31.97	35.72	39.99	44.87	50.42	56.76	64.00	81.70	104.8	118.8
22	24.47	27.30	30.54	34.25	38.51	43.39	49.01	55.46	62.87	71.40	92.50	120.4	137.6
23	25.72	28.85	32.45	36.62	41.43	47.00	53.44	60.89	69.53	79.54	104.6	138.3	159.3
24	26.97	30.42	34.43	39.08	44.50	50.82	58.18	66.76	76.79	88.50	118.2	158.7	184.2
25	28.24	32.03	36.46	41.65	47.73	54.86	63.25	73.11	84.70	98.35	133.3	181.9	212.8
26	29.53	33.67	38.55	44.31	51.11	59.16	68.68	79.95	93.32	109.2	150.3	208.3	245.7
27	30.82	35.34	40.71	47.08	54.67	63.71	74.48	87.35	102.7	121.1	169.4	238.5	283.6
28	32.13	37.05	42.93	49.97	58.40	68.53	80.70	95.34	113.0	134.2	190.7	272.9	327.1
29	33.45	38.79	45.22	52.97	62.32	73.64	87.35	104.0	124.1	148.6	214.6	312.1	377.2
30	34.78	40.57	47.58	56.08	66.44	79.06	94.46	113.3	136.3	164.5	241.3	356.8	434.7
40	48.89	60.40	75.40	95.03	120.8	154.8	199.6	259.1	337.9	442.6	767.1	1,342	1,779
50	64.46	84.58	112.8	152.7	209.3	290.3	406.5	573.8	815.1	1,164	2,400	4,995	7,218

Photo Credits

Chapter 1, *Pages 2–3,* Courtesy of www.istockphoto.com. iStock Photo International/Royalty Free.

Chapter 2, *Pages 60–61,* © Gary Houlder/CORBIS. All Rights Reserved.

Chapter 3, *Pages 126–127,* Courtesy of PhotoEdit Inc.

Chapter 4, *Pages 198–199,* Courtesy of Howard Koby Photography.

Chapter 5, *Pages 256–257,* Courtesy of Getty Images–Stockbyte.

Chapter 6, *Pages 314–315,* Courtesy of Corbis Royalty Free.

Chapter 7, *Pages 356–357,* Courtesy of Corbis Royalty Free.

Chapter 8, *Pages 404–405,* Courtesy of Getty Images–Stockbyte.

Chapter 9, *Pages 454–455,* Courtesy of The Image Works.

Chapter 10, *Pages 498–499,* Courtesy of Getty Images–Stockbyte.

Chapter 11, *Pages 544–545,* Courtesy of PhotoEdit Inc.

Chapter 12, *Pages 596–597,* Courtesy of Joel Gordon Photography.

Chapter 13, *Pages 640–641,* Courtesy of www.istockphoto.com. iStock Photo International/Royalty Free.

Chapter 14, *Pages 690–691,* Courtesy of Getty Images, Inc.

Chapter 15, *Pages 754–755,* Courtesy of Alamy Images.

Chapter 16, *Pages 806–807,* Courtesy of www.istockphoto.com. iStock Photo International/Royalty Free.

Chapter 17, *Pages 850–851,* Courtesy of Corbis Royalty Free.

Chapter 18, *Pages 900–901,* Courtesy of Corbis Royalty Free.

Chapter 19, *Pages 958–959,* Courtesy of Getty Images–Stockbyte.

Chapter 20, *Pages 1006–1007,* Courtesy of PhotoEdit Inc.

Chapter 21, *Pages 1056–1057,* Courtesy of Tim Boyle, Getty Images, Inc.

Chapter 22, *Pages 1110–1111,* Courtesy of Karl Weatherly, © Karl Weatherly/CORBIS, all rights reserved.

Chapter 23, *Pages 1168–1169,* Courtesy of Amazon.com®.

Chapter 24, *Pages 1220–1221,* Courtesy of Corbis Royalty Free.

Chapter 25, *Pages 1266–1267,* Courtesy of Myrleen Ferguson Cate, FotoEdit Inc.

Glindex *A Combined Glossary/Subject Index*

A

Absorption costing *The costing method that assigns both variable and fixed manufacturing costs to products,* 1049
  and manager incentives, 1052
  and variable costing, differences between, 1049, 1049E20A-1
  applying, *vs.* variable costing, 1050–1051, 1051E20A-2
  excrcises, 1052–1053
  problems, 1053–1054
  team project, 1054–1055
Accelerated depreciation method *A depreciation method that writes off more of the asset's cost near the start of its useful life than the straight-line method does,* 463
Account *The detailed record of the changes in a particular asset, liability, or owner's equity during a period. The basic summary device of accounting,* 62
  balance of, normal, 64–65, 71, 71E2-9
  numbers, 64–65
Account form, 212
Accounting *The information system that measures business activities, processes that information into reports, and communicates the results to decision makers,* 4
  concepts and principles of, 11–12
  financial *vs.* management, 5, 5E1-2
  users of, 4–5, 4E1-1
Accounting concepts and principles
  in the adjusting process, 128–132
  in the business environment, 11–12
Accounting cycle *Process by which companies produce their financial statements for a specific period,* 199, 200, 200E4-1
Accounting cycle, completing, 206E4-7
  accounting ratios, 214
  accounting vocabulary, 220
  adjusting entries, recording, 207, 207E4-8
  applying your knowledge
    decision case, 240
    ethical issue, 240–241
    financial statement case, 241
    team project, 241–242
  assessing your progress
    exercises, 223–229
    problems, 229–239
  assets and liabilities, classifying, 211–212
  balance sheet
    classified, 212
    forms, 212, 213E4-12–13
  closing the accounts, 208, 208E4-9
    net income, 209–210, 209E4-10
    net loss, 210
  decision guidelines, 215
  financial statements, preparing, 207
  postclosing trial balance, 210–211, 211E4-11
  review questions (quick check), 221–222
  summary problems, 204–205, 216–219
Accounting data, flow of, 71–72, 72E2-10
Accounting equation *The basic tool of accounting, measuring the resources of the business and the claims to those resources: Assets = Liabilities + Owner's Equity,* 13, 13E1-6
  assets and liabilities, 13

  debit and credit, rules of, 67, 67E2-3, 68E2-4
  owners' equity, 13–14
  retained earnings, components of, 14, 14E1-7
  revenues and expenses, 70E2-7
Accounting period, 129–130
Accounting profession
  ethics in, 6–7
  governing organizations, 6, 7E1-3
  professional conduct, standards of, 7
Accounting rate of return *A measure of profitability computed by dividing the average annual operating income from an asset by the average amount invested in the asset,* 1117E25-14
  decision rule for, 1119
  investments with no residual value and, 1117–1118, 1118E22-4
  investments with residual value and, 1118–1119
  net book value of B2B and Z80 portals, 1118E22-4
Accounting ratios, 214
Accounting records, 358
Accounting, and the business environment
  accounting vocabulary, 28–29
  applying your knowledge
    decision cases, 47–48
    ethical issues, 48–49
    financial statement case, 49
    team projects, 49–50
  assessing your progress
    exercises, 32–37
    problems, 38–46
  business organizations, types of, 8–9, 9E1-4
  concepts and principles of, 11–12
  language of, 4–5
  major business decisions, guidelines for, 25
  profession of, 6–7
  review questions (quick check), 30–31
  summary problem, 26–27
  transactions in, 15–19
    analysis (demo docs), 51–59
    and financial statements used, 21–24, 22E1-9
    evaluating, user perspective of, 19–21, 20E1-8
Accounts payable *A liability backed by the general reputation and credit standing of the debtor,* 63, 500
Accounts receivable *A promise to receive cash from customers to whom the business has sold goods or for whom the business has performed services,* 62–63, 406
  computers and, 24
Accounts receivable turnover *Measure a company's ability to collect cash from credit customers. To computer accounts receivable turnover, divide net credit sales by average net accounts receivable,* 770
Accrual accounting *Accounting that records the impact of a business event as it occurs irrespective of whether the transaction affected cash,* 128
  ethical issues in, 148
  vs. cash-basis accounting, 128–129, 129E3-1
Accrued expense *An expense that the business has incurred but not yet paid. Also called accrued liability,* 138, 503

  accounting for, 243–244
  accruing interest income, 139
  accruing salary expense, 138–139
  adjustments, 142E3-7
Accrued liability *An expense that the business has not yet paid. Also called accrued expense,* 63, 503
Accrued revenue *A revenue that has been earned but not yet collected in cash,* 140
Accumulated depreciation *The cumulative sum of all depreciation expense recorded for an asset,* 136
Acid-test ratio *Ratio of the sum of cash plus short-term investments plus net current receivables, to total current liabilities. Tells whether the entity could pay all its current liabilities if they came due immediately. Also called the quick ratio,* 426, 767
Activity-based costing (ABC) *Focuses on activities as the fundamental cost objects. The costs of those activities become building blocks for compiling the indirect costs of products, services, and customers,* 961
  accounting vocabulary, 982
  activity-based management, using ABC for decision making, 966
  for cutting costs, 967–969, 969E19-11
  for pricing and product mix, 965E19-8, 966–967, 966E19-9
  applying your knowledge
    decision cases, 1002–1003
    ethical issue, 1003
    team project, 1003–1005
  assessing your progress
    exercises, 985–994
    problems, 994–1001
  cost drivers, E19-3
  decision guidelines, 970
  refining cost systems, 960–961, 960E19-1, 961E19-2
  review questions (quick check), 983–984
  summary problems, 971–972, 981
  system of, 964–965, 965E19-7–8
    vs. traditional cost system, 962–964, 963E19-5, 964E42-6
  developing, 961, 962E19-3–4
  see also Just-in-time (JIT)
Activity-based management (ABM) *Using activity-based cost information to make decisions that increase profits while satisfying customers' needs,* 966
  cutting costs, 967–969, 967E19-10, 969E19-11
  pricing and product mix decisions, 966–967, 966E19-9
  see also Activity-based costing
Additional paid-in capital *The paid-in capital in excess of par, common plus other accounts combined for reporting on the balance sheet,* 555, 557
Adjusted trial balance *A list of all the accounts with their adjusted balances,* 145
  preparing, 145E3-10
    demo doc, 185–195

G-1

Adjusting entry *Entry made at the end of the period to assign revenues to the period in which they are earned and expenses to the period in which they are incurred. Adjusting entries help measure the period's income and bring the related asset and liability accounts to correct balances for the financial statements,* 128, 132–133
   categories of, 133
   preparing (demo doc), 185–195
   recording, 207
Adjusting process
   accounting concepts and principles, 128–132
   accounting process (decision guidelines), 149
   accounting vocabulary, 154
   accruals, ethical issues in, 148
   adjusted trial balance, 145, 145E3-10
   applying your knowledge
      decision cases, 177–178
      ethical issues, 178–179
      financial statement case, 179
      team project, 179–180
   assessing your progress
      exercises, 157–164
      problems, 164–176
   financial statements, 146, 147E3-11–13
   of accounts, 132–133
   prepaids, 133–135
   review questions (quick check), 155–156
   summary of, 141, 142E3-7, 143–144E3-9, 143E3-8
   problem, 150–153
Adjusting the books, 128
Advanced information systems, 811
Aging-of-accounts methods *A way to estimate bad debts by analyzing individual accounts receivable according to the length of time they have been receivable from the customer. Also called the balance-sheet approach,* 412–414, 413E8-2, 414E8-3
AICPA Code of Professional Conduct for Accountants, 7, 381
Allocation base *A common denominator that links indirect costs to cost objects. Ideally, the allocation base is the primary cost driver of the indirect method,* 863
Allowance method *A method of recording collection losses on the basis of estimates instead of waiting to see which customers the company will not collect from,* 410–411
Allowances
   purchase, 262
   recording, 309
   sales, 266, 267
Almanac of Business and Industrial Financial Ratios (Troy), 349
American Institute of Certified Public Accountants (AICPA), 6
   Code of Professional Conduct for Accountants, 7
Amortization *Systematic reduction of the asset's carrying value on the books. Expense that applies to intangibles in the same way depreciation applies to plant assets and depletion to natural resources,* 475, 647
   straight-line method of, 647
Annual Statement Studies (Risk Management Association), 764
Annuity *A stream of equal installments made at equal time intervals,* 681
Appraisal costs *Costs incurred to detect poor-quality goods or services,* 977
Appropriation of retained earnings *Restriction of retained earnings that is recorded by a formal journal entry,* 606, 607E12-7

Asset *An economic resource that is expected to be of benefit in the future,* 62
   classifying, 211–212
   rate of return on, 567
   safeguarding, 358
   types of, 62–63
   see also Plant assets
Audit *An examination of a company's financial statements and the accounting system,* 6, 362
Audit committee *A subcommittee of the board of directors that is responsible for overseeing both the internal audit function and the annual financial statement audit by independent CPAs,* 547
Authorization of stock *Provision in a corporate charter that gives the state's permission for the corporation to issue—that is, to sell—a certain number of shares of stock,* 9
Average cost *The total cost divided by the number of units,* 317–319
Average-cost method *Inventory costing method based on the average cost of inventory during the period. Average cost is determined by dividing the cost of goods available for sale by the number of units available,* 322–323, 322E6-6, 351–352
   comparing to FIFO, LIFO, 324, 324E6-7–8

B

Backflush costing *A standard costing system that starts with output completed and then assigns manufacturing costs to units sold and to inventories. Also called just-in-time costing,* 973
Bad-debt expense *Cost to the seller of extending credit. Arises from the failure to collect from credit customers. Also called doubtful-account expense or uncollectible-account expense,* 410
Balance sheet *An entity's assets, liabilities, and owner's equity as of a specific date. Also called the statement of financial position,* 21
   classified, 212
   forms, 212, 213E4-12–13
   of merchandiser, 273
   trial balance and, 79
Balanced scorecard, 1273–1273
   perspectives of, 1273, 1274E25-4
      customer, 1275
      financial, 1273–1274
      internal business, 1276
      learning and growth, 1276–1277
   see also Performance evaluation and the balanced scorecard
Bank check, 72
Bank collection *Collection of money by the bank on behalf of a depositor,* 369
Bank deposit ticket, 72
Bank errors, 368
Bank reconciliation *Document explaining the reasons for the difference between a depositor's cash records and the depositor's cash balance in its bank account,* 367, 370E7-6
   preparing
      bank side of, 368
      book side of, 369
      illustrated, 368E7-4, 369E7-5, 370E7-6
      journalizing transactions, 370E7–6, 371
Bank statement *Document the bank uses to report what it did with the depositor's cash. Shows the bank account beginning and ending balance and lists the month's cash transactions conducted through the bank,* 366–367, 367E7-3, 368E7-4

Bankcards, 417
Benchmarking *Using standards based on "best practice." Best practice may be an internal benchmark or an external benchmark from other companies,* 762, 1230, 1271
   against a key competitor, 763, 763E15-6–7
   against industry average, 764
   as budget performance target, 1173, 1173E23-4
Benefits, 508, 512, 516
Board of directors *Group elected by the stockholders to set policy and to appoint the officers,* 10–11, 547
Bond discount *Excess of a bond's maturity value over its issue price. Also called a discount on a bond,* 647
Bond premium *Excess of a bond's issue price over its maturity value. Also called a premium,* 652
Bonds payable *Groups of notes payable issued to multiple lenders called bondholders,* 642
   vs. stock, advantages and disadvantages of, 656–657, 657E13-4
   adjusting entries for, 652
   amortization, effective-interest method of, 683
      of a bond discount, 683–685, 684E13A-3
      of a bond premium, 685–685, 686E13A-4
   amortization, straight-line
      of discount, 647–648
      of premium, 651–652
   convertible, 655
   interest expense on
      with a discount, 647
      with a premium, 651
   interest rates of, 645, 645E13-3
   issuing between interest dates, 653–654
   issuing to borrow money, 645
      at a discount, 646–648
      at a premium, 651–652
      at maturity (Par) value, 646
   liabilities, reporting on balance sheet, 655–656
   present value of, 644, 679, 681
      an annuity, 681, 682E13A-2
      discount price, 682–683
      of $1, 679
      premium price, 683
      tables, 680
   prices of, 643–644, 644E13-2
   retirement of, 654–655
   types of, 642–643
   see also Liabilities, long-term
Bonus, 508
Book errors, 369
Book value *Amount of owners' equity on the company's books for each share of its stock,* 136–137, 565–566, 566E11-9
Book value per share of common stock *Common stockholders' equity divided by the number of shares of common stock outstanding. The recorded amount for each share of common stock outstanding,* 775
Bottom line, 273
Brand names *Assets that represent distinctive identifications of a product or service,* 476
Breakeven point *The sales level at which operating income is zero: Total revenues equal total expenses,* 1013–1014
   finding, using CVP analysis, 1013–1014
      income statement approach, 1014
      short-cut approach, using contribution margin, 1014–1015
      short-cut approach, using contribution margin ratio, 1016, 1016E20-5

Budget *Quantitative expression of a plan that helps managers coordinate and implement the plan,* 809
 benefits of, 1172–1173, 1172E23-3
 managers use of, reasons for, 1170–1171, 1171E23-1
 to plan and control, 1171–1172, 1172E23-2
 see also Master Budget
Budgeted balance sheet, 1185, 1186E23-15
Budgeted income statement, 1179, 1179E23-10
Budgeted overhead rate *Estimated manufacturing overhead allocation rate computed at the beginning of the year, calculated as the total estimated quantity of the manufacturing overhead allocation base. Also called the predetermined manufacturing overhead rate,* 863
Budgeted statement of cash flows, 1185, 1187E23-16
Building account, 63
Buildings, as assets, 458
Burglar alarms, 364
Business organizations, types of, 8–9
 comparison of, 9E1-4
Bylaws *Constitution for governing a corporation,* 10

C

Cafeteria plans, 510–511
Callable bonds *Bonds that the issuer may call or pay off at a specified price whenever the issuer wants,* 654
Capital *The claim of a business owner to the assets of the business,* 14
Capital assets, 1112
Capital budgeting *The process of making capital investment decisions. Companies make capital investments when they acquire capital assets-assets used for a long period of time,* 1112
 decision guidelines, 1120, 1148
 discounted cash-flow models, using to make decisions, 1129–1130, 1129E22-8
 capital rationing and the profitability index, 1138–1139, 1138E22-11
 net present value, 1130
 with equal periodic net cash flows, 1130–1131, 1131E22-9
 with unequal periodic cash flows, 1131–1138, 1132E22-10
 sensitivity analysis, 1139
 internal rate of return, 1140
 with equal periodic net cash inflows, 1140–1141, 1141E22-13
 with unequal periodic net cash inflows, 1142–1146, 1142E22-14
 methods of
 analysis, 1112–1114
 comparing, 1146–1148, 1147E22-15-16
 summary problem, 1149
Capital expenditure *Expenditure that increases the capacity or efficiency of an asset or extends its useful life. Capital expenditures are debited to an asset account,* 459, 460E9-3
Capital expenditures budget *A company's plan for purchases of property, plant, equipment, and other long-term assets,* 1175
Capital investment decisions
 accounting rate of return, 1117
 investments with no residual value, 1117–1118, 1118E22-4
 investments with residual value, 1118–1120
 accounting vocabulary, 1150
 apply your knowledge
 decision case, 1163
 assessing your progress
 exercises, 1153–1159
 problems, 1159–1162
 payback period, 1114
 criticism of, 1116–1117, 1117E22-3
 with equal annual net cash inflows, 1114–1115, 1115E22-1
 with unequal annual net cash inflows, 1115–1116, 1116E22-2
 review questions (quick check), 1151–1152
 summary problems, 1121, 1149
 see also Capital budgeting; Discounted cash-flow models; Time value of money
Capital investments, 1112
Capital rationing *Choosing among alternative capital investments due to limited funds,* 1114
Capital stock, 548
Capital turnover *The amount of sales revenue generated for every dollar of invested assets; a component of the ROI calculation, computed as sales divided by total assets,* 1285
Cash account, 62
Cash budget *Details how the business expects to go from the beginning cash balance to the desired ending balance. Also called the statement of budgeted cash receipts and payments,* 1182
 preparing, 1184–1185, 1184E23-14
 cash collections from customers, 1182, 1182E23-11
 cash payments for operating expenses, 1183–1184, 1183E23-13
 cash payments for purchases, 1182, 1183E23-12
Cash dividends, accounting for
 dates, 562
 declaring and paying, 562–563
 on cumulative and noncumulative preferred, 564–565
 preferred and common, dividing, 563–564, 563E11-8
Cash equivalents *Highly liquid short-term investments that can be readily converted into cash,* 693
Cash flows *Cash receipts and cash payments,* 1113
 see also Statement of cash flows
Cash payments, 23
 by check, controls over, 376
 purchase and payment, 376–377, 377E7-11
 streamlined procedures, 378
 voucher system, 377–378, 3787E-12
 petty cash payments, 378
 replenishing the petty cash fund, 379–380
 setting up the petty cash fund, 379
 ticket, 379E7-13
Cash payments journal *Special journal used to record cash payments by check. Also called the check register or cash disbursements journal,* 378, 513
Cash receipts
 by mail, 375–376, 376E7-9
 over the counter, 375, 375E7-8
Cash sales, 264, 265E5-5, 266
Cash-basis accounting *Accounting that records transitions only when cash is received or paid,* 128
 vs. accrual accounting, 128–129, 129E3-1
Cells, in spreadsheets

Centralized companies *Companies in which all major planning and operating decisions are made by top management*
Centralized decision making, 1268
Certificate of deposit (CD), 645, 1122
Certified management accountant (CMA) *A licensed accountant who works for a single company,* 6
Certified management accountant (CMA) *A professional certification issued by the IMA to designate expertise in the areas of managerial accounting, economics, and business finance,* 6
Certified public accountant (CPA) *A licensed accountant who serves the general public rather than one particular company,* 6
Chairperson *Elected by a corporation's board of directors, the most powerful person in the corporation,* 11
Chart of accounts *A list of all of the business's account titles and account numbers assigned to those titles,* 64–65, 65E2-1-2
Charter *Document that gives the state's permission to form a corporation,* 9, 546
Check *Document that instructs a bank to pay the designated person or business a specified amount of money,* 366
Check register *Special journal used to record cash payments by check. Also called the cash disbursements journal or cash payments journal,* 378
Chief executive officer (CEO) *The position hired by the board of directors to oversee the company on a daily basis,* 792
Chief financial officer (CFO) *The position responsible for all of the company's financial concerns,* 6, 49
Chief operating officer (COO) *The position responsible for overseeing the company's operations,* 11
Closing entries *Entries that transfer the revenue, expense, and owner withdrawal balances to the capital account,* 208
Closing the accounts *Step in the accounting cycle at the end of the period. Closing the accounts consists of journalizing and posting the closing entries to set the balances of the revenue, expense, and withdrawal accounts to zero for the next period,* 208, 208E4-9
 net income, 209–210, 209E4-10
 net loss, 210
 of a merchandiser, E5-6
Collection period *Ratio of average net accounts receivable to one day's sale. Indicates how many days' sales remain in Accounts Receivable awaiting collection. Also called the days' sales in receivables,* 426
Commission, 508
Common stock *The class of stock that represents the basic ownership of the corporation,* 14, 64, 550, 552
 declaring and paying, 562–563
 dividends, dividing between preferred and common stock, 563–564, 563E11-8
 issuing
 at a premium, 554–555
 at par, 554
Common-size statement *A financial statement that reports only percentages (no dollar amounts),* 761
Common-size treatment *A financial statement that reports only percentages (no dollar amounts),* 761–762

Company policies, 358
Comprehensive income *Company's change in total stockholders' equity from all sources other than from the owners,* 616, 617E12-11
Comprehensive problems
  for chapters 1–4, 246–247
  for chapters 1–5, 312–313
  for chapters 11–13, 689
  for chapters 14–15, 804–805
  for chapters 7–10, 542–543
Computer virus *A malicious program that (a) reproduces itself, (b) enters program code without consent, and (c) performs destructive actions,* 364
Conduct, standards of professional, 7
Conservatism *Reporting the least favorable figures in the financial statements,* 328
Consistency principle *A business should use the same accounting methods and procedures from period to period,* 328
Constraint *A factor that restricts production or sale of a product,* 1076
  and product mix, 1076–1077, 1077E21-17–18
Contingent liability, 505, 505E10-2
Continuous life, 546
Contra account *An account that always has a companion account and whose normal balance is opposite that of the companion account,* 136
Contra equity, 603
Contributed capital *Capital from investment by the stockholders. Also called paid-in capital,* 14
Contribution margin *Sales revenue minus variable expenses,* 1014
Contribution margin income statement *Income statement that groups costs by behavior—variable costs or fixed costs—and highlights the contribution margin,* 1015
Contribution margin per unit *The excess of the unit sales price over the variable cost per unit,* 1077
Contribution margin ratio *Ratio of contribution margin to sales revenue,* 1016
Control account *An account whose balance equals the sum of the balances in a group of related accounts in a subsidiary ledger,* 406
Control procedures, 360
Controller *The position responsible for general financial accounting, managerial accounting, and tax reporting,* 361
Controlling *One of management's primary responsibilities; evaluating the results of business operations against the plan and making adjustments to keep the company pressing toward its goals,* 809
Conversion costs *The combination of direct labor and manufacturing overhead costs,* 906
Convertible bonds *Bonds that may be converted into the common stock of the issuing company at the option of the investor,* 655
Copyright *Exclusive right to reproduce and sell a book, musical composition, film, other work of art, or computer program. Issued by the federal government, copyrights extend 70 years beyond the author's life,* 476
Corporate taxation, 547
Corporation (Corp.) *A business owned by stockholders; it begins when the state approves its articles of incorporation. A corporation is a legal entity, an "artificial person," in the eyes of the law,* 8, 546

advantages *vs.* disadvantages of, 547E11-1
capital stock, 548, 549 11–3
characteristics of, 9–10, 546–547, 547 11-1
income taxes, accounting for, 568–569
operations, evaluating, 567–568
organizing, 10–11, 547–548, 548E11-2
structure of, 11E1-5
see also Cash dividends, accounting for; Corporations, paid-in capital and the balance sheet; Corporations, retained earnings, treasury stock, and the income statement; Stockholders' equity
Corporations, paid-in capital and the balance sheet
  accounting vocabulary, 573–574
  applying your knowledge
    decision case, 593
    ethical issue, 594
    financial statement case, 594
    team project, 595
  assessing your progress
    exercises, 577–583
    problems, 583–592
  review questions (quick check), 757–576
  summary problems, 560–561, 571–572
Corporations, retained earnings, treasury stock, and the income statement
  accounting for (decision guidelines), 608
  accounting vocabulary, 621
  applying your knowledge
    decision case, 637
    ethical issue, 637–638
    financial statement case, 638
    team project, 638–639
  assessing your progress
    exercises, 624–629
    problems, 630–636
  review questions (quick check), 622–623
  summary problems, 609–610, 619–620
  see also Income statement; Retained earnings
Cost of a plant asset. *See* Plant assets
Cost of sales *The cost of the inventory that the business has sold to customers. Also called cost of goods sold,* 131, 264, 268
Cost allocation *Assigning indirect costs (such as manufacturing overhead) to cost objects (such as jobs or production processes),* 853
Cost behavior *Describes how costs change as volume changes,* 1008
  fixed costs, 1009–1010, 1009E20-2
  high-low method to separate fixed and variable costs, 1010–1012
  mixed costs, 1010, 1010E20-3
  relevant range, 1012, 1012E20-4
  variable costs, 1008–1009, 1009E20-1
Cost center *A subunit responsible only for controlling costs,* 1280
Cost driver *The primary factor that causes a cost,* 863
Cost object *Anything for which managers want a separate measurement of costs,* 817
Cost of goods manufactured *The manufacturing (or plant-related) cost of the goods that finished the production process this period,* 819–820
  calculating, 820, 820E2-16–9, 821E16-10
Cost of goods sold *The cost of the inventory that the business has sold to customers. Also called cost of sales,* 131, 264, 268
  in a period inventory system, 277
Cost of printed checks, 369
Cost principle, 12, 456
Cost tracing *Assigning direct costs (such as direct materials and direct labor) to cost objects (such as jobs or production processes) that used those costs,* 853
Cost-plus pricing, 1068–1069, 1069E21-12
Cost-volume-profit (CVP) analysis *Expresses the relationships among costs, volume, and profit or loss,* 1008
  accounting vocabulary, 1032
  applying your knowledge
    decision cases, 1047
    ethical issue, 1047–1048
  assessing your progress
    exercises, 1035–1040
    problems, 1040–1046
  break-even analysis, 1013
    assumptions, 1013
    contribution margin approach, 1014–1015
    contribution margin ratio, 1016, 1016E20-5
    income statement approach, 1014
  decision guidelines for, 1028–1029
  profit planning
    and target operating income, determining, 1017
    graphing CVP relations, 1017–1019, 1018E20-6
  review questions (quick check), 1033–1034
  sales mix, effect of, 1025–1027
  summary problems, 1020–1021, 1030–1031
  see also Cost behavior; Sensitivity analysis
Cost/benefit analysis *Weighing costs against benefits to help make decisions,* 810
Credit *The right side of an account,* 67
Credit-balance accounts, 71
Credit-cards
  sales, 416
  stolen numbers, 364
Creditor *The party to a credit transaction who sells goods or a service and obtains a receivable,* 13, 420
Cumulative preferred stock *Preferred stock whose owners must receive all dividends in arrears before the corporation pays dividends to the common stockholders,* 564
Current asset *An asset that is expected to be converted to cash, sold, or consumed during the next 12 months, or within the business's normal operating cycle if the cycle is longer than a year,* 211
Current liabilities and payroll
  accounting vocabulary, 522
  applying your knowledge
    decision cases, 539
    ethical issue, 539
    financial statement, 540
    team projects, 540–541
  assessing your progress
    exercises, 525–530
    problems, 531–538
  review questions (quick check), 523–524
  see also Liabilities, current; Payroll, accounting for
Current liability *A debt due to be paid with cash or with goods and services within one year or within the entity's operating cycle if the cycle is longer than a year,* 212, 500
  see also Liabilities, current
Current maturity *Amount of the principal that is payable within one year. Also called current portion of notes payable,* 502
Current portion of notes payable *Amount of the principal that is payable within one year. Also called current maturity,* 502

Current ratio *Current assets divided by current liabilities. Measures ability to pay current liabilities with current assets,* 214, 767
Current replacement cost, 329

D
Date of record, 562
Days' sales in receivables *Ratio of average net accounts receivable to one day's sale. Indicates how many days' sales remain in Accounts Receivable awaiting collection. Also called the collection period,* 770
Debentures *Unsecured bonds backed only by the good faith of the borrower,* 643
Debit *The left side of an account,* 67
  see also Debit and credit, rules of
Debit and credit, rules of
  accounting equation and, 67, 67E2-3, 68E2-4
  revenues and expenses, 69–70, 70E2-6-8
  and normal balances, 71, 71E2-9
  transaction analysis (demo doc), 116–125, 116E2-15
Debit-balance accounts, 71
Debit-cards, 417
Debt ratio *Ratio of total liabilities to total assets. Shows the proportion of a company's assets that is financed with debt,* 214, 771
Debtor *The party to a credit transaction who makes a purchase and has a payable,* 420
Decentralization, 1268
  advantages and disadvantages of, 1268–1269, 1270E25-1
  responsibility centers and, 1269, 1270E25-2
Decentralized companies *Companies that are segmented into smaller operating units; unit managers make planning and operating decisions for their unit,* 1268
  performance measurements of
    key performance indicators, E12-3
    responsibility centers for, E12-2
Declaration date, 562
Deductions. *See* withholding deductions
Deferred revenue *A liability created when a business collects cash from customers in advance of doing work. Also called unearned revenue,* 140–141, 503
Depletion expense *Portion of a natural resource's cost used up in a particular period. Computed in the same way as units-of-production depreciation,* 474
Deposit in transit *A deposit recorded by the company but not yet by its bank,* 368
Deposit ticket, 366
Depreciation *The allocation of plant asset's cost to expense over its useful life,* 135, 460
  accumulated depreciation account, 136
  and income tax, 469
  and matching expense with revenue, 460–461, 460E9-4
  assets (*see also* Plant assets)
    disposing of, 471–474
    fully depreciated, using, 471
    useful life of, changing, 470–471
  book value, 136–137, 137E3-5-6
  causes of, 461
  for partial years, 469–470
  measuring, 461
  prepaid expenses, similarity to, 135–136
  see also Depreciation, methods of
Depreciation, methods of, 461, 462E9-5
  comparing, 464–466, 465E8-10, 466E9-10
  double-declining balance, 463–464, 464E9-8, 465

MACRS, 469, 469E9-11
straight-line, 462–463, 462E9-6, 465, 466
  switchover to, 464
summary problem, 467–468
units-of-production, 463, 463E9-7, 465
Direct cost *A cost that can be specifically traced to a cost object,* 817
Direct labor *The compensating of employees who physically convert materials not the company's products' labor costs that are directly traceable to finished products,* 817
Direct labor efficiency variance, 1236
Direct labor variances, 1235–1236, 1235E24-10
  see also Flexible budget variance
Direct material variances, 1232
  efficiency variance, 1234
  price variance, 1232
  summary of, 1234 1234E24-9
Direct materials *Materials that become a physical part of a finished product and whose costs are traceable to the finished product,* 817
Direct method *Format of the operating activities section of the statement of cash flows; lists the major categories of operating cash receipts and cash payments,* 694
Direct write-off method *A method of accounting for uncollectible receivables, in which the company waits until the credit department decides that a customer's account receivable is uncollectible and then debits Uncollectible-Account Expense and credits the customer's Account Receivable,* 415
Disclosure principle *A business's financial statements must report enough information for outsiders to make knowledgeable decisions about the company,* 328
Discontinued operations, 611–612, 612E12-8
Discount (on a bond) *Excess of a bond's maturity value over its issue price. Also called a bond discount,* 643
Discounts
  purchase, 262
  recording, 309
  sales, 266, 267
Dividend dates, 562
Dividend revenue, 14
Dividend yield *Ratio of dividends per share of stock to the stock's market price per share. Tells the percentage of a stock's market value that the company returns to stockholders annually as dividends,* 775
Dividends *Distributions by a corporation to its stockholders,* 14, 64, 552
Documents, 363
Double taxation *Corporations pay their own income taxes on corporate income. Then the stockholders pay personal income tax on the cash dividends they receive from corporations,* 10, 547
Double-declining-balance (DDB) method *An accelerated depreciation method that computes annual depreciation by multiplying the asset's decreasing book value by a constant percent that is two times the straight-line rate,* 463–464, 464E9-8, 465
Double-entry accounting, 66
  increases and decreases in, 66–67, 67E2-3
  posting from journal to the ledger, 69, 70E2-6
  recording transactions in journal, 68–69, 69E2-5
  T-account, 66
Due date *The date when final payment of the note is due. Also called the maturity date,* 420

E
E-commerce, 811
  internal controls for
    pitfalls, 364
    security measures, 364–365
Earnings per share (EPS) *Amount of a company's net income for each share of its outstanding common stock,* 613–614, 774
  advantage of borrowing, 657, 65713–4
  basic and diluted, 614
  effect of preferred dividends on, 614
Earnings record, 514, 516E10-9
Economic value added (EVA) *A residual income measure calculating the amount of wealth generated by the company or its divisions for stockholders and long-term creditors,* 1283, 1288–1289
Effective interest rate *Interest rate that investors demand in order to loan their money. Also called the market interest rate,* 645
Effective-interest method of amortization, 683
  of a bond discount, 683–685, 684E13A-3
  of a bond premium, 685–685, 686E13A-4
Efficiency (quantity) variance *Measure whether the quantity of materials or labor use to make the actual number of outputs is within the standard allowed for that number of outputs. This is computed as the difference in quantities (actual quantity of input used minus standard quantity of input allowed for the actual number of outputs) multiplied by the standard price per unit of the input,* 1231
Electronic Data Interchange (EDI), 378
Electronic devices, 363
Electronic funds transfer (EFT) *System that transfers cash by electronic communication rather than by paper documents,* 367, 369
Employee compensation *A major expense. Also called payroll,* 503
Encryption *Rearranging plain-text messages by a mathematical process, the primary method of achieving confidentiality in e-commerce,* 365
Enterprise resource planning (ERP) *Software systems that can integrate all of a company's worldwide functions, departments, and data into a single system,* 811
Entity *An organization or a section of an organization that, for accounting purposes, stands apart from other organizations and individuals as a separate economic unit,* 11–12
Equipment account, 63
Equivalent units *Express the amount of work done during a period in terms of fully complete units of output,* 906–907
Estimated residual value *Expected cash value of an asset at the end of its useful life. Also called salvage value,* 461
Estimated useful life *Length of the service period expected from an asset. May be expressed in years, units of output, miles, or another measure,* 471
Estimated warranty payable, 504
Ethics in accounting and business, 6–7
  corporate and professional codes of ethics, 381
  issues in, 381–382
  judgments, making (decision guidelines), 383
Evaluated Receipts Settlement (ERS), 378
Expense *Decrease in owner's equity that occurs from using assets or increasing liabilities in the course of delivering goods or services to customers,* 14, 15, 64

External auditors, 363
External failure costs *Costs incurred when the company does not detect poor-quality goods or services until after delivery to customers,* 977
Extraordinary gains and losses *A gain or loss that is both unusual for the company and infrequent. Also called extraordinary items,* 612–613

F

Factory overhead *All manufacturing costs other than direct materials and direct labor. Also called manufacturing overhead or indirect manufacturing costs,* 817
Federal Insurance Contributions Act. *See* FICA tax
Federal Trade Commission (FTC), 809
FICA tax *Federal Insurance Contributions Act (FICA) tax, which is withheld from employees' pay. Also called Social Security tax,* 509–510, 511
Fidelity bonds, 364
Financial accounting *The branch of accounting that focuses on information for people outside the firm,* 5, 808
  vs. management accounting, 5E1-2
Financial Accounting Standards Board (FASB) *The private organization that determines how accounting is practiced in the United States,* 6, 736
Financial budget *The case budget (cash inflows and outflows), the budgeted period-end balance sheet, and the budgeted statement of cash flows,* 1175
Financial budget, preparing
  budgeted balance sheet, 1185, 1186E23-15
  budgeted statement of cash flows, 1185
  employee acceptance of, getting, 1185
  see also Cash budget
Financial statement analysis, methods of
  accounting vocabulary, 781–782
  applying your knowledge
    decision cases, 802–803
    ethical issue, 802–803
    financial statement, 803
    team project, 803
  assessing your progress
    exercises, 785–791
    problems, 791–801
  benchmarking, 762, 763E15-6
    against a key competitor, 763, 763E15-7
    against the industry average, 763, 763E15-7764
  horizontal, 757
    illustration, Google Inc., 758, 758E15-2, 759E15-3
    of balance sheet, 759–760
    of income statement, 759
    trend percentages, 760
  red flags in, 776
  review questions (quick check), 783–784
  summary problems, 765–766, 779–780
  vertical, 760
    comparing one company to another, 761–762, 762E15-5
    illustration, Google Inc., 761, 761E15-4
    see also Ratios, using in financial statement analysis
Financial statements *Documents that report on a business in monetary amounts, providing information to help people make informed business decisions,* 4
  of a service company and merchandiser, 258E5-1
    demo doc, 185–195

headings of, 23
preparing, to complete the accounting cycle, 207
types of, 21, 22E1-9, 23
  relationships among, 23–24, 146, 147E3-11–3-13, 196
Financing activities *Activities that obtain the cash needed to launch and sustain the business; a section of the statement of cash flows,* 694, 694E14-2
Fireproof vaults, 364
Firewalls *Devices that enable members of a local network to access the Internet but keep nonmembers out of the network,* 365
First-in, first-out (FIFO) inventory costing method *Inventory costing method: The first costs into inventory are the first costs out to cost of goods sold. Ending inventory is based on the costs of the most recent purchases,* 319, 320E6-4, 351, 950
  comparing to LIFO and average cost, 324, 324E6-7–8
  see also Process costing
Fiscal year, 129
Fixed asset *Another name for property, plant, and equipment,* 212
Fixed costs *Costs that stay constant in total despite wide changes in volume,* 1009–1010, 1009E20-2
Flexible budget *A summarized budget that managers can easily compute for several different volume levels. Flexible budgets separate variable costs from fixed costs; it is the variable costs that put the "flex" in the flexible budget,* 1223
  actual results *vs.* static budget, 1222, 1222E24-1, 1224–1225, 1225E24-4
  decision guidelines, 1222–1223, 1223E24-2, 1226
  how managers use, 1222
  summary problem, 1227
Flexible budget variance *The difference arising because the company actually earned more or less revenue, or incurred more or less cost, than expected for the actual level of output,* 1224, 1224E24-3
Flexible budget variance, analyzing
  direct labor variances, 1235, 1235E24-10
    efficiency variance, 1235–1236
    price variance, 1235
    summary of, 1236
  direct material variances
    efficiency variance, 1234
    price variance, 1232, 1233E24-8, 1234
    summary of, 1234–1235, 1234E24-9
Flexible budgets and standard costs
  accounting vocabulary, 1247
  applying your knowledge
    decision cases, 1263–1264
    ethical issues, 1264–1265
    team project, 1265
  assessing your progress
    exercises, 1250–1255
    problems, 1255, 1262
  income statement performance report, E23-4
  review questions (quick check), 1248–1249
  see also Flexible budgets; Standard cost
FOB terms (free on board), 262–263, 263E5-4
Form 941, 514, 515E10-8
Form W-4, 509, 510E10-3
Form W-2 (wage and tax statement), 514E10-9, 516E10-10
Four-column account, 82, 82E2-14

Franchise *Privileges granted by a private business or a government to sell a product or service under specified conditions,* 476
Free cash flow *The amount of cash available from operations after paying for planned investments in plant, equipment, and other long-term assets,* 743
Free on board terms (FOB), 262–263, 263E5-4
Freight in, 263
Freight out, 264
Fully-depreciated asset, 463, 471
Furniture and fixture accounts, 63
Furniture and fixtures, as assets, 458
Future value tables, 1166, 1167
  of an annuity, 1167

G

General expenses, 273
Generally accepted accounting principles (GAAP) *Accounting guidelines, formulated by the Financial Accounting Standards Board, that govern how accountants measure, process, and communicate financial information,* 11, 813
  reversing entries and, 243
Global competition, 811
Going-concern concept, 12
Goodwill *Excess of the cost of an acquired company over the sum of the market values of its net assets (assets minus liabilities),* 476–477
Government regulation, 547
Gross margin *Excess of net sales revenue over cost of goods sold. Also called gross profit,* 268
Gross margin percentage *Gross profit divided by net sales revenue. A measure of profitability. Also called gross profit percentage,* 276
Gross pay *Total amount of salary, wages, commissions, or any other employee compensation before taxes and other deductions,* 508
Gross profit *Excess of net sales revenue over cost of goods sold. Also called gross margin,* 268
Gross profit method *A way to estimate inventory on the basis of the cost-of-goods-sold model: Beginning inventory + Net purchases = Cost of goods available for sale. Cost of goods available for sale–Cost of goods sold = Ending inventory,* 332, 332E6—11
Gross profit percentage *Gross profit divided by net sales revenue. A measure of profitability. Also called gross margin percentage,* 276, 332

H

High-low method *A method for determining cost behavior that is based on two historical data points: the highest and lowest volume of activity,* 1010–1011
Historical cost, 12
Horizontal analysis *Study of percentage changes in comparative financial statements,* 757
  illustration, Google Inc., 758, 758E11-2, 759E15-3
  of balance sheet, 759, 759E15-3
  of income statement, 759
  trend percentages as form of, 760

I

In arrears, 564, 565
Income from operations *Gross profit minus operating expenses plus any other operating revenues. Also called operating income,* 273

Income statement *Summary of an entity's revenues, expenses, and net income or net loss for a specific period. Also called the statement of earnings or the statement of operations,* 19
   for merchandising company, 273
   multi-step, 275
   single-step, 275, 275E5-8
Income summary *A temporary "holding tank" account into which revenues and expenses are transferred prior to their final transfer to the capital account,* 208
Income taxes, accounting for, 568–569
Income-statement approach *A method of estimating uncollectible receivables that calculates uncollectible account expense. Also called the percent-of-sales method,* 411
Incorporated (Inc.), 546
Incorporators, 10, 547–548
Indirect cost *A cost that relates to the cost object, but cannot be traced to it,* 817
Indirect labor *Labor costs that are difficult to trace to specific products,* 818
Indirect manufacturing cost *All manufacturing costs other than direct materials and direct labor. Also called factory overhead or manufacturing overhead,* 817
Indirect materials *Materials whose costs cannot conveniently be directly traced to particular finished products,* 818
Indirect method *Format of the operating activities section of the statement of cash flows; starts with net income and reconciles to net cash provided by operating activities,* 694
   see also Statement of cash flows
Inflation, 12
Information system, 360
Institute of Management Accountants (IMA), 6, 823
   Standards of Ethical Conduct for Management Accountants, 823, 823E16-2
Intangibles *Assets with no physical form. Valuable because of the special rights they carry. Examples are patents and copyrights,* 456
   accounting for, 475
      research and development, 477
      specific, 475–477
   see also Plant assets
Interest *The revenue to the payee for loaning money; the expense to the debtor,* 420
   computing, 421
Interest period *The period of time during which interest is computed. It extends from the original date of the note to the maturity date. Also called the note term, or simply time period,* 420
Interest rate *The percentage rate of interest specified by the note. Interest rates are almost always stated for a period of one year,* 420
Interest revenue, 14, 369
   accruing, 423
Interim period *The period of time during which interest is computed. It extends from the original date of the note to the maturity date. Also called the note term, or simply time period,* 130, 420
Interim statements, 414
Internal auditors *The corporate function charged with assessing the effectiveness of the company's internal controls and risk management policies,* 362

Internal control *Organizational plan and all the related measures adopted by an entity to safeguard assets, encourage employees to follow company policy, promote operational efficiency, and ensure accurate and reliable accounting records,* 358
   over cash payments, 376
      by checks, 376–378, 377E7-10–11
      petty, 378–380, 379E7-13
   over cash receipts, 375–376, 375E7-8, 376E7-9
   accounting vocabulary, 385
   applying your knowledge
      decision cases, 401
      ethical issues, 402
      financial statement case, 402
      team project, 402–403
   assessing your progress
      exercises, 388–393
      problems, 393–400
   bank account as a control device, 366–367, 367E7-3 (*see also* Bank reconciliation)
   online banking, 371–372, 372E7-7
   components of, 359–360, 360E7-2
   for e-commerce, 364–365
   limitations of, costs and benefits, 365–366
   procedures
      audits, 362–363
      documents, 363
      electronic devices, 363
      other controls, 364
      personnel and, 361
      responsibilities, assignment of, 361
      separation of duties, 361–362
   reporting cash on the balance sheet, 380–381
   review questions (quick check), 386–387
   SOX and, 358–359, 359E7-1
Internal failure costs *Costs incurred when the company detects and corrects poor-quality goods or services before delivery to customers,* 977
Internal rate of return (IRR) *The rate of return (based on discounted cash flows) that a company can expect to earn by investing in the project. The interest rate that makes the NPV of the project's net cash inflows equal to zero,* 1139–1140
   with equal periodic cash flows, 1140, 1141E22-13
   with unequal periodic cash flows, 1142–1146, 1142E22-14
Internal Revenue Service (IRS), 809
Inventoriable product costs *All costs of a product that GAAP requires companies to treat as an asset for external financial reporting. These costs are not expensed until the product is sold,* 813, 817
Inventory *All the goods that the company owns and expects to sell in the normal course of operations,* 258
   adjusting, based on physical count, 271
   perpetual and periodic systems of, 259–260
   recording sale of, 310
Investing activities *Activities that increase or decrease long-term assets; a section of the statement of cash flows,* 693, 694E14-2
Investment center *A subunit responsible for generating profits and efficiently managing the division's invested capital (assets),* 1283
   financial performance of, measuring, 1283
      economic value added, 1288–1289
      limitations of, 1289–1291, 1290E25-9
      residual income, 1287–1288
      return on investment, 1284–1286

      short-term focus, 1291
      summary performance measures, 1283, 1284E25-8
Invoice *A seller's request for cash from the purchaser,* 72, 261, 261E5-3
Issue price, 553

J

Job cost record *Document that accumulates the direct materials, direct labor, and manufacturing overhead costs assigned to each individual job,* 853
Job cost sheet, 923
Job order costing *A system that accumulates costs for each batch, or job. Law firms, music studios, healthcare providers, mail-order catalog companies, building contractors, and custom furniture manufacturers are examples of companies that use job order costing systems,* 852
   accounting vocabulary, 876
   and process costing, differences between, 903, 904E18-1, 905, 905E18-2
   applying your knowledge
      decision cases, 896–897
      ethical issue, 897
      team project, 897–899
   assessing your progress
      exercises, 879–885
      problems, 885–895
   decision guidelines in, 872
   direct materials and direct labor, tracing (decision guidelines), 859
   for manufacturing products, 853, 853E17-1
   in a service company, 868, 869E17-9, 870–871, 870E17-10
      employee time record, E17-10
   in manufacturing company, E17-8
   labor, accounting for
      job cost record, 856, 856E17-4
      labor time record, 856–858, 856E17-5, 857E17-6
   materials, accounting for
      purchasing, 853–854, 854E17-2
      using materials, 854–855, 856E17-4
   review questions (quick check), 877–878
   summary problems, 860–861, 873–875
   see also Manufacturing overhead
Job rotation, 364
Journal *The chronological accounting record of an entity's transactions,* 62, 68
   details in, 80, 81E2-13
   FIFO entries, 320
   posting, 69, 70E2-6
   recording entries in, 68–69, E692-5
Journal reference (Jrnl. Ref.), 81
Just-in-time (JIT) *A system in which a company produces just in time to satisfy needs. Suppliers deliver materials just in time to begin production, and finished units are completed just in time for delivery to customers,* 811, 973
   vs. traditional costing systems, 973–974, 974E19-12, 975E19-13
   and quality costs
      decision guidelines, 980
      types of, 977, 978E19-15
      and quality programs, adopting, 978–979, 979E19-16
   illustrated, Mintel Company, 975–977, 976E19-14
   summary problem, 981
Just-in-time costing, 973

K

Key performance indicator (KPI) *Summary performance measures that help managers assess whether the company is achieving its long-term and short-term goals,* 1273

L

Labor time record *Identifies the employee, the amount of time spent on a particular job, and the labor cost charged to the job; a record used to assign direct labor cost to specific jobs*, 856–858, 856E17-5, 857E17-6

Lag indicators *Performance measures that indicate past performance,* 1272

Land account, 63

Land improvements, 457, 457E9-2

Last-in, first-out (LIFO) inventory costing method *Inventory costing method: The last costs into inventory are the first costs out to cost of goods sold. Leaves the oldest costs—those of beginning inventory and the earliest purchases of the period—in ending inventory,* 321, 321E6-5, 351
   comparing to FIFO and average cost, 324, 324E6-7–8

Lead indicators *Performance measures that forecast future performance,* 1272

Ledger *The record holding all the accounts,* 62
   details in, 81
   flow of accounting data, 71–72, 72E2-10
   journalizing transactions and posting to, 72–78, 79E2-11

Legal capital *The portion of stockholders' equity that cannot be used for dividends,* 552

Liabilities, current
   accounting for (decision guidelines), 506
   of known amount
     accounts payable, 500–501, 500E10-1
     accrued expenses (accrued liabilities), 503
     long-term notes payable, current portion of, 502
     sales tax payable, 502
     short-term notes payable, 501
     unearned revenues, 503
   reporting, 518, 518E10-11
     ethical issues in, 518
   summary problems, 507
   that must be estimated
     contingent liabilities, 505, 505E10-2
     estimated warranty payable, 504
   see also Current liabilities and payroll

Liabilities, long-term, 212
   accounting vocabulary, 661
   applying your knowledge
     decision case, 677
     ethical issue, 677
     financial statement, 677
     team project, 677
   assessing your progress
     appendix assignments, 686–688
     exercises, 664–670
     problems, 670–676
   decision guidelines, 658
   reporting of, on balance sheet
   review questions (quick check), 662–663
   summary problems, 659–660
   see also Bonds payable

Liability *An economic obligation (a debt) payable to an individual or an organization outside the business,* 13, 63
   types of, 63

Licenses *Privileges granted by a private business or a government to sell a product or service under specified conditions,* 476

Limited liability *No personal obligation of a stockholder for corporation debts. A stockholder can lose no more on an investment in a corporation's stock than the cost of the investment,* 10, 546

Limited liability companies (LLCs), 8

Limited liability partnerships (LLPs) *A form of partnership in which each partner's personal liability for the business's debts is limited to a certain amount. Also called LLPs,* 8, 547

Liquidation *The process of going out of business by selling the entity's assets and paying its liabilities. The final step in liquidation is the distribution of any remaining cash to the owner(s),* 129

Long-term asset *A liability other than a current liability,* 212

Long-term liability *A liability other than a current liability,* 212, 500

Loss-prevention specialists, 364

Lower-of-cost-or-market (LCM) *Rule that an asset should be reported in the financial statements at whichever is lower—its historical cost or its market value,* 329

Lump-sum (basket) purchase of assets, 458

M

Machinery and equipment, as assets, 458

Maker of a note *The person or business that signs the note and promises to pay the amount required by the note agreement: the debtor,* 420

Management accountability *The manager's fiduciary responsibility to manage the resources of an organization,* 808
   to stakeholders, 808–809, 808E16-1, 809E16-2

Management accounting *The branch of accounting that focuses on information for internal decision makers of a business,* 5, 5E1-2, 809
   vs. financial accounting, 810E16-3
   accounting vocabulary, 828–829
   applying your knowledge
     decision cases, 846–847
     ethical issue, 847
     financial statement case, 847
     team project, 848
   assessing your progress
     exercises, 832–839
     problems, 840–845
   building blocks of (decision guidelines), 825–826
   business environment trends and, 811
   ethical standards, 823–824, 823E16-2
   manufacturing companies, 817
     cost of goods manufactured, calculating, 820–821, 821E16-10
     flow of costs through inventory accounts, 822, 822E16-11
     income statement for, 819E16-7
     inventoriable product costs, 817, 818E16-6, 819E16-8
     overhead, 818–822
     unit product cost, calculating, 822
   merchandising companies, 813–814, 814E16-5, 819E16-8
   review questions (quick check), 830–831
   service companies, 812–813, 812E16-4, 819E16-8
   summary problems, 815–816, 827

Management by exception *Directs management's attention to important differences between actual and budgeted amounts,* 1193, 1280

Manufacturing company *A company that uses labor, plant, and equipment to convert raw materials into new finished products,* 817
   inventoriable product costs, 817, 818E16-6

Manufacturing overhead *All manufacturing costs other than direct materials and direct labor. Also called factory overhead or indirect manufacturing cost,* 817

Manufacturing overhead *All manufacturing costs other than direct materials and direct labor. Also called factory overhead or indirect manufacturing costs,* 817, 818
   accounting for, summary of, 867E17-8
   adjusting
     for completion and sale of finished goods, 865–866
     for underallocated or overallocated, at the end of the period, 866–867
   allocating, 862
     in a standard cost system, 1236–1237
     to jobs, 863–865, 864E17-7
   cost of goods manufactured, calculating, 820–821, 820E16-9, 821E16-10
   flow of costs through inventory accounts, 822, 822E16-11
   variances, 1236, 1238E24-11
     overhead flexible budget, 1237–1238
     production volume, 1238
     summary of, 1239

Manufacturing processes, 903

Margin of safety *Excess of expected sales over breakeven sales. Drop in sales a company can absorb without incurring an operating loss,* 1023–1024

Market interest rate *Interest rate that investors demand in order to loan their money. Also called the effective interest rate,* 645

Market price *Price for which a person could buy or sell a share of stock,* 329, 565, 566E11-9

Market value *Price for which a person could buy or sell a share of stock,* 329, 565, 566E11-9

Master budget *The set of budgeted financial statements and supporting schedules for the entire organization. Includes the operating budget, the capital expenditures budget, and the financial budget,* 1174

Master budget, and responsibility accounting
   accounting vocabulary, 1199
   applying your knowledge
     decision cases, 1215–1216
     ethical issue, 1216–1217
     team project, 1217–1219
   assessing your progress
     exercises, 1202–1207
     problems, 1207–1214
   components of, 1174–1175, 1174E23-5
   preparing, 1175–1177, 1175E23-6
   responsibility accounting (decision guidelines), 1194
   review questions (quick check), 1200–1201
   summary problems, 1180–1181, 1195–1197
   see also Financial budget, preparing; Operating budget, preparing

Matching principle *Guide to accounting for expenses. Identify all expenses incurred during the period, measure the expenses, and match them against the revenues earned during that same time period,* 131, 131E3-3

Materiality concept *A company must perform strictly proper accounting only for items that* *are significant to the business's financial situations,* 328

Materials requisition *Request for the transfer of both direct and indirect materials from Raw Materials Inventory to the production floor,* 855, 855E17-3

Maturity (par) value *A bond issued at par has no discount on premium,* 642, 643

Maturity date *The date when final payment of the note is due. Also called the due date,* 420, 642
   identifying, 420–421

Maturity value *The sum of the principal plus interest due at maturity,* 420

Medicare, 509

Merchandise inventory
   accounting for, in a periodic system, 350–352
   accounting principles and, 328
   accounting vocabulary, 335
   adjusting, based on a physical count, 271
   affects of, on a company, 316E6-1
   applying your knowledge
      decision cases, 348
      ethical issue, 348
      financial statement case, 349
      team project, 349
   assessing your progress
      exercises, 338–343
      problems, 343–347
   decision guidelines for
      inventory costing methods, 316–319, 317E6-2, 318E6-3 (*see also* Perpetual inventory system)
   issues in inventory, other, 329
      errors, effect of, 329–330, 331E6-9-10
      estimating ending inventory, 332, 332E6-11
      ethical issues, 330, 332
      lower-of-cost-or-market rule, 329
   management guidelines for (decision guidelines), 333
   review questions (quick check), 336–337
   summary problems, 334

Merchandising company *A company that resells tangible products previously bought from suppliers,* 814

Merchandising operations
   accounting vocabulary, 285
   adjusting and closing the accounts, 271–273, 272E5-6
   and accounting cycle (decision guidelines), 279
   applying your knowledge
      decision cases, 305–306
      ethical issues, 306
      financial statement case, 306–307
      team project, 307
   assessing your progress
      exercises, 288–294
      problems, 294–304
   financial statements, preparing, 273–275, 274E5-7, 275E5-8
   merchandiser *vs.* service entity, 258E5-1
   operating cycle of, 259, 259E5-2
   ratios for decision making, 275
      gross profit percentage, 276, 276E5-9
      rate of inventory turnover, 276–277, 277E5-10
   review questions (quick check), 286–287
   summary problems, 269–270, 279–282
   worksheet for, 283–284, 283E5A-1
   see also Perpetual inventory system

Mixed costs *Costs that have both variable and fixed components,* 1010, 1010E20-3

Modified accelerated cost recovery system (MACRS), 446, 469E9-11

Monitoring of controls, 360

Multi-step income statement *Format that contains subtotals to highlight significant relationships. In addition to net income, it reports gross profit and operating income,* 275

Mutual agency
   no mutual agency, 9, 546–547

N

Natural resources, accounting for, 474–475

Net (take-home) pay *Gross pay minus all deductions. The amount of compensation that the employee actually takes home,* 508, 515, 516, 517

Net income *Excess of total revenue over total expenses. Also called net earnings or net profit,* 21
   cash flows from operating activities, 696
   closing, 209–210, 209E4-10
   entering on worksheet, 203
   under/overstating, 415

Net loss *Excess of total expense over total revenues,* 21
   closing, 210
   entering on worksheet, 203

Net present value (NPV) *The decision model that brings cash inflows an outflows back to a common time period by discounting these expected future cash flows to their present value, using a minimum desired rate of return,* 1112, 1130
   of a project with residual value, 1139, 1139E22-12
   capital rationing and the profitability index, 1138, 1138E22-11
   positive/negative, 1131
   with equal periodic net cash inflows, 1130, 1131E22-9
   with unequal periodic net cash inflows, 1131–1138, 1132E22-10

Net realizable value, 414

No-par stock, 553
   issuing, 556

Noncash investing and financing activities, 703–704, 704E14-10, 740

Noncumulative preferred stock, 564

Nonsufficient funds (NSF) check *A "hot" check; one for which the maker's bank account has insufficient money to pay the check,* 369

Normal balance *The balance that appears on the side of an account—debit or credit—where we record increases,* 71, 71E2-9

Note term *The period of time during which interest is computed. It extends from the original date of the note to the maturity date. Also called the interest period, or simply time period,* 420

Notes receivable *A written promise for future collection of cash,* 63, 406
   accounting for
      accruing interest revenue, 423
      computers and accounts receivable, 424, 424E8-5
      dishonored, 423
      recording, 422
      reporting on balance sheet, 424
   discounting, 452–453, 452E8A-1
      exercise, 453
      problem, 453
   interest on, computing, 421
   maturity date, identifying, 420–421, 420E8-4

overview of, 420–421, 420E8-4
NSF check. *See* Nonsufficient funds (NSF) check

O

OASDI (old age, survivors', and disability insurance), 509–510

Online banking, 371–372, 372E7-7

Operating activities *Activities that create revenue or expense in the entity's major line of business; a section of the statement of cash flows. Operating activities affect the income statement,* 693, 694E14-2
   formats of, 694

Operating budget *Projects sales revenue, cost of goods sold, and operating expenses, leading to the budgeted income statement that projects operating income for the period,* 1174
   preparing, 1177
      the budgeted income statement, 1179, 1179E23-10
      the inventory, purchases, and cost of goods sold budget, 1178, 1178E23-8
      the operating expense budget, 1178, 1179E23-9
      the sales budget, 1177, 1177E23-7

Operating costs. *See* Period costs

Operating cycle *Time span during which cash is paid for goods and services, which are then sold to customers from whom the business collects cash,* 211

Operating expense budget, 1178, 1179E23-9

Operating expenses *Expenses, other than cost of goods sold, that are incurred in the entity's major line of business. Examples include rent, depreciation, salaries, wages, utilities, and supplies expense,* 273

Operating income *Gross profit minus operating expenses plus any other operating revenues. Also called income from operations,* 273

Operational efficiency, 358

Opportunity cost *The benefit forgone by not choosing an alternative course of action,* 1082, 1082E21-21

Other expense *Expense that is outside the main operations of a business, such as a loss on the sale of plant assets,* 273

Other revenue *Revenue that is outside the main operations of a business, such as gain on the sale of plant assets,* 273

Outsourcing *A make-or-buy decision: Managers decide whether to buy a component product or service or produce it in-house,* 1079
   considerations, 1080E21-19
   decision rule for, 1081
   incremental analysis for, 1080E21-20

Outstanding check *A check issued by the company and recorded on its books but not yet paid by its bank,* 368

Outstanding shares, 604

Outstanding stocks *Stock in the hands of stockholders,* 614

Overallocated manufacturing overhead *The manufacturing overhead allocated to Work in Process Inventory is more than the amount of manufacturing overhead costs actually incurred,* 867

Overhead flexible budget variance *Shows how well management has controlled overhead costs. It is the difference between the actual overhead cost and the flexible budget overhead for the actual number of outputs,* 1237, 1238E24-11

Overhead production volume variance, 1238
Overtime, 508
Owner's equity *The claim of a business owner to the assets of the business. also called capital,* 13

P

Paid-in capital *Capital from investment by the stockholders. Also called contributed capital,* 14, 557
Par value *Arbitrary amount assigned to a share of stock,* 553
Partnership *An association of two or more persons who co-own a business for profit,* 8, 517
Passing the dividend, 564
Patent *A federal government grant giving the holder the exclusive right to produce and sell an invention for 20 years,* 475, 476
Payback period *The length of time it takes to recover, in net cash inflows, the cost of a capital outlay,* 1112, 1114
   criticism of, 1116, 1117E22-3
   decision rules for, 1117
   with equal annual net cash inflows, 1114–1115, 1115E22-1
   with unequal net cash inflows, 1115–1116, 1116E22-2
Paycheck, 514, 514E10-7
Payee of note *The person or business to whom the maker of a note promises future payment: the creditor,* 420
Payment date, 562
Payroll *A major expense. Also called employee compensation,* 503
Payroll record, 513, 513E10-6
Payroll system, 513
   earnings record, 514, 514E10-8, 516E10-9-10
   internal control over, 517
      for efficiency, 517
      to safeguard payroll disbursements, 517
   paying the payroll, 514
      benefits paid to insurance companies and investment companies, 516
      net (take-home) pay to employees, 513E10-6, 515
      payroll taxes and other deductions, 513E10-6, 517
   payroll checks, 513E10-6, 514, 514E10-7
   payroll record, 513, 513E10-6
Payroll tax expense, 513
Payroll tax return, 514, 515E10-8
Payroll, accounting for, 508, 512–513, 512E10-5
   decision guidelines, 519
   employer payroll taxes, 511
      FICA, 511
      unemployment compensation taxes, 511, 512E10-4
   gross pay and net (take-home) pay, 508
   optional, 510–511
   summary of, 511
   summary problems, 520–521
   see also Current liabilities and payroll; Payroll system; Withholding deductions
Percent-of-sales method *A method of estimating uncollectible receivables that calculates uncollectible-account expense. Also called the income-statement approach,* 411–412, 414E8-3
Performance evaluation and the balanced scorecard
   accounting vocabulary, 1297
   apply your knowledge
      decision case, 1311
   assessing your progress
      exercises, 1300–1305
      problems, 1305–1310
   balanced scorecard, 1273–1273
      perspectives of, 1273, 1274E25-4
         customer, 1275
         financial, 1273–1274
         internal business, 1276
         learning and growth, 1276–1277
   decision guidelines, 1278, 1292
   evaluation systems, goals of, 1270–1271
   key performance indicators, 1273
   limitations of, 1272
   responsibility accounting performance reports, 1280–1282
      cost center, 1280, 1280E25-5
      management by exception and, 1280–1281
      profit center, 1281–1281, 1281E25-7
      revenue center, 1281, 1281E25-6
   review questions (quick check), 1298–1299
   service department costs, allocating, 1295–1296
   summary problems, 1279, 1293–1294
   see also Decentralization; Investment center
Periodic inventory system *A system in which the business does not keep a continuous record of inventory on hand. At the end of the period, it makes a physical count of on-hand inventory and uses this information to prepare the financial statements,* 260
   accounting for merchandise in
      vs. perpetual, 352, 353–354E6A-1
      costing methods, 351–352
      exercises, 311, 354–355
      problems, 355
      purchases, recording, 308–309, 308E5B-1
      sale of, recording, 310, 310E5B-2
      transportation costs, recording, 309
   cost of goods sold in, 277–278, 278E5-11
Permanent accounts *Accounts that are not closed at the end of the period—the asset, liability, and capital accounts,* 208
Perpetual inventory system *The accounting inventory system in which the business keeps a running record of inventory and cost of goods sold,* 260
   accounting for inventory in, 260–261
      purchases, 261, 261E5-3
         discounts, 262
         returns and allowances, 262
         summary of, 264
         transportation costs, 262–263, 263E5-4
      sales
         cash sale, 264–266, 265E5-5
         discounts, returns, and allowances, 266–267
         on account, 266
         sales revenue, cost of goods sold, and gross profit, 268
   costing methods
      average-cost, 322–323, 322E6-6
      comparing, 324, 342E6-7-8
      FIFO, 319–320, 320E6-4
      LIFO, 321–322, 321E6-5
      summary problem, 325–327
   purchase of inventory, 261, 261E5-3
      discounts, 262
      returns and allowances, 262
      summary of, 264
      transportation costs, 262–263, 263E5-4
   sale of inventory
      cash sale, 264–266, 265E5-5
      discounts, returns, and allowances, 266–267
      on account, 266
      sales revenue, cost of goods sold, and gross profit, 268
Phishing expeditions, 364
Planning *Choosing goals and deciding how to achieve them,* 809
Plant assets *Long-lived tangible assets, such as land, buildings, and equipment, used to operate a business,* 135
   accounting vocabulary, 481
   applying your knowledge
      decision case, 496
      ethical issue, 496–497
      financial statement case, 497
      team project, 497
   assessing your progress
      exercises, 484–488
      problems, 489–495
   cost of, measuring
      buildings, 458
      capital expenditures, 459–460, 460E9-3
      furniture and fixtures, 458
      land and land improvements, 457–458, 457E9-2
      lump-sum (basket) purchases of assets, 458–459
      machinery and equipment, 458
   disposing of, 471
      by exchanging (trade-ins), 473–474
      by selling, 472–473
   ethical issues, 478
   expenses of, related, 456E9-1
      accounting for (decision guidelines), 479
   review questions (quick check), 482–483
   summary problems, 480
   see also Depreciation; Intangibles
Post-audits *Comparing a capital investment's actual net cash inflows to its projected net cash inflows,* 1114
Postclosing trial balance *List of the accounts and their balances at the end of the period after journalizing and posting the closing entries. This last step of the accounting cycle ensures that the ledger is in balance to start the next accounting period,* 210–211, 211E4-11
Posting *Copying amounts from the journal to the ledger,* 69, 70E2-6, 81, 81E2-13
Posting reference (Post. Ref), 81
Preferred stock *Stock that gives its owners certain advantages over common stockholders, such as the right to receive dividends before the common stockholders and the right to receive assets before the common stockholders if the corporation liquidates,* 552, 553E11-5, 562
   issuing, 557
   noncumulative, 564
Preferred stockholders, 775
Premium *Excess of a bond's issue price over its maturity value. Also called bond premium,* 643
Prepaid expense *Advance payments of expenses. Examples include prepaid rent, prepaid insurance, and supplies,* 63, 133
   adjustments, 142E3-7
   depreciation and, similarities to, 135
   recorded initially as an expense, 181–182
   rent, 133
   supplies, 134
Prepaid rent expense, 133–134

Present value *Amount a person would invest now to receive a greater amount in the future,* 644
  tables, 1164
    of an annuity, 1165
Present value index. *See* Profitability index
Prevention costs *Costs incurred to avoid poor-quality goods or services,* 977
Price standards, 1228, 1228E24-5
Price variance *The difference in prices (actual price per unit minus standard price per unit) of an input multiplied by the actual quantity of the input,* 1231
Price/earnings (P/E) ratio *Ratio of the market price of a share of common stock to the company's earnings per share. Measures the value that the stock market places on $1 of a company's earnings,* 774–775
Principal *The amount loaned out by the payee and borrowed by the maker of the note,* 420
Principle amount *The amount loaned out by the payee and borrowed by the maker of the note,* 642
Prior-period adjustment *A correction to retained earnings for an error of an earlier period,* 616
Proceeds, 452
Process costing *System for assigning costs to large numbers of identical units that usually proceed in a continuous fashion through a series of uniform productions steps or processes,* 902–903
  accounting vocabulary, 929
  and job order costing, differences between, 903, 904E18-1, 905, 905E18-2
  applying your knowledge
    decision case, 946–947
    ethical issue, 947
    team project, 947–949
  assessing your progress
    appendix assignments, 955–957
    exercises, 932–938
    problems, 939–945
  conversion costs, 906
  equivalent units of production, 906–907, 907E18-3
  FIFO method, 950
    computing equivalent units, 952
    conversion costs, equivalent units of, 953
    costs, assigning to units completed and in ending work, 954–955, 955E18A-4
    direct materials, equivalent units of, 953
    flow of physical units, summarizing, 950–952, 951E18A-1, 952E18A-2
    total costs per equivalent unit, summarizing and computing, 953, 954E18A-3
    transferred in equivalent units, 953
  in first department, with no beginning inventory, 907, 908E18-4
    added costs, 908–909
    assigning costs to units completed and in ending work, 912–913, 913E18-9
    cost per equivalent unit, computing, 911–912, 911E18-7
    decision guidelines, 914
    flow of physical units, summarizing, 909, 911E18-6
    output, computing in terms of equivalent units, 910, 910E18-5
    production processes, E18-4
  in second department, 917, 917E18-10
    costs, assigning to units completed and in end work, 921–923, 921E18-14, 922E18-15
    decision guidelines, 925
    equivalent units, computing, 919–920, 920E18-12
    flow of physical units, summarizing, 919
    total costs per equivalent unit, summarizing and computing, 920–921, 921E18-13
    weighted-average process costing method, 917–918, 918E18-11
  production cost report, how managers use, 923–924, 924E18-16
  review questions (quick check), 930–931
  summary problems, 915–916, 926–928
Processes, 902
Product costing, 902
Production cost report *Summarizes a processing department's operations for a period,* 923, 924E18-16
Profit center *A subunit responsible for generating revenue and controlling costs,* 1280
Profit margin, 1285
Profitability index *An index that computes the number of dollars returned for every dollar invested, with all calculations performed in present value dollars. Computed as present value of net cash inflows divided by investment,* 1138
Promissory note *A written promise to pay a specified amount of money at a particular future date,* 406, 420, 420E8-4
Public Company Accounting Oversight Board, 6
Purchase invoice. *See* Invoice

Q
Quantity standards, 1229–1230
Quantity variance. *See* Efficiency (quantity) variance
Quick ratio *Ratio of the sum of cash plus short-term investments plus net current receivables to total current liabilities. Tells whether the entity can pay all its current liabilities if they come due immediately. Also called the acid-test ratio,* 425

R
Rate of return on common stockholders' equity *Net income minus preferred dividends, divided by average common stockholders' equity. A measure of profitability. Also called return on equity,* 567–568, 773–774
Rate of return on net sales *Ratio of net income to net sales. A measure of profitability. Also called return on sales,* 772
Rate of return on total assets *Net income plus interest expense, divided by average total assets. This ratio measures a company's success in using its assets to earn income for the persons who finance the business. Also called return on assets,* 567, 773
Ratios, using in financial statement analysis
  current liabilities, measuring ability to pay
    acid-test ratio, 769
    current ratio, 767, 768E15-8, 769
  decision guidelines for, 777–778
  inventory and receivables, measuring ability to sell and collect
    accounts receivable turnover, 770
    days' sales in receivables, 770–771
    inventory turnover, 769–770
  long-term debt, measuring ability to pay debt ratio, 771
    times-interest-earned ratio, 772
  profitability, measuring
    common stockholders' equity, rate of return on, 773–774
    earnings per share of common stock, 774
    net sales, rate of return on, 772
    total assets, rate of return on, 773
  stock investments, analyzing
    book value per share of common stock, 775–776
    dividend yield, 775
    price/earnings ratio, 774–775
  see also Financial statements analysis
Ratios, using to make decisions
  gross profit percentage, 276, 276E5-9
  inventory turnover, rate of, 276–277, 277E5-10
Receivables *Monetary claims against a business or an individual,* 406
  accounting vocabulary, 429–430
  applying your knowledge
    decision cases, 449
    ethical issue, 450
    financial statement case, 450
    team project, 450–451
  assessing your progress
    exercises, 433–439
    problems, 439–448
  bankcard sales, 417
  collection of, establishing internal control over, 407
  controlling, managing, and accounting for (decision guidelines), 409
  credit card sales, 416
  credit department, 408
  debit card sales, 417
  decision making in, using accounting information, 424–425, E8-6
    accounting for (decision guidelines), 427
    acid-test (or quick) ratio, 425
    days' sales in receivables, 426
  review questions (quick check), 431–432
  summary problems, 418–419, 428
  types of, 406, 407E8-1
  see also Notes receivable; Uncollectables, accounting for
Recovery of a bad account, 415
Red flags, 776
Regular prices, how to set
  considerations, 1064–1065, 1065E21-7
  cost-plus, 1068–1069E21-12
  price-takers *vs.* price-setters, 1065, 1065E21-8
  see also Target pricing
Relative-sales-value method, 458
Relevant information *Expected future data that differs among alternatives,* 1059–1060, 1059E21-2
  nonfinancial, 1060
  to special business decision, 1060–1061, 1061E21-3
Relevant range *The band of volume where total fixed costs remain constant and the variable cost per unit remains constant,* 1012, 1012E20-4
Reliability (objectivity) principle, 12
Report form, 212
Research and development (R&D) *Researching and developing new or improved products or services, or the processes for producing them,* 477
Residual income (RI) *A measure of profitability and efficiency, computed as the excess of actual income over a specified minimum acceptable income,* 1283, 1287–1288
Responsibilities, assignment of, 361
Responsibility accounting *A system for evaluating the performance of each responsibility center and its manager,* 1189

blame, not a question of, 1193
management by exception, 1193
master budget and (decision guidelines), 1194
performance reports, 1191–1193, 1280–1282
 at various levels, 1192E23-20
 cost center, 1280, 1280E25-5
 management by exception and, 1280–1281
 organization chart, partial, 1191E23-19
 performance measures, other, 1193
 profit center, 1281–1281, 128125-7
 revenue center, 1281, 1281E25-6
see also Master budget, and responsibility accounting

Responsibility center *A part or subunit of an organization whose manager is accountable for specific activities,* 1189
 decentralization and, 1269, 1270E25-2
 types of, 1189–1190, 1190E23-18

Retained earnings *Capital earned through profitable operation of the business,* 14, 64, 550–551, 598
 components of, 14E1-7
 deficit, 551
 statement of, 615, 615E12-9
  combined with income, 615, 615E12-10
 see also corporations, retained earnings, treasury stock, and the income statement

Return on assets *Net income plus interest expense, divided by average total assets. This ratio measure a company's success in using its assets to earn income for the persons who finance the business. Also called rate of return on total assets,* 567

Return on investment (ROI) *A measure of profitability and efficiency, computed as operating income divided by total assets,* 1283, 1284–1287

Returns
 purchase, 262
 recording, 309
 sales, 266, 267

Revenue *Amounts earned by delivering goods or services to customers. Revenues increase owner's equity,* 14, 64

Revenue center *A subunit responsible only for generating revenue,* 1280

Revenue principle *The basis for recording revenues; tells accountants when to record revenue and the amount of revenue to record,* 130, 130E3-2

Reversing entries *Special journal entries that ease the burden of accounting for transactions in the next period,* 211, 243, 244
 accounting without, 244
 accrued expenses, accounting for, 243–244
 making, 244–245
 problem, 245
Residual value, 462
Risk assessment, 360
Risk Management Association, 764, 769, 772
Rolling up unit budgets, 1188–1189, 1188E23-17
Rules of debit and credit, 67
 accounting equation and, 67E2-3
 revenues and expenses, 69–70, 70E2-8
 and normal balances, 71, 71E2-9

S

Salary, 508
Salary expense, 512
Sale on account, 266

Sales *The amount that a merchandiser earns from selling its inventory,* 14, 264

Sales budget *A detailed plan that shows the estimated sales revenue for a future period,* 1177, 1177E23-6

Sales discount *Reduction in the amount receivable from a customer, offered by the seller as an incentive for the customer to pay promptly. A contra account to sales revenue,* 266
Sales invoice, 72

Sales mix *Combination of products that make up total sales,* 1025–1027

Sales returns and allowances *Decreases in the seller's receivable from a customer's return of merchandise or from granting the customer an allowance from the amount owed to the seller. A contra account to sales revenue,* 266

Sales revenue *The amount that a merchandiser earns from selling its inventory. Also called sales,* 14, 264, 268
Sales tax payable, 502

Sales volume variance *The difference arising only because the number of units actually sold differs from the static budget units. This equals the difference between a static budget amount and a flexible budget amount,* 1224, 1224E24-3

Salvage value *Expected cash value of an asset at the end of its useful life. Also called estimated residual value,* 461

Sarbanes-Oxley Act of 2000 (SOX) *A congressional act that enhances internal control and financial reporting requirements, and establishes new regulatory requirements for publicly traded companies and their independent auditors,* 7, 358–359, 547

Secured bonds *Bonds that give bondholders the right to take specified assets of the issuer if the issuer fails to pay principal or interest,* 643

Securities and Exchange Commission (SEC), 6, 809
Security cameras, 364
Selling expenses, 273

Sensitivity analysis *A "what if" technique that asks what results will be if actual prices or costs change, or if an underlying assumption changes,* 1022
 and capital budgeting decisions, 1139
 fixed costs, changing, 1023
 impact of changes, summary of, E20-7
 information technology and, 1024, 1187–1188
 margin of safety, 1023–1024, 1024E20-7
 selling price, changing, 1022
 variable costs, changing, 1022–1023
Separation of duties, 361–362

Serial bonds *Bonds that mature in installments over a period of time,* 642, 656
Service charge, 369
Service department costs, allocating, 1295–1296
Service economy, shift towards, 811
Service revenue, 14

Shareholder *A person who owns stock in a corporation. Also called stockholder,* 8
Shareholders' equity. *See* Stockholder's equity
Short-term business decisions
 accounting vocabulary, 1088
 apply your knowledge
  decision case, 1107
  ethical issue, 1107–1108
  team project, 1108–1109
 assessing your progress
  exercises, 1091–1099
  problems, 1100–1106
 for dropping products, departments, territories
  considerations for, 1073E21-13, 1074E21-14
  direct fixed costs that can be avoided, 1074–1075, 1075E21-16
  fixed costs that exist and will not change, 1074, 1075E21-15
  other, 1075–1076
 making
  by managers, 1058, 1058E21-1
  keys to, 1060–1061, 1061E21-3
 on outsourcing, 1079–1082, 1080E21-19–20, 1082E21-21
 on selling as is or processing further, 1082–1085, 1083E21-22–23, 1085E21-24
 product mix, and constraints, 1076–1079, 1077E21-17–18
 relevant information, 1059–1060, 1059E21-2
  decision guidelines, 1070
 relevant nonfinancial information and, 1060
 review questions (quick check), 1089–1090
 special (decision guidelines), 1085
 special sales orders, 1061–1062
  when to accept, 1062–1064, 1062E21-4, 1063E21-5, 1064E21-6
 summary problems, 1071–1073, 1086–1087
 see also Regular prices, how to set; Target price

Short-term note payable *Promissory note payable due within one year, a common form of financing,* 501
Signature card, 366

Single-step income statement *Format that groups all revenues together and then lists and deducts all expenses together without drawing any subtotals,* 275, 275E5-8
Slide, 80
Social Security Act, 509
Social Security Tax, 509, 511
Source documents, 72
 journalizing transactions and posting, 72–78
 ledger accounts after posting, 78
 see also Trial balance
Special orders
 short-term business decisions, 1061–1062
  accepting, 1062–1064, 1062E21-4, 1063E21-5, 1064E21-6

Spreadsheet *A computer program that links data by means of formulas and functions; an electronic work sheet*
 for statement of cash flows, 748
 noninvesting and financing activities on, 750, 750E14B-2
 transaction analysis on, indirect method, 748, 749E14B-1, 750
 transaction analysis on, direct method, 752, 751E14B-3
Stable-monetary-unit concept, 12
Stakeholders, management accountability to, 808–809, 808E16-1, 809E16-2

Standard cost *A budget for a single unit,* 1228
 accounting systems
  income statement for management, 1241–1242, E24-13
  journal entries, 1239–1241, 1241E24-12
 application, 1229

price standards, 1228, 1228E24-5
quantity standards, 1229–1230
summary problem, 1244–1246
use of by companies, reasons for, 1230
variance analysis, 1231–1232, 1231E24-6, 1232E24-7
    decision guidelines, 1243
see also Flexible budget; Flexible budgets and standard costs

Stated interest rate *Interest rate that determines the amount of cash interest the borrower pays and the investor receives each year,* 642, 645

Stated value *An arbitrary amount that accountants treat as though it were par value,* 553, 556

Statement of budgeted cash receipts and payments *Details how the business expects to go from the beginning cash balance to the desired ending balance. Also called the cash budget,* 1182

Statement of cash flows *Report of cash receipts and cash payments during a period,* 21, 692
  accounting vocabulary, 709
  applying your knowledge
    decision cases, 733–734
    ethical issue, 734
    financial statement, 735
    team projects, 735
  assessing your progress
    appendix assignments, 752–753
    exercises, 712–722
    problems, 723–732
  cash equivalents, 693
  direct method of preparing statements, 736–737
    comparative balance sheet, 73714A-2
    for financing activities, 739–740
    for investing activities, 739
    for investing and financing, computing, 743
    for noncash investing and financing activities, 740
    for operating activities, 737–739, 73814A-3
    for operating cash flows, computing, 740, 741E14A-4–5, 743, 742E14A-6
    for payments to employees and payments for interest and income tax, computing, 743
    format of, 73614A-1
  financing activities, 694, 694E14-2
  free cash flows, measuring cash adequacy, 704, 743
  indirect method of preparing statements, 695–696
    comparative balance sheet, 696E14-4
    for financing activities, 701–703, 703E14-9
    for investing activities, 700–701, 701E14-8
    for noncash investing and financing activities, 703–704, 704E14-10
    for operating activities, 694E14-2, 696, 697E14-5–6, 698–699, 699E14-7
    formats of, 694 (*see also* Direct method; Indirect method)
    format of, 695E14-3 (*see also* Direct method; Indirect method)
  investing activities, 693, 694E14-2
  investments, evaluating (decision guidelines), 705, 744
  review questions (quick check), 710–711
  spreadsheets
    preparing, using direct method, 750, 751E14B-3, 752

    preparing, using indirect method, 748, 750, 74914B-1
    using to prepare statement, 748
  summary problems, 706–708, 745–747
  timing of, 692, 693E14-1

Statement of earnings *Summary of an entity's revenues, expenses, and net income or net loss for a specific period. Also called the income statement or the statement of operations,* 21

Statement of financial position, 21
Statement of retained earnings, 21, 273

Static budget *The budget prepared for only one level of sales volume. Also called the master budget,* 1222, 1222E24-1

Stock *Shares into which the owners' equity of a corporation is divided,* 552
  vs. bonds, advantages and disadvantages of, 656–657, 657E13-4
  classes of, 552
    common and preferred, 552, 553E11-5
    par, stated value, and no-par, 553
  common, issuing, 553–554, 554E11-6
    at a premium, 554–555
    at par, 554
    for assets other than cash, 556
    no-par, 556
    no-par, with stated value, 556
  ethical considerations, 557
  preferred, issuing, 557
  values of, 565–566, 566E11-9
Stock certificates, 548, 549E11-3

Stock dividend *A distribution by a corporation of its own to stockholders,* 599, 599E12-1
  accounting for, 600E12-2
  and splits, compared, 602, 602E12-5
  issuing, reasons for, 599
  recording, 599–600, 600E12-2, 600E12-3
    large, 601
    small, 600
  stockholders' equity after, 600, 601E12-3

Stock split *An increase in the number of outstanding share of stock coupled with a proportionate reduction in the value of the stock,* 601
  2-for-1, 601, 601E12-4
  and dividends, compared, 602, 602E12-5
Stock values, 565

Stockholder *A person who owns stock in a corporation. Also called a shareholder. Also called shareholder,* 8
  limited liability of, 10
  rights of, 552

Stockholders' equity *Owners' equity of a corporation,* 13, 64, 549, 549E11-4, 598
  dividends paid to, by a corporation, 552
  issues
    reporting variations, 606, 607E12-7
    retained earnings, restrictions on, 605–606, 607E12-7
    stock, retirement of, 605
  of a corporation (decision guidelines), 559
  paid-in capital, 550, 557, 558E11-7
  retained earnings, 550–551
    deficit in, 551
  return on, 567–568
  stockholders' rights, 552
  summary problem, 560–562
  total assets, rate of return on, 567
  types of, 64
  see also Stock

Straight-line (SL) depreciation method *Depreciation method in which an equal amount of depreciation expense is assigned to each year of asset use,* 462–463, 462E9-6, 465
Straight-line amortization, 647, 651–652
  of discount, 647–648
  of premium, 651–652
Streamlined procedures, 378

Subsidiary ledger *Record of accounts that provides supporting details on individual balances, the total of which appears in a general ledger account,* 406

Sunk cost *A past cost that cannot be changed regardless of which future action is taken,* 1059

Suppliers, 738
Supplies expense, 134–135

T

T-account, 66

Take-home pay *Gross pay minus all deductions. The amount of compensation that the employee actually takes home,* 508, 515, 516, 517

Target cost *Allowable cost to develop, produce, and deliver the product or service. Equals target price minus desired profit,* 968

Target full cost *The full cost to develop, produce, and deliver the product or service,* 1066, 1066E21-9

Target price *What customers are willing to pay for the product or service,* 967
  calculating
    fixed cost, 1067, 1067E21-10
    full cost, 1066–1067, 1066E21-9
    unit variable cost, 10671067E21-11
  increasing sales, 1068
  vs. traditional cost-based pricing, 967E19-10

Temporary accounts *The revenue and expense accounts that relate to a particular accounting period and are closed at the end of the period. For a proprietorship, the owner withdrawal account is also temporary,* 208

Term bonds *Bonds that all mature at the same time for a particular lease,* 642

Time period *The period of time during which interest is computed. It extends from the original date of the note to the maturity date. Also called the note term or interest period,* 420

Time record *Source document used to trace direct labor to specific jobs,* 868, 870E17-10

Time value of money *The fact that money can be invested to earn income over time,* 644, 1122
  and discounted cash-flow models, comparing, E9-15–16
  factors affecting, 1122, 1123E22-5
  future/present value factors, 1124–1126
  future/present values, along the time continuum, 1123–1124, 1123E22-6
  single sums and annuities, calculating present values of using PV factors, 1126–1128, 1128E22-7
  see also Bonds payable; Capital investment decisions
Time-based competition, 811

Time-period concept *Ensures that information is reported at regular intervals,* 131–132

Times-interest-earned ratio *Ratio of income from operations to interest expense. Measures the number of times that operating income can cover interest expense. Also called the interest-coverage ratio,* 772

Tombstones, 553–554, 554E11-6
Total fixed costs *Costs that do not change in total despite wide changes in volume,* 1009, 1009E20-2
Total manufacturing costs *Costs that include direct materials, direct labor and manufacturing overhead,* 821
Total quality management (TQM) *A philosophy of delighting customers by providing them with superior products and services. Requires improving quality and eliminating defects and waste throughout the value chain,* 811, 977
Total variable costs *Costs that change in total in direct proportion to changes in volume,* 1008, 1009E20-1
Trade receivable. *See* Note receivable
Trademarks *Assets that represent distinctive identifications of a product or service,* 476
Transaction *An event that affects the financial position of a particular entity and can be recorded reliably,* 15
  accounting vocabulary, 89
  analyzing
    debit/credit (demo docs), 116–125
    decision guidelines for, 84
  applying your knowledge
    decision cases, 113
    ethical issue, 114
    financial statement case, 114
    team project, 114–115
  assessing your progress
    exercises, 92–101
    problems, 101–112
  business, 15–19
  double-entry accounting
  evaluating, 19–21, 20E1-8
  from actual business documents, 82–83, 82E2-15, 83E2-16
  review questions (quick check), 90–91
Transferred-in costs *Costs incurred in a previous process that are carried forward as part of the product's cost when it moves to the next process,* 920
Transportation costs, 262
  FOB terms, 262–263, 263E5-4
  freight-in, 263
  freight-out, 264
  recording, 309
Transposition, 80
Treasurer *In a large company, the person in charge of writing checks,* 361
Treasury stock *A corporation's own stock that it has issued and later reacquired,* 602
  basics of, 603–604
  purchase of, 602–60

  sale of, 604–605, 605E12-6
  see also Corporations, retained earnings, treasury stock, and the income statement
Trend percentages *A form of horizontal analysis in which percentages are computed by selecting a base year as 100% and expressing amounts for following years as a percentage of the base amount,* 760
Trial balance *A list of all accounts with their balances,* 78–79, 79E2-11-12
  balance sheet and, 79
  errors in, correcting, 80
  summary problem, 85–88
  unadjusted, 132–133, 132E3-4
  see also Adjusted trial balance
Trojan *A malicious program that hides inside a legitimate program and works like a virus,* 364

U

Uncollectibles, accounting for
  allowance method, 410–411
  estimating, 411
    aging-of-accounts-receivable method, 412–413, 413E8-2
    percent-of-sales method, 411–412
    using percent-of-sales and aging methods together, 414, 414E8-3
  writing off, 414
    direct write-off method, 415
    recovery of, 415
Underallocated manufacturing overhead *The manufacturing overhead allocated to work in Process Inventory is less than the amount of manufacturing overhead costs actually incurred,* 867
Underwriters, 553
Unearned revenue *A liability created when a business collects cash from customers in advance of doing work. Also called deferred revenue,* 140–141, 503
  recorded initially as a revenue, 182–183
Unemployment compensation tax *Payroll tax paid by employers to the government, which uses the money to pay unemployment benefits to people who are out of work,* 511
Unit of output, 463
Units-of-production (UOP) depreciation method *Depreciation method by which a fixed amount of depreciation is assigned to each unit of output produced by an asset,* 463, 463E9-7, 465

V

Vacations, mandatory, 364
Value engineering *Reevaluating activities to reduce costs while satisfying customer needs,* 967

Variable costing *The costing method that assigns only variable manufacturing costs to products,* 1049
  and absorption costing, differences between, 1049, 1049E20A-1
  applying, *vs.* absorption costing, 1050–1051, 1051E20A-2
Variable costs *Costs that change in total in direct proportion to changes in volume,* 1008–1009, 1009E20-1
Vertical analysis *Analysis of a financial statement that reveals the relationship of each statement item to a specified base, which is the 100% figure,* 760, 1231
  illustration, Google Inc., 761, 761E15-4
  of balance sheet, 762E15-5
Voucher *Instrument authorizing a cash payment,* 378, 378E7-12

W

Wages, 508
Warranty expense, 504
Weighted average cost of capital (WACC) *The company's cost of capital; the target return used in EVA calculations to denote the return expected by stockholders and long-term creditors,* 1288
Weighted-average process costing method *A process costing method that costs all equivalent units of work with a weighted average of the previous period's and the current period's cost per equivalent unit,* 918
Withholding allowances, 509
Withholding deductions, 508, 509
  for employee income tax, 509–510, 510E10-3, 511
  optional, 510–511, 517
Work sheet *A columnar document designed to help move data from the trial balance to their financial statements,* 145, 201
  for closing entries (demo doc), 248–255
  for completing the accounting cycle, 202E4-2, 206, 206E4-7, 207E4-8
  summary problem, 204–205
  for merchandising business, 283–284, 283E5A-1
Working capital *Current assets minus current liabilities; measures a business's ability to meet its short-term obligations with its current assets,* 767

Company Index

A

Abalone Seafood, 1104–1105
Abbey Co., 384
ABC, 393
Abercrombie and Fitch, 1066
Abraham Woody, CPA, PC, 38
Abram Technology, 998
Accent Photography, Inc., 39
ACDelco, 1062–1064, 1066–1068, 1073–1076, 1091
Acme Petroleum, 1106
ADP, 1282
Advanced Audio Productions, 399–400
Advanced Automotive Corp., 33, 101
Advanced Design, 1095
A.G. Edwards, 801
Aguilar Outsourcing Solutions, 440–441
Air & Sea Travel, 32, 485
Air West Airlines, 641, 642, 643E13-1, 644–646, 644E13-2, 649, 651, 653, 654, 656, 658, 682, 683, 685
Alamo, Inc., 987–988
Alamo Co., 891–892
Alba Foundry, 883–884
Alden Group, Inc., 752–753
Alert Defensive Driving, Inc., 97–98
Alioto Corp., 785–786
Allegra, 1130–1132, 1138–1143
Allen Samuel Road Service, 36
Alliance Printing of Baltimore, 1208–1210
Allied Electronics Corp., 611–615, 622–623
Allied Telecom, 664
Allison Landscaping, 34
Allstate, 611
Alpha Graphics, Inc., 789
Alpha Graphics Corp., 237–238, 300
Amazon.com, 6, 38, 49, 114, 179, 241, 260, 276, 277, 306–307, 315, 318, 349, 402, 450, 497, 540, 545, 594, 638, 655, 678, 735, 803, 811, 813, 1085, 1120, 1148, 1169, 1170–1171, 1173, 1174, 1187, 1194, 1200–1201
American Airlines, 360, 458, 459–462, 469, 470, 642
American Express, 416, 434, 961
American Reserve Rare Coins (ARRC), 723, 726–727
America Online (AOL), 475
A-Mobile, Inc., 727
A-Mobile Wireless, 584
Amy Fisk, Attorney, PC., 42
Anchor Corp., 692, 695–697, 699–703, 736–741, 743, 748–752
Anderson Winery, 936–937
Annita Maxwell Co., 714
AOL4Free.com, 364
A-1 Accounting Service, 32
A-1 Publishers Co., 296
A-1 Rentals, 34–35
A-1 Security Consultants, 487
Apache Motors, 689
A ;aa; Fire & Safety Co., 106–107
Aqua Pure, 1205
Arctic Cat RVs, Inc., 301–302
Ariba Corp., 581
Arthur Andersen, 358, 383
Astro Antenna Corp., 986–987
Athens Academy Surplus, 629
Audio Forest stereo shop, 1210
Audiology Associates, Inc., 636
Audio Manufacturers, 936
Audio-Video, 347
Augusta National golf course, 1210
Aussie Travel, 1038
Austin Driving School, Inc., 627
Austin Sound Center, 258, 260–279, 283, 286–287, 308–310, 308E5B-1, 315, 590
Auto Components, 1094
Automax, 839
Avant Garde Clothiers, 435
Avery Trucking Co., 437
Avis Rent A Car, 476
Axiom Sports Co., 677
Azalea Technology, Inc., 293–294
Azbell Electronics, 796–797
Aziz, 1086

B

Baker Electric Co., 294
Baker Publishing Co., 400
Banc One Corp., 634
Banfield DVDs, Inc., 799–780
Bank Compliance Consultants, 588
Bank of America, 382, 1208, 1209
Bank of Nashville, 446
Barnett Associates, 870E17-10
Baseball Hall of Fame, 1095
Bass Shoe Co., 842
Battery Power, 1205
Baylor Associates, 373–374
Bed Bath & Beyond, 348
Beechcraft, Inc., 587
Bell South, 1190
Bennett Builders, 1096
Bernard Associates, 723
Best Buy, 348
Best Foot Forward, Inc., 38–39
Best Yet Catering, 159
Best Yet Electronic Center, 355
Beta North America, Inc., 675
Betsy Ross Flag Co., 802–803
Better Days Ahead, 114
Bevil Industries, 1158
Big Bend Picture Frames, 790
Big Daddy Music Co., 297–298
Big Tex Toys, 453
Big Time Investment Group, 1042
Billy's Worm Farm, 946–947
Binney and Smith, 901
BKFin.com, 1107
Blackwell Engineering, 96
Blinko Copy Center, Inc., 44, 172–173
Bloomingdale's, 1203
Bluebird Design, Inc., 889–890
Blume Irrigation Systems, 233
Blumenthal's, 513–514, 513E10-6, 514E10-7, 516E10-10, 526
BMS Pharmaceuticals, 295
Bobby's Bagels, 637–638
Bob's Cream Soda, Inc., 96
Body Studio, 155–156
Boeing Co., 7, 460, 477, 482, 484, 902, 1171–1172
Boise-Cascade, 1213
Boje, Inc, 1250–1251
Bombadier Industries, 539
Bonaparte, 790
Boozer Jewelers, 291
Boston Enterprises, 880
Boston Police Department, 1213
Bowen Electric Co., 169–170
BP (British Petroleum), 485, 1207
Brett Kaufman Enterprises, 223
Brett Wilkinson, Attorney, PC, 91
Bria, 1257–1258
Brian Corp., 881
Brigadier Homebuilders, 675–676
British Productions, 1041
Broadway Shows, 1044
Bronson Shrimp Farms, 1003–1005
Broyhill, 1213
Brun, 1102
Buchanan Corp., 672–673
Budget Business Systems Co., 292–293
Bull & Bear, Inc., 663
Buoy, 1100
Burpee.com, 1207
Butler Supply Co., 407, 409

C

Cadillac (of GM), 595
Caesar Salad Dressings, 396
Calenergy Corp., 619–620
Cameron, 992
Campbell Appliance, 348
Campbell Soup Co., 1190–1191, 1207
see also International Soups and Sauces (division of Campbell Soup)
Campus Apartment Locators, 26–27
Candy Creations, 291–292
Cannon Photographic Supplies, Inc., 628
Capital One, 1066
Capitol Hill Corp., 721–722
Captain Billy Whizbang Hamburgers, Inc., 671
Carl Redmon Consulting, 46, 112, 175–176, 239, 304
Carlson Corp., 728–729
Carolina Communications Corp., 289–290
Carolina Home Improvements, 537
Carolina Sound, 800–801
Carolina Sports Consulting Corp., 39
Carpetmaster, 339
Carrier Corp., 967
Casey Carpet, 940–941
Casey Computer Co., 823
Caterpillar Inc., 760
Cavender's Boot City, 392
CBS, 476
Cellular Technologies, 1255–1256
Centennial Construction Co., 401
Central Forwarding, 397
Central Jersey Bancorp, 548
Central States Telecom, 491–492
Centroplex Service, Inc., 585
Century 21 Real Estate Co., 1213
Champs Sporting Goods, 393
Changing Seasons Health Spa, 672
Chase Financial Services, 727
Chase Home Finance, 632–633
Chazz, 1076–1079
Checkpoint Systems, 363
Cherokee Carpets, 438–439
Chevrolet, 318, 476, 499
Chevron, 852, 1083–1085
Chewning Corp., 575
Chicago Acoustics, 1035
Chicago Cubs, 485
Chicago O'Hare Airport, 469
Chick Landscaping and Nursery, 343
Chili's, 434
China Spring, 932–933
Chocolate Inc., 714
Chocolite, 1094
Chrome Accessories, 944
Chrysler, 1112
Chupa Chups, 930–931
Ciliotta Design Studio, Inc., 36–37
Cimmaron Co., 525
Cincinnati Corp., 664
Cisco Systems, 1210
Citadel Sporting Goods, 527
Citibank, 1210
City National Bank, 391
Claire Hunter Floral Designs, 32
Clason, Inc., 993
Classic Poster Co., 883
Clay Employment Services, 150, 204, 216

I-1

Company Index

Clear Spring Co., 938, 955
Cloud Break Consulting, 185, 248
Clyde's Pets, 840–841
CNN, 393
Cobra Golf Club Corp., 627
Coca-Cola, 6, 8, 63, 128, 212, 545, 553, 566, 579, 593, 611, 618, 961, 1098, 1213, 1289, 1310
Coldwell Banker, 41, 1210
Colgate-Palmolive, 1311
College of St. Mary, 526
Collins Consignment Sales, 240
Colorado Corp., 577
Columbus, Inc., 667
Community Bank, 487–488
Community One Bank, 158
Compaq, 595
Compass Bookstores, Inc., 675
Compass Software, 731
Computer Solutions, 493, 494
CompWest.com, 897
Concentra Medical Center, 435
Concert Enterprises, 50
Concilio Video Productions, 527
Connor Health Foods, 576
Conseco Oil Co., 491
Continental Airlines, 1107
Cookie Lapp Travel Design, 15–16, 18–19, 20E1-8, 21, 22E1-9, 23, 33, 63, 64–69, 68E2-4, 71–72, 77–80, 82–83, 94, 128–141, 142–144E3-7-3-9, 146, 148, 155, 158, 200–201, 206, 206E4-7, 207, 207E4-8, 208, 210, 212, 213E4-12, 214, 215, 243, 257, 279
Cookies By Design, 834
Cool Gyrations, 400
Cosmo Coffee, 1045–1046
Costco, 1221
Covenant Trucking Co., 488
Crawford-Austin Properties, 589–590
Crayola, 901–906, 907E18-3
Creative Communications, 591
Crescent City Music Co., 797–798
Crestview Pool Supply, 624
Cromwell Co., 590
Crop-Paper-Scissors, 348
Crossroads Bank, 535–536
Curves International, 479
CVS, 1286
CVZ, 1309
Cycle World, 1215

D

Daily Corp., 985
DaimlerChrysler, 802, 811
Dairymaid, 1099
Dairy Queen, 528
Daisy Dog Collars, 991–992
Dale Corp., 576
Dalton Carpets, 1210
Damon Air Conditioning Service, 183
Dan Bell, M.D., PC, 107–108
Datapoint Corp., 331
Datsun, Inc., 724
Dave Lundy Tax Service, Inc., 45–46
Dawkins Co., 1260
Dean Witter, 553
Dearborn Manufacturing Co., 630
Dee Electronics, 938
Deere & Co., 553
Deer Valley Ski Resort, 1111–1113, 1129, 1147, 1151, 1153–1155
DeFilippo Catering, 3–7, 5E1-2, 13–15, 32, 47, 61–63, 127, 128, 199, 215, 257–258, 286–287
DefTone, 1079–1082, 1080E21-20, 1082E21-21, 1099
De Graff Corp., 616
Dell, 5, 46, 47, 112, 157, 406, 485, 499, 595, 852, 877–878, 902, 903, 904E18-1, 960–961, 961E19-2, 970, 973, 977, 980, 983–984, 1076, 1210, 1270
DellNet, 1107
Delphian Corp., 560
Delta Airlines, 461, 897–899, 1057–1058, 1079, 1112, 1213, 1270
Denim Bones, 841
Dent Fixers, 842–843
Denver Corp., 664
Department of Defense, 363, 364
Deutsche Bank, 1213
Deutsch Limited, 666
Dialex Watches, 445
Diehard, 1024
Digital Cable Co., 485
Digital Subscriptions, Inc., 725–726, 727
Dimension Networks, Inc., 720–721
Discount Pharmacy, 390
Discount Tire Co., 290
Discover Card, 416
Disneyland, 1210
DisneyWorld, 1035
Ditto Clothing Consignments, 487
Dobbs Wholesale Antiques, 306
Domino's Pizza, 473
Donnie's Frozen Pizzas, 956
Dorman Builders, 422, 452–453
Doubletree Hotels, 1269
Dow Jones News Retrieval Service, 767
DR Painting, Inc., 51–59
Drugstore.com, 1210
DuBois Furniture Co., 388
Duck Associates, 1107–1108
Duncan and Noble, 833
Duncan Brooks Co., 677
Dunlap Dollar Stores, 398–399
Durango Ceramics, 528
Dvorak Interiors, 442
DVR Equipment, Inc., 712
Dwyer Delivery Service, 246–247
Dwyer Minerals Corp., 591–592
Dynaclean Air Purification Systems, Inc., 166–167

E

Eagle Mountain Flagpoles, 436
Eagle Resources, 341
Earthlink Wireless, 672
Eason Co., 990–991
East Terrace Medical Center (EMC), 445
Easy Card, 436–437
Easy Living, 1105
EBay, 33, 42, 63, 128, 475, 583, 691, 812
Educators Credit Union (ECU), 670
El Conquistador, Inc., 671
Elevator Service Co., 238
Elite Mobile Homes, 722
Email Designers, 677
EMusic.com, 364
Enchanted Designs, 788, 789
Engineered Products, 1156
EnginePro, Inc., 890
Ennis DVD Co., 1254
Enron Corp., 7, 358, 359, 382–383, 767, 823
Environmental Concerns Limited (ECL), 670
E-Prep MBA, 1039–1040
ErgoNow, 1253
Eric O'Neill Associates, 530
Este;fe; and Lauder, 593
Etown, 1214
E*Trade, 1213
Expo Stores, 1073
Exxel, Inc., 686–687
Exxon, 361, 417
ExxonMobil, 391
E-Z Loan Co., 450

F

Fabricut, 1095
Farley, Inc., 897
FASTPACK Manufacturing, 1054–1055
Fat Cat Furniture, 1025–1026
Federal Credit Bank, 396
Federal Express (FedEx), 451, 482, 485, 492, 583, 811, 830, 852, 960, 1230
see also Kinko's Copies (FedEx)
FHA Loan Co., 591
Fiber Systems, 1098
Fidelity Medical Supply, 724–725
Fido Grooming, 836–837
First Central Bank, 1212, 1213
First City Bank, 452
First Fidelity Bank, 428
Fischer Chemical, 963
Fitzwater Co., 729–730
Fleet Management Services, 1093–1094
Fleet Truck Wash, Inc., 227
Fleetwood Homebuilders, 667
Flexon Prosthetics, 355
Flips Gymnastics Center, 487
Flores Co., 981
Florida Orange, 932
Footlocker, 813
Forbes magazine, 13, 1160, 1168
Ford Motor Co., 595, 802, 811, 971, 1213
Fortune magazine, 1160, 1170, 1268
Fossil, 30–31, 137, 137E3-6, 324, 325
4th Gear Website Design, 443
FOX, 393
Fox Club Clothiers, 1040–1041
Foxey Flowers, 579
Frazier Corp., 90
Frederick, Inc., 989
Frito-Lay, 63, 932, 1268, 1283
Fun City Amusement Park, 390
Fuzzy Dice Auto Parts, 720

G

Galaxy Theater Production Co., 167, 365
Galena Park Fitness Gym, 663
Gangbuster Video, 35
Gap, 288, 310, 415
Garfield Co., 672–673
Gateway, 595, 960, 1171
Gatorade, 1203
General Electric (GE), 64, 324, 422, 452, 476, 477, 523–524, 686
General Mills, 1066
General Motors (GM), 6, 381, 499–500, 500E10-1, 503, 504, 505, 510–511, 519, 595, 802, 811, 967, 1190
Georgia Tea & Coffee Company, 531–532
Get Wired, Inc., 729–730, 731
Gia's Foods, 1053
Glass Doctor, 833
Glenn Real Estate Appraisal Co., 231–232
Global Link, 1035
Gloria's Grooming, 837
Georgia-Pacific, 881
Golden Bear Construction Co., 539
Golden Oaks Retirement Homes, 611
Goldman Co., 944–945
Gold Rush Resorts, 542–543
Golf America, Inc., 733
Good Times Express Co., 629
Goodyear Tire and Rubber Co., 340, 1210
Google Inc., 553, 691, 755–764, 756E15-1, 758E15-2, 759E15-3, 761E15-4, 762E15-5, 763E15-6-7, 770, 776, 811
Gordon's Steel Parts, 1039
Go Spirit, 1044–1045
Go Sports, 1211–1212
Graco, 1073
Grandma Jones Cookie Co., 1302
Granite Shoals Corp., 745–747
Grant Film Productions, 240–241
Grayson Architecture, Inc., 42–43
Great Fender, 1254
Great Lips, 942
Great Southern Furniture Co., 942–943
Green Bay Packers, 476
GreenThumb, 1100–1101
Gretta Chun Associates, 489–490
Grippers, 1202, 1203
GSK Inc., 726
GTE, 1107
Guadalupe Corp., 589
Guatemalan Imports, 634

H

Habitat for Humanity, 506, 512, 1171, 1210

Company Index

HAL, Inc., 551
Haley-Davis Printing Co., 493
Hallmark Cards, 834, 1066
Hall's Exteriors, 940
Hampton Pharmaceuticals, 996
Hanes Textiles, 376–377, 378
Hang Ten Co., 1038
Happy Feet, 1020, 1030
Harley-Davidson, 525, 906
Harley's of Chicago, Inc., 298–299
Harris Systems, 1002–1003
Harry, Inc., 989
Hartley Manufacturing, 885
Havens Corp., 666
Hawaiian Airlines, 551
Hawkeye Gymnastics Equipment, Inc., 718–719
Hayes RV Center, Inc., 289
HeadSmart, 1258
Healthy Foods, 933
Heart of Texas Telecom, 224–225
Heirloom Mills, 787–788
Hershey Foods, 378
Hewitt Corp., 669–670
Hewlett-Packard (HP), 488, 825, 960
Hiebert Chocolate Ltd., 896
Highland Academy, 164
High Mountain Lumber, 947
High Performance Cell Phones, 437
High-Pressure Steam Cleaning, 438
High Range, 996–997
Hillcrest Corp., 577–578
Hobart Sign Co., 345–346
Holiday Inn, 476, 1300
Holze Music Co., 674–675
Homart, 611
Home Depot, 212, 294, 973, 1073, 1108, 1210, 1306
Honda, 499, 1007
House and Garden Depot, 1280–1283, 1280E25-5, 1281E25-6-7, 1293, 1295
Houston, Inc., 664
H&R Block, 812
Hueske Electric Co., 224
Hughes Law Firm, 93
Hummer Limo Service Co., 168–169
Hunter Corp., 664
Hyatt Magic, 339–340

I

IBM, 334, 595, 1079
Idaho Food Processors, 947–949
Igourmet.com, 1213
IHOP Corp., 545–546, 549–551, 549E11-4, 553–555, 554E11-6, 565, 567–570, 575, 577, 597, 599–601, 601E12-3-4, 602, 611, 618, 622
IMAX, Inc., 687
Indianapolis Auto Parts (IAP), 971
Ink Jet Printing, 224
In Motion, 357–358, 361–362, 366–369, 368E7-4, 369E7-5, 371, 376–377, 377E7-10–11, 378–379, 378E7-12, 380, 381, 405, 409, 411, 412–415, 413E8-2, 424, 425, 425E8-6, 426–427, 455, 457–458, 461, 470, 484, 641
Intel, 475, 477, 546, 852, 960
Intergem Jewels, 311
International Publishing Co., 581
International Soups and Sauces (division of Campbell Soup), 1190, 1193
Internet Solutions, 397
Interstate Marble Importers, 433–434
In Touch, 1207
Investors Brokerage Co., 235
IPod, 212, 765, 1276
Ireland Limited, 389
I70 RV Park, 798

J

Jackson, Inc., 815
Jackson Auto Glass, Inc., 292
Jackson Lighting Co., 100
Jacobs-Cathey Co., 585
Jaguar (of Ford Motor Co.), 595, 692
Jake's Roasted Peanuts, 34
Jane's Preschool, Inc., 234–235
Jan Featherston, Realtor, PC, 41
Jan King Distributing Co., 280
Java Caf;fe;, 1161–1162
Java Co., 578
Java Inc., 779–780
JCPenney, 129, 1289
J.D. Hunter, 391
JDC, 286
Jennifer Vera, Inc., 630–631
Jen Weaver Insurance Co., 235–236
JetBlue, 641, 897–899
Jim's Shopping Bags, 340
JoAnn's Bridal Shops, 714
Job Link Employment Service, Inc., 162
Joe Griffin Photography, 494
Joe's Delivery Service, 812–813, 812E16-4
John Deere tractors, 553
John Eagle, CPA, PC, 163
John Hilton, CPA, PC, 104–105
Johnstone Corp., 986–987
Jolly Giant, 943–944
Jon Spelman Co., 687
Joy McDowell Tutoring Service, Inc., 99
Joy's Dance Studio, 392
Juniper Cove Music Store, 346–347
Jupiter Cable Co., 602–606, 605E12-6
Jupiter Co., 37
Just Do It!, 1086–1087

K

Kahn Corp., 556
Keaton, 994
Kellogg's, 838, 1105–1106
Kelly Realty, 441–442
Kettle Chips, 488
Kimball Corp., 765–766
Kincaid Co., 1042
Kindler Orthopedics, 393
King Burger, 338
Kingston Brush Co., 837
Kinko's Copies (FedEx), 91, 451, 458, 483, 485, 583
Knight Fashion, 1092
Knightsbridge, Inc., 633
Kohler Faucets, 1298–1299
Kool Kayaks, 885
KPMG, 526
Kraft Food, 109, 360, 852, 1083
Krazy Kustard Donuts, 1043
Kristi's Divinity Co., 937–938
Kroger, 417, 1073
KXAS-TV, 580
Kyler Industries, 1253

L

Lafferty Trailers, 537–538
Lagos Toy Co., 715
Lake Air Carpets, 344–345
Lake Air Interiors, Inc., 163
Lakeside Copy Center, 451
Lakewood Co., 667
Lakewood Occupational Therapy, Inc., 626–627
Lamar Scuba Center, 346
Lancer Bank, 400
Lancer Copy Center, 238–239
Land's End, 1213
Lane & Goble Bookstore, 389
Lantana Bank & Trust Co., 434
Largo Toys, 1000–1001
La Salle Exploration Co., 582–583
La Tapatía's Mexican Foods, 346
Laura Knipper, Attorney, PC, 108–109
Lawton, Inc., 995
La-Z Recliner Chairs, 447
Leather Goods Co., 339
Lee Bovina, CPA, PC, 99
Lee & Dunham, 397
LeMar Packaging, Inc., 1003
Lennox Health Foods, 630
Leno, 1204
Lexington Corp., 171–172
Lexington Pharmacies, 531
Lexis/Nexis, 767
Lexite Laminated, 389
Lexus, 12, 393, 595
LG, 932
Liberty Corp., 783–784
Liberty Sales Co., 269
Lieberman Manufacturing, Inc., 884–885
Lifemaster, 1097
Lille Corp., 565–566
Lima Manufacturing Co., 844
Limonade, 1050–1052, 1051E20A-2
Lindsey Landscaping, 165
Little People Learning Center (LPLC), 714–715
L.L. Bean, 1210, 1302
L&M Electronics, 344–345
Lockheed-Martin, 364
Lockridge-Priest, Inc., 584
Locos, 1160
Lomax Cosmetic Supply, 447–448
Lone Star Landscaping, Inc., 41
Longman, Inc., 1251–1253
Lonyx Telecom, 888–889
Lowe's Companies, 786–787
LubeNGo, 1037
Lucenay Interiors, 728, 731
Luxor, Inc., 992
Lyndon Olson Political Consultants, 535
Lynx Corp., 1265

M

Mackey Home Center, Inc., 301
Macy's, 363, 375, 864, 864E17-7
Mail.com, 1107
Mailmax Direct, 588
Mail Plus, 439
Mancini, 1260
Mane Event Styling Salons, Inc., 580
Manor House Restaurants, 580
Maple Leaf Capital Corp., 580–581
Maria's Birthday Cakes, 812, 813, 818, 822
Marie Lange, M.D., PC, 35–36
Marine.com, 1206
Mark Brown, M.D., PC, 93
Mark Todd Wireless, Inc., 582
Martial Arts Schools, Inc., 627
Martin Realtors, 884–885
MasterCard, 45, 417, 438, 449
Master Suites Hotels, 666
Maui Jane Sunglasses, 1095–1096
Max-Fli Golf Co., 835
Maxfli Hot Air Balloons, Inc., 633
Max's Beach Hut, 1098
Mayfield Dairies, 1213
Mayflower Moving Co., 98
MBC Television, 495
MC, Inc., 593
McAdam Co., 337
McDonald's, 133, 200, 425, 476, 502, 948, 949, 1213
MC Electronics, 668
MCI (WorldCom), 7, 358, 359, 478, 767, 823
Media Enterprises, 788
Medicare, 509, 510, 517
MediShare Precision Instruments, 668
Mediterranean Importers, 437
MedTech Corp., 557, 558E11-7
Meg Grayson, Architect, 160
Meijer's, 390
Menards, 1108–1109
Mercedes Benz, 595
Merrill Lynch, 553
Merry-Go-Round Sales Consultants, 93
Merry Maids Co., 161–162
Metro Bank, 33, 771
MG Corp., 625
Miami Co., 664
Micatin Corp., 785
Michael Riggs, M. D., 397
Microsoft Corp., 13, 361, 476, 539, 1107, 1123, 1124, 1132, 1134, 1143, 1145
Mid America Amusements Corp., 628
Mid-America Water Park, 170–171

Company Index

Millan & Co., 993
Milliken, 1213
MiniScribe, 331–332
Minnesota Music Makers (MMM), 800–801
Mintel Co., 975–977
Missing Link Exploration Co., 111
Mi Tierra's Driving School, 1033, 1040
M&M Mars, 424, 424E8-5, 427
Mobile Motorsports, Inc., 632
Moe's Mowing, 116
Monarch Map Co., 418
Money Line, 772
Money Tree, 881
Monterrey Co., 476–477
Monterrey Enterprises, Inc., 589
Moonwalk Tanning Salons, 532
Morgan Stanley, 553
Morning Grain, 1105–1106
Morrisey Management Consulting, Inc., 631
Morrison's Gifts, 534
Moss Exports, 734
Movies Galore, 1262–1263
Mueller Imports, 847
Multi-Plex Healthcare, 395
Multiplex Medical Clinic, 170
The Music Box, 1212–1213
Mustang Properties, 579–580
M_z-Art, 1079–1082

Naman Howell Law Firm, 157
Nambe Clay, Inc., 1259
National Football League, 476
Nature's Health Foods, 789
Nature's Own, 896–897
Navasota Video Productions, 533–534
NBC, 393, 1107
Neiderhoffer Corp., 688
Networking Systems, 294
Newell Rubbermaid, 1073
Newfoundland Corp., 629
Newmarket Corp., 665
New York Optical Corp., 586
Nexus, 1066
Nick Spanos Antiques, 663
Niehbur Manufacturing Co., 994–995
Night Software, Inc., 842
Nike, Inc., 546, 1065–1066, 1070–1072, 1203
Nissan Motor Co., 967, 1059
Noodles restaurant, 1039
North American Sauces and Beverages Division of Campbell Soup Co., 1190–1193, 1191E23-19, 1192E23-20, 1203–1204
Northeast Electronics Co., 296–297
Northland Press, 1210
Northwood Inn, 536–537
Northwood Properties, 486
Nottingham, England, City of, 1060
Nutriset Foods, 341

Odessa Outfitters, 1255
Ogden, Inc., 664
Old Navy, 264
Olive Garden Restaurant, 1093
Omni Instruments, 1047–1048
One Way Cellular, 713
Onstar Communication, 665
Optical Dispensary, 529
Oracle, 1024
Oriental Rug Co., 529–530, 634–635
Ornamental Iron Works, 343
Outdoor Adventures, 1205–1206
Outdoor Living, 1264
Owens-Illinois, Inc., 626

Pablo's Mexican Restaurants, 528–529
Pace Foods, 930
Pacifica, Inc., 665
Pacific International, 163–164
Pack-N-Ship, 532–533
PackRite, 879
Paint My World, 934–936
Paladin Investment Advisors, Inc., 230
Paladin Security Services, 530
Palestine Corp., 628–629
Palisades Furniture, 755, 767–775, 768E15-8
Palm Pilot, 1203
Pan-American Paper Co., 534–535
Paramount Color Engraving, 716–717
Parisian Department Store, 528
Park and Fly, 489
Park Place Porsche, 490
Parties on Demand, 579
Party Planners, Inc., 168
Party Time Costumes, 345
Party-Time T-Shirts, 305–306
Passport Photography, 227
Patio Furniture, 289
Paychex, 1282
Pecos Pecan Buds, 1261–1262
Pellegrini Electronics Corp., 43–44
Pendleton Woolen Mills, 1060
Pendley Productions, 395–396
People Magazine, 158
PeopleSoft, 1024
Peppertree Copy Center, 711
PepsiCo, Inc., 128, 488, 495, 704, 743, 830, 852, 960, 1268, 1283, 1298, 1307
Petra's Music, 1260
Pfizer, 553
Philip Morris, 49
Phil Mickelson Systems, 496
Phoenix Magazine, 157
Picture Perfect, 843–844
Pier1 Imports, 529, 575, 624
Pikasso Party Planning, 227
Pilot Co., 711
Pizza Inns, Inc., 1213
Planet Beach Tanning Salon, 229
Playtime Park, 1035–1036
Pluto Corp., 667
Pluto Pools, 1222–1225, 1222E24-1, 1223E24-2, 1225E24-4, 1227–1228, 1229, 1232, 1233E24-8, 1234E24-9, 1235E24-10, 1236, 1238E24-11, 1239, 1241, 1241E24-12, 1242E24-13, 1243, 1244, 1245
Poiláne Bakery, 342
Polo Co., 834–835
Poppa Rollo's Pizza, Inc., 305
PowerSwitch, Inc., 846–847
Priceline.com, 540
PriceWaterhouseCoopers, 902
Prince George's Community College, 32
Procter & Gamble (P&G), 103, 299–300, 477, 852, 1213
ProNet Systems, 1248–1249
Providence Medical Supply, 311
Prudential Bache, 796
Publix supermarket, 1207
Pule, 934
Pulley-Bone Fried Chicken, 487
Puzzle Me, 907–914, 910E18-5, 911E18-6-7, 912E18-8, 913E18-9, 917–921, 917E18-10, 918E18-11, 920E18-12, 921E18-13-14, 923, 924E18-16, 925, 930, 950–952, 951E18A-1, 952E18A-2, 954E18A-3, 955E18A-4
PWC Corp., 625–626

Quail Creek Kennel, Inc., 33, 49–50
Quaker Foods, 1298
Quaker Oats, 1203
QuickBooks, 84
Quick Car Inspection, 1038
Quicksilver, 1156

Racer Sports Co., 1301–1302, 1303–1304, 1305
Rainbow Bakery, 933–934
Rainbow International Corp., 635–636
Randstad, 812
Ranger Pro Co., 1253
Ranger Security Systems, 388
Raycor, 1138, 1138E22-11
Raytheon, 364
Redbird Floor Coverings, Inc., 94
Red Lobster, 416
Reebok, 1190
Reed Paper Co., 939–940
Reed's Home Care Corp., 98
Reflection Redwood Corp., 587
Regal Co., 892
Reitmeier Service Center, 85
Renschler Communications, 446–447
Residence Suites, 1216–1217
Retirement Investors, 1045
Rick Spinn Optical Dispensary, 93
Riley Insurance Agency, 224
Risk Management Association, 764, 769, 771, 772, 803
Rite-Way Applications, 393
Ritter Razors, 1158
Ritz-Carlton, 1230
Riverside Hospital (Columbus, Ohio), 1230
RKI Properties, 494

Road Runner Internet, Inc., 232–233
Robbie's Repair Shop, 1040
Robert Morris Associates, 349
Roberto's Bakery, 812–813, 818–821, 822
Robins Corp., 706–707
Rocky Mountain Corp., 556
Rocky Mountain Sportswear (RMS), 315–316, 316E6-1, 319, 324, 329–330, 332, 337, 351
Rocky Recliners, 1256–1257
Rohr Chassis Co., 882–883
Rosetree Floral Supply, 444
Round Rock Corp., 711
Rountree TV Service, 36
Roxi, Inc., 997
Rubbermaid plastics, 1073
Rustic Elegance, Inc., 303

Safeway, 390
Saffron Restaurant Supply, 1043–1044
Sagebrush Software, 527
St. Charles & LaDue, 594
St. James Technology, Inc., 312
Sally's Day Care, 1035
Salon Products, 1157, 1158
Samantha's Shades, 1257
Sanchez, Inc., 785–786
Sanchez Hardwoods, 393
San Diego Harbor Tours, 401
San Diego Zoo, 1203
SAP, 1024
Sarah Lou Bakery, Inc., 629
Saturn Corp., 667
Saturn (dance club), 802
Saturn (division of General Motors), 1190
Saturn Solartech, 529
Sautter Advertising, 881
Scissors Hair Stylists, Inc., 158–159
Scoopy's ice cream parlor, 1263, 1264
Scotty's Scooters, 1040
Scribbles Stationery, 449
Seams Co., 1052–1053
Sears, 212, 611, 1024, 1213, 1306
Seasons Greeting, 853–857, 859, 862–870, 902
Seattle Crystal, 880
SeaWorthy, 941–942
Security Systems Corp., 40, 1101
Serenity, Inc., 687
Serrano Carpet Installers, Inc., 110–111
Shamalay Automotive, 847
Shamrock State Bank, 790
Sharpie, 1073
Shawnee Mission Corp., 791
Shea Law Firm, PC, 101–102
Sheffield Manufacturing, 1158–1159
Shell Oil Co., 704, 743, 902
Shepherd Cycles, 338
Sherman Lawn Service, 4, 6, 11–12, 14, 32, 47, 61, 62, 64, 127, 149, 199, 200, 215, 222, 241, 242, 257

Sherwin-Wilkens, 1306–1307
Showbiz Sportswear, 441
Showcase Cinemas, 734
Showtime Amusements Co., 102–103
Sierra Corp., 525
Sierra Mountain Mining, 488
Signature Lamp Co., 433
Sikes Hardware, 1156
Simms Advertising, 894–895
Simon & Schuster, 476
Simons Realty, 665
Simplicity Graphics, 609
Singular Corp., 795–796
Skippy Scooters, 873
Sloan's Seats, 882
Smartpages.com, 577
SmartPages Media Corp., 715–716
SnowDreams, 1091
Snow Park Lodge, 1111, 1112, 1153–1154, 1155
Snyder Corp., 839
Snyder Piano Service, Inc., 173
Softies, 1104
Solar Energy Co., 174
Sonic Drive-Ins, 664
Sonny's BBQ restaurant, 1209
Sony, 499, 504, 902
Source Today, 710
Southwest Airlines, 540
Speedo Paint Co., 442–443
Speedway Delivery Service, 491
Speegleville Marina, 666
Spice Inc., 663
Sports-Cardz, 1095
Sports Illustrated (SI), 503
Stained Glass Crafters, 443–444
Stanley & Weaver Jewelers, 311
Starbucks, 1066
Star Media, 710
Starstruck Theater, 396
State Farm Insurance Companies, 1207
State Street Bank, 1205
Statistical Research Services, Inc. (SRSI), 626
Steinborn Construction, Inc., 886
Stephanie Stouse, Registered Dietician, PC, 109–110
Steppin' Out Night Club, 393
Sterling Trust, 578
Steubs Environmental Solutions Co., 300–301
Stop-n-Go, 390
StoreAll, 1092–1093
Studio Gallery, Inc., 44
Subway Construction Co., 396–397
Sunburst Technology, 397

Sunoco, 1188
Sun West Media Corp., 713–714
Superhero Industries, 668
Super Saver Stores, Inc., 791
Swaim, 838
Swift Media Sign Company, 439
Swift Sign Co., 228
Synergy Bank, 437
Szigety Industries, 1071–1072

T
Target, 260, 276, 288, 363, 392, 393, 417, 1210
Teak Outdoor Furniture, 880
Tee's Golf School, 164–165
Telluride Railway, 1033–1034
Terry's Amusements, 295
Texaco, 852
Texas Aero, 484
Texas Telecom, 224–225
Theater by Design, 734
Thousand Oaks Realty, 788
The Thrifty Nickel, 485
Thrifty Trailers, 882
Tierra Firma, 1114–1115, 1119, 1141
Tiger Woods Enterprises, 495
Timekeepers, 1000
Time Warner, 475
Tinto Manufacturing Co., 841
Todd Department Stores, Inc., 792–793
Todd McKinney Magic Shows, 226
Toll-Free Calling, 732
Tom Baker, 860–861
Top Dog Running Shoes, 438
Top-Flight, 823
Toshiba Printers, 628
Total Placement Service (TPS), 673
Town & Country Realty, Inc., 44–45
Toyota, 12, 128, 131, 343, 436, 967, 973, 977, 1059
Toys "R" Us, 288, 340
Toy World, 343–344
Trader Bay, 1024
Tradewinds Sailing Supplies, 439
Trane Comfort Specialists, Inc., 585
Transnet, 440
TransWorld Publishing, 527–528
Trautschold Furniture Co., 486
Tree Doctors, 840
Tres Amigos Bed and Breakfast, 48
Tristate Recreation Park (TRP), 674
Triumph Corp., 712

True Discount Furniture, Inc., 624–625
Tru-Value Insurance, 394–395
T-Shirts Plus, Inc., 32, 637
Tulsa Paint Co., 1254
Turbo Champs Corp., 989–990
T Wholesale Co., 290
Tyco, 359
Tylenol, 1066

U
Underwood Co., 635
United Packaging, 1103
United Parcel Service (UPS), 37, 546, 1267–1268, 1272, 1277, 1278, 1292
United Rent-Alls, 611
U.S. Census Bureau, 811
U.S. Department of Defense, 363, 364
U.S. Food, 1093–1094
United Way, 509, 510, 1209
University Cycle Shop, 434
University of Utah, 1163
University of Wisconsin, 1213
Urieta, Inc., 1253–1254
URNO.1 Child Care, Inc., 106
US Ultracom, 673–674

V
Vacation Homes, 891
Valley Mills Construction, Inc., 637
Vance Design, 845
Vandergiff Jewelry, 492–493
Van Dyke Copier, 338
Van Dyke Diamonds, 290
Very Zone, Inc., 795–796
Victor Advertising, 485
Victoria Motors, Inc., 229–230
Video Avenue, 1096–1097
Video King, 1053–1054
Vinning Office Supply, 1207–1208
Virgin Airways, 641
Virtuoso Transportation, 667–668
VISA, 417, 434, 449
Vision Chemical, 1103
Vitamins Plus, Inc., 717–718
Viva, Inc., 956–957
Vivace, 1098
Vogue Skincare, 586
Volvo Marketing Corp., 582

W
Waddell & Reed, Inc., 581–582
Walgreen's, 311
Wallace, Inc., 999–1000
Wallace Farms, 1103

The Wall Street Journal, 553, 669, 774, 1213
Wal-Mart, 129, 258, 315, 363, 366, 378, 415, 417, 425, 447, 476–477, 813, 1076, 1112
Ward's Supercenter, 399
Washington Mutual Insurance Co., 665
Water World, 1160
Webvan, 440
Weddings on Demand, 449
Weekly Corp., 986
Weinstein, Inc., 794–795
Weiters Woods, 887–888
Wendy's restaurant, 34
Western Bank & Trust, 496–497
Westgate Wireless, 389
Westinghouse, 687
Westinghouse Air Brakes, 1229–1230
West Virginia Power Co., 650
WetNWild Swim Park, 1036–1037
Wheels, 1204
Whirlpool Corp., 553
Whitewater Sporting Goods, 1202–1203
Whole Foods Grocery, 342–343
Wholesale Distributors, Inc., 290
William Smith, M.D., 233–234
Willis Realty Co., 688
Wills Consulting Co., 104–105
Winnie's World, 1210
WireComm, 893–894
Wireless Solutions, Inc., 225–226
Woodward Technology Solutions, Inc., 96–97
Woodway Furniture, 998–999
WorldCom (MCI), 7, 358, 359, 478, 767, 823
Worldview Magazine, Inc., 668
Wrangler Co., 844–845
WRS Athletic Clubs, 625

X
Xeno Products, 988
Xerox Corp., 450
Xiaping Trading Co., 48
X-Perience, 1102

Y
Yahoo!, 757, 762–763, 763E15-6-7, 764
Yankee Traveler Magazine, 793
Yu Technology Co., 886–887

Z
Zetamax, 1121, 1149
Zippi, 1161
Zoro, 1304–1305, 1308